VIATOR

Medieval and Renaissance Studies

VOLUME 1

VIATOR

MEDIEVAL AND RENAISSANCE STUDIES

Volume 1 (1970)

PUBLISHED UNDER THE AUSPICES OF
THE CENTER FOR MEDIEVAL AND RENAISSANCE STUDIES
UNIVERSITY OF CALIFORNIA, LOS ANGELES

UNIVERSITY OF CALIFORNIA PRESS
BERKELEY, LOS ANGELES, LONDON 1970

VIATOR

Medieval and Renaissance Studies

EDITOR

Lynn White, jr.

Assistant Editors

H. A. Kelly   R. H. Rouse

BOARD OF EDITORS:

Milton V. Anastos   Gerhart B. Ladner
William Bowsky   Philip Levine
Robert Brentano   Lauro Martines
Carlo Cipolla   William Matthews
C. Warren Hollister   Ernest A. Moody
Charles Jones   Gilbert Reaney
Gustave von Grunebaum

EDITORIAL CONSULTANTS:

Marshall Clagett
(*Institute for Advanced Study*)
Felix Gilbert
(*Institute for Advanced Study*)
Sholomo Y. D. Goitein
(*Pennsylvania*)
Paul Oskar Kristeller
(*Columbia*)
Frederick C. Lane
(*Johns Hopkins*)
Robert S. Lopez
(*Yale*)
Edward Lowinsky
(*Chicago*)

Robert M. Lumiansky
(*Pennsylvania*)
Millard Meiss
(*Institute for Advanced Study*)
Johannes Quasten
(*Catholic University of America*)
Meyer Schapiro
(*Columbia*)
Kenneth Setton
(*Institute for Advanced Study*)
Joseph R. Strayer
(*Princeton*)
Brian Tierney
(*Cornell*)

University of California Press
Berkeley and Los Angeles, California
University of California Press, Ltd.
London, England
Copyright © 1971 by The Regents of the University of California
ISBN: 0-520-01702-1
Library of Congress Catalog Card Number: 71-111417

INTRODUCING
VIATOR

Viator is man on his way. The word implies direction, dedication, movement, and disregard of frontiers. The annual volumes of *Viator* will embrace all aspects of medieval and renaissance studies between late Antiquity and A.D. 1600, particularly, but not exclusively, stressing inter-
disciplinary and intercultural research. They will be concerned not only
with problems internal to the West, but also with relations among the
West, Byzantium, the Slavs, Islam, and the various Jewish and smaller
Christian groups, and even, occasionally, with radiations to and from
more distant regions.

Such catholicity is the essence of humanistic scholarship in our time.
Men whose feet have touched the moon must learn to join hands on earth.
Those who detect vibrations coming from beyond the visible galaxies
must discover the abyss within. We invite the collaboration in *Viator*
of scholars who, as they probe the past, share this sense of the present.

Manuscripts should be addressed to the Editor, the Center for Medieval
and Renaissance Studies, University of California, Los Angeles, California 90024, U.S.A. *Viator* is open to contributions from all sources.
Manuscripts should be typed entirely with double spacing, the footnotes
being numbered consecutively and typed with double spacing on sheets
following the text. Bibliographical references must be complete, but cited
with a minimum of punctuation. All abbreviations, with the exception
of AS (*Acta sanctorum*) PG and PL (J. P. Migne, *Patrologia graeca* and
Patrologia latina), and MGH (*Monumenta Germaniae historica*), must be
indicated in the notes of each article. Texts, illustrations, maps, diagrams,
musical examples and the like, will be published when they are necessary
to the documentation. Articles that have been, or soon will be, printed
elsewhere in any language in substantially the same form are not acceptable.

Inquiries concerning subscriptions should be addressed to the University
of California Press, 2223 Fulton Street, Berkeley, California 94720, U.S.A.
or 25 West 45th Street, New York, New York 10036.

THE EDITORS

CONTENTS

THE SHAPING
OF THE EARLY MEDIEVAL KINGDOM

•

by Herwig Wolfram

About the year 500 the western part of the Roman empire was split into several kingdoms obviously built upon Roman and non-Roman bases alike. These new states were nearly identical in development. Despite numerous setbacks, despite destruction and decline, they provided the prototypes of medieval statehood which were to spread all over Europe, following a series of, more often than not, painful transformations. By way of contrast, an almost complete break of political continuity occurred in former Roman Britain when the Anglo-Saxons founded their largely Germanic kingdoms. Thus it is safe to confine to Continental Europe and Roman Africa the treatment of the early medieval kingdom as the forerunner of the European type of state. Here, a distinctive type of Latin statehood came into being in the course of the fifth and sixth centuries.

The new states were established by the kings of a rich variety of ethnic and linguistic groups. Only scarce evidence of documents and semi-official sources, such as inscriptions and legends on coins and medallions, remains. But all of them betray the same fact, namely that these very kings carried Latin titles, issued laws, diplomas, and all kinds of administrative acts in Latin, and used what I would propose to label a "Latin state vocabulary." [1]

[1] I thank Professor Wayne S. Vucinich of Stanford University, and various members of the Department of History at UCLA, which I joined for the academic year 1968-69 as a visiting professor, for informal discussion of a subject on which I have been working for several years: a reevaluation of the concept of medieval rulership. The tools and methods that I apply are mainly those of semantics, diplomatics, and institutional history, as these are the specialty of the Institut für österreichische Geschichtsforschung to which I belong. Cf. Herwig Wolfram, *Intitulatio I. Lateinische Königs- und Fürstentitel bis zum Ende des 8. Jahrhunderts*, in the series Mitteilungen des Instituts für österreichische Geschichtsforschung (MIÖG) supp. 21 (1967); *Splendor imperii*, MIÖG supp. 20.3 (1963); "Mittelalterliche Politik und adelige Staatssprache," MIÖG 76 (1968) 1-22; "Fortuna in mittelalterlichen Stammesgeschichten," MIÖG 72 (1964) 1-33; "Constantin als Vorbild für den Herrscher des hochmittelalterlichen Reiches," MIÖG 68 (1960) 226-242; "Das Fürstentum Tassilos III, Herzogs der Bayern (748-788)," *Jahrbuch für salzburger Landeskunde* 108 (1968) 157-179. I would also like to express my gratitude to Professors Gerhart

In Carthage a *Rex Vandalorum et Alanorum* reigned over the remains of former Roman Africa,[2] while in the outlying districts of the old provinces several Berber kings had established their Moorish-Roman dominions. One of them was hailed as *Rex Masuna gentium Maurorum et Romanorum*.[3] In this part of the Roman world at least four tribal units were represented by kingdoms: the Vandals, an East-Germanic nation;[4] the Alans, a non-Germanic Indo-European people;[5] the Berber Moors; and the Romans themselves, who were considered to be just a gens, one tribe among others.[6]

A *Rex Sueborum* ruled over the northwestern territories of Spain, while the heartland of the peninsula and vast areas south of the Loire in Gaul stood under the sway of the Visigothic *Rex Gothorum*. The *Rex Francorum* and the *Rex Burgundionum* also ruled over the former Gallic provinces.[7]

In Italy a Gothic king reigned, yet he was no "King of the Goths". The Ostrogoth Theodoric called himself *Flavius Theodericus rex*. The philosophy behind this title might have been derived from, or rather connected with, political ideas developed by Theodoric's predecessor Odovakar. But we are sure at least that this political theory was adopted later by Theodoric's Gothic and Lombard successors in both Italy and Spain in imitation of the Ostrogoth, who was soon to become a model king among the Germanic tribes within and without the boundaries of the former empire.[8] The title *Flavius rex*, significantly, referred to the gens Flavia or, in other words, to the imperial family.

Constantine the Great, to legitimize and strengthen his claim for the throne, had established what we would now call a fictitious relationship between his father and the famous Flavian emperors of the first century after Christ. From the time of Constantine's reign, the former family name Flavius was used as an imperial *praenomen* in addition to *Imperator*,

---

B. Ladner and Richard H. Rouse, both of UCLA, to Professor Henry Myers of Madison College, and to UCLA graduate students Charles Braver and Michael Metzger.

[2] Wolfram, *Intitulatio* 79ff.

[3] *Ibid.* 82ff. A. H. M. Jones, *The Later Roman Empire* (Oxford 1964) 2.1023.

[4] By far the best work on the Vandals in Africa is C. Courtois, *Les Vandales et l'Afrique* (Paris 1955).

[5] Cf. B. S. Bachrach, "The Alans in Gaul," *Traditio* 23 (1967) 476-489. G. Vernadsky, "The Eurasian Nomads and their Impact on Medieval Europe," *Studi medievali* 34 (1963) 1-34. See also Courtois (n. 4 above).

[6] This change in thinking, according to which the universal concept "Romanus" was shrinking to a particular tribal connotation, is, for example, documented by the title of that odd fourth-century pamphlet "Origo gentis romanae." Cf. H. Beumann, "Zur Entwicklung transpersonaler Staatsvorstellungen," *Vorträge und Forschungen* 3 (1956) 218ff., esp. 223.

[7] Wolfram, *Intitulatio* (n. 1 above) 77f., 87ff., and 108ff.

[8] *Ibid.* 56ff.; O. Höfler, *Germanisches Sakralkönigtum* 1 (1952).

which had been introduced under Augustus.[9] Any member of the imperial family could use the honorific name Flavius as could "barbarian" military officials when they obtained Roman citizenship; *Imperator*, which was both title and *praenomen*, was, of course, reserved for the emperor himself.[10]

With the title *Flavius rex*, Theodoric was able to express his special position as ruler of Italy in place of an emperor to whose family he belonged in theory. This important relationship was reflected in many contemporary utterances, not the least in the pragmatic approach of Procopius, the Greek historian of the sixth century who is our major source for the conflicts between Justinian and the Persians, Vandals, and Goths. Procopius wondered why Theodoric simply called himself ῥήξ (pronounced *rhix*), "as the barbarians used to name their leaders," although the Ostrogoth reigned like any true emperor.[11]

As the barbarians used to name their laeders! What does this comment on *rhix* mean to us, since we have just stated that those "leaders" themselves used Latin titles? First of all, we would answer that ῥήξ is the Greek equivalent of *rex*, and it is evident that the Latin term was used in Greek from the second century onward.[12] But this answer is not sufficient. The Latin title *rex* was certainly not the original Germanic word for king with which "the barbarians used to name their leaders." As a Latin term it was quite naturally used by Roman speakers of both Latin and Greek. There is, however, an important source that provides a possible explanation for Procopius's statement, and for the absence about the year 500 of any East-Germanic word to denote a king. Bishop Ulfilas wrote the Gothic version of the Scriptures in the second half of the fourth century. To translate the Greek word ἄρχων ("commander," "governor," "military official"), Ulfilas used the Gothic term *reiks* (pronounced *rix*). At the same time, however, he rendered the famous question of Pontius Pilate to Jesus, "Art Thou the King of the Jews?" by *"Thu is thiudans Iudaie?"*[13]

Thiudans means "king of the people," both tribal and sacred, since tribe and king alike were held to have a divine ancestor, perhaps the same one. The word itself evidently derives from *thiod*, people, thus making the *thiudans* the people's representative par excellence.

---

[9] E. Rosenberg, "Imperator," in Pauly-Wissowa, *Real-Encyclopädie der classischen Altertumswissenschaft* 9 (1916) 1145; R. Syme, "Imperator Caesar," *Historia* 7 (1958) 172-188; A. E. Gordon, "Notes on the *Res Gestae* of Augustus," *California Studies in Classical Antiquity* 1 (1968) 136.

[10] Wolfram, *Intitulatio* 57.

[11] *De bell. goth.* 1.1.26; cf. 29.

[12] Wolfram, *Intitulatio* 40.

[13] Ulfilas, trans., John 18.33.

Reiks, however, is not a Germanic word, although it is obviously akin to Latin *rex*, Celtic *rigs*, and Sanskrit *rāj*. We do not know how and why the Germanic languages lost that element of their Indo-European heritage. We can simply state that the Celtic word *rigs* and its derivation **rikja* ("realm," "*Reich*") was to become a loanword with the Germanic peoples when the Celtic nations prevailed in Europe. These peoples then founded the first bodies politic larger than small tribal units whose religious and political center was the royal family that provided the tribal king. For the transmission of the word *reiks* it is significant that the first Germanic king to carry a name compounded with *-rix*, a form of *reiks*, was the Cimbrian Boiorix, which literally meant King of the Boii. The Boii were the famous Celtic tribe living in Bohemia who gave the country its name in the Germanic tongues. The Boii actually supported the first Germanic avalanche of peoples to hit the ancient world, or, in other words, the first Germanic **rikja*.[14] Yet the Goth Ulfilas still used *thiudans* for king and understood by the term *reiks* only a rank inferior to king, although the loanword *reiks* had originally meant not only "king," but "greater king."

This seeming contradiction can be resolved by a relatively well-founded explanation. From Caesar and Tacitus through Ammianus Marcellinus and Jordanes to Widukind of Corvey and even more recent authors, there exists evidence for two different kinds of Germanic king,[15] one popular, one military.

The king of the people, whom a great many of the sources call *thiudans*, *theoden*, *thiodan*, or the like, was chosen from the royal family; he was the archetype of a tribal king, elected because of his noble origins—*ex nobilitate*. He was the king of the "establishment" of a relatively stable and isolated society. The king of the victorious army started his career as the leader of his followers. He could have been either of nonroyal or of royal stock; the latter would have actually eased his start. The criterion for his election, which was carried out by his retainers, was not his origins but a decisive victory, or an outstanding success in settling newly won territories—in sum, a glorious heroic effort that proved his kingly qualities. He was chosen *ex virtute*.[16] He was the king of a socially mobile society. In other words, the king of the warrior retinue was the "founder king," creating both a new royal family and a new tribe; the king of the people was the successor of kings who had ruled the tribe since "time immemorial."

It was Georges Dumézil who, in systematizing the Indo-European pantheon, discovered this polarity of royal authority in a pair of complementary gods

[14] J. de Vries, "Das Königtum bei den Germanen," *Saeculum* 7 (1956) 303ff. R. Wenskus, *Stammesbildung und Verfassung* (Cologne 1961) 419.

[15] W. Schlesinger, "Lord and Follower in Germanic Institutional History," *Lordship and Community in Medieval Europe*, ed. F. L. Cheyette (New York 1968) 64ff., esp. 72-79. Wenskus (n. 14 above) 576ff.

[16] Schlesinger (n. 15 above) 72, according to Tacitus, *Germania* 7.

like Mitra-Varuna in the Rg Veda religion, and Tiwaz-Woden among the Germanic peoples. There was, on the one hand, a beneficent god who stood for a stable social order as a guarantor of laws and conventions, fertility and peace; and, on the other hand, there was a violent, dangerous, and even chaotic god who acted as a leader of the warrior retinues dedicated to him. Within the Teutonic pantheon, Woden embodied the principle that broke down the somewhat petrified sytem of the stable *thiudans* society. Woden was to become the god of warlords and their retinues who destroyed the pre-Migration tribes to build new bodies politic.

There is, however, some good reason to assume that the replacement of the tribal kings by warrior kings was not a historical phenomenon confined to the period of the Great Migrations. There is enough evidence for this dialectical process of succession before and after that period of time. Most of the royal families that we know revered mystical or semimystical "founder kings" as their ancestors, and each new founder king was all too eager to meet the needs of rulership by following the sacred patterns of a tribal king. That a victorious battle could even be considered an ordeal eased the new king's attempt to appear as a divine incarnation, and this actually justified his kingship.[17]

The North-Germanic tribes, isolated as they were, maintained a relatively stable society for a considerably longer period of time than the Continental Teutons.[18] The former still clung to the traditional form of sacred kingship even after Tacitus had written his *Germania*. Except for the Franks and Lombards, all the Germanic nations who founded kingdoms on Roman soil were of East-Germanic stock. The East-Germanic Goths, Vandals, Burgundians, Rugians, Herulians, and others derived their origins or, more important, their prevailing political traditions, from Scandinavia, that is to say, from the North-Germanic environment. This is the reason the Gothic version of the Bible still used the old term *thiudans* for king. The relatively new loanword *reiks* came to apply to the *dux*-stratum of warlords who were only potential kings.[19] These leaders seized their opportunity when the Great Migrations began; it is possible to prove that the *reiks* eventually became identical with the East-Germanic kings who founded the first kingdoms on Roman soil.

Although the concept *reiks* must have reached the north and east through West-Germanic routes, the word itself had been forgotten among the West-Germanic peoples by the time the Migrations began. At the same time, the

[17] J. de Vries, "The Present State of Studies on Germanic Religion," *Diogenes* 18 (1957) 86, discusses Georges Dumézil's findings. On the kingly couple *sinistus* and *hendinos* see Wenskus (n. 14 above) 576ff. I consider Jordanes's account of the accession of the Amals, Theodoric's royal family, to be the most striking example of the political philosophy cited above: Jordanes, *Getica* 76ff. Cf. Wolfram, *Intitulatio* (n. 1 above) 99ff.

[18] Cf. Wenskus (n. 14 above) 410.

[19] De Vries (n. 14 above) 301ff. Wenskus (n. 14 above) 322ff.

term *thiudans* was also fading or even died out in the center of the Continental West-Germanic areas where tribal kingship long since had been abandoned.[20] The old term *theoden* exists in Anglo-Saxon poetry and occurs as *thiodan* in related Continental Saxon sources. It is, however, assumed that this word was re-introduced by the Anglo-Saxon mission to honor Christ, while the original political concept had already been given up by the *Saxones antiqui*.[21] In official sources, diplomas, and documents, the Anglo-Saxons themselves had long since adopted the Frankish words and concepts of king and kingship.

The Anglo-Saxon king was the *cyning* or *kyning* as the Merovingian king was the *kuning*; the term derived from Germanic **kuningaz* but cannot be found in East-Germanic sources. This title was actually the West-Germanic counterpart of *reiks* and developed the way the *reiks-king* did in the East. Beowulf is commonly referred to as *thiod-cyning*.[22] In my opinion, this title connotes and means exactly the same as Theodoric's personal name **thiuda-reiks*: the new type of king has replaced the tribal *thiudans* by assuming his responsibility for the creation and maintainance of a given *thiod*, or people.[23] It was, however, the greater Frankish kingdom that finally gave the word "king" the medieval substance and broader meaning that could be adopted by the Anglo-Saxons, the Scandinavians (including the non-Germanic Finns), and the Slavs. The Merovingian *kuning* created the largest and most enduring realm; he destroyed petty kingdoms in his tribal zone of influence and conquered large foreign kingdoms such as the "Roman" kingdom of Syagrius, the Burgundian kingdom, and parts of both Gothic kingdoms. Thereby the Merovingian king elevated the term *kuning* to a formerly inconceivable degree. The Carolingian successors completed this impressive policy by incorporating the Lombard kingdom into the "Frankish commonwealth" and thus becoming the only Latin kings in Continental Europe.[24]

Most Slavic languages still reflect the rise of the nonroyal king. For example, Russian князб (knyaz'), which derives from **kuningaz*, means *princeps*, nonroyal lord, whereas королб (korol') stands for (foreign) king. It is a commonplace that this term *korol'* derives from the personal name of Charles

[20] Wenskus (n. 14 above) 409ff.

[21] De Vries (n. 17 above) 301. The only known exception to this rule is the archaic alliterative phrase "eorl and ceorl, thegn and theoden" which occurs once in the Anglo-Saxon laws (Felix Liebermann, *Die Gesetze der Angelsachsen* 1 [Halle an der Salle 1903] 456) and does not mean the king, as two Latin versions of the eleventh century indicate. See *ibid*. 457; cf. also 2.1 (Halle an der Salle 1906) 220.

[22] *Beowulf* 2579, for example.

[23] Cf. Ammianus Marcellinus 28.5.14, where the author distinguished between the Burgundian kings whose name was *hendinos*, and a single *rex sacrorum* (with only priestly functions) whom they called *sinistus*. See n. 17 above. Cf. Wolfram, *Intitulatio* 40.

[24] D. H. Green, *The Carolingian Lord* (Cambridge, Eng. 1965) 347f., 507. H. D. Kahl, "Europäische Wortschatzbewegungen im Bereich der Verfassungsgeschichte," *Zeitschrift für Rechtsgeschichte, Germanistische Abteilung* 77 (1960) 202ff., 239.

the Great, thus following, for instance, the pattern of *Caesar-kaisar-Kaiser-tsar*. Henrik Birnbaum, who kindly advised me on this difficult topic, points out that *korol'* is not the equivalent of *Carolus* or *Karolus* but of **Carolius*; it is not a noun but an adjective. The next question, of course, is: to which noun might this adjective have belonged? Birnbaum considers the possibility that it was *knyaz'*. If he is right, the Slavs redefined the **kuningaz-knyaz'* of princely but not royal rank as a *korol'-knyaz'*, that is to say, a Carolingian lord. This is in keeping with the development of the Carolingian rulers and is consistent with the concept and notion of the medieval *kuning* at the height of his power.[25]

As mentioned before, there is strong evidence that the *thiudans* disappeared as a ruling type among the West-Germanic tribes. The reason for this institutional shift is that tribal kingship had been given up by the West-Germanic peoples even before Caesar arrived in Gaul. It is again significant that they followed their Celtic neighbors in abandoning tribal kingship. The attempts to restore this kind of kingship were answered most often by successful resistance, as the fates of Orgetorix, Dumnorix, and Vercingetorix, on the one hand, and Arminius and Civilis, on the other, clearly indicate.[26] The widespread shaping of larger-than-tribal units during the third and fourth centuries[27] and the obvious success of war leaders during the fourth century at the latest brought "everlasting" royal rank to the former.[28] Thus Alaric, the conqueror of Rome in 410, became the *reiks*-king par excellence. He was of noble but nonroyal stock and had to start his career as a nonroyal war leader, as a *dux*, to use the expression of Tacitus.[29] Like Theodoric[30] and Geiseric[31] and many contemporary royal and nonroyal war leaders, he bore a personal name compounded with this very syllable *-rix* that significantly described his *reiks* quality. His victories over the Roman armies proved him to be a true king and his followers made him king. These were Visigoths, of course, but also Ostrogothic groups and other "barbarians," as the sources put it.[32]

In each of the cited cases, those avalanchelike bands of warriors led by a successful, "charismatic" personality would have turned to dust unless the process of consolidation and settlement has been initiated. To achieve this

[25] V. Kiparsky, "Die gemeinslavischen Lehnwörter aus dem Germanischen," *Annales Academiae scientiarum fennicae* B 32.2 (1939) 181f., 240ff. Cf. Kahl (n. 24 above) 176ff., 239.

[26] Cf. de Vries (n. 14 above) 304. Wenskus (n. 14 above) 416f., concerning the three Celtic "chieftains," 423, concerning Arminius and Civilis.

[27] Wenskus (n. 14 above) 435ff.

[28] Wolfram, *Splendor imperii* 108ff.

[29] Cf. his *Germania* 7.

[30] Wenskus (n. 14 above) 482ff.

[31] Courtois (n. 4 above) 217f. Wolfram, *Intitulatio* 86.

[32] Wenskus (n. 14 above) 476f.; cf. 322.

state of affairs, it took a central political figure, called king,[33] and a given
territory wealthy enough to provide the necessary economic base, a kingdom.
In other words the king had to turn his kingship into a kingdom, adding the
territorial principle to the theoretically still prevailing personal link between
himself and his retainers,[34] who had to become a new people.[35] This process
of institutional change, however, badly needed the active support of the
Romans.

Diplomatic and numismatic sources indicate that about the year 500 the
East-Germanic *reiks* and Latin *rex* (both pronounced and often written *rix*)
were considered to be homophones or homonyms. Still, the substantial meaning of the two words with quite a different history probably came to be one
and the same.[36] The Roman emperor Flavius Claudius Iulianus, better known
as Julian the Apostate, was proclaimed Augustus in 361 by his Gallic army,
like any Germanic war king or king of the victorious army. The soldiers,
who were almost all Germanic "barbarians,"[37] elevated him on a warrior's
shield after his overwhelming victories over successive waves of Germanic
invaders.[38] The Flavian house of Constantine was for the last time able to
produce an imperial war leader who was successful and respected enough
by the heavily Germanized "Roman" army to use the current trends for
reestablishing Rome's physical boundaries and political prestige.[39] With the
next generation, the situation started to change radically. The Roman emperors lost their credibility as successful war leaders. Around 400, the East-
Germanic *reiks* succeeded in offering himself as the desirable alternative for
the Germanic warrior to follow. A hundred years later, the *reiks*-king came
to be the king of Romans and Teutons alike. Procopius was actually correct

---

[33] One of the greatest merits of Wenskus's *Stammesbildung und Verfassung* is to have
shown the imperative necessity of kingship for the existence of early medieval tribes and
peoples: cf. 485.

[34] Except for the Flavian king title (see above nn. 8, 9), all early medieval royal titles
followed the same type, namely "*N. rex gentis/gentium* X(Y)." This gave expression to
the political theory that the king is a king of *people(s)* rather than territory. It was not
until the beginning of the later Middle Ages that, for example, *Franciae* began to replace
Francorum: see C. T. Wood, "*Regnum Franciae*: A Problem in Capetian Administrative
Usage," *Traditio* 23 (1967) 117-147. See also n. 35 below.

[35] This process, of course, implied what I would call the "territorialization" of the tribe
for which the Visigothic transmission provides the earliest evidence: King Leowigild, for
example, expressed the theory that he reigned the *patria vel gens Gotorum*. This double
concept tended to become Spania. Wolfram, *Intitulatio* 70.

[36] Wolfram, *Intitulatio* 41ff.

[37] Cf. Jones, *Later Empire* (n. 3 above) 284-602. For our particular problems, I still
prefer E. Stein, *Histoire du bas-empire*, 2 vols. (Paris 1959); cf. esp. 1.124.

[38] Stein (n. 37 above) 155.

[39] *Ibid.* 142ff., attributes this to the enormous victories won by Julian over various
Germanic peoples. Julian even crossed the Rhine to attack the bases of potential and actual
enemies.

when he mentioned that the barbarians used to call their leader "rhix." He simply failed to add that so did the Romans of Latin and Greek tongues: since about 500 the syllable *rix* (*rhix*) meant almost the same to all of them.[40]

But is this semantic evidence enough to conclude that the Romans supported the new bodies politic, even if we can buttress semantics by historical facts? What was the Roman attitude toward the concepts of "king," "kingship," and "kingdom" and how did it apply to their new rulers and political systems?

This question is threefold:

First, Roman political tradition was antiroyal. Hellenistic anti-Roman propaganda explained Roman politics as almost exclusively determined by hatred of kings.[41] Caesar's fate supported this conviction.[42] The Greek historian Appian, native of Alexandria and born about A.D. 95, notes that the Romans were bound by an old oath not to accept kings as their rulers.[43] How did this attitude change?

Second, the Diocletian reform separated the military power from civil authority and established two kinds of public careers. The military hierarchy, especially of the West, became more and more the exclusive province of barbarians, while the civil bureaucracy, by far the more important means to consolidate and organize a state, for quite obvious reasons remained Roman and intact.[44] How could the king overcome this difficulty and establish himself as head of both powers?

Third, everybody agrees that the tribal units that founded kingdoms were heavily outnumbered by the Roman population. Five percent of the total population might have been non-Roman; in some kingdoms the percentage of newcomers may have been even lower.[45] This has always caused me to wonder why the Romans did not drive out the intruders. How could a Germanic king and his primitive tribal organization get along with that seemingly overwhelming majority of potential enemies?

The three subquestions could be answered as follows:

First, concerning the antiroyal tradition: Appian not only indicates that the Romans might have cursed the name of king, but also states "they [the emperors] are very kings in fact."[46] Cassius Dio (d. 235), a Greek observer

[40] Wolfram, *Intitulatio* 41ff.

[41] H. Fuchs, *Der geistige Widerstand gegen Rom in der antiken Welt*, ed. 2 (Berlin 1964) 16f.

[42] Cf. G. Dobesch, *Caesars Apotheose zu Lebzeiten und sein Ringen um den Königstitel* (Vienna 1966).

[43] *Romaike* 53.17.1f.

[44] Stein (n. 37 above) 1.69ff.

[45] S. Katz, *The Decline of Rome and the Rise of Medieval Europe* (Ithaca 1958) 115. L. Schmidt, "Das germanische Volkstum in den Reichen der Völkerwanderung," *Historische Vierteljahrsschrift* 29 (1935).

[46] *Romaike* 53.17.1f.

of Roman history and policy and Roman high official and consul, interpreted the Roman polity since Augustus: "The word monarchy, to be sure, the Romans so detested that they called their emperors neither dictators nor king nor anything of the sort; yet, since the final authority for the government devolves upon them, they must needs be kings."[47] This logical conclusion was in keeping with the traditional theory in both Greek and Latin. We have only to recall Cicero's definition of king and kingdom: "When the direction of all depends on one person, we call this individual a king, and this form of political constitution a kingdom."[48]

We keep in mind that the Greek-Hellenistic interpretation of the Roman monarchy was pragmatical: Augustus' construction could not conceal the reality that authors such as Appian and Cassius Dio described in the proper terms. But the Greek-Hellenistic approach was not only pragmatical, it was also based upon an old philosophical conception of the philosopher king, the ideal monarch. The application of the venerable Platonic concept to the Roman emperor became more and more common as time went on. Marcus Aurelius is the best known of those whom the term philosopher king could actually fit. The final reevaluation of royal rulership was certainly one of the most important features of the general process described as the Hellenization of the Roman political theory.[49]

On the eve of the fourth century, the leading and educated strata of Roman society, we may assume, must have been theoretically well prepared to accept the idea of royal government. Furthermore, the imperial government as established by Diocletian and Constantine must have looked like any Hellenistic kingdom in practice. Little wonder that Constantine took the first step of which we know from theory (writing, reading, and feeling) to institutional realization, when he determined the imperial succession.

Diocletian had organized the empire in four administrative districts, headed by two *Augusti*, full-fledged emperors, and two *Caesares*, second-rank emperors with the right of succession after the *Augusti* to whom they were subject. Constantine tried to fill this tetrarchy with his own descendants, but thanks to his aggressive fatherly love, he had only three sons left. He chose the elder son of his brother to be the second Caesar. But this man had a younger brother, called Hannibalianus. Constantine, to indemnify Hannibalianus, married him to his daughter and made her Augusta. Then Constantine ordered that Hannibalianus should be "King of the Kings and Pontic nations."[50] This title betrays a good deal of political philosophy. Hannibalianus assumed the title of the Persian king, and he was obviously supposed

[47] Cited by F. Dvornik, "Early Christian and Byzantine Political Philosophy," *Dumbarton Oaks Studies* 9.2 (1966) 519.

[48] *De Rep.* 1.26.

[49] Dvornik (n. 47 above) 453ff.

[50] Wolfram, *Intitulatio* 34f.

to become a king of nations. Therefore, I would say, he was supposed to rule over Christian Armenia, which was continuously disputed between Persians and Romans, or to establish a Roman dynasty in the kingdom of Persia, after having conquered it, of course. There are indications that Roman territory was also to be added to his dominion. If we are right in this, the Roman emperor himself considered the Romans to be a gens, a tribe, a nation like any other in the world, and, of necessity, to be ruled by a king.[51]

None of those plans actually materialized. Constantine's sons killed their cousins, and the final conquest of Armenia or of Persia remained as impossible as ever. Kingdoms were not established on Roman soil until the approach of the next century. In 382, Theodosius the Great came to an agreement with the victorious Visigoths along the lines of the traditional federate system after, however, having changed one most important condition. Up to that time, the Roman government had concluded treaties with tribal units who lived outside the boundaries. The tribes had to provide troops and were allowed to keep their own political organization. It sometimes even looks as if the Romans supported the accession of kings ruling over federates, since it was obviously easier to deal with one dependent king, recognized by a given federate people, than with a plurality of noblemen and chieftains, who would consider themselves to be each other's peers and equals.[52]

In 382, however, the emperor was forced to allow the Visigoths to maintain their political and socioeconomic identity within the Roman polity. At that very moment, the Visigoths did not have a king as a central political figure. But they were soon to make Alaric their king.[53]

The emperor reached the settlement with the tribe, not with a territory called Gothia or Visigothia. But, despite the personal principles according to which the agreement was made, the Visigoths lived in a territory that was populated by Roman citizens. Little wonder that Alaric's successor, Athaulf, already considered the possibility of replacing Romania by Gothia: he did, however, reject the idea as utopian.[54]

In the years to come, more and more Roman citizens were subjected by imperial decision and recognition to Germanic kingdoms.[55] In sum, we can

[51] *Ibid.* Cf. Salvian, *De gubernatione Dei* 5.15: ". . . barbari, qui sunt unius gentis et regis."

[52] Cf. Tacitus, *Germania* 42: "sed vis et potentia regibus ex auctoritate Romana." Italicus, Arminius' nephew, was invested as king over his tribe by the Roman government and upon the request of a strong Cheruscan party; the same group which opposed his uncle's kingship, however, also resisted the emperor-sent king. Tacitus, *Annal.* 11.16. Wenskus (n. 14 above) 421ff.

[53] *Ibid.* 477ff.

[54] Orosius, *Hist.* 7.43.3. Cf. G. B. Ladner, "Religious Renewal and Ethnic-Social Pressures as Forms of Life in Christian History," *Theology of Renewal* 2 (1968) 333.

[55] Cf. Procopius, *De bell. goth.* 1.1.9: "It was about this same time that the Goths also, who were dwelling in Thrace with the permission of the emperor, took arms against the

say that the imperial policy along with a changed political theory prepared Roman citizens to accept royal government.

Also, we have to consider the role of the Roman bureaucracy. A Sicilian-Vespers-like revolt occurred in Byzantium in July 400 in the course of which the Gothophile government was overthrown and most of its Germanic supporters were eliminated and destroyed. The victory of that "national" Roman movement allowed the thorough reorganization of the army. The results were the following: First, federates were no longer recruited from tribes within the empire. The commanders of those troops were usually Roman natives. For instance, among the twenty-two commanding officers of Belisarius's army were eighteen Roman natives (most of them from Thracia), three Huns, and only one of Germanic origin. Second, the high military command of the eastern empire was decentralized and divided among a college of equals. Third, the emperor had still a certain cadre of crack troops under his immediate command.[56]

By way of contrast, the western government could not or would not take advantage of a similar movement that destroyed the almighty general Stilicho and a great many of his Germanic followers. The Vandal Stilicho, to be sure, had an immediate successor of Germanic stock; but this man could not keep his position either. His fall paved the way for a Roman native to become *magister peditum praesentalis*, that is to say, commander-in-chief of the western Roman army in the "presence" of the emperor. This important shift, however, was not exploited to achieve the same reorganization and decentralization of the high command as had been one decade before in the East. Instead, a cautious reading of the sources reveals that it was this very Roman officer, Constantius, who definitely assumed the office for which Stilicho had failed to receive final imperial recognition. It is even more suprising and against Roman political experience that Constantius, having become the third emperor of this name, did not abolish this "superoffice" that so obviously paved the way to become Augustus.

Constantius was the first to be called *patricius et magister peditum praesentalis*. This position allowed interference in civil affairs, although Constantius was primarily a military officer. Until then, "patrician," meaning "father of the emperor," was a title usually given to top civil officials. Now things had completely changed: a new superoffice came into being, which semiofficial sources called "patriciate of the West," and this was the antecedent and prelude to the Italian kingdoms and the Exarchate of Ravenna directly, and of the Gallic kingdoms indirectly. In Gaul, the head of the army was the *magister equitum Galliarum*; he certainly was inferior to the Italy-

---

Romans under the leadership of Theodoric, a man who was of patrician rank and had attained the consular office in Byzantium."

[56] Stein (n. 37 above) 1.235-241.

stationed commander-in-chief in the presence of the emperor, but he became eligible for the desirable patrician dignity in the course of the fifth century.[57]

As time went on, the Gallic patriciate as well as the higher Italian patriciate of the West was reopened to Germanic war leaders, among whom Rikimer was the most effective and famous general. He ruled over the shrinking territories of the western empire, which were without a resident emperor, with a single Augustus in faraway Constantinople. Rikimer's nephew Gundobad, who was to become his successor, had yet to leave Italy. On his return to his Burgundian tribe in the Rhone valley, he was made king. Thus he was the first to show the links between patriciate and kingship, between office and royal rulership.[58]

Odovakar stressed that mutual relationship even more. He deposed the emperor Augustulus and killed the patrician of the West, who was the real father of the emperor; Odovakar was then made king by mostly-Germanic federates, called the Italian army. But although he was of royal blood, the new king considered his kingship only a valuable object of bargaining for imperial recognition. He offered his kingship to the emperor in Constantinople in exchange for investiture as patrician of the West under the same conditions granted to Rikimer. Odovakar could not fully make the bargain with the emperor; yet Theodoric, who by imperial command set out for Italy to fight the Italian king, considered a *tyrannus* by the imperial policy, did so not as a king of the Goths but as an imperial officer, as *consul et patricius*.[59] The theory behind this imperial construction, however, was clearly outdated, at least as far as the Germanic polity and its need for kingship was concerned.[60] For the third time in his life, Theodoric was made king by an ad hoc body of retainers; this time his *comitatus* felt that the final victory over Odovakar was just a matter of time. They elected him king without awaiting the permission of the new emperor.[61]

Now it was up to the imperial government to keep pace with the creation of kingdoms by bestowing imperial offices upon the kings, especially if they were as powerful and successful as Clovis, the king of the united Frankish peoples. Clovis was formally invested as patrician by imperial grant and privilege after he destroyed and conquered Visigothic Gaul. Although there are doubts about the nature of the office bestowed upon Clovis, most recent research has shown that it was the patriciate.[62] Among other evi-

---

[57] Wolfram, *Intitulatio* 45ff. Stein (n. 37 above) 265ff. A. H. M. Jones, "The Constitutional Position of Odoacer and Theoderic," *The Journal of Roman Studies* 52 (1962) 126-130.

[58] Wolfram, *Intitulatio* 87ff.

[59] Stein (n. 37 above) 1.398, 2.54ff. Cf. n. 55 above.

[60] See n. 33 above.

[61] Anonymous Valesianus, in MGH Auct. ant. 9.306ff.

[62] Gregory of Tours, *Hist. Franc.* 2.38, interpreted by K. Hauck, "Von einer spätantiken Randkultur zum karolingischen Europa," *Frühmittelalterliche Studien* 1 (1967) 30ff. See

dence[63] there is the famous Theodoric letter, written to the emperor in Constantinople immediately after the day at Tours in 508 when Clovis was invested as patrician. In the letter the Gothic king judges the step taken by the imperial government to be very unfriendly, and blames the emperor for having broken the special state of confidence and peace prevailing between the empire and its *imago*, its copy, the kingdom of Italy. Theodoric's kingship implies precedence among the "kings of the nations" by virtue of its specific political tradition and base—that is to say, in succession of the patriciate of the West. This means, further, that Italy was ruled by a Flavian king instead of the Flavian emperor, and not by the king of any tribe. It is evident that this political theory must have been heavily threatened by the imperial investiture of Clovis with the patrician title. But it was not only theory which was at stake. Theodoric, a patrician king of Italy who had destroyed another patrician king of Italy, must have realized the real dangers which could come from that victorious Frankish patrician king Clovis.[64]

Throughout the fifth, sixth, and even seventh and eighth centuries, the mutual relationship between Latin kingship and western patriciate came to be one of the most important political and theoretical factors. Finally, it was still a patriciate—even if modified—of the West which paved Charlemagne's way toward his imperial coronation on Christmas Day 800.[65]

To sum up the second point of the investigation of the Roman attitude toward kingship, we can say: The imperial recognition of federate kingship on Roman soil was originally valid for the tribal unit alone. This kingship necessarily combined military command and civil authority. The tribal unit occupied Roman soil; among the Romans, the tribe and its king often were the only effective executive power in a given area. Thus, the territorial principle was quickly introduced; the king became the only authority in a given territory to be supported by imperial recognition and decision. The kings of the federates were automatically high Roman military officials. In Gaul and especially in Italy, the king's Roman military office merged with a new Roman superoffice, the patriciate of the West, established against Diocletian reform principles in the civil bureaucracy.

The third of these considerations concerns the lack of resistance from the Roman population. As mentioned before, the "national" reaction against

---

Wolfram, *Intitulatio* 126, where I have submitted my questioning the whole "honorary consulate" theory. Now I would stress my doubts even more. Perhaps we would do more justice to Gregory's account if we understand Clovis as "consul et patricius" by which formula the Frankish king could have reached the Ostrogoth, Theodoric, against whom the Byzantine-Frankish alliance was devised.

[63] In the table of contents of the second book of his *History of the Franks*, Gregory calls chap. 38 "De patriciato Chlodovechi regis."

[64] Cassiodorus, *Variae* 1.1.1. Wolfram, *Intitulatio* 54 n. 103, concerning "Theoderich."

[65] *Ibid.* 45-54, 225ff.

the Germanic infiltration succeeded in the East and failed in the West. Many scholars see this inability of the western half of the empire as a sufficient indication of the critical conditions in those areas. Nobody can deny the difference between West and East. The eastern half of the empire was better off economically, geographically, and demographically. But the Germanic intruders were only five percent of the total population. Moreover, it is simply a fairy tale that the Romans were unable to fight and to become soldiers. There has remained, for example, the Frankish tribal saga according to which King Childerich, Clovis's father, was driven out for his unseemly behavior with the Frankish ladies. In his place, the Franks chose the "emperor-sent Roman commander-in-chief and patrician Aegidius" as their king. This account is rather confusing, but it sufficiently indicates the high prestige of a Roman warrior and general with the Germanic allies of the empire that he represented.[66]

In contrast, it took the armies of Justinian twenty years to reconquer Italy, because the support by the "Romans" of the peninsula was so poor. Isidore of Seville belonged to a Roman family who rejected the Byzantine reconquest of parts of Spain as invasion. Isidore's literary production justifies the Gothic rule over Spain.[67] The Vandal kingdom, moreover, was overthrown by the Moors rather than by Belisarius's army, as the late Christian Courtois showed in his brilliant *Les Vandales et l'Afrique*.[68]

The Germanic invasions were, of course, invasions and not polite occupations. It would be a romantic glorification in terms of the "noble savage" pattern of yesteryear to call those invasions liberation from the yoke of slavery that the late Roman empire had imposed upon its own subjects. Furthermore, there was a strong religious conflict between the Catholic Romans and the Germanic Arians that was successfully avoided only by the Franks, who converted directly from heathendom to Catholicism. We know of anti-Germanic Roman movements active under Germanic rule as late as the end of

---

[66] Gregory of Tours, *Hist. Franc.* 2.12. R. Wenskus, "Bemerkungen zum Thunginus der Lex Salica," *Festschrift Percy Ernst Schramm* (1964) 217ff., tries successfully to explain this strange account. Aegidius was, however, not the only Roman representative considered worthy and able to become a Germanic king. After his first victories on Italian soil, a large group of the Ostrogoths offered Belisarius the Gothic-Italian kingship and kingdom. Procopius, *De bell. goth.* 2.29.17-27. Cf. Wolfram, *Intitulatio* 47f.

[67] Cf. Procopius, *De bell. goth.* 3.11.10: "So spoke Belisarius. But no one of the enemy came over to him, neither Goth nor Roman." 3.12.8: "And this also you must know well, my master, that the majority of those serving in your army have deserted to the enemy" (Belisarius to Justinian). On Isidore of Seville, see H. Messmer, "Hispania-Idee und Goten-mythos," *Geist und Werk der Zeiten* 5 (1960). Jones (n. 3 above) 2.1059, contradicts his own statement, 2.1022.

[68] Courtois (n. 4 above) 353ff.

the sixth century.[69] But we have to admit that all those efforts must have gained weak support, since they failed everywhere before long.

Yet there are indications that the "process of acculturation" worked the other way. Throughout the Migrations, conservative Roman patriots complained that their fellow Romans, especially the aristocratic youth, spoke Germanic tongues, wore Germanic clothes, and had Germanic hairstyles— they had a sort of Germanic hippie outlook, we would say nowadays.[70]

The conclusion remains that the Romans cooperated with the intruders at an early stage. Maybe there is no perfect solution to the problem of a lack of resistance. But I think that what might be called the "process of re-archaization" worked faster and more radically in the West than in the East. By the term "re-archaization" I mean:

1. Particularism and provincialism, alienation, and detachment from the empire as political reality grew with fatal speed in the course of the fifth century.[71] The Gallic senatorial class, for instance, was finally frustrated by the fall of "their" emperor Avitus.[72]

2. Destruction of the citystructure of the empire and thereby of those classes who identified themselves with the empire, was caused mainly by a mistaken tax policy toward the cities.[73]

3. The converse growth of huge holdings anticipated the medieval dominion over land and dependent people. Incidentally, those vast holdings of the leading senatorial class were actually called *regna*, "kingdoms," in contemporary sources. The same term *regna* was also applied to the whole empire, which the contemporaries could no longer consider to be a monolithic entity.[74] The classic Roman theory according to which the empire was a confederation of cities came to be replaced by the interpretation of the empire as a plurality of *regna*.[75]

---

[69] E. Zöllner, "Die politische Stellung der Völker im Frankenreich," *Veröffentlichungen des Instituts für österreichische Geschichtsforschung* 13 (1950) 94. Wolfram, *Intitulatio* 52.

[70] K. F. Stroheker, *Der senatorische Adel im spätantiken Gallien* (1948), provides sufficient evidence beyond the one-sided statement of Salvian, *De gubernatione Dei* 5.23: "quam quod plerique et honesti et nobiles et quibus Romanus status summo et splendori esse debuit et honori, . . . compulsi sunt, ut nolint esse Romani." Cf. 5.37. See also Claudius Claudianus, *In Rufinum* 2.11.78-85. D. Sinor, "The Barbarians," *Diogenes* 18 (1957) 51. Wenskus (n. 14 above) 537. Zöllner (n. 69 above) 107ff.

[71] Gerhart B. Ladner, *The Idea of Reform* (Cambridge, Mass. 1959) 251ff. One of the scholars who saw this phenomenon of alienation clearly is M. Rostovtzeff in his famous work *Social and Economic History of the Roman Empire*, ed. 2 (Oxford 1963) 1.534ff. In my opinion, however, he overstresses the "class" conflict, which no doubt existed, at the expense of the particularistic tendencies prevailing in various parts of the empire, which came to be called *regna*.

[72] Stein (n. 37 above) 1.368-373.

[73] M. Rostovtzeff (n. 71 above) 1.513ff. Jones (n. 3 above) 2.734ff.

[74] Wolfram, *Intitulatio* 35.

[75] Jones (n. 3 above) 2.712. Rostovtzeff (n. 71 above) 1.533ff.

4. This simplification of Roman political theory and philosophy reflected the simplification and change of the Roman institutions and vice versa. Irrational and mystical concepts of blood, innate power, and virtue became more and more important with the Roman ruling class itself, and not just with the Germanic kings and noblemen who were considered to be incarnations of, or at least derived from, Woden and other pagan gods. Cassiodorus, Theodoric's "prime minister," devised a genealogy of the Gothic kings of Italy which, modeled on the pattern of the mystical seventeen kings of Alba Longa from Aeneas to Romulus, named Gaut-Woden as the first king of the Goths. This was presented to the Roman senators with the following justification: "As you believe yourselves to be of old and venerable stock, so, too, are the kings who have to rule over you." This seventeen-king succession was of such a strong appeal that even a Lombard king of the seventh century used it for legitimization.[76]

Furthermore, the Holy Scriptures stressed the non-Roman concepts of king, nation, and the God-chosen state. The Scriptures also provided strong anti-Roman traditions that could easily merge with the popular anti-Roman feelings still alive in the western provinces of Spain and Gaul.[77] On a lower level, the Roman veneer was ripped off. Saint Jerome noted that the people in the countryside around Trier, one of the four imperial capitals at this time, spoke a Celtic idiom, not Latin.[78] The "rebirth" of nonclassical traditions and modes is reflected by the "name fashion" that favored non-Roman and nonurban rustic names.[79]

In sum, it was this very process labeled "re-archaization" that prepared the economically, geographically, and demographically weak West to lose its political identity; or to find a new identity in the smaller dimensions[80] of a

[76] Wolfram, *Intitulatio* 99ff.

[77] Fuchs (n. 41 above) 19ff.

[78] Jones (n. 3 above) 992f. J. B. Russell, "Celt and Teuton," *The Transformation of the Roman World*, ed. L. T. White, jr., UCLA Center for Medieval and Renaissance Studies: Contributions 3 (Berkeley 1966) 240.

[79] See "Prosopographie" in Stroheker (n. 70 above).

[80] The following consideration is more a feeling as yet than something known or even proved by sufficient evidence. But, considering the succession of centralization and decentralization in European history, on one hand, and refuting the rather primitive but popular description of this phenomenon as succession of order and chaos, on the other, I would say that one "trend" in European history has been the "thorough organization of the smaller space" after the universal body politic had failed to provide sufficient external protection and internal prosperity. From this point of view, the rise of the Frankish principalities during the dismemberment of the Carolingian empire could be much better explained as replacement of ineffective forms of government rather than as mere usurpation, as aristocratic chaos, and so on. The same would hold true for the territorial principalities in Germany, Italy, and elsewhere. Certainly, to assume this point of view, it was necessary to abandon the nineteenth-century belief in the growing, centralized, and universal national state as a "good thing."

Germanic kingdom that in turn largely depended on the cooperation of the Romans, especially of the senatorial class. It is also true that the senatorial class in Italy, Spain, and Gaul was courted by the new rulers. With royal support and permission, the senators achieved even more power and prestige than they had known before under the Roman emperors. This order became the backbone of the ecclesiastical organization, which transmitted a sort of administrative continuity to the new bodies politic; and, although theoretically not represented, it was in fact responsible for the kingdoms of the Franks, Burgundians, Goths, Lombards, and, to some extent, even for the African Vandals virtually becoming Latin kingdoms.[81]

The conclusion of all those considerations concerning the shaping of the Latin kingdom of the early Middle Ages could read as follows: The early medieval kingdom was founded by a *reiks* or *kuning*, a king of a victorious warrior retinue, whose rulership was institutionalized and incorporated into the western Latin half of the Roman empire by means of the federate system. This was actually an old Roman institution. It, however, was modified in favor of the king involved when the emperors or their representatives lost the image and credibility of being successful leaders of warrior retinues by themselves. The treaty of 382, settled between Theodosius and the Visigoths, made way for the maintainance and organization of non-Roman political structures on Roman soil. In the following decades, one king after another was allowed by imperial order and recognition to establish his kingdom on Roman soil. As leader of a federation, the king was automatically the highest military official in a given area. In Italy and Gaul, the king was able to occupy (or at least to attach himself to) the late Roman position of the patrician and commander-in-chief in the presence of the emperor. This highest magistrate abolished the Diocletian system that had separated military command from civil authority. Thus, it provided the best possible foothold for the king to become the head of the civil bureaucracy of each dominion. The kings in Spain and Roman Africa did not have this institutional link, but despite this disadvantage, their kingdoms followed the same patterns as did those in the north. Thus we are able to speak of the early medieval kingdom as a specific type of institution.

According to the treaties concluded by the Vandal and Spanish-Gothic kings with the empire, the local bureaucracy was required to obey the kings. The lack of the patriciate in Africa and Spain, however, decreased the loyalty of the kings involved to the empire. The kings of Roman Africa and Spain were the first to "shake off the yoke of the treaty," to become completely independent, almost sovereigns in the modern sense of the word. This evaluation, however, must not be considered to express a contemporary value judgment, since it is evident that Theodoric, who observed the closest relations

---

[81] See "Prosopographie" in Stroheker (n. 70 above).

to the empire, enjoyed the highest esteem among his contemporaries and fellow kings.[82]

An early medieval kingdom was a multitribal or polyethnic, yet Latin, successor state of the empire. It was called, to be sure, after the prevailing tribal element or elements. Except in the little-known Berber kingdom in and around Altava, the Romans were theoretically not represented. Personal law and right, however, secured their special status and national identity as it did for the other ethnic groups. The prevailing tribal element provided pre-Christian sacred traditions concerning king and kingship, and these were familiar and general enough that the Romans and other ethnic groups could identify with them. Christianization of the king and the inner circle of his people by no means abolished or weakened those traditions.[83]

The kingdoms were Latin, since the official language for expressing political, legal, and socioeconomic matters was usually Latin.[84] This fact mirrored the conviction of the newcomers that Latin was the only adequate means of communication for effective statehood; or, in other words, that Roman statehood, modified and re-archaized though it was, could be the only possible form of government and administration.[85] This image of "Romania" as a plurality of *regna*, ruled by powerful kings to whom one might belong one day, must have been established with the ruling class of the Germanic peoples when the majority of them were still outside the empire and before the final effort was made to create a kingdom on Roman soil.[86] Such a kingdom, finally,

---

[82] Wolfram, *Splendor imperii* (n. 1 above) 108ff.

[83] *Ibid.* 126.

[84] To Jones (n. 3 above) 2.992, must be added Wolfram, *Intitulatio* 42, as far as the Gothic language is concerned; Gothic was used for legal texts of which, however, nothing has remained.

[85] See n. 54, above.

[86] I consider the following evidence to be very important proof for this assertion. In 1927 a solid gold medallion, weighing one pound, was found at the Russian-Polish border. On the obverse it showed two crudely rendered emperors on horseback and a legend: REGIS ROMANORUM. I wrote to Philip Grierson, the expert in this field, about this strange legend on a strange piece of gold. He answered that the medallion was a contemporary Germanic copy of a Roman medallion of which no specimens are known. Since an inscription REGIS ROMANORUM on the original was quite inconceivable, Grierson imagined that the obverse of the original had no inscription at all, and that the legend on the Germanic imitation was an invention of the Germanic and—evidently—Latin-writing copyist. Finally, Grierson concluded on certain convincing grounds that this medallion was made from the plunder taken at Adrianople in 378. This piece of heavy gold still stems from the fourth century; it received its final shape by and for men to whom Roman statehood was important. They must have understood Latin, although they were no longer prepared to accept those "Latin" emperors as more than kings of nations, kings of the Romans, as this fit their own political experience and tradition; that is to say, with the memory of the vast and powerful Ermanaric kingdom still in mind. The kings of the Romans were interpreted as if they were kings of the Goths. They were, moreover, two kings fitting the patterns of age-old

was the expression of the trends of the period in which the reality of the Mediterranean empire was buried forever, although the ideas and hopes involved have never died.

University of Vienna
A-1010 Vienna 1
Austria

---

sacred kingship (see Wenskus [n. 14 above] 321). Yet these equations did not mean that one would or could conceive of any language but Latin to express terms of statehood connected with the Roman world. Cf. Wolfram, *Intitulatio* 36ff. K. Hauck, *Goldbrakteaten aus Sievern*, Münstersche Mittelalter-Schriften 1 (Munich 1970) 398.

PROCOPIUS AND THE CHRONOLOGY
OF CLOVIS'S REIGN

•

by Bernard S. Bachrach

The history of early medieval Europe is plagued by uncertain chronology, and the reign of Clovis (481-511) is one of the most serious examples of this problem. Some of the very important events of his reign, including his marriage, his victory over the Alamans, and his conversion, are variously dated. Other events such as the Frankish acquisition of the area between the Seine and the Loire and the elimination of the Frankish *reguli*, who ruled small warrior bands throughout northern Gaul, remain undated owing to lack of evidence.[1]

Despite an abundance of contested dates, scholars now seem to embrace one of two systems: the long chronology or the short chronology. The creator and champion of the former, André van de Vyver, supports the dates 503, 506, and 506 for the marriage, the victory over the Alamans and his conversion, respectively. The key to this chronology is the rejection of the dates found in the *History* of Gregory of Tours (the traditional chronology), especially 496 for the battle of Tolbiac, and the acceptance of the date 506 for the battle, on the basis of a letter written to Clovis by Cassiodorus for his ruler, the Ostrogothic king, Theodoric.[2] The most effective supporter of the short chronology has been Ferdinand Lot. In general, Lot argues for the acceptance of the traditional chronology (pre-496 for the marriage, 496 for the battle of Tolbiac, and 496-497 for the conversion). He does, however, contend that the Franks fought more than one battle against the Alamans

---

[1] For their help in the preparation of this paper I thank Professor Richard W. Emery of Queens College and Professor Walter Goffart of the University of Toronto. The problem of Frankish expansion is discussed by Lucien Mussett, *Les invasions: les vagues germaniques* ed. 2 (Paris 1969) 125-130, 300-303.

[2] André van de Vyver, "La victoire contre les Alamans et la conversion de Clovis," *Revue belge de philologie et d'histoire* 15 (1936) 859-914; 16 (1937) 35-94; "Clovis et la politique méditerranéanne," *Études d'histoire dédiée à la mémoire de Henri Pirenne* (Brussells 1937) 367-388; "L'unique victoire contre les Alamans et la conversion de Clovis en 506," *Revue belge de philologie et d'histoire* 17 (1939) 793-813; "La chronologie du règne de Clovis d'après la légende et d'après l'histoire," *Moyen Age* 53 (1947) 177-196. The problem is reviewed by Georges Tessier, *Le baptême de Clovis* (Paris 1964) chaps. 4, 5.

—one in 496 resulting in Clovis's conversion, and a final one in 506 which elicited Theodoric's letter.[3]

This approach to the chronology of Clovis's reign emphasizes certain important events but passes over others. One of the neglected events is the Frankish acquisition of the area between the Seine and the Loire, which is seemingly described in some detail by Procopius in his *Gothic Wars* (1.12. 13ff). During the past generation, however, scholars interested in the chronology of Clovis's reign have tended to ignore this text largely because of Ferdinand Lot's effort to discredit it.[4] In this paper I show that Procopius's description is a reasonably accurate account of Frankish expansion into the area between the Seine and the Loire, and that by utilizing this account some of the problems of the chronology of Clovis's reign may be solved.

In the twelfth chapter of his first book on the Gothic Wars, Procopius attempts to describe the barbarian conquest of Roman Gaul and in particular the rise to dominance of the Franks. After some general remarks on geography, he tries to indicate the location of the tribes that inhabited Gaul:

> The Rhine empties into the ocean. And there are many lakes in that region, and this is where the Germans lived of old, a barbarous nation, not of much consequence in the beginning, who are now called Franks. Next to these lived the Arborychi, who, together with all the rest of Gaul, and, indeed, Spain also, were subjects of the Romans from of old. And beyond them toward the east were settled the Thuringian barbarians, Augustus, the first emperor, having given them this country. And the Burgundians lived not far from them toward the south, and the Suevi also lived beyond the Thuringians, and the Alamanni, powerful nations. All these were settled there as independent peoples in earlier times.
>
> But as time went on, the Visigoths forced their way into the Roman empire and seized all Spain and the portion of Gaul lying beyond the Rhone River and made them subject and tributary to themselves. By that time it so happened that the Arborychi had become soldiers of the Romans. And the Germans, wishing to make this people subject to themselves, since their territory adjoined their own and they had changed the government under which they had lived from of old, began to plunder their land and, being eager to make war, marched

---

[3] Ferdinand Lot, "La victoire sur les Alamans et la conversion de Clovis," *Revue belge de philologie et d'histoire* 17 (1938) 63-69. Other attacks on van de Vyver's position have been made by J. Calmette, "Observations sur la chronologie du règne de Clovis," *Académie des inscriptions et belles-lettres, comptes rendus* (1946) 193-202 and C. Courtois, "L'avènement de Clovis II et règles d'accession au trône chez les Merovingiens," *Mélanges d'histoire du Moyen Age dédiée à la mémoire de Louis Halphen* (Paris 1951) 163-164. Cf. M. Chaume, "Francs et Burgundes," *Recherches d'histoire chrétienne et médiévale* (Dijon 1947) 147-162.

[4] Ferdinand Lot, "La conquête du pays d'entre Seine-et-Loire par les Francs," *Revue historique* 165 (1930) 241-253.

against them with their whole people. But the Arborychi proved
their valour and loyalty to the Romans and showed themselves
brave men in this war, and since the Germans were not able to overcome them by force, they wished to win them over and make the
two peoples kin by intermarriage. This suggestion the Arborychi
received not at all unwillingly; for both, as it happened, were Christians. And in this way they were united into one people, and came
to have great power.

Now other Roman soldiers also had been stationed at the frontiers of Gaul to serve as guards. And these soldiers, having no
means of returning to Rome, and at the same time being unwilling to
yield to their enemy who were Arians, gave themselves, together with
their military standards and the land which they had long been
guarding for the Romans, to the Arborychi and Germans; and they
handed down to their offspring all the customs of their fathers,
which were thus preserved, and this people has held them in sufficient reverence to guard them even up to my time. For even at the
present day they are clearly recognized as belonging to the legions
to which they were assigned when they served in ancient times. and
they always follow the customs of their fathers. And they preserve the
dress of the Romans in every particular, even as regards their shoes.[5]

Lot attacks Procopius's description on three counts. First he summarizes
the geographical description:

> Ainsi, dans l'idée de Procope, les Arboryques habitaient au sud des
> Francs, alors que ceux-ci étaient aux bouches du Rhin, et ils avaient
> pour voisins, à l'est, les Thuringiens, auxquels Auguste avait permis
> de s'établir en cette contrée. Au sud des Thuringiens étaient les
> provinces que tenaient le Bourguignons.[6]

Lot seems to misinterpret Procopius. Where Procopius indicates that the
Arborychi live "next to" (τούτων) the Franks, Lot contends that they lived
"au sud." Yet if the *Arborychi* are to be identified with the *Armorici* as scholars have done for some two centuries,[7] then clearly Procopius is correct in
stating that they lived "next to" the Franks, since they inhabited the *Tractus
armoricani*, which included the provinces of *Lugdunensis senona* and *Lugdunensis secunda*; both of these ran to the western or southwestern limits of
Belgica secunda, where Clovis had held sway as early as 486. But Lot's primary objection to Procopius's geography is his placing of the Thuringians

---

[5] Procopius, *History of the Wars* 5.12.8ff., trans. H. B. Dewing, Loeb Classical Library
3 (London 1919) 119ff. Cf. *Procopii Caesariensis opera omnia*, ed. J. Haury and G. Wirth
(Leipzig 1963) 2.64ff.

[6] Lot (n. 4 above) 243.

[7] *Ibid.* 242, esp. n. 2.

north of the Burgundians. Lot argues that while this may have been true between 413 and 436, it was not the case toward the end of the fifth century, the period Procopius claims to be describing. In short, Lot recognizes the validity of Procopius's description except for the location of the Thuringians. "La localisation de ces derniers en Gaule est certainement le résultat d'une méprise," he writes.[8] It seems clear that the main group of Thuringians was not located in the area Procopius indicated, but the Byzantine writer never says that he is describing the main group. Procopius qualifies his description of the Thuringians only by noting that they were settled by the Emperor Augustus. Although no other source confirms the origin of this settlement, it may well be that Augustus (or, more probably, some later emperor) settled a small group of Thuringians along the middle course of the Rhine. These may have been the same Thuringians whom Jordanes, describing events of the late fifth century, locates north of the Burgundians and east of the Franks.[9] It may also be the group that Clovis conquered in 491;[10] it is scarcely likely that he subdued the main body of Thuringians so early in his career. Gregory clearly indicates that the Thuringians did not fall under Frankish domination until 531 when Clovis's sons subjected them.[11]

Lot's second argument against Procopius's description is based upon the meaning of the word *Arborychi*. As noted above, scholars have considered the *Arborychi* to have been the *Armorici*. Lot, however, insists that "par *Arboryques*, Procope entend l'ensemble des Gallo-Romains du nord de la Gaule, les *Aborigènes*."[12] On philological grounds *Aborigènes* surely has no more validity as a corruption of *Arborychi* than does *Armorici*. Again, on historical grounds it is clear that the inhabitants of the *Tractus armoricani*, the *Armorici*, lived next to the Franks.[13]

Third, Lot argues against Procopius's contention that Roman soldiers remained in Gaul and that they preserved imperial military customs.[14] Procopius surely exaggerates the exactness with which the descendants of Rome's military contingents in Gaul preserved the formal military aspect of their forebears; it is equally clear that erstwhile units of the Roman army and their descendants lived and served in Gaul during the second half of the fifth

[8] *Ibid.* 244.

[9] Jordanes, *Getica* 55, ed. T. Mommsen, MGH Auct. ant. 5.1 (Berlin 1882) 130: "ab occidente Francos, a meridie Bergundzones, a septentrione Thuringos."

[10] Gregory of Tours, *Historia* 2.27, ed. Bruno Krusch and W. Levison, MGH Scr. rer. merov., 1.1, ed. 2 (Hannover 1937-1951) 73.

[11] *Ibid.* 3.7.103ff.

[12] Lot (n. 4 above) 244.

[13] Marc Bloch, "Observations sur la conquête de la Gaule romaine par les rois francs," *Revue historique* 154 (1927) 175 n. 1, accepts the identity of the *Arborychi* with the Armorici and concluded, "La confusion *Apbopuxoi* pour Armorici semble indiquer un renseignement oral." E. Zöllner, *Geschichte der Franken* (Munich 1970) 51ff. adds nothing new.

[14] Lot (n. 4 above) 245.

century. At the battle of Chalons in 451 there were enough Roman troops in Gaul to hold the right wing of the Roman line. The *alites* who served in Majorian's army in Gaul about 457 were probably the descendants of the *equites Mauri alites* listed in the *Notitia dignitatum* about 425 as serving in Gaul. Roman fighting men were expected to support Riothamus against the Visigoths about 467, and Count Paul was leading a force of Romans when he was killed at Angers about 470.[15] It would thus be hardly surprising if Roman troops remained in Gaul in Clovis's day. The continued use of Roman armor by the descendants of Roman soldiers (or for that matter by anyone who could get it) would be usual, for armor was hard to come by and very costly. For arms and armor to stay in use for several generations or even centuries was common.[16] Concerning the use of Roman shoes, however, Procopius was probably exaggerating.

While it would be rash to accept the accuracy of every word of Procopius's account, there seems to be no reason to disregard it completely, especially that part of his text which apparently equates the *Arborychi* with the *Armorici* and describes their relations with the Franks. Procopius's account of the union of the Franks with the inhabitants of the area between the Seine and the Loire can be of help in solving some of the chronological mysteries of Clovis's reign[17] According to Procopius, the Franks were Christians when they joined with the *Armorici*. He notes further that Frankish

[15] Jordanes (n. 9 above) 38.109 for the battle of Chalons; Sidonius Appollinaris, *Carmina* 5.476, ed. C. Luetjohann, MGH Auct. ant. 8 (Berlin, 1887) 199; and *Notitia dignitatum*, Oc. 6.53 and 7.177, ed. Otto Seeck (Berlin 1876) for the *Alites*. For Riothamus see Jordanes (n. 9 above) 45.118 and for Count Paul, Gregory (n. 10 above) 2.18.65. Bloch (n. 13 above) 175 n. 2, seems to defend Procopius on this point. See also E. Meyer, "Die Entstehung der Vasallität," *Festgabe für Rudolph Sohm* (Munich 1914) 46. See also my "A Note on Alites," *Byzantinische Zeitschrift* 61 (1968) 35.

[16] From the archaeological evidence it can be seen that armor was often repaired and refurbished and sometimes remained in use for as long as three hundred years. The survival of armor in reasonably good condition for some three thousand years is evidenced by archaeological finds and museum collections. Among the barbarians it was traditional to pass armor from generation to generation and this may account for the paucity of body armor in otherwise richly adorned graves. For the handing on of body armor see *Beowulf* 2036-2056, 2155-2162, and 2190-2193. For the archaeological evidence, see J. B. Thordeman, *Armor from the Battle of Wisby, 1361* (Stockholm 1939-1940) 1.24 and J. K. Anderson, *Ancient Greek Horsemanship* (Berkeley 1961) 215 n. 7.

[17] Ludwig Schmidt, "Aus den Anfängen des salfränkischen Königstums," *Klio* (1942) 34, 318ff., admits that Procopius's remarks under consideration here are not free of error, but he argues that Lot goes too far in rejecting them entirely. Curiously enough, Schmidt, while dealing with chronology (admittedly in a cursory manner), ignores the problem of Clovis's conversion and fails to deal with van de Vyver's arguments. Bertoald Rubin, "Prokopios von Kaisareia," Pauly-Wissowa, *Real-Encyclopädie der classischen Altertumswissenschaft* 23 (Stuttgart 1957) 438, also accepts the general import of Procopius's description and perceptively concludes that the fact that both the Franks and the Armoricans were Christians at the time of the union is "ein wichtiges Indiz für die Datierung."

raids were made into Armorica before there was a definitive attempt at conquest, but the campaign came to naught largely because the military forces of the *Armorici* were too strong for the Franks. Procopius's account contains more than a hint that subsequent Frankish success owed much to the union of the Franks and the *Armorici*.

Three dates in Clovis's reign are generally accepted by scholars. His victory over Syagrius in 486 gave him control over the kingdom of Soissons; his victory at Vouillé in 507 destroyed Visigothic power in Gaul; and his death occurred in 511.[18] The first two events are specifically related to the extension of Frankish power into the area between the Seine and the Loire. Only after the defeat of Syagrius in 486 did Clovis's territory border upon the lands of the *Armorici*. It is highly unlikely that Clovis would have mounted a campaign into Armorica before 486, thus passing through the potentially or actively hostile area ruled by Syagrius. It must be concluded that Clovis's major campaign against Armorica and the subsequent Frankish-Armorican alliance thus took place after 486. Similarly, Clovis would hardly have undertaken an extensive campaign against the Visigoths south of the Loire before having reached some agreement with the *Armorici* north of the Loire, whose powerful forces stood between the Franks and the Visigothic kingdom of Toulouse.[19]

When Clovis conquered Syagrius he and his followers were pagans, but the Franks were Christians when they allied with the *Armorici*. Clovis' conversion to Christianity has always been closely connected with the Frankish victory over the Alamans at Tolbiac,[20] and the date of this battle is the most disputed event in the entire Clovis chronology.[21] If Tolbiac took place in 506 as the proponents of the long chronology contend, Clovis would have had to be converted to Christianity, campaign against the *Armorici*, suffer a

---

[18] Mussett (n. 1 above) 128.

[19] In the Copenhagen continuation of Prosper's chronicles it is noted that the Franks took Bordeaux in 498. *Continuatio Haviensis Prosperi*, ed. T. Mommsen, MGH Auct. ant. 9 (Berlin 1902) 331: "Ann. XIIII Alarici Franci Burdigalam obtinuerunt et a potestate Gotharum in possessionem sui redegerunt capto Suatrio Gothorum duce." This makes no reference to Clovis and his followers. Since Bordeaux is accessible from the sea, it seems more than likely that it was taken for a short time by pirates who may have been Franks. It is unlikely that Bordeaux was held until 507 because Gregory, *Hist.*, 2.37.85ff., in describing Clovis's campaign against the Visigoths, makes no mention of Frankish warriors moving from the South (Bordeaux) to help Clovis catch the Visigoths in a pincer at Vouillé. If the Franks (Clovis) had held Bordeaux in 507 then this would probably have been their course of action to secure victory at Vouillé. The chronicler, however may be in error; the taking of Bordeaux may have been a venture of Saxon pirates settled in the Loire area or the date may have been wrong and may refer to Clovis's taking of the city in 507-508. Cf. J. M. Wallace-Hadrill, *The Long-haired Kings and Other Studies in Frankish History* (London 1962) 173-174.

[20] Wallace-Hadrill (n. 19 above) 169ff.

[21] Mussett (n. 1 above) 300-302.

defeat at their hands, negotiate an alliance, raise a new army, and campaign against the Visigoths all within one year; the area between the Seine and the Loire had to be secure before the Visigothic campaign could be undertaken.[22]

Such an effort would seem too difficult even for a warrior of Clovis's herioc energy and ability. If, however, the battle of Tolbiac took place in 496 and Clovis was converted shortly thereafter, then a decade still remained for the Armorican venture and the conquest of the Visigoths. Procopius's description tends to support the traditional short chronology found in the work of his contemporary, Gregory of Tours.

If Clovis defeated the Alamans at Tolbiac in 496, how soon therafter did he try to conquer the *Armorici* and fail? At Tolbiac Clovis probably led almost all the Franks as well as the non-Frankish followers of Syagrius. At that time "he was a 'Bretwalda' if ever there was one."[23] But when Clovis went against the *Armorici* he found them too strong for him. In 500-501 Clovis intervened in Burgundy and was unsuccessful. In short, after the great victory at Tolbiac in 496 and his conversion to orthodox Christianity, Clovis's power seems to have declined. Quite possibly his conversion, however greatly it pleased the Gallic bishops, antagonized some of his Frankish followers. That not all the Franks followed Clovis to the baptismal font may even be deduced from Gregory's account, which has significant omissions. Gregory writes that somewhat more than three thousand of Clovis's followers were converted with him.[24] Scholars have argued that this figure is not to be trusted since Gregory was following a biblical text (Acts 2.42);[25] it may be asked, however, why Gregory chose this particular biblical parallel. There are numerous other texts relating to mass conversions for example, Luke 3.21; John 3.23; Acts 8.12, 16.33, 18.8; Romans 10.2, 12.13); only the one used here by Gregory mentions a number. If all Clovis's followers had accepted conversion, one would expect Gregory to have proclaimed the fact to the world; even had only a bare majority done so, Gregory might probably have announced that "the Lord won a majority of the Franks that day." But Gregory does not make such a boast, as was his wont.[26] By choosing the number three thousand as represented in Acts 2.42, Gregory at once avoids indicating the percentage of Clovis's followers who were converted

---

[22] Wallace-Hadrill (n. 19 above) 173.

[23] *Ibid.* 169.

[24] Gregory, *Hist.* 2.34.76ff. Sir Francis Oppenheimer, *Frankish Themes and Problems* (London 1952) 56, says that "Gregory does not tell us of the *leudes* who seceded. We have here yet another of Gregory's omissions in favour of his orthodox *parti pris.*" See Wallace-Hadrill (n. 19 above) 104-105.

[25] Wallace-Hadrill (n. 19 above) 170.

[26] For examples of Gregory's boasting about conversions see *Historiae* 6.17, and 9.15.286 and 439.

and gives his readers a figure for the numerical strength of Clovis's forces which they would not think unreasonable.[27]

It may be noted that Hincmar, in his *Vita Remigii*, gives a rather modest account of the conversion, one that may reflect a surviving tradition: he relates that only about half of Clovis's warriors accepted conversion and that only after Clovis had defeated Ragnachar, the last of the *reguli* to be subdued, was the conversion of the Franks in Gaul completed.[28]

That Clovis feared that the Franks would react adversely to his conversion is explicitly stated by Gregory himself.[29] I suggest that there was indeed a sizable group of Franks who did not accept Christianity at that time and who were thereby estranged from Clovis, who in consequence commanded fewer warriors after his conversion than before. Such a development could well account for his failures against the Burgundians and the *Arorici*.

The major Armorican campaign appears to have been undertaken after the Burgundian venture (501), because the unsuccessful Armorican campaign was followed by an Armorican alliance which greatly strengthened Clovis's forces. The Franco-Armorican force that crushed the Visigoths at Vouillé in 507 would surely have been able to defeat the weaker Burgundians in 501 if such a force had then existed. Thus it would seem that the Armorican campaign took place some time after the Burgundian venture (501) and before the Visigothic campaign (507).

In 506, a decade after the first victory at Tolbiac, Clovis fought another campaign against the Alamans and soundly defeated them.[30] Some time after the Franco-Armorican alliance, Clovis met with Alaric II, the Visigothic

[27] This figure as well as the evidence given by Hincmar (see n. 28 below) is accepted by Robert Brentano, *The Early Middle Ages* (New York 1964) 13. It is difficult not to agree with the judgment of Wallace-Hadrill (n. 19 above) 153 that Hincmar knew more about the Franks than we do.

[28] Hincmar, *Vita Remigii* 30, ed. Bruno Krusch, MGH Scr. rer. merov. 3 (Leipzig 1910) 297ff. For Ragnachar's defeat see Gregory (n. 10 above) 2.42.92-93. Wallace-Hadrill (n. 19 above) 104-105.

[29] Gregory (n. 10 above) 2.31.76. The Burgundian king, Gundobad, Clovis's neighbor and contemporary, found himself in a similar position. Gundobad secretely professed orthodox Christianity but he was afraid to admit it because he feared that he would lose the support of his Arian followers if he did so. The possibility that Clovis's conversion met with serious resistance from his followers may well have influenced Gundobad's feelings and kept him from going against his people; this, despite Bishop Avitus's admonition that the people should follow the king and that the king should not follow the people. It is interesting that Gundobad's son Sygibert did accept orthodox Christianity, but only after Clovis had subdued the remainder of the Frankish *reguli* and united his people. Clovis's ultimate victory may have been viewed by Sygibert as the result of the power of the orthodox God; thus the Burgundian ruler was encouraged to adopt the orthodox way. For this episode see Gregory, *Hist.* 2.34.81-82. This is discussed in some detail by Lot (n. 3 above) 66ff.

[30] Lot (n. 3 above) 65.

king, to discuss ways of keeping the peace now that the two peoples had a common border.[31] This meeting would seem to have taken place not later than 505. Clovis's major campaign into Armorica, his defeat, and the subsequent negotiations probably consumed much of the period between 502 (or perhaps 503) and 504-505.

My interpretation of the sources helps to clear up some of the chronological problems of the decade preceding the Frankish victory over the Visigoths; and it may be of some help also in ascertaining the course of events in the last years of Clovis's reign. Clovis lost the support of many of his followers as a result of his conversion, and it seems that he did not reassert control over the Franks who had deserted him until after 507. It seems unlikely that very many of the *reguli* had returned to Clovis's banner by 501, when his Burgundian venture failed; nor had they returned for the Armorican campaign shortly thereafter. In the Visigothic campaign of 507, Chloderic, the son of Sygibert of Cologne, fought at Clovis's side but no mention of the other *reguli* is made in the sources.[32] For the campaign of 507 Clovis issued specific orders for the securing of fodder and water for his warriors' mounts.[33] Since it is generally agreed that the majority of the Franks were footmen,[34] it would seem that Clovis's concern about fodder reflects the needs of his new Armorican allies, among whom were the descendants of the Alan settlers of the Orléanais and the area to the north. The Alans, who had been settled in Armorica toward the middle of the fifth century, were horsemen.[35] In short, Procopius's contention that the Armorican alliance was a key to Frankish success seems reasonable, for the mounted Alan warriors assimilated into Christian Gallo-Roman Armorican society were worthy opponents for the Visigothic cavalry. Only a half century earlier between four and seven thousand Alan horseman from Armorica held the center of the Roman line against the Huns at Chalons.[36] If Clovis's Frankish followers numbered only about three thousand in the years immediately following 496, then it is clear that they could not defeat the *Armorici*, who must have been composed not only of the descendants of the *Armorici* who had fought at Chalons,[37] but also of the descendants of those Alans who had likewise fought there, and who had in the following half-century been assimilated into the *Armorici*. And it becomes clear too why this group was to play a significant role in subsequent Frankish expansion, as suggested by Procopius.

[31] Gregory *Hist.* 2.35.84.

[32] *Ibid.* 2.37.87-88.

[33] *Ibid.* 2.37.88.

[34] E. A. Thompson, *The Early Germans* (Oxford 1965) 130ff.

[35] See my article, "The Alans in Gaul," *Traditio* 23 (1967) 486ff.

[36] *Ibid.* 487-488.

[37] Jordanes (n. 9 above) 38.108.

After the campaign of 507 Clovis saw to it that Sygibert of Cologne and his son Chloderic were killed. After this he did away with Chararic and his son, then he destroyed Ragnachar and his brothers. With the elimination of the Frankish *reguli* in Gaul, the conversion of the remaining Franks was completed.[38] Having secured his position over the Franks by murder and conversion, Clovis turned his attention in what was to be the last year of his reign to the task of formalizing the affairs of his kingdom, through the recording of the *lex salica* and the approval of the acts of the Council of Orléans. In these efforts the hand of Clovis's Roman friends, both lay and ecclesiastical, lawyers and bishops, may clearly be seen.[39]

To conclude, the chronology of Clovis's reign begins about 481 with his accession to the throne of Tournai. In 486, with the help of Ragnachar but presumably without the aid of many of the other *reguli*, Clovis defeated Syagrius and conquered the kingdom of Soissons. In 491 Clovis conquered what seems to have been a small group of Thuringians east of his territory. Five years later, with the help of most of the Frankish *reguli* (who had probably recognized him as overlord), Clovis defeated the Alamans at Tolbiac. Shortly thereafter, probably, Clovis was converted to Christianity. This would seem to have encouraged many of the *reguli* to renounce his overlordship. With his power weakened and his army reduced to half its former size, Clovis ventured unsuccessfully into Burgundian affairs in 500-501 and shortly thereafter mounted an unsuccessful campaign into Armorica. But an alliance with the *Armorici* enabled Clovis to recover his position and strength. This, however, brought the Franks into direct contact with the Visigoths, and around 505 Clovis met with Alaric II at Amboise to discuss ways of keeping the peace between the two peoples. In 506 Clovis won another victory over the Alamans, who had probably regained some of their former strength during the decade of Frankish disunity that followed Clovis's conversion. In 507 Clovis and his Armorican allies moved against the Visigoths and defeated them decisively at Vouillé. Clovis devoted the remaining years of his life to eliminating the *reguli*, whose very existence he seems to have regarded as a threat to his position. Once all the *reguli* had been liquidated and the remaining Franks in Gaul had been converted, Clovis seems to have felt sufficiently secure to regularize his relations with the church and to have the laws of the Franks written down in an official compilation. Clovis died in

---

[38] Gregory treats the Visigothic campaign in chapter 37 of his *Historiae*, the murders of Sygibert of Cologne and Chloderic in Chapter 40. Chararic and his son are dealt with in chapter 41, and Ragnachar and his brothers are treated in chapter 42. See Mussett (n. 1 above) 130 and Oppenheimer (n. 24 above) 56 n. 5. It seems clear that Gregory's order of treating these events represents their chronological order. For the later conversion of Ragnachar's followers, see Hincmar (n. 28 above) 300.

[39] Both these developments are discussed by Wallace-Hadrill (n. 19 above) 77ff.

511 at about forty-five years of age. His power during the early stages of his career was based upon the war bands of the Frankish *reguli* in northern Gaul, but after his conversion many of the *reguli* deserted him, and it was the "Roman" elements in Gaul who supported him. With their help, he was able to achieve military success and to develop the institutions that were to provide the basis for more than two centuries of Merovingian rule in Gaul.

Dept. of History
University of Minnesota
Minneapolis, Minnesota 55455, U.S.A.

SAGENA PISCATORIS: PETER DAMIANI AND THE PAPAL ELECTION DECREE OF 1059

•

by Kennerly M. Woody

In the spring of 1059 a council assembled at Rome by the newly seated Nicholas II adopted a number of measures designed to reform the discipline of the church. Among them was a decree dealing with papal elections and sanctioning retrospectively certain departures from traditional practices which had been made when Nicholas II was elected in opposition to a prior claimant of the office (Benedict X). Peter Damiani[1] tells us that the cardinal bishops opposed Benedict energetically, and the prominent role in papal elections assigned to them by the decree is an uncontested landmark in the development of the cardinal college. More controversial is the decree's provision "saving the due honor" of Henry IV; this has been taken by some to contain, by deliberate vagueness, an attack on the dominant part that the Germanic emperors had played in papal elections of the past, and the decree has not infrequently been regarded as a papal declaration of independence from imperial control.[2] In recent years the attempt of Anton Michel to assign the decree to the pen of the fiery and intransigent author of the period's first major attack on lay investiture, Cardinal Bishop Humbert of Silva Candida, has enjoyed a wide popularity. The claims of the more moderate Damiani to at least a share in its preparation, however, have also been urged; in this paper I pursue evidence that supports those claims.

---

[1] See his ep. 3.4, PL 144.291. On Damiani, who was a cardinal bishop of recent date at the time of Nicholas II's election, see the two excellent biographies by F. Dressler, *Petrus Damiani: Leben und Werk*, Studia anselmiana 34 (Rome 1954) and J. Leclercq, *Saint Pierre Damien: ermite et homme d'église*, Uomini e dottrine 8 (Rome 1960). Cf. also the "Bibliografia su San Pier Damiano" in *Studi su San Pier Damiano in onore del Cardinale Amleto Giovanni Cicognani*, Biblioteca Cardinale Gaetano Cicognani 5 (Faenza 1961) xxi-xxiv. I hope to be able to publish soon a dissertation on Damiani, prepared under the direction of John H. Mundy, of which this article originally formed a part.

[2] On this question see the dissenting work of H. G. Krause, *Das Papstwahldekret von 1059 und seine Rolle im Investiturstreit*, Studi gregoriani 7 (Rome 1960). Krause's position has been accepted in the main in a careful review by H. E. Feine, *Zeitschrift der Savigny-Stiftung für Rechtsgeschichte, kanonistische Abteilung* (ZSSR) 48 (1962) 391-397 and by Friedrich Kempf, "Pier Damiani und das Papstwahldekret von 1059," *Archivum historiae pontificiae* 2 (1964) 73-89.

The literature on the decree is notoriously large and hard to deal with.[3] This is to be explained not merely by the importance of the subject itself, but also by the uncertainty that attaches to such preliminary questions as the establishment of the decree's text, the translation of the text once established, and the identification of its author.

The first of these questions was settled, definitively it seems, by Scheffer-Boichorst in 1879. Scheffer-Boichorst showed that neither of the two quite different versions of the decree that have come down to us are good copies of the original; that the "papal" and the "imperial" versions go back to different copies of the decree, both of them faulty; but that the parent manuscript of the imperial version was the less faulty of the two, except of course for these portions which were deliberately altered, presumably by some partisan of Henry IV. His arguments have been weakened in some regards and strengthened in others by later works, notably that of Grauert,[4] and there seems no reason to try to reopen the question, nor to revise Scheffer-Boichorst's solution as suggested by Pflugk-Harttung[5] and Michel[6] (namely, that the papal version has also been deliberately altered, or "forged").

In 1936 Michel provided what seemed an answer to both the second and third questions, by attempting to show that only Humbert of Silva Candida could have written the decree. (Since a sizable corpus of other writings of Humbert is available, Michel's thesis also provided a sort of lexicon to the decree, which could help to establish what meaning, or how precise a meaning, should be given to the words themselves—and also, of course, to the decree as a whole.[7]

Although Michel's designation of the decree as a concordat between papacy and empire was widely rejected,[8] his identification of its author as Humbert has been accepted almost eagerly, and was not seriously contested until 1960, when Krause reexamined Michel's supposed stylistic parallels between the decree and the works of Humbert, and countered them with even more striking parallels between the decree and the works of Peter Damiani.

Krause concluded that there is nothing striking or individual enough about the style of the decree to enable the stylistic method to say anything definite

[3] Scheffer-Boichorst was already making this complaint in 1879; see his *Die Neuordnung der Papstwahl durch Nicholas II* (Strassburg 1879) 4.

[4] H. Grauert, "Das Dekret Nicholas II von 1059," *Historisches Jahrbuch* 1 (1880) 501-602.

[5] J. von Pflugk-Harttung, "Das Papstwahldekret des Jahres 1059," *Mitteilungen des Instituts für österreichische Geschichtsforschung* (MIÖG) 27 (1906) 11-53.

[6] A. Michel, "Das Papstwahlpactum von 1059," *Historisches Jahrbuch* 59 (1939) 332-333. Against Michel: Krause (see n. 2 above) 14f., 75, 114ff.

[7] A. Michel, *Papstwahl und Königsrecht oder das Papstwahl-Konkordat von 1059* (Munich 1936).

[8] Cf. the reviews of Michel's works by W. Holtzmann, ZSSR 26 (1937) 541; R. Holtzmann, ZSSR 27 (1938) 150-153; H. W. Klewitz, ZSSR 30 (1941) 423; C. Erdmann, *Deutsches Archiv* 4 (1941) 536.

about its author. He accepted the parallels from Humbert and those from Damiani as of equal value, and, since both men were in the service of the curia and since the introductory protocol is similar to those of other conciliar decrees emanating from the curia, he argued that its style is simply the style of the curia.[9]

Although this is undoubtedly true of the protocol, and although the body of the decree—the *dispositio*—has nothing very unusual about its style, it is hardly true of the *narratio* with which the pope himself prefaced the body of the decree at the Roman Council of 1059. This *narratio*, as is often the case in medieval documents, fairly sparkles with rare words used in rare senses, with rather awkward and tortured images, and with the emotions that are suppressed in the *dispositio*—in short, with the individual. To anyone who asks who wrote this decree, the *narratio*, even on first reading, is very promising of an answer.[10]

In fact, in its way, this *narratio* was so impressive that it was later separated from the decree proper and appropriated by other writers. We find this being done only a few decades after the writing of the decree, by the author of the similar decree issued in 1087 by Victor III,[11] and, some centuries later, Dietrich of Niem repeated the complaints of Nicholas and Victor about their times, and found them appropriate at the Council of Constance.[12]

I think, therefore, that there is no reason to abandon entirely the search for the man who put the decree (or at least its *narratio*) into writing. My own hopes of being able to bring this search to an end may be ill-founded: the search is old, and has led from the assertion made in 1076 by the Council of Worms that Hildebrand was its author,[13] through the assumption of the canonists that its author was the pope to whom its protocol assigns it,[14] to the reassertion of Hildebrand's claims in the nineteenth century,[15] down to Michel's suggestion of Humbert, and Krause's contention that it is simply in the style of the curia (which seems to be another form of the "official" view of the canonists).

There seems no one left now but Damiani; Friedrich Kempf has argued that Damiani probably participated in the dictation of the decree,[16] and I

---

[9] Krause (n. 2 above) 257-270.

[10] See pp. 52-54 for the text of the decree.

[11] MGH Script. 7.751ff.

[12] Heinrich Finke, *Acta concilii constanciensis* 3 (Münster 1926) 123.

[13] MGH Const. 1.108.

[14] Gratian, *Distinction* 23, chap. 1: "Unde Nicholaus papa II in concilio lateranensi."

[15] See W. von Giesebrecht, *Geschichte der deutschen Kaiserzeit* 3 (Braunschweig 1848) 40: "Hildebrand—denn er ist der Verfasser des berühmten Decrets." Cf. Scheffer-Boichorst (n. 3 above): "die Papstwahlordnung vom Jahre 1059, welche Nicholaus II oder vielmehr der hinter ihm stehende Mönch Hildebrand . . . erliess."

[16] Kempf (n. 2 above) 81-82. Kempf based this suggestion on the "unusual" description of the simoniacs "als Geldpräger (*trapezitae*) mit Hämmern und Ambossschlagen" in the

contend that there are, in fact, very good reasons for ascribing the *narratio*, at least, to Damiani.

It seems, thus far, to have escaped comment that in the decree's *narratio* the word *sagena*, which ordinarily means "net," is used in the sense of "ship." It is true that there has been some uncertainty as to how this passage is to be translated, and Meyer von Knonau did translate the word as "Netz."[17] A net, however, can hardly be "shipwrecked," it is no great misfortune for it to be "submerged," and Ducange does give some examples of the use of this word in the sense of "navicula."[18] Krause is therefore correct, I think, when he translates it as "Schifflein," noting that Damiani (but not Humbert!) repeatedly used the expression *sagena piscatoris* to refer to Rome.[19]

Decree's *narratio* and by Damiani, PL 144.291, 145.95, 443; the similarity of these passages was also noted by Meyer von Knonau, *Jahrbücher des deutschen Reiches unter Heinrich IV und Heinrich V* 1 (Leipzig 1890) 87 and by Krause (n. 2 above) 266 and 269, but they failed to draw Kempf's conclusion: "entweder war er am Diktat direkt beteiligt, oder man hat sich von einem der 1058 geschriebenen Briefe (etwa dem an Nikolaus und Hildebrand gerichteten PL 145.443) inspirieren lassen ... Wahrscheinlicher ist unmittelbare Diktatbeteiligung." The association of the word *trapezita* with simony is not, however, unparalleled; cf. Benzo de Alba's *Liber ad Heinricum* 2.2, MGH script. 11.613: "Prandellus Sarabaita, filius Symonis, tuusque [i.e., Alexander II's] trapezita."

[17] G. Meyer von Knonau (n. 17 above) 1.135: "Die Säule sei wankend geworden und das Netz des Fischers durch die Stürme dem Schiffbruche preisgegeben."

[18] *Glossarium mediae et infimae latinitatis* 7 (Niort 1886) 265.

[19] Krause (n. 2 above) 265, cites the following examples of this use of *sagena* by Damiani: ep. 7.8, PL 144.447: "Ingerat tibi [Agneti] nauseam aula regalis imperii, sola tuis naribus sagena redolcat piscatoris," and ep. 2.1, PL 144.255-256: "Unicus et singularis portus romana patet Ecclesia: et, ut ita fatear, pauperculi piscatoris est parata sagena, quae omnes ad se sincere confugientes de procellarum intumescentium fluctibus eripit, et in littore salutiferae quietis exponit." There are, to my knowledge, six other places where Damiani uses the word this way: *Disceptatio synodalis*, MGH Libelli de lite (LL) 1.93: "Agamus illi gratias, qui prius sagenam Petri periclitari permisit, et turbine ventorum, et procellis undarum: sed ecce, ut regrediens manum tetendit, Petrum erexit." *Liber gratissimus*, MGH LL 1.69: "Immo qui vice Petri claves tenet aeclesiae ... et qui clavum sagenae regit, quae piscatoribus est commissa, malos pisces a bonis sub hac studeat dispensatione secernere, ut cum eis simul etiam bonos non adiciat reprobare." Opusc. 19, PL 145.423: "Nunc autem te in sagena Petri clavum regente, sub tranquilla pace tota Christi gratulatur Ecclesia." Opusc. 36, PL 145.595: "Qui solus de marini fluctus procellis eripitur, dum sagenam adhuc inter rupes et scopulos, inter minaces atque intumescentes undarum cumulos periclitari considerat." Sermo 15, PL 144.582-583: "Ad hoc itaque sidus sagenam mentis nostrae certi cursus linea dirigat." Opusc. 5 in PL 145.92: "[Ambrosius] quos corrigere non potuit, velut scatentem vermibus sentinam ex urbis huius [Mediolanensis] sagena projecit." Michel, *Papstwahl* 8, was unable to find parallels to this use of *sagena:* the "parallels" to this passage which he found in Humbert's work are: 1) a reference to the apostles in general as "piscatores": ep. 1 ad Cerularium, ed. Cornelius Will, *Acta et scripta* (Leipzig 1861) 118, and PL 143.745, "per piscatores et simplices [Deus] piscatus est sophistas"; 2) a comparison of simoniacs to someone trying to catch fish where there are none, *Adversus simoniacos* (Adv. sim.) 1.15, MGH LL 1.125; a statement that the simoniacs have "shipwrecked" their faith, Adv. sim. 1.20, MGH LL 1.134.

Since I first noticed this similarity between the use of *sagena* in Damiani's works and in the decree (in 1959, oddly enough), I have been unable to find any other instance, either in writings of the time or in earlier works, where the *navicula Petri* is called a *sagena*.[20] Moreover, as I have already indicated, there are other similarities between the language of the election decree, particularly of its *narratio*, and that of Damiani. This similarity was first noticed by Meyer von Knonau, who commented on a passage in Damiani's letter of 1058 to Archbishop Henry of Ravenna[21] that "in bemerkenswerter Weise klingen Wendungen der Einleitung des Papstwahldekretes von 1059 an wie: quot per simoniacae heresis trapezitas malleis crebrisque tunsionibus subjacuerit."[22] Krause, who made a more systematic comparison of Damiani's works with the decree, found enough other resemblances to make Damiani a much more likely candidate than Humbert. He is only prevented from taking the final step and nominating Damiani by his conviction that the stylistic method cannot prove anything, and that the style of the decree is simply that of the papal chancery.[23]

The only document that Krause adduced to prove this anonymity of the decree's style is the protocol from the synod of 769. The corresponding protocol of the decree of 1059 is naturally in this same chancery style. But it need hardly be said that this protocol does not form part of the decree itself, which is in the form of a speech delivered by the pope before the council; the protocol is a description of what went on there. Aside from this, all the documents that Krause produced to prove this "chancery style" thesis were written by Peter Damiani.

The further fact that the expression *sagena piscatoris* is so rare as almost to seem Damiani's personal seal not only argues against this chancery thesis and for Kempf's suggestion of *Diktatbeteiligung*, but calls for a careful examination of the expression itself. It is clearly impossible to *prove* that no one

[20] A number of examples of the use of the *navicula Petri* image in this period are given by H. Rahner, "Navicula Petri," *Zeitschrift für katholische Theologie* 69 (1947) 33-35. It would be futile to try to list more—one meets Peter's *navicula* almost as often as Peter himself—but it may deserve mention that Victor II referred to it in his motto: "Tu pro me navem liquisti, suscipe clavem" (PL 143.803).

[21] Ep. 3.4 in PL 144.291: "sicque per totam urbem velut officinam male fabricantis Simonis factam, vix aliud quam, ut ita loquar, malleorum atque incudum tinnitus auditur."

[22] Meyer von Kronau (n. 16 above) 1.87. Cf. Krause (n. 2 above) 266 and 269, who also compares the "ut eum ad apostolatus culmen proveheret" of this letter to the "ad apostolici culminis apicem provehunt" in chap. 4 of the decree (although there is nothing particularly unusual about this phrase).

[23] Krause (n. 2 above) 267ff.: "so konnte man mit dem gleichen Recht, mit dem Michel dem Kardinalbischof Humbert das Papstwahldekret zugeschrieben hat, den Kardinalbischof Petrus Damian für den Verfasser erklären, wenn sich eben mit dieser Methode überhaupt solch ein Beweis führen liesse." But Krause immediately uses the same method to prove that the style is that of the chancery!

else but Peter Damiani ever used the expression. Even if I were able to canvass all the literature of this period and answer that it contains no other *sagenae piscatoris*, the possibility would remain that some document now lost, or some conversation unrecorded, was the common source of both Damiani's and the decree's use of the expression.[24] I must, then, in the absence of absolute proof that no one else but Damiani ever used the expression, explore the probability that someone else *might* have done so.

That calls, first, for a careful study of the word *sagena* itself: how it may have come to have the meaning "ship," and when and where it was used with this meaning. But here the only literature to cite seems to be Ducange and his successors: to my knowledge, the ship *sagena* has never been the subject of any monograph, or even of a paragraph, outside the notice in Ducange, which badly needs to be resifted and elaborated.[25]

To work then: it is plain I think that the word could not have been used in the sense of "ship in general"; it must have referred to some specific type or types of ship. And since ships come and go (and since their names do not necessarily survive them), we may hope to discover not only what sort of ship a *sagena* was, but also the approximate dates of its birth and death.

Ducange lists three uses of *sagena* in the sense of "ship" which are prior to the ninth century. The first of these is in what Ducange calls the *Encomium sancti Basilei episcopi et martyris* 18.[26] The passage which he quotes, however, occurs in chapter 18 of what Godfried Henschen calls the *Passio sancti Basilei episcopi Amaseae*, and not in the *Encomium*.[27] Ducange

---

[24] Baronius also treated Damiani's *sagena piscatoris* as his "seal" in ascribing the *Disceptatio synodalis* to him: see *Annales ecclesiastici, ad annum* 1062, chap. 67: "sagena pro navicula superius usurpata a Petro Damiani, quibus intelligas eius esse hoc opus." For some reason he failed to use this argument where the election decree was concerned.

[25] The *Bulletin Ducange* 28 (1958) 38 adds nothing but the text of the passage from the *Vita Romuli* (see n. 41 below). The Byzantine use of *sagena* (ship) is discussed briefly, however, by H. Ahrweiler, *Byzance et la mer: La marine de guerre, la politique et les institutions maritimes de Byzance aux VII<e>-XV<e> siècles*, Bibliothèque byzantine, Études 5 (Paris 1966) 414. Ahrweiler groups it with the words *saktoura* and *katèna* as designating a class of rounded, heavy vessels, powered by sail rather than oar, used by the Byzantine navy to carry supplies but employed as warships by the Arabs and Dalmatians.

[26] Ducange, *Glossarium ad scriptores mediae et infimae graecitatis* (Lyon 1688). This is Saint Basil of Amasia (Pontus), who was martyred in Nicomedia by order of Licinius. His body was thrown into the Black Sea, and was recovered in the nets of some fishermen off Sinope. His disciples, who were present when the body was found, took it back to Amasia, and one of them (a deacon named John) wrote an account of the affair under the title: Μαρτύριον τοῦ ἁγίου Βασιλείου, επισκόπου ᾽Αμασείας.

[27] The passage runs as follows: Οὕτως οὖν γενομένου, ἀῤῥήτῳ τινὶ συμπλοκῇ τὸ σῶμα τοῦ ἐνδόξου ᾽επισκόπου καὶ μάρτυρος Βασιλείου ταῖς σαγίναις ἐνσπαργανοῦται. Αἰσθόμενοι τοιγαροῦν ἐν τῷ ἀνέλκεσθαι τὰς σαγίνας ἔχειν πλείονα φόρτον. Henschen, in AS Apr. 3.420, furnished a translation of this by Guilielmo Sirleto: "Hoc igitur facto, gloriosi episcopi et martyris Basilei corpus, admirabili quodam modo et supra quam dici possit, in sagena illa complicatum fuit. Cum igitur piscatores sagenam extrahentes, multum onus

evidently took his notes here rather hastily, and while it may be possible to translate this particular passage in such a way that *sagena* means ship or boat,[28] this does not seem to have occurred to Sirleto or to Henschen. The martyr's body is described as being "swaddled"[29] in the σαγίναις, and if Ducange had read the preceding chapter more carefully he would have found *sagena* used twice there in its ordinary sense of "net."[30] Moreover, it is always used in the plural, as a synonym for δίκτυα, while it is evident that the fishers have only one boat (a κάραβος).

Moreover, it was shown by Le Cointe that the *Diploma Chilperici*, in which Ducange's second early example of *sagena* as "ship" occurs, is a spurious one, dating at the earliest from the ninth century.[31] And in this case, although the translation as "boat" is possible, it is not necessary; the charter confers on the bishop of Tournai the "teloneum de navibus super fluvium Scalt . . . de quolibet commertio seu et de carrigio vel de saginis necnon de ponte super flumine Scalt, vel de omnibus venalibus ubicumque vendantur." These are different sorts of *telonea*, the words "navibus . . . carrigio . . . saginis . . . ponte . . . omnibus venalibus" are not a piling up of synonyms, and the "teloneum . . . de saginis" may be either a tax on netloads of fish taken, or the word may be used in the sense of "tractus sagenae" (fishing license), which Ducange gives under "Sagena 1" and defines as "ius piscationis." The same holds true of the other example of this sort which he gives, a charter of immunity granted in 859 by Charles the Bald in favor of the monastery of Beaulieu in the Limousin, according to which "nullus exactor vel judex publicus, nec de navibus, nec de saginatibus, vel carris, seu quibuslibet exactionibus . . . quicquam ab eis accipiat."[32]

With the elimination of the *Encomium Basilei* and of the spurious charter of Chilperic, we are left with the use of the word in the *Strategicon* of "Maurice" as the only example that is earlier than the ninth century. Here the word clearly means "ship"; a supply or transport ship used with the "other heavier

---

in illa esse praesensissent." Ducange may have been confused by the fact that Henschen translated part of the "Encomium" (whose text he was the first to print: *ibid.*, app. lvi-lx) and used it as a sort of preface (416-417) to Sirleto's translation of the "Passio," which he gave under the title of *Acta martyrii* in 417-422. The heading *"Pars encomii"* is set in much larger type than the *"Acta martyrii"* on the facing page, so that the latter looks like a subtitle.

[28] Ducange may have been misled by the fact that φόρτος can mean "ballast," and by the impression that when *sagena* was spelled with an iota it meant ship (Cf. his appendix col. 166: *"Lexicon Ms. ex Cod. Reg. 3183.* σαγένη, τὸ δίκτυον, σαγίνη . . . τὸ ὅπλον ί. Leg. τὸ πλοῖον.") The reference in the lexicon, however, is probably to the net of the gladiator.

[29] Ἐνσπαργανοῦται ; cf. Luke 2.7, 12.

[30] App. lii: ἡ δευτέρα . . . τῶν σαγίνων βαλή; . . . τὰς σαγίνας . . . ῥίψαι . . . εἰς θάλασσαν.

[31] Charles Le Cointe, *Annales ecclesiastici Francorum* 2, chap. 5 *ad annum* 575 (Paris 1666) 156f. Cf. MGH Dipl. imp. 1.130 n. 22.

[32] Maximin Deloche, *Cartulaire de l'abbaye de Beaulieu* (Paris 1859) 15f.

ships" ($\beta\alpha\varrho\upsilon\tau\acute{\epsilon}\varrho\omega\nu$ $\sigma\varkappa\epsilon\upsilon\tilde{\omega}\nu$) in support of the faster warships (the *dro-monia*).[33] Unfortunately, the *Strategicon* of Maurice has not been edited since 1664, and as yet neither its date, nor its author, nor its exact relation to similar Byzantine tactical works have been established with certainty. The datings given range from the time of Urbicius (early sixth century) all the way to the ninth century.[34] But the earlier datings, especially the traditional one of the time of the emperor Maurice (582-602), have received the wider recognition,[35] and this dating is also supported by the possibility that the ship meant by Maurice may have been of a different sort from what was meant by *sagena* in the ninth and tenth centuries.

Most of the other uses of *sagena* (ship) fall roughly between 870 and 950, and from these it becomes clear that a *sagena* was a small, fast ship used by Saracen pirates, by residents of the maritime cities of Italy, and by the inhabitants of the Dalmatian coast. It is first mentioned during this period in a letter from Emperor Louis II to Basil I which was written in 871.[36] Louis, who had captured Bari the year before, and who was now trying to take Tarentum from the Saracens, asked Basil to send a fleet to cut off the Saracens in Tarentum and Calabria from North Africa, and also to prevent the Neapolitans from supporting the *sagena* raids of the Saracens of Palermo and Calabria.[37]

[33] Mauricii, *Ars militaris* 12.8.21, ed. J. Scheffer (Upsala 1664) 347. The versions of this passage included in what A. Dain, *Naumachica* (Paris 1943) 11 calls the *Ambrosiana collectio* of Byzantine works on naval tactics associates the *sagenae* with "the transport and heavier ships" ($\alpha\tilde{\iota}$ $\sigma\alpha\gamma\tilde{\eta}\nu\alpha\iota$ $\varkappa\alpha\grave{\iota}$ $\tau\grave{\alpha}$ $\varphi\omega\varrho\tau\eta\gamma\acute{\alpha}$ $\pi\lambda o\tilde{\iota}\alpha$ $\varkappa\alpha\grave{\iota}$ $\beta\alpha\varrho\acute{\upsilon}\tau\epsilon\varrho\alpha$, *ibid.* 41, 101).

[34] The literature favoring a later date is summarized by Lynn White, jr., *Medieval Technology and Social Change* (New York 1962) 144. The work seems to be a compilation, so that an early date for one portion cannot exclude a later date for others; cf. Carl Krumbacher, *Geschichte der byzantinischen Literatur* 1, ed. 2 (Munich 1958) 636: "eine ziemlich unselbständige Kompilation." According to R. Vari, "Zur Überlieferung mittelgriechischer Taktiker," *Byzantinische Zeitschrift* 15 (1906) 71f., 82f., the prologue and bk. 12 (in which the *sagenae* are mentioned) are later than the rest of the work.

[35] Gyula Moravcsik, *Byzantinoturcica*, ed. 2 (Berlin 1958) 1.417-419 defends a date in the time of Maurice. Dain (n. 33 above) 39 dates it even earlier, in the time of Justinian. Since the *sagena* passage is meant for large rivers like the Rhine, Danube and Euphrates, rather than the smaller rivers of Italy and Greece (which he suggests would be the only ones involved at that time). Dain argues that it derives from some earlier source; however, an earlier section of Maurice (11.5.272ff.) deals with warfare against the Slavs along the Danube and with the same problem (river crossings under fire) as the *sagena* passage; I fail to follow him.

[36] The letter is quoted in the *Chronicon salernitanum* written in the second half of the tenth century by a monk of Salerno (ed. Waitz, MGH Script. 3.527). The passage where *sagena* occurs (chap. 107) was also given by Baronius, *Annales ecclesiastici, ad annum* 871, chap. 70. On the authenticity of this letter, which was first questioned by Michele Amari, *Storia dei Musulmanni di Sicilia* 1 (Florence 1854) 381, see Jules Gay, *L'Italie méridionale et l'empire byzantin* 1 (Paris 1904) 84-88. Gay defends its authenticity and the 871 date, and ascribes it to Anastasius Bibliothecarius.

[37] "Et quia nonnulli Saracenorum Panormi latrunculi cum sagenis, solatio et refugio iam memoratorum Neapolitanorum freti, per Tirrenum mare debachantur, oportet ut et

One would expect the ships used by these Arab "latrunculi" to be especially fast, and this can also be gathered from an incident that occurred slightly before Louis's letter and which is reported in the nearly contemporary *Vita s. Athanasii episcopi neapolitani*.[38] There we find the prefect of Amalfi, Marinus, using twenty *sagenae* to run a blockade of Nisita established by the Neapolitans and Saracens. The author fails to identify the ships used by the latter. I assume that they are also *sagenae*; at any rate, Marinus was unable to outdistance them, and had to fight his way out.[39]

It appears, then, that both the Saracens and the Christians of Southern Italy were using this ship, and a somewhat later source, the anonymous author of the *Vita s. Romuli*,[40] tells us that the Saracens from Spain who established themselves toward the end of the century (about 890) in Le Freinet also arrived in *sagenae*.[41]

We learn most about the *sagena* from the *De administrando imperio* of Constantine Porphyrogenitus, who tells us in chapter 31 that the navy of the Croats on the Dalmatian coast includes small *kondourai* carrying ten

---

hoc [*sic*] capiendos tuae fraternitatis stolus sine dilatione mittatur. Isti [Neapolitani] sunt qui et Calabritanis Saracenis indefesse stipendia praebent, et hiis qui Panormi sunt auxilia cotidiana ministrant; unde si capiantur, sagenae maxima ex parte Saracenorum tam Panormi quam Calabriae constringuntur."

[38] Ed. B. Capasso, *Monumenta ad neapolitani ducatus historiam spectantia* 1 (Naples 1881) 96: *Bibliotheca hagiographica latina* (BHL) (Brussels 1898-1901) 735. The Bollandist editor, G. Cuperus, dated this life between the death of Athanasius in 872 and the translation of his body to Naples in 877 (AS Jul. 4.83). There have since been two attempts to assign it to the twelfth century: the first by A. S. Mazzochi, *De sanctorum neapolitanae ecclesiae episcoporum cultu* (Naples 1753) 363ff., and the second by Erich Caspar, *Petrus Diaconus und die Monte Cassineser Fälschungen* (Berlin 1909) 93-104. The author's repeated references to himself as a contemporary of Athanasius, however, and the fact that one of the manuscripts containing this life has been dated at the end of the tenth century or the beginning of the eleventh, support the date given by Cuperus, or at least one near the turn of the tenth century. Against Mazzochi, cf. Waitz, MGH Script. rer. lang. 1.401 n. 6, and Capasso 1.84 n. 3 and 213 n. 3; against Caspar, cf. H. Moretus (Review of Caspar), *Analecta bollandiana* (AB) 29 (1910) 169; Hippolyte Delehaye, "Hagiographie napolitaine," AB 59 (1941) 21. On the dating of the manuscript, Moretus says: "écrit, pour cette partie du moins, à la fin du xe siècle ou peu après." Cf. A. Poncelet, AB 30 (1911) 167: "saec. XI in."

[39] "Lodoycus imperator Benevento degens, nondum capta Bari, doluit ex intimo corde una cum augusta, et concite miserunt Marino, Prefecto Amalphi, ut veniret, et tolleret sanctum virum ex iam praefata insula, et sanum duceret Beneventum. At ille iussis obtemperans Augustorum, venit cum viginti sagenis, et tulit inde sanctum virum. Hoc audientes Neapolites exierunt super eos navaliter una cum Saracenis, persecutique sunt eum procul ab urbe. Sed Deus, qui subvertit Pharaonis currus, confregit et illorum tunc superbiam, et in fugam versi sunt; Saracenis captis ibidem et occisis."

[40] The Premonstratensian editor, Cornelius Byeus, dates this life of "San Remo" (BHL 7335) about 930: AS Oct. 6 (Tongerloo 1794) 206.

[41] "Saracenorum autem gens . . . sagenis ascensis, pro more piraticam exercens Arelatem urbem invasit, provincialesque depopulans usque ad Fraxenetum pervenit. Quo latibulo latrocinandi invento resedit" (*ibid.* 209).

men, larger ones carrying twenty men, and *sagenae* carrying forty men.[42]
His description of these *sagenae* as warships may be contradicted by his statement a few lines above that the pacific, "baptized" Croats do not use their
kondourai and *sagenae* for war, but that those of the Croats who went to engage
in commerce go around in them from town to town in "Pagania" (that is,
the Narentan territory), the gulf of Dalmatia, and as far as Venice. Constantine, however, obviously regards the *sagenae* as primarily warships, since
some lines later he distinguishes *kondourai* and *sagenae* from "merchant ships"
(ἐμπορευτικὰ πλοῖα),[43] and in chapter 30 he describes the ships of the Narentan pirates as *sagenae*.[44]

To judge from these scraps of information, it would seem that the *sagena*
was some fast cargo ship that could double as a raiding or transport ship
and could carry forty men. This versatility would explain its popularity
with the pirates of Le Freinet, Palermo, and Dalmatia.

Since the appearance of the word *kondoura* indicates that the emperor
is relying in this section on some sort of intelligence report using the indigenous
terminology,[45] and since the word *sagena* does not appear in the other portions
of his work, it would seem that *sagenae* were not a part of the Byzantine fleet
in his time. It is true that Ducange also lists Constantine's *De thematibus*
2.1 and 6 as examples of the use of *sagena* (ship).[46] But in this case the translation "net" seems preferable: the emperor describes the Romans' conquest
of their empire by saying that they "unfolded [or "stretched"] their *sagena*
to all the limits of the cosmos,[47] and that all Greece "came under" this *sagena*.[48]
Since ships cannot be unfolded or stretched, and since things are put *in* them
rather than *under* them, it would seem that Constantine has in mind the net
of a gladiator. At any rate, it did not occur to Banduri to translate the word
as "ship" in either passage.[49] Ducange's translation may have been suggested

---

[42] Constantine Porphyrogenitus, *De administrando imperio*, ed. Gyula Moravcsik and
trans. R. J. H. Jenkins (Budapest 1949) 1.150.

[43] *Ibid.* 152, concerning the "unbaptized" Croats and their lack of a navy: Ἀλλ' οὐδὲ σαγή-
νας κέκτηνται, οὔτε κονδούρας, οὔτε ἐμπορευτικὰ πλοῖα.

[44] *Ibid.* 144.

[45] Cf. F. Dvornik, in *De administrando imperio 2, Commentary*, ed. R. J. H. Jenkins
(London 1962) 128. He suggests that Constantine's source may have been "a Latin document read by Constantine's informant in one of the Latin coastal cities or deposited in the
imperial archieves."

[46] Ed. A. Pertusi, in *Studi e testi* 160 (Vatican City 1952). On Pertusi's attempt to date
book two at the end of the tenth century see G. Ostrogorsky, "Sur la date de la composition du Livre des Thèmes," *Byzantion* 23 (1953) 44. Ostrogorsky dates it ca. 934-935.

[47] 2. 1 (84): Ἀφ οὖ γὰρ ἡ τῶν Ῥωμαίων ἀρχὴ τὴν ἑαυτῆς σαγήνην ἐξήπλωσεν εἰς πάντα
τὰ ιοῦ κόσμου τέρματα.

[48] 2.6 (91) : πᾶσα ἡ Ἑλλάς . . . ὑπὸ τὴν τῶν Ῥωμαίων σαγήνην ἐγένετο.

[49] PG 113.110: "Etenim ex quo Romanorum principatus sagenam suam ad omnes mundi
limites expandit"; 126: "omnis Graecia . . . Romanorum sagenae jugum subierunt."

by the use of verbs that contain the root σκευ-; but σκεῦος is a word of many meanings.

The relative infrequency of the word *sagena* (ship) in Byzantine sources as compared with those from the West is striking. In addition to Constantine's notice on Dalmatia the only other Byzantine writer to use the word is Maurice, and he was probably thinking in this "river-crossing" passage of the fighting against the Slavs along the Danube which he describes in 11.5(272ff.).

This apparent absence of a ship called *sagena* in the eastern Mediterranean may be explained by its comparative smallness, since the fleets of the East would probably have been larger and more specialized than those of the West, where the political fragmentation on both sides, Saracen and Christian, meant warfare on a smaller scale, approaching piracy.

The use of the word by Constantine is the last we meet with for a long time. After a gap of over a century and a half, during which *sagena* (ship) appears only as a symbol, in Damiani and in the election decree of 1059, it suddenly crops up twice more, at the turn of the twelfth century, and then disappears forever (except, of course, in works influenced by the decree, like that of Dietrich of Niem). We meet it once in an epic poem celebrating Pisa's conquest of Majorca in 1115, which was written soon afterwards by a participant, Henry of Pisa; and it occurs again, in the diminutive form *sagenula*, in the life of Saint Aldhelm (the first abbot of Malmesbury), which was written shortly before 1100 by an Italian monk at Malmesbury named Faricius (d. 1117). Henry of Pisa puts it at the end of a list of the ships prepared by the Pisans for their Majorcan expedition.[50] Faricius tells us that Aldhelm was taken out to the *scapha* of some merchants at Dover in a *sagenula*.[51] It is conceivable that the word has been brought back to life by its use in the election decree; but this is hardly probable, especially since both of these writers, as Italians, hail from what seem to have been the home waters of the ship. (It may be of significance that when William of Malmesbury described the same incident in the life of Aldhelm, he did not use the word *sagenula*; according to William, the saint was taken out to the *navis* of the merchants

---

[50] Carlo Calisse, *Liber maiolichinus de gestis Pisanorum illustribus* (Rome 1904):

> Ceditur omne nemus, cesum descendit ad undas.
> Hoc varie fiunt diviso robore naves,
> Gatti, drumones, garabi, celeresque galee,
> Barce, currabii, lintres, grandesque sagene.

Ducange suggested that *sagene* might be a mistake for *sagittae*, but all the manuscripts have *sagene*. On Henry, see M. Manitius, *Geschichte der lateinischen Literatur des Mittelalters* 3 (Munich 1931) 674.

[51] PL 89.73B: "Rogant mercatores quod ad eos venire . . . non differat, eorumque inspicere scapham . . . non recuset. Tunc Dei famulus . . . sagenulam ascendit, et eos continuo . . . adivit" BHL 256. On Faricius, who nearly succeeded Anselm as archbishop of Canterbury, and who died as abbot of Abingdon, see W. Dugdale, *Monasticon anglicanum* 1 (London 1846) 508.

in a *scapha*).[52] To Faricius, it is clearly not much more than a rowboat. Henry of Pisa may have in mind something not much larger: although he says "grandes sagene," his list of ships seems to proceed from the larger to the smaller, and the *sagenae* come last, after the *lintres* (which are, literally, "washtubs").

It is quite puzzling that (with the exceptions of the references to a *sagena piscatoris* made by Damiani and the election decree, and—possibly—of the *sagenula* of Faricius) there is no indication that a *sagena* (ship) had anything to do with fishing. Why then was it named after *sagena* (net)? There is a remote possibility that the name was borrowed from some other language, and it is possible that Italian sailors, when they heard the Saracens refer to their ships as *sefine*, corrupted this to *sagenae* (this being their only nauticial term with a similar pronunciation).[53] This possibility is unlikely, however, since Maurice (whatever his date is) never mentions the Saracens, and the only naval tactics he describes are meant for rivers.[54]

That leaves two other explanations: either the word was borrowed from some language other than Arabic, or else it originally described a fishing boat and only began to find literary mention after it had been put to other uses. It remains somewhat surprising, however, that only the "symbolic" *sagena* of Damiani and the election decree belongs to a fisherman.

A second mystery is the fact that the ship *sagena* almost disappears from the sources after the middle of the tenth century. The reason, perhaps, is that as the Byzantine-Arab struggle intensified in the central Mediterranean during the ninth and tenth centuries, the day passed to larger ships. In 827, the headquarters of the western naval theme, Sicily, had to be rescued by the eastern fleet,[55] and Venice lost consistently to the Saracens until she began copying the Byzantine *chelandia* in the 850s.[56] In the early tenth century, under Romanus Lecapenus, the Byzantine navy seems to have gone in for even larger ships.[57] At any rate, when Nicephoros Phocas retook Crete in 960-961, he was using ships with as many as 250 rowers,[58] and the Cretan expedition of 910 already included battleships (*dromonia*) with 230 rowers

---

[52] *De gestis pontificum anglorum* 5, PL 179.1644, BHL 257.

[53] *Sefine* seems the only similar Arabic word for ship, since *sage* means a sort of canoe. Cf. Hans Kindermann, *"Schiff" im Arabischen* (Bonn dissertation 1934) 38, 40.

[54] See n. 35 above. R. Vari (n. 34 above) 71-72, argues that Maurice refers to the Saracens under the pedantic name of "Persians."

[55] See Archibald R. Lewis, *Naval Power and Trade in the Mediterranean, A.D. 500-1100* (Princeton 1951) 133 and 157.

[56] John the Deacon, *Cronaca veneziana*, ed. G. Monticolo (Rome 1890) 115: "duces ad sua tuenda loca eo tempore duas bellicosas naves tales perficere studuerunt, quales numquam apud Veneciam antea fuit, que greca lingua zalandriae dicuntur."

[57] Lewis (n. 55 above) 158.

[58] *Ibid*. 184.

and 60 marines.[59] By the time of Constantine Porphyrogenitus the Croatian navy's largest vessels were forty-man *sagenae*; this may have been as much a sign of their military decadence as the fact that the number of their *sagenae* had decreased from eighty in the time of Kresimir II (928-945) to thirty in that of Michael Kresimir II (949-969);[60] it is possible, however, that the use of the smaller ships was favored by the intricacies of the Dalmatian archipelago, and that the *sagena* continued to be "the ship" in this region longer than elsewhere for that reason. In Constantine's time, the Croats were explaining their nonaggressive ways (and the weakness of their navy?) by the myth that they had been sworn to them when they were converted to Christianity under Basil I; hence, they said, they used their *sagenae* only for peaceful purposes. But their troublesome neighbors, the Narentans, continued their piracy without much opposition throughout the tenth century, until they were defeated by Doge Pietro Orseolo II in 998—and the *sagena* is the only Narentan ship mentioned by Constantine Porphyrogenitus. This continued use of the *sagena* off the Dalmatian coast might, however, explain the deciveness of their defeat by Orseolo. In any case, the use and importance of the *sagena* must have declined sharply between 949, when Constantine described its use along Dalmatia, and 1115, when Henry of Pisa mentions it last (and almost as an afterthought) in the list of ships prepared for the Majorcan expedition.

In conclusion, the use of the word in this sense must still have been *familiar* to the Italian audiences of Damiani in the 1050s. But probably it is only along the Dalmatian coast that one might expect to encounter the word in this period as a current synonym for *navis* or *navicula*, which could be used interchangeably for one or the other.

This leads me to chance the conjecture that it was Damiani's contact with Dalmatia (along with his penchant for esoteric, Greek-sounding terms in general) which led to his use of the word. The location of Ravenna naturally involved it with Dalmatia, and Orseolo's conquest of the coast cities there had led Romuald to settle for a while in Istria, where (as Mittarelli notes)[61] he had some influence on Bishop Gaudentius of Ossero, just to the south of Istria. Damiani also had contacts with Gaudentius, who resigned his office to live as a monk in the monastery of Santa Maria Portusnovi near Ancona about 1042, and died there in 1045. Damiani refers to Gaudentius twice,[62]

---

[59] L. Bréhier, "La marine de Byzance du VIII e au XI e siècle," *Byzantion* 19 (1949) 14; cf. *ibid*. 11: the *Taktica Leonis* 19.4 gives the normal complement of a dromon as 130 men, of whom 100 were rowers. This work has been assigned both to Leo III (717-741) and to Leo VI (886-911); Bréhier assumes the former; the latter is favored by Moravcsik (n. 35 above) 1.401-406.

[60] *De administrando imperio* 1.151. Cf. Dvornik's remark in 2.129-130.

[61] J. B. Mittarelli and D. A. Costadoni, *Annales camaldulenses* 1 (Venice 1755) 258.

[62] Both times in the same context, opusc. 19 PL 145.425, opusc. 20, PL 145.446.

and it may even have been in the conversations he says he had with him that the use of *sagena* as a synonym for ship was impressed on his mind.

With this suggestion I broach a third (and final) mystery: why did Damiani *misuse* the word as he did? It has to be called a misuse not only because none of the other sources (except, of course, the election decree) describe this ship as a fishing boat, but also because, in Damiani's first use of it in the *Liber gratissimus*, he has clearly mistranslated the *sagena* (net) of Matthew 13.47.[63]

The reason, I suspect, is that Damiani was not even conscious that the word *could* mean net. So far as I can discover, he never uses it in that sense: in the one dubious place where he may have done so,[64] he simply quotes Job 40.26: "Nunquid implebis sagenam pelle eius, et gurgustium piscium capite illius?" Here it could very easily be translated "boat," and, in any case, the whole passage is one that Damiani has taken over more or less bodily from Gregory the Great.[65] (And it *is* possible, with the idea in your head that the word means boat, to translate it that way in Matthew 13.47.)

This brings me to an obvious remark: the reason that this use of the expression *sagena Petri* is so rare is not only that the *sagena* (ship) was apparently becoming obsolete in this period, and in any case was apparently not a fishing boat; but also that, in the intensely conservative vocabulary of allegorical exegesis, *sagena* already had a symbolic function of its own, which was independent of that of *navicula*.[66] The Bible, needless to say, always uses the word in its original and ordinary sense of "net," and the same naturally holds true of those who went to the Bible for their ideas. In fact, it would seem to require a very particular set of circumstances for anyone to read the commentaries on the various scriptural passages in which *sagena* appears—as Damiani undoubtedly did—and emerge with the unshaken faith that the word meant "ship" there.

---

[63] Opusc. 6, MGH LL 1.69: "Immo qui vice Petri claves tenet aecclesiae . . . et qui clavum sagenae regit, quae piscatoribus est commissa, malos pisces a bonis sub hac studeat dispensatione secernere, ut cum eis simul etiam bonos non adiciat reprobare." Cf. Matthew 13.47: "Iterum simile est regnum caelorum sagenae missae in mare, et ex omni genere piscium congreganti. Quam cum impleta esset, educentes, et secus littus sedentes, elegerunt bonos in vasa, malos autem foras miserunt. Sic erit in comsummatione saeculi."

[64] Opusc. 52, PL 145.766.

[65] Cf. Gregory I, *Hom. in Ev.* 2.31.8, PL 76.1232.

[66] See Albert Blaise, *Dictionnaire latin-français des auteurs chrétiens* (Strasbourg 1954) 733. To the examples of the patristic use of the word or image of *sagena* (net) collected there and in PL 219.269 the following can be added:

   Augustine: PL 35.1964; PL 39.1612; PL 41.611.

   Gregory I: PL 76.695.

   Jerome: PL 25.307, 677 (= PG 13.558), 703-704; PL 26.834.

   Origen: PL 13.861-865: the Benedictine editor Delarue commented that this passage was imitated by Jerome.

The possibility is not entirely excluded that someone else might have done the same thing. But I think there is little likelihood of it. The facts that *sagena* (ship) was becoming obsolete by Damiani's time and that it was not a fishing boat, together with the facts that the biblical and patristic use of the word was always in the sense of "net" and that it was necessary to mis-read these passages in order to use the word the way Damiani and the election decree used it; these combined make it rather improbable that two members of the curia would suddenly make the identical blunder. Someone else might have imitated Damiani; but this would be an unnecessary hypo-thesis.

The use of *sagena* in the decree's *narratio*, then, argues strongly for Damiani's authorship of this part of the decree. So far as the rest of the decree is con-cerned, however, it is difficult to go so far. Krause has rightly emphasized that there must have been open discussion of the questions it dealt with, just as there was of others on which the council reached agreement.[67] The decree's *dispositio* may well have behind it a number of drafts and suggested amendments. Its wording is awkward in places (notably, where the "salvo" clause is tacked on as a long, parenthetical ablative absolute at the end of a sentence), which is what one would expect if its composition had been a collective affair.

There is, so far as I can see, only one verbal pecularity in the *dispositio* which might be of help. In chapter 4 of the decree (chapter 3 in Michel's edition) we have the clause: "nimirum ne venalitatis morbus qualibet oc-casione surripiat." This is the reading of most manuscripts of both versions. *Surripiat*, however, is obviously incorrect; it should be *surrepat*. Gratian and the copyists of four of the manuscripts of the decree make this correction, and Scheffer-Boichorst concluded that *subrepat* must have stood in the original and have been corrupted to *surripiat* in some manuscript that is the common source of both the papal and imperial versions.[68]

This, however, is not necessarily the case. Michel was able to find such incorrect *surripiat*'s in some of the manuscripts of Gregory of Tours, and used Humbert's familiarity with this passage of Gregory as an argument for Hum-bert's authorship—despite the fact that Humbert himself never used *surripiat* incorrectly.[69]

---

[67] Krause (n. 2 above) 18-20.

[68] Scheffer-Boichorst (n. 3 above) 34.

[69] Michel (n. 7 above) 34 n. 28c; cf. 157-158. Wieland, MGH Const 1.542, accepts *subre-pat* in his text of the "imperial" version, although the great majority of the manuscripts he cites have *subripiat* or *surripiat*. There is another "Merovingian" example of *surripere* in the manuscripts of Venantius Fortunatus, *Miscellanea* 10.2, PL 88.323. Cf. Caesarius of Arles, *sermo* 60.1, Corpus Christianorum, series latina 103.263: "minuta peccata quae cotidie subripiunt redimat."

But it seems hardly a coincidence that Damiani was in the habit of using *surripere* where he ought to have used *surrepere*.[70] The mistake may have been a more common one than Scheffer-Boichorst supposed; although everyone would know that words in *-ripio* are compounds of *rapio*, and appreciate the distance between the violence of the one and the stealth of the other, the difference may not have been felt so strongly in this sort of context. (Whether a fault has crept up on me, or whether some external agent has "wrested" it from me—the result is about the same.)[71]

There is no assurance, then, that *surripiai* did not stand in the original of the election decree. Scheffer-Boichorst's assumption that it did not flies in the face of the manuscript evidence and given the other indications that Damiani at least put the decree into its final form, the decree's *surripiat* seems fair evidence that this holds for the *dispositio* as well as for the *narratio*.

Some hope of identifying the author of the *dispositio* may be held out by the version of Leo I's canon *Nulla ratio sinit* that it contains. The canon was a very popular one, however, and there must have been a large number of manuscripts containing it in circulation. Humbert himself quotes from two different versions of it in his *Adversus simoniacos*.[77] The first differs from the version in the decree in that it has "provincialibus episcopis" rather than the "comprovincialibus episcopis" of the decree. (But two manuscripts of the decree have the same reading as Humbert's first version). His second version does have "comprovincialibus," but has "a plebibus sunt expetiti" where all the manuscripts of the decree have "a plebibus expetiti." Damiani gives the canon in the *Liber gratissimus*, and his version is identical with Humbert's first version.[73]

---

[70] Cf. opusc. 20, PL 145.445: "Sic itaque ne deceptio potuisset forte subripere" (repreated in PL 145.425). I have checked these passages with the reading in the most highly regarded of the manuscripts of Damiani's works, Cod. vat. lat. 3797 (V), which reads "surripere" (fols. 167v and 302). On this manuscript see K. Reindel, "Studien zur Überlieferung der Werke des Petrus Damiani" 1, *Deutsches Archiv* 15 (1959) 68-79; *ibid.* 3, 18 (1962) 329-331. Further on in opusc. 20 (written shortly before the election decree), Migne's edition, PL 145.454, has "Mox enim, ut verba conserimus, paulatim quaedam lenocinia confabulationis alternae subrepunt." However, V fol. 178v reads "surripiunt." Cf. also Damiani's letter to the Florentine clerics, ep. 5.8, PL 144.352: "Quod si hoc laicis indulgetur, ut peccata sua eleemosynis redimant, ne subripiente mortis articulo, ex hac vita sine reatus sui, quod absit, absolutione recedunt" (this portion of the letter is lacking in V).

[71] The confusion might have been more difficult in classical Latin, but medieval Latin was familiar with usages of *surripere* which are sometimes difficult to distinguish from that of *subrepere*: cf. Gregory I, ep. 3.49, PL 77.644: "ut dignos huic officio adhibere possitis, non vobis potentia aut supplicatio quarumlibet surripiat personarum. Ante omnia cautos vos esse oportet, ut nulla proveniat in ordinatione venalitas," and Deusdedit, *Contra invas.*, MGH LL 2.312: "Homo quippe fuit [Nicholaus] eique, ut contra fas ageret, surripi potuit."

[72] 1.2, MGH LL 1.104, and 3.5, MGH LL 1.204.

[73] Opusc. 6.24, MGH LL 1.52.

The variants of this canon can tell us nothing, then. The *way* in which it is used in the election decree, however, may be an indication that the final part in its preparation was taken by Damiani rather than by Humbert.

One of Michel's main arguments for Humbert's authorship was that Humbert also used this canon in laying down the law concerning episcopal elections, and that, like the author of the election decree, Humbert used it to argue that the clergy should have the decisive, though not exclusive, voice in such elections.

Borino[74] and Krause[75] have argued against Michel here that Humbert never says anything about *papal* elections in his three books against the simoniacs. Michel's reply,[76] that this argument "bedarf . . . wie jede Argumentum ex silentio grosser Vorsicht" seems a good one.

That does not mean, however, that Humbert would have used this canon in precisely the way it is presented in the election decree. The canon is used in the election decree to justify the priority of the cardinals as "religiosi viri" in papal elections—a priority that, the author says, is necessary because of the danger of simony ("ne venalitatis morbus qualibet occasione surripiat"). He has already had the pope say in the *narratio* that he has been prompted to make the decree because after the death of his predecessor, the counterfeiting *trapezita* Simon had almost destroyed the Roman church, and he now wants to preclude the possibility of this happening again. At the same time, he is implicitly justifying his own election as one in which the cardinals and Italian bishops had played a dominant part (while only a part of the Roman people could be present) by charging that the simony of Benedict X or his supporters had made an election at Rome impossible. Nicholas goes on to say that an "ordo electionis" in which simony is precluded by entrusting the leadership to these "religiosi viri," the cardinal bishops and clergy, is justified by the authority of his predecessor Leo, who had insisted that no one could be bishop who was not chosen by the clergy, requested by the people, and consecrated by the comprovincial bishops at the "judicium" of the metropolitan. He then adds the explanation that, where papal elections are concerned, the cardinal bishops must be thought of as acting (collectively) as metropolitan. Since the cardinal bishops come first in his own list of electing factors, but correspond to the metropolitan who comes *last* in Leo's canon, he must be assuming that Leo was listing the most decisive voice last.

Such an assumption has not always been shared by modern critics, who have questioned the aptness of the canon for the purpose of the decree. But Krause[77] has rightly argued, I think, that the point here was not so much

---

[74] Borino, *Studi gregoriani* 3 (1948) 504ff.

[75] Krause (n. 2 above) 123f.

[76] "Humbert and Hildebrand bei Nikolaus II (1059/61)," *Historisches Jahrbuch der Görresgesellschaft* 72 (1953) 144.

[77] Krause (n. 2 above) 82f.

to lay down a strict temporal sequence of votes, as to emphasize the absolute
necessity of the participation of the cardinal bishops in a papal election (partly
because one of the main weaknesses of Benedict's election was that he was
opposed by most of the cardinal bishops, and had not been consecrated by
the cardinal bishop of Ostia). Krause rightly points out, therefore, that
he is supporting the authority of this canon by an appeal to the ecclesiastical
custom that made cardinal bishops the consecrators of popes, with the "innere
Begründung" that a canonical election must also be free of simony.

In short, in using this canon, the decree's author seems to be assuming
that it was directed against simoniac elections: if an election in violation of
the canon is not regarded as a simoniac election, then it is not of much use
in justifying the thesis "ut . . . nimirum ne venalitatis morbus qualibet oc-
casione surripiat . . . religiosi viri [cardinales episcopi = metropolitani]
praeduces sint."[78] But that was an assumption that Humbert did not share.
The canon, in fact, goes on to say that although persons not elected in the
way it describes are not bishops, the ordinations they perform are still valid.
As a result of this provision, the canon had been used by Auxilius to defend
the ordination of Formosus, and by Damiani to defend the ordinations performed by simoniacs (arguing that anyone elected against the "vota" of
clergy, people, comprovincial bishops, and metropolitans *must* have had
the help of simony).[79]

Damiani was wrong, of course; Humbert demonstrated this clearly in
the first six chapters of his first book against the simoniacs.[80] But Humbert
was forced to do so, since he could hardly afford to have Leo the Great against
him on the question, and so he made it his first business to show that this
canon had nothing to do with simoniacs, or any other "heretical" ordinations

---

[78] It seems possible that the reason this canon was chosen was that the author felt it
served both of his purposes—that is, that it stressed adequately the rights of metropolitans
(with whom he wanted to equate the cardinal bishops), and was also directed against simoniac elections. If he had wanted one which simply stressed the rights of metropolitans,
there were other canons at his disposal, which did not have the inconvenient pecularity
of putting the metropolitan last (cf. Gratian's Distinction 65).

[79] Damiani interprets the decree as follows in his *Liber gratissimus*, MGH LL 1.53: "Ecce
autentico Leonis papae iudicio . . . ut is, qui ad episcopatus officium cum tanta usurpatione
prorupit, ut adversus eum omnium fere vota concurrant, et sibi, quod accepit, prodesse
nil valeat . . . et aliis prosit, quatinus qui ab eo promoti sunt, a suis nequaquam honoribus
arceantur. Sed quis neget potuisse illic etiam venale intervenire commercium, ubi ad
honoris culmen tam obstinata, tam inopportuna fuerit ambitione subreptum?" (Auxilius
uses a different version of the canon, PL 129.1066).

[80] MGH LL 1.103-110. Humbert was also wrong, however, since Leo was referring to
ordinations by bishops who had never been ordained as bishops themselves: cf. the *In-
quisitio* of Rusticus of Narbonne to which Leo's canon is the answer (Mansi 6.400): "De
presbytero, vel diacono, qui se episcopos esse mentiti sunt; et de his quos ipsi clericos
ordinarunt."

but referred to "catholics" whose elections had been, for some reason, irregular (in terms of the forms that held in the time of Leo).[81]

This is not to say that Humbert would have opposed the use of *Nulla ratio sinit* to defend an "ordo electionis" in which "religiosi viri" are the leaders. When he cites the canon in his third book, Humbert is arguing that it is the violation of this canon and "ordo" which has led to the despoiling of the church and the prevalence of simony. According to his own interpretation of the rest of the canon it permitted a translation similar to that of Nicholas (though he argued against this "liberty"), and fitted the occasion.

But its proximity to the justification "ne venalitatis morbus . . . surripiat" connects Leo's *Nulla ratio sinit* with simony more closely than Humbert might have wished; conceivably, it even leaves the door open to defending some of the ordinations of the "simoniac" Benedict. If the "surripiat" is Damiani's, then, it and the inclusion of *Nulla ratio sinit* may represent his retouching of a "collectively" composed *dispositio* to suit his own ideas.[82]

In conclusion, I would like to stress that I would regard it as a mistake to go as far in urging Damiani's authorship of the decree as Michel went in urging Humbert's. It is, by the nature of the case, impossible to know how many persons contributed to its wording. If there are good grounds, as I think there are, for holding that Damiani wrote the *narratio* and perhaps even contributed a portion of the *dispositio*, it is quite possible that he drew

---

[81] Humbert, in order to show that there had been "catholic" elections that violated the forms set down by Leo, said that he would appeal to the examples of the ordinations of the apostles and their disciples, if it were not for the fact that there could be no laws "ubi benedictionem, gratiam et gloriam dedit legislator et naturarum Dominus" (1.6.109). But he had also found, in the *Historia tripartita* of Cassiodorus, examples of bishops named by popes and patriarchs, whose flocks had refused them, but who retained the title of bishops and were later sent to other sees. He quotes Cassiodorus concerning irregularities permitted "primitus propter persecutionis tempus" and ends with the caution that these exceptions to the rules were excused by the "necessitas et sua libertas" of the ancients, but cannot be allowed to the "moderni." His position contrasts strangely with that of Damiani, who defended the irregular election of Nicholas II by writing, PL 145.443, "Et quia vos (Nicholas II and Hildebrand) apostolica sedes, vos romana estis ecclesia, ad deponendum reddendumque quod bajulare nequiveram, integrum mihi visum est non adire fabricam lapidum; sed eos potius, in quibus viget ipsius Ecclesiae sacramentum. Sub persecutione quippe judaica ubicunque erant apostoli, illic esse primitiva dicebatur ecclesia. Nunc autem cum Simon ille . . . romanam urbem velut officinam sibi . . . usurpat, quo vos Petrus vobiscum fugiens attrahit, illic esse romanam ecclesiam omnibus indubitanter ostendit." It seems doutful that Humbert would have accepted this appeal to what the apostles did during the "judaica persecutio," since he hesitated to appeal to the freedom of the time of the apostles, and refused to appeal to the necessity of the time of persecutions (particularly in reference to translations—such as that of Nicholas II). On this passage in Damiani and its relation to the later rule of the decretists "ubi papa, ibi ecclesia," cf. Kempf (n. 2 above) 73-75.

[82] On the harmony of the canons of the Lateran Synod of 1059 with Damiani's ideas see Krause (n. 2 above) 119-120.

up the entire document. I doubt that this could be shown conclusively, however; even if it could be, it would not exclude the probability that the decree's contents were the result of discussion and agreement between the pope and other figures besides Damiani. There are, however, sufficient signs that Damiani's pen was at work on the decree, especially in its use of the word *sagena*, to make it very probable that he supported it.

APPENDIX

The Text of the Papal Election Decree of 1059

I give here the papal version of the decree (P), omitting the "comminatio" and "eschatocol"; I have added emendations in square brackets from the imperial version (R). Although the arabic numbering of the paragraph is that of Weiland, MGH Const. 1.538ff., I follow Krause's division, (n. 2 above) 271-275, in the indentation and in the italicised analytic titles that I have added to the text.

Protocol

1) In nomine Domini Dei salvatoris nostri Iesu Christi, anno ab incarnatione eius MLIX, mense Aprili indictione XII, propositis sacrosanctis evangeliis, praesidente quoque reverendissimo ac beatissimo Nicolao apostolico papa, in basilica Lateranensis patriarchii que cognominatur Constantiniana, considentibus etiam reverendissimis archiepiscopis, episcopis, abbatibus seu venerabilibus presbyteris atque diaconibus, idem venerabilis pontifex auctoritate apostolica decernens de electione summi pontificis inquit:

Context

Narratio

2) Novit beatitudo vestra, dilectissimi fratres et coepiscopi, inferiora quoque membra [Christi][83] non latuit, defuncto piae memoriae domino Stephano decessore nostro, haec apostolica sedes cui auctore Deo deservio, quot adversa pertulerit, quot denique per simoniacae haeresis trapezitas malleis crebrisque tunsionibus subiacuerit, adeo ut columna Dei viventis iamiam paene videretur [concussa][84] nutare et sagena summi piscatoris procellis intumescentibus cogeretur in naufragii profunda submergi. Unde, si placet fraternitati vestrae, debemus auxiliante Deo futuris casibus prudenter occurrere et ecclesiastico statui, ne rediviva—quod absit—mala praevaleant, in posterum praevidere.

[83] P omits.
[84] P omits.

Dispositio

Quapropter instructi praedecessorum nostrorum aliorumque sanctorum patrum auctoritate decernimus atque statuimus: (3) Ut, obeunte huius Romanae universalis ecclesiae pontifice, inprimis cardinales episcopi,[85] diligentissima simul consideratione tractantes,[86] mox sibi clericos cardinales adhibeant; sicque reliquus clerus et populus ad consensum novae electionis accedant. (4) Ut—nimirum ne venalitatis morbus qualibet occasione surripiat[87]—religiosi viri[88] praeduces sint in promovendi pontificis electione, reliqui autem sequaces.

Et[89] certe rectus atque legitimus hic electionis ordo perpenditur, si perspectis diversorum patrum regulis sive gestis, etiam illa beati praedecessoris Leonis sententia recolatur: "Nulla," inquit, "ratio sinit, ut inter episcopos habeantur, qui nec a clericis sunt electi, nec a plebibus expetiti, nec a comprovincialibus episcopis cum metropolitani iudicio consecrati."[90] Quia vero sedes apostolica cunctis in orbe terrarum praefertur ecclesiis atque ideo super se metropolitanum habere non potest, cardinales episcopi procul dubio metropolitani vice funguntur, qui videlicet electum antistitem ad apostolici culminis apicem provehunt.

5) Eligant autem de ipsius ecclesiae gremio, si reperitur idoneus, vel si de ipsa non invenitur ex alia assumatur.[91] (6) Salvo debito honore et reverentia dilecti filii nostri Henrici, qui inpraesentiarum rex habetur et futurus imperator Deo concedente speratur sicut iam sibi [mediante eius nuntius Longobardiae cancellario W.][92] concessimus et successorum illius, qui ab hac apostolica sede personaliter hoc ius impetraverint.

7) Quodsi pravorum atque iniquorum hominum ita perversitas invaluerit, ut pura, sincera atque gratuita electio fieri in Urbe non possit, cardinales[93] episcopi cum religiosis clericis catholicisque laicis, licet paucis, ius potestatis obtineant eligere apostolicae sedis pontificem, ubi[94] congruentius iudicaverint.

---

[85] R omits "episcopi."

[86] R replaces the words "mox sibi . . . clerus et populus" with the "salvo" clause: "salvo debito honore et reverentia dilectissimi filii nostri Heinrici, qui in presentiarum rex habetur et futurus imperator Deo concedente speratur, sicut iam sibi mediante eius nuntio Longobardie cancellario W. concessimus, et successorum illius, qui ab hac apostolica sede personaliter hoc ius impetraverint."

[87] See n. 69.

[88] R adds "cum serenissimo filio nostro rege Heinrico."

[89] R omits this paragraph.

[90] Gratian, Distinction 62, chap. 1.

[91] Cf. *ibid.* 61, chap. 13.

[92] I follow Michel (n. 7 above) 29, in assuming that this reference to the Italian chancellor Wibert was omitted by P through negligence. Cf. Krause (n. 2 above) 97-98.

[93] R replaces the words "cardinales . . . licet paucis" with "licet pauci sint."

[94] R adds "cum invictissimo rege H."

8) Plane postquam electio fuerit facta, si bellica tempestas vel qualiscunque hominum conatus malignitatis studio restiterit, ut is qui electus est in apostlica sede iuxta consuetudinem intronizari non valeat, electus tamen sicut papa auctoritatem obtineat regendi sanctam Romanam ecclesiam et disponendi omnes facultates illius, quod beatum Gregorium ante consecrationem suam fecisse cognoscimus.

Princeton University Library
Princeton, New Jersey 08540, U.S.A.

THE FUNCTION AND EVOLUTION
OF BYZANTINE RHETORIC

•

by George L. Kustas

In his *Prolegomena to Rhetoric* a fifth-century anonymous author remarks that the function of rhetoric varies with the type of polity. Among the ancient Lacedaemonians rhetoric served the aims of oligarchy; among the Athenians, democracy; "*we* practice it in faith and orthodoxy under an empire."[1] The statement expresses in concise terms the new role that rhetoric had come to play in Byzantine life. Not only had the system of government changed; it had assumed a religious habit. The devices of rhetoric must be adapted to serve not merely an empire but the Christian Empire of the East, with its political roots in its Roman past and its cultural heritage the educational ideals and techniques of late Antiquity. My purpose is to review the bases of the Byzantine rhetorical tradition as it arose in the early Christian centuries, to indicate the interplay between it and the forms of Byzantine literature, and to trace the changes that were rung on this pagan legacy in response to the evolving patterns and challenges of Byzantine civilization.

Byzantine rhetoric is throughout its history the heir of the Second Sophistic, that movement in thought and letters which extends from the time of Augustus to the end of the ancient world. Within the movement there are wide variations, and in its later history it exists side by side with the literature of Christianity which drew on it. If the Christian Chrysostom is the student of the pagan Libanius, sophist from Antioch, it is equally notable that the school of Gaza in the sixth century is peopled by Christian sophists. The Second Sophistic has in fact no clear terminus. One should rather say that it shades off into the Byzantine world of letters. In rhetoric as in other fields there can have been little awareness of the break, so useful to modern analysis, between late antique and Byzantine. Precisely because the tradition remained alive there never developed in Byzantium a uniquely Christian

---

[1] *Prolegomenon Sylloge*, ed. H. Rabe (Leipzig 1925) 41.7-9: Ἀθηναῖοι δὲ καὶ ἡ τῶν ῥητόρων δεκὰς ἐπολιτεύσατο μὲν ὡς ἐν δημοκρατίᾳ. Λακεδαιμόνιοι δέ, ὡς ἐν ἀριστοκρατίᾳ · ἡμεῖς δὲ νῦν εὐτυχῶς ἐν βασιλείᾳ πιστῶς καὶ ὀρθοδόξως. Cf. also 38.8: ἡμεῖς σὺν θεῷ μετερχόμεθα τὴν τρίτην (i.e. type of rhetoric). I wish to thank my colleague Professor Westerink for many helpful suggestions in the writing of this paper.

rhetoric existing as an entity apart and distinct from its Sophistic for-
bears. The changes within this received framework are slow and sometimes
subtle, but, for all that, there is, as we shall see, a clear pattern of development.

Starting from the latter part of the second century the literary practices
and ideals of the Second Sophistic begin to be codified into the systems or
textbooks that are henceforth to form the subject of instruction and the
basis of literary performance and analysis for the succeeding centuries. These
are the treatises that make up the Byzantine rhetorical tradition; they are
copied many times over down to the late Middle Ages, commented upon,
excerpted from, and on occasion altered in response to Christian demand.
I mention two authors in particular: first, Hermogenes, the second- and
third-century rhetorician from Tarsus, and second, the fourth- and fifth-century figure, Aphthonius of Antioch.[2] Byzantium knew and used other handbooks. One can trace the influence of Theon, Hermagoras, and Menander,
and record the use of rhetorical masters such as Dionysius of Halicarnassus,
Demetrius, Synesius, and Aristides, particularly after the tenth century; but
they come much less to the fore than the ever present and ever used outlines
of Hermogenes and his commentator, Aphthonius.[3]

The corpus of Hermogenic writings offers little that is original in the creative sense of the word. Hermogenes' works, however, have the virtue of
clear exposition and arrangement of the subject matter, from which a large
element of their appeal must derive. At the same time the five treatises in
the corpus[4] were the only attempt to cover the whole of rhetoric. The Second
Sophistic had seen a trend away from the practical application of rhetoric
for the law courts and political ceremonies of the empire. Rhetoric was now
cultivated more and more as an academic subject, meant to supply the curriculum of higher education. Hermogenes' work suited the purpose admirably.
The text is well written and its content, by no means easy—it was meant after
all for the higher schools—has the virtue of a studied simplicity, a quality that

---

[2] Much of the Walzian corpus is a selection from some of these commentaries on these
two authors. The wealth of the manuscript tradition may be inferred from the massive
lists in the introduction to the Teubner text: *Hermogenis Opera, Rhetores graeci* 6, and
Aphthonii Progymnasmata, Rhetores graeci 10, both ed. H. Rabe (Leipzig 1913, 1926).
Rabe's two introductions should be supplemented by the valuable accounts of Radermacher and Brzoska in Pauly-Wissowa, *Real-Encyclopädie*.

[3] In focusing on Hermogenes and Aphthonius I do not wish to underestimate other
contributions. The study of Byzantine rhetoric is in its infancy, and in this paper I do not
propose more than a sketch of its main outlines. Future research must work in part towards
tracing the fortunes of other figures through specialized studies on their rhetorical methods
and vocabulary.

[4] *Προγυμνάσματα, Περὶ στάσεων, Περὶ εὑρέσεως, Περὶ ἰδεῶν, Περὶ μεθόδου δεινό-
τητος.* Rabe considers the *Προγυμνάσματα* and the *Περὶ εὑρέσεως* spurious.

was to strike a very sympathetic Byzantine nerve and one that the author actually holds out as an ideal of style in his writings.[5]

Hermogenes had the good fortune to be received not long after his death into the bosom of the Neoplatonists. The earliest commentary of which we hear is by the third-century philosopher, Metrophanes of Phrygia, and no less a person than Iamblichus further enhanced Hermogenes' reputation by declaring in his favor over the claims of rival systems.[6] Our earliest extant commentary is by Syrianus, the fifth-century Athenian scholar.[7]

Before we trace the later fortunes of Hermogenes, let us consider his partner, Aphthonius. The work by which Byzantium knew him was the *Progymnasmata*. The word refers to those school exercises, *praeexercitamenta* in Latin, which had since Hellenistic times formed part of the instruction in the ancient tongues. A progymnasma is essentially a set composition, in which one could presumably exercise the techniques of style laid down in such textbooks as those of Hermogenes.[8] There is an inner logic in the fact that Aphthonius, through whom the Christian world was to learn so much of its rhetoric, was, like Chrysostom, a student of the pagan Libanius. Libanius also wrote progymnasmata. The special success of Aphthonius lies in the simplicity of his exposition as well as in his inclusion of examples for each of the types under discussion. His examples are hardly his own creation. As in the case of most rhetorical works, we can hardly ever hope to trace such formulas back to their origins, and we can only console ourselves that it would be little gain to the history of ideas to know the name of the schoolmaster who first thought of asking his pupils to write a composition reproducing Ajax's thoughts before his suicide or Danaë's reaction to Zeus's golden shower.[9]

The standard number of progymnasmata is fourteen. They are divided by the scholiasts on Aphthonius into three categories, symbouleutic, dicanic, and panegyrical, the tripartite arrangement that is at least as old as Aristotle.[10] Under the first are ranged 1) μῦθος, myth; 2) χρεία, ethical thought;

---

[5] Note the heavy emphasis in the Περὶ ἰδεῶν on such concepts as καθαρότης, εὐκρίνεια, σαφήνεια, ἐπιείκεια, ἀφέλεια, ἀλήθεια, and how to achieve each.

[6] For the relation of these and other figures of the time to Hermogenes see Christ-Schmid-Stählin, *Geschichte der griechischen Litteratur* 7.2.2, ed. 6 (Munich 1924) 934-936.

[7] *Syriani in Hermogenem commentaria*, ed. H. Rabe (Leipzig 1892-1893) 2 vols.

[8] Τὰ δὲ τοῦ Ἀφθονίου προγυμνάσματα εἰσαγωγή τις ὄντα πρὸς ἐκεῖνα (i.e., τὰ τοῦ Ἑρμογένους βιβλία): *Rhetores graeci* 2.566.23.

[9] Ajax: *Libanii opera*, ed. R. Foerster (Leipzig 1925), 8.384ff.; Danaë: Nicephorus Basilaces, *Rhetores graeci* 1.476.

[10] *Rhetores graeci* 2.567.7. See also Matthew Camariotes, *Epitome*, *Rhetores graeci* 1.120. 10; Anonymous on Aphthonius, *Rhetores graeci* 1.127.16. For other, albeit basically similar ways of dividing the progymnasmata, see the chart provided by Stegemann, *s.v.* "Theon" in Pauly-Wissowa, *Real-Encylopädie*, cols. 2043, 2044.

and 3) γνώμη, a maxim or saying.[11] Four others are dicanic: 1) ἀνασκευή, the refutation of a given statement; 2) κατασκευή, its opposite, or confirmation; 3) εἰσφορὰ νόμου, a discussion whether a given law is good or bad; and 4) κοινὸς τόπος, *communis locus*, by which is meant the amplification of a given topic. These judicial types were among the first to be affected by the decline of political oratory under the Roman Empire. At the same time that they were, on one level, retained as school exercises, they took a new lease on life by lending their resources to new purposes. Ἀνασκευή and κατασκευή were early turned into weapons of historical criticism. The Christian apologists used the techniques to counter the myths of the pagans, and Byzantine theological literature followed suit.[12] Cicero tells us that the *communis locus* plays on two emotions in particular: *indignatio* and *misericordia*.[13] Like the εἰσφορὰ νόμου,[14] it had comparatively little independent existence in Byzantium, but, insofar as the appeal of many a homily and epistle rests on the evocation of just these two states of mind, it had a long and vibrant echo through the whole of the Middle Ages.

The panegyrical types are four: 1) ἐγκώμιον, encomium; 2) its opposite, ψόγος, which censure, helped supply the long vocabulary of Byzantine invective before which one can only stand back in amazement; 3) σύγκρισις, comparison; and 4) ἠθοποιΐα, characterization. Ἔκφρασις, description (of people, places, and things), and διήγημα, narrative, are common to all three types, while θέσις, the posing of a question of general interest, partakes of both the symbouleutic and the panegyrical. Although all the progymnasmata were current throughout Byzantine history, Byzantium paid more attention to the symbouleutic and the panegyrical than to the dicanic. The clear correlation between these preferences and the main categories of Byzantine literature is striking proof of their vitality.

Letter writing had not been particularly developed as a genre in ancient Greece. Its heyday belongs rather to the Roman age and goes hand in hand with the emphasis on individual portraiture and character expression that

---

[11] Apthonius's definitions, which are not original with him, are as follows: χρεία ἐστὶν ἀπομνημόνευμα σύντομον εὐστόχως ἐπί τι πρόσωπον ἀναφέρουσα: 3.21; γνώμη ἐστὶ λόγος ἐν ἀποφάνσεσι κεφαλαιώδης ἐπί τι προτρέπων ἢ ἀποτρέπων: 7.2. See also Theon, the oldest of the writers on progymnasmata available to us (second century of our era), *Progymnasmata*, ed. L. Spengel, *Rhetores graeci* (Leipzig 1854) 2.96.19: χρεία ἐστὶ σύντομος ἀπόφασις ἢ πρᾶξις μετ᾽ εὐστοχίας ἀναφερομένη εἴς τι ὡρισμένον πρόσωπον ἢ ἀναλογοῦν προσώπῳ · παράκειται δὲ αὐτῇ γνώμη καὶ ἀπομνημονεύματα · πᾶσα γὰρ γνώμη σύντομος εἰς πρόσωπον ἀναφερομένη χρείαν ποιεῖ.

[12] H. Lausberg, *Handbuch der literarischen Rhetorik* (Munich 1960) sect. 1125.

[13] *De inn.* 2.16.51.

[14] This particular progymnasma, as a matter of fact, was from the beginning not quite on a par with the rest. See Hermogenes 26.11: καὶ τὴν τοῦ νόμου εἰσφορὰν τάττουσί τινες ἐν γυμνάσμασι. Similarly Aphthonius 46.20. One of the commentators, *Rhetores graeci* 1.597-648, omits it altogether.

is so marked a feature of Roman portrait art. During the Second Sophistic epistolography invaded Greek literature more and more: we need only think of such large collections as the letters of Alciphron and of Libanius. In the process, rhetoricians undertook to distinguish its various forms and to define the rules of composition. By the fifth century the pseudo- Libanius tradition recognized 41 distinct types of letter,[15] but even this number was to prove inadequate to express the variegated refinements of the Byzantine mind. A late tradition lists 113 different possibilities.[16] There is hardly a Byzantine author without his collection of letters. Epistolography is one of the most widely used and most successful of medieval literary forms. From the point of view of rhetorical theory, it falls under the heading of ἠθο- ποιία,[17] the progymnasma par excellence which gave the freest scope to the expression of personality traits.

This particular legacy of the Second Sophistic, however, did not reach Byzantium only through pagan channels. Christianity had introduced itself to the world in the form of a letter.[18] The importance of Saint Paul's Epistles, as witness the extensive and frequent byzantine commentaries, cannot be exaggerated. The religion of Jesus had accentuated the sense of the individual person or circumstance by emphasizing the private and unique relationship of the human soul to its Creator. In addition, the development of Christian theology had demanded of the Fathers a clear and close exposition of views by way of refining orthodox belief and combating heretical opinion. It is not without reason that Gregory of Nazianzus, Gregory of Nyssa, Basil, and Chrysostom are incorporated into a Christian canon of epistolography and frequently cited by the rhetoricians of the later centuries together with their pagan predecessors. The Cappadocians gave to epistolography its eminently practical Christian character,[19] and the lesson was not lost among that long parade of emperors and priests who chose to express themselves on a limitless range of subjects through the medium of their letters.

What is more, this emphasis on the personal was not restricted to letter writing. Many other literary forms, such as general histories, theological treatises, or even scientific tracts, come to be not merely dedicated, as in Antiquity, but now addressed to some particular person. The influence that ἠθοποιία exercised upon other forms of literature and the high esteem in which it was held in Byzantine circles are nowhere better illustrated than in an anonymous scholium on Aphthonius that ἠθοποιία is the perfect kind of progymnasma and in this capacity contributes to the ἐπιστολιμαῖος χα-

---

[15] Ἐπιστολιμαῖοι χαρακτῆρες, ed. V. Weichert (Leipzig 1910) 14.

[16] Ibid. 34.

[17] See Nicolaus, Progymnasmata, ed. J. Felten (Leipzig 1913) 67.2.

[18] J. Sykutris, Pauly-Wissowa, Real-Encyclopädie supp. 5 s.v. "Epistolographie" col. 219.24.

[19] Ibid. 219.39.

ϱακτήϱ.[20] Not only the epistle but the homily as well had a large stake in it. Originally, under the Second Sophistic, the person of the orator displaying his virtuosity had become more prominent as against the virtuosity of the production. The Christian homilist through his address to his congregation now achieved the same effect as the pagan sophist.

At the same time, ἠθοποιΐα is practiced extensively as a form of literature in its own right. Here we can distinguish two types of compositions: those that followed the old pagan models and those that adopted Christian themes. The origin of the Christian topics is as obscure as that of their pagan equivalents. It is clear, however, that the techniques of Christian education were elaborated in the fourth century and developed and multiplied throughout the fifth and sixth centuries. That the school of Gaza played an important role is more than likely.[21] The writings of the Gazaeans continued very popular in Byzantium, and in their texts one will find quotations from Homer side by side with passages from Isaiah. The pious Christian could now release his imagination to ponder not Ajax, but what Samson said upon being blinded, what the Virgin might have remarked upon seeing her son change the water into wine, or—a mixture of pagan and Christian—Hades's remarks on learning of Lazarus's resurrection.[22] The most that can be said for these pursuits is that they may have promoted the cause of Christian piety. Yet behind the ἠθοποιΐα, as well as behind the forms of literature it affected, lurks the informing presence of Aphthonius, rhetorician from Antioch.

Just as with the ἠθοποιΐα, so too in the encomium one can detect three different levels of transmission from Rome to Byzantium. The first keeps to the letter of the old tradition. Encomia continue to be formed on the basis of the pagan prescriptions. In the second, the outer structure is again retained, but the author heaps his praise on Christian models. The third is the most fruitful, for it uses the resources of the encomium to guide and adorn other forms of literature. One thinks of the panegyrics composed by the Cappadocians and later Fathers in honor of Christian martyrs; the catalogues of praise that are a vital ingredient of the saints' lives; the appreciation, often in the form of a letter, of the virtues of the Fathers and, in the secular sphere, of

---

[20] *Rhetores graeci* 2.52.1.

[21] Much work still needs to be done to clarify the text tradition and to assess the contribution of the Gazaean authors. See the old but useful account by K. Seitz, *Die Schule von Gaza* (Heidelberg 1892), as well as Aly's recent discussion of Procopius in Pauly-Wissowa, *Real-Encyclopädie*; also G. Downey, "The Christian Schools of Palestine," *Harvard Library Bulletin* 12 (1958) 297-319.

[22] One of the more interesting treatments of such topics is by Nicephorus Basilaces in the middle of the twelfth century, *Rhetores graeci* 1.466ff., where such ἠθοποιΐαι are presented side by side with those of pagan themes, whether mythological (Zeus, Ajax) or historical (Xerxes 487).

learned or otherwise distinguished contemporaries; the admiration and reverence with which the Byzantine exegete approached the Gospel text; and, not least commonly, the praise of the Lord of Heaven and other persons of the Christian pantheon through homily or hymn. The attitudes and functions that define this religious literature were nourished early in the career of the schoolboy and later university student by rhetorical handbooks, of which the summary of Aphthonius was the most popular. I do not mean to suggest that the Byzantines owed the nobility of their religious vision or their cultural achievements to what is admittedly a thoroughly pedestrian compendium of rhetorical rules. Rather, the retention of such legacies came about because they had a certain natural affinity with Byzantium's own interests. We cannot hope to decide at any given point whether we are dealing with the Christianization of Hellenism[23] or the Hellenization of Christianity; so intimately entwined are the two strands and so inseparable a complement do they form to one another in the tapestry of medieval culture.

The third of the panegyrical forms is the σύγκρισις. It cuts across the other rhetorical types and affects them all. A simile is one of its simplest expressions. A Plutarchian parallel *Life* is another. Σύγκρισις is indispensable to the encomium (how better to stress the virtues of your subject than by comparing him to a lesser man), and it is common in the ἔκφρασις (how much better this mosaic is than that of Zeuxis; this icon puts Pheidias to shame).[24] The habit of the comparison is built into the system of progymnasmata itself: ἀνασκευή is followed by κατασκευή, encomium by ψόγος, and θέσις suggests ἀντίθεσις. Although the comparison appears in many of the genres of Byzantine literature, it is particularly effective in the homilies with their exhortations to the good life: the works of the devil are contrasted with the works of God, the grossness of heathenism with the beauty of the Christian revelation, the way of the sinner with the way of the pious. The technique of comparison is already biblical: witness the parable of the foolish virgins, and the same sense of contrast must have impressed itself on the early Fathers who saw themselves ranged on opposite sides of a dogmatic issue or against the power of Rome as they sought to develop a scheme of Christian doctrine. In one of his letters, Gregory of Nazianzus, instructing a friend in the principles of effective writing, encourages the use of mythology as a form of σύγκρισις.[25] Finally, the technique finds its most fruitful and

[23] Nothing better illustrates the impact of religion upon the progymnasmata than the fortunes of the ψόγος, the opposite of the encomium. In their original secular functions, the two would be on a par and each had a purely human reference that derived ultimately from the equal rights of plaintiff and defendant in the courtroom. In a religious society whose instruments are devoted to the celebration of the Deity, ψόγος often appears as part of the encomium, serving to attack heretics and nonbelievers.

[24] See M. Guignet, *St. Grégoire de Nazianze et la rhétorique* (Paris 1911) 189.

[25] Letter 46, PG 37.96A.

original development in literary criticism. The many comparisons to be found among the literary notices in Photius's *Bibliotheca* are guided by his sense of historical fitness. He will compare only works of literature which are legitimately matched and will use a critical vocabulary carefully chosen so as to be generally contemporary with the authors under review.[26]

Although the ἔκφρασις could apply as well to people as to things, some of our best examples describe the realm of nature and, as a special category, works of art. In the general decline of poetry during the Second Sophistic and in some periods of Byzantine history, it supplied a kind of lyric in prose in which the word-painter could give rein to his talents. The ἔκφρασις has given us some of the most beautiful passages in Byzantine literature. The particular attraction that it had for the medieval mind is not difficult to see. As Guignet points out, the immobility and fixity of form of a work of art permitted the unhampered pursuit of detail and made possible, at least theoretically, the attainment of perfection in the genre.[27] At the same time that it served the cause of art, the ἔκφρασις in its larger sense aided the cause of religion. The descriptions of the heavenly majesty in the religious poetry of Byzantium, the inspired variety of address to the Deity, the deeply felt recital of the mercy and providence of God, must have been initially fostered in the Byzantine classroom. Further, the ἔκφρασις is one of the most Christianized of forms. Between the sixth and the eleventh centuries practically all the examples we have are devoted to Christian works. Then, with the revival of interest in pagan subjects, we begin to find ἐκφράσεις of classical art. Psellus's description of two representations of the Circe episode in Homer and Constantine Manasses's of an antique relief of Odysseus and Polyphemus are among the earliest.[28]

Aphthonius defines the μῦθος as "a false saying which mirrors the truth,"[29] the same definition that appears in the lexica of Hesychius, Photius, and the Suda. The extensive use of the fable is a continuation from the period of the Second Sophistic, when the collections of fables in prose and verse that have come down to us were originally compiled. In Byzantium the μῦθος answered the ethical demands of the religious mind, and its popularity may be due in part to the momentary freedom that its fictional appeal gave from the confinements of dogma and the strictures of doctrina prescription.

---

[26] This subject has been treated *in extenso* in my "The literary criticism of Photius, a Christian definition of style," Ἑλληνικά 17 (1962) 132-169.

[27] *St. Grégoire* 207.

[28] Psellus: *Tzetzae allegoriae Iliadis*; *accedunt Pselli allegoriae*, ed. J. Boissonade (Paris 1851) 363-365; *M. Pselli scripta minora* 2: *Epistulae*, ed. E. Kurtz (Milan 1941) letter 188, 207-209. For Manasses see C. Mango, "Antique statuary and the Byzantine beholder," *Dumbarton Oaks Papers* 17 (Washington 1963) 65.

[29] 1.6: ἔστι δὲ μῦθος λόγος ψευδὴς εἰκονίζων τὴν ἀλήθειαν.

$X\varrho\varepsilon i\alpha$ and $\gamma\nu\acute{\omega}\mu\eta$ also fall in the symbouleutic category,[30] the one a specific quotation from a given author, the other a general maxim. Some of the texts continue to be taken from the ancient tradition. Nicephorus Basilaces, a twelfth-century writer, professor of Gospel exegesis and author of a rhetorical manual, urges Sophocles as a model for the $\chi\varrho\varepsilon i\alpha$; and an anonymous scholiast cites a Demosthenic $\gamma\nu\acute{\omega}\mu\eta$.[31] The $\chi\varrho\varepsilon i\alpha$ has its Christian echoes in the exegetical commentaries of Byzantium, with their investigations of scriptural meaning, as well as in the quotations from the early Fathers and in the vast body of catenae literature.

The predilection for the important saying, the mot juste, the epigrammatic, has its other side as well. The lexicographers are an instance of the fragmentation of learning in pursuit of the subtle and unique. The extensive collections of the paroemiographers and the excerpts from classical and Christian works that begin in the ninth century and continue apace through the scholarly labors of Constantine Porphyrogenitus are affected by the same spirit. In judging all these efforts, however, we have to make a distinction between the interest in the unique and in the uniquely representative. When the Byzantines pursued the former, they often degenerated into mere purism; when they sought the latter, we see them at their best, as in the great periods of their art. Both possibilities derive from the same source and for both rhetoric had a significant role to play.

The highest achievement of the Christian prose literature is the homily. Many of the techniques of rhetoric contribute to its formation and lend their resources to its power and beauty. One of the best illustrations is the recently edited and translated corpus of nineteen Photian homilies.[32] The selection of the canon, made probably by the author himself, is such as to give representation to the major categories we have been discussing: two of the homilies are in the form of an $\check{\varepsilon}\varkappa\varphi\varrho\alpha\sigma\iota\varsigma$; two are encomia; one has extensive citations from the pagan myths in condemnation of those who prefer them to the Christian revelation; two are narratives of the history of the Arian controversy; and throughout them all we see a free use of scriptural quotation, folk proverb, as well as character description. The author knew Hermogenes intimately,[33] and his acquaintance with Aphthonius is evident from the notice in the *Bibliotheca* codex 133.[34] To be sure, the corpus of the homilies was not compiled with them in mind; but it is clear that one of the most splendid monu-

---

[30] See n. 11 above.

[31] *Rhetores graeci* 1.445, 605.

[32] $\Phi\omega\tau\iota\sigma\upsilon$ $\dot{\sigma}\mu\iota\lambda\iota\alpha\iota$ ed. B. Laourdas (Thessalonike 1959), C. Mango, *The Homilies of Photius, Patriarch of Constantinople English Translation, Introduction, and Commentary*; (Cambridge, Mass. 1958).

[33] Photius's use of Hermogenes is analyzed in detail in the work cited above, n. 26.

[34] Photius prefers, however, the style of the fourth-century rhetorician, Palladius of Methone.

ments of Byzantine literature owes much of its outer form to the rhetorical tradition.

The influence of rhetoric is not limited to the literary arts. The Greek language has, built into it, a surprisingly large number of ways of saying "if." The system of progymnasmata can be regarded as in some ways a codification of this speculative spirit. It compels a consideration of all possibilities in a given instance. The encomium, for example, calls for ever new variations on the theme of praise; ἠθοποιΐα concerns itself with what so-and-so would have said if—;the χρεία asks for the exercise of the imagination on the possible meanings in a given phrase; the θέσις ponders such questions as εἰ πλευστέον, εἰ γαμητέον, should one take a trip, should one marry; the σύγκρισις, by juxtaposing parallels, enlarges the range of experience of the possibilities of life. This rhetorical education, in addition to marking the educated man, was the key to entering the imperial bureaucracy. If politics is the art of the possible, one may be justified in seeing a correlation between the educational system and the vaunted successes of Byzantine diplomacy, which by adroitly balancing one adversary against another, kept at bay the host of enemies that through so many centuries ringed the Empire on every side.

Rhetoric for the Byzantine was not simply an educational force but a way of life. παιδεία means both education *and* culture. Neither the Hellenistic nor the Byzantine world knew the set of associations which we give to a college "commencement." Life is one, under the guidance of Divine Providence. Such a philosophy could yield brilliant successes, but it had also its pitfalls in irrelevance and retreat before new challenge. The fortunes of poetry are a case in point: on the one hand the sublimity of a religious ode; on the other, poetry as merely an aid to the work of prose. The failure of secular poetry comes about not because, as is sometimes said, Byzantium could not appreciate it, but because prose, not poetry, was the proper medium of education, and education was all in all.

The prescribed style in which the literature we have been examining was to be written continued to be Attic. The definition of the term, however, changes as we move down in time. The basic distinction is between ἀττικῶς (or ῥητορικῶς) and κοινῶς.[35] Starting about the middle of the tenth century, the scribes of the Byzantine renaissance begin to copy not only prose works but poetry as well. As a result the compass of Attic style expands so as to include the ancient tragic poets. Böhlig's recent study has shown that much of what earlier lexica call poetic, Tzetzes by the twelfth century calls Attic.[36] This tendency pushed into the background the difference between prose and poetry and helped continue the hegemony of prose. The introduction

---

[35] G. Böhlig, *Untersuchungen zum rhetorischen Sprachgebrauch der Byzantiner* (Berlin 1956) 3ff.

[36] *Ibid.* 14.

of poetry into the definition of Attic meant that more and more the literary tradition was intended for the discriminating few. Since poetry and prose together become opposed to what is κοινόν, and since κοινόν means "ordinary" as well as "in general use," its opposite is therefore "extraordinary" or Attic.[37]

Concurrent with the introduction of poetry Byzantium witnesses the steady enlargement of the canon of Attic prose. The scholars of the Renaissance turn their attention to manuscripts not only of the classical authors but of later Greek literature as well. The *Bibliotheca*, for example, reviews not only the old canon of the ten Athenian orators but records another list, created probably in the fourth century, which includes Dio, Herodes, Philostratus, and Aristides.[38] Into this continuum there is fitted by the ninth century a third canon of Christian authors. The models of Christian epistolography come to be Basil, Gregory of Nazianzus, and Isidore.[39] Beginning with the ninth century, a kind of Christian classicism appears, engendered in part by the triumph of orthodoxy over iconoclasm, which comes to be thought of as the last heresy to plague the Faith. Hence the need to hold out what is orthodox becomes apparent not merely in dogma but in literature as well. By the twelfth century there is added to this curious mixture of classical and early Christian figures a Byzantine name. Joseph Rhacendytes's *Rhetorical Synopsis* lists as model epistolographers the three Cappadocians, Synesius, Libanius, and "the most learned Psellus."[40] Another writer gives as models of the panegyrical form Basil, Aristides, Themistius, Procopius of Gaza, Choricius, and, he says, particularly Psellus. In epistolography, his exemplars are the three Cappadocians, Synesius, Libanius, and Psellus.[41] Indeed, Psellus became the prime model for all types. Thus, if Homer *and* Demosthenes *and* Chrysostom *and* Psellus are Attic, the word has come by the twelfth century to refer to any author worthy of imitation, contemporary or ancient.[42]

The way to achieve Attic style was to follow the precepts of Hermogenes. His Περὶ ἰδεῶν recognizes seven qualities of style: σαφήνεια (clarity); ἀξίωμα λόγου (loftiness); κάλλος (beauty); γοργότης (conciseness); ἦθος; ἀλήθεια (sincerity); and, the pinnacle of stylistic excellence, δεινότης (force).

---

[37] *Ibid.* 16. See also T. Hedberg, *Eusthathios als Attizist* (Uppsala 1935), and P. Wirth, *Untersuchungen zum byzantinischen Rhetorik des zwölften Jahrhunderts* (Munich 1960).

[38] See A. Mayer, "Psellos' Rede über den rhetorischen Charakter des Gregorios von Nazianz," *Byzantinische Zeitschrift* 20 (1911) 82.

[39] See B. Laourdas, "Παρατηρήσεις ἐπὶ τοῦ χαρακτῆρος τῶν ἐπιστολῶν τοῦ Φωτίου," Ἐπετηρὶς Ἑταιρείας Βυζαντινῶν Σπουδῶν 21 (1951) 74-109.

[40] *Rhetores graeci* 3.559.12.

[41] *Rhetores graeci* 3.572.25ff.

[42] Böhlig (n. 35 above) 16.

Not all of these are equally emphasized at every period, but inasmuch as
their selection defines the over-all pattern of Byzantine literary culture, the
fortunes of Hermogenes are a good guide for tracing the evolution of rhetoric.

We can distinguish four periods. After Syrianus our information about
Hermogenes is scanty. The school of Gaza made little use of him. His influence, it would seem, was particularly felt in Athens and Alexandria; with
the closing of the Athenian school in 529 and with the Arab conquest of Antioch and Alexandria his fortunes faded. Constantinople must have initially been least aware of him, and he does not figure in the works of such
writers as Nicephorus and John of Damascus. The manuscript tradition,
however, may perhaps be interpreted as bearing witness to an undercurrent
of use in the schools. The present corpus of five treatises was first put together
in the late fifth or early sixth century, and many progymnasmata written at
the time became attached to his name.[43] That Photius relies heavily on Hermogenic concepts without ever citing the name of the rhetor suggests that Hermogenes continued to form a staple of the educational system. The systematic
search for manuscripts following the Arab defeat in 868 and the expansionist
policies of the Byzantine court no doubt helped bring him once again to the
fore.

With the ninth century begins the second period of Byzantine rhetorical history. The direction it takes and the principles it espouses are the immediate result of the iconoclastic age. The struggle had ended with the triumph of image
worship. The questions that had for centuries been pressing for solution had
now to be resolved. One of the major contributions of the opponents of images
had been to substitute for religious art a cycle of representations drawn from
the ancient tradition. In so doing they gave strong reinforcement to the
classical elements in Byzantine life. The pagan tradition had, however,
through the use of such textbooks as Hermogenes, rigidified the lay sector
of Byzantium, and in its realm Christianity had done the same. Nothing
could be clearer than the prescription of the Trullan Synod of 692, which
requires homilists to draw from the Fathers rather than compose their own
sermons.[44] Thus iconoclasm challenged the Church on its home ground, and
with the victory of the iconophiles the stage was set for defining the relationship between Christianity and classical culture. Photius offers a synthesis in which Christianity is the ruling element, effecting itself in concert
with a carefully culled classicism.

---

[43] *Praefatio* to Rabe's edition of Aphthonius, xiv. See n. 2 above.

[44] *Sacrorum conciliorum nova et amplissima collectio*, ed. J. D. Mansi (Graz 1960)
11.952CD: οἱ τῶν ἐκκλησιῶν προεστῶτες μᾶλλον ἐν τούτοις (i.e., the Fathers) εὐδοκιμή-
τωσαν ἢ λόγους οἰκείους συντάττοντες.

This interaction of classical and Christian can be detected as well in the educational reforms of the day. The patriarchal school had existed in Constantinople side by side with the university. It had not dealt exclusively with theology or the training of the clergy, but obviously did less than the university with the profane disciplines. In 861 Photius restored instruction in the profane sciences along with theology. Two years later Caesar Bardas reorganized the university and, as a result, both institutions now supported profane studies. Before his elevation, Photius had been a professor at the university; thus his support of secular learning was natural.[45]

The style of writing practiced in both these schools no doubt followed the Photian principle of adaptation from a Hermogenic base. Selection is to be made of only those qualities of style which correspond to the ideal of Christian character. Photius calls for a gracious and noble simplicity—a Hermogenic concept—of both words and action and, in doing so, deliberately turns away from the cornerstone of Hermogenes' system, δεινότης, as well as from some of the means by which it is acquired, such as τραχύτης (ruggedness), σφοδρότης (intensity), and δριμύτης (pungency), all of which could suggest the very opposite of Christian modesty and humility. Like Hermogenes, he recommends a proper mixture of the ingredients of good style. This feeling for propriety (τὸ οἰκεῖον), which he shares with the Second Sophistic, is deepened in response to a profound historical sense in the judgment of life and letters; and, indeed, the mixture is of something far greater than stylistic effects. It is Christianity and classical culture itself.[46]

The tradition of letter writing must have played an important role in the formulation of the Photian ideal, for some of the terms that he retains are similar to the requirements laid down by Gregory of Nazianzus for epistolography: συντομία, σαφήνεια, χάρις, τὸ πρέπον and ἀττικισμός.[47] Isidore of Pelusium in the fifth century continues the tradition,[48] as does Photius in the ninth, listing βραχύτης, σαφήνεια, χάρις, and ἀπλότης as the qualities by which to convey the ethos of the letter writer and his subject.[49] So too, a

---

[45] See F. Dvornik, "Photius et la réorganisation de l'académie patriarcale," *Analecta bollandiana* 68 (1950) 108-125 *passim*.

[46] This paragraph is a summary from the detailed analyses to be found in the work cited in n. 26 above as well as in my "History and theology in Photius," *Greek Orthodox Theological Review* 10 (1964) 37-74.

[47] Letter 51, PG 37.105.

[48] Bk. 5.133, PG 78.1404B: ὁ ἐπιστολιμαῖος χαρακτὴρ μήτε παντάπασιν ἀκόσμητος ἔστω μήτε μὴν εἰς θρύψιν κεκοσμημένος ἢ τρυφήν. τὸ μὲν γὰρ εὐτελές, τὸ δὲ ἀπειρόκαλον · τὸ δὲ μετρίως κεκοσμῆσθαι καὶ πρὸς χρείαν καὶ πρὸς κάλλος ἀρκεῖ.

[49] B. Laourdas, "Παρατηρήσεις ἐπὶ τοῦ χαρακτῆρος τῶν ἐπιστολῶν τοῦ Φωτίου," Ἐπετηρὶς Ἑταιρείας Βυζαντινῶν Σπουδῶν 21 (1951) 81.

late anonymous writer reminds us that ἠθοποιΐα should be καθαρά, and
without ruggedness.[50]

The third period extends from the eleventh to the end of the twelfth
century. The Macedonian renaissance had introduced Christian scholarship
on a solid and equal footing with the classics. The succeeding centuries
saw an expansion of both. If nothing else, the sheer weight of the multi-
plication of knowledge may be enough to account for the dissolution of the
Photian synthesis. The period comes to be marked by a sharp polarity between the two traditions. The key figures of the age, Psellus, Tzetzes,
Eustathius, have in common a curious ambivalence that makes it possible
for our handbooks to divide their productions into two parts, those on pagan
versus those on Christian themes.

Psellus's works well illustrate this division. He has left us two different
treatments of the style of Gregory of Nazianzus. One cites him as part of the
Christian canon that includes Chrysostom and the other two Cappadocians,[51]
just as the ninth century had done. Psellus is here at pains to show that Gregory's prose and poetry meet the ancient criteria, that Gregory can stand on
an equal footing with the models of the Second Sophistic such as Aristides,
and in short, that he is the Christian equivalent, preferable for the Christian
because he writes about Christian things and writes about them well. This
is a legitimate appreciation of Gregory as a literary figure and as a Church
Father. In the other treatise[52] Psellus sees Gregory as the acme of a long,
unbroken tradition of Greek letters, superior to Sappho, Thucydides, and
others with whom Gregory could have nothing in common. Here, rhetorically
speaking, the σύγκρισις principle has gone awry. In an excess of pious zeal,
Psellus has failed to fit his subject into the proper literary and historical
context. Interestingly enough, the treatise that brings to bear the greater
amount of classical knowledge is not the first, which, despite the sounder
evaluation, is rather standard and restricted in its analysis, but the second.
Here the learned Psellus draws on wide resources. In addition to Hermogenes,
he makes critical use of the rhetorical vocabulary of Dionysius of Halicarnassus
(whose work *De compositione verborum* he had partially excerpted),[53] of

---

[50] *Rhetores graeci* 3.595.11: οὐδὲ καθαρὰν τὴν φράσιν ἐτήρησαν φλεγμαίνοντες τὰ πολλὰ
καὶ τραχυνόμενοι τῇ λέξει · καὶ τοῦτο δὲ δι᾽ ἐπίδειξιν, ὅμως οὐκ ἐμέμφθησαν τοῖς πολλοῖς
διὰ τὸ φιλότιμον τοῦ λόγου καὶ πόριμον, ἴσως δὲ καὶ ἡμεῖς ζηλώσομεν τούτους κατὰ
καιρόν.

[51] Χαρακτῆρες Γρηγορίου τοῦ θεολόγου, τοῦ μεγάλου Βασιλείου, τοῦ Χρυσοστόμου
καὶ Γρηγορίου τοῦ Νύσσης, ed. J. Boissonade in M. Psellus, *De operatione daemonum;
accedunt inedita opuscula* (Nuremberg 1838, repr. Amsterdam 1964) 124-131.

[52] Text and commentary by A. Mayer, "Psellos' Rede über den rhetorischen charakter
des Gregorios von Nazianz," *Byzantinische Zeitschrift* 20 (1911) 27-100.

[53] *Rhetores graeci* 5.598. Note also Hermogenes rendered into political verse, *Rhetores
graeci* 3.687, and Psellus's summary of the Περὶ Ἰδεῶν, *Rhetores graeci* 5.601.

Demetrius, and Longinus; and he borrows phrases in abundance from Philostratus and Synesius. The work displays a heightened interest in pagan rhetoric as such, side by side with a strong religiosity; but the discussion fails because the one does not inform or relate to the other.

Psellus's two main interests in the pagan tradition are rhetoric and philosophy. He pursues two objects, "to improve his stylistic eloquence through rhetoric and to purify his spirit through philosophy."[54] In an encomium on his teacher, John Mauropus, he remarks that philosophy without rhetoric has no grace, and rhetoric without philosophy no content.[55] He berates one of his correspondents with the remark, "Perhaps you know philosophy and rhetoric, but you do not know how to put them together; there is a philosophizing rhetoric as well as a rhetoricizing philosophy."[56] In another letter, he points out, "Just as Plato in the *Timaeus* combines theology with physical science, so I write philosophy by means of rhetoric and fit myself to both through the use of both."[57] He recognizes another kind of philosophy superior to the pagan,[58] and there are a number of passages such as the above which call for a synthesis of rhetoric and philosophy,[59] but the appeal is self-conscious and almost obsessive. The terms in which it is couched take us back into the atmosphere of late Antiquity and remind us of the Neoplatonic concern to relate philosophy to rhetoric in a meaningful way. Psellus's role as head of the philosophical school organized by Constantine IX in 1045 gave him the opportunity of exploring in these areas without strict reference to the Christian tradition.

At the same time, there is a Christian Psellus. We are not yet in a position to date the mass of his works so as to establish a pattern of intellectual development, but it is clear that he was active in both traditions and that

---

[54] *The History of Psellus* 36, ed. C. Sathas (London 1899) 6.107.15: ῥητορικοῖς μὲν λόγοις τὴν γλῶτταν πλάσασθαι πρὸς εὐπρέπειαν καὶ φιλοσοφίᾳ καθᾶραι τὸν νοῦν.

[55] *Bibliotheca graeca medii aevi*, ed. C. Sathas (Paris 1876) 5.148: ὦτα νοῦ προεστῶτες γλῶτταν ἀδιανόητον ἔχουσιν—ὅ τε γὰρ μόνως φιλόσοφος ἄχαρις καὶ ὁ τὴν τέχνην διῃρημένως κομπάζων τοῦ κοσμοῦντος ἐστέρηται σχήματος—κατώρθωσε συνάψας τὰ διαστῆναι δοκοῦντα καὶ τὸν νοῦν καθηδύνας τοῖς ἀπὸ τῆς ῥητορικῆς χάρισι τήν τε γλῶτταν σεμνύνας τοῖς φιλοσόφοις νοήμασι.

[56] *Ibid.* 442: σὺ μὲν οὖν ἴσως φιλοσοφίαν ἐπίστασαι καὶ ῥητορικήν, τὸ δ' ἐξ ἀμφοῖν σύνθετον ἀγνοεῖς · ἔστι δέ, ὦ λῷστε, καὶ φιλοσοφίας ῥητορικὴ καὶ ῥητορεία φιλόσοφος. The passage forms part of a discussion of Hermogenes.

[57] *Ibid.* 476: καὶ ὥσπερ ὁ Πλάτων τῇ φυσιολογίᾳ μίγνυσι Τιμαιογραφῶν κατὰ τὸν σιλογράφον οὕτω δὴ κἀγὼ τῇ ῥητορικῇ τὴν φιλοσοφίαν συντίθημι καὶ πρὸς ἀμφοτέρας δι' ἀμφοτέρων ἁρμόζομαι.

[58] *The History of Psellus* 42, ed. C. Sathas 6.109.26: ἐστί τις καὶ ὑπὲρ ταύτην ἑτέρα φιλοσοφία.

[59] *Ibid.* 41; *Bibliotheca graeca* 5.480; Encomium on Symeon Metaphrastes, PG 114.188A: ἔμφωνον ἵν' οὕτως εἴπω τὸν νοῦν καὶ ἔννουν τὴν γλῶτταν εἰργάσατο; Letter 241, ed. Kurtz (n. 28 above); et al.

rhetoric is a vital force in both. Hermogenes is still the key figure.[60] Psellus, like Tzetzes, renders the text into political verse. Of particular interest is his *Synopsis* of the rhetorician. One way of achieving σεμνότης, says Hermogenes, is to talk about the gods (τῶν θεῶν). Psellus keeps the outline but makes the phrase singular, τοῦ θεοῦ.[61] The frame of the text is received without question, and only that portion changed which stands in glaring contrast to Christian concerns. Of roughly the same date must be a set of anonymous scholia on the *Περὶ ἰδεῶν*.[62] Once again, the treatment of δεινότης follows Hermogenes' pattern. Besides the gods, Hermogenes suggests 1) a discussion of divine matters (τὰ θεῖα πράγματα), that is, cosmology (his examples are taken from Plato's *Timaeus*); 2) things with a divine connection that men care about, such as the immortality of the soul or the cardinal virtues; and 3) important but exclusively mortal things, like the battles of Plataea, Marathon, or Salamis.[63] The Paris manuscript adds to these same scholia a note to the effect that Christians have many citations not available to the ancient writers, such as the beginning of the Fourth Gospel, and that writers on the Hexaëmeron achieve σεμνότης by their reference to creation and the works of God.[64] Another curious manuscript from the twelfth or thirteenth century gives an ordinary analysis of Hermogenes' text, but the scribe into whose hands it fell erased the examples from Demosthenes and substituted where he could quotations from Gregory of Nazianzus.[65]

The last period in the rhetorical history of Byzantium is the Palaeologan age. Here we have come full circle. The scholia of Maximus Planudes on Hermogenes do little more than elaborate the text.[66] Pletho's synopsis also follows the rhetorician, although one detects here a more original mind, going beyond the traditional scheme by citing other handbooks, calling attention to Hermogenes' sources, and occasionally being slightly critical of him.[67] The literary quarrel between Theodore Metochites and Nicephorus Chumnus in the fourteenth century has recently been the subject of a monograph by Ševčenko.[68] Metochites is attacked by Chumnus because his style is ἀσαφής (unclear), the opposite of the Hermogenic ideal, and also lacks κάλλος and ἦθος.

[60] See n. 53 above.

[61] *Rhetores graeci* 5.602.2. σεμνότης is a subdivision of ἀξίωμα λόγον in Hermogenes' scheme. Tzetzes: *Rhetores graeci* 3.671ff.

[62] *Rhetores graeci* 7.2.861ff.

[63] Hermogenes, 219ff.

[64] *Rhetores graeci* 7.2.954ff., esp. 956, 957.

[65] See V. de Falco, *Trattato retorico bizantino (Rhetorica marciana) (Pavia* 1930).

[66] The passage on σεμνότης for example, restores the plural, τῶν θεῶν: *Rhetores graeci* 5.480-481.

[67] *Rhetores graeci* 6.546-598.

[68] I. Ševčenko, *Études sur la polémique entre Théodore Métochite et Nicéphore Choumnos* (Brussels 1962).

In his defense Metochites says that his aim is δεινότης, also recommended by Hermogenes, and notes that this recognized excellence is acquired in part by τραχύτης and σφοδρότης, the very qualities which the ninth century had tended to exclude. Thus Metochites cultivates ἀσάφεια deliberately and can cite in his defense Hermogenes' own condemnation of excessive clarity.[69]

This peculiar state of affairs, which elevates obscurity into a literary virtue, explains the direction of much of Byzantine writing. No one who reads Byzantine literature at all need be told that, whereas the ideal constantly being held forth is clarity and simplicity, clear and simple is precisely what the literature is often not. The secular reasons for this can be seen in the set of associations that come to be attached to the word "Attic." One must, however, look also for a Christian explanation. As early as the latter part of the ninth century, Arethas had written an answer to those who had accused him of obscurity.[70] Like Metochites, he defends himself by saying that his writing appears obscure not because he has abandoned the rhetorical rules, but because his contemporaries do not understand him. Obscurity has the virtue of keeping out the crowd. The source for such a sentiment is probably to be found in the admonition by Photius (his teacher):

> I answer in a few words your question, as to just why it is that prophecy is overshadowed by the devices of obscurity. Prophecy is not history. The virtue of history is assuredly to speak clearly and not to contrive. It teaches events done in our midst, which we all alike, the prominent and the ordinary, experienced at the time and may learn about now. For prophecy, on the other hand, the function of which is to reveal the hidden to those who are worthy, but to keep it from the uninitiated, that is most fitting which is obscure and enigmatic and screened from view. So I think your difficulty is solved: to wit, if we did not need to learn, we should not be obliged to speak at all; but if we are to learn, then prophecy should not be unclear and practically the same as not speaking at all. My remarks have now established that it is both proper to learn and necessary not to speak wantonly and commonly. Things should rather be said in clarity to the initiated but kept inaccessible and unapproachable to the profane.[71]

---

[69] *Ibid.* 57.

[70] Πρὸς τοὺς εἰς ἀσάφειαν ἡμᾶς ἐπισκώψαντας, ἐν ᾧ καὶ τίς ἡ ἰδέα οὗ μέτιμεν λόγου, ed. L. Westerink, *Arethae scripta minora* (Leipzig 1968) 186-191. See Ševčenko (n. 68 above) 169 n. 2.

[71] PG, 101.948B, C: πυθομένῳ δέ σοι τί δήποτε ἡ προφητεία τοῖς τῆς ἀσαφείας τρόποις συνεσκίασται, διὰ βραχέων ἀμείβομαι. Διότι οὐκ ἔστιν ἱστορία ἡ προφητεία. ἱστορίας μὲν γάρ, εἴπερ τι ἄλλο, ἀρετὴ σαφῶς τε εἰπεῖν καὶ μηδὲν περινενοημένον ἐξεργάσασθαι. Τὰ γὰρ ἐν τῷ μέσῳ γεγενημένα διδάσκει, καὶ ἃ πάντες ὁμοίως καὶ σπουδαῖοι καὶ φαῦλοι κατ' ἐκεῖνο καιροῦ ἠπίσταντο, καὶ νῦν εἰδέναι οὐκ ἀπείργονται. προφητεία δέ, ἧς ἔργον τοῖς ἀξίοις ἀποκαλύπτειν τὰ ἄδηλα, τοῖς δὲ βεβήλοις ἄβατα ποιεῖν, τὸ συνεσκιασμένον

Photius's remarks proceeds from a reading of the famous text of Saint
Paul on the prophecy of tongues (1 Corinthians 13.4-14.40). They are prompted
more by a religious than a literary feeling. The sentiment, however, could
and did give him and his student biblical authority for cultivating deliberate
obscurity in the name of both Christianity and of the classical tradition as seen
through the medium of Hermogenes. Psellus was later to say that a man
who does not have the proper combination of rhetoric, philosophy, and political action is as tinkling cymbal.[72] The phrase comes from precisely the
same scriptural context. It was to serve Byzantium well. The Pauline text
that inspired the translation of the liturgy into foreign tongues and the conversion of the heathen and revealed Byzantium in her most glorious and successful role might also sustain the most serious shortcomings of her literature.[73]

Such were the rhetorical patterns that Byzantium inherited from her Greco-
Roman past and the uses to which they were put. The history of accommoda-
tion to rhetoric is the history of Byzantine culture itself. Byzantium contended
throughout her history with the challenge implicit in her very birththright.
There are moments when the two claimants to her soul, Christianity and
classical culture, stand apart, but in the very dualism of her nature there
lay hope for a union and harmony such as the ninth century proffered. The
grand tragedy of Byzantium lies in the fact that the expanded conscious-
ness of both the Christian and the classical traditions in the ninth century
facilitated the selection of one *or* the other on the part of succeeding generations.

Rhetoric was one of the few elements of Byzantine life to survive the wreck-
age of 1453. Many of the rhetorical ideals of Hermogenes are adapted by the
Italian Renaissance, and in the later sixteenth and seventeenth centuries
exert an even greater influence on English letters. Aphthonius, through even
more numerous editions and translations, passed into the educational habits
of Europe. Indeed, the techniques of composition practiced in our schools
ultimately owe much to the tradition that he represents, while among the
more conservative quarters of modern seminary education, the retention of

---

καὶ αἰνιγματῶδες καὶ τὸ διὰ παραπετασμάτων, πρεπωδέστατον. Ἐξ ὧν οἶμαι λελῦσθαί
σοι τὸ ἄπορον, ὡς, εἰ μὴ ἔδει μαθεῖν, οὐδ' ὅλως ἐχρῆν εἰπεῖν, εἰ δ' ἐκρίθη μαθεῖν, οὐκ ἀσα-
φῶς ἔχειν τὴν προφητείαν, καὶ ἐν ἴσῳ σχεδὸν τοῦ μηδὲ εἰρῆσθαι. διῃτήθη γὰρ ἐκ τῶν εἰρη-
μένων, ὅτι καὶ μαθεῖν προσῆκον ἦν καὶ ἀναγκαῖον μὴ βεβήλως καὶ κοινῶς εἰπεῖν, ἀλλὰ
τοῖς μὲν μύσταις εἰρῆσθαι σαφῆ, ἄδυτα δὲ τοῖς ἀμυήτοις διατηρηθῆναι καὶ οὐκ ἐφικτά.

[72] *Bibliotheca graeca* 5.148.

[73] It would be a useful and rewarding task to trace the history of this difficult and at
some points obscure text in Byzantine thought. The passage is crucial to the understanding
of some of the most basic manifestations of Byzantine culture.

[74] Hermongenes' contribution to English literature forms the subject of a book by Professor A. M. Endicott of the University of Toronto, to appear shortly under the auspices
of the Princeton University Press.

rhetorical forms such as the θέσις, one of the most common of the medieval progymnasmata, gives proof of the continuing vitality of ancient forms.[75]

Department of Classics
State University of New York at Buffalo
Buffalo, New York 14214, U.S.A.

[75] See Brzoska *s.v.* "Aphthonios" in Pauly-Wissowa, *Real-Encylopädie*, for relevant bibliography. I do not wish to depreciate other more important elements, such as Aristotle and Cicero, but only to call attention to a neglected aspect of the rhetorical tradition. The *editio princeps* of both Aphthonius and Hermogenes (except for his *Progymnasmata*, not printed until 1790, ed. Heeren, Göttingen) is volume 1 of the Aldine *Rhetorum graecorum collectio* (Venice 1508). The first Latin translation of Aphthonius appeared as early as 1513 (Aldine, ed. J. Catanaeus). After that his editions are very frequent and widespread throughout Europe. Some were to become very popular and influential, as for example, the Latin version by R. Agricola (Paris 1549). In addition to the lists provided in the introductions in Rabe's editions, consult J. Fabricius, *Bibliotheca graeca* 6 (Hamburg 1797) 69ff., 95ff.; also Brzoska, *loc. cit.* For the history of rhetoric among Greek speakers after 1453, particularly as regards homiletics, two recent works are indispensable: K. Kourkoulas, ʿΗ Θεωρία τοῦ κηρύγματος κατὰ τοὺς χρόνους τῆς Τουρκοκρατίας (Athens 1957), and P. Trempelas, ʿΟμιλητικὴ ἢ ʿΙστορία καὶ θεωρία τοῦ κηρύγματος (Athens 1950). I wish to thank Mr. Laourdas for calling my attention to these two works.

ASPECTS OF THE HISTORY OF LITERARY RHETORIC AND POETICS IN ARABIC LITERATURE*

•

by S. A. Bonebakker

The title of my paper reflects, I hope, my hesitation in approaching a subject on which very little research has been done and one that deals with material that consists for the greater part of unpublished manuscripts, most of them uncatalogued. In years of work, I have only been able to glimpse the vast material on this subject, and am far from finding an answer to some of the fascinating questions that have recently been raised in connection with it. I have asked myself whether there is any point in trying to outline the history of this branch of Arabic literature; any attempt may be frustrated tomorrow by the discovery of new texts.

By using the term "literary rhetoric" in the title, I have tried to indicate that the theory of style in Arabic literature is concerned almost exclusively with poetry and artistic prose, rarely with oratory. The theory of style of the Arabs does not seem to have any roots in the art of oratory as does that of the Greeks. For example, the term in Arabic which comes closest to what we would call rhetoric is *balāgha*. The word *balāgha* is derived from a root *balagha* meaning "to reach" and the etymology is explained by interpreting the *balāgha* as the art of reaching the listener in attempting to convey one's ideas to him, or the art of reaching the utmost perfection in the style and content of a composition. In the classical period it is applied indiscriminately to poetry, ornate prose, and oratory.[1] In contrast, the Arabic term for oratory, *khiṭāba*, is

---

* Since I wrote this paper in 1965, my views, notably on the relations between the poets and the philologists of the early Abbasid period, have undergone some changes, and new evidence has come to my attention. See my paper "Reflections on the *Kitāb al-Badīʿ* of Ibn al-Muʿtazz" in *Atti del III Congresso di studi arabi e islamici* (Naples 1967) 191-209, and my paper "Poets and Critics in the Third Century A.H." in *Logic in Classical Islamic Culture*, ed. G. E. von Grunebaum (Wiesbaden 1970) 85-111. For the question of Aristotelian influence on Arabic poetics see the important work by W. Heinrichs, *Arabische Dichtung und griechische Poetik* (Beirut 1969).

[1] The first interpretation is given by Abū Hilāl al-ʿAskarī (d. 395/1005) in his *Kitāb aṣ-Ṣināʿatayn* (Cairo 1952) 6, the second by Ibn al-Athīr (d. 637/1239) in his *al-Mathal as-Sāʾir* (Cairo 1939) 1.69. Earlier sources, as far as they are known to me, though characterizing the *balāgha* in various ways, neither offer a clear definition of the term nor ex-

applied strictly to the spoken word in public addresses, and is not used in any wider sense.[2]

By this distinction I do not mean to say that the Arabs had no theory of oratory. A theory of oratory definitely existed, but it did not have much chance to develop. It soon came to be incorporated as a branch of the *balāgha* and only some Aristotelian philosophers continued to treat it independently. Nor does the art of oratory appear to have made any significant contribution to the theory of the *balāgha*. The reasons for the somewhat shadowy existence of the art of oratory should be sought in the religious and political structure of Islamic society. Islam, regulating as it did both public and private life even to the smallest details, gave a place to public speaking only in the Friday sermon in the mosque. The establishment of the Umayyad caliphate in 41/661,[3] soon after the death of Muhammad, brought with it a rapid decline of the primitive tribal democracy of the Arabs. The last traces of this tribal democracy disappeared in the beginning of the Abbasid period, that is, soon after 132/750, and with it, apparently, whatever tendency might otherwise have existed to discuss oratory either independently or as an important branch of the *balāgha*.

Finally, I have tried to indicate that in my view Arabic rhetoric cannot be separated from the study of poetry. In the classical period at least, rhetoric is little more than a theory of the poetic art. I will return to this point later, but mention it here to justify not only saying a few words on the character of early Arabic poetry, but also to justify dealing with the criticism of poetry as our most important source for the study of what we may call rhetoric in Arabic literature.

Compared to other branches of Arabic literature, Arabic rhetoric (as well as Persian and Turkish rhetoric, which are based on it) attracted the interest of Western scholars at a comparatively early date. As early as 1801, F. Gladwin wrote his *Dissertation on the Rhetoric, Prosody and Rhyme of the Persians*; this was followed in 1853 by Mehren's *Rhetorik der Araber* and in 1873 and 1874 by similar works by Garcin de Tassy[4] and by the German poet, Rückert,[5]

---

plain its etymology. It seems clear, however, that whatever meaning was attributed to the term *balāgha* in these early sources, the term was rarely if ever applied to oratory alone. For the term *balāgha* in late medieval sources and the difference between this term and the term *faṣāḥa* ("chastity," "euphony"), see A. F. Mehren, *Die Rhetorik der Araber* 15-18.

[2] The only exception known to me is a passage in ʿAbdalqāhir al-Jurjānī's *Asrār al-Balāgha*, ed. H. Ritter, 368 = 428 of Ritter's translation, where the term is perhaps used in a wider sense.

[3] Here and elsewhere in this paper, whenever two dates are given, the first refers to the Muslim and the second to the Christian era.

[4] J. H. S. V. Garcin de Tassy, *Rhétorique et prosodie des langeus de l'orient musulman* (Paris 1873).

[5] F. Rückert, *Grammatik, Poetik und Rhetorik der Perser*, ed. W. Pertsch (Gotha 1874). The Turkish system is, according to E. J. W. Gibb, based entirely on the Persian and Arab

the author of a famous German translation of a collection of ancient Arabic poetry known as the *Ḥamāsa*. These books were without exception descriptive; all were based on textbooks dating from the late Middle Ages and they gave almost no attention to the history of this branch of literature or to its place among similar types of literature in other languages, though occasionally their authors attempted to render some of the technical terms used by the Arabs for certain figures of speech by Western equivalents. The chief purpose of these books was to further the understanding of Islamic poetry; their authors may have felt that the time was not yet ripe for a study of Arabic rhetoric from a historical point of view, or for a comparison of Arabic rhetoric to the systems of other languages, especially Greek and Latin.

In 1896, however, the study of Arabic rhetoric and literary criticism was put on a different level. Goldziher, in an article that has hardly been outdated by recent work, analyzed the attitude of early medieval critics on the question of the superiority of pre-Islamic over Islamic poetry.[6] Important editions of texts, monographs and articles followed: the edition by Tkatsch of Abū Bishr's Arabic translation of Aristotle's *Poetics* (1928-1932), Kratchkovsky's edition of Ibn al-Muʿtazz's *Kitāb al-Badīʿ* (1935), Ritter's edition and translation of al-Jurjānī's *Asrār al Balāgha* (1954, 1959), and the numerous books and articles by von Grunebaum, to mention only a few. One of the most spectacular contributions, though by no means one of the best, was a paper presented by the well-known Egyptian scholar, Ṭāhā Ḥusayn at the Congress of Orientalists in Leiden in 1931, in which he claimed to see a relation between the *Rhetoric* of Aristotle and Arabic poetics, a possible relationship which has been occasionally discussed since, but has not yet been clarified.[7]

The small amount of work that has been done on Arabic poetics still compares favorably with the work that has been done on Arabic poetry itself. Though excellent monographs on the poetry of particular periods or areas exist, there is as yet no study of the history of Arabic poetry as a whole; one of the cornerstones of the study of the history of Arabic poetics is still missing.

I will nevertheless try to say a few words on one of the most typical forms of Arabic poetry, the *qaṣīda*, and on one of the most important periods of Arabic poetry in general, that of the early Abbasids. In doing so in the con-

---

systems. For a brief discussion of this system see Gibb's *History of Ottoman Poetry* (London 1900-1909) 1.111-124.

[6] I. Goldziher, *Abhandlungen zur arabischen Philologie* (Leiden 1896-1899) 1.122-176.

[7] Ṭāhā Ḥusayn, "Le rapport entre la rhétorique arabe et la rhétorique grecque." A brief summary of this paper has been published in *Actes du XVIII⁰ congrès international des orientalistes* (Leiden 1931) 241-242. An Arabic translation of the full text, under the title *al-Bayān al-ʿArabī min al-Jāḥiẓ ilā ʿAbdalqāhir*, appeared as a preface to the edition by Ṭāhā Ḥusayn and ʿAbdalḥamīd al-ʿAbbādī of the so-called *Naqd an-Nathr* of Qudāma (see n. 37 below).

text of this brief paper I shall, of course, be unable to avoid a great deal of oversimplification.[8]

The *qaṣīda* is a poem of pre-Islamic origin. It conforms to the complex rules of a set number of different meters and to the even more complex rules of the rhyme, which must be maintained throughout. Further characteristics of its form are the use of an archaic language, rich in apparent synonyms, and the frequent independence, both grammatical and thematic, of each line of the poem, a characteristic that accounts for a certain lack of cohesion. The poet's purpose, broadly stated, is to assert himself as a warrior, horseman, and hunter, as a member of a distinguished tribe, and as a man of noble character who does not fail to show his gratitude when receiving the help or protection of a patron.[9] This purpose manifests itself in a sequence of themes that from our point of view are often disjointed, the most characteristic of which is the *nasīb*, a sentimental opening theme in which the poet laments the loss of his beloved, who moved away with her tribe.

The sequence, or even the choice of the themes, seems to have been optional at first; it soon became fixed, at least theoretically, as a series beginning with a *nasīb*, followed by a set of descriptive themes (the poet's journey through the desert after his visit to the remains of the camp in which he had enjoyed the company of his beloved), and concluding with a panegyrical theme sometimes combined with satire.

The *qaṣīda* in this standardized form had a remarkable vitality and in Islamic times acquired an outspoken ceremonial function.[10] Even in the nineteenth century, as Goldziher tells us,[11] a number of *qaṣīdas* were dedicated by Arab scholars to Western monarchs at congresses of orientalists.[12] This vitality of the *qaṣīda* is the more astonishing if we keep in mind that within a century after Muhammad's death Arabic had become the language of the elite of a vast empire in which people of pure Arab stock rapidly lost prominence in favor of non-Arab subjects with a superior cultural background. They, one would think, could find little inspiration in a set of themes that had

---

[8] For an accurate and up-to-date account of the questions discussed in the following pages, see H. A. R. Gibb, *Arabic Literature*, ed. 2 (Oxford 1963) Chaps. 3, 4, 5, and R. Blachère, *Histoire de la littérature arabe* 2 (Paris 1964) 374ff.

[9] Blachère, *Histoire* 378; G. Richter in *Zeitschrift der deutschen morgenländischen Geselschaft* 92 (1938) 552-569.

[10] H. A. R. Gibb (n. 8 above) 61.

[11] I. Goldziher (n. 6 above) 173.

[12] These Arab scholars, of course, did not travel to Europe on camels; they traveled comfortably on steamers. All the same, they refer to the camel in their descriptions of means of transportation: "Da vergiesst der aus Kairo aufbrechende Delegirte Thränen des Schmerzes an den verödeten Wohnungsspuren [of the camp where he had once enjoyed the company of his beloved] und zieht auf schnellfüssigen Kamelen durch gefahrvolle Wüsten, bis dass er in Wien oder Stockholm anlangt, um den Ruhm der dort thronenden Fürsten zu besingen" (Goldziher).

no connection with the sedentary life of their Persian, Aramaean, Berber, or Greek ancestors, even though these originally non-Arab subjects had adopted the language of the conquerors as their medium of expression.

In spite of the predominance of the *qaṣīda* as the most characteristic form of poetry, there were nevertheless several independent genres. Dating from pre-Islamic times is the elegy with its own traditional form. In the age of the Umayyads (that is, during the first century of Islam, a peirod in which we find an empire almost exclusively ruled by an aristocracy of pure Arab descent that lived in the Fertile Crescent rather than on the Arabian peninsula), some other genres emerge: the independent love poem (different in purpose and theme from the sentimental prologue of the *qaṣīda*), the wine song (which, however, is said to have been an imitation of the pre-Islamic wine song), the hunting poem and the political poem. But these genres follow the same rules of prosody as the pre-Islamic *qaṣīda* and often show a close resemblance to it in language and in spirit.[13] A radical change does not occur until the beginning of the Abbasid period, the second Islamic century. This era, which begins with the fall of the Umayyads in 132/750, is marked, politically and socially, by the gradual transformation of a society in which aristocrats of pure Arab descent were almost the only governing power into a society in which people of non-Arab descent, but using Arabic as their official and literary language, were influential to the same or to an even greater degree. There is no doubt a connection between these social and political changes and those of both style and content that can be discerned in the poetry of the age. These transformations are as marked as they are difficult to define. The poets scrupulously observed the established rules of grammar and, with rare exceptions, those of meter and rhyme. At the same time, however, they attempted both to simplify the vocabulary and to handle old themes according to their own ideas by introducing skillful variations on these themes and new similes. In addition, they began deliberately, if we may believe the Arab critics, but still on a modest scale, to introduce rhetorical devices. These changes no doubt account for much of the freshness and the sometimes irresistible charm of early Abbasid poetry. Yet the early Abbasid age saw the emergence of only two new genres, the ascetic poem and the mystical poem. This, and the absence of new patterns of rhyme and meter, justifies us in characterizing early Abbasid poetry as the late blooming of an ancient art. It was bound henceforth to show a certain decline because of the lack of innovations that had any lasting appeal either to the poet or to his audience.[14]

---

[13] The hunting poem, however, uses the *rajaz* meter which is not counted among the classical meters of the *qaṣīda* ; see E. Wagner, *Abū Nuwās* (Wiesbaden 1965) 266ff. On the extended poems in the *rajaz* meter dating from the Umayyad period see M. Ullmann, *Untersuchungen zur Raǧazpoesie* (Wiesbaden 1966) 26-44.

[14] An exception must be made for certain forms of popular poetry, the most famous of which are the *muwashshaḥ* and the *zajal*, which originated in Spain in the fourth/tenth

This tendency towards a gradual stiffening of Arabic poetry may have been reinforced by the curious fact that the early Abbasid poets, in spite of their frequent open opposition to the philologists and their no less open ridicule of the traditional themes of pre-Islamic poetry admired by the philologists, were yet to a large extent dependent upon them. They accepted, whether willingly or not, the philologist's doctrine of the superiority of pre-Islamic poetry as the foundation on which all later achievements rested.

I will not try to explain this curious phenomenon in detail. Perhaps many poets of the Abbasid age did not speak Arabic as their mother tongue, or they spoke a dialect that was very far from the literary idiom. In either case they would have had to spend many years studying this literary idiom, which was almost exclusively represented by pre-Islamic poetry with its limited range of themes. It is not surprising that later Abbasid poets often slipped back into a kind of neoclassicism, imitating the language and, to some extent, the themes of the pre-Islamic era to a degree that makes their poetry artificial and unattractive to many Westerners despite its technical merits and occasional originality. We may say that the philologists emerged as victors, even though they were formally defeated, as we shall see later.[15]

As I have already noted, most studies on Arabic literary theory in Western languages are summaries of late medieval handbooks. Only recently have scholars become interested in the early history of Arabic literary criticism, particularly in two of its aspects: the attitude of early critics towards Islamic poetry, and the question whether or not these critics were influenced by Greek works on literary theory. I am convinced that much more can still be learned on these and other aspects, in spite of the fact that many texts have not come down to us. The difficulty is that information is scattered over many different sources: anthologies of pre-Islamic and Islamic poetry, works on grammar and lexicography, collections of biographies, and even works on the interpretation of the Koran. Many of these sources must be carefully examined since they may yield quotations from critics of the first two centuries of Islam on such subjects as poetic technique, classifications of the genres of poetry, and, most important of all, quotations that reveal attempts

---

and sixth/twelfth centuries, and spread thence to the East. In the late Middle Ages, these popular forms of poetry became the subject of special treatises. See, for instance, W. Hoenerbach, *Die vulgärarabische Poetik . . . des Ṣafiyaddin Ḥilli* (Wiesbaden 1956). The present survey does not take into account the numerous occasional pieces on various subjects which date as far back as the early Abbasid period. See Gibb (n. 15 below) 577.

[15] In discussing this phenomenon and in particular the survival of the *nasib* theme in Islamic poetry, H. A. R. Gibb, in *Bulletin of the School of Oriental and African Studies* 12 (1948) 574-578, offers a somewhat different explanation. He points to the "growing body of sociological observation which throws light on the perennial fascination which the old bedouin life and traditions have exercised upon the thought and imagination of the Arabs." In his opinion "both poet and philologist served, in their different ways, the same ends and shared the same ideals."

to create a technical vocabulary of the poetic art. I must admit that much of what has turned up is very far from enlightening on any of these matters. What we find most often, apart from philological explanations, are comments on a single line of poetry: the common remark among these early critics is that "the greatest among Arab poets is the one who has said such and such," or, that "the best line of elegy ever composed is such and such." Even in quite early times (first/seventh century), however, we find analytical criticism that is not limited to individual lines of poetry, but deals with the work of the poet seen as a whole.[16] There is even a tradition that attributes to the caliph ʿUmar (d. 23/644), the second successor of Muhammad, a fragment of literary criticism in which the technical terms *waḥshī* (var. *ḥūshī*, "unfamiliar, unintelligible language") and *muʿāẓala* ("sticking together," "discord," a term of uncertain meaning) occur. The poet Zuhayr, ʿUmar is reported to have said, avoided the *waḥshī* and the *muʿāẓala* and, in addition, distinguished himself by praising a man only according to the virtues he really possessed.[17] There is much to be said for rejecting this tradition as a forgery aimed, perhaps, at counterbalancing other traditions that describe ʿUmar's severity in dealing with poets who were guilty of composing defamatory poetry deemed detrimental to the unity of the Muslim community. Not until the first half of the second/eighth century do we find similar discussions of characteristics of style,[18] and not until the end of that century or the beginning of the next do we find any terms for what we should call figures of speech.[19] Still there exist from the second half of the first century examples of technical terms, used probably for certain defects of the rhyme, which terms are undoubtedly authentic.[20] It would not be surprising, therefore, if further in-

---

[16] See A. Trabulsi, *La critique poétique des Arabes jusqu'au Vᵉ siècle de l'hégire* (Damascus 1956) 5f., 146, 220.

[17] See al-Jumaḥī, *Die Klassen der Dichter*, ed. J. Hell (Leiden 1916) 18; Ibn Qutayba, *Liber poësis et poëtarum*, ed. de Goeje (Leiden 1902) 57; Qudāma ibn Jaʿfar, *Naqd ash-Shiʿr*, ed. S. A. Bonebakker (Leiden 1956), 100, 103; Abu 'l-Faraj al-Iṣfahānī, *Kitāb al-Aghānī* (Cairo A.H. 1285) 9.147, lines 2-3, 21-22; al-Marzubānī, *al-Muwashshaḥ* (Cairo A.H. 1343) 354; Abū Hilāl al-ʿAskarī (n. 1 above) 162; Ibn Rashīq, *al-ʿUmda* (Cairo 1325/1907) 1.62; al-Khafājī, *Sirr al-Faṣāḥa* (Cairo 1952) 183f.; Ibn al-Athīr (n. 1 above) 1.292.

[18] See, for instance, Ibn al-Muqaffaʿ's (d. 142/759) characterization of the *balāgha* quoted by al-Jāḥiẓ, *al-Bayān wa 't-Tabyīn*, ed. ʿAbdassalām Muḥ. Hārūn (Cairo 1948-1950) 1.115f.; Abū Hilāl al-ʿAskarī (n. 1 above) 14; al-Ḥuṣrī, *Zahr al-Ādāb* (Cairo 1953) 1.104f., and the poet Bashshār's (d. 167/784 or 168/785) discussion of his own work as quoted by al-Ḥuṣrī 1.110 and Ibn Rashīq (n. 17 above) 2.185f.

[19] See below nn. 25, 30. If, however, we accept as authentic two traditions quoted by al-Bāqillānī, *Iʿjāz al-Qurʾān*, ed. Aḥmad Ṣaqr (Cairo 1954) 108 and Ibn Rashīq (n. 17 above) 1.181, the term *istiʿāra* ("metaphor") would have been known to the philologists Abū ʿAmr ibn al-ʿAlāʾ (d. about 154/770) and Ḥammād ar-Rāwiya (d. after 155/771) and would have existed at least half a century earlier.

[20] See my edition of Qudāma ibn Jaʿfar's *Naqd ash-Shiʿr*, Introduction, 34f.; Blachère in *Arabica* 6 (1959) 132-151.

vestigations prove that technical terms for certain characteristics of style and even for certain figures of speech also existed at a very early date, if not as early as the reign of the caliph ʿUmar.

Characteristic of the second and early third centuries of Islam are the discussions on the question whether poetry composed after the advent of Islam could be equal in merit to pre-Islamic poetry. In this controversy, which attracted Goldziher's attention some seventy years ago, the conservative side was taken by the philologists, who had been engaged for a long time in collecting and expounding the meaning of pre-Islamic poetry and the verse composed by the contemporaries of Muhammad. The motives behind this activity were twofold. First, these philologists were bent on handing down and preserving the monuments of native Arab tradition to a society that used Arabic as its official language, but was not always of Arab stock, and had often lost contact with this tradition. Second, they felt that they had to use the pre-Islamic poetry of the desert Arabs as a base if they were to succeed in compiling a grammar and a lexicon that could claim to describe the language in its purest form. Some philologists went so far as to forge poems to prove certain points.

With this background of philogical studies in mind, it is not difficult to understand that the grammarians and the lexicographers were opposed to accepting contemporary poetry, that is poetry composed by early Abbasid poets, as equal in quality to pre-Islamic poetry.[21] In their eyes the poets of the second and third centuries, who were often not of pure Arab descent, could not be expected to compose good poetry, but were to be counted among those who needed grammatical training based on pre-Islamic models. But the philologists went a step further and rejected early Islamic poetry by poets of Arab descent. The early Islamic poets, they felt, might well possess a certain competence in the language but would no longer be familiar with the Bedouin environment that had inspired the themes of pre-Islamic poetry. Pushing this doctrine to its extreme consequences, one of them even expressed the view that Islam had introduced a code of ethics which had destroyed the background necessary for composing good poetry.[22]

---

[21] An amusing anecdote involving the famous philologist Ibn al-Aʿrābī (d. between 230/844 and 232/846) is quoted by Goldziher (n. 6 above) 165. It is also quoted in various forms by aṣ-Ṣūlī, *Akhbār Abī Tammām* (Cairo 1937) 175f., Abū Hilāl al-ʿAskarī (n. 17 above) 45, and al-Khafājī (n. 17 above) 328. According to this anecdote, Ibn al-Aʿrābī was made to believe that a certain poem was pre-Islamic. It greatly pleased him, and he ordered one of his pupils to write it down on a sheet of paper. But when it was revealed to him that the poem was by the contemporary poet, Abū Tammām (d. 231/845 or 232/846), he ordered the sheet of paper to be torn up. A similar anecdote, in which the same Ibn al-Aʿrābī unwittingly pronounces a favorable judgment on a poem by Abū Nuwās (d. between 198/813 and 200/815), is related by al-Ḥuṣrī (n. 18 above) 1.241.f., on the authoridy of Abū Hiffān (d. 255/868 or 257/870).

[22] Goldziher (n. 6 above) 136. The tradition also occurs in Ibn Qutayba's *Liber poësis* (n. 17 above) 170, and in a different form in al-Marzubānī's *al-Muwashshaḥ* (n. 17 above) 62.

The attitude of the second- and early third-century philologists is understandable from still another point of view. Their chief concern was to give a firm foundation to history and philology. Aesthetic criticism was a mere byproduct of their activity. This, in my view, also explains the fact that this negative attitude towards Islamic and, in particular, Abbasid poetry (whatever its motives) died out as grammar and lexicography slowly reached maturity and scholars began to be interested in literary criticism for its own sake. Scholars were eventually forced to abandon their rigid attitude and to adopt more liberal views simply because the rulers of the Abbasid age continued to give generous support to contemporary poets without regard for the objections of the scholars. So too, did many members of the newly emerging class of Persian Muslims who used Arabic as a medium of expression and to whom the Abbasids granted a status equal to that of Muslims of pure Arab descent.

I think there is evidence that the views on contemporary poetry of at least some philologists took a new turn no later than the first half of the third/ninth century. It is possible, moreover, that the conflict between philologists and poets may sometimes have been more apparent than real, and it is possible that some of them were quite able to make a distinction between their use of a line of poetry as a *locus probans* and their appreciation of its literary merits.[23]

---

[23] The reports are often contradictory. According to a tradition quoted by Goldziher (n. 6 above) 141, from the *Kitāb al-Aghānī* of Abu 'l-Faraj al-Iṣfahānī (n. 17 above) 17.12, Abū ʿUbayda's (d. around 210/825) dislike of Islamic poetry was feared by his contemporary, the poet Ibn Munādhir. Abū ʿUbayda, however, is reported to have favored another of his contemporaries, the poet Abū Nuwās. See Abū Nuwās, *Dīwān*, ed. E. Wagner (Wiesbaden 1958) 11. Al-Aṣmaʿī (d. 216/831), whom Goldziher (n. 22 above) cites as the author of one of the most extreme statements on the comparative merits of pre-Islamic and Islamic poetry and who, like his contemporary Ibn al-Aʿrābī, was characterized as a conservative by the fifth/eleventh-century rhetorician Ibn Rashīq (n. 17 above) 1.57, admired, according to other traditions, the poet Bashshār (d. 167/784 or 168/785) and compared him to some pre-Islamic poets. See Abu 'l-Faraj al-Iṣfahānī (n. 17 above) 3.25; al-Marzubānī (n. 17 above) 251-252. He and Ibn al-Aʿrābī are also reported to have shown their admiration for Abū Nuwās. See Ibn al-Muʿtazz, *Ṭabaqāt ash-Shuʿarāʾ al-Muḥdathīn*, ed. ʿAbdassattār Aḥmad Farrāj (Cairo 1357/1956) 215-217; Abū Nuwās (n. 23 above) 11-12, 22; Abu 'l-Faraj al-Iṣfahānī (n. 17 above) 18.16; al-Ḥuṣrī (n. 18 above) 2.1088. Ibn al-Aʿrābī, however, in the anecdote quoted above (n. 21) showed his embarrassment over a favorable judgment that he had accidentally pronounced on this poet; he attributed to incidental good fortune some lines by Abū Nuwās which had won the recognition of others (al-Marzubānī [n. 17 above] 275). To assume that these scholars "contradicted themselves frequently and often unconsciously" or "improvised their judgments orally," as suggested by Trabulsi (n. 16 above) 4, hardly seems an adequate explanation. To my knowledge no such contradictions exist in the case of al-Aṣmaʿī's pupil, Abū Ḥātim as-Sijistānī (d. 255/869). In a long passage quoted in Ḥamza al-Iṣfahānī's commentary on the *Dīwān* of Abū Nuwās (14-16), this famous philologist gives an appreciation of twenty-five younger poets. Though his judgments are by no means always favorable, he appears to be seriously interested in contemporary poetry, and the passage clearly reflects the new trend in literary criticism.

We also find, however, the Arab rhetoricians of later generations defending Islamic poetry against the attacks of these early philologists. In doing so, they cannot have been following a mere convention, and Goldziher is no doubt correct in assuming that many educated Muslims remained convinced that pre-Islamic poetry could not be equaled by early Abbasid poetry, let alone the poetry of later periods.

We now come to the emergence of literary theory as an independent branch of literature. This took place about the middle of the third/ninth century or possibly somewhat earlier, in the first half of the century.[24] The new branch of literature, so far as we can judge from surviving evidence, is of two types, synthetic and analytic. In the first, the writer takes an interest in such questions as the quality of Islamic as compared to pre-Islamic poetry, the relation of content to form, poetic inspiration, talent and affectation, and the borrowing of themes by one poet from another. This type sometimes shows an attempt to arrive at a kind of synthesis between philology and aesthetic criticism. The second could be called the analytical method of criticism and it is more specifically concerned with themes, figures of speech, and characteristics of style. Though the synthetic would appear to us to be the more promising, in time, the analytic branch of criticism became the more typical and the more influential. The authors from the third century whose works have come down to us were no longer exclusively grammarians and lexicographers; and one of them, Ibn al-Muʿtazz, was a poet of considerable merit. Accordingly, the question arises whether the poets themselves had any influence on the genesis of Arabic poetical theory. This question has not been properly investigated. I have found evidence that there were poets around the year 200 of the Islamic era who discussed the meaning of three technical terms for figures of speech. These figures of speech were later included among those regularly discussed by the theorists and two of the three terms became part of accepted terminology.[25] I would not, however, conclude on the basis of this evidence that Arabic poetical theory owes its origin exclusively to the

---

[24] Of the several books on poets and poetry composed near the end of the second/eighth or the beginning of the third/ninth century, most are only known by their titles, and most are collections of poetry and biographies of poets. They may well have contained occasional critical remarks, but probably their authors did not discuss questions of literary theory either in the context of the biographies or in a separate chapter.

[25] See Abū ʿAlī al-Muẓaffar ibn al-Faḍl al-ʿAlawī al-Ḥusayni (fl. in the first half of the seventh/thirteenth century), *Naḍrat al-Ighrīḍ fi Nuṣrat al-Qarīḍ*, MS Istanbul, Damat Ibrahim 963, fol. 42b, where the poet ʿUmāra (still alive during the reign of the caliph al-Mutawakkil, 232/847-247/861) is quoted as using the term *raddāt* (= *tajnīs*, "paronomasia"); *ibid*. f. 58a, where the poet Abū Tammām (d. 231/845 or 232/846) uses the term *tardīd* ("using a word twice in the same line, but in relation to different concepts"); Ibn Rashīq (n. 17 above) 2.33, and Usāma ibn Munqidh, *al-Badīʿ fī Naqd ash-Shiʿr* (Cairo 1960) 75, where Abū Tammām discusses with his pupil, the poet al-Buḥturī (d. 284/897), the meaning of the term *istiṭrād* ("digression").

poets. It may well be that what we see in this new branch of literature is
the merging of the ideas of some independent minds (independence as well
as encyclopedic interests are very characteristic of the third century) with
a tradition of poetic craftsmanship that had been using its own terminology
for an as yet undetermined period of time and that now came into the open.
The assumption that Arabic poetic theory owes its origin exclusively to the
poets finds some support in a passage in the famous *Kitāb al-Badīʿ* of Ibn
al-Muʿtazz (d. 296/908). This *Kitāb al-Badīʿ, The Book of the Ornate Style*,
as the title says, deals with embellishments of style. The author successfully
shows that certain of these embellisments, claimed by early Abbasid poets
to be their invention, were in fact already used by the ancient Bedouin poets
and were used in the Koran. That Ibn al-Muʿtazz defended this claim does
not mean that he was in any way hostile to contemporary poetry. As I have
said he was himself a poet and at the same time a distinguished philologist.
Moreover, such an attitude would have been incompatible with the fact that
he edited a collection of such contemporary poetry. The fact that Ibn al-
Muʿtazz does not find it necessary to mention the controversy over ancient
and contemporary poetry shows that, in his circle at least, the discussion
on this matter had long been settled.

Ibn al-Muʿtazz devotes the first part of his book to pointing out, in both
contemporary and pre-Islamic poetry and prose, including the Koran, the
existence of metaphor, paronomasia, antithesis (all approximate translations),
repetition in the rhyme of a word that has occurred earlier in the line (sometimes identical with the ἐπαναδίπλωσις of the Greeks and the *redditio* of
the Romans), and an embellishment called "proceeding by logical argument"
(not, of course, a figure of speech in the sense we give to the term). He observes that this style is what certain early Abbasid poets call *badīʿ* (a term
by which Ibn al-Muʿtazz probably understands "unusual," or "ornate" style,
not "new" style as the editor, Kratchkovsky, thought).[26] He then points
out that people may disagree as to the number of existing categories of this
badīʿ and adds twelve categories of *maḥāsin* or "beauties" of style, so that
nobody can accuse him of having only a limited knowledge of the existing
figures of speech. The distinction between *badīʿ*-figures and "beauties" of
style has puzzled scholars, but probably "beauties" is a generic term, that is,
all figures are "beauties" but some of these "beauties" are to be considered
as peculiar to the style of modern poets, the *badīʿ*, and one can of course
easily disagree on their number. To forestall such criticism in an even more
emphatic manner and at the same time to stress his originality in dealing
with this problem of literary history, Ibn al-Muʿtazz observes that few are
competent to define the number of *badīʿ* figures, as *badīʿ* is a technical term
for certain types of poetry (this must mean: figures of speech in poetry) men-

---

[26] See I. Guidi in *Rivista degli studi orientali* 16 (1936) 410f.

tioned by *the poets and the educated critics among them. As for the students
of the language and of ancient poetry, they do not know this term and what it
stands for.*[27]

Other early texts support Ibn al-Muʿtazz's statement and likewise associate
the term *badīʿ* with the early Abbasid poets, actually attributing the creation
of the term to one of them, the poet Muslim (d. 208/823).[28] One passage attributes the term to the "transmitters of poetry,"[29] but these "transmitters"
need not necessarily be identical with the "students of the language and of
ancient poetry" whom Ibn al-Muʿtazz has in mind. Nor does this statement
exclude the poets from using the term.

It seems clear, however, that when Ibn al-Muʿtazz speaks of "students
of the language and of ancient poetry," he does not mean a contemporary
generation of philologists. He must be describing an older generation, perhaps
the generation that was still hostile to contemporary poetry. For Ibn al-
Muʿtazz must have known that his teacher Thaʿlab (d. 291/904), who no
doubt belongs to the category of "students of language and of ancient poetry,"
was interested in figures of speech and discussed them in a treatise. Moreover,
we find that at least three quarters of a century earlier the famous philologist
al-Aṣmaʿī uses three terms for figures of speech in a context that leaves no
doubt about his understanding of these terms.[30] The negative part of Ibn
al-Muʿtazz's statement cannot therefore be accepted unconditionally, and
it is likely that the philologists were at least acquainted with the terminology
of the *badīʿ*. The possibilities should not be ruled out that they elaborated
the system of rhetoric originally invented by the poets, or even that they were
themselves responsible for this system.

Apart from the passage just quoted and an introductory paragraph at
the beginning of the book, the *Kitāb al-Badīʿ* consists of technical terms,
with or without definition, followed by examples from the Koran, the sayings
of Muhammad and his companions, and ancient and modern poetry and
prose. Ibn al-Muʿtazz does not limit himself to giving examples of happily

[27] See Ibn al-Muʿtazz, *Kitāb al-Badīʿ*, ed Kratchkovsky (London 1935) 57f.

[28] See Muslim ibn al-Walīd, *Dīwān*, ed. de Goeje (Leiden 1875) 228-229; *idem*, ed. Sāmī
ad-Dahhān, 364f.

[29] Al-Jaḥiẓ (n. 18 above) 4.55.

[30] See Abū ʿAlī al-Muẓaffar (n. 25 above) fol. 49a-b, where al-Aṣmaʿī illustrates the term
taṣdīr (= *radd al-aʿjāz ʿala 'ṣ-ṣudūr*, the repetition in the rhyme of a word that has occurred
earlier in the line; see above, p. 85). See Ibn Rashīq (n. 17 above) 2.7, where al-Aṣmaʿī
explains the etymology of the term *muṭābaqa*, "antithesis" (see above, p. 85) and quotes
an example, and Abū Hilāl al-ʿAskarī (n. 1 above) 392, and Ibn Rashīq (n. 17 above) 2.37-38,
where he illustrates the *iltifāt* ("apostrophe") in the poetry of al-Jarīr. With regard to these
and similar traditions (see nn. 18, 23, 25 above), one should bear in mind that their authenticity cannot be satisfactorily proved even though (as in two of the three al-Aṣmaʿī traditions) an authority for the tradition is expressly mentioned.

phrased figures, but also quotes examples of their improper use.[31] Unfortunately, he rarely quotes arguments to support his judgments, and it is
therefore difficult to draw any conclusions as to his standards of criticism
except by inference.

A work that is often mentioned along with Ibn al-Muʿtazz's *Kitāb al-Badīʿ*
as one of the most important of its kind is the *Kitāb Naqd ash-Shiʿr*, the
Book of the Criticism of Poetry, of Qudāma ibn Jaʿfar.[32] The author died after
320/932 and was, therefore, a younger contemporary of Ibn al Muʿtazz. Qudāma's book was to some degree inspired by that of Ibn al-Muʿtazz, though
the name of Ibn al-Muʿtazz and the term *badīʿ* are nowhere mentioned.
The purpose and the framework of the *Criticism of Poetry*, however, are completely different. Qudāma asserts on the very first page that no work has
yet been written which would enable people to distinguish good from bad
poetry, a claim that is hardly justified even if we look only at the book
of Ibn al-Muʿtazz. Qudāma goes on to define poetry as "metrical rhymed
speech expressing a certain meaning." This definition in itself, he says, cannot
be used as a standard for distinguishing good poetry from bad. It is necessary,
therefore, to enumerate both the good qualities that, if the poet could combine them, would make his poem sublime, and the bad qualities that, if they
were found together, would make a poem utterly bad. These good and bad
qualities, as he wishes to make clear to his readers, do not depend on the
moral value of the ideas the poet chooses to express, or on praise given a
subject in one poem and criticism given it in another, but rather on the poet's
skill in the use of the four constituent elements of poetry: "word," "meaning,"
"meter," and "use of rhyme," which are implicit in his earlier definition,
and on his combination of these four elements two by two.

In accordance with this thesis, Qudāma then discusses themes in poetry,
questions of poetic technique and figures of speech under the headings "word,"
"meaning," "meter," "use of rhyme," or under the headings "combining word
and meaning," "combining meaning and meter," and the like. Following
much the same method as Ibn al-Muʿtazz, Qudāma makes each of the chapters
carry a technical term as its title. If necessary, this technical term is briefly
defined and several examples follow. The same arrangement is followed
in the second section dealing with errors in the description of themes, errors
in poetic technique and wrongly phrased figures of speech, the difference
being, of course, that Qudāma attributes such errors to a wrong use of the
constituent elements of poetry.

Qudāma's approach strikes us as very scholastic. The scheme of four elements which he devised no doubt helped him to arrange his material in an

[31] For a synopsis of the contents of the *Kitāb al-Badīʿ* see the introduction to Kratchkovsky's edition, 10-13.

[32] Ed. S. A. Bonebakker (Leiden 1956). For a brief synopsis of the contents of the *Kitāb
Naqd ash-Shiʿr*, see the introduction, 8ff.

orderly fashion. But it could not possibly be accepted as a basis for a sound theory of literature. It is not surprising, therefore, that this four-element scheme was rarely taken over by others and never in its complete form. In spite of this, we find hardly an author among those dealing with literary theory in succeeding generations down to the nineteenth century who does not owe something to Qudāma's terminology and definitions. The same is true, though, I believe, to a lesser degree, of Ibn al-Muʿtazz. The influence of these two scholars is, of course, most clearly noticeable in treatises that emphasize the discussion of terminology. We have several such works that show all the shortcomings of Qudāma's and Ibn al-Muʿtazz's systems without any of their merits. Every chapter follows the same order: technical term, definition, and examples. By the sixth/twelfth century the term *badīʿ* is no longer restricted to rhetoric, and figures of speech and characteristics of style are discussed side by side with questions of literary history and even of syntax. This leads to a proliferation of chapters and, occasionally, to the complete absence of any system or order. The quotations appear at times to be more important than the explanation of a terminology that is no longer always correctly understood. The treatise is at times more interesting as an anthology than as a work on rhetoric.

In many of the better treatises, however, the influence of Qudāma and Ibn al-Muʿtazz is either superficial or limited to certain sections, while in other sections the author discusses the history and social function of poetry, the poet's dependence on inspiration, and a wide variety of other important questions that are not found in the *Kitāb al-Badīʿ* or the *Naqd ash-Shiʿr*.[33] Another fact that should be mentioned is that the classical treatises that I have been discussing, beginning with the *Kitāb al-Badīʿ* of Ibn al-Muʿtazz, deal either exclusively with poetry or with poetry and prose in one context. Dating from the time of Ibn al-Muʿtazz we have an independent treatise of some importance on the art of letter writing. On the whole, however, it is safe to say that the critics felt little need to set up separate rules for prose writing. It is scarcely an exaggeration to say that prose to them was no more than poetry without meter and without continuous rhyme. This attitude is easily understandable if one remembers that the use of rhymed prose became widespread in the fourth/tenth century.

---

[33] For a detailed discussion of the contents of the fourth/tenth and fifth/eleventh century treatises on rhetoric, see G. E. von Grunebaum in *Journal of the American Oriental Society* 61 (1941), 51-57; Trabulsi (n. 16 above), especially the second part. These studies also discuss some of the medieval treatises that apply the theories of Arab rhetoric in weighing the merits of one poet against another, or in defending individual poets, and some of the treatises that use rhetoric to support the doctrine of the inimitability of the Koran. On the last category see especially G. E. von Grunebaum, *A Tenth-Century Document of Arab Literary Theory and Criticism* (Chicago 1950).

The position of these critics is perhaps best illustrated by what Ibn al-Athīr (d. 637/1239) has to say on the subject. This author was himself a secretary and his book contains examples from prose—that is letters—which are at least as numerous as the examples from poetry. Yet, when he speaks of the numerous disciplines with which authors, poets as well as prose writers, should familiarize themselves, he sees only one that is peculiar to the poet: the use of meter and rhyme.[34] In another passage on the "foundations of prose-writing," he states that only one of these "foundations" is specifically characteristic of the prose writer, that is, the secretary (or at least much easier for him than it is for the poet): the introduction of passages paraphrased the Koran and the Hadith. He encourages the student of letter writing to memorize good poetry and to paraphrase this poetry in his epistles.[35] This means, in his own words, that poetry is the substance (mādda) of prose. He finds a historical justification for this view in the fact that Arabic literature, through the ages, has consisted almost exclusively of poetry and that ancient prose, if it ever existed in any quantity, did not survive.[36] It seems that the poet Abū Tammām had the same idea in mind when, four centuries earlier, he somewhat unkindly called rhetoric the "fallen leaves" or "fallen fruit" (nafaḍ) of poetry.[37]

An important new approach to the art of rhetoric was introduced in the fifth/eleventh century by the appearance of two books by ʿAbdalqāhir al-Jurjānī (d. 471/1078), the Asrār al-Balāgha or Secrets of Eloquence[38] and the Dalāʾil al-Iʿjāz or Proofs of Stylistic Miraculousness (of the Koran).[39] He led a somewhat obscure existence in Jurjān, a province of Persia on the shore of the Caspian Sea, and his two books seem to have passed unnoticed at first. In the late sixth/twelfth or early seventh/thirteenth century, however, they were abridged by Fakhraddīn ar-Rāzī (d. 606/1209) and Sakkākī (d. 626/1229), both Persians. These digests spread outside Persia. An abstract of the rhetorical section of as-Sakkākī's work, the Talkhīṣ al-Miftāḥ of al-Qazwīnī (d. 739/1338), became the most popular textbook on rhetoric during the late Middle Ages and thereafter, and was the subject of countless commentaries.[40]

---

[34] Al-Mathal as-Sāʾir (see n. 1, above) 1.9-10.

[35] Ibid. 1.75.

[36] Ibid. 1.85.

[37] See Isḥāq ibn Ibrāhīm ibn Sulaymān ibn Wahb al-Kātib, Kitāb al-Burhān fī Wujūh al-Bayān, wrongly attributed to Qudāma and edited under the title Naqd an-Nathr by Ṭāhā Ḥusayn and ʿAbdalḥamīd al-ʿAbbādī (Cairo 1933 and 1938); see ʿAlī Ḥasan ʿAbdalqādir in Revue de l'académie arabe de Damas 24 (1949) 73-81. The passage occurs in the MS Dublin, Chester Beatty G 767 (see below n. 52) fol. 126b. A similar saying: "(prose) writing is taking poetry apart" (naqḍ) is quoted anonymously in Abū Hilāl al-ʿAskarī (n. 1 above) 222.

[38] Ed. H. Ritter (Istanbul 1954).

[39] Printed in Cairo in 1321/1903, 1331/1913, and 1366/1946.

[40] See Ritter's edition of the Asrār al-Balāgha, introduction 6-7. For editions of the Talkhīṣ al-Miftāḥ and commentaries, see C. Brockelmann, Geschichte der arabischen Literatur (Leiden 1939-1949) G 1.295-296; S 1.516-519.

The *Secrets* seem to have been little known except through abridgements, and several medieval authors state that the original was not accessible to them. One reason for the scarcity of the unabridged text may be that it was not easily understood, and contained ideas that could not so readily be put to practical use as, for instance, the catalogues of examples that were available elsewhere.

The original and uncompromising character of al-Jurjānī's work will be clear to anybody who cares to read a few pages of the *Secrets*, which is now available in an excellent German translation.[41] Al-Jurjānī brushes aside all the earlier writings on the subject and limits himself to those figures of speech which have the most striking effect in both poetry and prose: simile, metaphor, and analogy. In discussing these figures, he says, "his predecessors preferred not to send their minds too far afield, and God knows that is easier and saves trouble."[42] Though al-Jurjānī does not deign to mention these predecessors by name, there can be little doubt that he has in mind Ibn al-Muʿtazz and Qudāma, and the school created by these two authors. Al-Jurjānī has no use for their definitions and superficial analyses of the figures. Instead, he builds up a theory of his own, based mainly on a thorough analysis of the psychological effect of simile, metaphor, and analogy in their various forms. In the *Proofs of Stylistic Miraculousness*, as the title indicates, he tries to prove that the style of the Koran is inimitable. But actually he offers much more than just a proof of this dogma and gives a detailed discussion of syntax in its relation to style.[43]

The wide dissemination of epitomes of the *Secrets* and the *Proofs* led to a new division of the science of rhetoric which survives to the present day. This division puts the material of the *Proofs* in one category called "The Science of Notions," the material of the *Secrets* in a second category called "The Science of Exposition," and the remaining figures of speech in a third called by the ancient name "Science of the *Badīʿ*" (ornate style). Within this last section the figures are divided into those pertaining to "word" (or expression) and those pertaining to "sense" (or concept). Von Grunebaum[44] has recognized in this the Greek division into σχήματα λέξεως and σχήματα διανοίας, although, in my opinion, it may be that we have here a survival of part of the framework of Qudāma's treatise, or a division inspired by the discussions of the relation of "word" to "sense" (form to content) that are part of practically every treatise.

This brings us to a topic that I should like to mention very briefly before ending this paper: the possible influence of Greek literary theory on the creation and development of literary theory in Arabic. This question, as I have

---

[41] H. Ritter, *Die Geheimisse der Wortkunst des ʿAbdalqāhir al-Curcānī* (Wiesbaden 1959).

[42] I follow Ritter's translation in the introduction to his edition of the Arabic text, 9. This introduction contains a summary of the contents of the *Asrār al-Balāgha*.

[43] *Ibid.* 6. See also the analysis of this work by M. Weisweiler in *Oriens* 11 (1958) 77-121.

already remarked, was first raised by the Egyptian scholar Ṭāhā Ḥusayn, and, in my opinion, has never been answered satisfactorily simply because the early history of Arabic literary theory is still largely unknown. Comparisons between Greek and Arabic texts, therefore, lack cogency; hence, I will limit myself to calling attention to a few difficulties.

In an interesting passage in his *Criticism of Poetry*, Qudāma takes the side of those who prefer using the hyperbole in poetic expression to staying within reasonable limits. At the end of the passage he supports his views with the following statement: "The ancient authorities," he says, "who understood poetry and the poets held the same opinion. It is known to me that one of them said 'the best poetry is the most untruthful,' and this is also the view of poetry held by the Greek philosophers in keeping with the structure of their language."[45]

The significance of the passage, in my opinion, lies only in the direct reference to the Greek philosophers, not in the actual substance of Qudāma's statement. For he does not refer to any specific author and does not even assign the maxim, "the best poetry is the most untruthful," to any of the Greek philosophers. He rather suggests that an Arab invented this maxim. (That this may actually be so is borne out by a passage from Diʿbil's *Book of the Poets* quoted in Zolondek's dissertation.[46] Diʿbil lived from 148/765 to 246/860, a hundred years earlier than Qudāma, and the views he comments upon would therefore have been those of "ancient authorities" in Qudāma's time). Moreover, hyperbole is discussed often enough in Greek literature to make it difficult to identify Qudāma's source. Yet the passage undoubtedly proves that he had access to Greek sources either in the original or in translation, or that he had heard about them. And if this is true of one of the early theorists, it could be true of the others too. In fact the author of the so-called *Criticism of Prose*, a book wrongly attributed to Qudāma,[47] credits Aristotle with having said that poetry "contains more lies than truth,"[48] and Ibn al-Mudabbir, a critic of the third/ninth century, believes him to have stated that "eloquence consists of [using] beautiful metaphors."[49] Others, among them Abū Aḥmad al-ʿAskarī (d. 382/933) know that Plato attacked the poets and quote some examples and vague definitions of Greek eloquence.[50]

[44] G. E. von Grunebaum, *Medieval Islam* (Chicago 1946) 327, n.; *idem*, s.v. "BALĀGHA" in the *Encyclopaedia of Islam*, ed. 2.

[45] Qudāma (n. 32 above) 26 (see Introduction 36).

[46] L. Zolondek, *Diʿbil b. ʿAlī* (Lexington 1961) 133 (trans. 128b).

[47] See n. 37 above.

[48] Qudāma ibn Jaʿfar, *Naqd an-Nathr*, ed. Ṭāhā Ḥusayn and ʿAbdalhamīd al-ʿAbbādī (see n. 37 above) 90.

[49] See Muḥammad Kurd ʿAlī, *Rasāʾil al-Bulaghāʾ* (Cairo 1946) 251.

[50] Abū Aḥmad al-ʿAskarī, *Risāla fi 't-Tafḍīl bayn Balāghatay al-ʿArab wa-'l-ʿAjam*, MS Istanbul, Aṣir Efendi 433, fols. 1-11.

The problem, therefore, is not so much to determine whether there was any influence, but whether this influence went beyond the introduction of a few quotations and resulted in the integration of Greek rhetoric into the Arabic system or in its adoption as the model for the Arabic system. This question, which is not always clearly formulated, has been approached from the point of view of a possible influence of Aristotle's *Poetics* and *Rhetoric* on Arabic literary theory and on the basis of certain similarities between the subject matter of Greek and Arabic treatises on figures of speech. Let me quote a few opinions: Ṭāhā Ḥusayn asserts[51] that Aristotle's *Poetics* did not have any influence, but that the third part of his *Rhetoric* was used by Qudāma, the author of the *Criticism of Poetry*. Ṭāhā Ḥusayn gives examples but does not give specific references to either Aristotle or Qudāma, and I have been unable to identify with certainty the passages of Aristotle he has in mind. Nor do I always identify his allusions to Qudāma's *Criticism of Poetry*, though I edited this text myself. It is obvious that there are certain similarities. But, in my opinion, they do not offer any proof that there is a connection between the two authors and may even point to the opposite conclusion. It is true, for instance, that both Qudāma and Aristotle observe that simile and metaphor are close. But Qudāma says this in passing and as part of a chapter in which he speaks of the use of an inappropriate vocabulary; he points out that this is excusable only when it is clear that the poet intends to use a metaphor. In Aristotle, on the other hand, the metaphor takes a very important place in his discussion of style, and improper metaphors are mentioned only in passing. That both authors should defend hyperbole cannot possibly be quoted as a proof of Qudāma's dependence on Aristotle.[52]

A second scholar who defends the theory of Greek influence, though in a less emphatic way, is Trabulsi,[53] who holds that Aristotle's *Rhetoric*, in the translation by Isḥāq ibn Ḥunayn (d. 298/910 or 299/911)[54] may have prompted Ibn al-Muʿtazz to write his *Book of the Ornate Style*. Ibn al-Muʿtazz's pur-

---

[51] See n. 7 above.

[52] I have not attempted to determine whether there is any truth in Ṭāhā Ḥusayn's assertion that the so-called *Naqd an-Nathr* (see n. 37 above) shows the influence of Aristotle's *Rhetoric* and *Poetics*. The title *Naqd an-Nathr* [*The criticism* of *prose*], which this work carries in the Escorial MS 242 (the only manuscript known to the editors Ṭāhā Ḥusayn and ʿAbd-alḥamīd al-ʿAbbādī) wrongly suggests that it is a work on rhetoric. The text as it appears in the Escorial MS is incomplete. An examination of the complete text preserved in the Chester Beatty Collection shows that the work actually has a much wider scope, though rhetoric is one of the important subjects discussed. To my knowledge the *Naqd an-Nathr* did not influence the literary theorists of the author's own or of later generations and is never quoted.

[53] Trabulsi (n. 16 above) 78ff.

[54] Cf. Arisṭūṭālīs, *al-Khiṭāba*, ed. ʿAbdarraḥmān Badawī (Cairo 1959), Introduction. Badawī doubts if there really existed a translation by Isḥāq ibn Ḥunayn, but thinks that the old translation edited by him dates from the third/ninth century.

pose would have been not so much to discount the claim of modern poets to the invention of the "ornate style" as to emphasize that the Arabs of the desert were already acquainted with this style. For if this could be proved, then those who were inclined to give too much praise to this newly translated work of Greek antiquity, and who asserted that it introduced an art that was new to the Arabs, would be refuted. In other words, Trabulsi thinks that Ibn al-Mu'tazz was driven by a desire to disprove the arguments of those who held the culture and the language of the ancient Arabs to be inferior to those of the centers of civilization they subdued. What Trabulsi supposes to have been Ibn al-Mu'tazz's view was characteristic of the Shu'ūbiyya, a social and cultural movement that had many followers among the Persians in the second/eighth and third/ninth centuries.[55] The superiority of Greek culture, however, was also used as an argument in support of the Shu'ūbiyya doctrine. Accordingly, attempts to criticize the attitude of the Shu'ūbiyya would occasionally take an anti-Greek character.

Trabulsi's theory is ingenious, but at the same time difficult to accept, for the figures of speech which are the main subject of Ibn al-Mu'tazz's book are treated in Aristotle's *Rhetoric* only in passing and in a manner quite different from that of Ibn al-Mu'tazz. Trabulsi's theory becomes even less acceptable if we ask ourselves what the Arabs could have understood of Aristotle's *Rhetoric* and in what manner they could have used it, since political and forensic oratory had no place in their society. Only if the *Rhetoric* had been properly understood and applied, could it have been a challenge to the chauvinistic tendencies that Trabulsi ascribes to Ibn al-Mu'tazz's work. One may, however, choose to follow Ṭāhā Ḥusayn and Trabulsi, and admit that their argument is sound for the third part of the *Rhetoric*, the relevance of which extends beyond the limits of oratory. At the same time, it could be said that Ibn al-Mu'tazz might well have reacted against the *Rhetoric* of Aristotle without mentioning it specifically. But if so, one would expect other contemporary critics to have explained their attitude toward it or to have referred to it occasionally. This is particularly relevant to Qudāma, the author of the *Criticism of Poetry*, a book which, as far as I can see, shows no influence of either the *Rhetoric* or the *Poetics*. Yet this same Qudāma twice quotes from the *Categories* of Aristotle and appears to be acquainted with the works of other Greek philosophers as well.[56] Qudāma was certainly not opposed to the idea of using Aristotle. Moreover, the existence of Aristotle's *Rhetoric* could hardly have been unknown to him.

What has been said of the *Rhetoric* applies also to the *Poetics*. As Trabulsi rightly observes,[57] the *Poetics* is mainly a theory of drama, a genre unknown

---

[55] See I. Goldziher, *Muhammedanische Studien* (Halle 1889-1890) 1.147-216.
[56] See Qudāma (n. 32 above) Introduction 39ff.
[57] Trabulsi (n. 16 above) 74-75.

to the Arabs. Arabic poetry, by contrast as we have seen, centered on the *qaṣīda*, which was both in content and in form completely different from anything we find in Greek literature. The point is, therefore, that the Arabs could not use, and probably could not even properly understand, the book that would seem most likely (by virtue of its title) to have influenced their thinking on the subject of literary theory. One may counter that, in addition to a summary by al-Kindī (d. after 256/870) which is now lost, there were others by al-Fārābī (d. 339/950). Avicenna (d. 428/1037), and Averroes (d. 595/1198), the last of which is a serious attempt to apply Aristotle to Arabic poetry. It should be remembered, however, that al-Fārābī and Avicenna hardly make any attempt to illustrate the ideas of Aristotle by examples from Arabic literature, that Avicenna expresses serious doubts with regard to the use that could be made of Aristotle in discussing Arabic poetry, and lastly, that Averroes maintains many of his predecessor's reservations despite his own efforts to prove the contrary.[58] Moreover, these epitomes were completely disregarded by the Arab critics.[59]

Greek literary theory is of course not limited to Aristotle's *Rhetoric* and *Poetics*, nor is early Arabic literary theory limited to Ibn al-Muʿtazz and Qudāma. For this reason, von Grunebaum and Ritter have been looking for parallels between the terminology and examples of the Greeks and those of the Arabs without limiting themselves to any specific author on either side. They have made some fascinating discoveries. To mention only some of the most striking examples, the term *iltifāt* corresponds in meaning and

---

[58] These summaries are now available in a volume published by ʿAbdarraḥmān Badawī under the title Arisṭūṭālīs, *Fann ash-Shiʿr* (Cairo 1953). Of the earlier editions only that by A. J. Arberry of al-Fārābī's summary, published with an English translation in *Rivista degli studi orientali* 17 (1938) 266-278, is accessible to me. Avicenna's epitome was published by D. S. Margoliouth, *Analecta orientalia ad poeticam aristoteleam* (London 1887) 80-112, and Averroes's by F. Lasinio, *Il commento medio di Averroè alla Poetica di Aristotele* (*Annali della Università Toscana* 14 [Pisa 1872]). Badawī's book also contains the Arabic translation of the *Poetics* by Abū Bishr Mattā ibn Yūnus al-Qunnāʾī (d. 328/940), which was published first by Margoliouth in the above mentioned volume, 1-76, and again by J. Tkatsch, *Die arabische Übersetzung der Poetik des Aristoteles und die Grundlage der Kritik des griechischen Textes* (Vienna - Leipzig 1928-1932) 2 vols., as well as Badawī's own translation of the *Poetics*. The digests by Avicenna and Averroes were analysed by F. Gabrieli in *Rivista degli studi orientali* 12 (1929-1930) 291-331.

On the question of Aristotelian influence on Arabic rhetoric in general see also I. Kratchkovsky, in *Le monde oriental* 23 (1929) 24ff.; I. Guidi, in *Rivista degli studi orientali* 16 (1936) 412ff.; and Kratchkovsky's introduction to his edition of Ibn al-Muʿtazz's *Kitāb al-Badīʿ* (n. 27 above) 1f.

[59] Cf. Ibn al-Athīr's judgment on the summaries of the *Rhetoric* and the *Poetics* in Avicenna's *Kitāb ash-Shifāʾ*, translated by Kratchkovsky in his article in *Le monde oriental*, 27. The passage occurs in the *Mathal as-Sāʾir* of Ibn al-Athīr (Cairo 1939) 1.311.

derivation to the Greek ἀποστροφή,[60] *bārid* corresponds to ψυχρός,[61] *sūqī* to ἀγοραῖος.[62] The introduction of the expression "Zayd is a lion" as an example of a metaphor corresponds to "Achilles is a lion" in the discussion of the same figure in Aristotle's *Rhetoric*.[63]

Do we have reason, therefore, to believe that when al-Jāḥiẓ, an intelligent and well-informed critic living in the third/ninth century (that is, during the period in which Arabic rhetoric came into being as an independent branch of literature), said, "The *badīʿ* is limited to the Arabs. On account of it their language is superior to all other languages and stands above all other tongues,"[64] did not know what was going on in his own time; or did he choose deliberately to ignore it? That is, do we have enough of the kind of parallels I have just cited to convince ourselves that the system of the Arabs was influenced in any substantial way by Greek rhetoric? For the moment, I am more impressed by the differences that exist between the technical vocabularies of the two systems than I am by the agreements. I feel, moreover, that we ought to keep in mind that some technical terms are in themselves definitions and would therefore necessarily correspond in the two languages, and that many other questions have still to be considered, such as the extent to which non-Aristotelian rhetoric could have been known in the Near East in the first centuries of Islam.

Department of Near Eastern and African Languages
University of California
Los Angeles, California 90024, U.S.A.

[60] See the introduction to H. Ritter's edition of al-Jurjānī's *Asrār al-Balāgha* (n. 2 above) 4.
[61] See G. E. von Grunebaum, *Medieval Islam* (n. 44 above) 328.
[62] *Idem, A Tenth-century Document* (n. 33 above) 72.
[63] *Idem, Medieval Islam* (n. 44 above) 327.
[64] Al-Jāḥiẓ (n. 18 above) 4.55f.

LETALDUS, A WIT OF THE TENTH CENTURY

•

by Cora E. Lutz

Even Democritus could have found little to provoke his laughter in the tenth century. Whether a mirthful temperament, a hypersensitivity to the incongruous, or a sneering contempt for his fellowmen might explain the habitual behavior of the "laughing philosopher," he would surely have been sobered into a Heraclitus, the "weeping philosopher,"[1] by the brutality of endless wars, the ruthless havoc wrought by barbarian invasions, the utter annihilation of all hard-won cultural achievements, and the consequent demoralization and stultification of Western society in the tenth century. Yet so resilient is the human spirit that men of that age of "lead and iron"[2] were able themselves to find moments of laughter at the human comedy.

From the literature that has come from the tenth century, let me cite two examples as evidence that humor of a kind did exist even amid turbulence and violence. The first is a scene in the well-known play *Dulcitius*, which the nun Hroswitha of Gandersheim wrote for her young pupils to spare them the indelicacy of the comedies of Terence. In this tale of the martyrdom of three virgins, Dulcitius, a general of the emperor Diocletian, is ordered to question the maidens. Though reluctant to be a partner in this cruel business, yet captivated by their beauty, he has the maidens confined to the kitchen for the interrogation. There, under cover of darkness, he comes to them, but unable to see, he mistakes the pots and pans for the girls, and embraces and kisses them until he becomes so covered with dirt and soot that, when he leaves in chagrin, his own soldiers fail to recognize him. The humor of the scene lies not so much in Dulcitius's gaucherie and frustration as in the actions and remarks of the brave maiden Irene who is peering through a

---

[1] References to the legendary account of the contrasting reactions to life of the two philosophers were frequent in ancient literature, *e.g.* Seneca, *De ira* 2.10.5 and *De tranquillitate animi* 15.1-6.

[2] Lorenzo Valla's famous label has been succeeded by other equally harsh designations such as "that wastest place of European literature and of the human mind," R. Trench, *Sacred Latin Poetry* (London 1864) 46, and "the bad eminence, the nadir of the human intellect," H. Waddell, *The Wandering Scholars* (New York 1927) 69.

crack, reporting in scornful tones to her terror-paralyzed sisters the ludicrous behaviour of Dulcitius.[3]

The second is a scene that is equally familiar. It occurs in the epic poem *Waltharius*, a product of Saint Gall, now generally credited to Gerald.[4] The romantic tale of the flight of the valiant young hostages, Walter of Aquitaine and Hildegund of Burgundy, from the court of Attila, king of the Huns, is full of violence, suspence, and terror, but the poet finds an occasion for humor in the very critical episode of the escape. Under the pretext of celebrating a victory of the Huns, Walter invites Attila and his chieftains to a lavish banquet. There he supplies them so copiously with wine that the strong warriors can neither control their tongues nor manage their feet. The next morning, as the fugitives ride further and further from Pannonia, the Huns are deep in sleep; the mighty king emerges late from his bedroom, vanquished by his own weakness and unable to do more than hold up his head with his hands.[5]

In each of these episodes, the writer depends upon a single comic situation depicting simple physical actions to achieve his effect, hence he is inviting the most elementary type of humorous response. In general, one might say that such obvious humor was characteristic of literature written for an audience of very limited intellectual experience such as one might expect in a leaden age. But as a striking exception to this generality, there was a more subtle literary work of the tenth century which, I believe, would even have called forth the "silvery laughter" of Meredith's Comic Spirit. That is the poem entitled *Versus Letaldi de quodam piscatore quem ballena absorbuit*.[6]

---

[3] Cf. K. Strecker, *Hrosvithae Opera* (Leipzig 1906) 141:

Hirena Ecce, iste stultus, mente alienatus, aestimat, se nostris uti amplexibus.

Agapes Quid facit?

Hireno Nunc ollas molli fovet gremio, nunc sartagines et caccabos amplectitur, mitia
        libans oscula.

Chionia Ridiculum.

[4] Cf. K. Strecker, "Der Walthariusdichter," *Deutsches Archiv für Geschichte des Mittelalters* 4 (1941) 355-381. E. Duckett, *Life and Death in the Tenth Century* (Ann Arbor 1967), 237-238.

[5] Cf. J. W. Beck, *Ekkehards Waltharius* (Groningen 1908):

316-7 Balbutit madido facundia fusa palato,
      Heroas validos plantis titubare videres.

362-3 Attila nempe manu caput amplexatus utraque
      Egreditur thalamo rex.

[6] This poem was found in two manuscripts, Paris, Bibliothèque Nationale 5230 A of the eleventh century, *Catalogus codicum Bibliothecae Regiae* (Paris 1744) 4 app. 518, and Tours 890, *Catalogue général* 37, ed. M. Collon (Paris 1900) 641-643, of the late twelfth century, which was destroyed in 1940. It has been edited three times, first by B. Hauréau from the Paris manuscript, in an almost inaccessible publication, *Bulletin du Comité historique des monuments écrits de l'histoire de France* 1 (1849) 178-183; then by A. Wilmart, "Le poème héroïque de Létald sur Within le pêcheur," *Studi medievali* 9 (1936) 188-203 (text 195-199), from the Tours manuscript; finally by J. P. Bonnes, "Un lettré du xe siècle," *Revue Mabillon* 33 (1943) 23-47 (text 37-45), from the Paris manuscript.

Its author was Letaldus, a monk of the abbey of Micy in the diocese of Orléans.[7] In the absence of precise dates for his birth and death, it can only be determined that he lived in the second half of the tenth century. Almost certainly his whole life passed in the monasteries at Micy and at Le Mans. A man of keen intellectual endowment, he somehow managed to acquire a good education in the liberal arts and a love for Classical literature. It was his good fortune to count among his friends two outstanding men of learning, Abbo of Fleury[8] and Constantin of Micy,[9] both scholars and extraordinary teachers. Only one incident is recorded, and that very incompletely, to furnish evidence that Letaldus was a man of strong convictions. This provides the information that, under his leadership, the monks of Micy once drove out their unworthy abbot, and that when, for political reasons, he was restored, Letaldus could not accept this indignity and so retired to Le Mans, probably to the abbey of La Couture.[10] His fame rests on two hagiographical writings that reveal him as a scholar of sound critical judgment, unusual historical acumen, and exceptional facility in composition. His *Liber de miraculis s. Maximini*[11] relating the life and activities of Saint Mesmin, the first abbot of Micy, was written during his long residence at the abbey. His *Vita s. Juliani*,[12] composed at the request of his bishop, Avesgaud of Le Mans, superseded earlier, less reliable accounts of the first bishop of Le Mans and constitutes the authorized version of the early history of the abbey.

In marked contrast to the sober prose of these historical works,[13] Letaldus's poem is a purely literary creation, a charming imaginative fantasy.[14] We are fortunate that it has survived, for it is now preserved in only one manu-

---

[7] For the life of Letaldus, cf. *Histoire littéraire de la France* (Paris 1742) 6.528-537; B. Hauréau, *Histoire littéraire du Maine* 7 (Paris 1874) 188-200 ; A. Ledru, "Origine de Léthald," *Province du Maine* 16 (1908) 326-328; M. Manitius, *Geschichte der lateinischen Literatur des Mittelalters* (Munich 1923) 2.426-432; J. P. Bonnes (n. 6 above) 24-33.

[8] Cf. Abbo of Fleury, *Epistola* 11, PL 139.438: "Tandem ad te, mi quondam familiaris Letalde, nunc sermo dirigitur, cujus alias singularem scientiam mea parvitas amplecititur et summis laudibus extollere nititur."

[9] Of Constantin, the pupil of Abbo and later abbot of Micy, Gerbert, the most brilliant scholar of the period says, "nobilis scolasticus, adprime eruditus, michique in amicitia conjunctissimus," *Epistola* 92, ed. J. Havet (Paris, 1889) 85.

[10] The sources for this incident are chiefly Abbo of Fleury's *Apologeticus*, (PL 139.461-471), and his *Epistola* 11, PL 139.436-438.

[11] PL 137.795-824. It was written in 986-987.

[12] PL 137.781-796. It was written after 996. Cf. A. Ledru, "Saint Julien, Évêque du Mans," *Province du Maine* 12 (1904) 116-121.

[13] It has been conjectured that an anonymous poem of 40 lines, *Versus de eversione monasterii glomnensis*, published by E. Dümmler in *Poetae latini aevi carolini* 2.146-149, was the work of Letaldus. To me, the poetic craftsmanship, particularly the monotonous internal rhyme in every line, is inferior to Letaldus's work.

[14] This designation, the only appropriate word I know to characterize the poem, was happily applied to it by Bonnes (n. 6 above) 34.

script. Composed of 208 Latin hexameter lines, it reveals the poet's remarkable mastery of the standard classical verse form,[15] while at the same time it has a medieval flavor produced by the incorporation of several instances of internal rhyme.[16] The author represents his tale as a story told him by a venerable old man.[17] Actually, it gives the impression of being a bit of folklore, perhaps originating in Brittany.[18] It is recounted by Letaldus apparently for the sheer joy of the telling, with no thought of pointing a moral, furnishing an exemplum, or painting an allegory. Briefly, the poem tells the adventure of Within, an English fisherman, who with his boat was swallowed by a whale; after five days of horror, during which he managed to kill the whale by building a fire inside it, Within was rescued by his own townspeople in Rochester on the coast of Kent. Curiously, there are no parallels to the story in early European folklore; it was only after the use of the motif in one of the tales of the popular *Gesta Romanorum* in the thirteenth century that it appears in literature, chiefly in Italy.[19] The Pinocchio story seems to mark the end of this tradition. Yet, outside of Europe, the theme was known over a wide area of the earth, for anthropologists have found tales containing some of its features in legends of many of the islands of the East.[20]

---

[15] A. Wilmart (n. 6 above) 191 remarks: "Les mots, entre ses mains, s'arrangeaient sans effort dans la forme de l'hexamètre classique, mais cela même, au xe siècle, n'est-ce pas une sorte de miracle?" Cf. Bonnes (n. 6 above) 45-47.

[16] For example:
127 Presul ut audivit, mox limina sacra petivit.
167 Sic Anglo, reducem dum cernit ab equore lucem.
All references are to Bonnes' edition. A. Wilmart, (n. 6 above) 192, found twelve instances of this and thirty-nine in which only the final vowels are the same. He says: "On aperçoit assez nettement, dans une longue série d'hexamètres reguliers, l'entrée insidieuse du vers à rime interne, dit 'léonin,' cette déplorable invention du moyen âge."

[17] 9-10 Moribus hoc senior venerabilis et gravis aevo
        Retulit, os cuius rutilum splendescit ut aurum.
This may, of course, be no more than a simple poetic conceit to win credence for the story.

[18] Cf. B. Hauréeau (n. 7 above) 200 : "Cette fable, tirée de quelque légende bretonne, n'est pas d'une heureuse invention."

[19] Cf. *Gesta Romanorum*, ed. H. Oesterley (Berlin 1872) 655-657 n. 251. Here the daughter of an unnamed king, the fiancée of the son of the Emperor Honorius, is heroine of the tale. For the use of the motif in Renaissance literature, cf. C. Speroni, "More on the Sea-Monsters," *Italica* 35 (1958) 21-24.

[20] Cf. L. Radermacher, "Walfischmythen," *Archiv für Religionswissenschaft* 9 (1907) 248-252. A. Wilmart (n. 6 above) 190 n. 3 remarks: "La légende apparait un peu partout: en Océanie, Amérique, Afrique, Mongolie; elle est surtout remarquable dans l'histoire polynésienne de Rata et Nganaoo. En Europe ses traces sont plus rares; on la rencontre en Lithuanie. De là, en définitive, l'intérêt particulier et fort inattendu du récit recueilli par Létald; on peut croire qu'il fut importé des pays scandinaves en Angleterre, peut-être lors de l'invasion danoise." For a treatment of the aspects of the whale myth that apply to Letaldus's story, cf. H. Schmidt, *Jona* (Göttingen 1907) 38-60, 132-135. There are no close parallels.

Certainly it was not Clio, but some *musa iocosa* whom Letaldus must have invoked to inspire his poem. What he wrote cannot be strictly classified. It is not a parody comparable to the mock heroic *Battle of the Frogs and the Mice*, for there is no record of an ancient Moby Dick tale to provide his principal; neither can it be typed as a pastiche similar to Ermoldus Nigellus's ingenious Ovidian elegy to King Pippin,[21] for it is not at all a work of "scissors and paste." Rather it appears to be simply the intellectual pastime,[22] a kind of scholarly game, of a man who knew and loved the Latin language and literature. The complete lack of pedantry and affectation, as well as the absence of any satirical implication would suggest that it was composed solely for the poet's own amusement and for the entertainment of a small group of literary friends who could appreciate it.

The skill of the poet in treating his theme seems to lie, first of all, in his ability to sustain a pseudoepic framework. A brief prelude sets the tone of his heroic style when he declares that even if he had Pindar's lyre and Orpheus's voice, he would be unable to create poetry commensurate with his lofty theme. Appropriately, the epic opens by establishing the setting of the story with a eulogy of England and her stalwart, fair-haired people who, under the guidance of Saint Gregory, learned to sing praises to Christ in their rude language. Immediately one of these British people, the fisherman hero Within, is introduced suitably, not as a descendant of illustrious warriors, but as noble in his calling, a fearless explorer of river and ocean, whom neither fair weather nor storm can keep away from the sea. One memorable day, in his sturdy coracle laden with nets, gear, and food, Within sets out at dawn, alone, for the deep waters. Barely has he located a proper place to anchor his boat when the antagonist appears. He is a "belua enormis," a creature of overwhelming bulk, hideous to behold, and capable of devouring whole cities in his terrible jaws. Within starts for shore, but it is too late. There is no titanic struggle; the brute monster simply swallows Within and his boat at one gulp. Imprisoned but unscathed, the fisherman is carried about through the seas helplessly, until he is able to devise a plan of action. Finally, with wood and his oars, Within builds a fire that sends dense smoke gushing from the monster's eyes, ears, and mouth. The striken beast plunges madly, leaping and diving, in an effort to escape his torment, but with the fisherman chopping away at his vital organs, he finally gives a tremendous roar and dies. For five days and four nights of extreme anguish, inside the dead monster, Within maintains his life by eating the inner parts of his captor. At last the great body of the fish is cast upon the shores of Rochester where his townspeople, finding this unexpected windfall, rush upon it to obtain food.

[21] Cf. "Carmen Nigelli Ermoldi exulis in laudem gloriosissimi Pippini regis," *Poetae latini aevi carolini* 2.79-91.

[22] Cf. Bonnes (n. 6, above) 35: "un jeu désintéressé de l'intelligence." Bonnes alone among the critics appreciates the subtle humor of the poem.

Like a true epic poet, Letaldus gave his poem features of the drama. His cast of characters, in addition to Within and the whale, consists of the bishop, Within's wife, and a chorus of townspeople. Their essential qualities are revealed through their actions even though they are on the stage but briefly. The hero, Within, besides being a skillful, experienced, and brave fisherman, proves himself a veritable Odysseus, resourceful in executing a bold and imaginative plan for killing his enemy, as well as self-controlled enough to force himself to provide grisly food from the interior of the killer who has preyed on him. Since he is a man whose mettle has normally been pitted against the elements and the creatures of the sea, Within is unprepared for his role of hero to his fellow townsmen. When he staggers forth from the mutilated caracass of the whale, in a dazed condition, his moment of triumph has come, and his neighbors will not permit him to refuse his act. Blinded by the light, bald as an old eagle, lacking eyelashes and fingernails, exhausted by his ordeal, and harried by the press and questioning of the crowd, he yet manages to receive the welcome and praise of bishop, priests, and people, in the august manner of an emperor. Then, assuming the part of husband, he has a tearful reunion with his wife. His tale ends happily with the assurance of his restoration to his former handsome appearance.

The bishop, too, has a good role to play. Like Calchas of old, he can interpret the supernatural and knows how to protect his people against malign forces. As soon as he hears of the phenomenon of a beached whale that utters words, he knows what to do. Going to the cathedral, in a calm voice, he summons his clergy and all his people to pray to God that the evil menace may not harm the city. Then, selecting the most worthy of his flock to bear the sacred relics of the saints and the holy water, he leads a procession of the whole parish down to the beach to exorcise the demon. The priests raise a ladder and climb onto the great back of the whale, sprinkle it with holy water, and command the evil spirit to declare its name and power. At this awesome moment, out of the expectant silence comes the muffled voice of the fisherman, giving his name and imploring help. Later, when the flesh of the fish has been broken up, the largest portion is given to the clergy— but everyone receives his fair share. The holy relics are duly returned to the cathedral. Then, when Within's strange story is being related, the bishop stands in reverence before this man, a second Jonah, who had the awesome experience of being brought back from death.

Within's wife has a small but meaningful part to fill in the dramatic poem. One of the last to hear the news, she wanders in anxiety and despair all over the shore seeking her husband, calling him by name, until she is finally led into his presence. He is so changed, however, that his voice is the only means by which she can identify him. Overcome with weeping, she enters the house with him as the poet draws the curtain on what he forecasts as a happy ending.

The chorus of townspeople, even though composed of children, youths, women with their distaffs in their hands, and old men bent with years, acts as one. We see them first as they become aware of the unexpected booty that has been washed upon their shores. Greedily they attack the whale with axes and knives, each trying to secure some of the plunder. When the imprisoned Within, fearing lest they strike him with their weapons, calls out to them, as one they fall into headlong flight, in terror, pallid with fear, and incapable of speech. In their panic, they seek their spiritual advisor, the bishop. Then, at a word from him, these same townspeople all flock into the cathedral, listen to the wise priest, and join the procession back to the whale. When Within is freed, practical and thrifty as they are, they attend first to the division of their spoils. Only then do they surround the battered fisherman and force him to tell his adventure.

Of course, the plot is highly dramatic. The apparent destruction of a guiltless, a brave man by a vicious monster proves to be the effective cause of the actual destruction of the beast by its victim. Horror, pity, suspense, and relief are all here. The unfolding of the action is made vivid by direct quotation. We hear Within's cries for help as he begs his unsuspecting townsmen to release him. We hear the prayer that the bishop intones in the cathedral and the solemn adjuration of the demon in the whale. Within calls out from the whale, identifying himself and again imploring aid. His poor wife calls "Within, Within," to which only the echoing shores reply.

In all of this the poet, with no innuendoes, with no hint of anything but serious intent (but without, I feel, any desire to make sport of us), is enjoying himself as he is entertaining us when he presents an epic situation that is quite beyond credulity. The situation is dramatic and we feel tense concern, not to say pity and fear, but it is not tragic. The hero is almost a nonhero as he appears at what should be his great scene of triumph, dirty and dishevelled, looking like a moulting old eagle, barely able to stand. Further, his experience has produced no profound change in his life, no downfall, for as soon as his hair has grown out, he will be exactly as he was before it happened.

If Letaldus found amusement in working out his plot and manipulating his characters to form a story that the simplest person could understand, he must have given both himself and his educated readers greater intellectual pleasure in his language and rhetoric. First of all, the vocabulary sets the English tale in the realm of ancient epic by the use of references such as the Eumenides (77, 148), Scylla and Charybdis (40), Mount Aetna (75), and Aurora and Tithonus (23). Further, the abundance of words, phrases, and even a whole scene borrowed from the epic poets and applied to situations quite different from the original setting affords the reader the satisfaction of recognition often accompanied by an appreciation of a certain irony in the new application. The greatest number of such borrowings comes from the

works of Vergil.[23] For example, the confident hero sets forth (23-24) "Ti-
thoni croceum dum Aurora cubile liqueret," words that had been used to
mark the cruel day that dawned for Dido when she discovered Aeneas's
departure (*Aen.* 4.585). Again, when confronted by his unequal adversary (46),
Within "deserit inceptum," gives up his attempt to reach shore, as Turnus
abandoned his position in the field to charge the gates of Aeneas's camp
(9.694). Using Vergil's words describing the preparation of the venison
Aeneas had procured for his hungry men shipwrecked at Carthage (1.212),
"veribusque trementia figunt," Letaldus describes (97) the preparation of
Within's gruesome meal of whale meat. When Creusa's ghost appeared
to Aeneas (2.774), the same words, "vox faucibus haesit," are used (120)
to denote the speechless condition of the townspeople when they hear a
voice from inside the whale. Splendid Dido set forth for the fateful hunting
expedition accompanied by a great band of noble attendants (4.136), "magna
stipente caterva"; the motley crowd of people bringing up the procession
to the whale is identified (139) with the same words. Most conspicuous is
Letaldus's use of Vergil's description of Juturna in the disguise of her brother
as she darted about like a swallow through the enemy lines (12. 473-477).
Within's wife goes flying over the seashore (191-196) just as a multicolored
swallow passes through the high halls and cuts through the air over lakes
and resounding pools, gathering food for her chirping young ones. As the
distraught wife goes, her cries of "Within, Within" are returned from the
mountains even as the Argonauts' shouts for Hylas filled the resounding
shore (*Ec.* 6.44). In addition to these examples, there are other less striking
instances of Letaldus's use of Vergilian phrases,[24] as there are also phrases
reminiscent of Ovid,[25] Lucan,[26] Statius,[27] and Claudian.[28]

   Letaldus may have used these classical sources to give an atmosphere of
the heroic age to his saga, but he proves himself perfectly capable of mimicking
the poetic devices appropriate to the epic style. There is, for instance, an
interesting example of apostrophe (55-62) when the poet speaks to Within
as he sits bewildered in his boat inside the whale. He asks him what emotions
he is experiencing, he reminds him of his children waiting for him, he exhorts

[23] Both Wilmart (n. 6 above) and Bonnes (n. 6 above) have pointed out Letaldus's
borrowings from Vergil.

[24] Some that consist of a word or two may well be unconscious borrowings. This would
also seem to be true of many of the echoes from the later epic poets.

[25] Bonnes (n. 6 above) has noted thirteen instances of phrases similar to Ovid's. The
most striking is *Treicius vates* (4) from *Met.* 11.2.

[26] Bonnes cites three parallels to phrases in Lucan's *Pharsalia*, e.g. Letaldus 52 *cara-
basa ventis* and *Phars.* 5.560.

[27] Bonnes gives eleven phrases reminiscent of Statius's *Thebaid*, e.g. Letaldus 75 "Sul-
phureos velut ille fremens vomit Ethna vapores" and *Theb.* 8.327 "aetneos vapores."

[28] Bonnes supplies nine instances of echoes from the poems of Claudian, e.g. Letaldus
119 "tremor ossa ferit" and *De raptu Proserpinae* 2.152 "vibrat tremor ossa."

him (since he is alone in his extremity and beyond help) to use his wits and to exert all the strength he has to overcome the circumstances. Finally he suggests that courage usually does not manifest itself under favorable conditions, but it is adversity that tests and reveals a man's worth.

Several good metaphors are used by the poet. In the prelude, speaking disparagingly of his ability, he says, "Carmen rudibus fibris cudere conor" (8). He describes the interior of the whale as "ceco antro" (51), and Within calls the beast "faucibus angens Eumenides" (147). More extensive is the use of similes. For instance, the hideous fish is like Scylla and Charybdis (40). It swallows Within and his boat (49-50) just as a traveller parched by the summer heat gulps down water from a cool spring. When Within builds a fire inside him, the animal sends forth sulphurous smoke like Aetna (75), and rages like the Eumenides (77). Within emerges from the whale looking like a dove weatherbeaten by the wintry frost or an old bedraggled eagle (160-163). Even in his unfortunate condition, he receives the admiring people in the manner of an emperor accepting an ovation (178). He is like a second Jonah (187). Using the figure of paradox, the poet points out the interesting situation of the predator destroyed by his prey. (93-94) An instance of hyperbole has already been noted where the whale is described as capable of swallowing whole cities (42).

Letaldus also sustains the epic effect by his use of unusual phrases. One may cite the following: "carabo amico" (24), "fluctiugam puppim" (29), "maris undisoni" (32), "ancipiti discrimine" (59), "profani hostis" (73), "vindex pelagus" (90), "altisonas undas" (66), "rabidis faucibus" (147), and "versicolor hirundo" (191). Again, in the manner of the epic poet, he makes effective employ of anaphora. Three from a rather long list are:

> Qua Within natus, hamum qua ponere doctus. (106)
> Heu, parcite cives!
> Parcite, ait, misero! (117-8)
> Os, oculos Scille similis, similisque Caribdi. (40)

Alliteration is used in a restricted way, generally, though there are three striking exceptions:

> Transtra tenet teretesque tegunt tabulata rudentes. (30)
> Datque cibus mortem, rabidum vorat esca vorantem,
> Praedaque predonem versa vice sternit enormem. (93-94)
> Viscera visceribus curans et corpore corpus. (98)

Perhaps the fact that Letaldus's poem has been taken as a serious work even in modern times[29] may serve as a gauge of its success. Certainly there

---

[29] A. Wilmart, "Le Florilège de Saint-Gatien," *Revue bénédictine* 48 (1936) 15, calls the poem "une antique légende de foklore, que l'auteur rajeunissait, sans s'en douter, puisqu'il la conte sérieusement sur la foi d'un vieillard."

are no comic situations to raise a laugh. No buffoon has a place in the cast of characters. The poet admits no indecent, suggestive, or ludicrous language to insure a response of ribald laughter. Rather, the art of Letaldus is completely subtle. There is gentle irony in his presentation of ordinary, little people thrust into an epic situation. In dignifying his tale by casting it in the lofty style of Vergil, Letaldus with delicate skill maintains the heroic illusion. When he recalls to the minds of his readers who have had the training to appreciate them the very words of the great Roman poet in a totally foreign context, he is furnishing the most refined type of humor. Directing his scholarly *jeu d'esprit* to the intelligence of his readers, Letaldus most happily plays the role of a man of wit.[30]

Beinecke Rare Book and Manuscript Library
Yale University
New Haven, Connecticut 06520, U.S.A.

[30] A later fellow countryman of Letaldus who should understand the Gallic temperament, H. Bergson, says, "Il (le comique) s'addresse à l'intelligence pure," *Le rire* (Paris 1930) 6.

ABELARD AS IMITATOR OF CHRIST

•

by Donald K. Frank

Despite the fulness of comment upon Peter Abelard's autobiographical writings, including the recent and skillful presentation of Mary McLaughlin,[1] there is a significant aspect of the *Historia calamitatum* and Abelard's letters which has not, I believe, been properly emphasized. This involves the considerable extent to which the sense of self and individuality of the later Abelard, psychologically damaged by mutilation and misfortune, rested on a most unusual psychic foundation. Others have pointed out that Abelard's experience of mutilation would greatly intensify unstable emotional tendencies[2] and this should be borne in mind during the discussion to follow. This paper presents an interpretation of the Abelard of these letters which is derived to some extent from an appreciation of certain overtones in his writing as well as from his more specific comment.[3]

Abelard follows the standard medieval practice of identification with major religious figures. He refers often to Saint Jerome, whose heir Abelard is in calumny and detraction,[4] and points out, for example, that the hatred of the French drove Abelard westward[5] (to the monastery of Saint Gildas in Brittany) just as the hatred of the Romans drove Jerome to the East. Moreover, the monks at Saint Gildas sought to poison Abelard just as others had previously

---

[1] Mary McLaughlin, "Abelard as Autobiographer: The Motives and Meaning of his 'Story of Calamities,'" *Speculum* 42 (1967) 463.

[2] *Ibid.* 467 and Georg Misch, *Geschichte der Autobiographie* 3: *Das Mittelalter* 1: *Das Hochmittelalter im Angang* (Frankfurt 1959) 553.

[3] This paper proceeds on the assumption, of course, that the letters of Abelard and Heloise are genuine or, at most, were the result of a redaction by Abelard or even a later hand. Arguments that I find convincing on this score have been presented by both Gilson and Muckle. Thus: E. Gilson, *Heloise and Abelard*, trans. L. K. Shook (Ann Arbor 1960) 145, and "The Personal Letters of Abelard and Heloise," ed. J. T. Muckle, *Mediaeval Studies* 15 (1953) 48-67. Moreover, since the contioversy over authenticity focuses primarily on the letters of Heloise, in particular her first, the assumption of authenticity may be all the more readily utilized because I am dealing with what Abelard wrote.

[4] See Muckle's edition of the *Historia calamitatum* in *Mediaeval Studies* 12 (1950) 211; the translation by Muckle, *The Story of Abelard's Adversities* (Toronto 1954) 69.

[5] *Historia* 203; *Abelard's Adversities* 57.

attempted to poison Saint Benedict.[6] Abelard, however, proceeds beyond an identification with such as Benedict, Jerome, or Origen, to focus his sense of similar identity upon the human nature of Jesus: an imitation of Christ which sometimes hints at Abelard's possession of a stature in some fashion commensurate with that of the Bridegroom. McLaughlin speaks of a "sense of vocation or mission"[7] possessed by men such as Abelard, and in the *Historia calamitatum* Abelard presents Heloise's arguments against a marriage that would deny him to the whole world.[8] Moreover, we are reminded of the Gospel when we are told that he arrived at the Council of Soissons with but a few disciples, feared a stoning because of local hostility, and found his enemies authorized to judge him. His enemies sought for a condemnable comment from him and, nearly in vain, for a condemnable argument against him.[9] Yet the Bishop of Chartres, sympathetic to Abelard, pointed out that Abelard had many supporters and would simply have his reputation enhanced if dealt with harshly and unfairly in private.[10] The Bishop urged objectivity and a full opportunity for Abelard to reply to charges. As Abelard cites him: "At least such action will be in accordance with the statement of the blessed Nicodemus who, wanting to free the Lord himself, said: 'Does our law judge a man until it first give him a hearing and know what he does?'"[11] But Abelard's opponents raised a din, crying out against "the verbosity of a man whose arguments and sophisms the whole world could not gainsay,"[12] although Abelard modestly demurred that "surely it was much more difficult to argue against Christ."[13]

Abelard was condemned at Soissons, found temporary refuge at Saint Denis, provoked trouble by questioning the identity of the abbey's founder, was horrified at the villainy of the monks of Saint Denis and accordingly declared that "having suffered ill fortune so long I fell into deep despair, feeling that the whole world was conspiring against me."[14] He was able to retire to the wilderness and yet his rivals complained (secretly, declares Abelard): "Behold, the whole world has gone after him," a paraphrase of the complaint

---

[6] *Historia* 209; *Abelard's Adversities* 66.

[7] McLaughlin (n. 1 above) 481.

[8] *Historia* 186; *Abelard's Adversities* 29.

[9] John 8.59, 10.31; *Historia* 193, 195; *Abelard's Adversities* 40, 44.

[10] *Historia* 194; *Abelard's Adversities* 42; see Matthew 26.59-65, Mark 14.55-65.

[11] *Historia* 194: "iuxta illam saltem beati Nicodemi sententiam, qua Dominum ipsum liberare cupiens, aiebat: 'Numquid lex nostra iudicat hominem nisi audierit ab ipso prius et cognoverit quid faciat?'" (John 7.51); *Abelard's Adversities* 42.

[12] *Historia* 194: "contra eius verbositatem contendamus, cuius argumentis vel sophismatibus universus obsistere mundus non posset"; *Abelard's Adversities* 43.

[13] *Historia* 194: "Sed certe multo difficilius erat cum ipso contendere Christo"; *Abelard's Adversities* 43.

[14] *Historia* 198: "me universus coniurasset mundus"; *Abelard's Adversities* 49.

of the Pharisees against Jesus.[15] His rivals lamented that "we have got now-
where persecuting him and gained for him greater renown. We have tried to
blot out hi name and we ave made it better know ."[16]

When Heloise and her nuns were expelled from Argenteuil, Abelard perceived
that this was a God given opportunity for him to make new provision for his
oratory and, subsequently, for Heloise.[17] He invited Heloise and her nuns
to the Paraclete and rendered them the possessors thereof. He began to
visit them often for purposes of aid and, as a result, his calumniators accused him of still being swayed by carnal lust. Abelard's reply is instructive.
In addition to noting the physical impossibilities, he recalled similar malicious
detractions levied against Jerome and pointed out that the spite of enemies
like his would have accused Christ himself and the prophets because they
associated so closely with women. That Pharisee who criticized Jesus for
not taking note of the sinful nature of a particular woman "could have imagined much more easily, so far as human judgments go, wrongdoing on the
part of the Lord than they of me. Likewise with greater reason they could
have harbored suspicion if they had seen Christ's mother entrusted to a young
man"[18] or the prophets as guests of widows.

Moreover, in the third letter, Abelard to Heloise, he requests that she and
her community help him before God with their prayers. He emphasizes in
particular the value of prayers delivered by wives for their husbands. If
Heloise cannot by herself secure aid for Abelard before God, the holy convent
of virgins and widows with which she is associated will do so. Yet Abelard
does not doubt that the great sanctity of Heloise is effectual before the Lord
and that she is bound to do all that she can for him above all men. He trans-
mits a special prayer for their recitation which solicits God's protection for
him and which requests his restoration in safety "to Thy handmaids." Should
he perish, through the triumph of his enemies or otherwise, Abelard requests
that Heloise bring his body to the Paraclete, where his sepulcher may be
constantly attended and the nuns may pour out prayers for him to the Lord.
"Nor do I think," declares Abelard, "that there is a fitter place for Christian
burial among any of the faithful than among women devoted to Christ. Women
they were who, solicitous for the grave of our Lord Jesus Christ, came with
precious ointments, and went before and followed, watching diligently about

[15] See John 12.19.

[16] *Historia*, 200: "Ecce mundus totus post eum abiit, nihil persequendo profecimus, sed
magis eum gloriosum effecimus. Exstinguere nomen eius studuimus, sed magis accendimus";
Abelard's Adversities 52.

[17] *Historia* 205: "Quae eum diversis locis exules dispergerentur, oblatam mihi a Domino
intellexi occasionem qua nostro consulerem oratorio"; *Abelard's Adversities* 60.

[18] *Historia* 208 : "Multo commodiorem, quantum ad humanum iudicium spectat, turpi-
tudinis coniecturam de Domino concipere poterat, quam de nobis isti; aut qui matrem eius
iuveni commendatam"; *Abelard's Adversities* 64; Luke 7.39.

His sepulcher and lamenting with tears the death of the Bridegroom, as it
is written: 'The women sitting by the sepulcher lamented the Lord.'"[19]

In the fifth letter, Abelard to Heloise, while speaking of his mutilation and
its ultimate spiritual benefit for both of them, Abelard indicates that Heloise
was but a tool utilized by God to alter his destiny. Further, he counsels her
to grieve for his loss in the same spirit as she might lament the death of Christ.
In an interesting juxtaposition of the two thoughts, he enjoins: "Grieve not
that you are the cause of so great a good, for which you need not doubt that
you were principally created by God. Nor lament that I have borne this
loss, save when the blessings of the passions of the martyrs and the death
of our Lord Himself shall make you sad."[20] Moreover, in this letter Abelard
exhorts Heloise to hold Christ ever as her true spouse and urges her to "be
of the people, of the women who wailed and lamented for Him—Have deep
compassion upon Him, who suffered willingly for your redemption [as, in his
fashion, Abelard suffered for her] and who was crucified for you." Abelard
continues a favorite image : "Be present ever in your mind at His sepulcher,
and with the faithful women weep and lament—Prepare with them the ointments for His burial—"[21] and do so with the whole force of your devotion.
Indeed, in the seventh letter, Abelard to Heloise, he discourses at considerable
length on the holy women and true nuns who followed Christ, citing how they
ministered to Christ, nourished and anointed Him and prepared spices for
His burial. They won greater praise of Jesus than did the apostles. When
Peter denied Christ and the rest of the group scattered, these women stayed
fearless and would not be parted from Christ in either His passion or death.
The Evangelist Matthew diligently describes how they remained unmoved
by His sepulcher. "Passing a sleepless, tearful night by His sepulcher, the
women first deserved to see the glory of the Risen Lord. By their faithfulness after His death they showed Him not so much by words as by deeds

---

[19] Muckle (n. 3 above) 77: "Nec Christianae sepulturae locum rectius apud aliquos fi-
deles quam apud Christo devotas consistere censeo. Quae de Domini Jesu Christi sepultura
sollicitae eam unguentis pretiosis et praevenerunt et subsecutae sunt et circa eius sepulcrum
(studiose vigilantes et sponsi mortem lacrymabiliter) plangentes, sicut scriptum est : 'Mu-
lieres sedentes ad monumentum lamentabantur flentes Dominum.'"

Muckle reminds us that Abelard's quotation about the women lamenting is not in the
Scriptures. It is the antiphon for the *Benedictus* in the Roman Breviary for Holy Saturday. The bracketed Latin concerning the death of the Bridegroom is found in the Migne
and Muckle editions but not in the edition of Victor Cousin.

[20] Muckle (n. 3 above) 88 : "Nec te tanti boni causam esse doleas, ad quod te a Deo ma-z
xime creatam esse non dubites."

[21] *Ibid.* 91: "Esto de populo et mulieribus quae plangebant et lamentabantur eum . . .
Patienti sponte pro redemptione tua compatere et super crucifixo pro te compungere. Se-
pulcro eius mente semper assiste, et cum fidelibus feminis lamentare et luge . . . Para cum
illis sepulturae eius unguenta."

how greatly they had loved Him in life."[22] One thinks of the constancy of
Heloise and her nuns, Abelard's repairing for spiritual solace to the Paraclete[23]
and his often repeated request that these women pray over his sepulcher at
the Paraclete (as they did). Further, Abelard gives the impression of an
uninterrupted vigil by Christ's sepulcher, which is not the impression that
the Scriptures convey.[24] He would perhaps have the biblical circumstance
accord more readily with the type of vigil he wished Heloise and her nuns
to maintain.

In evaluating the Abelard of the *Historia* and the letters it is, of course,
instructive to contrast briefly the tone of Abelard's approach to Jesus with
that of Bernard of Clairvaux, a founder of western speculative mysticism[25]
and Abelard's greatest critic. It is also pertinent to glance at some twelfth-
century autobiography.

Whereas Bernard, in his *Sermons on the Canticle*, approaches the Lord in
fear and trembling, seeking a loving union of the Bridegroom (Jesus) and
the bride (soul), Abelard's *Historia* displays his sense of proud emulation
of the career of the earthly Jesus. While Bernard would interpret the ministrations and anointments of the female followers of Jesus in a spiritual and symbolic
sense,[26] Abelard would view the actions of Mary Magdalen and the others as

---

[22] PL 178.231: "Insomnem ad sepulcrum illius noctem in lacrymis feminae ducentes, re-
surgentis gloriam primae videre meruerumt. Cui fideliter in mortem quantum dilexerint
vivum, non tam verbis quam rebus exhibuerunt."

[23] *Historia* 209; *Abelard's Adversities* 66; see McLaughlin (n. 1 above) 483 : "For Abelard
the most essential facets of his now dominant sense of self came to be most harmoniously
integrated in the images, roles and relationships centered in the Paraclete." The earlier
Heloise had emphasized to her future bridegroom his universal "sacred and philosophical
responsibilities." Now they had been reunited in a collaboration "that made her, as abbess
of the Paraclete, the sharer and, in a sense, the agent of his vocation."

[24] See Matthew 27.61 and 28.1; Mark 15.47 and 16.1, 2; Luke 23.55, 56 and 24.1; John
19.41, 42 and 20.1.

[25] See E. Gilson, *History of Christian Philosophy in the Middle Ages* (New York 1955) 164.

[26] Saint Bernard of Clairvaux, *On the Song of Songs* (*Canticum canticorum*), trans. by a
Religious of C. S. M. U. (London 1951). Bernard mentions three spiritual perfumes proper
to the bride (soul). The first is Contrition, the second Devotion and the third Piety. Thus:
"This first most needful unguent of the sinful soul was typified by the actual ointment
wherewith the sinful woman anointed the bodily Feet of God. Of that ointment we are
told that 'the house was filled with the odour of it.' And the odour of penitence reaches
even to the mansions of the blessed. . . . Moreover, whereas the first ointment was proved
upon the Feet of Christ, this one anoints His Head. For 'whoso offereth Me thanks and
praise, he honoureth Me,' says God; and Paul says that 'the Head of Christ is God.' So
without doubt he who gives God thanks anoints Christ's Head. . . . Of the two former
perfumes we found mention in the Gospels; of the first, that a woman kissed the Lord's
Feet and anointed them with it; of the second, that she or another poured it upon His Head.
The passage which refers to the third perfume is this: 'Mary Magdalen and Mary of James
and Salome had brought sweet spices, that they might come and anoint Jesus.' Notice
that—they brought them to anoint Jesus, His whole Body, not a part only, as the Head or

indicative, in a certain historical sense, of the modus operandi to be followed by Heloise and her nuns in regard to the ministrations he requested. Bernard's emphasis is upon an exalted commingling and marriage with the Word. It calls for a descent of God into the soul and a certain loss of self in a higher unity.[27] Abelard's emphasis is on an individuality that is heightened by a sense of his similarity to Jesus.

As indicated by the *Historia*, the twelfth century is a period when one can find a positive affirmation of self in autobiography.[28] Thus the Abbot Guibert of Nogent, for example, presents a muted premonition of the stance taken a bit later by Abelard. Guibert prided himself on his intellectual skills, and in his youth had thought of fame through the acquisition of a literary distinction tied to "the worldly advantages of birth and a handsome person."[29] At the end of the century, Giraldus Cambrensis declared that, equalling the greatest of teachers, he had lectured at Paris "with wondrous art" and taught the Trivium there "most excellently."[30] Later he cited his "pure intent" and knew of the "praise and glory" he would gain "for all ages" in his efforts to secure the bishopric of Saint David.[31]

Feet. You also, if you study to do good to all men, as Paul enjoins, for God's sake not refusing service even to your enemies, you also will be fragrant with this perfume, and will have taken on yourself, so far as in you lies, to anoint the Lord's whole Body—that is to say, the Church" (35-38).

[27] *Ibid.* 90: "This commingling of the Word with tne soul is purely spiritual, and has nothing corporeal or concrete in it. The rapture of the pure soul into God, and God's most blessed descent into the soul, these constitute a union which takes place in the spirit, because God is a Spirit and He is moved with love towards the soul whom he knows to be walking in the spirit, especially if He sees it burning with love towards Himself. A soul in this condition, so loving and so loved, will not be satisfied with the sort of manifestation through created things that is given to everyone, nor even with the dreams and visions granted to the few. It will demand a special privilege—not an outward appearance but an inward inpouring. It will desire Him not merely to appear to it but to act upon it, and the more interior His operation is, the happier it will be. For He is the Word: He does not merely sound in ears, He enters hearts."

[28] Such an affirmation can also be found in other areas of twelfth-century literature. For example, if one looks beyond the conventions of the courtly lyric, it is apparent that the troubadour is ready to declare the value of his subjective reactions and, in particular, his quality and distinctly individual worth. See D. Frank, "On the Troubadour Sense of Merit," *Romance Notes* 8.2 (1967).

[29] Guibert of Nogent, *Autobiography (De vita sua)*, trans. C. C. Swinton-Bland (London 1926) 57, 64.

[30] See the *Autobiography of Giraldus Cambrensis*, ed. and trans. H. E. Butler (London 1937) 37-67.

[31] *Ibid.* 233. Giraldus was wont to say of himself: "In this struggle I am sustained and uplifted by two wings which lighten my toil and render it delightful. The right wing is the pure intent and the clear conscience with which I have undertaken a pious and without doubt a meritorious labour on behalf of the honor of St. David and the dignity of our Church. But the left wing is the praise and glory which I am sure to gain even on earth, both now and for all ages, because of this noble enterprise inspired by so firm a purpose."

Yet the quieter proclamation of Guibert and the steadier blast of Giraldus can be used as contrast to the shrill notes of Peter Abelard.[32] Assuredly, in the *Historia calamitatum* and his letters to Heloise, Abelard achieved an affirmation of self as well as an intensity of self-revelation. This affirmation of self, however, does not necessarily reflect a complete integration of personality, an entire individual. Rather it aquires much of its strength, I suggest, from Abelard's propensity to emulate and identify with the achievements of the earthly Jesus.

Department of History
C. W. Post College
Long Island University, Merriweather Campus
P. O. Greenvale, New York 11548, U.S.A.

[32] If such is the case, the Abelard who composed these letters could be less readily cited as a prime example of a waxing and maturing individuality, a harbinger of a later Renaissance, although the Heloise of the letters may be so cited. See Gilson's valuable discussion, *Heloise and Abelard* 134-144. Yet Gilson would include Abelard within the domain of Renaissance individuality: "If all we need for a Renaissance is to find individuals developed to the highest point, does not this pair suffice?" *Ibid.* 126.

ANOTHER LOOK AT THE "ANATOMIA PORCI"

•

by Ynez Violé O'Neill

Rarely in the history of medicine has a text been so variously evaluated and so seldom studied as the *Anatomia porci*. Moreover, to some extent, these characteristics appear to be interrelated. The paradox that this brief treatise is termed the earliest Western work on anatomy in one history of medieval science,[1] and yet is not mentioned at all in perhaps the most widely read history of pre-Harveian anatomy and physiology,[2] may well stem from the fact that comparatively little scholarly attention has ever been directed toward the *Anatomia porci*, and no attempt seems to have been made for over thirty years to assess its proper role in the history of anatomy. The purpose of this paper is to review the significant literature on this treatise, to examine some of the theories advanced concerning it, and to suggest a few possible sources both of its nomenclature and structure, and of certain distinctive concepts expressed in it.

A superficial glance at descriptions of this text in highly reputed histories of medicine affords, if little else, proof of the maxim that, though history may not repeat itself, historians certainly repeat each other. Fortunately this occupational reverence for authority is usually dull, but harmless. The ubiquitous misconception that the *Anatomia porci* was composed by a Salernitan named Copho, however, effectively impeded serious study of the text for decades, as a brief sketch of its origins and influence will illustrate.

The first known printed edition of the *Anatomia porci* appeared in the Latin edition of Galen's works issued at Venice in 1502. Subsequently, perhaps initially in a small book titled *Divi Mesue Vita*, published at Lyons in 1523, the untitled anatomical text was appended to the *De modo medendi* of Copho the Salernitan. In this form it was reprinted the following year by Valentin Kobian at Hagenau. Johann Eichmann or Dryander then included the *Anatomia porci* in his *Anatomia pars prior* of 1537, which was published

[1] A. C. Crombie, *Medieval and Early Modern Science*, ed. 2 (New York 1959) 1.68.

[2] Charles Singer, *A Short History of Anatomy and Physiology from the Greeks to Harvey* (New York 1957) 66-109.

at Marburg, but he entitled the short treatise, *Anatomia Cophonis*, and in consequence it appeared under this title in subsequent editions.[3]

The effects of this persistent error might have been trivial had not Salvatore De Renzi, who had never seen a manuscript copy of the text, become convinced that the *Anatomia porci* was in fact the *Anatomia Cophonis*, and made this conviction the keystone of his theory concerning the age of the work. Noting that statements in the *Anatomia porci* were contested or elaborated upon in in another treatise of anatomy, the *Demonstratio anatomica*, now more commonly known as the *Demonstratio anatomica corporis animalis*, De Renzi surmised that the two works were written about the same time. Since several writings known to have been unavailable in western Europe before the twelfth century were cited in the *Demonstratio anatomica corporis animalis*, De Renzi concluded that the *Anatomia porci* was written by a Salernitan master, Copho the younger, who lived during the first half of the twelfth century.[4]

Although De Renzi's syllogism was founded on rather tenuous premises, his conclusion that the *Anatomia porci* was composed early in the twelfth century is still generally accepted. One of the reasons for the theory's continued favor is the supportive evidence found in the nomenclature of the work. Certain words in the *Anatomia porci* were traced to the versions of Constantine the African, the enigmatic translator of Arabic medical works about whom little is known except that he died at Monte Cassino in 1087. If the nomenclature found in the *Anatomia porci* originated in the translations of Constantine, then the *Anatomia porci* could not have been composed before the last quarter of the eleventh or the first quarter of the twelfth century.[5]

An ardent advocate of this opinion was Ignaz Schwarz of Würzburg. In 1907 Schwarz published a version of the *Anatomia porci* he had found in a thirteenth-century manuscript of the University Library of Würzburg. As the Würzburg text was much longer and more elaborate than the previously known versions of the *Anatomia porci*, Schwarz believed that it was the original work of Copho, or as Sudhoff termed it, the *Urkopho*. Furthermore, as his manuscript contained numerous examples of Constantinian influences, Schwarz maintained that it must have been composed, as De Renzi had proposed, after the third quarter of the eleventh century.[6]

[3] George Washington Corner, *Anatomical Texts of the Earlier Middle Ages* (Washington, D. C. 1927) 19-21, and Karl Sudhoff, "Die erste Tieranatomie von Salerno und ein neuer salernitanischer Anatomietext," *Archiv für Geschichte der Mathematik, der Naturwissenschaften, und der Technik* 10 (1927) 137.

[4] Salvatore De Renzi, "Lezioni anatomiche della Scuola Salernitana," *Collectio Salernitana* 2 (Naples 1853) 387.

[5] George Sarton, *Introduction to the History of Science* 2 (Baltimore 1931) 1.237, and compare with *ibid.* 770, 742.

[6] Ignaz Schwarz, *Die medizinischen Handschriften der kgl. Universitätsbibliothek in Würzburg* (Würzburg 1907) 21 69-76.

Ten years after Schwarz published his findings along with a recension of the Würzburg text, Franz Redeker, having examined Schwarz's edition carefully, concluded that the so-called *Urkopho* was a composite work, that in fact it was not the pristine *Anatomia porci*, but an adulterated version. Redeker demonstrated also that the Constantinian influences observed in the Würzburg text had been drawn from a later anatomical writing, a copy of which he was fortunate enough to discover in Munich, and that such influences were rare in the *Anatomia porci*.[7]

Redeker's findings were later developed by his teacher, Karl Sudhoff, whose studies of Salernitan anatomy are fundamental to any consideration of the subject. Sudhoff had read most of the known manuscript copies of the *Anatomia porci*, and, since none of them bore the title *Anatomia Cophonis*, he was among the first to discard De Renzi's theory that the anatomical treatise was written by Copho the Salernitan.[8] Moreover, Sudhoff agreed with Redeker that the *Anatomia porci* contained little that derived from the Constantinian translations. Sudhoff also showed that even the most anatomical of Constantine's versions, his translations of ʿAli ibn ʿAbbas's *al-Maliki*, generally called the *Pantegni*, had little in common with the *Anatomia porci*.[9] Although he could not deny that a few terms in the latter work were Constantinian,[10] Sudhoff maintained that the impetus for the *Anatomia porci* antedated the recovery and translation of Arabic texts.

In order to follow Sudhoff's reasoning, let us examine the term in question. The initial sentences of the *Anatomia porci* appear to acknowledge its author's indebtedness to classical medicine. "Since the composition of the interior members of the human body was generally unknown, the ancient physicians, and Galen most of all, resolved to expose the positions of the internal organs by dissecting animals."[11] The following sentence seems to outline the purpose

[7] Franz Redeker, *Die "Anatomia magistri Nicolae phisici" und ihr Verhältnis zur Anatomia Chophonis [sic] und Richardi* (Leipzig 1917) 4-6.

[8] Sudhoff (n. 3 above) 137.

[9] *Ibid.* 148.

[10] The terms manifestly Constantinian are *sifac*, the peritoneum, and *zirbus*, the omentum, although as Sarton observed in *Introduction* 2.1.237, the classical term, omentum, also appears in the text of the *Anatomia porci*.

[11] "Quoniam interiorum membrorum humani corporis conpositiones omnes erant innotae, placuit veteribus medicis et maxime Galieno, ut per anathomiam brutorum animalium interiorum positiones manifestarentur," *Anatomia porci* in Sudhoff (n. 3 above) 141. 1-3 (henceforth this text will be cited as *Anatomia porci*; the line citations refer to this edition). Sudhoff stated that he prepared this edition of the *Anatomia porci* by collating the texts he found in these five manuscripts: Vatican City, Bibliotheca apostolica vaticana, Cod. lat. 2378 (12-13 century); Erfurt, Städtische Bücherei, Qu. 185 (13-14 century); Munich, Bayerische Staatsbibliothek, Cod. monac. lat. 4622 (12 century); Bamberg, Stadtbibliothek, Cod. L III 37 (15 century); and Paris, Bibliothèque Nationale, Cod. lat. 7030A (14 century). Missing from perhaps the oldest of these manuscripts, the Munich text, and from several other copies of the *Anatomia porci*, are the descriptions of the uterus and the brain that

of the treatise. "Although among the animals certain ones, such as the monkey, appear to resemble us externally, others such as the pig, internally, the internal structure of none appears to be more like ours than is that of the pig, and therefore we shall conduct an anatomy upon this animal."[12]

The *Anatomia porci*, then, appears to be a description of the dissection of a pig for didactic purposes. Sudhoff believed that it was the first composition designed to instruct medical students, based on the observation of a natural object and on the demonstration of information obtained from the body of a vertebrate animal.[13] He thought that the material in the *Anatomia porci* was obtained from observations of actual dissections that had been conducted, as he contended, long before the advent of the Constantinian texts. Sudhoff concluded, therefore, that although the *Anatomia porci* might date from the first quarter of the twelfth century, it represented a much older tradition.[14] It lies beyond the scope of this paper to inquire into the pre-Constantinian history of medical instruction at Salerno, but a question pertinent to our topic is whether or not written sources existed from which the distinctive material in the *Anatomia porci* could have been drawn. Identification of such sources would tend to refute Sudhoff's contention that the *Anatomia porci* was a dissection manual based upon observations of actual dissections.

One of the reasons Sudhoff discounted the importance of nomenclature in determining the age of the *Anatomia porci* was, very likely, that he and others had discovered that most of its anatomical terminology could be traced to two pre-Constantinian sources, Isidore of Seville's *Origines*, and Vindician's *Gynaecia*. Isidore wrote the *Origines*, often erroneously called the *Etymologiae*, during the first quarter of the seventh century, and, although his goal in writing this work was primarily lexicographic, he discussed and defined in it terms pertaining to the structure of the human body. Since the *Origines* was one of the capital books of the early Middle Ages, it could have served as a source for the *Anatomia porci*, as it did for many of the other medieval considerations of anatomy.[15]

Sudhoff included as the final sections of his edition. As they may have been appended to the treatise long after it was originally composed, these portions of Sudhoff's edition will not be considered in this paper.

[12] "Et cum bruta animalia quaedam ut simia in exterioribus, quaedam (ut porcus) in interioribus nobis videantur similia, secundum positionem interiorum nulla nobis inveniuntur (adeo) similia sicut porci, et ideo in eis anathomiam fieri destinavimus," *Anatomia porci* 141.3-7.

[13] "Erst spät erkannte man sie als das was sie ist; den ersten literarischen Niederschlag der nicht bloss gedächtnismässig erfassten, also memorierenden, sondern auch am Naturobjekt beobachtenden und demonstrierenden Kenntnisnahme vom Baue des Wirbeltierleibes als wichtigen Unterrichtsstoffes für den werdenden Arzt," Sudhoff (n. 3 above) 136.

[14] *Ibid.* 147-149.

[15] Robert von Töply, in his *Studien zur Geschichte der Anatomie im Mittelalter* (Leipzig 1898) 88-89, was among the first to note that some of the terms in the *Anatomia porci* could

Unlike Isidore, Vindician was a physician, and his purpose in writing a description of the human body was medical, or perhaps more precisely, obstetrical.[16] Although his work was composed toward the end of the fourth century, since he had been one of Saint Augustine's mentors[17] the *Gynaecia* was known throughout the medieval period, and its significance as a repository of Greco-Latin anatomical concepts and terminology has long been acknowledged.[18]

There is a striking difference, however, between the manner in which the anatomical material is presented in these texts and in the *Anatomia porci*. The section on anatomy in the *Origines* and in the *Gynaecia* begins with a description of the head. Thereafter the hair, forehead, eyebrows, eyes, and other structures of the body are discussed in a cephalocaudal order.[19] In contrast, the anatomical section of the *Anatomia porci* begins with instructions to incise the neck of the pig, and the cervical structures are the first described.[20] Because this appeared to be a logical method of beginning the dissection of a pig, it has been assumed that the *Anatomia porci* was the description of such a procedure. Furthermore, since it seemed similar to no previous text, it has been presumed that the original form of the *Anatomia porci* proved that its author had drawn his material from observation and experimentation rather than from traditional texts.[21]

What the proponents of this theory failed to recognize, however, was that these hypothetically original features of the *Anatomia porci* could have been derived from a description in a compendium of classical medicine. In the

---

be found in the works of Isidore. For a list of texts derived from Isidore's statements on anatomy and a short bibliography of the few modern writings to consider his influence upon the history of medieval medicine, see n. 3 in my "An *Exordium membrorum* written in the Tenth Century," *Sudhoffs Archiv* 51 (1967) 364.

[16] "De compagine hominis quomodo formatur in utero materno vel coteneatur. hanc epistolam disponere ex libris grecis in latinum sermonem. quibus ossibus vel quibus nervis, aut quibus compaginibus corpus humanum continetur. quomodo in utero materno formatur. cuius anathomi id est compaginis. ratione exponere non morabor," Vindician, *Gynaecia* in Cod. Paris. lat. 4883 (Colb. 2140) f. 5b 1, as cited by Valentin Rose in his edition of *Theodori Prisciani Euporiston libri III cum physicorum fragmento et additamentis. . . . Accedunt Vindiciani Afri quae feruntur reliquiae* (Leipzig 1894) 429.

[17] In the fourth book of his *Confessions*, Saint Augustine tells us how earnestly Vindician tried to dissuade the young teacher of rhetoric from believing in astrology (*Conf.* 4.3, PL 32.695).

[18] A brief bibliography is appended to the note on Vindician in Sarton, *Introduction* 1.374, but a more extensive account of the life and works of the fourth-century physician is in Josef Schipper's *Ein neuer Text der Gynaecia des Vindician* (Erlangen 1921).

[19] Isidore of Seville, *Etymologiae* 11.1, PL 82.397-415, and compare with Vindician, *Gynaecia*, ed. Rose 429-443.

[20] *Anatomia porci* 141-142.8-24.

[21] Sudhoff (n. 3 above) 145, also used the *modus procedendi* argument in his attempt to prove that the descriptions of the uterus and of the brain were intrinsic parts of the dissection manual.

first century of the Christian era, very likely during the reign of Tiberius (A.D. 14 to 37), A. Cornelius Celsus prepared a vast encyclopedia of the arts.[22] Of this great work, only a few fragments of the chapters on agriculture and rhetoric, and eight books of the medical section have survived.[23] As two manuscript copies of Celsus's *De medicina* dating from the ninth century and one of the tenth century are still extant, the work must have been known and read in Europe centuries before Constantine began to translate Arabic medical texts.[24]

In the *De medicina* is a description of the internal parts of the body, beginning with an account of the cervical structures and sketching the inferior members of the body precisely as they are dealt with in the *Anatomia porci*.[25] It seems likely that the unknown author of the latter work used Celsus's description as a model for his treatise. If this be true, then the contention that animal dissection was an intrinsic part of the pre-Constantinian Salernitan curriculum would rest on flimsy evidence. Moreover, the belief that the *De medicine*, though available in the ninth and tenth centuries, exerted little or no influence upon the development of medieval medicine,[26] would need to be reconsidered. Finally, positive demonstration that the *Anatomia porci* was patterned on *De medicina*'s anatomical section would further confirm the opinion that the influence exerted upon the history of anatomy by texts known in Europe prior to the twelfth century was more powerful than has hitherto been recognized.

If the nomenclature and form of the *Anatomia porci*, however, can be traced at least provisionally to such texts, certain concepts expressed in it cannot. The first of these is set forth directly after the introductory sentences mentioned in the paragraph above. Having instructed his readers to begin by cutting through the pig's neck, the author continues: "The first thing you encounter there is the tongue (*lingua*) bound on the left and right sides by certain nerves called *motivi*, and to the tongue itself come nerves from below which are called *reversivi*, and these passing from the brain to the lung, return to the tongue, by which it is moved producing the voice."[27]

---

[22] A brief biography of Celsus, and the history of the publication of his work, is in George Sarton's *The Appreciation of Ancient and Medieval Science during the Renaissance* (Philadephia 1955) 12-14.

[23] All of the surviving fragments together with a biography of Celsus are contained in the definitive edition of Celsus's works, *A. Cornelii Celsi quae supersunt opera omnia*, ed. Friedrich Marx (Leipzig 1915).

[24] The manuscripts are: Paris, Bibliothèque Nationale, MS lat. 7028 fol. 13rv; Florence, Bibl. medicea laurensiana plut. LXXIII MS 1, fol. 2-140; and Vatican City, Bibl. Apostolica Vaticana, MS lat. 5951 fol, 1-155v; these are described by Augusto Beccaria, *I codici di medicina del periodo presalernitana* (Rome 1956) 152-156, 277-281, 312-313.

[25] *Anatomia porci* 141-143; cf. Celsus, *De medicina* 4.1, Marx 147-151.

[26] C. H. Talbot, *Medicine in Medieval England* (London 1967) 13.

[27] "Et tunc lingua primo tibi occurret quae dextrorsum et sinistrorsum nervis quibusdam colligata est qui motivi dicuntur, et ad ipsam linguam ab inferioribus veniunt nervi qui

This passage is most reminiscent of Galen's account of the movement of the larynx. In *The Use of Parts*, Galen stated that because the recurrent laryngeal nerves appeared to arise below the larynx, they were believed by some investigators to originate not from the brain, but from a lower part. He then refuted this contention by showing that the recurrent laryngeal nerves were projections of the larger vagus nerves.[28] In the eleventh book of his *Anatomical Procedures*, Galen not only confirmed his earlier account of the laryngeal nerves, but advised the vivisection of pigs to demonstrate the distribution and function of these nerves. It is noteworthy that he also counseled against using apes in this demonstration.[29]

The fact that in the *Anatomia porci* the principal organ of phonation is termed a tongue (*lingua*) appears to be another indication of Galenic influence in the early medieval anatomical writing. In *The Use of Parts*, Galen called the most important instrument of the voice γλῶττις that is, tongue.[30] Although authorities differ on what structures Galen considered to be essential parts of this organ,[31] there is little doubt that a translated version of the Galenic term appears in the *Anatomia porci*.

Thus it seems that the author of the treatise was acquainted in some measure with material in Galen's anatomical writings. The problem posed by this finding is that there appears to be no channel by which he could have acquired this knowledge. Although a Latin abridgment of *The Use of Parts* is believed to have been made late in the thirteenth century, this work is thought not to have been completely translated until Nicholas of Reggio rendered it from Greek to Latin during the fourteenth century.[32]

That one of the later books of *Anatomical Procedures* could have served as a source for the *Anatomia porci* is even less likely. Complete Greek manuscripts of the fifteen books of this work were known to Hunain ibn Ishaq, the Nestorian translator, as late as the ninth century, but all Greek manuscripts in western Europe derive from one mutilated copy containing only the first eight books and the first part of the ninth book. This truncated version was published in the 1525 Aldine edition of Galen's works, and many times subsequently; but the remainder of book nine and all of books ten through

reveisivi dicuntur, quia cum ipsi a cerebro veniant ad pulmonem, revertuntur ad linguam, per quos lingua movetur ad voces," *Anatomia porci* 141.9-13.

[28] Galen, *On the Use of Parts* 7, *Opera omnia*, ed. Carolus Gottlob Kühn (Leipzig 1821-1833) 3.567-585; *Œuvres anatomiques, physiologiques, et médicales de Galien*, ed. and trans. Charles Daremberg (Paris 1854) 1.497-508.

[29] Galen, *on Anatomical Procedures* 11, *Galen on Anatomical Procedures—the Later Books*, trans. L. H. Duckworth, ed. M. C. Lyons and B. Towers, (Cambridge 1962) 80-87.

[30] Galen, *The Use of Parts* 7, Kühn 3.560-561; cf. Duckworth 84.

[31] Daremberg, 1.493 n. 1, believed that for Galen, the glottis was an instrument consisting of the true and false chords and their ventricles, but Hans Baumgarten, in his *Galen über die Stimme* (Göttingen 1962) 112, 172, disputed Daremberg's contention.

[32] Galen, *Anatomical Procedures*, trans. Charles Singer (London 1956) 238-239 n. 10.

fifteen were unknown in the West until discovered in two Arabic manuscripts, collated and published with a German translation by Max Simon in 1906.[33]

Since neither of the Galenic sources containing ideas similar to those found in the *Anatomia porci* seems to have been available in Europe when the *Anatomia porci* was composed, the question how the Galenic concepts found their way into that work must for the present remain an open one.

Another puzzling feature of the *Anatomia porci* is the account of the heart and its ancillary vessels: "And then you will see a vein, called the concave one, which comes from the liver through the middle of the diaphragm, and enters the auricle of the heart from below. Then it becomes an artery and from it are derived all of the other arteries which proceed to the parts, in which the pulse occurs."[34] From this passage it is evident that the author of the medieval anatomy believed that the aorta derived from the vena cava. This notion is extraordinary not only because it contradicts several of the basic tenets of Galenic physiology, but also because it seems to have sprung from a distinguished lineage.

According to Galen, blood was formed in the liver and distributed through the body in the veins. Some of it eventually reached the right ventricle of the heart where it followed one of three courses. The largest portion of the blood, having become purified, flowed back into the venous system. Believing that the right ventricle occurred only in those animals provided with lungs, and that its primary purpose was pulmonic alimentation, Galen maintained that a second portion of the blood was carried to the lungs by way of the pulmonary artery, and that the third and remaining part passed from right to left through the interventricular septum. The septum was believed to be porous, and the blood was further refined by percolating through this sievelike structure. Once in the left ventricle, a portion of this purified blood was made into vital spirits, which then effected the vital functions of the body, and flowed in the blood of the arteries.[35]

Clearly, to have believed in the existence of an intercardiac anastomosis between the veins and the arteries would have undermined the anatomical foundations upon which the Galenic theories concerning the operation of the cardiovascular system, as well as those explaining nervous function, were based. Whatever may have been the origins of the cardiac description in the *Anatomia porci*, therefore, it seems unlikely that they were Galenic.

To find a comparable cardiovascular description, we must turn to the works of one of Galen's predecessors. In his *Account of Animals*, Aristotle, who did

[33] Lyons and Towers, Introduction to the Duckworth translation, xi-xviii.

[34] "Et tunc videbis quandam venam, quae concava dicitur, quae ab epate venit per medium diafracmatis et subintrat auriculam cordis, et fit arteria, de quae fiunt omnes aliae arteriae, quae pocedunt ad membra in quibus fit pulsus," *Anatomia porci* 142.27-29. The auricle is the only division of the heart mentioned in this text.

[35] Galen, *The Use of Parts* 4-7 *passim*, Kühn 3.266-608, Daremberg 1.278-526.

not recognize a distinction between veins and arteries, maintained that all blood vessels derived from two principal ones originating in the heart. He called these fundamental vessels the great blood vessel and the aorta,[36] and further explained that as the heart lay between them, it was really part of the vascular system. Later in the same work, Aristotle indicated that the great blood vessel passed through the heart and joined the aorta.[37]

Authorities have long struggled with these passages, attempting to reconcile Aristotle's statements with anatomical facts.[38] Some have argued that the text is corrupt, or that Aristotle, whose interest in embryology is well known, may have referred to the ductus arteriosus, and others have contended that, although Aristotle was a careful observer, he was compelled by convention to ignore the evidence of his eyes, and to describe the heart as the superstitions of his time demanded.[39] But even more difficult than determining why Aristotle chose to maintain that the principal artery and the principal vein were united in the heart is the task of indicating how this idea was transmitted to the author of the *Anatomia porci*.

Recently scholars have begun to revise traditional judgments concerning the earliest dates that Aristotle's works became known in the West, but unfortunately, no evidence has been produced showing that their recovery antedated the middle of the twelfth century.[40] Since the earliest use of the

---

[36] Μεγάλη φλέψ, ἀορτή, Aristotle, *Historia animalium* 3, *Opera omnia quae extant graece et latine* (Paris 1619) 1.798.

[37] Aristotle, *Historia animalium* 3.3, trans. D'Arcy Wentworth Thompson in *The Works of Aristotle*, ed. J. A. Smith and W. A. Ross (Oxford 1908) 4.513ab.

[38] Perhaps the most famous of these discussions are the articles by T. H. Huxley, "On certain errors respecting the structure of the heart attributed to Aristotle," *Nature* 21 (London 1879) 1-5. and by Arthur Platt, "Aristotle on the heart," *Studies in the History and Method of Science*, ed. Charles Singer, (Oxford 1921) 2.521-532.

[39] D'Arcy Thompson reviewed many of these suggestions in his edition (513a35 n. 3). It would seem that Michael Scot, who rendered *The Account of Animals* from Arabic to Latin during the first decades of the thirteenth century, was also confused by Aristotle's discussion of the heart and its vessels. In Michael's influential and perhaps first Latin version of the Aristotelian biological treatise, one vessel called the *orti* (the word is undeclined) was described as originating in the heart, and another, the *adorti*, as joining the vena cava; there two new vessels were formed, one passing to the lungs, and the other to the spine. As the text of Michael's translation is as yet unpublished, these lines were compared in two thirteenth century manuscripts of the work: Cambridge, Gonville and Caius College MS 109 fol. 20v; and a copy in the private library of Mr. Robert B. Honeyman, Jr., of San Juan Capistrano, California, fol. 12rv. Mr. Honeyman's kindness in allowing me to use his manuscript as well as in providing me with a microfilm copy of the pages in question is most gratefully acknowledged.

[40] Alexander Birkenmajer's *Le rôle joué par les médecins et les naturalistes dans la reception d'Aristote au XIIᵉ et XIIIᵉ siècles*, in *La Pologne au VIᵉ congrès international des sciences historiques, Oslo, 1928*, (Warsaw 1930), is the basic work on this subject, but L. Minio-Paluello, in his "Jacobus Veneticus Grecus—Canonist and Translator of Aristotle," *Traditio* 8 (1952) 293-295, reported significant new findings concerning it.

Libri naturales was found in the writings of two twelfth-century Salernitan physicians,[41] and since notions expressed in Aristotle's biological writings reappear in what is considered to be the first Salernitan anatomical treatise, I suggest that the *Anatomia porci* in general, and its cardiac account in particular, ought to be studied by those interested in establishing when Aristotelian concepts first became incorporated into Western scientific writings.[42]

This study, although questioning that the origins of the *Anatomia porci* were primarily empirical, has failed to demonstrate that all of the ideas in the treatise were derived from written materials known to have been available in Europe during the twelfth century. Rather it has shown that certain Galenic and Aristotelian anatomical theories appear to have been perceived in the West, albeit imperfectly, before the works in which they were expounded are believed to have been translated into Latin. The only seemingly valid explanation for this phenomenon, in the absence of written materials that might serve as intermediaries, is the oral tradition long operative in certain Mediterranean enclaves. We know, for example, that from the late tenth, until the late thirteenth centuries many people in Southern Italy read, wrote, and even spoke not only Latin and Arabic, but also Greek. That anatomical ideas may have been discussed by at least a few of them is not inconceivable for one fact, if no other, about the metamorphosis of Western anatomy seems clear. Its chrysalis pupated, very likely, in the southern Italian alluvium.

241 South Windsor Boulevard

Los Angeles, California 90004, U.S.A.

---

[41] Birkenmajer (n. 40 above) 4-5.

[42] Martin Grabmann, in his "Aristoteles im zwölften Jahrhundert," *Mediaeval Studies* 12 (1950) 161-162, suggested that twelfth-century medical writings might hold the key to the knowledge and use of the "new Aristotle."

THE LION-KNIGHT LEGEND IN ICELAND AND THE VALÞJÓFSSTAÐIR DOOR

•

by Richard L. Harris

1. Introduction

Since the mid-nineteenth century, when the door from Valþjófsstaðir first came to the attention of the academic world, numerous attempts have been made to identify its carvings with episodes found in various sagas or in continental European literature. The carvings depict scenes related to the lion-knight legend, familiar to Arthurian scholars from the Y*vain* of Chrétien de Troyes but certainly current in late medieval Europe—and Iceland—in several other forms as well. The most recent investigation conducted in the search for the carvings' source has concentrated on versions of the story of Henry the Lion.[1] I believe, however, that everything of significance in the material on the door may be found in the Icelandic sagas themselves. It is necessary to examine these works thoroughly for a solution to the problem before ranging through areas of European literature and legend which may never even have been known in Iceland.

Unfortunately, despite the extended controversy over sources for the carvings, the sagas in which the lion-knight legend occurs have received but little attention, and no study has been made of the interrelationships between them with respect to the legend. Such a study is offered in the second part of this paper, and it is intended to serve as a basis for my own arguments regarding the Valþjófsstaðir door. It should also be useful as a preliminary consideration of materials which might be of interest to Arthurian specialists who have not been previously aware of the lion-knight's fame and popularity in thirteenth-century Iceland. The third part of the paper contains my proposal concerning the source of the carvings on the door.

The wooden door (Plate 1) from Valþjófsstaðir, in the east of Iceland, may be seen today in the National Museum of Iceland, where it has been

---

[1] Peter Paulsen, *Drachenkämpfer, Löwenritter und die Heinrichsage* (Cologne 1966) 179-196. See also H. Schneider, *Die Gedichte und die Sage von Wolfdietrich* (Munich 1913) 246-247, and K. Hoppe, *Die Sage von Heinrich dem Löwen* (Bremen 1952) 31.

since 1930 when it was returned to its native country with other objects by
the Danish government. It had been placed in the Royal Museum for Northern
Antiquities in Copenhagen in 1851.² At that time, the door was taken from
the church at Valþjófsstaðir, although there is vague and perhaps erroneous
information to the effect that it once was part of a grand hall there, decorated
with much more of the exquisite carving found on the door itself. The earliest
record of the door's existence is in Bishop Brynjólfur Sveinsson's *Visitation
Book*, dated 1641, in which there is no mention of the hall.³

The carvings on the door are contained within two large circular panels,
the lower of which (Plate 2) represents four closely knit dragons. The symmetrical nature of the pattern formed by these creatures might lead one to consider its possible relationship to the symbol of the cross within a circle, or
perhaps the knot. Such similarities and their potential significance are dealt
with by Paulsen in *Drachenkämpfer*.⁴ It is, however, difficult to see any
iconographic connection between the matter of the lower panel and the motif
that is presented in the upper panel (Plate 3). This latter is divided into two
halves. In the lower half is an armed knight or warrior astride a horse, attempting to save a lion from a dragon. In the upper left portion of the circle,
the lion follows the knight, who is still on horseback. In the upper right,
the lion appears to lie upon a grave with a cross at its head and with a runic
inscription, of which the first four or five letters have been lost with a piece
of the door. The inscription reads as follows:

. . . rikia konong her grapin er ua dreka þæna.

Anders Bæksted, in *Islands Runeindskrifter*, suggests this supplement and
normalization:

[Sé inn] ríkja konung hér grafinn er vá dreka þenna.⁵

A possible translation into English would be:

[See the] powerful king here $\frac{\text{carved}}{\text{buried}}$ who killed this dragon.

In the nineteenth century several attempts were made to establish the
date of the carvings. Captain O. Blom studied the weapons and armor used
by the hero and came to the conclusion, stated at a meeting of the Kongelige
Nordiske Oldskriftselskab in April, 1870, that the door could have been made
as early as 1100 and not later than 1150. Gísli Brynjólfsson contended at

² Anders Bæksted, *Islands Runeindskrifter*, Bibliotheca arnamagnæana 2 (Copenhagen
1942) 183.
³ Bæksted 194.
⁴ Paulsen 48-60.
⁵ Bæksted 192.

the same meeting that since the church at Valþjófsstaðir was built between 1186 and 1190, the door could reasonably have been made for that occasion and at that time. Brynjólfsson observed further that the Continental fashions of weapons and armor might not have reached Iceland immediately and that, at all events, current fashions probably would not have been considered appropriate for the representation of a story set in an earlier age.[6]

In 1884 Björn M. Ólsen examined the runic inscription in some detail, concluding that it could not have been made prior to 1200. Another matter that he found of interest was the possibility that the door might once have belonged to an old hall, remarkable for its decorative carvings. He noted that Eggert Ólafsson, who with Bjarni Pálsson wrote a travel book about Iceland in the 1760s, referred to such a hall at Valþjófsstaðir but added that it had been altered in later times. Ólsen included a description of the hall supposedly from a manuscript in the National Library of Iceland, written in the mid-eighteenth century, which does not mention a door, although other portions of the hall ornamented by carvings are enumerated.[7] This fits in with what might be expected if Bishop Brynjólfur's *Visitation Book* is actually speaking of the Valþjófsstaðir door.

Guðbrandur Jónsson's views on these matters were influenced by his awareness of a historical fact that apparently had not been given consideration previously. He pointed out that the church at Valþjófsstaðir had burned in 1361 and that it was unlikely that the door could have survived this event if it had been on the church at the time. Therefore, he concluded, the door must have originated later than 1361. He also believed there was no evidence in the carvings themselves that the door was made in Iceland to begin with.[8] It is difficult to see why, under these circumstances, the door must necessarily have been made so late. It could just as well have been taken from the hall to enhance the beauty of the new church built after the fire. In his study of Norse and Icelandic runes, published in 1910, Finnur Jónsson remarks briefly that the door is assumed to date from around 1200, or the first quarter of the thirteenth century, though it is possible that it is from the last quarter of the twelfth century.[9] Magnus Olsen states simply that the inscription was made around 1200.[10]

Dr. Kristján Eldjárn, president of Iceland and formerly curator of the National Museum of Iceland, has written in a letter to me that "it seems most

---

[6] For a report of the meeting see *Dags-Telegrafen*, April 25, 1870, 1.

[7] Björn M. Ólsen, "Valþjófsstaðahurðin," *Árbók hins íslenzka fornleifafélags* (1884-1885) 24-37.

[8] Bæksted 199.

[9] Finnur Jónsson, "Runerne i den norsk-islandske digtning og litteratur," *Aarboger for nordisk oldkyndighed og historie* 2.25 (1910) 298.

[10] Magnus Olsen, "De norröne runeinnskrifter," *Runorna*, ed. O. v. Friesen (Stockholm 1933) 104.

likely that it [the door] was carved about 1200 or maybe sometime in the two first decades of the 13th century." Regarding its place of origin, he is of the opinion that it is futile to search in other countries "when all the necessary conditions, material, spiritual, artistic, for its being made by Icelandic craftsmen" were available.[11] It seems to me that little could be added to such a conclusion. In the first chapter of *Drachenkämpfer*, Paulsen deals with various methods of dating the door and does not significantly disagree with Dr. Eldjárn in his findings.

   The story of the grateful lion apparently reached medieval Iceland only in its chivalric form, the lion-knight legend. It exists with variations in at least five sagas, and this count does not include *Ívens saga* or *Þiðriks saga af Bern*, which both have demonstrably close relationships to continental European works. The popular currency of the legend, evidenced by its repeated use in Icelandic literature, came about in part because of these two Old Norse saga romances which seem to have been made during the career of King Hákon IV Hákonarson of Norway (reigned 1217-1263). An additional Continental source of information available to Icelanders regarding the lion's character would have been one or another of the bestiaries. It has not as yet been established with certainty what other debts Old Norse literature owes to the South for its varied conceptions of the story of the lion-knight.

   The entrance of romance literature into Old Norse has been discussed in several places, and there is no need to examine the process here.[12] It is sufficient to say that King Hákon encouraged the translation of romances and related material into Old Norse, possibly in an attempt to raise the cultural level of his court. Likely enough, one of the first of these endeavors was *Tristrams saga*, rendered into Old Norse from the Anglo-Norman *Tristan* of Thomas by Brother Robert in 1226.[13] *Ívens saga*, the Old Norse translation of Chrétien's *Yvain*, was probably made during Hákon's time, possibly by Brother Robert, although the colophon mentioning him at the end of the saga is thought to have been added at a later time.[14] *Ívens saga*, then, coming after *Tristrams saga* but before 1263, must have been written in the second quarter or early part of the third quarter of the thirteenth century.

   The greater portion of *Þiðriks saga af Bern* is found in a parchment manuscript said to date from the latter half of the thirteenth century. It is a com-

   [11] In a letter dated November 17, 1964.

   [12] H. G. Leach, *Angevin Britain and Scandinavia* (Cambridge, Mass. 1921) 25-72; M. Schlauch, *Romance in Iceland* (New York 1934) 1-17; Einar Ól. Sveinsson, *The Age of the Sturlungs*, trans. Jóhann S. Hannesson, Islandica 36 (Ithaca, N. Y 1935) 35-42; Phillip M. Mitchell, "Scandinavian Literature," *Arthurian Literature in the Middle Ages*, ed. R. S. Loomis (London 1959) 462-471.

   [13] Mitchell 464.

   [14] *Ívens saga*, ed. E. Kölbing, Altnordische Saga-Bibliothek 7 (Halle 1898) xxi; Mitchell 466.

posite of a number of German stories, translated into Old Norse while King
Hákon ruled, or else a little later, soon after 1278, if Leach's conjectures are
valid.[15] That episode in the saga which is of interest here is more closely
related to *Wolfdietrich* than to any other known work.

There is evidence that the *Physiologus* was popular in Iceland for some
time before the writing of the two sagas whose dates of composition are discussed above. According to Halldór Hermannsson, it had been translated
twice into Icelandic by the end of the twelfth or the beginning of the thirteenth
century.[16] While nothing is said of a lion in the extant fragments, and while
the available Continental redactions of the *Physiologus* have nothing so elaborate in them as the lion-knight legend, the descriptions of the lion which
must once have been in the Icelandic versions could have provided another
basis for the animal's high reputation in the north.[17]

Since in the preceding material we find the earliest known sources of information about lions and the lion-knight legend in Iceland, we are faced in
the existence of the Valþjófsstaðir door with the necessity of positing an
even earlier source of the legend which is no longer recognizably extant.
In addition, as will be shown below, the legend represented in carvings on
the door differed in certain details from the story of the lion-knight as it is
found today either in *Ívens saga* or in *Þiðriks saga*. The legend may have
existed within a saga, or in a song, or in a folk tale, but in any case it was in
Iceland sometime in the first two decades of the thirteenth century, the time
during which the door was carved.

II. THE LION-KNIGHT LEGEND IN THE SAGAS

As was previously stated, the lion-knight legend appears in Old Norse
in varying forms, the interrelationships of which will be studied in detail
in this section. It has been obvious to those who have broached the subject
at all that the legend in *Ívens saga* and in *Þiðriks saga* was indebted to Continental works. Other sagas in which a knight encounters a dragon on a lion's
behalf are *Konráðs saga keisarasonar*, *Vilhjálms saga sjóðs*, *Sigurðar saga
þögla*, *Ectors saga*, and *Kára saga Kárasonar*.[18] Margaret Schlauch contended

[15] *Þiðriks saga af Bern*, ed. H. Bertelsen (Copenhagen 1905-1911) 1.viii; E. F. Halvorsen,
"*Didriks saga af Bern*," *Kulturhistorisk leksikon for nordisk middelalder* (Copenhagen
1958) 3.74; Leach (n. 12 above) 164.

[16] Halldór Hermannsson, *The Icelandic Physiologus*, Islandica 27 (Ithaca, N. Y. 1938) 4.

[17] For descriptions of the lion which are typical of the *Physiologus*, see Florence McCulloch,
Medieval Latin and French Bestiaries, University of North Carolina Studies in Romance
Languages and Literatures 33 (Chapel Hill 1960) 37.

[18] *Konráðs saga keisarasonar*, ed. Bjarni Vilhjálmsson, Riddarasögur 3 (Reykjavík 1949)
269-344; *Vilhjálms saga sjóðs*, ed. Agnete Loth, Late Medieval Icelandic Romances (LMIR)
4, Editiones arnamagnaeanae (EA) B 23 (Copenhagen 1964) 3-136; *Sigurðar saga þögla*,
ed. Loth, LMIR 2, EA B 21 (Copenhagen 1963) 95-259; *Ectors saga*, ed. Loth, LMIR 1,

that *Ívens saga* and perhaps the bestiaries were responsible for the inclusion of the legend in all of the latter narratives.[19] The following study shows that the situation is much more complex than Schlauch supposed. There is reason to believe another source was influential in the development of the lion-knight legend in Old Norse literature. Such a source could have been present in Iceland in the early thirteenth century, thus forming a part of the cultural milieu in which the carvings of the Valþjófsstaðir door were conceived and executed.

Ívens saga is the simplest early extant Norse version of the lion-knight story. The saga is shorter than Chrétien's *Yvain*, having undergone condensation especially in its later chapters, and the dragon episode has been affected by this. In the Norse translation, which differs little from the story in the French poem except as regards length, Íven rides along a deep valley, comes to a dense forest and, hearing distressing cries and noises, goes towards them. He sees a lion in the brushwood ("hrís"). A dragon is holding its tail and burning it with fire and poison ("af eldi ok eitri").[20] Íven's motivation to help the lion differs from that of Yvain: the French hero comes to the beast's assistance "Qu'a venimeus et felon / Ne doit l'an feire se mal non," whereas Íven fights for the lion because he has perceived that it cried to him for protection ("at leónit œpti á hann sér til náða").[21]

It is also interesting that although Yvain chops off some of the lion's tail in the rescue, Íven does not do so. He harms only the dragon, cutting it in half and then into little pieces.[22] The lion is thus freed, and Íven fears he will be attacked by it. He prepares to defend himself, but the creature crawls to him and turns up its stomach ("sneri þá upp á sér maganum").[23] After this curious action, for which it is difficult to find a specific source in Chrétien, the lion does something equally remarkable. It wets its snout with tears

---

EA B 20 (Copenhagen 1962) 81-186; *Sagan af Kára Kárasyni*, ed. Einar Þorðarson (Reykjavík 1886) 3-84. *Kára saga* must have been written quite late, and since the lion-knight episode in it is brief and vague it is not discussed in this paper. Two other sagas, both rather late, have lions that are befriended by heroes. Vígkænn, in *Sagan af Vígkæni kúahirði*, ed. Einar Þorðarson (Reykjavík 1886) 3-28, gains two lions as companions when he gives aid to a lioness having difficulty in labor. The hero in *Sagan af Hinríki heilráði* (Bessastaðir 1908) takes a young lion from its nest, tames it and teaches it to follow him as if it were a dog. Either or both of these sagas may be related to the Continental motif of the grateful lion more closely than to the lion-knight legend (see below 130, 143-144, and Brodeur's articles, n. 33). The friendly, or at least trained, lion was also familiar in later Icelandic folklore; see Jón Árnason, *Íslenzkar þjóðsögur og ævintýri* (Reykjavík 1955-1961) 2.403-405, 4.543-548, 559-560 5.198-199.

[19] Schlauch (n. 12 above) 167. Schlauch seems to háve overlooked *Vilhjálms saga*.

[20] *Ívens saga* 75.

[21] Chrétien de Troyes, *Sämtliche erhältene Werke*, ed. W. Foerster (Halle 1884) 2.139; *Ívens saga* 76.

[22] Chrétien 140; *Ívens saga* 76.

[23] *Ívens saga* 76.

("ok vætti sitt trýni með tárum"), which corresponds to this phrase in *Yvain*: "Et tote sa face moilloit / De lermes par humilité."[24] With that, the lion gives itself into Íven's power, and Íven thanks God for having sent him such a follower. Yvain does not thank God. The hunting scene in Chrétien's poem is summarized in *Ívens saga* with the laconic report that the lion hunted animal as food for them ("veiddi leónit þeim dýr til matar").[25]

Although the final representation on the door has been commonly interpreted as showing the lion mourning the death of its master, no such event occurs in any of the sagas containing the lion-knight legend. It must be observed here, though, that there is a mock death scene in *Yvain* and in *Ívens saga*. The hero and his companion are making their way through the forest when they come upon a spring, stone, and chapel where the central adventures of the romance began. Reminded of his fault in not having returned to his wife at an appointed time, the lion's master falls in a swoon. In so doing, he is pierced superficially in the neck by his sword. The lion thinks he is dead, mourns for him and wants to commit suicide, but the crisis comes to a sudden end when the hero recovers his senses.[26] The possibilities of a relationship between this episode and the final scene on the door will be discussed in the third part of this paper. *Ívens saga* follows Chrétien in making no statement regarding the ultimate fate of the lion. In this saga, a shortened and unimaginative translation made in Norway, there is no evidence of the writer's awareness of any other versions of the lion-knight legend.

Perhaps what is most extraordinary about the dragon fight recorded in *Þiðriks saga af Bern* is that þiðrik fails to save the lion. In *Wolfdietrich*, which contains an episode that is probably the source of this one in *Þiðriks saga*, there is also, later, a successful fight to save a lion from a diminutive dragon, a "saribant," which is attacking the lion beside a lake. The lion holds the serpent in its mouth, and Wolfdietrich hews it asunder. Afterwards, the lion becomes the hero's faithful companion.[27] Þiðrik's only dragon fight preserved in Old Norse takes a less fortunate turn. He is riding through the woods when he comes to a trail after having gone in the direction of some suspicious noises. The writer observes of the trail that a dragon must have made it. Þiðrik rides along the trail and sees a lion and a dragon fighting fiercely. Since he has a lion on his shield, he decides to aid the lion. This is the same motivation as that for Wolfdietrich's entrance into the melee.[28] In the German work, though, a precedent for such behavior has been set by Otnit, who bore an elephant on his shield and who for this reason once gave

---

[24] Chrétien 141; *Ívens saga* 76.

[25] Chrétien 142-144; *Ívens saga* 78.

[26] Chrétien 145-147; *Ívens saga* 78.

[27] *Das deutsche Heldenbuch*, ed. Adelbert von Keller, Bibliothek des litterarischen Vereins in Stuttgart 81 (Stuttgart 1867) 495-498.

[28] *Heldenbuch* 466-467; *Þiðriks saga* 2.362.

aid to an elephant under attack by a dragon.[29] Þiðrik strikes the dragon but breaks his sword in doing so. In *Wolfdietrich*, the lion understands the hero's speech and, at his request, holds the dragon off for a time to give the knight a chance to recuperate.[30]

Having been disarmed, Þiðrik prays to God and then pulls up a tree by the roots. The dragon is angered at this, takes the lion in its mouth, coils its tail about Þiðrik, and flies to its nest. The lion is consumed by the dragon and its offspring. When the dragon is full, it relaxes its grip on Þiðrik. He slips away and jumps under some clothes, groping around until he finds a sword. With this he strikes at rocks. The area is illuminated by the sparks so that he is able to discern the dragon and its young. He strides to the beast, cuts it in two and then chops at it many times until it is dead. Next he returns to and then leaves the valley. The escape of Wolfdietrich is not quite so easy. The dragons try to eat him but meet resistance and eat his horse instead. They stone Wolfdietrich and then fall asleep. After that, he also finds an effective sword and destroys his assailants.[31] Although no other extant versions of an unsuccessful attempt to save a lion in such a situation exist in Old Norse, several elements mentioned here have been preserved in other sagas, as will be seen below.

Leach contends that *Konráðs saga keisarasonar* came into Old Norse by way of the Hanseatic merchants, around the close of the thirteenth century. Bjarni Vilhjálmsson assigns the same general date to the work and suggests that it was composed in Iceland in its present form. He observes that there are similarities between it and some German romances, in particular *Loher und Maller*. Although all of the characters' names in *Konráðs saga* are German, the material itself has been said to be of oriental origin.[32]

The greater part of the narrative tells about the exposing of an unfaithful servant, Roðbert, who is remarkable both for his cunning and for his ability with languages. When Konráð, son of the king of Saxland, goes to Constantinople ("Miklagarðr") to propose to Princess Matthilda, Roðbert comes along as his fosterbrother and interpreter. Upon arriving there, however, Roðbert lets it be thought that he is Konráð, that Konráð is his subservient fosterbrother and that he, Roðbert, is interested in Matthilda. Numerous schemes are evolved to bring about Konráð's ultimate demise by sending him out on errands, which he is led to think are meant to impress the king and court. Konráð survives these missions and finally succeeds in establishing

---

[29] *Heldenbuch* 306.

[30] *Ibid.* 469; *Þiðriks saga* 2.362.

[31] *Heldenbuch* 472-477; *Þiðriks saga* 2.362-363.

[32] Leach (n. 12 above) 165, 268; Vilhjálmsson, in Formáli to Riddarasögur 3.ix-x; Jan de Vries, *Altnordische Literaturgeschichte*, Grundriss der germanischen Philologie 2.16 (Berlin 1964-1967) 2.497.

himself at the court through his courage and the good advice given him by Matthilda.

The lion is first encountered in an adventure that takes place when, at the contrivance of Roðbert, Konráð has been locked out of the city one night. He thinks he sees a fire on a mountain north of the city and rides toward it to see what it is. When he gets near the mountain he hears awful shrieks; he goes in the direction from which they come. Then he sees a huge dragon attacking a lion, its talons in the lion's shoulders and its tail coiled around the lion's body. The dragon is attempting to ascend the mountain with this load. Along the mountain slide, though, there is brushwood ("viðbrekkt"), which the lion spurns at in order to hinder their progress. It will be recalled that brushwood is incidentally mentioned in *Ívens saga*, but that the lion makes no use of it there. Without defining his motivation, Konráð hews the dragon's coil asunder beyond, or behind, the lion, presumably to avoid injuring the lion itself. The dragon frees the lion of its coil, but Konráð still has to chop off its talons above the claws. Then he loosens the claws from the lion's flesh as gently as possible.

This elaborate process of freeing the lion must bring to the reader's mind a story related to the lion-knight legend: the removal of a thorn or sharp bone from some part of a lion's body. Brodeur has demonstrated that such a story may have provided the origins of the European grateful lion motif, of which the lion-knight legend is a later, chivalric offshoot.[33] In this connection, it might be significant that the lion expresses pleasure not after the dragon is killed, but after the claws are taken out.

Konráð tells the lion he knows that it understands man's speech and is the wisest of all animals. He offers to heal it and be its master. The lion drops tears like a man and, again, crawls to him. Then, like Íven's lion, it turns up its stomach ("sneri upp maganum"). The fact that the lion shows pleasure and crawls to the hero twice may indicate that the writer was using different sources and that he switched from one to another at this point.

The dragon's attempt to ascend to its nest on the mountain has failed. It is not said that Konráð is motivated by further desire to discover the source of the light on the mountain, but for some reason he goes to the dragon's nest himself and kills the two young dragons that he finds there. He takes some gold away with him, either as a curiosity or as proof of his adventure ("til synis"). The writer discloses that it was the light from the gold which seemed to him to be a fire. Konráð puts a cord on the lion, gets his horse, takes the dragon's talons and returns to the city.[34]

---

[33] A. G. Brodeur, "Androcles and the Lion," *The Charles Mills Gayley Anniversary Papers* (Berkeley 1922) 197-213, and "The Grateful Lion," *Publications of the Modern Language Association* 39 (1924) 485-524.

[34] *Konráðs saga* 310-312.

The knight's new companion accompanies him on an expedition to the land of lions but is left behind at Matthilda's direction when Konráð proceeds to the land of serpents. The lion is not eager to be left behind but awaits him faithfully and greets him with joy upon his return. Konráð has the beast carry some of his possessions as they make their way back to Constantinople.[35] The lion is not mentioned in the saga after that. It may be appropriate to point out here that the temporary or permanent desertion of the lion by its master is another motif that has medieval Continental analogues.[36]

The legend as it appears in *Konráðs saga* is associated with the material of *Ívens saga* generally in that the dragon is killed when the lion is saved. Specific similarities such as the mere presence of the brushwood and the lion's means of expressing gratitude may be coincidental. It does not seem necessary to conclude that the composer of *Konráðs saga* was familiar with the text of *Ívens saga* or *Ývain*. It is much more likely that he was aware of the episode in *Þiðriks saga* or in *Wolfdietrich* or in material related to it. The existence of the nest to which the dragon attempts to take the lion, the slaying of the young dragons, and the plundering of the nest are events suggestive of some relationship to the material of *Wolfdietrich*.

Although *Vilhjálms saga sjóðs* is highly eclectic and abounds in folklore elements, little research has been done on this work. It is in an Icelandic manuscript from the fifteenth century, but it probably assumed its present form in the first half of the fourteenth century.[37] The plot of *Vilhjálms saga* is complex and is divided roughly into two parts. In the first part Vilhjálmr, son of Ríkarðr, King of England, effects the release of his father and several other kings who have been taken captive by trolls in the fabulous land of Eirs, in Africa. The second part is devoted to setting aright certain undesirable situations that have arisen while the hero was on his expedition. Most notable among these feats is the saving of Astrinomia, daughter of King Kirjalax of Constantinople, from the hands of an uncouth and aggressive suitor. Astrinomia, like Matthilda in *Konráðs saga*, gives Vilhjálmr valuable advice and eventually becomes his wife.

Vilhjálmr and the lion meet after the knight has begun his search for his father. He has set off through Saxland and Lombardy and stopped for the night at a forest called Lutwalld. He sets up his tent in preparing for sleep, when he hears cries and noises, goes out of the tent and sees a fire burning on the side of a mountain. He goes toward the noises until he comes to a slide in the mountain, where he sees a flying dragon with a lion in its clutches. The dragon's claws are in the lion's shoulders, and, while the attacker tries to fly up the mountain with its prey, the lion grasps at trees. The trees come

---

[35] *Ibid.* 317, 323, 330.
[36] Brodeur, "The Grateful Lion" 496-498.
[37] Loth, Introduction to LMIR 4, vii.

loose, and the dragon starts to take lion and all up to its nest. Vilhjálmr strikes at the dragon's coil, wrapped around the lion. As it comes apart the dragon falls forward and fire gushes from its nose and mouth. Vilhjálmr chops three times at the dragon's neck before its head comes off. Then he cuts off the talons at the lion's shoulders, and it crawls to him. He goes next to where the fire is, finds the dragon's nest and three of its offspring, described by the writer as much grown, and kills them all. He takes what gold he pleases and returns to his tent followed by the beast. As long as it lives, the lion never parts from him. He remains there several nights, healing his new-found companion.[38]

Similarities between *Konráðs saga* and *Vilhjálms saga* are so plentiful in this passage that a discussion of differences in the two narratives seems more to the point. First, Vilhjálmr has already stopped for the night and has set up his tent and prepared for sleep when he hears noises, goes out and sees a fire. Whereas Konráð's lion is successful with only brushwood to help anchor it, Vilhjálmr's lion holds trees in its grasp (the word used is cognate with "oak"), and even these do not deter the dragon's progress. Vilhjálmr does not worry over the lion's safety as he butchers its enemy, and when he at last cuts off the talons, without bothering to remove the claws, the lion's gratefulness is not described; it simply crawls towards its benefactor. There is no mention of the lion's ability to understand human speech. The leader learns later, again without explicit statement, of this ability. Vilhjálmr does not actually move towards the fire until after he has killed the dragon, and when he arrives at the nest he kills three partially matured offspring instead of the two of undetermined size which Konráð dispatches. When he takes what gold he pleases from the nest, no special motivation is given for his action.

On the other hand, *Vilhjálms saga* contains nothing that is in agreement with *Þiðriks saga* as opposed to *Konráðs saga*. While it is true that the name of the forest, Lutwalld, can be found in *Þiðriks saga*, it is not said that Þiðrik meets the dragon there, and the borrowing is thus of little significance in this discussion.[39] The closer resemblance generally to *Konráðs saga* is obvious.

One very singular event that occurs in this saga is the killing of a small dragon or serpent that attacked Vilhjálmr when he was unarmed. The lion's active part in this adventure and the fact that it takes place in a lake are two elements that render the scene reminiscent of Wolfdietrich's successful encounter with the saribant (see p. 131).[40] In addition, it is to be observed that the word used for this creature in Old Icelandic is *ormr*, whereas the lion's former adversary in this same saga is referred to only as a *dreki*. Of

---

[38] *Vilhjálms saga* 26-27.
[39] *Þiðriks saga*, 2.335.
[40] *Vilhjálms saga* 45-46.

the two terms, *ormr* would be the more likely translation of saribant. While these similarities are indicative of the writer's awareness of *Wolfdietrich* material that is not known to have been translated into Old Norse, the situation does differ from that in *Wolfdietrich* in some respects. In the saga, the lion itself kills the serpent with its powerful tail and its claws. Again, when it is unable to swim, Vilhjálmr, who cannot live without his companion, saves it from drowning.

Eventually, they come to a great river where Vilhjálmr, following Astrinomia's advice, parts with the lion for a time. He tells it to guard his weapons, horse, and saddle. Then he kisses it, and both cry as he leaves. Upon his return the lion is weeping, grieving the loss of its master. It rejoices when it sees him.[41] The sadness of the lion reminds the reader of the lion's reactions in the mock death scene in *Ívens saga*. The motif of the desertion of the lion by its master is recognizable, too, and it is interesting that in both this work and in *Konráðs saga* the lady giving advice has specified that the lion may not accompany the hero on one part of the journey.

The lion receives a mortal wound in the stomach in one of the saga's final battles while it is giving aid to a friend of Vilhjálmr. It continues to fight for a time, holding its entrails in with its tail. When it finally dies Vilhjálmr has its fur made into a cloak. He sees to the preparation of a stone coffin, puts the beast in it, and has gold letters inscribed on it, telling what lies below ("og liet skrifa med gullstaufum huat þar lægi under"). He makes Sjóðr, a coward, eat five bites from the lion's heart, thus causing the man to become brave. Vilhjálmr names his first son Leo, in memory of his dead companion.[42]

Two scenes in this saga are related in an as yet undefined way to *Konráðs saga*: the dragon fight and the desertion of the lion by its master. One episode, the fight with the serpent, shows a connection with some *Wolfdietrich* material that is not found in *Þiðriks saga*. Only one of the four chief events in which the lion is involved in *Vilhjálms saga* has no known relationship to another work. Under these circumstances it seems reasonable to assume that the writer could also have had a source in mind when he described the lion's death and burial.

Sigurðar saga þögla exists in two recensions of unequal length, the longer one having been written in the fifteenth century.[43] The shorter version, said by Einar Ó. Sveinsson to have been composed earlier, is found in two as yet unpublished fragments, one from around 1350, the other from around 1400. Sveinsson, in describing the relationship of the two recensions, says that the "author of the longer version of *Sigurðar saga* apparently used the shorter version as his basis but augmented it with all kinds of matter borrowed from

[41] *Ibid.* 57, 60-61, 74-75.
[42] *Ibid.* 114, 119-120, 128.
[43] Loth, Introduction to LMIR 2, viii.

here and there, which he scattered throughout the story."[44] A close comparison of the relevant passages of the shorter text, in AM 596, quarto, with the corresponding passages in the longer, published text has failed to reveal that the later writer used any other source than the shorter recension for his knowledge of the lion and its activities. The text referred to hereafter will be the longer one, since it is more readily available to the reader.

The saga tells of the adventures of Sigurðr, one of the three sons of Lodivikus, King of Saxland. When his two brothers have been chastised by Sedentiana, a "maiden king," merely because one of them wished to marry her, Sigurðr decides upon revenge. He is successful in carrying out his decision, and finally he marries her himself. Various irrelevant events are introduced along the way; the lion-knight legend is one of them.

The reader is made aware of the dragon in this story before Sigurðr protects the lion from it. His two brothers are journeying along the Rhine after their unfortunate experience with Sedentiana when they and their followers are attacked by a dragon. It eats one of their men and carries two more to a high mountain. At this time Sigurðr is eighteen.[45] He sets out on his first expedition as an armed knight. It is not said that he is aware of the damage inflicted on his brothers' company, nor that he even knows the dragon exists. He comes to a place on the Rhine, though, which is not far from where his brothers have been. He lies down and sleeps awhile before being awakened by violent noises and shrieks that he hears in the forest. He realizes that trees are being bent to the breaking point and that the noises result from this. He rises, puts on his armor, and goes out in the woods where he sees a frightful dragon flying. The dragon has a lion in its claws, and its coil is wound around its prey. The writer remarks that though the lion might be called king of all other animals it is powerless against the dragon. The dragon wants to fly to the high mountain, which Sigurðr's brothers saw and where its nest is, but the lion grasps at trees with its feet. This makes the dragon's claws dig deeper into its victim's flesh, so that it roars with pain. The dragon spews fire and poison, burning the surrounding woods.

Having a lion on his shield, Sigurðr realizes that he must take the animal's side against the dragon. Thus he follows the fighting beasts. He does not want to injure the lion, and at first he sees no opportunity for an assault. The lion looks at Sigurðr gently, as if it were pleading for relief, and the hero thrusts his spear into the dragon between its wing and the lion. Blood rushes from the dragon; it becomes weak and drops the lion, which falls to the ground. Then Sigurðr chops off the dragon's feet, and they also fall to earth. Sigurðr continues to dismember his opponent, protecting himself with his shield.

[44] Einar Ó. Sveinsson, "*Viktors saga ok Blávus*, sources and characteristics," in *Viktors saga ok Blávus*, ed. Jónas Kristjánsson, Riddarasögur 2 (Reykjavík 1964) cxviii-cxix, cxxxvii.
[45] *Sigurðar saga* 134-135.

He cuts off its coil, which forces the creature to descend, and then he beheads it. The writer observes that it is the hero's first deed of renown. The lion looks gently at Sigurðr, crawls to him, and he strokes it. He takes it to his tent, gives it food and spends three days there healing its wounds.

Only after the lion has recovered does Sigurðr think of going to the high mountain to which the dragon had tried to fly and where Sigurðr believes it had its nest. The nest is in a cleft above a high precipice. The hero can see a bright light shining from the cleft, but he is unable to climb to it. He realizes the lion must nearly understand human speech. The writer now pays extended tribute to the lion's abilities, noting first that if it girds itself with its tail there is no cliff so high that it will be injured by jumping from it. He apparently copies directly from a *Physiologus* three facts about the lion which are found traditionally in some versions of that book: it sleeps with its eyes open; the whelps are born dead and remain so for three days until the father comes and blows on them; and it covers its tracks by trailing its tail in the dust.[46] He refers to a Master Lucretius as having said that the lion injures no man who does not provoke it, unless it is extremely hungry.

The lion drags Sigurðr up the steep incline by means of a rope, and the hero then sees that the brightness comes from gold. He finds two young dragons, much grown, and kills them both as the lion watches with a fierce expression. He also finds weapons and human bones. The gold is in great crucibles, stuck to the cave's floor because some of the metal has overflowed and hardened. Sigurðr cuts out the crucibles with his sword. There is more than four horses could carry, but the lion is able to run down the slope with the whole load on its back. The knight lowers himself on the rope, and they return to the tent.[47]

The writer's interest in the lion seems to wane after this, and the beast is involved only briefly in later episodes of the saga. It is once mistaken for a dog by two troll women who attack Sigurðr's camp.[48] Although Konráð and Vilhjálmr both leave their lions behind by direction of advice-giving heroines, no one advises Sigurðr to desert his lion temporarily as he sets out to torment Sedentiana. No mention is made of the desertion, either, until the adventure is ended and the hero returns to his ships, where his men have been keeping the lion.[49] Nothing of the lion's sorrow is expressed. As in *Vilhjálms saga*, the writer includes a description of the death of the lion. The death occurs when an earl's son, Herburt, urges his men to kill the beast and then thrusts a spear at it himself. Sigurðr starts to exact revenge for the misdeed, but the two men are reconciled and Herburt marries Sigurðr's sister, Florencia.[50] The disposal of the lion's carcass is not dealt with.

[46] See above 129 and n. 16.
[47] *Sigurðar saga* 141-147.
[48] *Ibid.* 148-149.
[49] *Ibid.* 210.
[50] *Ibid.* 212-217.

The writer's love of words and his constant desire to show off his learning confuse the immediate impression of the legend so far as its relation to the parallel events in *Konráðs saga* and *Vilhjálms saga* is concerned. The events themselves, though, are quite simple and a comparison of them will serve to demonstrate the closeness of *Sigurðar saga* to the story in *Vilhjálms saga* as well as the relation of these two narratives to that in *Konráðs saga*. There are impressive similarities between the stories of Konráð and Vilhjálmr as opposed to that of Sigurðr. First, although the fire on the mountain is mentioned in both *Konráðs saga* and *Vilhjálms saga* at the start of the adventure, it is not until after the lion has been saved that Sigurðr notices a brightness coming from the mountain. Second, there is an example of an unresolved or blind element in Sigurðr's story which has a corresponding element with real purpose in the other two narratives. Konráð and Vilhjálmr both cut off the dragon's talons because the dragon is still holding the lion. Sigurðr's lion, however, has been freed and has dropped to the ground when the lance pierces the dragon's side. There is thus no reason for cutting off the dragon's feet. The writer overexercised either his imagination or his eclectic proclivities at this point. Another interesting feature in the history of Sigurðr is that the lion does not cry or turn up its stomach in gratitude at being saved. Because of these divergences on the part of *Sigurðar saga* from the other two works in question, it is not possible that *Sigurðar saga* provided a source for *Vilhjálms saga*. Chronological considerations, of course, preclude any possibility of material in *Konráðs saga* being derived from *Sigurðar saga*. A closer relationship between *Vilhjálms saga* and *Konráðs saga* has been shown to be likely. Either they shared a common source as opposed to *Sigurðar saga*, or the writer of *Vilhjálms saga* knew and used the story of Konráð, or both of these conclusions may be valid.

On several occasions, the adventures of Sigurðr and Vilhjálmr agree against the legend as it is found in *Konráðs saga*. While at the start of the episode Konráð is riding at night, both Vilhjálmr and Sigurðr have retired and Sigurðr has even gone to sleep. The lion resists the dragon's attempted flight in *Konráðs saga* by dragging its feet against brushwood. In both the other sagas, the lion grasps at trees. Again, although Konráð does not cut off the dragon's head, the other two heroes do. Finally, the writers of *Vilhjálms saga* and *Sigurðar saga* describe the deaths of the lions, although the two deaths are admittedly dissimilar. From this evidence it may be seen that the legend in *Sigurðar saga*, already proven not to be a source of the relevant material in *Vilhjálms saga*, is nevertheless closely related to it; Sigurðr's chronicler could, in fact, have used *Vilhjálms saga*. If he had taken his story from *Konráðs saga*, then there would probably be points at which he agreed with that saga but disagreed with *Vilhjálms saga*. This is the case in only one instance, where Vilhjálmr finds three young dragons in the nest, but the other heroes find only two. Here it is probably more important that the young dragons that Vilhjálmr and Sigurðr find are described as being much grown. Further evidence that *Sigurðar saga* is derived in part from the story of Vilhjálmr is found in the fact that one of Sigurðr's brothers, named Vilhjálmr, owns a ship that is called Leon because it bears a carved lion's head on its prow.[51]

There are at least two indications that the writer of *Sigurðar saga* was aware of *Þiðriks saga*. First, there is his use of the shield decorated with a lion as the hero's motivation for taking that beast's side against the dragon. Second, there is an episode much later in the saga in which Sedentiana, the maiden king, has a special stone house built for herself as protection against the hero. In an upper room she has the walls decorated with scenes from the sagas of Þiðrik and other heroes.[52]

My conclusions as to the relationship of the versions of the lion-knight legend within the sagas discussed are shown in the following diagram:

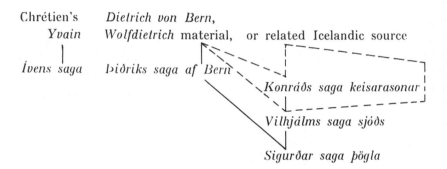

Presumably, the source related to the *Wolfdietrich* material was in Iceland at a very early time, in the first part of the thirteenth century. Evidence from *Vilhjálms saga* (see p. 136) suggests that it told of events that are not now found in *Þiðriks saga* but which are in *Wolfdietrich*. I believe that it was this source, related in some way to the *Wolfdietrich* material, which was used by the carver of the Valþjófsstaðir door.

Ectors saga appears in manuscripts from the fifteenth century, and its composition probably did not take place before that period.[53] Little scholarly work has been done on *Ectors saga*.[54] The writer uses a pseudoclassical setting, revealing his awareness of *Trójumanna saga* and *Alexanders saga*. Like the author of the later *Dínus saga dramblata*, he mentions a Master Galterus and often professes to use him as a source.[55] Galterus is actually Gautier

---

[51] *Ibid.* 108.

[52] *Ibid.* 182-183.

[53] Loth, Introduction to LMIR 1, ix.

[54] R. Meissner, "Zur isländischen Hectorsage," *Zeitschrift für deutsches Altertum* 37 (1894) 333-335.

[55] *Ectors saga* 185; *Dínus saga dramblata*, ed. Jónas Kristjánsson, Riddarasögur 1 (Reykjavík 1960) 99, 101.

de Chatillon, whose *Alexandreis* was translated into Old Icelandic in the second half of the thirteenth century.[56] The translator included the author's name in his work, and it then became the common property of writers who desired the dignity of a European source. The material of the saga is not classical, aside from references to the Troy legend. A survivor of the Trojan war, Karnotius, settles in the East and has a son who is named Ector and for whom great things are predicted. When he reaches early manhood his father gathers a retinue for him. In his company are six heroes who, with Ector, vow each to go off alone to a strange land and perform an exploit for fame. The rest of the saga deals with adventures that result from these oaths.

The lion enters the story in the fifth tale, which is about Trancival, son of King Translatius of Armenia. The knight is riding between a dense forest and the sea when he hears noises and cracking sounds in the woods. The earth quakes and the trees fall to the ground. He dismounts and sees a dreadful dragon come flying, a lion held in its claws with the dragon's coil wrapped around it. The lion grasps at trees so that they come up with their roots, and this makes the dragon move slowly and become tired. Trancival stands between two trees and strikes at the dragon's back, cutting the beast in two, so that each part falls separately. The lion is grateful for being saved and follows Trancival as long as it lives.[57]

It should be remarked first that the writer has created a blind element in having the dragon attempt to fly somewhere; there is no place for it to fly to. The writer used a source in which the dragon was trying to reach its nest. Second, while several elements in the story are reminiscent of *Sigurðar saga*, others are closer to *Vilhjálms saga*. Trees in *Sigurðar saga* are bent to breaking; in this work, they fall. When Vilhjálmr's lion grasps at trees everything comes up, as happens here. In addition, both *Vilhjálms saga* and *Ectors saga* state that the lion follows its savior, not to be parted from him as long as it lives—in anticipation, perhaps, of its death.

This episode in *Ectors saga* is so short that it is difficult to make conclusive decisions about its sources, but the writer's eclecticism and familiarity with literature would render it likely that he used both *Vilhjálms saga* and *Sigurðar saga*. The lion is mentioned again only in connection with its death, in a battle, at the hands of a giant named Atremon. Ector's reaction to the loss of his companion is not recorded, and the passage is no more revealing as to sources than is the dragon fight.[58] Little is added to this discussion of the lion-knight legend in the sagas by a consideration of the motif in *Ectors saga*. None of the conclusions reached in the preceding section are altered by what is found here.

[56] Kristjánsson 1.lxix.

[57] *Ectors saga* 123-124.

[58] *Ibid*. 132.

III. THE CARVINGS AND THEIR SOURCE

The study of the lion-knight legend in Old Norse saga literature has not only served to demonstrate the probable history of the motif in the north. It has also been useful for the purpose of representing that peculiar originality typical of the late saga: an originality not in the material itself, but in the eclectic choice of material and in its varied arrangement within individual works. The sources were many. Not only other sagas, written or oral, but folklore, Icelandic and Continental, provided a rich stock from which selections might be made.

In his studies of Celtic elements in Icelandic literature, Einar Ól. Sveinsson has on more than one occasion referred to the revolution that took place in saga style at the end of the thirteenth century. He observes in this great change a movement "in the direction of the baroque" with an increasing "predilection for exaggeration and the supernatural."[59] If, as Sveinsson supposes, it was only in this situation that Celtic motifs, current in Icelandic folklore since the Settlement, could first make their appearance in the sagas, then perhaps other motifs as well, long popular on a folk level, now gained literary expression. This could explain how the lion-knight legend as it is represented on the Valðjófsstaðir door was lost in its original form yet partially preserved in some later sagas. Further speculation as to the generic nature of the source used in the creation of *Konráðs saga*, *Vilhjálms saga* and the carvings on the door would probably not be fruitful here. It is more to the point to discuss the carvings themselves and to show how all the events depicted in them may be found in the relevant sagas.

In the scene depicting the fight with the dragon, the lion's hind quarters are held by its attacker's tail. The dragon has not grasped the lion's shoulders, but the carver might not have had sufficient room to portray that. The knight is cutting with his sword through the dragon's body between its wings and the part of its tail which holds the lion. An unidentified bird flies over the lion and the knight. In the upper right corner three heads peer out of what seems to be a hole; it has been suggested that they are the young dragons in the nest.[60]

In both *Konráðs saga* and *Vilhjálms saga*, the hero attacks the dragon initially with a sword, and the former narrative mentions that the stroke falls beyond the lion. The bird could be a part of the natural setting, as is the vegetation at the edge of the circle; it could also be the knight's hunting bird. I find no parallel to it in the sagas, and I am not certain that the bird is of any importance. The three young dragons whose heads may appear

---

[59] Einar Ó. Sveinsson, "Celtic Elements in Icelandic Tradition," *Béaloides* (1957) 15. See also Sveinsson, "Keltnesk áhríf á íslenzkar ýkjusögur," *Skírnir* 106 (1932) 113-114.
[60] Paulsen (n. 1 above) 131.

in the upper right are referred to in *Vilhjálms saga*. There is little in this section of the carvings to suggest a need for looking beyond the stories of Konráð and Vilhjálmr in the search for a literary representation of the source that the carver used.

The upper left portion of the circle shows the lion following its master. The bird apparently rests on the horse's mane. The hero holds the reins in his left hand; in his right hand he holds a mysterious, elongated object that is divided at its top into three leaflike projections. Paulsen calls this a lily stalk and discusses its symbolic importance in Icelandic and Germanic culture.[61] It could just as well be one of the dragon's claws which Konráð took with him. The collar about the lion's neck may be related to the cord Konráð put on his lion before returning to the city. As was true of the carvings in the lower half of the circle, there is little in this scene which is of distinguishing significance in an attempt to define the source.

The situation of the lion on the tablet with its inscription and the cross and small building has been traditionally interpreted as a scene of mourning for the fallen knight. No such event occurs in any of the sagas, although Óláfr Tryggvason is said to have left behind a dog, Vigi, who lay in sorrow on his master's grave and finally died of starvation.[62] There are also the stories that built up around the famous historical figure, Henry the Lion, who was supposedly thus mourned by his lion when he died. His death occurred, however, in 1195, and the time between then and the execution of the carvings probably was not long enough for such an impressive legend about him to have formed and made its way to Iceland.[63]

It may be that there is some vague connection between the carved mourning scene, if it is one of mourning, the mock death scene in *Ívens saga*, and the temporary desertion of the lion by Konráð and Vilhjálmr. Konráð's lion does not want to be left behind; Vilhjálmr's lion is grieving for him when he returns. Such displays of emotion are not typically Icelandic, and I believe it is safe to assume that the lion's reaction in *Vilhjálms saga* is indicative of a source that is essentially Continental. Instances in which the grateful lion is deserted by its master, voluntarily or through necessity, are discussed in Brodeur's article referred to previously (see p. 133). In these sagas the mock death scene and the desertions may be suggestive of a more serious event in some other Continental story that came to Iceland and is illustrated in the last part of the circle, but such a story has not survived in literary form.

It seems possible and much more reasonable to interpret the picture in a different way, to assume that the coffin is the lion's and that the figure of the lion on it is the beast's effigy. The practice of mounting an effigy of

---

[61] Paulsen 139-140.

[62] Oddr Snorrason, *Saga Óláfs Tryggvasonar*, ed. Finnur Jónsson (Copenhagen 1932) 259.

[63] See above 139 and n. 1.

the deceased on the sarcophagus was still common on the Continent in the thirteenth century and it is thus not remarkable if the carver included such a figure without its being mentioned in his source. The small building could have been an innovation on the part of the carver; it might be a chapel or the cover for the sarcophagus. It may be objected at this point that a scene in which a lion lies entombed with a cross at its head would render the door unacceptable for use in a church. Such an objection might be seriously considered if it could be proved that the ecclesiastical establishment of thirteenth-century Iceland was aware of, and on guard against, all manifestations of heresy.

The inscription describes a powerful king who killed a dragon. It will be remembered that Vilhjálmr had a stone coffin or sarcophagus made for his lion and that on it he had inscribed in gold letters what lay beneath. As for the inscription's reference to a king, it can be seen from *Sigurðar saga* that the lion was known in Iceland as the king of beasts (see p. 137). The only serious objection to the whole hypothesis could be raised on the basis of the specific statement that the king killed "this dragon" (see p. 126). If the lower picture has been correctly interpreted, then it is the hero himself who is responsible for the dragon's death there. Although the lion, too, becomes a dragonkiller in *Vilhjálms saga*, there is nothing to indicate that it is the lion's accomplishment that is celebrated in the lower illustration. In an attempt to solve this problem it may be conjectured that the source of the legend that the carver knew could have been imperfect here, or that the carver himself misunderstood the story. It seems to me most likely that the lion-knight legend as the carver knew it resembled more the relevant episodes in *Konráðs saga* and especially in *Vilhjálms saga* than any other known work incorporating such material. From this it might be concluded that the common source of those two sagas, perhaps related to the *Wolfdietrich* stories, was also essentially the source of the carvings on the Valþjófsstaðir door.

IV. CONCLUSION

The theory that an episode representative of the carved grave scene might be found in *Vilhjálms saga* seems to have been proposed first before the academic world by Gísli Brynjólfsson in his paper delivered in Copenhagen in 1870, as we saw at the beginning. Unfortunately, Brynjólfsson was at least understood as contending, and may actually have meant, that the saga itself was the source of the carvings. While Julius Lange objected in a curiously ill-founded statement that the lion on the door was not dead but "emaciated and dying" ("udtæret og døende"), Svend Grundtvig raised his voice in denunciation of *Vilhjálms saga* itself—"a tasteless, semilearned hodgepodge of Greek-Roman-Jewish-Gothic legendary writings, most certainly . . . not older than the fourteenth century" ("et smagløst halvlærd Sammensurium

Plate 1. The Valþjófsstaðir door

Plate 2. Lower panel of the Valpjófsstadir door

Plate 3. Upper panel of the Valpjófsstadir door

af græsk-romersk-jødisk-gotisk Sagndigtning, ganske vist ikke er ældre end det 14de Aarhundrede"). Grundtvig held that the door had been made in Norway in the twelfth century, and this excluded any possibility of a relationship to *Vilhjálms saga*.[64] So far as I am aware, no one has mentioned Brynjólfsson's theory after Grundtvig.

It would, of course, be absurd to contend that *Vilhjálms saga* itself provided the carver with the legend that he knew. If the estimates adopted here are correct, then the saga assumed its present form a century or so after the door was carved. As has been shown in the second part of this paper, however, there is reason to suppose that the lion-knight legend came to Iceland in at least one version other than those incorporated in *Ívens saga* and *Þiðriks saga*. It is the version found with variations in *Konráðs saga* and *Vilhjálms saga* and used also in both recensions of *Sigurðar saga*.

One episode in *Vilhjálms saga*—the slaying of the small dragon by the lion—demonstrates a connection between that saga and material associated with *Wolfdietrich* but not found in *Þiðriks saga*. I take this to suggest that the version of the legend used in the stories of Konráð and Vilhjálmr may have been related to the German poem. Such a version could have told of the lion's grave and could thus have been used both by the writer of *Vilhjálms saga* and the carver of the Valþjófsstaðir door.

Department of English
University of Iowa
Iowa City, Iowa 52240, U.S.A.

---

[64] Svend Grundtvig, Tillæg til Nr. 9, *Danmarks gamle Folkeviser*, ed. S. Grundtvig and A. Olrik (Copenhagen 1853-1919) 4.684.

GESETZ UND GESCHICHTE:
ZUR HISTORISIERENDEN HERMENEUTIK
BEI MOSES MAIMONIDES UND THOMAS VON AQUIN[1]

•

von Amos Funkenstein

Meinem verehrten Lehrer
Herrn Professor Wilhelm Berges
zum sechzigsten Geburtstag
in Dankbarkeit

1. DIE RATIO PRAECEPTORUM (TA'AME HAMITSVOT) BEI SA'ADIA UND MAIMONIDES

In der Auseinandersetzung mit dem Christentum und mit dem Islam um die ewige Gültigkeit des "Mosaischen Gesetzes" entwickelte die jüdische Religionsphilosophie seit Sa'adia Gaon (883-945) systematische Lehren der Vernunftsgründe der Gebote.[2] Gestützt auf mehrere zerstreute Hinweise in der exegetischen Tradition (der auch der Name dieser Disziplin entnommen wurde)[3] unterschied Sa'adia zwischen den "Vernunftsgeboten" (מצוות שכליות) und "Gehorsamsgeboten" (מצוות שמעיות),[4] wobei die Rationalisierungsmethode

---

[1] Für ihre wichtigen Hinweise bin ich meinen Kollegen, den Herren Professoren H. Davidson und M. Perlmann, zu grossem Dank verpflichtet.

[2] Grundlegend ist die zusammenfassende Übersicht von I. Heinemann, טעמי המצוות בספרות ישראל; frz.: *La loi dans la pensée juive* (Paris 1962). Vgl. auch S. Baron, *A Social and Religious History of the Jews* (SRH) 6.141ff. Auch die Polemik gegen Skeptikei wie Hivi habalki darf in diesem Zusammenhang nicht übersehen werden; über ihn J. Rosenthal, "Hiwi ha-Balkhi," *Jewish Quarterly Review* NS 38 (1947-1948) 317ff.; Baron, SRH 6.299ff., 478f.

[3] Z.B. Bab. Tal. Jona 76b; Numeri Rabba 16.1.147ff, insbes. 149a: ר' יהושוע מסכנין בשם רבי לוי אמר ד' דברים יצה"ו משיב עליהם דכתיב בהם חוקה .... sowie weiter fol. 149a: א"ר יוסי ב"ר חנינא א"ל הקב"ה למשה אני מגלה לך טעם פרה אדומה אבל לאחד חוקה חוקים. Vgl. Heinemann 20ff. sowie neuerdings E. E. Urbach, חז"ל: פנקי אמונות ודעות (Jerusalem 1969) 320-347.

[4] *Kitab al-Amanāt wa'l-I'tikadāt* 3, ed. S. Landauer (Leiden 1880) 11ᵉ ff.; hebr. ספר האמונות והדעות in der Übers. Ibn-Tibbons (Jerusalem 1962) 109f. Dt. (unzulängliche) Übertragung von J. Fürst, *Emunot We-dëot, oder Glaubenslehre und Philosophie* (Leipzig 1845) 193ff. Vgl. Heinemann, 51ff., sowie A. Altmann," Saadya's Conception of the law, **The John Rylands Library** (1934) 320-339 und neuerdings Y. Elstein, תורת המצוות במשנת ר' סעדיה [The precepts in the philosophical teachings of Sa'adya Gaon], *Tarbits* 38.2 (1968) 120ff.

durchgehend aktualisierend oder, negativ ausgedrückt, durch das völlige
Fehlen der historischen Dimension gekennzeichnet war. "Vernunftsgebote"
sind solche, deren aktuelle Notwendigkeit oder Vernünftigkeit bei jeder Person
oder jedem Gemeinschaftsverband, aus politischen, ethischen oder medizinischen Gründen, bewiesen werden kann. Aus dem gleichen Grunde war daher
in diesem Deutungstypus die Gegenüberstellung von Vernunft und Gehorsam
disjunktiv und ging sein Bemühen dahin, die Anzahl der "Gehorsamsgebote"
auf ein Minimum zu beschränken.

Offenkundig war die Frage nach den *ta'ame hamitsvot* in der philosophischen
Literatur insgesamt eine Variante der Suche nach den Übereinstimmungs-
punkten der Offenbarung mit der (natürlichen) Vernunft. Dass diese Übereinstimmung nahtlos sei, stand für Sa'adia *a priori* fest. Er selbst stellte sich
jedoch (im Eingang seines *Buches der Glauben und Meinungen*) die Frage,
warum trotz dieser Übereinstimmung Offenbarung und Propheten überhaupt
nötig gewesen seien, könnte doch das Menschengeschlecht deren Inhalte
aus eigenem Vermögen entwickelt haben; und er antwortete mit einer
historischen Überlegung. Gewiss könnte die Menschheit aus eigenen Kräf-
ten zu den Offenbarungswahrheiten gelangen, doch nur wenigen gelänge
es, und dies nach langen Mühen und vielen Irrwegen. "Doch bewahrte uns
der Schöpfer vor allen diesen Mühen von Anbeginn und sandte uns seine
Gesandten und sprach zu uns in seiner Lehre und gab uns Beweiszeichen
um sie ... Und wenn die Zeit, die man benötigt, um sich in sie zu vertie-
fen, auch lang ist, so ist sie jedoch nicht eine Zeit ohne jegliche Unterwei-
sung"[5] (wie sie sonst eine auf sich selbst angewiesene Gemeinschaft erfahren
müsste).

Übereinstimmend damit konstruierte Sa'adia seine Epistemologie. Von
den vier Evidenzquellen (משכי האמת) sind drei allgemein bindend: Sinnes-
wahrnehmung, Intuition und deduktive Erkenntnis: die vierte aber, das
"beglaubigte Wort" (ההגדה הנאמנת)ist auf die "Gemeinschaft der Gottes-
gläubigen" (קהל המייחדים) beschränkt und begründet ihre Gültigkeit durch

---

[5] Sa'adia אמינות ודעית, Vorwort, und unmittelbar voraufgehend: "Denn er wusste
in seiner Weisheit, dass das mit der Arbeit des Verstandes zu erlangende nur in einem bestimmten Zeitmass vervollständigt werden kann ... vielleicht könnten viele die Arbeit
nicht vollenden wegen eines (ihnen) innewohnenden Mangels ... oder weil ihn Zweifel
befallen ... und Gott bewahrte uns vor allen diesen Mühen ... und sandte uns seine Gesandten" (Aus dem heb. übersetzt). Das liest sich wei eine Umkehrung des alten, schon bei
Xenophanes belegbaren Motivs: οὗτοι ἀπ' ἀρχῆς πάντα θεοὶ θνητοῖς ὑπεδειξαν, ἀλλὰ
χρόνῳ ξητοῦντες ἐφευρίσκουσιν ἄμεινον. (Fragm. B18; Diels-Kranz, *Fragm. der Vor-
sokratiker*, ed. 6, Berlin 1934). Doch wäre es methodisch zweifelhaft, wie Ephrat (unten
Anm. 6) direkt auf vermeintliche Antike Bezugsquellen ohne Hinweis aus Vermittlungs-
möglichkeiten hinzuweisen. Im übrigen ist, in diesem Abschnitt, die "historische" Begründung von der "soziologischen" (die Beschränktheit der Menge) noch nicht unterschieden.
Vgl. J. Guttmann, *Philosophie des Judentums* hebr. Aus. (Jerusalem 1951) 64.

die Kontinuität der Tradition.[6] Sa'adia bleibt bei dieser engeren Begriffs-
bestimmung nicht. In der Tradition sieht er zwar nicht einen neuen Erkennt-
nismodus, wohl aber eine komplementäre Stütze der übrigen Erkenntnismodi,
eine Erkenntnisquelle, die in unserem Wissen *in praxi* dominiert. Ohne sich auf
die Aussage anderer zu verlassen, käme keine Kommunikation und kein Gesetz
zustande, und noch mehr: unser Wissen (denn auch die Erinnerung ist sekun-
käre Erkenntnisquelle) wäre auf momentane Sinnesgewissheiten reduziert.[7]

Anhand dieser grundsäztlichen Überlegung Sa'adias liesse sich eine alternative Denkmöglichkeit zur Deutung der (scheinbar undeutbaren) "Gehorsamsgebote" ausarbeiten: wenn die Offenbarung Erkenntnisinhalte und Konstitution der perfekten (auserwählten) Gemeinschaft vorwegnahm, so könnten
—oder müssten gar—in ihr auch solche Redewendungen und Verfügungen
eingebaut worden sein, die pädagogischer Natur sind, d.h. der Fassungskraft
der Menge zur Zeit ihrer Verkündigung angepasst waren; denn zweifellos,
könnte argumentiert werden, musste die Kluft zwischen der Gemeinschaft,
welcher die Offenbarung vorweg gegeben wurde, und der Idealgemeinschaft,
in welcher die Offenbarung immanente Vernunftsinhalte ausdrücken wird,
überbrückt werden. Sa'adia hat von dieser Deutungsmöglichkeit, die sich
dem aufmerksamen Leser des Vorwortes seiner philosophischen Propädeutik
auftut, bewusst keinen Gebrauch gemacht; würde sie doch die Ewigkeit
solcher "pädagogischen" Massnahmen in Frage stellen.[8] Zwar bestimmt Sa'adia

---

[6] *Ibid.* hat hier die Bedeutung von "Materie": vgl. D. Kaufmann, *Geschichte der Attri-
butenlehre in der jüdischen Religions-philosophie von Sa'adia bis Maimuni* (Gotha 1877, Neudr.
1967) 1ff., insbes. Anm. 1. Über Sa'adias Erkenntnislehre, A. Heschel, *The Quest for
Certainty in Sa'adias Philosophy* (New York 1944); und zuletzt G. Vajda, "Autour de la
théorie de la connaissance chez Sa'adia," *Review des études juives* 126 (1967) 135ff., 375ff.,
sowie (הפילוסופיה); in ר, אפרת, שיטתו הפילוסופית של ר' סעדיה גאון
שיטות וסוגיות ·(היהודית בימי הביניים) שיטות וסוגיות (Tel-Aviv 1965) 88f. (Ünglucklich der
Vergleich mit den necessariae rationes Anselm's von Canterbury; vgl. mein Aufsatz "Changes in the Patterns of Christian Anti-Jewish Polemics in the 12th Century," *Zion* 33 (1969)
131; vgl. auch Elstein 124ff.

[7] Sa'adia, *Emunot*, Vorwort; 3 (Arab. 12ff.; hebr. 9, 79f.); vgl. Guttmann 65. Über die
arabischen Quellen Sa'adia's. Vajda, *ibid.* Die antike Quelle dieser Gedankengänge ist
mir unbekannt; ich vermute sie in den Diskussionen innerhalb der griechischen Skepsis
und gegen sie. In der spätscholastischen Diskussion sind sie wichtig (dazu A. L. Maier,
"Das Problem der Evidenz in der Philosophe des 14. Jahrhunderts," *Scholastik* 38 [1963]
183-225), und noch bei Descartes erscheinen sie in einer besonderen Funktion. Er muss
nicht nur die Gewissheit einzelner Erkenntnisse in Zweifel ziehen, sondern auch deren Zusammenhang im diskursiven Denken: die Kontinuität einer Argumentation und die Siche-
rung des schon Bewiesenen stützen sich auf die Erinnerung. Dem Gottesbegriff fällt so die
Aufgabe zu, den Gang des diskursiven Denkens, die Gültigkeit der Deduktionen, zu sichern
(Principia 1.13, ed. Thanery).

[8] Sa'adia, *Emunot* 3: "Oder er setzt sie (die Tora) in einen bestimmten Zeitabschnit
(חלק מהזמן) als sage er: tut dies hundert Jahre und es sei in weniger als hundert aufgehoben" usf. (Arab. 128f.; hebr. 80). Auch das mosaische Gesetz hat dem Gesetz Abrahams
nur hinzugefügt, es nicht ersetzt.

ausdrücklich, dass auch "Vernunftsgebote" der Konkretion vermittels der Gesandten Gottes bedürfen; und andererseits setzt er eine vernünftige Struktur voraus auch bei den Gehorsamsgeboten—oder er postuliert "zusammengesetzte" Gebote:[9] auch diesen Ansatz wird Maimonides später erweitern und modifizieren. Dennoch blieben für Sa'adia die einzig gültigen Vernunftsgründe der Gebote die ewigen, unveränderlichen.[10] Der Sinn der "Gehorsamsgebote" ist vornehmlich dieser, dass sich der Gläubige durch ihre Befolgung umso grössere Verdienste erwirbt, als sie ihm unbegreiflich bleiben—ein Beweis der Intensität seines Gottvertrauens.[11]

So blieb bei Sa'adia die durchgängige Vernünftigkeit des geoffenbarten Gesetzes notwendigerweise eine nicht restlos zu beweisende Behauptung. Das gilt auch von allen Nachfolgern, die die sa'adianische Disjunktion übernommen haben. Unter ihnen ist Bahjah ibn Pakuda von besonderem Interesse, nicht weil ihm eine bessere Lösung vorschwebte, sondern weil er deutlicher als Sa'adia die Vorstellungen von der göttlichen Pädagogie artikuliert hatte, und zwar mit ähnlichen Redewendungen wie später Maimonides. Dass die Offenbarung auch Gehorsamsgebote einfügte, deren Sinn verborgen war, geschah "weil das Volk in jener Zeit (בעת ההיא), in der die Offenbarung gegeben wurde, von animalischen Begierden beherrscht war."[12] Die Begründung der Gebote wurde dem intellektuellen Stand Israels angepasst.[13] Wie später Maimonides, bevorzugt Bahja organologische Metaphern.[14] Doch zum einen meint Bahja mit seiner Anpassungstheorie eher die Begründung der Gebote (Lohn und Strafe) denn die Gebote selbst; sodann hat er allenfalls Hinweise für weitere Überlegungen (die sich ohnehin in der exegetischen Tradition befanden)[15] gegeben, nicht aber eine Lösung.

Maimonides hatte diese immanente Schwäche der Position Sa'adias und seiner Nachfolger wohl im Auge, als er die alternative, "historisierende"[16] Deu-

---

[9] Sa'adia, *Emunot* 3 (Arab. 114ff., 118f; hebr. 73ff., 81). Hierzu Elstein 129ff.

[10] In der Sache könnte man hier ein Naturrechtsdenken postulieren; der Begriff jedoch fehlt in der jüdischen Philosophie bis auf das späte Mittelalter. Bgl. unten Anm. 26.

[11] *Ibid.* 9 (Arab. 114f., hebr. 72): "Und die zweite Gruppe enthält Dinge, die der Verstand nicht als gut oder verächtlich an sich beurteilt. Ihnen hat der Schöpfer Befehl und Warnung hinzugefügt, um unseren Lohn und unseren Nutzen durch sie zu mehren, wie es heisst (Is. 42.21): 'Gott hat es gefallen ob seiner Gerechtigkeit.'"

[12] Bahja ben Josef ibn Pakuda, *Buch der Herzenspflichten* (ספר חובות הלבבות) in der hebr. Übers. des Ibn Tibbon 3.3, ed. A. Zifroni (Tel-Aviv, Mahbarot Lesafrut) 228. Zum Ganzen G. Golinski, *Das Wesen des Religionsgesetzes in der Philosophie des Bachja ibn Pakuda* (Würzburg 1935) und Heinemann 57ff. Im Zusammenhang mit der Gesetzeslehre Rambams bei Baron, SRH 6.398 Anm. 172, erwähnt.

[13] 4.4 (ed. Zifroni 330).

[14] Vgl. unten, 15ff.

[15] Siehe unten, 19f.

[16] Von einer "historischen Betrachtungsweise" spricht u.a. auch J. Guttmann, *Die Philosophie des Judentums*, hebr. Ausgabe (Jerusalem 1951) 168. Vom "historischen Moment," der "in die Auffassung M.s hineinkommt" spricht C. Neuburger, *Das Wesen des Gesetzes in*

tungsmöglichkeit systematisch entwickelte. Im *More Nebukim* versucht er zunächst, die seit Sa'adia eingebürgerte Disjunktion von "Vernunfts"—und "Gehorsamsgeboten" aufzuheben.[17] Methodisch versucht er das zu definieren, wonach man eigentlich fragt, wenn man Vernunftsgründe der Gebote sucht, oder (was dasselbe ist) was man meinen kann, wenn man einem Gebot Vernunftsgründe abspricht. Der Gang der Argumentation ist komplex und halb verschlüsselt, hier wie so oft im *More Nebukim*. Den bisherigen Stellungnahmen in der philosophischen Literatur scheint Maimonides (nicht expressis verbis) voreilige Begriffsbildung vorzuwerfen. "Gehorsamsgebote," das setzt er bei denen voraus, die diese Bezeichnung gebrauchen, sind nicht arbiträr: ihr Sinn ist bloss verborgen.[18] Dass damit nicht nur ein von der Tradition unterstütztes Postulat aufgestellt wird, dass die Vernünftigkeit auch der unverständlichen Gebote grundsätzlich beweisbar ist, wird Maimonides nur dann begreiflich machen können, wenn er mit der Begründung einer Gebotsgruppe zugleich auch zeigen wird, aus welchem Grund der Sinn einiger Gebote verborgen bleiben muss. Um ein solches hermeneutisches Prinzip zu erreichen, radikalisiert Maimonides seine Fragestellung. Heisst es nicht in der Tradition von einigen Geboten, sie seien nur um des Gebotes willen, der "Läuterung der Menschen" wegen, gegeben worden? Das widerspricht dem bisher Gesagten und kann nicht (wiederum stellt sich Maimonides lautlos gegen Sa'adia)[19] auf die Gebote bezogen werden. In der Tat sind jeder Suche nach Vernunftsgründen Grenzen gesetzt; oftmals muss sie bei den "Gebotsteilen" halten. Gesetzt, man habe einen Vernunftsgrund für das Opfergesetz gefunden: "dass aber das eine Opfer ein Lamm, das andere ein Widder, und dass ihre Zahl eine bestimmte ist—diesem Tatbestand kann kein besonderer Grund zugeschrieben werden, und wer sich um eine derart detaillierte Begründung

---

der Philosophie des Maimonides, Diss. Breslau 1932 (Danzig 1933) 43. Er unterscheidet richtig zwischen dem—hier fehlenden—historischen Entwicklungsgedanken und dem Entwicklungsgedanken Maimonides', der die göttliche Pädagogie ausdrücken will. Von "unusually modernistic explanations" spricht Baron, SHR 6.148. Zugleich weist Baron auf einige Vorläufer hin (vgl. *ibid.* 6 Anm. 13), fragt aber nicht, was Maimonides von ihnen unterscheidet—in dessen eigener Schätzung und für den heutigen Betrachter. Zum "Bild der Geschichte" bei M. siehe Baron, "The Historical Outlook of Maimonids," *Proceedings of the American Academy of Jewish Research* 6 (1935) 5ff., oder in: *History and Jewish Historians* (Philadelphia 1964) 109ff.

[17] Vgl. Neuburger 33ff., insbes. 34f; ebd. lit.

[18] *More Nebukim* (MN) 3.26 Anfang: Maimonides verweist selbst auf seine Diskussion der Vorsehung im allgemeinen, an die sich diese Kapitel anschliessen. Zur Stellung dieser Kapitel im Gesamtbau des Werkes siehe S. Rawidowicz, "The Structure of the 'More Nebukim'" in: *The Maimonides Book of Tarbits* tr. hebr. (Jerusalem 1935) 80ff. Wo wir den arabischen Text benutzen, ist es in der Edition von S. Munk, *Moise ben Maimon, Dalālat al Ḥā'irīn* (1856-1866 repr. 1964).

[19] Siehe oben, 4 Anm. 11.

bemüht, verfällt dem Wahnsinn."[20] Das heisst: Die Differenzierung der Gebotsprinzipien muss oftmals eine Grenze erreichen, bei der die Konkretion
dieses oder jenes untergeordneten Prinzips nur noch durch die Wahl zwischen
gleichrangigen Möglichkeiten geschehen kann; ist doch unsere (nicht nur sub-
luneare) Welt kontingent, und im allgemeinen Materie, d. h. Potentiali-
tätsprinzip, zugleich Individuationsgrund. Schon Aristoteles hatte so die
Grenzen der teleologischen Principiierung abgesteckt.[21] Es scheint, dass
Maimonides das Verhältnis zwischen den Gebotsprinzipien und dem mate-
riellen Objekt, an dem sie sich verwirklichen, in der Analogie der Naturgesetze zu den individuellen Akzidentien begreift.[22] Die Suche nach Vernunftsgründen der Gebote hat also nur dann einen Sinn, wenn genau
zwischen dem generellen und dem partikulären Prinzip der Einzelverfü-
gung einerseits und ihren Teilen, d.h. ihre kontingente Konkretion, unterschieden wird (כלל המצוות, כלל המצווה, חלקי המצווה). Das konnte,
so darf man ergänzen, die bisherige aktualisierende Rationalisierung nicht
leisten, denn sie hatte kein Kriterium, um zwischen der allgemeinen und partikulären Absicht der Gebote zu unterscheiden und wiederum zwischen der
partikulären Absicht und ihrer kontingenten Vergegenständlichung. Ihre Begründungen musste sie aus der Natur—oder besser der "Materie"—der Gebote
holen, und so lag es in ihrem Wesen, dass zie zur detaillierten Begründung
gezwungen war. Das methodische Problem, welches sich Maimonides daher
setzte, könnte so formuliert werden: ein hermeneutisches Prinzip zu finden,
welches zwischen Gebotsgruppen, einzelnen Geboten und ihrer Konkretion
hinsichtlich ihrer Intention so zu unterscheiden vermag, dass 1) die Einteilung
und Funktion der verschiedenen Gebotsgruppen durchsichtig wird; dass 2)
der Zwang zum Detail aus demselben Vernunftsgrund, der der Gebotsgruppe
zusteht, zuweilen aufgehoben werden kann und 3) in vielen Fällen, die schliess-
liche Konkretion der Gebote unbefragt bleiben kann, insofern es nachweisbar
ist, dass sie hinsichtlich der Intention des Gebots gleichgültig ist. (Maimonides scheint wohl zu meinen, dass meistens das Einzelgebot die äusserste
Grenze der partikulären Prinzipierung ist).

Dieses hermeneutische Prinzip konnte nicht konsequent aktualisierend
sein: es bestand, im Gegensatz zur bisherigen Suche nach permanenten Ur-

---

[20] MN, loc. cit. Es handelt sich nicht, wie Heinemann 92f. meint, bloss um eine methodische Einschränkung. Vgl. auch Neuburger 32f.

[21] Arist. *De generatione animalium* 4.3, 778b16-18; Ross 124. Über Kontingenz in der
Kosmologie und Epistemologie Maimunis s. J. Guttmann, "Das Problem der Kontingenz in
der Philosophie des Maimonides," *Monatsschrift für Gesch. und Wiss. des Judentums* 83
(1939) 406ff. Über die Funktion des Partikularisationsprinzips auch bei Maimonides, s. H.
Davidson, "Arguments from the Concept of Particularisation," *Philosophy East and West*
18 (1968) 299ff., insbes. 311ff. u. 313 Anm. 50.

[22] Vgl. auch MN 3.34 (Zur Frage, ob die Tora für jeden denkbaren individuellen Fall oder
individuelle Veranlagung vorgesorgt hat).

sachen allein, aus der weitgehenden Historisierung vornehmlich des Zeremonialgesetzes, dergestalt, dass Maimonides die der eigenen Zeit am wenigsten
verständlichen Gebote als "List Gottes" zur Überwindung der abscheulichen
Praktiken jenes politheistischen Volkes der "sa'aba" (Sabbäer) im Umkreis
des entstehenden Judentums erklärte. Dass diese Teile des Gesetzes keine
aktuelle Funktion haben können, beweist Maimonides im *More Nebukim* 3.27.
Alle Gebote fügen sich in einen *ordo finium*. Dieser besteht aus der primären
Intention der Vollendung der Seele und der mittelbaren Intention der Körper-
vollendung. Die Vollendung der Seele (שלמות הנפש) wird erreicht durch
die richtigen Meinungen, durch spezielle Gebote hinsichtlich des Glaubens-
inhalts, oder durch das allgemeine Gebot, Gott zu lieben: *amor Dei intellectualis* ist für Maimonides das oberste Gebot. Der intellektuellen Vervollkommnung untergeordnet und auf sie gerichtet ist die Vollendung des Körpers,
welche (und hier verlässt Maimonides den Rahmen dieses Topos, wie er etwa
von Bahja abgesteckt war) in der Veredelung der Sitten und der Ausrichtung
der zwischenmenschlichen Handlungen erreicht wird, also zunächst durch
die adäquate Staatsverfassung, "ist doch der Mensch seiner Natur nach poli-
tisch."[23] Diese sekundäre Intention des Gesetzes ist im Gebot der Gottes-
furcht subsumiert.[24] Es scheint, hier wie aus anderen Zusammenhängen,
dass Maimonides die sa'adianische Disjunktion zum Verständnis der Gebot-
struktur überhaupt diente: Jedes Gebot ist vernünfigt und dennoch nicht
bloss um seiner Vernünftigkeit willen, sondern als Befehl Gottes, aus "Furcht,"
einzuhalten;[25] Maimonides kennt den Begriff der *lex naturalis* nicht.[26] Die

---

[23] MN 3.25; vgl. 2.40. Vgl. L. Strauss, *Philosophie und Gesetz; Beiträge zum Verständnis Maimunis und seiner Vorläufer* (Berlin 1935) 109; Heinemann 93ff.; Neuburger 37ff.

[24] MN 3.27; ויצונו ה' לעשות את כל החוקים האלה ליראה את ה' אלהינו
(Deut. 6.24).

[25] Bekanntlich definiert M. die "Gerechten unter den Völkern" (חסידי אומות העולם)
als jene, die die "Sieben Gebote der Noachiden" (שבע מצוות בני-נוח) belolgen, und
zwar nicht nur wegen deren Vernunftgehalt, sondern als von Gott gegeben, als Offenbarung
akzeptieren. Von einer ähnlichen juridischen Eindeutigkeit ist sein Offenbarungsbegriff
des mosaischen Gesetzes: Auch die Gebote, die Abraham gegeben wurde, mussten in Sinai
wiederholt werden, um gültig zu sein. (Dazu J. Levinger, *Maimonides' Techniques of Codification*, hebr.: דרכי המחשבה ההלכתית של הרמב"ם, Jerusalem 1965 insbes.
37f.) Das heisst: Die Begründung der Gebote ist durch und durch vernünftig; ihre Gültigkeit
aber beziehen sie aus der blossen Tatsache der Offenbarung an diejenigen, für die die
Gebote bestimmt waren (ähnlich Baron, SRH 6.397 Anm. 168).

[26] Hierzu J. Paur, מקור חיובן של המצוות לפ' דעת הרמב"ם [The Basis for the
Authority of the Divine Commandments According to Maimonides], *Tarbits* 38.1 (1969)
43ff. Paur versucht, das Gesetzesverständnis Maimunis von dem Sa'adias so abzuheben,
als habe Maimunis die Naturgesetzlehre Sa'adias bewusst abgelehnt. Paur betont zu recht,
dass Maimuni die sa'adianische Disjunktion von Vernunfts- und Gehorsamsgebote ablehnt;
und dass er keinen Naturgesetzesbegriff entwickeln mochte, hängt durchaus hiermit zusammen; doch bedeutet es nicht, dass er den Begriff nicht entwickeln konnte: auch in der
thomistischen Lehre z. B. war Naturgesetz stets auf die Konkretion durch die *lex divina*

Gebote richten sich daher ausschliesslich auf "Meinungen, Sitten und politische Führung" (דעות, מידות, הנהגה מדינית),[27] und es ist zunächst unmöglich, die Opfer-wie viele der Reinigungsgesetze in diese notwendige
Systematik einzuführen. Der Hinweis auf ihren "Läuterungseffekt" hilft
nur dann—dies ist seine neue Interpretation dieses Topos—wenn man "Läuterung" als zeitliche Propädeutik begreift.

Maimonides fährt fort mit einer ausführlichen Beschreibung der sabbäischen
Sitten und Gebräuche.[28] Er beschreibt, er rekonstruiert die konkrete Umgebung,
in der Israel vor und zur Zeit der Gesetzgebung gewesen ist: die geoffenbarten
Gesetze und Verfügungen, dies wird Maimonides danach beweisen wollen,
waren dieser Entwicklungsphase angemessen. Mithin hat Maimonides das
gesuchte hermeneutische Prinzip gefunden. Indem es ein Prinzip ist, das
genau die positiven und die bloss negierenden Intentionen des Gesetzes gegeneinander abzustufen vermag, leistet es das Gewünschte: die spezifische Intention der unverständlichen Teile des Zeremonialgesetzes (Opferung, Tempel)
wird im allgemeinen durchsichtig; und dennoch kann ruhig das eine oder
andere Detail unverständlich bleiben: man kann dieses den Lücken in unserem historischen Wissen zuzuschreiben. Solche Lücken sind sogar notwendig:
hat doch dieser Teil des geoffenbarten Gesetzes seine Funktion weitgehend
erfüllt. Die Gegenwart versteht vieles an diesen Geboten nicht, weil ihr die
Praktiken, die diese Gebote bekämpfen sollten, längst fremd geworden sind.
Gerade das Unwissen ist ein Zeichen des Erziehungserfolges. "Und die meisten
von uns erklärten Gebote galten nur um jene Meinungen zu entfernen—,uns
die grosse Mühsal und Pein und Bürde, die jene Menschen an ihrem Gottes-
dienst hatten, zu erleichtern. Und jedes Handels- oder Unterlassungsgebot,
dessen Sinn du nicht begreifst, ist bloss die Heilung für eine dieser Krank-
heiten, die wir nicht mehr kennen müssen, gelobt sei der Name hierfür."[29]
Die Wirklichkeit, die diesen Gesetzen zugrunde lag, musste vergessen werden

---

oder *adinventio humanae rationis* angewiesen (siehe unten), also mehr verbindliche Struktur
denn konkrete Verfassung: Paur orientiert sich zu sehr am stoischen Begriff. Weder hatte
Sa'adia einen bewussten Naturgesetzesbegriff (obzwar natürlich die מצוות שכליות so
gedeutet werden könnten), noch hat Maimuni diessn Begriff, den er nicht kannte, ab-
lehnen wollen oder müssen.

[27] MN 3.31 (ed. Munk 68b: באלארא ואלאכלאך ובאלאעמאל אלסיאסיה
אלמדניה).

[28] MN 3.28.31. Vgl. unten Anm. 50.

[29] MN 3.49 (Ende). Etwas vorher vermutet Maimonides dass, wüsste er mehr über
die Ansichten der Sa'aba—Buchwissen gleicht nie einem Augenzeugen—so würde ihm
auch der Sinn der Gebotsteile klar werden. Heisst es, dass er nunmehr jedes Detail für
sinnvoll hält? Das würde dem oben angeführten Gedanken (3.26) widersprechen, dass
jede Konkretion schliesslich die Auswahl zwischen indifferenten Möglichkeiten treffen muss.
Oder unterscheidet Maimonides vielleicht zwischen der logischen Begründung und der
historischen so, dass die historische Begründung auch für das aufkommt, was vom Standpunkt der strikten Gesetzmässigkeit kontingent bleiben muss?

und verlangt eben darum, rekonstruiert zu werden. Mit diesem Prinzip hebt
Maimonides sein Interpretationsmodell über den blossen Akkommodationsgedanken hinaus, wie ihn die mittelalterliche Exegese, insbesondere die christliche, kannte. Schliesslich hebt die historische Begründung, doch nicht nur
sie allein, auch den Zwang auf, jeden Teil eines Gebotes als positive, einzig
mögliche Determination zu deuten.

Die Gebote werden in vierzehn Gruppen eingeteilt, von denen einige als Heil-
mittel gegen das Heidentum gedacht sind (3.35-49), und mit einer allgemeinen
Reflexion darüber, wie man die göttliche Anpassung an die Notwendigkeit der
Zeiten und an die Fassungskraft der auserwählten Gemeinschaft begreifen
soll, eingeleitet. Diese Überlegung (3.31-34) steht zwischen der Beschreibung
des Sa'aba und der konkreten Begründung der Gebote. Diese Teile des göttlichen Gesetzes hatten eine doppelte Funktion. Sie sollten sowohl den unüber-
brückbaren Gegensatz zwischen Israel und seiner Umgebung unterstreichen als
auch die Schärfe dieses Gegensatzes im Bewusstsein derer, die dem Gesetz
folgen sollten, mildern. Um das junge Israel von den abscheulichen Ver-
ehrungsriten der Umgebung abzulenken ohne einen totalen Bruch mit den
bisherigen Gewohnheiten abzuverlangen, konzedierte Gott einige, sinnver-
änderte Opferungsformen und andere der bisherigen Gewohnheiten, um die
übrigen umso wirksamer verbieten zu können; auch die Gegenmassnahmen
waren von der Art dessen, was sie bekämpfen sollten. Dieser pädagogische
"Umweg"—Maimonides vergleicht ihn mit dem Umweg des aus Ägypten
Ziehenden über die Wüste Sinai[30]—ist als notwendig gedacht, da Gott nicht
contra naturam handeln will, und die nur allmähliche Umwandlung von einem
Gegensatz ins Andere das Naturgesetz alles Organischen ist.[31] "Darum wäre
der plötzliche Verzicht auf alles Gewohnte der Natur des Menschen zuwider."
Mit pädagogischer "List" entschärfte Gott die paganen Gewohnheiten,
indem er andere, auf sich gerichtete, an ihre Statt setzte.

Maimonides spricht hier von der "List Gottes"[32] in einer ähnlichen Weise,
in der Hegel von der "List der Vernunft" reden wird. Gewiss nicht schon

---

[30] "Und ähnliches bringt schon die Tora, wo es heisst: "und Gott führte sie nicht durch
das Land der Philister . . . Und Gott führte das Volk über einen Umweg . . . (Ex. 13.17-18):
So wie Gott sie vom geraden Weg abführte, aus Rücksicht auf dass, was es von Natur aus
nicht zu erleiden vermochte, um die erste Absicht auszuführen" (MN 3.32). Maimonides
wiederholt die Listmetapher wie auch den Hinweis auf Ex. 13 an einer anderen Stelle, im
מאמר תחית המתים. Dort geht es um die Frage, warum die Tora die Gewissheit der
Auferstehung nicht explizit vermittelte: Gottes pädagogische List überliess dies den Propheten.

[31] MN 3.32. Munk, in der frz. Übers. 250 Anm. 2, verweist auf die Quellen (Galen, Ibn
Sina). Vgl. auch Ibn Pakuda, Ḥobot ha-Lebabot 2.5, und die folgende Anm.

[32] MN 3.32 passim; ed. Munk 69: תלט׳ף אלאלאה והכמתה פי כלק אלחיואן
ותדר׳ג חרכאת אלאעצֹא ומג׳אורה בעצֹההא לבעצֹ . . . ; הכמתה ותלט׳פה
פי תדריג׳ האלאת ג׳מלה האלה אלשכֹע האלה בעד האלה . . .
In seiner Untersuchung der Quellen des Maimonides führt S. Pines, *The Guide of the
Perplexed* (Chicago 1963), die Listmetapher bei M. (talaṭṭuf, von ihm mit "graciousness"

darum, weil ein ähnlicher Ausdruck gebraucht wird: von der Kriegslist Gottes
sprach der Koran,[33] aus der Bibel konnte man ihn herauslesen.[34] Bei Maimonides aber dient diese Metapher zur Verdeutlichung der Problematik, die
allen Vorstellungen von der Pädagogie Gottes zugrunde liegt. Neu akzentuiert
in der maimonideischen Version des Erziehungsplans Gottes ist die Dialektik
von Offenbarkeit und Verborgenheit in der teleologischen Geschichtsstruktur.
Der Begriff 'List,' so heisst es bei Maimonides später,[35] umschreibt die prak-
tische Vernunft, die an sich wertfrei ist, d. h. auch im Besitz des Ungerechten
sein kann. Es ist die Kunst, Gedanken praktisch einzusetzen; man könnte
ergänzen: Ziel und Gegebenheiten aneinander zu messen. Über den Umweg
der menschlichen Natur, die er nicht mit einem blossen Willkürsakt verändern
will, verbessert Gott den Menschen. Die Vorsehung in der sublunearen Welt
mit der Ausnahme des Menschen—diese Ausnahme vorausgesetzt stimmt
Maimonides der "aristotelischen Meinung" zu[36]—ist eine indirekte, durch
die Naturgesetze vermittelte: die Natur ist schlechthin sich selbts überlassen.
Dagegen ist die Vorsehung in der Geschichte (besser: in den menschlichen
Angelegenheiten) zwar eine direkte und individuelle, zugleich aber sind ihre
Mittel indirekte und verborgene. Die von Gott gewollte Freiheit und Mündigkeit des Menschen schliesst den direkten Eingriff in seine Natur aus und
verlangt eben diesen "Umweg" über seine Natur beim Versuch, den Menschen
zu erhöhen.[37]

   Im befremdenden Gebrauch der Listmetapher bei Hegel ist diese Dialektik
thematisch geworden, umso mehr, als Natur und Vernunft nicht mehr durchgängig gegeneinander bestimmbar sind. "Das ist die List der Vernunft zu
nennen, dass sie die Leidenschaften für sich wirken lässt, wobei das, durch

---

übersetzt) auf Alexander von Aphrodisias zurück, (der sich aber nicht auf die Geschichte,
sondern auf die kosmische Ordnung bezog) und bemerkt auch kurz die Ähnlichkeit mit
Hegels Listmetapher (S. 71ff. n. 32) ohne sie näher zu begründen. Über die Sabbäer ebd. 123ff.

[33] Hierzu I. Goldziher, *Vorlesungen über den Islam* (Heidelberg 1910) 23 (*kejd* und *makr*,
Kriegslist); 31 Anm. 4. Mein verehrter Kollege, Herr Professor M. Perlmann, informierte
mich, dass Maimonides ein anderes Wort als das, womit der Koran die List Gottes kenn-
zeichnet (*makr*), beforzugt (*talaṭṭuf*).

[34] Ps. 18.27 (Goldziher ebd. Anm. 3).

[35] MN 3.54 (Munk 132): ויקע עלי אקתנא אלפצّאיל אלבלّקיה . . . ויקע עלי
אלתלّטّﭏ ואלאﭏת'יאﭏ הבה נתחכמה לי . . . (In der Unterscheidung der verschiedenen Bedeutungen des hebräischen Wortes חכמה, Weisheit).

[36] MN 3.17, insbes. die "fünfte Meinung." Es ist die Frage nach der individuellen Pro-
videnz.

[37] MN 3.32: "Doch die Natur der Menschen ändert Gott nicht durch Wundertaten . . .
Dieses sage ich nicht, weil ich glaube, dass die Veränderung der Natur eines jeden einzelnen
Menschen Ihm, er sei erhaben, schwer fiele . . . sondern er wollte es nicht, und wird es nie
wollen, gemäss den Grundlagen des Gesetzes. Denn wäre es sein Wille, die Natur jedes
einzelnen Menschen ob dessen, was Er, er sei erhaben, von ihm will, zu verändern, wäre
die Sendung der Propheten wie der Gesetzgebung zwecklos."

was sie sich in Existenz setzt, einbüsst und Schaden erleidet."[38] In Existenz
setzt sich die Vernunft vermittels der Individuen und ihrer Triebkräfte. Diese
müssen als Mittel und Zweck zugleich gedacht werden, wenn der Gang der
Weltgeschichte mit Notwendigkeit als "Fortschritt im Bewusstsein der Freiheit"[39] bestimmt werden soll. Denn die subjektive Freiheit des Handelnden,
sein "unendliches Recht,"[40] ist ebenso eine Voraussetzung dieser Notwendigkeit wie es das Gegensätzliche ist, die objektive des Geschichtsverlaufs. Freiheit und Notwendigkeit schliessen sich im subjektiven Bewusstsein aus,
wenn ihm nicht die Triebfeder seiner Handlungen entzogen sein soll.[41] Ihre
Übereinstimmung im tatsächlichen Geschichtsgang ist die List der Vernunft,
die sich mit und trotz der Würde und Mündigkeit des Handelnden ausdrücken
muss. Auch hier bedient sich die Vernunft des Umweges über die "Natur"
im uneigentlichen Sprachgebrauch. Es sei damit nicht suggeriert, dass Hegel
den *More Nebukim* kannte, wohl aber, dass sich Maimonides der Problematik des Pädagogiegedankens deutlich bewusst war.

Die Gefahren der historisierenden Deutung des Gesetzes für das jüdische
Selbstverständnis waren den Zeitgenossen Maimunis nicht entgangen: in der
Polemik gegen Maimonides, in der Provence entfacht, spielten sie eine grosse
Rolle.[42] Wir haben gesehen, dass Maimonides seine Methode mit tatsächlich
vorhandenen Ansätzen der antiken Tradition zu legitimieren wusste. Solche
Ansätze befinden sich zahlreicher, als Maimonides von ihnen Gebrauch machte,
im Midrasch; die besten Belegstellen hat er nicht erwähnt, obgleich er sie
gewiss kannte. So heisst er im Leviticus Rabba, Gott habe die Opferwerke
eingeführt, um Israel vom Teufelsdienst, an das es sich in der ägyptischen
Umgebung gewöhnt hatte, abzulenken und die Gesundung seines Geistes

---

[38] Hegel, *Philosophie der Geschichte*, ed. F. Brunstäd (Reclam 1961) 78ff.

[39] *Ibid.* 61.

[40] *Ibid.* 65.

[41] *Ibid.*, insbes. 69f. "Vernunft" und geschichtlicher Fortschritt verhalten sich bei Hegel
so wie Natur und Geschichte bei Kant; "Das Mittel, dessen sich die Natur bedient, die
Entwicklung aller ihrer Anlagen zustande zu bringen, ist der Antagonismus derselben in der
Gesellschaft sofern dieser doch am Ende die Ursache einer gesetzmässigen Ordnung der-
selben wird." So wird die "Geschichte der Menschengattung" zur "Vollziehung eines ver-
borgenen Plans der Natur." *Ideen zu einer allgemeinen Geschichte, Werke*, ed. W. Weischedel
(Frankfurt 1964) 37, 45. Für "Vorsehung" kann leicht "List der Natur" eingesetzt werden.
Eine Interpretation der Entwicklung der Kantschen Geschichtstheorie von diesem früheren
Standpunkt zum Begriff der bewussten, historischen Verwirklichung des *summum bonum*
versucht, am Leitfaden Hegels, J. Yovel, "The *Summum Bonum* and History in Kant,"
Iyyun [A Hebrew Philosophical Quarterly] 16 (1965) 11ff. (hebr.), 129 (englische Zusammen-
fassung). Über den ähnlich gefassen Providenzbegriff Vico's siehe B. Croce, *La filosofia
di Giambattista Vico* (Bari 1911) Kap. 10. Und neuerdings den (ebenfalls zu einseitig
an Hegel orientierten) Interpretationsversuch von A. R. Caponigri, *Time and Idea: The
Theory of History in Giambattista Vico* (London 1953) 91ff.

[42] Hierüber zuletzt D. J. Silver, *Maimonides' Criticism and the Maimonidean Controversy
1180-1240* (Leiden 1965) 148ff., insbes. 157ff.

herbeizuführen.[43] Ähnliche Deutungen, die sich zum Eindruck einer konsequenten Methode verdichten, werden zuweilen an die "Schule R. Jishmaels" geknüpft.[44] Allerdings wird man in diesen und ähnlichen tanaitischen Hinweisen auf keinen Fall relativisierende Tendenzen entdecken dürfen; den Opfergeboten wurde nur eine Dimension hinzugefügt,[45] die andere Gebote wegen ihrer primären Reminiszenzfunktion schon längst hatten. Die Frage ihrer historischen Permanenz lag gänzlich ausserhalb des Diskussionshorizonts, es sei denn in der eschatologischen Spekulation über die Aufhebung der Gebote im kommenden αἰών.[46] Anders bei Maimonides. Ihm galt, wie der rationali-

---

[43] Vajikra Rabba 22.6, ed. Margulies (Jerusalem 1956) 3.517ff.: ר' פנחס בשם ר'
לוי: לבן מלך שנזז (נ"א' גס) לבו עליו והיה למוד לאכול נבלות וטרפות.
אמר המלך זה יהיה תדיר על שולחני ומעצמו הוא נידור. כך לפי שהיו
ישראל להוטים אחרי עבודה זרה במצרים והיו מביאים קרבנותיהם לשעי-
רים, ואין שעירים אלא שדים שנאמר "יזבחו לשדים" (דברים ל"כ, ר,"ז),
ואין שדים אלא שעירים שנאמר "ושעירים ירקדו שם" (ישעיהו ר"ג, כ"א) ;
והיו ישראל מקריבים קרבנותיהם באיסור במה ופורענות באה עליהם.
אמר הקב"ה יהיו מקריבים לפני בכל עת קרבנותיהם באוהל מועד והם
נפרשים מעבודה זרה והם ניצולים.
Auf diese Stelle (die eine Reflexion auf Lev. 17.7 ist) im Zusammenhang der Gesetzesinterpretation Maimunis macht u.a. A. Weiss in der (unzulänglichen) deutschen Übersetzung des MN 3 aufmerksam (Philos. Bibliothek 184b, Leipzig 1924, 197f.) Vgl. Baron, SRH 6.397 Anm. 169.

[44] Hierüber (in einiger Überspitzung) zuletzt A. J. Heschel, *Theology of Ancient Judaism* (London 1962) 10ff., insbes. 41ff. (hebr.). Als negative Parallele solcher Lehren könnte man die weitverbreiteten antijüdischen hellenistischen Interpretationen der Entsehung des mosaischen Gesetzes sehen. Es handelt sich um die gleichen Erklärungen mit umgekehrten Vorzeichen. Bei Manetho hiess es (Josephus, *Con. Apionem* 1.237ff., ed. Thackeray, Loeb Classical Library 260ff.): Osarsiph (Moses), ein entlaufener ägyptischer Priester, der sich den verbannten Leprosen hinzugesellt hatte, gab ihnen eine Konstitution und einen Kult, der in allen Stücken dem herrschenden Ägyptischen entgegengesetzt war: ὁ δὲ πρῶτον αὐτοῖς νόμος ἔθετο μήτε προκυνεῖν θεοὺς μήτε τῶν μάλιστα ἐν' Αἰγύπτῳ θεμιστευμένων ἱερῶν ξῴων ἀπέχεσθαι μηδενός etc.: Vgl. auch Tacitus, *Hist.* V.3: profana illic omnia quae apud nos sacra, rursum concessa apud illos quae nobis incesta. Die Bedeutung solcher Stellen ist klar: die Ethnizität und eine genuine (und alte) *Politeia*, beides Zeichen der Ehrwürdigkeit und Legitimität in der römischen Welt und die wirkliche Basis für die jüdische Autonomie, sollte den Juden abgesprochen werden. Der "antike Antisemitismus" ist schon darum keiner, weil er den Juden die genuine Ethnizität absprach.

[45] Der Tendenz zur Entsymbolisierung, die in diesen Deutungen Ausdruck findet, entspricht im juristischen die von R. Jishmael gehandhabte Regel: דברה תורה כלשון
בני-אדם (gegen die juristische Interpretation jedes Jota des Gesetzes in der Schule R. Akkiba). Erst das Mittelalter (und vielleicht auch schon die antike christliche Exegese) hatte dieses Prinzip auch auf die biblische Metaphorik ausgedehnt, es als die Akkommodation der Tora an die Fassungskraft der Menschen verstanden אנציקלו-פדיה תלמודית.
s. v. (דברה תורה) Einen sadduzäischen Ursprung dieser Maxime vermutet (ohne zwingende Beweise) J. Z. Lauterbach, "The Sadducees and Pharisees," *Rabbinic Essays* (Cincinnati 1951) 31f. u. Anm. 11.

[46] Gegen Heschel 43. Man merke, dass hier eher von עולם הבא als von ימות המשיח die Rede ist, zu einer Zeit, da beide schon unterschieden wurden: aus dem 3. Jh. stammt

sierenden Tradition seit Philo überhaupt, das biblische Gesetzeswerk als politische Idealverfassung. Nur wurde es ihm entgegen der bisherigen Tradition zur methodischen Gewissheit, dass *auch eine Idealverfassung die historischen Bedingungen ihrer Konkretion reflektieren muss*, dass wegen dieser Bedingtheit auch nicht von einer Idealverfassung per se, sondern von Idealverfassungen, der jeweiligen politischen Situation entsprechend, die Rede sein kann. Die irrationalen Gebote waren ihm nicht ein entbehrlicher, wenn auch nützlicher, Zusatz zu den "systematisierbaren" Geboten,[47] sondern die Voraussetzung für die Verwirklichung des Offenbarungsgesetzes überhaupt. Die Bekämpfung des heidnischen Ritus und der heidnischen Meinungen ist in der letzten Analyse "die Wurzel und die Achse, um die sich unsere *tora* dreht"[48]—und dieses ist der tiefere Sinn des tanaitischen dictums: "Wer Götzendienst ablehnt, gilt, als habe er die ganze *tora* angenommen."[49]

Wird somit die Gültigkeit der Offenbarung, insbesondere aber der diskutierten Partien des Zeremonialgesetzes, nicht letztlich doch relativiert? Hat sich doch Maimonides dazu um das Argument gebracht, auch heute noch existiere der verderbende Einfluss der Vielgötterei auf das auserwählte Volk. Man erinnere sich, dass Maimonides den Erziehungszweck der Offenbarung in dieser Hinsicht als nahezu vollendet betrachtete. Die Vielgötterei, so meint er an einer anderen Stelle, existiere nur noch an der Peripherie der bewohnten Welt; ihre Träger seien "halb Affen, halb Menschen," Nomaden (Türken), Neger und einige Inder. Die Sabbäer existieren nur noch als Restgemeinde.[50] Maimonides wirft im *More Nebukim* die Frage nach dem Sinn der Fortdauer der von ihm als zeitgebunden gedeuteten Gebote nicht ausdrücklich auf. Seine Antwort lässt sich nur aus versteckten Hinweisen konstruieren.

Die eine Antwortmöglichkeit wäre konservativ und bestünde im Hinweis auf die stets latente wenn auch nicht aktuelle Gefahr des Götzendienstes im Hinblick auf die Menge der Ungebildeten. Maimonides begnügte sich nicht mit einer Phänomenologie des Götzendienstes: er entwickelte auch, vor allem im *Mishne Tora*, eine religionshistorische Theorie seiner Natur

---

das (für Maimonides' Eschatologie entscheidende) dictum: Nichts unterscheidet diese Welt von den messianischen Tagen ausser der Knechtschaft unter den Herrschaften.

[47] Sieh oben, 13.

[48] MN 3.29.

[49] *Ibid.*; vgl. Mischne Tora, Hilkhot Avodat Kochavim 2.4. (Quellenverweise: Heschel 35; es ist ein Grundprinzip der Schule R. Jischmaels).

[50] MN 3.51; 3.29. Die arabischen Quellen Maimunis wurden schon von D. Chwolson, *Die Ssabier und der Ssabismus* (Petersburg 1856) untersucht; ibid. 689ff. über Maimonides; zur neuen Literatur und zum Sprachgebrauch Maimunis, Baron, *The Historical Outlook* 114ff. und Pines a.a.O. Zweierlei mag entscheidend gewesen sein bei der Verketzerung der Sa'aba; zunächst ihr Wohnort in der Umgebung, in der Abraham aufwuchs; sodann die Vorstellung, dass die Sabbäer nicht einem naiven Polytheismus huldigten, sondern einem theoretisch begründeten.

und Entstehung. Inbegriff des Götzendienstes—seine sublimste, begreif-lichste, und darum gefährlichste Erscheinungsform—ist die Sternanbetung, עבודת כוכבים. "In den Tagen des Enosch begingen die Menschen einen verhängnisvollen Irrtum ... und Enosch selbst war unter den Irrenden. Sie meinten, da Gott die Sterne und Sphären (גלגלים) erschuf um die Welt zu leiten, sie zuoberst fixierte und ihnen Ehre erteilte, so gezieme es sich, sie zu loben und ihnen zu huldigen. ... Sie begannen, den Sternen Tempel zu errichten und ihnen Opfer darzubringen und im Wort zu huldigen und vor ihnen zu knien, um, gemäss ihrer fehlgeleiteten Meinung, den Willen des Schöpfers zu erfüllen. Dieses ist der Wesensinhalt des Sternendienstes."[51] Gottesleugnung war dies keinesfalls, nur eine fortschreitende Hintansetzung seiner Verehrung. Erst allmählich habe sich aus der Verehrung der vermeint-lichen Vermittlungsinstanzen ihre Verehrung um ihrer selbst willen entwickelt; der Name Gottes ward vergessen. Abraham, der kein Gesetzgeber, wohl aber ein Lehrer gewesen ist,[52] gelang es, den monotheistischen Glauben mit Ver-nunftsargumenten bei einigen Tausenden zu verbreiten. Die Nachkommen seiner Gefolgschaft, in der heidnischen Umgebung Ägyptens, verfielen er-neut dem Irrtum; die Wiederherstellung des Monotheismus durch Moses ge-schah diesmal nicht bloss durch Lehre, sondern vermittels einer umfassenden Gesetzgebung, die nicht nur aktuelle Formen des Götzendienstes verbietet (oder umwandelt), sondern auch alles, was dazu führen kann.[53] Es ist das Gesetz, das die Wiederholung des Irrtumswegens versperrt: auf die Einsicht der Menge ist kein Verlass. Sie ist auch heute für Aberglauben empfänglich.[54] Es läge dem Maimonides durchaus nahe, zu behaupten, dass, wäre die Menge ohne genaue Kultvorschriften sich selbst überlassen, so würde sich ebenso wie schon zweimal in der bisherigen Geschichte ihr (heute gewiss verwandelter, monotheistischer) Glaube allmählich und unmerklich verflüchtigen. Mai-monides war kein Entwicklungsoptimist. Noch stärker als andere mittel-alterliche Philosophen bringt Maimonides eine tiefe Verachtung gegenüber der unaufklärbaren "Masse" zum Ausdruck, eine Verachtung, die vielleicht

---

[51] Mishne Tora, Av. Kochavim 1.1-3. Theorien über die Depravation des "Urmonotheis-mus" liegen jeder biblizistischen Spekulation nahe; man vergleiche etwa Eusebius, *Kirchen-geschichte* 1.2.19ff. (ed. Schwartz 8) sowie F. E. Cranz, "Kingdom and Policy in Eusebius of Caesarea," *Harvard Theological Review* 45 (1952).

[52] *Ibid.* sowie (pointierter) MN 3.29: "Und wir haben bereits in unserem grossen Werk, Mischne Tora, dargelegt, dass Abraham unser Vater begonnen hatte, diese Meinungen *mit Argumenten und sanfter Predigt* zu widerlegen, durch die Versöhnung seiner Mitmenschen und durch Wohltat sie zur Gottesarbeit zu bekehren versuchend: bis dann der Meister der Propheten kam ... und diese Absicht verwirklichte und *befahl*, die Ketzer zu töten."

[53] MN 3.29.

[54] *Ibid.*: "Und von dem, wozu die Seele der Menge neigt und anhangt ..." und weiter unten: "Denn vielmals neigt die Menge dazu, Unsinniges zu glauben"; u.ö.

das deutlichste Unterscheidungsmerkmal zwischen der mittelalterlichen Philosophie und den Idealen neuzeitlicher Aufklärung ist.[55]

Eine andere, gewagtere Antwort liesse sich ebenfalls aus den Attributen der Masse entwickeln. Maimonides unterscheidet vier Menschengruppen hinsichtlich ihrer Nähe zu Gott. An der Peripherie der zivilisierten Welt gibt es noch Heiden: sie sind ungefährlich und ohne Einfluss.[56] Sodann existiert die grosse Gruppe der "Irrenden," weitaus verdammungswürdiger als die erste: hierzu gehören das Christentum und der Islam, die (negativen) Wegbereiter des Messias. Die nächste Kategorie, die "Menge der Gottesfürchtigen," muss sich mit dem blinden Befolgen des Gesetzes begnügen. Die wahre Gotteserkenntnis (und mithin, so darf man aus dem Zusammenhang ergänzen, die Einsicht in die *ta'ame hamitsvot*) ist auf die wenigen Weisen beschränkt. Schon am Eingang seiner Erörterungen meinte Maimonides, dass die (sa'adianische) Disjunktion von "Vernunfts" —und "Gehorsamsgeboten" nur für die Menge gelten könne.[57] In diesen Bemerkungen mag man auch eine weitere Antwort Maimunis auf das Relativierungsproblem suchen: der unverständigen Menge muss und soll das Offenbarungsgesetz als unveränderbar erscheinen, obgleich viele seiner Einzelverfügungen anachronistisch sein mögen. Die legitimierten Weisen, denen die historische Bedingtheit des Gesetzes begreiflich ist, haben auch die Möglichkeit, es unmerklich zu verändern.

Mit Hilfe dieser Deutungsstruktur versuchte jüngst J. Levinger in einer überzeugenden Analyse widersprechende Positionen in den verschiedenen Schriften Maimunis zur Übereinstimmung zu bringen.[58] Im "Mishne Tora," dem Kodifizierungswerk, das mit dem Anspruch auftrat, über das gesamte mündliche Gesetz so zu informieren, dass "kein anderes Buch" zwischen

---

[55] Vgl. L. Strauss, *Philosophie des Gesetzes* 51ff., 88ff.; ähnlich J. Taubes, *Glauben und Meinungen in der Theologie des 19. Jahrhunderts* (hebr.: אמונות ודעות בתיאולוגיה 19-ה המאה של) in ערכי היהדות (Tel-Aviv 1950, 92f.) letzlich, so ist Taubes, *ibid.* 104 zu korrigieren, war das Dilemma des Maimonides nicht gänzlich anderer Natur als das Krochmals.

[56] MN 3.51; die Kategorie: כל איש מבני אדם שאין לו אמונת דת (unter die Christen und Mohammedaner eindeutig nicht zu rechnen sind) erinnert an die Unterscheidungen des *Hameiri* später (אומות הגדורות בדרכי הדתות): er kannte ja den *More* in der Übersetzung. Über ihn J. Katz, *Exclusiveness and Tolerance; Jewish-Gentile Relations in Medieval and Modern Times* (New York 1962) 114ff. Von Maimonides (doch nicht unbedingt) mag auch Raymundus Martini (vgl. unten, 44) seine Unterscheidung zwischen legem habentes (Juden, Christen, Moslems) und legem non habentes (Heiden, Philosophen) genommen haben: *Pugio fidei adversus Mauros et Judaeos* (Leipzig 1687).

[57] MN 3.32. Darum enthält das Gesetz nicht immer zugleich seine Begründungen: neben den משפטים (*sententia, iudicia*) hat es auch חוקים, unbegründete Gesetze. Vgl. Mischne Tora, Meila (Ende) und Heinemann 98ff., sowie unten, Anm. 87.

[58] J. Levinger, "The Oral Law in Maimonides' Thought" (hebr.: המחשבה ההלכתית של הרמב"ם), *Tarbits* [A Quarterly for Jewish Studies] 37.3 (1968) 282ff., insbes. 288ff. Vorsichtiger und unbestimmter in der gleichen Richtung, Neuburger 71ff.

ihm und der *tora* gelesen werden muss,[59] betrachtet Maimonides das Religions-
gesetz "statisch." Denn diese Schrift ist nicht eine argumentierend-philo-
sophische, sondern für die Menge bestimmt und darum apodiktisch. Hier
erscheinen auch die späteren Verfügungen der "mündlichen Tora" häufig
als blosse Explikation des geschriebenen Gesetzes. Der *More Nebukim* hingegen war für die Philosophiekundigen bestimmt, und um ihn dem Miss-
verständnis der Masse zu entziehen, unsystematisch-argumentativ geschrieben.
In ihm vertritt Maimonides (so Levinger) eine "dynamische" Auffassung der
Religionsgeschichte. Darum werden hier viele der rabbinischen Verfügungen,
die Maimonides im *Mischne Tora* als Explikation des geschriebenen Gesetzes
ansah, als selbständige Anpassung an die Zeitnotwendigkeiten gedeutet.[60]

Ob man diese Interpretation in dieser Eindeutigkeit durchhalten kann,
weiss ich nicht. Zweifellos aber ist im dritten Teil des *More Nebukim* ein

[59] Mischne Tora, Haqdamat ha-Rambam. Das gilt natürlich nur vom bestehenden Gesetz, nicht von seiner Begründung in der halachitischen Diskussion. Demgemäss wird
Maimonides in der Formulierung der Halacha sehr sorgfältig verfahren, weniger Sorgfalt
bei der Begründung zeigen (Levinger a. a. O.). Es ist ein Buch für die Menge: aber auch
das geoffenbarte Gesetz war für die Menge bestimmt, weswegen es nicht alle Gebote begründete (oben, Anm. 57).

[60] Eine ähnliche, aber weitaus radikalere Interpretation legt L. Strauss (im einführenden
Essay zur englischen Maimonides-Übersetzung, oben, Anm. 27) vor. Er versucht, im MN
eine ausgeprägte Fortschrittslehre nachzuweisen. Demnach waren nicht nur die Opferge-
bote, sondern der Gebrauch anthropomorphisierender Metaphern in der Bibel überhaupt
auf das Niveau der Zeit der Offenbarung zurückzuführen, als Konzession und Ablenkung
zugleich usw. (Doch ist dies keinesfalls überzeugend: von Konzession an die Zeit spricht
M. nur bei den erwähnten Gebotsgruppen; דברה תורה כלשׁוי בני־אדם hingegen—die
Tatsache, dass die Bibel die Wirkungen Gottes versinnbildlicht—scheint M. eher auf die immer beschränkte Auffasungskraft der Menge zurückzuführen). Strauss baut seine Prämisse
konsequent auf. Wenn die ganze Offenbarung mit zeitgebundenen Mitteln operiert, so
muss seither ein Fortschritt des religiösen Bewusstseins stattgefunden haben; von der
Tora zu den Propheten, und wiederum in der nachbiblischen Zeit (wiederum sind seine Belege
bestenfalls zweideutig). Schliesslich bietet Strauss einen äusserst bestechenden Gedanken-
gang an: dass für Maimonides die "Residuen der Götzenanbetung" (Verkörperlichung),
die die Offenbarung benutzte, um vom Götzendienst abzubringen, und deren Genese notwendigerweise (eben weil die "List" Gottes wirksam war) vergessen wurden, wieder aufgedeckt werden müssen, um zu einer vollkommenen Erkenntnis zu gelangen. Es ist nun an
der Zeit, die Residuen der הגשמה aufzuräumen, nachden sie ihren Zweck erfüllt haben,
und dies kann nur (und erst in der Gegenwart) geschehen, indem man ihre (mit Bedacht
bisher verborgene) Herkunft aufdeckt. Aber keine explizite Äusserung Maimuni's recht-
fertigt ein derartiges Interpretationsmodell. Im Gegensatz zur Aufklärung ist ihm die
Beschränktheit der Masse eine konstante Grösse; ihr Bewusstseinsfortschritt zuzuschreiben,
läge ihm fern. Wohl können die Objekte ihrer Phantasie und Verehrungspraktiken kon-
trolliert—doch nicht ihre Mechanismen geändert werden. Nicht einmal ein Fortschritt
in der Erkenntnis der wenigen Weisen jeder Generation—von Abraham über Moses, die
Propheten, die Tanaim bis zur Gegenwart deutet M. an. Was er z. B. über Abraham sagt,
erweckt den Eindruck, dass dieser schon im Besitz der höchstmöglichen gereinigten Gotters-
erkenntnis war, und es ist die Aufgabe der Weisen jeder Generation, diese gereinigte Erkenntnis insgeheim (d. h. so, dass sie nicht die Masse verwirrt) weiterzutradieren.

Höhepunkt historischer Argumentation erreicht worden, desgleichen man in der mittelalterlichen Literatur selten findet.[61] Nicht nur darum, weil Maimonides vom Akkommodationsgedanken Gebrauch macht, sondern weil er in der konsequenten Ausführung dieses Prinzips zur Einsicht gelangte, dass die Rekonstruktion des Vergangenen die Rekonstruktion eines gänzlich fremdgewordenen Teiles der eigenen Kultur bedeutet. Darin hat Maimonides, vielleicht als einziger im Mittelalter, ein Grundprinzip der historischen Kritik seit dem 16. Jahrhundert vorweggenommen und beeinflusst.

2. Die historische Begründung der alttestamentlichen Gebote in der christlichen Tradition und die Rezeption der Maimonideischen Gesetzestheorie bei Thomas von Aquin

In seiner Analyse der *lex vetus*, vornehmlich in der *Summa*, benutzte Thomas den dritten Teil des *More Nebukim* durchgehend, beruft sich aber ausdrücklich auf "Rabbi Moyses" nur dort, wo es um den *sensus litteralis* der Gebote geht.[62] Das Ausmass der Maimonides-Rezeption, hier wie in anderen Lehrstücken des Aquinaten, hat schon J. Guttmann untersucht.[63] Nach Absicht und Art der Rezeption, nach den Veränderungen, die Maimunis Methode und Grundbegriffe bei Thomas erfahren haben, fragte Guttmann kaum— hinsichtlich der Gesetzestheorie noch seltener als in anderen Abschnitten.

Die Frage, warum sich Thomas, wie schon andere Theologen vor ihm, in der historischen Begründung der Gebote derart an Maimonides anlehnte, scheint leicht beantwortbar. Er fand in der frühen christlichen Exegese nichts Vergleichbares. In der westlichen Theologie des 12. und 13. Jahrhunderts, so erfahren wir in der vorbildlichen Untersuchung B. Smalleys,[64] wurde die systematisch historische Deutung des Alten Testaments wiederbelebt aus eigenen Stücken, denn der Antiochener Ansatz war nahezu vergessen. Das setzte ein neues Verhältnis dessen voraus, was vom *sensus litteralis* zu erwarten ist; Thomas gab diesem neuen Verständnis den prägnantesten Ausdruck: "Illa ergo prima significatio, qua voces significant res pertinet ad primum sensum, qui est sensus historicus vel litteralis. Illa vero significatio, qua res significatae per voces iterum res alias significant, dicitur sensus spiritualis, qui super litteralem fundatur et eum supponit."[65] Das Schriftwort

---

[61] Über die Grenzen der historischen Methode bei Maimonides treffend Baron, SRH 6.

[62] *Summa theol.* (ST) 12-1.2.99.3, 4, 5; 101.1, 3; 102.3-6; 105.2, ed. Caramello, Marietti (Turin 1952).

[63] J. Guttmann, *Das Verhältnis des Thomas von Aquino zum Judentum und zur jüdischen Literatur* (Göttingen 1891) insbes. 80ff. (Die Erklärung der biblischen Gebote); 82ff. (Opferlehre).

[64] B. Smalley, *The Study of the Bible in the Middle Ages* (Notre Dame 1964).

[65] ST 1.1.10. Über die Interpretationsschwierigkeiten siehe H. de Lubac, *Exégèse médiévale: les quatres sens de l'écriture* 2.2 (Lyon 1964) 272ff., 285ff. Eine Vorform dieser

—ob es unmittelbar begreiflich oder als Parabel erscheint—bezieht sich stets auf ein Ereignis oder eine Sache, und dieser Bezug wird vom Litteralverständnis aufgedeckt. Nur das Ereignis, der sächliche Inhalt selbst, auf das sich das Schriftwort bezieht, hat weitere Bezüge und verlangt weitere Ebenen des Verständnisses. Daher muss konsequent nach dem *sensus historicus* gefragt werden: in den historischen und prophetischen Schriften, aber auch hinsichtlich der Gebote. Den Bruch mit der bisherigen exegetischen Tradition, der die Unverständlichkeit vieler Gebote oftmals als Argument für die Notwendigkeit ihrer Aufhebung diente, sieht Smalley am deutlichsten in der historisierenden Interpretation des Zeremonialgesetzes bei Thomas.[66] Nach den Modifikationen der Gesetzestheorie Maimunis bei Thomas fragt auch sie nicht. Ihre Erklärung der Tatsache der Maimonidesrezeption bleibt aber auch dann gültig wenn, entgegen ihrer Meinung, eine gewisse Kontinuität in der historisierenden Gesetzesdeutung auch vor Thomas nachzuweisen wäre. Wenn ich mich im folgenden um diesen Nachweis bemühe, so nur darum, weil er helfen kann, die objektive Stellung Thomas' in der exegetischen Tradition zu bestimmen. Letztlich, so wird sich zeigen, hat Thomas den Ansatz Maimunis auf das reduziert, was in der christlichen Exegese potentialiter und in allgemeinen, fragmentären Hinweisen schon je dagewesen ist.

Von Anbeginn war das christliche Gesetzesverständnis von entgegengesetzten Positionen bestimmt. Je nach der polemischen Situation wurde die Kontinuität vom Alten zum Neuen Testament betont oder beschränkt. In der Auseinandersetzung mit Juden und Judenchristen konnte das Gesetz als verhängnisvolle Bürde dargestellt werden, die Israel "im Fleische" ob seiner Sündhaftigkeit auferlegt wurde;[67] unbegreiflich und unverwirklichbar und nur der allegorischen oder typologischen Deutung offen. Je entschiedener die Unverständlichkeit der Gebote hervorgekehrt wurde, umso deutlicher konnte die Notwendigkeit ihrer Aufgabe bewiesen werden. Seit dem Barnabasstreit diente insbesondere das Zeremonialgesetz als topisches Beispiel dieser negativen *praeparatio evangelica*. Es ist diese Tradition, die

---

Lehre entwickelte, mit Wilhelm von Auvergne, Alexander von Hales, ST p. 2 inq. 3 tract. 2 sec. 3 q. 1 c. 2 (*Quaracchi* 1948) 4.760ff. Es ist interessant zu beobachten, wie solche Lehren gelegentlich auf das Judentum rückwirken. Vgl., z.B., Ramban (Nachmanides), פרוש התורה zu Gen. 36.39: כי היו המקרים ראשונים רמז לזרעם (vgl. auch seinen Kommentar zu Gen 2.2 mit seinem ausgearbeiteten System der Präfigurationen und Weltperioden, von Augustin über Isidor v. Sevilla und Abraham bar Chija entlehnt; hierüber mein *Heilsplan* 129 Anm. 27; siehe unten, Anm. 74).

[66] Smalley 303ff. Dieses Beispiel ist nicht richtig gewählt, wenn es Smalley darum ging, andere Deutungsansätze des Zeremonialgesetzes auszuschliessen; da wäre die Exegese zu Lev. 17.7 charakteristischer. Unbedingt ist ihr jedoch zuzustimmen, dass es für die allgemeine Deutungstendenz repräsentativ ist.

[67] Z.B. Gal. 3.19; siehe M. Werner, *Die Entstehung des christlichen Dogmas*, Aufl. 2 (Bern 1953) 201ff., 207.

die christliche Exegese bis in 12. Jahrhundert bestimmt hat und von der *Glossa ordinaria* übernommen wurde.[68]

Doch zu Leviticus 17.7 heisst es in der *Glossa*: "lex ergo, quasi paedagogos eorum, praecipit Deo sacrificare (Ex. 32) ut in hoc occupati abstinerent se a sacrificio idolatriae. Tamen sanctivicavit sacrificia, quibus mysteria significantur futura."[69] Ähnliche Bemerkungen finden sich bei Hieronymus, (hier mit einem Seitenhieb auf die Ebioniten), Augustin, Origenes, Irenaeus,[70] —häufig als Exegese der genannten Leviticusstelle, von der auch R. Jishmael die Legitimation seiner Deutung der Ofpergebote als pädagogische Konzession Gottes bezog. Zum hermeneutischen Prinzip wurde in der antiken Exegese dieser Gedanke, soweit ich sehen kann, nur bei Theodoret von Cyrrhus. In seinem Leviticuskommentar fasst er das, was er "vielerorts expliziert hatte," zusammen : "Ἐπειδὴ δὲ χρόνον συχνὸν ἐν Αἰγύπτῳ διατετελικὼς ὁ λαὸς θύειν δαίμοσιν ἐδιδάχθη, συνεχώρησε τὰς θυσίας, ἵνα τῆς δεισιδαιμονίας ἐλευθερώσῃ. . . . Πρὸς δὲ τούτοις · καὶ ἕτερον αὐτοῖς ἀλεξίκακον διὰ τούτου κατεσκεύασε φάρμακον. θέσθαι γὰρ αὐτῷ προσέταξε τὰ παρ᾽ Αἰγυπτίων θεοποιούμενα[71], usf." Es handelt sich nicht um gelegentliche Beobachtungen, sondern um eine systematische Interpretationsmethode. Ob eine direkte Anlehnung an bestimmte Richtungen im Midrash vorliegt, ist schwer zu bestimmen. Wie R. Jischmael interpretiert auch Theodoret z. B. den Tabernakelbau als Antwort Gottes auf die sündhafte Verehrung des goldenen Kalbes—entgegen der Erzählungsfolge in Exodus.[72] Auch sonst ist ihm der Midrasch geläufig.[73]

---

[68] Levit., Praef., PL 113.295ff; vgl. z. B. Hesychius *in Lev.* 1, PG 93.792 (vgl. sogar seine Deutung zu Lev. 17.7, ebd. 1002f.; weitere Beispiele, Smalley, a. a. o.).

[69] PL 113.344-345.

[70] Origenes, *In Lev.* (Praef.), PG 12.398; Hieron., *In Lev.* (zu Lev. 17.7); *In Esaiam* 1.1.11 (Corpus Christianorum, series latina 70.16f.): An beiden Stellen polemisiert H. gegen die Ebioniten. Sollte ihre Eschatologie die Wiederherstellung des Tempelsdienstes enthalten haben? Bei Augustin finden sich nur allgemeine Andeutungen, z.B. *Contra Faustum* 18.6, PL 42.346. Eine Einzeldeutung dieser Richtung findet sich auch beim Ps. Hieronymus; vgl. L. Ginzberg, *Die Haggada bei den Kirchenvätern* (Amsterdam 1899) 25. Über ähnliche Belege bei Origenes, in den Clementischen Recognitionen, bei Irenaeus siehe L. Diestel, *Geschichte des Alten Testament in der christlichen Kirche* (Jena 1869) 36f. 45ff., 52, 56ff.

[71] Theodoretus Cyrensis, *Quest. in Lev.*, PG 80.300. Vgl. *in Isaia* 1.2, PG 81.226. Ausführlich wieder in: *Graecorum affectionum curatio* 7: *De sacrificiis*, PG 83.991ff., insbes. 995ff. (Hier u. a. auch die starke Betonung der Fleischgier, die auch im Midrasch nicht fehlt).

[72] Theodoret, *Quaest. in Exod.*, inter. 60, PG 80.280f.; vgl. (zum Midrasch) Heschel 36ff. Allerdings ist hier die Begründung (Zeichen des Vergebens) eine andere als bei Theodoret. Im übrigen basiert die Änderung der Erzählungsfolge auf der Regel: אין מוקדם ומאוחר בתורה. Von allen Regeln, die Tychonius in *De septem regulis* aufstellte, ist diese (bei ihm die sechste: De recapitulatione) die einzige, die, wirklich in der jüd. Exegese als מכילתא) מידה, Mass) vorkommt: H. Grundmann, *Studien über Joachim von Fiore* (Leipzig 1827, Neudruk 1966) 25 Anm. 2-3, und die dort angegebene Literatur.

[73] Z.B. *Quaest. in Gen.* inter. 12, PL 80.93 (συναγωγὰς) = Gen. Rabba 5.8 (מקווה מים). Auf den Einfluss des Midrasch auf die Patristik wurde oft hingewiesen, am ausführlichsten

Gelegentlich diente auch ausserhalb der Exegese gerade das Opfergesetz als Beispiel der göttlichen Pädagogie, als Beweis der Akkommodation der Offenbarung an die menschliche Fassungskraft.[74] So z. B. bei Gregor von Nazianz, in einer Stelle, die Anselm von Havelberg im 12. Jahrhundert im Zusammenhang seiner kirchenhistorischen Betrachtung extensiv benutzte.[75] In einem ähnlichen Argumentationskontext benutzte schon Walafrid Strabo ähnliche Gedankengänge. Beweisziel seines Traktats *De exordiis et incrementis quarundam in observationibus ecclesiasticis rerum* war die Notwendigkeit und Fruchtbarkeit der Anpassung der Kirche (und ihrer Liturgie) an Zeitnotwendigkeiten und Ortsbedingungen. Gott selbst gibt ein Beispiel ähnlicher Wandlungen. *Ante legem* verbreitete sich allmählich der Dämonenkult; das Opfergesetz war eine Konzession an das gewohnte Opfergesetz und zugleich seine Umdeutung und Bekämpfung: "omnipotens et patiens creator facturae suae volens undecumque consulere, quia vero propter fragilitatem carnalium omnes consuetudines pariter tolli non posse sciebat."[76]

Es liessen sich wohl weitere Beispiele dieser rationalisierend-historischen Begründung des Zeremonialgesetzes auch im Westen vor dem 13. Jahrhundert sammeln. Sie bleiben aber insgesamt fragmentär, die Betonung der Unverständlichkeit des Zeremonialgesetzes dominiert. Allerdings liesse sich auch aus der historischen Sinngebung, nicht minder als aus ihrer schlechthinnigen Negation, die Aufhebung des Gesetzes verdeutlichen; und zwar ohne die Gefahren, welche die durchgängige Allegorisierung der Offenbarung heraufbeschwor. Denn je mehr der konkrete Sinn und die historische Funktion der Offenbarung in den Hintergrund gedrängt wurden, je deutlicher die historische Diskontinuität vom Alten zum Neuen Testament hervorgehoben wurde, umso schwieriger wurde es, die historische Tatsache der Offenbarung zu begründen. Das antike Christentum begegnete diesen Gefahren nicht nur mit dem allgemeinen Pädagogiegedanken und immer neuen Definitionen der Kontinuität vom Alten zum Neuen Testament, sondern auch mit dem häufigen Rekurs auf die Literalexegese. Im Hintergrund der konsequenten Wiederherstellung des Litteralsinns vor und beim Aquinaten steht ebenfalls

---

bei L. Ginzberg, *Die Haggada bei den Kirchenvätern*; doch nach dem Einfluss einer *bestimmten* exegetischen Richtung (von Philo, der ohne Einfluss im Horizont des "normativen Judentums" blieb, abgesehen), wurde m. W. nicht gefragt; es fehlt auch eine systematische Untersuchung der Antiochener Exegese aus dieser Perspektive.

[74] In meiner Dissertation, *Heilsplan und natürliche Entwicklung* (München 1965) habe ich versucht, die Geschichte dieser Vorstellung und ihre Bedeutung für das historische Denken kurz zu umreissen.

[75] Gregor von Nazianz, Oratio 5.25 (*Orat. theologicae* 3.2ff.), ed. J. Barbel, *Testimonia*; *Schriften der altchristlichen Zeit* 3 (Düsseldorf 1963) 261ff. = Anselm von Havelberg, *Dialogi* 1.5, PL 188.1147; hierzu *Annuaire de l'Université de Louvain* (1936-1939) 750ff. und mein *Heilsplan* 65ff. Anm. 67a, 75.

[76] Walafrid Strabo, *De exordiis*, ed. A. Boretius, K. Krause, MGH Capit. 2.476; vgl. Augustin (oben Anm. 70) und mein *Hielsplan* 62 (ebd. Lit.).

nicht nur eine Tradition, die etwa mit Hugo von St. Victor begann, sondern wohl auch die Notwendigkeit, Extremstellungen und Häresien seiner Zeit zu begegnen, von denen viele und voneinander verschiedene dieses gemeinsam hatten, dass sie an der Notwendigkeit und Gerechtigkeit der alttestamentlichen Dispensation zweifelten.[77]

Ähnliche Motive mögen schon in der vorthomistischen Scholastik, besonders bei Wilhelm von Auvergne und Alexander von Hales, das Interesse für die Gesetzeslehre Maimunis mitbestimmt haben.[78] Bei Wilhelm von Auvergne ist sogar, verglichen mit Thomas, die Anlehnung an den *More Nebukim* 3 weitaus stärker im Detail. In vielen seiner Einzelbegründungen konnte er den methodischen Ansatz Maimunis insofern bereichern, als er Belege aus der klassischen Literatur zur Unterstützung brachte; Maimonides war in seinem Versuch, eine anschauliche Beschreibung des "Heidentums" zu geben, auf die "sabbäische" Literatur angewiesen.[79] Auch zeichnete sich schon vor Thomas die prinzipielle Frage ab: wie weit darf man den radikal genetischen Ansatz Maimunis, und sei es bloss bei den Opfer und Reinigungsgesetzen, als ausschliessliche Methode der Literalexegese akzeptieren? Wilhelm von Auvergne schränkte die Anwendung dieses Prinzips grundsätzlich ein, während Alexander von Hales mit Maimonides zumindest den Opfergesetzen eine nur mittelbare Ausrichtung auf das Moralgesetz zuzubilligen scheint.[80] Erst dem Aquinaten gelang eine neue, sinnvolle Vermittlung zwischen der historischen und der figuralen Deutung, sowie zwischen den verschiedenen Rationalisierungsprinzipien auf der literalen Deutungsebene selbst.

---

[77] ST 1-2.98 kann als eine Widerlegung solcher, z. T. aktueller Häresien gelesen werden.

[78] Bei Alexander von Hales heisst es ausdrücklich: "Et primo, contra Manichaeos ostendendum est quod lex Moysi sit lata a bono et a solo Deo" (ST p.2 inq. 3 tr. 1.9.1.5 [Quaracchi] 4.374; cf. 375 col. 2). Über beide Jacob Guttmann, "Der Einfluss der maimonideischen Philosophie auf das christliche Abendland," *Moses ben Maimon, sein Leben, seine Werke und sein Einfluss*, hg. J. Guttman (Leipzig 1908) 1.144ff., 152ff. Auch hier geht Guttmann auf die Rezeptionsarten nicht ein. Die Ansicht, Thomas habe sich "der maimonidäischen Gesetzesauslegung nahezu rückhaltlos" angeschlossen (163), hoffen wir im folgenden zu modifizieren.

[79] Diese Praxis hat ein späterer Benutzer des More, Spencer, erweitert (Julius Guttman, unten Anm. 101). Man muss sich vergegenwärtigen, wie wenig und fragmentär die faktische Kenntnis des Heidentums auf Grund jüdischer und arabischer Literatur, einschliesslich der Bibel, bleiben muss.

[80] *Guilelmi Alverni episcopi Parisiensis* ... *Opera* (Paris 1674) 1 (*Tractatus de fide et legibus*) 2, p. 29 col. 2: Septem de causis ante legem, et etiam sub lege sacrificia huiusmodi sibi offerri voluit Deus, non solum propter consuetudinem idolatriae, ut quidam opinati sunt. Haec enim causa in Cain et Abel locum non habet (zitiert auch bei Guttmann, *Der Einfluss*, a. a. O.). Alexander von Hales: unten Anm. 83. Es ist die durchgehende Praxis Wilhelms, verschiedene *causae* aufzuzählem, um die *honestas* und *utilitas* der Gebote nachzuweisen. Auch gehen er und Alexander, wie Maimonides, von der Frage der Vielfalt der Gebote, die dennoch unter wenige Maximen fallen, aus (*ibid.* 24 col. 1-2).

Wie Thomas verschiedene Ebenen des Literalverständnisses aufeinander abstimmt, zeigt seine Deutung des Zeremonialgesetzes und mithin die Art und Weise, wie er Maimonides' Ausführungen rezipierte. Die oben aus dem *More Nebukim* angeführte Zurückweisung der disjunktiven Unterscheidung zwischen "Vernunfts" und (undeutbaren) "Gehorsamsgeboten" zitiert Thomas zwar so, als handle es sich um eine von Maimonides selbst vertretene Ansicht;[81] mit Maimonides wird er jedoch versuchen, sie zu widerlegen. "Unverständlich" ist ihm das Zeremonialgesetz nur, insofern seine figurale Bedeutung zur Zeit seiner "buchstäblichen" Geltung nicht begreiflich war (*non est adeo manifesta ratio*); Thomas wird die durchgängige Vernünftigkeit, oder exakter: Angemessenheit, des Gesetzes auch *litteraliter* beweisen müssen. Was übernimmt er vom *More Nebukim*? Eine gesonderte Begründung erfahren bei Thomas, Alexander von Hales und Wilhelm von Auvergne die vier Gebotsgruppen des Zeremonialgesetzes (*sacrificia, sacra, sacramenta, observantia*): sie entsprechen den Gebotsgruppen 10-12 bei Maimonides.[82] Gleich Maimonides gilt auch ihnen das Opfergesetz als pädagogische Konzession an den *corporalis cultus* und zugleich als seine Sublimierung; es war notwendig, damit "aliqui ad idolatriam proni . . . ab idolatriae cultu per praecepta caeremonialia revocarentur ad cultum dei"; "per huiusmodi homines retrahebantur a sacrificiis idolorum."[83] Doch nicht nur gelegentliche Bestätigungen oder Beispiele suchte Thomas im *Dux dubitantium*: solche konnte er, mit einiger Anstrengung, auch in der christlichen exegetischen Tradition finden. Er übertrug aber, wie wir zunächst zeigen möchten, die hermeneutische Methode und einen Teil der Voraussetzungen der maimonideischen Gesetzestheorie in den Zusammenhang seiner eigenen Systematik.

Sodann werden wir nach den Grenzen dieser Anlehnung fragen. Denn durchgängig wie die Berufung auf Maimonides in den Einzelbegründungen ist, bleiben die Hinweise des Thomas auf die Entstehungsbedingungen des Zeremonialgesetzes weit hinter der Radikalität Maimunis zurück. Von der Sa'aba und ihren Gebräuchen, über die Maimonides nahezu mit Entdeckerfreude berichtet, hören wir bei Thomas nichts; auch von den zusätzlichen Illustrationen Wilhelms von Auvergne bringt er nur wenige. Anders ausgedrückt: es fehlt bei Thomas der Ansatz zur chronologischen Präzisierung der historischen Umstände der Gebote. Damit entgeht ihm auch Maimonides' Einsicht in

---

[81] ST 1-2.101.1: "Rabbi Moyses dicit, quod praecepta caerimonialia dicuntur quorum ratio non est manifesta. Sed multa pertinentia ad cultum Dei habent rationem manifestam: sicut observatione sabbati. . . . Ergo caerimonialia non sunt quae pertinent ad cultum Dei." Wir haben gesehen, dass es sich bei Maimonides um eine vorläufige Bestimmung handelte.

[82] Vgl. Wilhelm von Auvergne, *De leg.* 28, p. 94a; Alexander von Hales, ST p. 2 inq. 3 sec.3 q.3 c.2.

[83] ST 1-2.101.3; 102.3. Alexander von Hales (unter Berufung auf Lev. 17.7) p.2 inq.3 tr. 1 q. 2 c. 2 ad 3 (392 col. 2; cf. 768 col. 2); Wilhelm von Auvergne, oben, Anm. 82.

die Fremdheit der zur rekonstruierenden Vergangenheit. Verzichtet Thomas
auf einen derartigen Beweis für die Zeitgebundenheit des *lex vetus* bloss aus
Gründen der Darstellungsökonomie?

Mit Maimonides teilen Thomas und seine Vorgänger die methodische Einsicht, dass eine rationale Deutung des Zeremonialgesetzes auch die Tatsache
seiner Vielfalt, seiner konkreten Gestalt, begründen muss.[84] Maimonides
sprach von der "primären" und "sekundären" Intention des Zeremonialgesetzes: Die primäre Intention, "Dass ihr mich erkennt und keinen anderen
Gott verehrt, so dass 'ich Euch zum Gott und ihr mit zum Volkè' werdet,"[85]
schreibt gewiss nicht diese oder jene Zeremonien und Opfer vor, und zöge
man sie allein in Betracht, müsste man dem Gebet den Vorrang über den
Opferdienst einräumen. Eine historische Notwendigkeit war es aber, die
das Opfern zur adäquaten Verehrungsform machte: um vorerst einen Teil-
zweck zu verwirklichen, die Abwenddng vom tief eingewurzelten Götzendienst. "Erste" und "Zweite" Intention verhalten sich zueinander wie Wesens-
bestimmung und Partikularisationsprinzip. Ähnlich sind wohl auch die verr-
schiedenen *causae*, die bei Wilhelm von Auvergne unvermittelt nebeneinander
standen, bei Thomas aufeinander bezogen. Figürlich weist das Opfergesetz
auf das *sacrificium Christi* hin: hiervon kann der *sensus historicus* absehen.
Historice wurde es *ad cultum Dei* aus einem doppelten Grund eingerichtet:
einmal, denn "ad rectam ordinationem mentis in Deum pertinet quod omnia
quae homo habet, recognoscet a Deo tanquam a primo principio et ordinet
in Deum tanquam in ultimum finem. Et hoc repraesentabatur in oblationibus
et sacrificiis." In beiden Fällen—in der Figur wie auf dieser ersten Ebene
der *historice*-Exegese—geht es um den Symbolcharakter des Opfers. Eine
Analogie lässt sich aber vermittels verschiedener *res* ausdrücken; sie kann
nicht endgültig ihre materielle Konkretion bestimmen. Determiniert wird
das Opfer als Opfer durch eine weitere *causa*: "Ex hoc quod homines retrahebantur a sacrificiis idolatrorum"; das Opfergesetz gestaltet eine gegebene
Verehrungsform um. So gesehen wird es verständlich, warum Thomas die
doppelte *historice* Begründung durchweg in der Deutung des Zeremonialgesetzes behält, und bei der "Zweiten" Ursache sich stets an Maimonides an-
lehnt: wie diesem ist sie ihm Individuationsprinzip.

Aber während bei Thomas—viel klarer als bei Wilhelm oder Alexander
von Hales—beide Intentionen des Gesetzgebers in einem und demselben
Gebot vermittelt sind, scheinen sich beide Intentionen bei Maimonides nicht
gleichzeitig, sondern in einer chronologischen Sukzession zu verwirklichen.
Bei Thomas ergänzen sich Symbolcharakter und historische Umstände in
der Gestaltung des Zeremonialgesetzes.[86] Maimonides betrachtete symbolische

---

[84] ST 1-2. 101.3. Davon gingen auch Wilhelm von Auvergne und Alexander von Hales aus.

[85] MN 3.32.

[86] So etwa das candelabrum (מנורה): seine Arme und Position repräsentieren die Planeten

Auslegungen, wie sie etwa Ibn Ezra reichlich brachte, mit grosser Skepsis. Er beschränkt sich auf die Darlegung der Umwelteinflüsse, die mit dem Gesetz überlistet werden sollen—nur mittelbar, in seinem zeitlichen Erfolg nämlich, dient das Gesetz, in der Ansicht Maimunis, auch der rechten Einsicht. Darum konnte Thomas auf den komplizierten historischen Apparat Maimunis durchaus verzichten: hatte doch dieser zur Aufgabe, jede Einzelheit der Kultgebote aus der Notwendigkeit eines bestimmten Zeitpunktes und einer bestimmten Umgebung verständlich zu machen. Innerhalb seiner Zeit war in der Ansicht Thomas' das Gesetz, auch das Zeremonialgesetz, von mehr oder minder gleichmässiger Relevanz. Die Zeitgebundenheit der *lex vetus* liegt, in der Anschauung Thomas, nicht etwa an den Umständen, unter denen er gegeben wurde (eine Ansicht, die er ohne Anstrengung aus dem *More Nebukim* herauszupräparieren vermocht hätte), sondern an der Notwendigkeit der Überwindung des Gesetzes überhaupt, in allen seinen Teilen als Gesetz.

Das verdeutlicht die Systematik. Die Unterscheidung der *lex divina* nach *moralia*, *caerimonialia*, und *iudicialia*[87] basiert zwar auf bewusste Unter-

---

und deren Richtung (ST 1-2. 102.4 ad 6). Ähnlich Wilhelm von Auvergne, *De fide et legibus* 31 col. 2, ebenfalls mit der Berufung auf Josephus; im Unterschied zu Wilhelm, begnügt sich Thomas jedoch mit zwei Begründungsmodi.

[87] Zur Systematik R. P. Chenu, "La théologie de la Loi Ancienne selon S. Thomas," *Revue Thom.* 61 (1961) 485ff. Die Tradition dieser Begriffe ist in der Tat aus der biblischen Terminologie verständlich (מצוות, חוקים, משפטים).

Ursprünglich mag es ein Unterschied nicht nur des Geltungsbereiches (Gerichtswesen, Kultisches), sondern auch der Rezeptionsquellen gewesen sein (doch siehe, gegen A. Alt, J. Meek, *Hebrew Origins* [New York 1963] 72ff). Für den Midrasch gilt חוק als unbefragbare גזירה, gleich dem Naturgesetz (חוקים שחקקתי בהם שמים וארץ)— in einer umgekehrten Bedeutung dessen, was das Mittelalter unter Naturgesetz versteht (Numeri Rabba 16.1, ed. Mirkin [Jerusalem 1960] 147ff.; Lev. Rabba 35.4 zu Lev. 26.3). משפטים = דינים (begründete Urteilssprüche, Gesetze) Exod. Rabba 30; ebd. f. 16a auch die Gleichsetzung תורה = דברות im engeren Sinne. Diese Tradition mag Hieronymus beeinflusst haben. Er übersetzt תורה mit *lex*, Gebote (oder Verfügungen), מצוות mit *praecepta* (Lev. 27.34; Deut. 7.11) oder *mandata* (Ex. 14.12)—letzteres dort, wo davon die Rede ist, dass die Gebote Moses "übergeben" werden. משפטים (Urteile) übersetzt er stets mit *iudicia*: der terminus ist in jedem Kontext deutlich abgrenzbar. Nicht immer deutlich übersetzbar ist das Wort חוקים (Gesetze). Je nach der inhaltlichen Bestimmbarkeit wird es übersetzt: *lex*, *leges* (Ex. 28.43; Lev. 26.15); *praecepta* (Lev. 18.4; 25.18; so insbesondere in der spezifischen Verbindung חוקים ומשפטים). An einigen Stellen, die sich auf das Kultische beziehen, ist חוקים mit *caerimoniae* übersetzt (Num. 9.3). Das gleiche gilt bei Geboten der Gottesverehrung zur Bekämpfung des Götzendienstes (Deut. 6.24; 7.11; 8.11). Aus dieser Übersetzungspraxis gewinnt man den Eindruck, dass Hieronymus die Deutung des Zeremonialgesetzes als Mittel zur Bekämpfung des Heidentums—eine Deutung, die er kannte (oben Anm. 70)—durchaus akzeptierte. Die Unterscheidung zwischen den Gesetzesgattungen blieb fester Bestandteil der christlichen Exegese. Die *Glossa ord.* führt aus (zu Deut. 8.11, PL 113.461D mit Berufung auf den Ps.-Ambrosius): "'Iudicia': Quae per Moysen post legem datam diversis temporibus populo praecepta sunt, quae in Exodo iustificationes appellantur. 'Et Caeremonias': Circumcisionem, ritus sacrificiorum. Unde Ambrosius super Epistolam ad Romanos: Triplex (inquit) est lex, prima

scheidungen zwischen den alttestamentlichen Gebotskategorien, die schon
längst Bestandteil der christlichen Exegese wurden und auch die Wortwahl
der Vulgata bestimmt hatten. Doch zeigt die inhaltliche Bestimmung dieser
Kategorien bei Thomas seine Vertrautheit mit dem *More* auch dort, wo er
von ihm abweicht. Auch für ihn gilt: "Intentio legis divinae est ut constituat
principaliter amicitiam hominis ad Deum,"[88] und zwar auch dort, wo zwischen-
menschliche Beziehungen genormt werden. Gemeinsam ist auch die Unterscheidung zwischen *moralia* und *iudicialia*, nicht aber die Funktionsbestim-
mung der Moralgesetztes: Thomas (in der Tradition der christlichen Exegese)
identifiziert es mit dem Naturgesetz (aus welchem Grunde der Dekalog all-
gemeingültig ist, und zwar "non quia erant de veteri lege, sed quia erant de
lege natura").[89] Sowohl die *iudicialia* als auch die *caerimonialia* sind nur
zeitgebundene, positive Bestimmungen des Moralgesetzes.[90] Diese weitaus
allgemeinere Definition (im Vergleich zu תקון המידות bei Maimuni) muss
im Zusammenhang mit der Tatsache interpretiert werden, dass andererseits Thomas keine besondere Kategorie der "Meinungsgebote" kennt: für
Maimonides war sie die oberste.[91] Für Thomas bilden die Zeremonialgesetze
eine besondere Gruppe; bei Maimonides waren sie insgesamt eine negative
und positive Vorbereitung auf "wahre Meinungen," auf die wahre Gotteserkenntnis, (wobei es für beide von Bestimmungen handelt, die ihre Begründungen nicht aus sich selbst haben, sondern *ex ordine ad aliud*). Diese Funktion hatte dagegen das mosaische Gesetz für Thomas insgesamt—sofern es
über sich selbst hinausweist.

Die Unterschiede in den Angaben über die Strukturprinzipien reflektieren
daher, jenseits jeder Übereinstimmung im Detail wie in der Methode, die
unterschiedlichen Auffassungen hinsichtlich des mosaischen Gesetzes. Für
Maimonides enthält das mosaische Gesetz sowohl die zeitlose Zielsetzung
der intellektuellen Vervollkommnung als auch die jeder Gemeinschaft gezie-
menden Normen und, als notwendige Vorbereitung und Konkretisierung beider,
auch zeitgebundene Verfügungen. Von solcher Art ist auch das Zeremonialgesetz (im Gegensatz zum Gebet, zum Gemeinschaftsgottesdienst). Besser als
seine christlichen Vorgänger begründet Thomas hingegen, dass das gesamte
Gesetz vorbereitender Natur ist und auf ein anderes hinweist. Zwar nicht
so, als wäre es aus sich selbst schlechthin unverständlich: wohl aber, insofern
seine letztliche Verwirklichung nicht in seinem Horizont geschehen kann.

Die Widersprüchlichkeit der maimonideischen Gesetzestheorie rührte daher,
dass Maimonides an der Ewigkeit des mosaischen Gesetzes festhalten muss;

---

pars de sacramento divinitatis; secunda congruit legi naturali, quae peccatum interdicit;
tertia festorum legis, id est, sabbata, neomeniae, et circumcisio."

[88] ST 1-2.99.2.

[89] ST 1-2.98.5. Der Naturbegriff war Maimonides fremd; vgl. oben Anm. 26.

[90] ST 1-2.99.4 ad 2; 100.11.

[91] Siehe oben S. 153

es ist für ihn eine allgemeine, je nach Ort und Zeit zu bestimmende Formel
sowie ein nach örtlichen und zeitlichen Bedingungen schon bestimmtes Gesetz.
Die Aufgabe des Aquinaten ist eine viel einfachere. Er muss bloss die Übereinstimmung der *lex divina* mit der *lex naturalis* so aufweisen, dass die letztere als die einmal bestimmte Form des ersteren esrcheint. Das wird besonders deutlich in der Diskussion der politischen Verfassung *(iudicialia)*,
wo Thomas ohnehin mit anderen Kategorien als Maimonides operiert, da
ihm die aristotelische Politik bereits vertraut war. Als "bestgeordnet" erscheint ihm die alttestamentliche Herrschaftsstruktur, weil sie (der ursprüng-
lichen Verfassung nach) ein wirkliches *regimen mixtum* darstellt;[92] (nur) *suffi-
cienter* erscheint ihm die *communicatio hominum ad invicem* genormt.[93] Wenn
im Naturgesetz nur die Notwendigkeit der *distinctio possessionum* und ihre
Aufhebung im Gemeinnutzen *(commune quoad usum)* festgelegt ist, so hat
das bestimmte, positive oder göttliche Gesetz die Aufgabe, diese Bestimmung
materiell zu determinieren, sie zu einem individuellen Gesetz zu machen.
Dass dies auch in der *lex vetus* geschah, beweist Thomas, nicht aber, dass es
eine für alle Zeiten verbindliche, und nicht einmal, dass es die best denkbare
Konkretion war. Was die *iudicialia* anbelangt; ist ihm das alttestamentliche
Gesetz zwar eine Erfahrungsquelle, keinesfalls aber ein Ersatz für die *adinventio humanae rationis*, der es obliegt, durch steten Erfahrungswachstum
behutsam neue Gesetze einzuführen; auf solche situationsgebundene Kon-
kretionen ist das Naturgesetz angewiesen, wie umgekehrt sich das positive
Gesetz stets durch das natürliche legitimieren muss.[94]

Thomas, wie einige seiner unmittelbaren Vorgänger, rezipierte also die maimonideische Gesetzeslehre so, dass der radikal historisierende Ansatz Maimunis stark gemildert wurde. Zwar hätte man annehmen können, die christliche Exegese müsste für zusätzliche Beweise für die Zeitgebundenheit der
lex vetus stets empfänglich sein; das stimmt aber für die Exegese vor dem
13. Jahrhundert nicht, und auch für Thomas nur bedingt. Noch weniger
war er bereit, die umgekehrte Position zu beziehen, und in der historischen
Begründung des Alten Testaments bloss ein Hindernis im Wege des figürlichen Verständnisses zu sehen. Ihm war es klar, dass die historische Begründung eine unerlässliche Vorbedingung der *intelligentia spiritualis* sein
muss, wenn diese sich nicht in Spekulationen verlieren will. Aber ebenso
war es ihm bewusst, dass die historische Begründung, um als plausible und

---

[92] ST 1-2.105.1; zur Lehre vom regimen mixtum bei Thomas; W. Berges, *Die Fürsten-
spiegel des hohen und späten Mittelalters*, Aufl. 2, Schriften der MGH 2 (Stuttgart 1952)
198ff.

[93] ST 1-2.105.2.

[94] Auf die Bedeutung der Erfahrungslehre im politischen Denken des Aquinaten hat
Berges 196ff. hingewiesen.

genügende Basis der figuralen dienen zu können,[95] nicht bloss aus *einem* Abschnitt der Zeit *sub lege* bezogen werden kann: und letzten Endes beweist Maimonides seine Deutungen des Ritualgesetzes aus der Zeit vor Moses. Aus der Art und Weise, in der Thomas die Gesetzesdeutung Maimunis rezipierte, ablehnte oder umdeutete, können wir in die subtile Synthese zwischen der litteralen und figürlichen Deutung der *vetus lex*, die ihm vorschwebte, Einblick gewinnen.

Gänzlich unreflektiert erscheint dagegen wieder der Gebrauch, den Raimundus Martini—Zeitgenosse und Ordensbruder des Aquinaten—von Maimunis Gesetzeslehre macht.[96] Sein *Pugio fidei* blieb die gelehrteste und bestdokumentierte Polemik gegen das Judentum, die das Mittelalter hervorbrachte; Er kannte die jüdische Literatur aus erster Quelle, und benutzte sie auf zweierlei Ebenen. Im ersten Teil seiner Schrift zeigt er die einmütige Haltung der Christen wie der Irrenden, die dennoch "legem habentes," gegenüber Heiden und "philosophi": So wird er z. B. den Unterschied zwischen der diskursiven menschlichen Erkenntnis und der intuitiven Erkenntnis Gottes mit einem Midrasch-Zitat belegen,[97] und so benutzt er die Argumente Maimunis in der Diskussion um die Ewigkeit der Welt. In den Auseinandersetzungen mit dem Judentum hingegen dient ihm die jüdische Literatur als Beweis dafür, dass auch die nachbiblische jüdische Tradition Hinweise auf die Wahrheit des Dogmas enthält. So beruft er sich auch auf die Gesetzeslehre Maimunis, um den Ewigkeitsanspruch der *vetus lex* aus jüdischen Quellen zu widerlegen. Ausführlicher als Thomas zitiert er aus dem dritten Teil des *More Nebukim*[98] —daneben aber, in scheinbarer Ergänzung, stellt er die figurale Schriftdeutung. Es fehlt auch hier gänzlich der Versuch, verschiedene Interpretationsebenen der Schrift gegeneinander zu bestimmen: erst bei einem derartigen Versuch wären ihm, ähnlich wie Thomas, die Schwierigkeiten aufgegangen, die in der zunächst bestechenden historisierenden Hermeneutik Maimunis enthalten sind.

[95] ST 1-2.104.4: "Similiter etiam status veteris legis, sicut dictum est, institutus erat ad figurandum mysterium Christi, oportet autem esse aliquid determinatum id per quod aliud figurari debet, ut scilicet eius aliquam similitudinem repraesentet." Vgl. 102.3: "Rationes sacrificiorum figuralium veteris legis sunt summendae ex vero sacrificio Christi."

[96] Auf die Schrift Martinis, wie auf die spätmittelalterliche christliche Exegese, geht Guttmann, *Der Einfluss der Maimonid. Philosophie* (oben Anm. 78) nicht ein.

[97] *Pugio fidei* 1.23, p. 246f.; über "legem habentes vel sibi legis vocabulum arrogantes" (letzterer charakterisiert wohl den Islam) oben Anm. 56. Über seine jüdische Quellen vgl. Liebermann, שְׁקִיעִין מדרשׁיו המווירפים (Jerusalem 1938) sowie (dagegen.) I. Baer, קל"ן (ירושלים) 1942.). של ריימונדוס מדטיני, ספר הזכרון לא· גולאק, וש. קל"

[98] *Pugio fidei* 3.12 (809f.): "Et nota quod iste Rabi Moseh . . . ostendit, qualiter Deus pie curat de omnibus animantibus et ideo quia ab unaquaque re in suum contrarium difficilis est semper egressus, nunquam mutat aliquam ex iis subito naturaliter ex uno statu totaliter ad contrarium" etc: es folgen ausführliche Zitate.

SCHLUSSBEMERKUNGEN

Von den Gemeinsamkeiten in der Gesetzesinterpretation bei Maimonides und Thomas erscheint dem heutigen Leser die historische Begrenzung des Idealcharakters des Alten Testament als politische Verfassung wohl als die interessanteste. Doch enthielt, wie wir zu zeigen versuchten, der "historisierende" Ansatz Maimunis vergleichsweise mehr Reibungspunkte mit der bisherigen Tradition als seine Umwandlung im "Figuralen Realismus"[99] des Aquinaten. Darum wurde dieser Teil von Maimunis Lehre im Mittelalter weitgehend verändert, bekämpft, oder ignoriert;[100] und darum spielt er eine nicht unbedeutende Rolle in den Anfängen der neuzeitlichen Bibelkritik.

Doch dieses allein erklärt seinen Einfluss auf die historische Kritik seit dem 16. Jahrhundert noch nicht. Überschaut man die Nuancen seiner Rezeption bei Spinoza und Simon, bei den englischen Deisten,[101] bei Mendelssohn,[102] so lassen sich deutlich die ungewandelten Intentionen von der vertieften Methode unterscheiden. In dieser oder anderer Form ist allen gemeinsam, dass sie bei Maimonides einen Beleg für die Interpretation des Judentums (oder zumindest eines Teiles seiner Gesetze) als blosse Staatsverfassung, und insofern historisch bedingt, finden. Sodann aber, was von weitaus grösserer Wichtigkeit ist, stand Maimonides im Einklang mit einem der wichtigsten Prinzipien der neuzeitlichen historischen Kritik—mit der Einsicht dass Vergangenheit, und sei sie ein Teil der eigenen Kultur, als fremd begriffen und darum aus versteckten Hinweisen rekonstruiert werden muss.[103]

1) Für die Umkehrung der Intentionen ist Spinoza das radikalste Beispiel. Für Maimonides' radikale Historisierung interessiert er sich nur insofern sie seiner Kritik der institutionellen Religion und Bibelauslegung dienlich ist.

---

[99] Mit diesem Ausdruck hat E. Auerbach den Realismus Dantes charakterisiert: *Mimesis; Dastellungen der Wirklichkeit in der abendländischen Literatur*, 2 ed. (Bern 1959) 185ff. Die Bezeichnung liesse sich mit gutem Recht auf die methodische Synthese des Thomas übertragen: Realgrundlage und figura verhalten sich wie Potenz zur Aktualisierung.

[100] Eine besondere Rolle spielte das maimonideische Interpretationsmodell auch weiterhin in der Polemik. Die Reflexion zur Entwicklung der Offenbarung bei Alfunso von Valladolid (Abner von Burgos) ist eine Inversion des maimonideischen Interpretations-models; über ihn siehe J. Baer, *A History of the Jews in Christian Spain*, hebr. (Tel-Aviv 1959) 192ff., insbes. 200ff. Über die Rezeption des Maimonides in der antijüdischen Polemik hoffe ich an einer anderen Stelle zu berichten. In diesen Zusammenhang gehört auch die Kritik Albos.

[101] Hierzu J. Guttmann, "John Spencers Erklärung der biblischen Gesetze in ihrer Beziehung zu Maimonides," *Festschrift für D. Simosen* (Kopenhagen 1923) 258ff. sowie S. Ettinger, "Jews and Judaism as seen by the English Deists of the Eighteenth Century," *Zion* 29 (1964) 182ff.

[102] Über Mendelssohn und Spinoza, J. Guttmann, "Mendelssohns Jerusalem und Spinozas theologisch-politischer Traktat," *48ter Bericht der Hochschule für die Wissenschaft des Judentums* (Berlin 1931) 31ff.

[103] Siehe unten, Anm. 111.

Spinoza's Sinnentlehrung des Offenbarungsbegriffes wurde von Strauss ana-
lysiert;[104] implizit folgt hieraus die Destruktion aller Vorstellungen von der
göttlichen Pädagogie, explizit die Destruktion des Auserwähltheitsbegriffes.
Dass Gott nicht unmittelbar in die Geschichte eingreifen will, wo sein Eingreifen die Aufhebung der menschlichen Natur zur Folge hätte: das war die
Voraussetzung des maimonideischen Pädagogieprinzips, das umschrieb er
mit der Listmetapher. Dass ein solches Eingreifen eine *contradictio in ad-
jecto*, sozusagen auch *potestate dei absoluta*[105] unmöglich sei, ist Spinozas Voraussetzung; eine spezielle Offenbarung als göttlicher Willensakt kann es nicht
geben.[106] Folglich muss auch der Begriff der "Auserwähltheit" auf das, was
er immanent historisch-politisch bedeuten kann, reduziert werden. Auserwähltheit ist keine *qualitas obscura* (wie sie z. T. Jehuda Halevi begründete)
und kann auch kein Zeichen der besonderen Fürsorge Gottes sein. Sie ist
nur das, was sie *prima facie* zu sein scheint—metaphorische Bezeichnung
für den politischen Erfolg eines Gemeinschaftsverbandes während einer
begrenzten Zeitspanne, gesichert durch eine angemessene Verfassung. So
gesehen, waren auch die Kena' aniter "Auserwählte"[107] gleich jedem Gemeinschaftsverband hinsichtlich seiner Leistungen.

Darum kann auch die "Übertragung" der Auserwähltheit auf das spirituelle
Israel keinen konkreten Sinn haben. Eine ähnliche Sinnentlehrung vermittels
einer Reduktion auf den bloss politischen Inhalt erfuhr zuvor, seit der Renaissance, ein anderer Translationsbegriff—die Vorstellung von der *translatio imperii*.[108] Aber auch die methodische Suche nach Präfigurationen der

---

[104] Leo Strauss, *Spinoza's Critique of Religion* (New York 1965), englische Übersetzung
des 1930 im Akademischen Verlag erschienenen Buches *Die Religionskritik Spinozas*,
insbes. 147ff., 165ff. Vgl. neuerdings A. Malet, *Le traité theologico-politique de Spinoza
et la pensée biblique* (Paris 1966) 19-70.

[105] Die Unterscheidung zwischen *potentia dei absoluta et ordinata* benutzt Spinoza in
Cogitata metaphysia 2.9 (ed. Vloten 4.219). Er setzt *potentia absoluta* mit der Macht,
Naturgesetze zu brechen, gleich, bezweifelt die Legimität der Unterscheidung (wohl gegen Descartes) und schliesst (sehr im kartesischen Geist): "Verum hoc decernere theolo-
gis relinquimus." In der Ethik hat er diese Unterscheidung längst aufgehoben und braucht
sie nicht. Auf die möglichen spätscholastischen Quellen Spinozas geht H. Wolfson, *The
Philosophy of Spinoza* (1934, Neudruck New York 1969) kaum ein.

[106] *Tractatus theologico-politicus*, ed. Vloten (Haag 1882) 1.407ff.

[107] *Ibid.* 3.418. Im Zusammenhang seines Auserwähltheitsbegriffes ist auch die berühmte
Erwägung zu sehen, dass bei gegebener politischer Konstellation und wenn die Juden in
ihrer Isolation "unverweichlicht" beharren werden, sie die politische Souveränität wieder-
erlangen könnten. Über die jüdische mittelalterliche Quelle solcher Gedankengänge siehe
S. Pines, "Joseph Ibn Kaspi's and Spinoza's Opinions on the Probability of a Restoration
of the Jewish State," *Iyyun* 14-15 (1963-1964) 289ff.

[108] Über Machiavellis Vorstellung von der Übertragung der *virtus*, die er in der nach-
antiken Zeit auf viele Nationen verteilt sieht, siehe F. Meinecke, *Die Idee der Staatsraison*,
Werke, hrsg. W. Hofer, ed. 2, 1 (München 1960) 37ff., insbes. 40f. (und die dort zitierte Arbeit E. W. Mayers). Zur *Regna*-Lehre Bodins siehe A. Klempt, *Die Säkularisierung der
universalhistorischen Auffassung* (Göttingen 1960) 67f.

Kirchengeschichte in der vorchristlichen Geschichte Israels und seinen In-
stitutionen verliert ihre Legitimation. Überlegen ist das Christentum dem
Gesetz Moses allein darum, weil das letztere den Menschen in seiner Unmündig-
keit beliess. Demgemäss überträgt Spinoza Maimonides' Interpretation des
Ritualgesetzes aus dem Niveau der Zeit, in der es gegeben wurde, auf das
Gesetz überhaupt. Schlüsselbegriff der historischen Deutung ist ihm allerdings nicht der zu überwindende Götzendienst, sondern die Sklavennatur
und Sklavengewohnheiten der Juden zur Zeit der Gesetzesstiftung. Schon
darum kann das Gesetzeswerk Moses nicht als Idealverfassung gelten, sondern
als bewunderswerte Anpassung des Ziels an die Gegebenheiten.

Diese Interessenverschiebung macht es deutlich, warum Spinoza an Maimuni's Rekonstruktionsversuchen nicht sonderlich interessiert war, und
ebensowenig an ähnlichen Gedankengängen seiner eigenen Zeit. Von einer
"Entwicklung" Israels während der biblischen Zeit, und sei es nur (wie bei
Maimonides) von einer fortschreitenden Aufhebung des Aberglaubens, kann
bei ihm nicht die Rede sein. Die Bibelgeschichte interessiert ihn vor allem
als Substrat der kritischen Textgeschichte.[109] Das Alte Testament will keine
"rechten Meinungen" vermitteln. Apodiktisch ist nur sein (mittlerweile
überholter) Gesetzesteil, als Staatsverfassung eines mittlerweiler aufgelösten
Staatsverbandes. Darüber hinaus enthält die Schrift nur Hinweise für das
ethisch-religiöse Verhalten, dem Niveau ihrer Zeit angepasst. So gesehen,
ist zwar die Bibel (anders, als Hobbes es haben wollte) "aus sich selbst" verständlich, doch nur als ein vielschichtiger Text, von verschiedenen Mentali-
täten zu verschiedenen Zeiten verfasst. Erst der Verfall, i.e. die Institutiona-
lisierung der Religion, brachte es mit sich, dass die Schrift dogmatisiert wurde.
Da also die Kanonisierung als historischer Prozess (und nicht die historischen
Entwicklungen als solche) im Mittelpunkt des Beweiszusammenhanges des
theologisch-politischen Traktats steht, ist Spinoza natürlich der Tradition
der biblischen Textkritik, deren Ansätze er bis zurück zu Ibn Ezra's zerstreuten
Hinweisen überschaute, weitaus mehr als Maimonides verpflichtet.

2) Die unmittelbare Rolle des Maimonides war auch in einer anderen
Hinsicht eine beschränkte. In den verschieden Theorien hinsichtlich der
"ägyptischen" Ursprünge der mosaischen Gesetzgebung kam es dabei zu
einer kuriosen Synthese zwischen seinem Ansatz und den über Josephus
bekannten Fragmenten der antiken antijüdischen Polemik.[110] Die Triebfeder
solcher Überlegungen war wiederum, ähnlich wie in der humanistischen
Kritik des römischen Rechts, die Irrelevanz oder gar Rückständigkeit einer
angeblichen Idealverfassung aufzuzeigen. Als dieser polemische Impetus abebb-

---

[109] Hierüber, neben Strauss, neuerdings Y. Yovel, "Critique of Religion and Scriptural
Interpretation in Spinoza and Kant," *Iyyun* 17.4 (1968) 240ff. Der Verfasser betont zu
Recht den eigentlich ahistorischen Charakter der Ausführungen Spinoza's.
[110] Siehe oben Anm. 44.

te, und als die rationalistische Vorliebe für Stifterfiguren durch Theorien anonymer Ursprünge ersetzt wurde, verlor die Gesetzesdeutung Maimuni's auch diese Funktion als älteste Bestätigung der eigenen historisch-kritischen Ansätze. Es ist also vornehmlich um des methodischen Prinzips willen, dass es sich verlohnen würde, seine mittelbare und unmittelbare Stellung in der neuzeitlichen Literatur zu verfolgen.

Denn in seiner Rekonstruktionsmethode des sabäischen *Kontext* des entstehenden Judentums hatte Maimonides ein Grundprinzip der neuzeitlichen historischen Kritik vorweggenommen—ihre Aufforderung, Vergangenheit nicht aus ihrer Ähnlichkeit mit dem Gegenwärtigen und nicht in ihrer Relevanz zum Gegenwärtigen zu verstehen, sondern in ihrer Andersartigkeit zu rekonstruieren.[111] Ein derartiges *Verstehen durch Entfremdung* (des zuverstehenden) hatte sich in der Kritik der römischen Rechtsquellen, in den Altertumswissenschaften, in der Religionskunde[112] wie in der Bibelkritik seit dem 16. Jahrhundert manifestiert,[113] längst ehe es in die Praxis der Geschichtsschreibung eindrang.

Vico's Verdienst war es nicht, diese Methode entdeckt zu haben. Er hat die Ansätze seiner Vorgänger vertieft und zu einer Entwicklungstheorie ausgestaltet: ihr lag ein neuer Periodenbegriff zugrunde, die Vorstellung einer (idealen) Zeiteinheit, deren Gestaltungsprinzipien in ihr selbst liegen und zugleich ihre Aufhebung bedingen. Darüber hinaus gab er der historischen Hermeneutik, dem Instrument seiner "neuen Wissenschaft," eine tragfähige epistemologische Begründung. "Verum et factum convertuntur"[114] bedeutet

---

[111] Darauf hat vor allem J. G. A. Pocock, *The Ancient Constituuion and the Feudal Law; A Study of English Historical Thought in the Seventeenth Century* (Cambridge 1957) 1ff., hingewiesen.

[112] Hierüber (neben der oben Anm. genannten lit.), F. E. Manuel, *The Eighteenth Century Confronts the Gods* (New York 1967). Zum Einfluss Maimunis (vor allem des Tractats Avoda Zara aus den Mishne Tora) ebd. 8, 48, 130.

[113] Als ein Gemeinplatz erscheint z. B. diese Einsicht bereits in der Kirchengeschichte Franz Budde's: "Saepius animadverti, plurimis mortalium, etiam praestantissimis viris, contingere, ut de rebus antiquissimis secundum sui tempoiis conditionem notiones animo forment. Quo ipso non tantum in errores gravissimos probabuntur, sed figurentis quamplurimis, saepius ineptissimis, campum latissimum aperiunt." *Historia ecclesiastica* (Jena 1715 u. 1719, 3. Aufl. 1726) Praef.; bei Diestel, *Geschichte des Alten Testaments* 463.

[114] Über das Prinzip "Verum et factum convertuntui," und über Vico's Erkenntnislehre überhaupt, siehe (neben Croce's klassischen Untersuchung) neuerdings die Aufsätze von L. Berlin und N. Baldoni in: *Giambattista Vico; an International Symposium* ed. G. Toglia Cozzo and H. V. White (Baltimore 1969) 379ff, 391ff. Dass Vico eine mittelbare Kenntnis des Maimonides hatte, ist unwahrscheinlich. Das gleiche gilt von der Bibelkritik. Sollte er sie auch gekannt haben, so hatte ei sie mittels der Unterscheidung zwischen der Geschichte der *gentes* und der Heilsgeschichte aus seinen Betrachtungen verbannen können. Er stand eher in der unmittelbaren Tiadition der historischen Rechtskiitik und Altertumswissenschaft. Es ist meine Absicht, den in dei Schlussbemerkung angedeuteten Fragenkomplex an einer anderen Stelle ausführlich zu behandeln.

nicht zuletzt, dass in der Arbeit des Verstehen der seine spontane Inhalte rekapitulierende menschliche Geist zur Selbstkenntnis kommt. Man könnte sagen: die Entfremdung der Vergangenen, die Voraussetzung dieses Bemühens, wird als Ergebnis seines Gelingens wieder überwunden.

Department of History
University of California
Los Angeles, California 90024, U.S.A.

THE SOURCE AND MEANING OF CONJOINTURE IN CHRETIEN'S EREC 14

•

by Douglas Kelly

Por ce dist Crestïens de Troies
que reisons est que totevoies
doit chascuns panser et antandre
a bien dire et a bien aprandre;
et tret d'un conte d'avanture
une molt bele conjointure
par qu'an puet prover et savoir
que cil ne fet mie savoir
qui s'escïence n'abandone
tant con Dex la grasce l'an done:
d'Erec, le fil Lac, est li contes,
que devant rois et devant contes
depecier et corronpre suelent
cil qui de conter vivre vuelent.[1]

There has been no systematic effort to determine the precise meaning of *conjointure* as it appears in the beginning of Chrétien's *Erec*, and to fit the term into a poetic tradition. There are of course many who have proposed a "definition" of it,[2] and most scholars do agree that for Chrétien *conjointure* more or less describes narrative structure. W. A. Nitze, in a number of separate studies, set forth what is perhaps the most authoritative commentary on the term. He derives it from *iunctura* in Horace's *Ars poetica* (*Ad Pisones*), verse 242;[3] but Horace uses *iunctura* in reference not to plot or narrative

---

[1] *Erec et Enide* 9-22, ed. Mario Roques, Classiques français du Moyen Âge (CFMA) (Paris 1955).

[2] See Erich Köhler, "Zur Selbstauffassung des höfischen Dichters," in *Trobadorlyrik und höfischer Roman* (Berlin 1962) 14-15.

[3] *Q. Horati Flacci opera*, ed. E. C. Wickham and H. W. Garrod, ed. 2 (Oxford 1959). See, for example, W. A. Nitze, "The Romance of Erec, Son of Lac," *Modern Philology* (MP) 11 (1913-1914) 487; "'Sans et matière' dans les œuvres de Chrétien de Troyes," *Romania* 44 (1915-1917) 16 n. 1; "Arthurian Problems," *Bulletin bibliographique de la Société internationale arthurienne* (BBSIA) 5 (1953) 76-79; "Conjointure in *Erec*, vs. 14," *Modern*

structure, but rather to artful and elegant syntax.[4] Since Nitze failed to explain *iunctura*, *conjointure* remained in itself an unknown. He was therefore able to attribute to the term a variety of meanings. In some places, *conjointure* is identified with a basic story pattern contained in Chrétien's source, a pattern fundamental to all his poems. Elsewhere Nitze makes it equivalent to Chrétien's own arrangement of disparate material in the composition of the poem. In the article on *Perlesvaus* in *Arthurian Literature in the Middle Ages*, Nitze equates *conjointure* with the principle of *entrelacement*, composition by interlacing of different episodes or tales as Ferdinand Lot and Professor Vinaver have used the term for French and English prose romance. It is true that interlacing is used in the structure of *Perlesvaus*; but are we justified in equating the principle of interlacing with Chrétien's term *conjointure*? In other words, did Chrétien use interlacing in *Erec* and his other poems? And does Chrétien's Celtic story pattern or a Celtic story pattern lie behind the composition of works where interlacing is obvious, such as *Perlesvaus* and the Lancelot in Prose? Nitze offers no answer to these questions. The confusion arises largely from the fact that Nitze speaks on the one hand of a *conjointure* in Chrétien's source, on the other of *conjointure* as the disposition given to that work by Chrétien himself. The failure to make a sharp distinction between *matière* and arrangement of *matière* is hardly conducive to an understanding of what Chrétien meant by the term in *Erec*.

D. W. Robertson, Jr., has called attention to a passage in Alan of Lille's *De planctu Naturae* containing an example of *coniunctura* in the sense of narrative structure:[5] "When Chrétien says that his poem is 'une mout bele conjointure,' he implies (1) that it is a fable as opposed to an actual sequence of events, a *conjunctura* of events not joined in nature; (2) that this *conjunctura* is 'bele,' that is, that it is made 'cum decore aliquo'; and (3) that this pleasing *cortex* covers a *nucleus* of truth."[6] Mario Roques criticized Robertson's interpretation of *conjointure*: "Par les vers si souvent cités du prologue d'*Erec* . . . Chrétien voudrait faire entendre [according to Robert-

---

Language Notes (MLN) 69 (1954) 180-181; "Perlesvaus," *Arthurian Literature in the Middle Ages*, ed. R. S. Loomis (Oxford 1959) 270-273.

[4] "Tantum series iuncturaque pollet, / tantum de medio sumptis accedit honoris" (vv. 242-243). The term also appears earlier, although not in precisely the same sense as in v. 242: "dixeris egregie notum si callida verbum / reddiderit iunctura novum" (vv. 47-48). In the latter instance, Horace is speaking of the *callida iunctura*, the combination of current words in an unexpected or unusual way; in the former instance, of elegant syntax in general. On this distinction, see Adolf Kiessling and Richard Heinze, *Q. Horatius Flaccus: Briefe*, ed. 6 (Berlin 1959) 296-297, 332; A. Rostagni, *Arte poetica di Orazio* (Turin 1930) 14-15, 69-70; and especially M. Ruch, "Horace et les fondements de la 'iunctura' dans l'ordre de la création poétique (AP 46-72)," *Revue des études latines* 41 (1963) 246-269.

[5] "Some Medieval Literary Terminology, with Special Reference to Chrétien de Troyes," *Studies in Philology* (SP) 48 (1951) 669-692; see esp. 670-671, 684-686.

[6] *Ibid.* 685.

son] que, d'un récit plus ou moins authentique, il a tiré une très belle combinaison faite avec des éléments fabuleux. Mais la proportion du fabuleux est bien réduite dans cette combinaison, et l'emploi du verbe *tret* serait peu exact s'appliquant à un seul des éléments de cette combinaison." Roques asked: "La combinaison ne peut-elle pas se comprendre comme l'arrangement d'éléments divers, de scènes décousues et sans lien, telles que les présentent les jongleurs?"[7] But this is precisely how Robertson does understand the term: "The poet . . . uses diverse materials from various places. The persons, places, or events he describes may or may not be actual persons, places, or events, but the sequence in which he places them is his own. The new sequence is the *conjunctura*."[8] There is, therefore, no problem with Chrétien's use of *tret* with *conjointure* as Robertson interprets the term.

Although Robertson appears to accept Nitze's derivation of *conjointure* from Horace's *iunctura*, he disallows a passage from Philippe Mousket cited by Nitze in support of that derivation:[9]

> [Grammar] nos ensegne en quel manière
> on doit escrire les figures
> et asambler les congointures.[10]

Robertson objects that here *congointure* "is concerned with the elements of composition." Nitze responds by asking: "Are not Horace and Alain [in the *De planctu Naturae*] . . . speaking about 'composition?'"[11] In fact Robertson's criticism is well founded. Nitze commits the same error in reading *congointure* in Mousket that he does in reading *iunctura* in Horace. Both these authors are speaking about composition in the sentence (*compositio*), whereas Alan and Chrétien are plainly speaking about narrative composition.

The passage cited by Robertson from the *De planctu Naturae* demands some textual comment. Robertson cites Alan from Migne's *Patrologia latina* (210.451). It reads somewhat differently in Thomas Wright's more reliable edition in the Rolls Series,[12] and the differences are useful for the discussion to follow. I shall cite the relevant passage, including significant variations and commentary in the notes.

---

[7] Review of Robertson's article, *Romania* 73 (1952) 551. Cf. Nitze, MLN 69.181; BBSIA 5.77 n. 13.

[8] Robertson 684. Thus Robertson concurs in Nitze's earliest formulation: "the combination of features or motifs taken from that [i.e. the poem's] source" (MP 11.487).

[9] Robertson 670 n. 7.

[10] Philippe Mousket, *Chronique rimée* 9703-9705, ed. Baron de Reiffenberg, 2 vols. (Brussels 1836-38). Cf. v. 9705 note: "*Congointures*, les divers membres de la phrase."

[11] MLN 69.181 n. 1.

[12] *The Anglo-Latin Satirical Poets and Epigrammatists of the Twelfth Century*, Rolls Series 59 (Oxford 1872) 2.465-466.

> Poetae aliquando historiales eventus joculationibus fabulosis, quasi quadam eleganti structura,[13] confoederant, ut ex diversorum competenti junctura[14] ipsius narrationis elegantior pictura resultet.

Thus the more probable reading of the term in Alan si not *coniunctura* but *iunctura*, as in Horace.

Robertson's and Nitze's studies raise a question that must be answered if we are to understand what Chrétien meant by *conjointure*: what if any relation is there between Horace's use of *iunctura* and Mousket's of *congointure* on the one hand, and Chrétien's *conjointure* and Alan's *iunctura* on the other? The question is fundamental: If two important twelfth-century authors, the one writing in Latin, the other in French, employ the same term to describe narrative composition, an understanding of how they used that term will certainly help us better to appreciate the composition of medieval narrative literature. Let us look first at commentaries on Horace's *Ars poetica* which have survived from late Roman and medieval times.

Porphyrion's is the earliest surviving commentary on Horace's poetry.[15] His gloss for *iunctura*, verse 48 (there is none for verse 242) merely confirms the interpretations of modern scholars to the effect that the term describes the disposition of words: "*Dixeris egregie notum si callida verbum.* Exponit nunc de uerbis ueteribus ac nouis, quo modo poetica sint. Nam licet aliqua uulgaria sint, ait tamen illa cum aliqua conpositione splendescere."[16] Dependent in part on Porphyrion's commentary, the *Scholia* of the so-called pseudo-Acro dates from the fifth century, but contains additions and revisions made down to the end of the medieval period; it sccms to have been the most widely used and respected commentary on Horace's poetry during the Middle Ages. In it we discover the key to the two interpretations of *iunctura*, the one used in Horace, verses 48 and 242, the other in Alan's *De planctu Naturae*. The glosses to verses 47-48 follow essentially the interpretation in Porphyrion;[18] but to verse 242 the pseudo-Acro glosses: "*Tantum series*: Idest ordo

---

[13] Vars.: *sutura, fictura* [*fictura* the reading in Migne].

[14] *Coniunctura* in Migne not found in Wright's variants.

[15] *Pomponii Porphyrionis commentarii in Q. Horatium Flaccum*, ed. Wilhelm Meyer (Leipzig 1874); Meyer dates the commentary at before the end of the fourth century (p. vi).

[16] Meyer 346.

[17] *Pseudacronis scholia in Horatium vetustioria*, ed. Otto Keller, 2 vols. (Leipzig 1902-1904) 2.ix-x; on the ascription to Acro, see ix, and on the dates and relationships among the manuscripts, i-viii.

[18] Keller 2.316: "*Dixeris egregie.* Et cum laude dicis uerbum uulgare, si illud bene composueris.

"Exponit de uerbis ueteribus et nouis, quomodo poetica licentia fiant. Nam aliqua licet uulgaria sint, dicit tamen ea cum aliqua conpositione posse splendescere." The ninth-century *Scholia vindobonensia ad Horatii artem poeticam*, ed. J. Zechmeister (Vienna 1879) 5-6, 29, adds little to what is found in Porphyrion, despite the fact that it derives in part from the pseudo-Acro; see Zechmeister xiv-xviii and Keller 2.xiv.

rerum, diuisio operis, ordo uerborum, *oikonomia*, compositio uerborum, idest tantum ualet ordo et compositio, ut eas difficile sit imitari."[19] This gloss indicates at once the variety of contexts that both *series* and *iunctura* may fit, and the common factor underlying their use in all those contexts: disposition—whether arrangement and disposition of narrative material ("ordo rerum, diuisio operis") or arrangement and disposition of words and phrases in the sentence ("ordo uerborum," etc.). The glossator goes on to make specific application of *series* and *iunctura* within the context of verse 242 in the *Ars poetica* to *compositio*, that is to elegant and artful syntax in the line of verse. In this passage Chrétien's *conjointure* and Alan's *iunctura* find a link with Horace's *iunctura* and Philippe Mousket's *congointure* in the common notion of disposition. Nitze's connection of *conjointure* and *iunctura* is, in this context, not only correct; it is also meaningful.

Series and *iunctura* in verse 242 are not exactly synonymous. The *Scholia vindobonensia* distinguishes between them in the following way: "Nam *tantum pollet series*, id est, ordo verborum *et iunctura* sententiarum."[20] Rostagni clarifies the distinction: "Or[azio] non allude [in v. 242] soltanto alla *synthesis tès lexeōs* in generale (*series*), ma a quell'artificio per cui la parola comune, *applicandosi a una parola o a un'idea* cui non è comunemente riferita, diventa metaforica, e quindi nuova (*iunctura*)."[21] Horace is therefore speaking not only of the order and disposition of words (*series*); he is stressing in particular the way in which words, phrases, and sentences are linked (*iunctura*). For it is precisely the linking that gives distinction and elegance to the style and renders it most effective in communicating ideas and sentiments. Is one justified in transferring this concept of disposition and linking to, respectively, *series* and *iunctura* as they are used to describe narrative composition?

One is indeed, and the justification for doing so is contained in the *Ars poetica* itself (vv. 1-9).

> Humano capiti cervicem pictor equinam
> iungere si velit, et varias inducere plumas
> undique collatis membris, ut turpiter atrum
> desinat in piscem mulier formosa superne,
> spectatum admissi risum teneatis, amici?
> Credite, Pisones, isti tabulae fore librum
> persimilem cuius, velut aegri somnia, vanae
> fingentur species, ut nec pes nec caput uni
> reddatur formae.

[19] Keller 2.350.

[20] Zechmeister 29. The context makes it clear that for the scholiast *sententia* = "phrase, sentence."

[21] *Ibid*. 69-70 (Italian italics mine).

Through verse 45 Horace elaborates upon narrative composition, stressing the care necessary in joining different narrative components. The discussion concludes as follows (vv. 42-45):

> Ordinis haec virtus erit et venus, aut ego fallor,
> ut iam nunc dicat iam nunc debentia dici,
> pleraque differat et praesens in tempus omittat;
> hoc amet, hoc spernat promissi carminis auctor.

Whereupon he applies the *same principles* to the arrangement of words, and introduces the first mention of *iunctura* (cf. the verb form, *iungere*, v. 2):

> In verbis *etiam* tenuis cautusque serendis
> dixeris egregie.[22]

In short, in the entire section on order and disposition (vv. 1-45), Horace stresses appropriate linking or joining of different elements, what should be retained, what left out, what changed from one place to another—in other words, he is describing *series* and *iunctura* in narrative.

There is adequate evidence that *iunctura* retained its sense of linking different elements, at all stages of composition, in the time of Chrétien and Alan of Lille. Conrad of Hirsau uses the term *iunctura* to designate the process of composition envisaged in the first 45 lines of the *Ars poetica*:

> In ipsa operis sui fronte quadam comparatione irrationabilis monstri
> vitiosa poemata detegens et dampnans opus debito carens ordine,
> ubi pulcrae materiae propositae consequens sententiarum ordo
> non responderet, velut si membra capitis humani formis variis ani-
> malium diversorum in se receptis solida iunctura non constarent.
> Ad quam formulam somniantis egri vanas imagines coaptasse videtur,
> qui rerum corporalium imaginaria ludificatione dementatus hoc
> putat esse veritatis quod est vanitatis. Qua similitudine mentem

---

[22] Italics mine. For a discussion of Horace's transition, see Kiessling and Heinze 296-297. The commentaries accord with their interpretation; cf. *Scholia vindobonensia* 5: "*In verbis etiam*. Hactenus de ordine. Nunc de facundia dicit.*"* Not only in Roman and medieval times did the terms *series* and *iunctura* apply to both narrative disposition and composition in the sentence; Corneille used them to describe the composition of *Horace*: "Elle [Sabine] ne sert pas davantage à l'action que l'Infante à celle du *Cid*, et ne fait que se laisser toucher diversement, comme elle, à la diversité des événements. Néanmoins on a généralement approuvé celle-ci, et condamné l'autre. J'en ai cherché la raison, et j'en ai trouvé deux. L'une est la liaison des scènes, qui semble, s'il m'est permis de parler ainsi, incorporer Sabine dans cette pièce, au lieu que, dans le *Cid*, toutes celles de l'Infante sont détachées et paroissent hors d'œuvre: . . . *Tantum series juncturaque pollet!*" *Œuvres de P. Corneille*, ed. M. C. Marty-Laveaux (Paris 1862) 3.277.

solidae scientiae vel poeticae artis penitus vacuum damnavit, quae sibi arrogat quod ignorat.[23]

The extensive commentary he devotes to the beginning of Horace's work evinces considerable concern for the proper arrangement and combination of the different parts of the poem.[24] Yet Conrad is also aware of *iunctura* in the sense of appropriate rhetorical embellishment and elegant syntax: "Iuncturas etiam verborum et sententiarum figuras studiosis rhetoricae convenit advertere."[25]

Conrad alludes in the foregoing passage to the value of training in the art and craft of writing for learning how to fashion a good *iunctura*. Appropriately, the twelfth- and thirteenth-century arts of poetry use the term *iunctura* to designate disposition and linking on all levels of composition. The most extensive and advanced of these treatises, Geoffrey of Vinsauf's *Poetria nova*, offers these examples of the use of the term or of the concept:

1) Simile as a means of amplification (*collatio aperta*) (vv. 242-246):

> Respice quaedam
> juncta satis lepide; sed quaedam signa revelant
> nodum juncturae: collatio quae fit aperte
> se gerit in specie simili, quam signa revelant
> expresse.[26]

2) Metaphor as a means of amplification (*collatio occulta*) (vv. 256-262):

> Hoc genus est genus plantae, quod si plantetur in horto
> materiae, tractatus erit jocundior; hic est
> rivus fontis, ubi currit fons purior; hic est
> formula subtilis juncturae, res ubi junctae
> sic coeunt et sic se contingunt, quasi non sint
> contiguae, *sed* continuae quasi non manus artis
> junxerit, immo manus naturae.[27]

---

[23] Conrad of Hirsau, *Dialogus super auctores*, ed. G. Schepss (Würzburg 1889) 64. The edition of R. B. C. Huygens, Collection Latomus 17 (Brussels 1955), gives Schepss's pagination; cf. also p. 48: "Nonne et mos scripturarum est secundum vulgi opinionem aliquando texere orationis seriem?" On *texere* and similar expressions, see John Leyerle, "The Interlace Structure of *Beowulf*," *University of Toronto Quarterly* 37 (1967) 4.

[24] *Dialogus* 63-65.

[25] *Dialogus* 77.

[26] Geoffrey of Vinsauf, *Poetria nova*, ed. Edmond Faral, *Les arts poétiques du XII*ᵉ *et du XIII*ᵉ *siècle* (Paris 1924).

[27] Italicized words represent emendations on Faral's text proposed by W. B. Sedgwick, "Notes and Emendations on Faral's *Les arts poétiques*," *Speculum* 2 (1927) 337. Note the *iunctura* of a metaphor "in serie," vv. 248-253, recalling Horace's terminology ("series iuncturaque," v. 242).

3) The discussion of *ornatus facilis* and *difficilis* applies the principles Horace does in speaking of the *callida iunctura* (vv. 756-762):

> Ut res ergo sibi pretiosum sumat amictum,
> si vetus est verbum, sis physicus et veteranum
> redde novum. Noli semper concedere verbo
> in proprio residere loco: residentia talis
> dedecus est ipsi verbo; loca propria vitet
> et peregrinetur alibi sedemque placentem
> fundet in alterius fundo.

Subsequently, in discussing metaphor (*transsumptio*, *translatio*) as a variety of *ornatus difficilis*, Geoffrey employs the term *iunctura* (vv. 777-779):

> Et, quia lucet ibi junctura simillima rerum,
> si de quo loqueris sit non homo, lora retorque
> mentis ad id quod homo.

On the arrangement of words so as to give them a sense different from their original or usual meaning, Geoffrey states (vv. 840-843):

> Sic ergo loquaris,
> sic grave junge levi, ne res haec detrahat illi,
> sed sibi conveniant et sede fruantur eadem
> pacificetque suam concors discordia litem.[28]

These and other varieties of *iunctura* are subsumed under the general problem of disposition in Geoffrey's *Documentum de modo et arte dictandi et versificandi*.

> Si . . . diffuse tractare velimus et amplum tractatum construere,
> in primis consideremus universum corpus materiae, et omnia lina-
> menta corporis illius prosequamur, vel directe secundum natura-
> lem ordinem, vel indirecte secundum artificialem, ut in tractatu
> materiae diffusae omnes partes materiae sibi cohaereant, scilicet
> principium, medium et finis.[29]

The authority for these words is the beginning of the *Ars poetica*.[30] This passage permits us to link Chrétien's *conjointure* to the discussion of order

---

[28] The use of this *callida iunctura* is significant in the light of Ruch's analysis of *iunctura* in Horace. *Concors discordia* is a Horatian concept, and has its roots through Horace in Classical religious and philosophical thought; see Ruch's discussion of *concordia discors*, "Horace" (n. 4 above) 260-267.

[29] Faral 314 par. 154.

[30] *Ibid.* 314-315, pars. 155-156; in general, see 309-317; and Franz Quadlbauer *Die antike Theorie der genera dicendi im lateinischen Mittelalter*, Österreichische Akademie der Wissenschaften, philosophisch-historische Klasse 241.2 (Graz 1962) 102-104 no. 44 o 1.

at the outset of Geoffrey's *Poetria nova*.[31] After urging careful thought in
the planning of the poem's *materia*, thought that must precede putting the
materia into verse, Geoffrey proceeds (vv. 58-67):

> Opus totum prudens in pectoris arcem
> contrahe, sitque prius in pectore quam sit in ore.
> Mentis in arcano cum rem digesserit ordo,
> materiam verbis veniat vestire poesis.
> Quando tamen servire venit, se praeparet aptam
> obsequio dominae: caveat sibi, ne caput hirtis
> crinibus, aut corpus pannosa veste, vel *illa*
> ultima displiceant, *aliunde* nec inquinet *illam*
> hanc poliens partem: pars si qua sedebit inepte,
> tota trahet series ex illa parte pudorem.[32]

Here again, faulty joining of any part of the narrative to another destroys
the beauty of the poem. Geoffrey's concern for *series* and *iunctura* plainly
reflects the preoccupations we have found in Horace's *Ars poetica* and in late
Roman and medieval commentaries and *accessus* to that work.[33]

Turning now to French romance, we find, if not the term, at least the principle of *iunctura* expressed in passages like the following:

> Pour ce pri tous ceus qui cest oevre
> verront, quant en leur mains charra,
> qui male fachon i verra
> que il ne veille ma rudesce
> reprendre par trop grant apresce,
> ainz me deport courtoisement
> se j'ai parlé trop rudement
> et se l'uevre est mal acoutree.[34]
> Du roi Dagonbert uos larrai,
> mais molt par tans i reuenroi,
> quant tans sera de retorner.

---

[31] As I did in *Sens and Conjointure in the Chevalier de la charrette* (The Hague 1966)
90-91, without adducing any evidence to justify the comparison.

[32] Italicized words represent emendations on Faral's text proposed by Sedgwick 2.336.

[33] A somewhat earlier example of this principle is found in the following passage from
Bernard of Utrecht's eleventh-century commentary on the *Eclogue* of Theodulus: "in
serie autem continuationes, id est, ut praecedentia conueniant sequentibus"; see J. Frey,
*Über das mittelalterliche Gedicht "Theoduli ecloga" und den Kommentar des Bernhardus
ultraiectensis*, 84. Jahresbericht über das Königliche paulinische Gymnasium zu Münster i.
W. für das Schuljahr 1903-1904 (Münster 1904) 18; on Bernard, see Max Manitius, *Geschichte
der lateinischen Literatur des Mittelalters* (Munich 1911-1931) 3.194-196.

[34] Jehan Maillart, *Le Roman du Comte d'Anjou* 8076-8083, ed. Mario Roques, CFMA
(Paris 1931).

> Mais ancois uos uorroi conter
> vne auenture perilleuse.[35]
>
> Huimès orrés chançon bone et bien agencie,
> car a l'onneur d'amours la matiére est traitie.[36]

Lengthier romances in both verse and prose link the adventures and quests
of one knight to those of another by an abrupt but simple transition; the
following passage from *Claris et Laris* will suffice to illustrate this technique:

> Atant l'estoire de lui laisse,
> si vos redirai une laisse
> de Gaheriez.[37]

Other romances resembling *Claris et Laris* use the same overt method of
linking adventures: *Les merveilles de Rigomer*, *Durmart le gallois*, Girard
d'Amien's *Escanor*, Chrétien's *Perceval* and its continuations, and Arthurian
prose romance in general, including the Lancelot-Grail cycle and, as Nitze
pointed out, *Perlesvaus*.

Thus far it has been possible, from an analysis of Horace's term *iunctura*,
to define Chrétien's *conjointure* as the arrangement and linking of narrative
material into an orderly poem. But it is possible to define more explicitly
the exact nature of the formal narrative disposition Chrétien and his contemporaries had in mind in using *iunctura* and *conjointure*.

The passage cited above from *Claris et Laris* provides a hint as to the form
some of the *iuncturae* took and to the terminology used to distinguish one
narrative component from another. A new sequence of adventures is referred
to there as a *laisse* (v. 11662); elsewhere in the same romance a sequence is
designated a *vers* (vv. 9774-9776):

> Si con nos raconte cist vers,
> ja estoit passez li yvers;
> li Laiz Hardiz erroit sa voie.

Such continuations, sequels, and interruptions abound in the prose romances:

> Et bohors entre en son chemin tout seus & dist quil ne retornera mie
> a la cort le roy artu deuant .j. an ains ira par tot querant auentures
> Si se taist ore li contes a parler vn poi de lui . et retorne a parler de
> patrides au cercle dor qui sen uait a la cort le roy baudemagu . ensi
> com lancelot li ot commande.

---

[35] *Octavian* 71-75, ed. Karl Vollmöller, Altfranzösische Bibliothek 3 (Heilbronn 1883).
[36] *Brun de la Montaigne* 243-244, ed. Paul Meyer, Société des anciens textes français
(SATF) (Paris 1875).
[37] *Li romans de Claris et Laris* 11661-11663, ed. Johann Alton, Bibliothek des litterarischen
Vereins in Stuttgart 169 (Tübingen 1884).

Or dist li contes que quant patrides se fu partis de lancelot ensi
com li contes uous a deuise . si erra toute ior ensi naures comme il
estoit.[38]

In its simplest form, the separate *laisse* or *vers* relates the exploits of a particular knight or company of knights, or transpires in a particular environment,
for example a forest or a court. The change from the adventures of one knight
to those of another, or from one setting to another (as from a crossroads to
a court) provides the *iunctura*. Furthermore, the author usually advises
his public of what he intends to do, at the same time warning that the story
will return later to take up the episode where he is leaving it. *Vers* in this
sense—a sequence of adventures or episodes—may be meant as well in the
following lines from Gerbert de Montreuil's *Roman de la violette*:

> Lors commencha, si com moi samble,
> con chil qui molt estoit senés,
> un ver de Guillaume au court nes,
> a clere vois et a douch son.[39]

Gerbert is hardly referring to a single line of verse from a poem about Guillaume, although he could mean a *laisse* as this term is used to designate the
assonanced stanzas in *chansons de geste*. But only four *vers* are sung in all
(v. 1429), and yet the entire four are meant as entertainment during a meal.
Since it is unlikely that even four very long *laisses* would have sufficed for
a complete meal, it seems more likely that Gerbert's *vers* is a series of adventures in the cycle of Guillaume. This and related terms—*laisse, branche,
ambages, aventures*—designate separate narrative components or sequences;
and the *iunctura* is precisely the linking of two or more of these elements
together in a particular poem or romance. The deliberate and artificial breaking and linking of narrative sequence we may call *iunctura aperta*. Corres-
pondingly, Chrétien's reference in *Erec* to a *premiers vers* (v. 1796) is a reference to the first narrative sequence in that poem.

Now, the *iunctura* of the *premiers vers* in *Erec* is not at all so sharply defined as in the preceding examples, despite Chrétien's comment. The conclusion of the *premiers vers* coincides with Arthur's bestowal of the kiss of
the white stag on Enide, and precedes the celebration of the marriage of

---

[38] *The Vulgate Version of the Arthurian Romances*, ed. H. Oskar Sommer (Washington,
D.C. 1908-1916) 4.300. To the terminology for different *vers* may be added the references
to the seven "gardes" or "souviestement" in *The Elucidation: A Prologue to the Conte del
Graal*, ed. A. W. Thompson (New York 1931), vv. 14-24 and 317-382.

[39] Gerbert de Montreuil, *Le Roman de la violette ou de Gerart de Nevers* 1403-1406, ed.
D. L. Buffum, SATF (Paris 1928); cf. also v. 6164: "Ou il canta les quatre vers" and v.
6243: "La ou les quatre vers cantai." The passage cited from his song in the text is really
from *Aliscans*; see Buffum lxxxvi.

Erec and Enide; no extraneous material separates the marriage from the conclusion of the white stag episode. The abruptness of Chrétien's statement is obvious in context (vv. 1793-1802).

> Li rois, par itele avanture,
> randi l'usage et la droiture
> qu'a sa cort devoit li blans cers:
> ici fenist li premiers vers.
> Quant li beisiers del cerf fu pris
> a la costume del païs,
> Erec, come cortois et frans,
> fu de son povre oste [Enide's father] an espans:
> de ce que promis li avoit
> covant mantir ne li voloit.

Erec's gift to his father-in-law to be and his marriage to Enide are prepared in the narrative preceding the mention of the *premiers vers*; they are thus necessary consequences of what has gone before and constitute a proper conclusion to the foregoing narrative. The appropriate division between the *premiers vers* and what follows would therefore seem to belong after the marriage, when Erec and Enide leave Arthur's court.

To resolve this problem, it will first be necessary to consider the definition of *materia* and *narratio* in Conrad of Mure's *Summa de arte prosandi*; we must also return to Horace's *Ars poetica* to consider more carefully the relation between *series* and *iunctura*, and the implications of that relation for narrative composition.

Conrad of Mure distinguishes between two kinds of *materia: materia remota* and *materia propinqua*.

> Set aliud est materia remota, aliud propinqua. materia remota sunt
> rudes lapides et inexpoliti, et ligna nondum dolata nondum leuigata.
> set materia propinqua sunt lapides et ligna bene preparata, ut in
> structura domus prout expedit conponantur.[40]

---

[40] Conrad of Mure, *Summa de arte prosandi*, ed. Ludwig Rockinger, *Briefsteller und Formelbücher des eilften bis vierzehnten Jahrhunderts*, Ben Franklin Research and Source Works Series 10 (New York 1961) 441 [reprinted from *Quellen und Erörterungen zur bayerischen und deutschen Geschichte* 9.1 (Munich 1863)]. Conrad's treatise is concerned primarily with epistolary style; he does, however, base his instruction in part on general conceptions of composition derived from Horace's *Ars poetica* and from Geoffrey's *Poetria nova* (415, 418, 428); we may therefore consider his general remarks on composition applicable, *mutatis mutandis*, to poetry as well as to *dictamina*. For more detailed analysis of this passage, see D. Kelly, "*En uni dire* (*Tristan* Douce 839) and the Composition of Thomas's *Tristan*," MP 66 (1969) 12-13.

The different elements that make up the *materia remota* are polished and shaped to fit into, to be linked together in, the completed work. But the author must take care that each element in the combination be whole and consistent, both within itself and in combination with the rest of the *materia*; otherwise the *series* will not hang together well. This is the fault Geoffrey of Vinsauf is anxious to prevent by counseling careful planning in the initial stages of composition (vv. 62-70). Matthew of Vendôme inveighs against the same fault in the Prologue to his *Ars versificatoria*: "Pannorum assutores ab inspectione hujus operis excludantur . . . qui . . . nugarum aggregationem nituntur in unum compilare."[41]

The narrative may of course be composed of homogeneous or heterogeneous material:

> Narrationum alia simplex, alia multiplex.
> Simplex est, in qua unum solum narratur.
> Multiplex est, in qua plura narrantur. ibi prosator
> debet uidere, qualiter diuersas orationes ordinet et
> coniungat: scilicet quid in primo, quid in medio, quid
> in fine decenter ordinetur.[42]

The distinction between *narratio simplex* and *multiplex* goes back to a passage in the *Ars poetica* in which Horace treats unity and disunity (vv. 21-23).

> Amphora coepit
> institui: currente rota cur urceus exit?
> Denique sit quodvis, simplex dumtaxat et unum.

The pseudo-Acro contains the following gloss to these lines: "*Simplex*: Idest coeptae materiae et nondum finitae non debes aliam adiungere."[43] This becomes in Conrad's treatise the idea of *narratio simplex*. If a variety of material is brought together, the *narratio* becomes, in Conrad's terminology, *multiplex*. Yet he insists that it must be unified. As the *amphora-urceus* image in Horace implies, the *narratio multiplex* would otherwise be a *nugarum aggregatio*, and this Conrad is anxious to avoid. Like the *contes d'avan-*

---

[41] Faral 110 par. 7.

[42] A similar distinction is contained in a legal *accessus*: "Materia in hoc opere duplex est: alia promulgationis, alia compositionis. Promulgare est quasi ex occulto nature aliquid novum elicere, id est illud quod est rude et informe ad formam et ad actum reducere. Compositio est ex multis rebus unam efficere, sicut ex tecto et fundamento et pariete domus efficitur, vel sicuti ex aqua et farina efficitur panis. Materia promulgationis in omnibus libris legum est eadem, materia compositionis est diversa"; cited from Bruno Sandkühler, *Die frühen Dantekommentare und ihr Verhältnis zur mittelalterlichen Kommentartradition*, Münchner romanistische Arbeiten 19 (Munich 1967) 29.

[43] Keller 2.312.

ture, whose faults Chrétien condemns in the *Erec* Prologue, such a work is incomplete; the different parts do not link together properly into a unified whole.

There is another type of narrative that is *multiplex* but not unified in the Horatian sense. Horace disallows this type when he compares, unfavorably, the cyclic poets with Homer (vv. 146-152):

> nec reditum Diomedis ab interitu Meleagri,
> nec gemino bellum Troianum orditur ab ovo:
> semper ad eventum festinat et in medias res
> non secus ac notas auditorem rapit, et quae
> desperat tractata nitescere posse, relinquit,
> atque ita mentitur, sic veris falsa remiscet,
> primo ne medium, medio ne discrepet imum.

Cyclic poetry resembles what Conrad calls *narratio multiplex*, without being the same thing. For Conrad, like Horace, insists on internal unity even in *narratio multiplex* ("quid in primo, quid in medio, quid in fine decenter ordinetur"), whereas the cyclic poets lack precisely such organic unity. "Ai due poemi omerici già in qualche modo descritti ed esaltati... contrappone qui [in vv. 146-147] rispettivamente due poemi nei quali la materia, per se stesso, era analoga a quella dei due poemi omerici, ma vi era trattata... in tutte le sue *ambagi*."[44] The late Roman and medieval commentators on Horace are aware of this distinction. At verse 146 of the *Ars poetica*, Porphyrion glosses: "Antimachus fuit cyclicus poeta. Hic adgressus est materiam, quam sic extendit, ut uiginti quattuor uolumina impleuerit, antequam septem duces usque ad Thebas perduceret."[45] Likewise the pseudo-Acro comments: "Antimachus poeta reditum Diomedis narrans coepit ab exordio primae originis, idest coepit ab interitu Meleagri. Hic ergo praecipit longo prooemio non esse utendum."[46] Cyclic poems may indeed lack formal unity; they need not for all that be incoherent. They do not seem to have been held in disesteem in thirteenth-century France, as we may observe in Arthurian prose romance. This fact suggests the emergence of a taste different from, or at least broader than Horace's.

Medieval writers often distinguished poetry from oratory and letter writing because of its complexity.

---

[44] Rostagni 45 (italics Rostagni's); see in general 41-48, and Kiessling and Heinze 313-315.
[45] W. Meyer 351.
[46] Keller 2.333. See also *idem*: "148 *Semper ad euentum*. Idest ad id, unde oriendum est . . . aut semper ad finem festinat, idest odit longa prooemia. *Semper ad euentum festinat*, cogitans fastidium lectoris ad exitum operis properat; ideoque non est longius opus ab origine inchoandum"; cf. also the *Scholia vindobonensia* 16-18.

> Huiusmodi sunt omnia poetarum carmina, ut sunt tragoediae, co-
> moediae, satirae, heroica quoque et lyrica, et iambica, et didascalica
> quaedam, fabulae quoque et historiae, illorum etiam scripta quos
> nunc philosophos appellare solemus, qui et brevem materiam longis
> verborum ambagibus extendere consueverunt, et facilem sensum
> perplexis sermonibus obscurare, vel etiam diversa simul compi-
> lantes, quasi de multis coloribus et formis, unam picturam facere.[47]

Hugh of Saint Victor is describing two kinds of *narratio multiplex*. First,
like Conrad of Mure, he envisages the combination of diverse materials into
a single unified work ("diversa simul compilantes . . . unam picturam facere");
the words are also reminiscent of Horace's comparison of composition in
painting and poetry, an image that runs through the first 45 lines of the *Ars
poetica*. But, unlike Horace and Conrad of Mure, Hugh also allows the complex narrative of cyclic poetry, wherein the usual standards of narrative
unity no longer obtain ("brevem materiam longis verborum ambagibus ex-
tendere . . . facilem sensum perplexis sermonibus obscurare"). Dante shows
the same willingness to accept cyclic poetry of the thirteenth-century French
type when he refers to the "Arturi regis ambages pulcerrime."[48] Now such
narrative is obviously not, in the mind of Dante, the incoherent mass of material we might suppose from Horace's words; rather it presupposes a different
formal principle, and may possess its own special beauty. As Professor Vinaver
has described it: "Far from being a mosaic from which any one stone could
be removed without upsetting the rest, the Cycle turned out to be remark-
ably like the fabric of matting or tapestry; a single cut across it, made at any
point, would unravel it all. And yet it was clearly not a unified body of material: it consisted of a variety of themes, independent of, but inseparable
from, one another."[49] Within themselves, the various branches and sequences
of medieval cyclic romance might well possess organic unity in the Horatian
sense; but the interlacing often made them appear incomplete or inconsistent
to prejudiced or inattentive readers.[50] Dante demonstrated keener perception
and finer taste.

The terms *narratio simplex* and *narratio multiplex* are convenient and
appropriate to designate the two principal structural forms of twelfth- and
thirteenth century narrative. Under *narratio multiplex* it is necessary to

---

[47] Hugh of Saint Victor, *Didascalicon de studio legendi*, ed. C. H. Buttimer, Catholic
University of America Studies in Medieval and Renaissance Latin 10 (Washington, D.C.
1939) 54.

[48] *De vulgari eloquentia* 1.10, ed. Aristide Marigo (Florence 1957) 76.

[49] *Form and Meaning in Medieval Romance*, The Presidential Address of the Modern
Humanities Research Association, 1966 (Leeds 1966) 10.

[50] Eugène Vinaver, Introduction to *Le roman de Balain*, ed. M. Dominica Legge (Manchester 1942) xi-xxii; Fanni Bogdanow, *The Romance of the Grail* (Manchester 1966) 15-16;
Janet M. Ferrier, *Forerunners of the French Novel* (Manchester 1954) 8-10.

make an important division: either the narrative unifies the heterogeneous material in the sense Horace understood this expression (*multiplex* and *unum*), or it interlaces it in the sense Dante used in speaking of the *ambages* of French prose romance. There is, however, a principle of composition fundamental to all these varieties of *narratio*, a principle that goes beyond the mere distinction between beginning, middle, and end—or the lack of them—and which indeed gives to the terms beginning, middle, and end a special sense that one might not at first suspect. To understand this principle we must look again at Horace's discussion of *series* and *iunctura* in verses 48 and 242.

In those lines Horace is speaking of *compositio*, the artful sentence known as the Latin period. The period, which we associate with the best Roman oratory and poetry, is not subject to the rules of word order that tend to determine the arrangement of parts of speech in the English or French sentence. The basic subject-verb-object pattern is superseded by interlacing of words in an effort to attain a particular effect by that very arrangement, as well as to indicate the relative importance of different parts of the sentence by their location in the entire statement. What comes at the beginning, middle, and end of a period, and what is expressed in principal and subordinate clauses in the beginning, middle, and end of the sentence depends as much on aesthetic, rhetorical, or logical considerations as on rules of grammar; indeed, often more so. Thus the *iuncturae* are extremely important, just as Horace said they are. "Or il est bien évident," to cite Ruch again, "que pour Horace... il s'agit [in a *iunctura* in *series*] de la réunion de *deux* termes antithétiques, donc de ce que nous appelons une 'alliance de termes' impliquant une relation bilatérale antinomique.... Ce sens indiscutable du mot *iunctura* et son association avec *series* (*Art poétique*, vers 242) interdisent de penser que le verbe *sero* (*in uerbis serendis*, vers 46) pourrait signifier 'semer,' donc 'créer' et non pas 'associer,' 'entrelacer.' Voilà tout ce que peut nous apprendre le contexte de l'*Art poétique*."[51] Here we encounter familiar terminology. The *entrelacement*, interlacing of words in the Latin period, becomes

---

[51] Ruch (n. 4 above) 255; cf. also Leyerle (n. 23 above) 4-5. The interlacing was within a unified sentence, that is that it contained a logical beginning, middle, and end. A correlation between syntax and narrative composition of the cyclic type may derive from nonclassical sources; see for example the discussion of syntax and narrative structure in *Beowulf* in Leyerle 7-15. In one respect only I cannot agree with Professor Leyerle's otherwise valuable contribution to the discussion of interlacing, and that is in his derivation of the principle from the notion of natural and artificial order (5-7). The arts of poetry regard this arrangement as essentially the disposition of narrative that is already organized, coherent, and unified: artificial order is simply the relocation of beginning, middle, and end of narrative in a different formal pattern. The result may be interlacing; but the theoreticians of the twelfth- and thirteenth-centuries certainly did not envisage students evolving cyclic poetry from the principle. Natural and artificial order may indeed be an elementary application for beginning writers of one simple side of the more complicated process of interlacing, but I know of no direct evidence that this is so.

on the level of the arrangement of different parts of the poem's *materia*, an interlacing of different narrative components from the *materia* in an appropriate and pleasing manner. The analogy is confirmed by the parallel we have already noted between the first 45 lines of the *Ars poetica* and the *iunctura* passage in verse 48. Indeed, we find interlacing in the structure of the *Ars poetica* itself. Many readers in the past have considered the poem's arrangement of themes perplexing because there is no readily apparent order in the sequence of parts. There is of course a very broad three-part division that has been generally recognized, and which one may call beginning, middle, and end;[52] but within this division, Horace has interlaced his themes in such a way that the disagreeable regularity and dry formality of the treatise are eliminated, and replaced by an urbane, elegant, and artfully constructed commentary on the poem, poetry, and the poet. The *Ars poetica* was not conceived as the classroom treatise it became in the Middle Ages. What such a treatise would be we may judge from Geoffrey of Vinsauf's *Poetria nova*, with its carefully objective plan, clear and logical subordination, and orderly progression, after the fashion of rhetorical treatises, from invention and disposition through ornamentation and memory to delivery.[53] But the lesson in arrangement offered by the disposition of Horace's poem was not lost on medieval writers; the use of "gliding transitions" and "brusque abruptness" (the latter narrative principle corresponds to the syntactical *iunctura* as defined by Ruch: "une 'alliance de termes' impliquant une relation bilatérale antinomique") in changing from one subject to another is familiar to all readers of French prose romance.[54] The example of Horace's poem reveals that not only for the cyclic poets, but for poets who, like Horace himself, demanded unified composition, the principle of arrangement within the poem was interlacing. We may illustrate this for the Middle Ages by returning to the perplexing allusion to the *premiers vers* in *Erec*.

The *premiers vers* is complete when Arthur bestows the kiss of the white stag on Enide. As the word *premiers* suggests, the *vers* begins the romance, for the hunt for the white stag precedes even the appearance of Enide and Erec in the poem (vv. 27-76). And Chrétien returns to the subject at various

---

[52] See Rostagni 3; C. O. Brink, *Horace on Poetry* (Cambridge 1963) 13, 232-233, who adds an Introduction, vv. 1-45. There is of course no complete agreement among modern scholars regarding the precise disposition of the *Ars poetica*, but that is of no consequence for the discussion here; for an *état présent* of the problem, see Brink 15-40.

[53] See D. Kelly, "The Scope of the Treatment of Composition in the Twelfth- and Thirteenth-Century Arts of Poetry," *Speculum* 41 (1966) 271-273; in the *Poetria nova*, see especially vv. 77-86, where Geoffrey outlines the plan of his treatise. The same arrangement is found in the *Rhetorica ad Herennium* and, by implication, in Cicero's *De inventione*— both textbooks.

[54] See P. Cauer, "Zur Abgrenzung und Verbindung der Theile in Horazens *Ars poetica*," *Rheinisches Museum für Philologie* 61 (1906) 232-243; and Brink 26-28 and 244-271.

intervals in the intervening narrative. From the Prologue we learn that those
who previously told the story of Erec had not told it well. Rather than link
their *matière* in a way both pleasing and instructive, those storytellers botched
up the whole matter, tearing apart what belongs together (*depecier*) and leaving
out important episodes (*corronpre*). The following lines from Aimon de Va-
renne's *Florimont* help to clarify this interpretation of *corronpre*:

> Si lairons des .II. rois a tant,
> si vos dirons d'un atre avant
> dont li contes est conronpus,
> que primes nen fut menteüs:
> se fut li muedres des millors
> des rois et des empereors
> que en cel tens ierent en terre
> por pris et por honor conquerre;
> mai on ne le poroit savoir.
> Qui ne[l] conteroit d'oir en oir,
> nen seroit l'istoire seüe;
> por ce nen est pas conronpue.[55]

The story of King Phelipe of Macedonia was incomplete because the legend
of his son-in-law and successor Florimont had heretofore been omitted; by
adding Florimont's life to the narration Aimon sought to make the story
complete and whole. Similarly, the tales told about Erec were faulty and
incomplete. For his own poem, Chrétien asserts that he has drawn from a
"conte d'avanture" his "molt bele conjointure"; by implication, then, his
poem is unified and complete. He has taken a congeries of narrative material
(Conrad of Mure's *materia remota*) and arranged these elements and fashioned
them into the shape they have in the poem (*materia propinqua*). One of these
elements was the adventure of the White Stag; the romance, as Chrétien
put it together, begins with this adventure, and that adventure concludes
at the point Chrétien indicates in his allusion to the *premiers vers*. This *vers*
is in turn interlaced and intertwined with other elements drawn from the
matière—the insult to Guenevere and Erec, the sparrow-hawk episode, Erec's
courtship of Enide—and linked to material that comes up afterwards, particularly the marriage, the tournament, and the quest. The basis for the
linking of separate elements is the figure of Enide herself, as R. S. Loomis
has pointed out: "The romance of Erec and Enide, up to the marriage of the
two, consists of a series of episodes which, whatever their original purport,
have been skillfully recast in order to bring out the supreme beauty and

---

[55] Aimon de Varennes, *Florimont* 1673-1684 ed. Alfons Hilka, Gesellschaft für romanische
Literatur 48 (Göttingen 1932).

franchise of Enide."[56] Enide gives meaning to the disparate elements and binds them together by the significant role she plays in each one.

Loomis attributes the happy arrangement and linking of the diverse parts of the narrative to Chrétien's source. In speaking specifically about the sparrow-hawk episode, he concludes: "By skillful changes, omissions, and dovetailing, the author of X [= Chrétien's source] succeeded in the difficult task of making a coherent, well-motivated narrative out of four distinct patterns— the abduction of Guenievre, the insolent dwarf, the venerable host and his beautiful daughter, and the sparrow-hawk contest. He was an artist of a high order."[57] It is not likely that he was an "artist of a high order," since Chrétien criticizes all those who told the tale before him; at least, the author of X (if there ever were an X) was certainly not an artist in the sense Chrétien understood that term. But Chrétien's *matière* may indeed have been in one piece, as Loomis implies, since *Erec et Enide* is said to derive from "*un* conte d'avanture." This fact would not preclude Chrétien's introducing changes into the arrangement of episodes and the significance of that tale, or even omitting parts and adding others; Hartmann von Aue did as much with his *Erec*, which is based, in large part at least, on Chrétien's version.[58] On the other hand, Chrétien may have used *conte d'avanture* as a generic term to cover the multifarious tales he refers to in verses 19-22. It is impossible to resolve this problem, and in any case it makes little difference for our analysis of *conjointure*. Chrétien extracted his version from a single *conte d'avanture*, linking the separate elements into a particular interlacing pattern, or he joined various elements from a number of *contes corrompus* in the same way ("diversa simul compilantes . . . unam picturam facere").

Interlacing is not unique to *Erec* among Chrétien's poems. The parallel adventures (parallel in sequence if not in chronology) of Perceval and Gauvain in the *Conte du graal* have already been alluded to; there Chrétien indicates the *iuncturae* (vv. 4813-4815, 6212-6216, 6514-6518)[59] just as do the

---

[56] Loomis, *Arthurian Tradition and Chrétien de Troyes* (New York 1949) 68.

[57] *Arthurian Tradition* 84.

[58] See Hugo Kuhn, *Dichtung und Welt im Mittelalter* (Stuttgart 1959) 133-136. Hartmann may have used another version of *Erec* along with Chrétien's, but this problem has still not been resolved satisfactorily; see Peter Wapnewski, *Hartmann von Aue* (Stuttgart 1962) 39-41.

[59] *Le roman de Perceval*, ed. William Roach, Textes littéraires français (Geneva 1959). Wolfram von Eschenbach employs the same technique in interlacing the quests, and does so more artfully than Chrétien; this is, of course, because Chrétien did not complete that part of his poem. Another example supporting this interpretation of *vers* is contained in *Claris et Laris*: "Tant jut Laris, qu'il fu garis / dont grant joie mainne Claris / et li rois et tuit li baron, / mes d'euls ici vous laisseron; / revenir nous covient arriere / a nostre premiere matiere. / Roys Ladon iert durement viax, / molt avoit fet de ses aviax," etc. (vv. 13457-64). King Ladon is in fact the principal figure of the first episode of the poem, that is, of the *première matière*. The distinction between the terminology in *Claris et Laris* and *Erec*

authors of *Claris et Laris* and the prose romances, and as he did in the allusion to the *premiers vers* in *Erec*. More frequently than such "brusque abruptness" in changing from one part to another, Chrétien uses "gliding transitions," or what we may call *iuncturae subtiles*. In the first part of *Cligés*, Arthur's travels and the revolt of Angrés bind together Alexandre's chivalric and courtly achievements on the one hand and the story of his romance with Soredamors on the other into an interlacing pattern. In *Yvain*, Chrétien links by means of the figure of Yvain a variety of elements that were once independent: the quest of Calogrenant, the defense of the storm fountain, the romance with the recent widow. The quests too, although they advance in a definite linear progression, sometimes interlock episodes according to an ABABA pattern, or some variation of this pattern. And other twelfth- and thirteenth-century romances exemplify variations of *iuncturae subtiles*. The author of *L'atre périlleux*, to cite one example, claims to have taken his poem from a book.[60] Some scholars doubt the veracity of this assertion, or at least its implied exclusion of secondary sources, because of resemblances in persons and events in *L'atre périlleux* with other romances.[61] Nonetheless, the arrangement of material in the poem is, in Alexandre Micha's words, "unusually coherent"; and, he elaborates, "this is not a *roman à tiroirs*, in which the episodes are separate and do not connect with each other; rather it is a *roman à tirettes*, constructed like a telescope, in which one event slides into another."[62] This happy formulation describes aptly and precisely the "gliding transitions" that shape the *bele conjointure* of both *L'atre périlleux* and of *Erec et Enide*— the skillful interlacing and linking of separate elements in the narrative sequence. In these poems the authors have knitted their material into a unified whole: the plots are either *simplex* and *unum*, as in *Erec*, or they are *multiplex* and *unum*, as in *Perceval*.

To these two we may add the "open-ended" structure of cyclic poetry and thirteenth-century prose romance. Unlike their predecessors, these authors did not strive for a unified whole. Rather they sought to combine ever more tales and developments into a continually expanding but coherent narrative. The separate tales, might, as Professor Vinaver has shown, possess internal unity; but they are linked to other tales, either in fact or by implication in a potentially expanding sequence.[63] The implied links would become true

---

is one of emphasis: Chrétien uses *vers* to designate a structural component, the author of *Claris et Laris* uses *matière* to designate the deversified content of the narrative.

[60] *L'atre périlleux* 3396, 4728-29, ed. Brian Woledge, CFMA (Paris 1936); elsewhere the author refers to his source as simply his *conte* (vv. 2580, 3479, 4729), his *estoire* (v. 6430), and as *ma matire* (v. 4026).

[61] Alexandre Micha, "Miscellaneous French Romances in Verse," in Loomis, *Arthurian Literature* 367-368.

[62] *Ibid.* 368.

[63] *Form and Meaning in Medieval Romance* 12.

links if later writers added to the work begun by their predecessors. This is in fact what happened in Arthurian prose romance. Such romance is also valid *narratio multiplex*.

The varieties of interlacing which we have designated *narratio simplex* and *narratio multiplex* (whether by combination into a unified whole or in an open narrative) exhaust the possible forms of *conjointure*. Of course, they do not account for the multifarious single *conjointures* illustrated by each separate work; nor do they imply that each *conjointure* was as successful as that for Chrétien's *Erec* or the Lancelot-Grail cycle. To appreciate this principle of composition in all its manifestations, both in its formal beauty and as it is used to give meaning to the narrative, we require careful critical study of narrative writing throughout the twelfth and thirteenth centuries. Such study may even bring to light further formal possibilities besides the three defined in this paper. For example, thirteenth-century verse romance like *Claris et Laris* has characteristics in common with the type of interlacing found in the prose romances and in Chrétien's poems. The development of the *nouvelle* form from prose romance in the later Middle Ages may in turn have influenced the development of prose romance itself during this period.[64]

It is now possible to summarize the findings of this paper and to propose a succinct explanation of the term *conjointure*. Robertson correctly defined *conjointure* as the arrangement of different elements found in the poet's *matière*;[65]

---

[64] Ferrier, *Forerunners of the French Novel.*

[65] This is not to say that I agree with Robertson's argument as to what meaning the *conjointure* may or must give to the work. The bulk of his article in *SP* is indeed given over to this question—that is, in his terminology, the meaning of the *cortex* and, especially, of the *nucleus* of the narrative. This is the question of *sens* in Chrétien's poems, as this term is used in the *Chevalier de la charrete* 26 ed. Mario Roques, CFMA (Paris 1958). But that is another problem, whose solution is not directly relevant to the meaning of *conjointure* as a purely formal concept. In this context, it is appropriate to cite the recent article of Jean Rychner, "Le Prologue du 'Chevalier de la charrette,'" *Vox romanica* 26 (1967) 1-23, in which he denies, on syntactic evidence, that *sens* even has the sense of "meaning, signification" in *Charrette* 26. It is noteworthy that Matthew of Vendôme treats *sensus* as if it were content (*Inhalt*, not *Gehalt*), and thus equivalent to *materia*: "Adhuc multa dicenda restant de exsecutione materiae; sed quia ad metam nostrum suspirat curriculum, ne taedium suppullulet, sequatur de permutatione materiae, quae quidem pertinet ad exsecutionem. Est autem permutatio materiae bipertita; una est verborum et sententiarum, sed retenta sensus aequipollentia; alia verborum et non sententiarum" (*Ars versificatoria* 185 par. 20; cf. also pars. 21-22). In this sense, Marie de Champagne, in providing Chrétien with the *matière* and *sens* of the *Charrette*, gave him in fact the material content of the poem. Did Chrétien mean by *antancion*, v. 29, what we have, since Nitze's article in *Romania* (see n. 3, above), taken *sens* to mean, that is meaning or signification of the work (whatever the *precise* meaning of signification may or must be)? See Robertson, SP 48.690. In any case, to return to Rychner's article, there are in Chrétien other passages that suggest he was intent both on pleasing and instructing his public (cf. for example *Erec* 9-12, cited at the beginning of this paper). Clearly, the question regarding the meaning of *sens* is still open; see the note of Félix Lecoy, *Romania* 89 (1968) 571-573.

but this explanation does not go far enough. The meaning of *iunctura* in the Latin period, the arrangement of material in Horace's *Ars poetica* and in medieval romance, indicate that the *conjointure* is specifically the result of the interlacing of different elements derived from the source or sources (or, for that matter, from the author's imagination). Such *matière* may be a single tale, or it may comprise heterogeneous material brought together by the poet; this material, the *materia remota* of the proposed work, is prepared for inclusion in the completed work, and becomes by this process *materia propinqua*. The product may be a unified tale in the Horatian sense (*narratio simplex*) or the skillful interlacing of diverse material into either a unified or a coherently expanding narrative (*narratio multiplex*). But the mere combination of the material is not by itself either good or bad. Rather the particular manner in which it is arranged and joined, the quality of the particular *iuncturae*, determines the beauty of each combination; and the quality of the total combination makes the overall *conjointure* beautiful or not beautiful: "ex diversorum *competenti* junctura ipsius narrationis *elegantior* pictura," to cite Alan of Lille again. Arrangement and linking of narrative elements are therefore the essential objects of composition; even amplification and abbreviation and ornamentation are subordinate to that process.[66] In the light of these findings, the comparative analysis of works treating the same or similar themes, with especial attention to additions and to changes in arrangement from one work to the other, is a paramount desideratum of future studies of composition in medieval romance.

Department of French and Italian
The University of Wisconsin
Madison, Wisconsin 53706, U.S.A.

[66] *Speculum* 41.272-274.

DANTE AND BERNARD SILVESTRIS

•

by David Thompson

Modern scholarly discussions of the *Commedia* have tended to take place in a sort of literary vacuum: the *poema sacro* is deemed a unique work, comparable not to other poetic fictions but only to writings of a theological cast. Dante is God's writer; his poem embodies a distinctively scriptural mode of figure or allegory; and our best *accessus* to it is via a study of the Bible and of patristic exegesis.[1]

But Dante's was not the first *poema sacro*: Macrobius had used just these words of the *Aeneid* (*Saturnalia* 1.24.13). Dante calls Vergil his *maestro* and his *autore* (*Inferno* 1.85); as an authority Vergil had his commentators;[2] and a consideration of the *Aeneid*, along with medieval interpretations of it, can tell us a good deal about what sort of poem Dante wrote and about where he stands in the European literary tradition.[3]

Some years ago Theodore Silverstein studied Dante's "indebtedness to the *Aeneid* as it was transformed by both the allegorical commentaries and the mythographers." He gave special attention to a commentary by the twelfth-century Platonist, Bernard Silvestris; and having shown how Bernard transformed Aeneas's descent into "an ascent to the divine," Silverstein concluded that "Dante evidently conned [Vergil's] volume even better than we have hitherto observed. Among the number of those who describe the experience of the soul rising through the spheres to its Creator, among Augustine and Macrobius and Thomas Aquinas, among Saint Bernard and Hugh of Saint

---

[1] Such approaches have had considerable heuristic usefulness; indeed, they have revolutionized our understanding of the *Commedia*. But for some reservations about the theories of Erich Auerbach and Charles Singleton, see my essay on "Figure and Allegory in the *Commedia*" in a forthcoming volume of of *Dante Studies*.

[2] A convenient survey is afforded by the Rev. Terrence A. McVeigh, "The Allegory of the Poets: A Study of Classical Tradition in Medieval Interpretation of Virgil" (Ph.D. diss. Fordham University 1964).

[3] The most recent work in this line, with excellent bibliography, is by Robert Hollander, "Dante's Use of *Aeneid* I in *Inferno* I and II," *Comparative Literature* 20 (1968) 142-156. Especially relevant in this context is Hollander's illuminating discussion of Dante's attitude toward Vergil and the *Aeneid* (144-145). For the influence of Vergil upon Dante's view of history, see Charles Till Davis, *Dante and the Idea of Rome* (Oxford 1957) esp. 100-138.

Victor and all the other mystics whom Dante knew, we must not fail to include Vergil the mystic, that Vergil who was Dante's master."[4] My own
study starts from this insight and attempts a more specific statement of the
relationship between Bernard Silvestris and Dante. I wish to show that as
allegorized by Bernard, the *Aeneid* afforded Dante not only a literary precedent for his physical journey to the other world but also a possible paradigm
for his major allegorical mode and for the first part of his spiritual itinerary.[5]

Before entering upon the "altro viaggio" along which Vergil proposes to
lead him, Dante protests his unworthiness for such an undertaking:

> Tu dici che di Silvio lo parente,
> Corruttibile ancora, ad immortale
> Secolo andó, e fu sensibilmente.
>
> . . . .
>
> Andovvi poi lo Vas d'elezione
> Per recarne conforto a quella fede
> Che è principio alla via di salvazione.
> Ma io perchè venirvi? o chi'l concede?
> Io non Enea, io non Paolo sono:
> Me degno a ciò nè io nè altri 'l crede.
> (*Inferno* 2.13-15, 28-33)

The relevance of Paul is obvious enough: in 2 Corinthians 12.2-4 he had
said: "I knew a man in Christ above fourteen years ago (whether in the body,
I cannot tell; or whether out of the body, I cannot tell: God knoweth); such
an one caught up to the third heaven. And I knew such a man ... How
that he was caught up into paradise, and heard unspeakable words, which
it is not lawful for a man to utter." This was generally taken as a reference
to Paul's own experience; and in Augustine's and Aquinas's interpretation the
raptus Pauli became the great exemplar of *visio intellectualis*, the direct,

---

[4] H. Theodore Silverstein, "Dante and Vergil the Mystic," *Harvard Studies and Notes
in Philology and Literature* 14 (1932) 51-82. The only edition of Bernard thus far was
based on a single Paris manuscript: *Commentum Bernardi Silvestris super sex libros Eneidos
Virgilii*, ed. Guilielmus Riedel (Greifswald 1924). For an excellent survey of work on Bernard, see Giorgio Padoan, "Tradizione e fortuna del commento all' 'Eneide' di Bernardo
Silvestre," *Italia medioevale e umanistica* 3 (1960) 227-240, esp. n. 4. To this should now be
added J. Reginald O'Donnell, "The Sources and Meaning of Bernard Silvester's Commentary
on the Aeneid," *Mediaeval Studies* 24 (1962) 233-249; and McVeigh 142-183.

[5] It is not my intention to depict Dante as merely another footnote to Plato; but there
is a good deal of Plato behind, if not always in, the *Commedia*. See particularly the various
studies of John Freccero: e.g., "Dante's Firm Foot and the Journey Without a Guide,"
Harvard Theological Review 52 (1959) 245-281; and "Dante's Pilgrim in a Gyre," *Publications of the Modern Language Association* 76 (1961) 168-181.

unmediated and indescribable knowledge of God which Dante himself attains at the end of the poem.[6]

As for Aeneas, his *descensus ad inferos* was of course the major literary precedent for a physical journey to the other world by a man still in this life, "in the body" as Dante is when he makes his journey. But as allegorized by Bernard Silvestris, the *Aeneid* was more than just a history of physical events: it also represented a literary precedent for Dante's spiritual itinerary, the journey of the soul to God.

Bernard prefaces his commentary with a discussion of Vergil as poet and philosopher: "'Geminae doctrinae observationem' perpendimus in sola Eneide Maronem habuisse, teste namque Macrobio: 'qui et veritatem philosophiae docuit et figmentum poeticum non praetermisit.'" In his capacity as poet, Vergil employs an *ordo artificialis*, beginning *a media narratione* and recurring *ad principium*; and his purpose is twofold, for he writes *causa delectationis* and *causa utilitatis*.[7] Moreover, his work has a twofold usefulness: "Si quis vero haec omnia studeat imitari, maximam scribendi peritiam consequitur, maxima etiam exempla et excitationes aggrediendi honesta et fugiendi illicita per ea quae narrantur habentur" (2).

However, Bernard's real interest lies not in Vergil the stylist or Vergil the moralist, but in Vergil the philosopher: "Scribit enim in quantum est philosophus humanae vitae naturam. Modus vero agendi talis est: sub integumento describit quid agat vel quid patiatur humanus spiritus in humano corpore temporaliter positus. Atque in hoc scribendo naturali utitur ordine, atque ita utrumque narrationis ordinem observat, artificialem poeta, naturalem philosophus" (3). Without thinking to distinguish between *ordo artificialis* and *ordo naturalis*, Fulgentius had read the *Aeneid* as an allegory depicting the ages of man. Bernard retains Fulgentius's basic scheme, reading Book I as a story of *infantia*, II as *pueritia*, and so on; but he adds a new dimension, for in his interpretation the poem becomes a Platonic allegory, the story of the human soul imprisoned in its mortal body.[8] Aeneas he glosses as "ennos demas i.e. habitator corporis" (10), and Aeneas's adventures are interpreted as the spirit's erring but finally successful journey to its true goal: "Per Italiam vero quae incrementum interpretatur naturam animi accipimus quae est rationalitas et immortalitas, virtus, scientia" (20). Of this spiritual *iter* Bernard says: "in hac vita itur ad contemplationem, in alia ad ora i.e. ad videndum facie ad faciem" (52). Here Bernard of course echoes Corinthians 13.12: "Videmus nunc per speculum in aenigmate; tunc autem

---

[6] See Francis X. Newman, "St. Augustine's Three Visions and the Structure of the *Commedia*," *Modern Language Notes* 82 (1967) 56-78.

[7] Bernard quotes Horace, *Ars poetica* 333-334: "aut prodesse volunt aut delectare poetae aut simul atque iocunda et idonea dicere vitae."

[8] On similar Neoplatonic interpretations of the *Odyssey*, see Félix Buffière, *Les Mythes d'Homère et la Pensée Grecque* (Paris 1956) 588-589.

facie ad faciem." And by assimilating the *Aeneid* to the whole Platonic-Christian tradition of spiritual progress, Bernard makes the *Aeneid* an allegory structurally very like what we find in the *Commedia*, where Dante's physical journey, the literal level of the poem, figures another journey, a spiritual itinerary that takes place in this life. Thus the allegorized epic afforded Dante a close paradigm for his major allegorical mode, and Vergil may have been Dante's *maestro* in a way we had not heretofore realized.

Bernard's interpretation of Aeneas's *iter* may also be relevant to the specific configuration of Dante's journey. Glossing Aeneas's vision near the end of Book V, Bernard says: "Monetur imagine patris ad inferos descendere visurus patrem ibi i.e. cogitatione quadam imaginaria quam de creatore habet. Non enim perfectam potest habere, cum deus incircumscripturus sit cogitatione. In qua ille monetur, ut ad mundana per cognitionem descendat, ibique videbit patrem quia quamvis in creaturis non sit, cognitione tamen creaturarum cognoscitur. Ideoque iubetur apud inferos quaerere patrem licet celsa inhabitat" (27-28).[9] Then in the introduction to his word-by-word commentary on Book VI, Bernard explains that there are four kinds of descent, the most important of which in this context is type two: "Est autem alius virtutis qui fit dum sapiens aliquis ad mundana per considerationem descendit, non ut in eis intentionem ponat sed ut eorum cognita fragilitate eis abiectis ad invisibilia penitus *se convertat* et creaturarum cognitione creatorem evidentius agnoscat" (30: emphasis added).[10] Bernard later glosses *iter* as *ascensiones per creaturarum agnitiones*, explaining that the first step is from inanimate to insensible animate things, thence to irrational animals, rational animals ("i.e. ad homines," Bernard adds, with the optimism of an earlier age), the celestial orders, and finally to God: "Itaque per ordinem creaturarum itum est ad creatorem" (52).

---

[9] Bernard draws upon Macrobius's discussion of the soul's descent. A *descensus ad inferos* may simply signify the soul's descent into the body: "Antequam philosophia ad id vigoris adolesceret, theologiae professores aliud esse inferos quam corpora humana negaverunt, inferos autem corpora dixerunt eo quod in rebus nichil aliud inferius invenerunt" (28; cf. *Commentarium in Somnium Scipionis* 1.10.9). Or—and Bernard prefers this more general interpretation—*inferi* may have a wider reference, to this "caducem et inferiorem regionem" (29).

[10] The Sibyl who guides Aeneas represents *intelligentia*, and in glossing her prophecy Bernard says: "Intelligentia namque divina praecipue docet, divinis vero integumenta praecipue congruunt, quia ut ait Martianus cuniculis verborum divina sunt tegenda. Unde Plato et alii philosophi cum de anima vel alio theologico aliquid dicunt ad integumentum se convertunt: ut Maro in hoc opere" (51). Although Bernard's is not a Christianizing interpretation of the *Aeneid*, and there are some elements in his commentary which would be difficult to square with Christian doctrine, he had good patristic sanction for the idea that pagans could know God through His creation. For example, in discussing the similarity between Platonism and Christianity Augustine three times (*De civitate Dei* 8.6, 10, 12) quotes Romans 1.19-20: "Quia quod notum est Dei, manifestum est in illis; Deus enim illis manifestavit. Invisibilia enim ipsius, a creatura mundi, per ea quae facta sunt, intellecta, conspiciuntur; sempiterna quoque eius virtus, et divinitas."

Charles Singleton has glossed the three lights in the *Commedia* with the following comment by Aquinas: "There is a kind of vision for which the natural light of intellect suffices, such as the contemplation of invisible things according to the principles of reason; and the philosophers placed the highest happiness of man in this contemplation; there is yet another kind of contemplation to which man is raised by the light of faith . . . and there is that contemplation of the blessed in Heaven [*in patria*] to which the intellect is uplifted by the light of Glory"—which sometimes happens, as in Paul's case, to a man still in this life.[11] These three lights do not correspond to the tripartite division of the *Commedia*, for it is Beatrice who gives Dante wings for flight (*Paradiso* 10.53-54), and his whole flight to God is a transhumanizing, a going beyond the human (*Paradiso* 1.70: "trasumanar"), while his movement under Vergil's guidance was by the natural light of intellect.[12] *Inferno* and *Purgatorio* mark a first ontological stage, *Paradiso* a second.

In discussing man's threefold knowledge of divine things, Aquinas said: "Prima est secundum quod homo naturali lumine rationis per creaturas in Dei cognitionem ascendit"[13]—exactly the mediated, partial vision to which Bernard refers, vision that is not yet *facie ad faciem*. Thus, if Aquinas's whole formulation is a fair gloss upon the *Commedia*, Bernard's allegorized *Aeneid* assumes a striking resemblance to the Vergilian first stage of Dante's journey.

Vergil can lead Dante only so far: then Beatrice must take over. At this crucial point in the poem, as if to underline the parallelism between his own *iter* and that of Aeneas, Dante quotes from the climactic episode of *Aeneid* 6:

> Tutti dicean: *Benedictus qui venis,*
> E fior gittando di sopra e dintorno,
> *Manibus o date lilia plenis.*
> (*Purgatorio* 30.19-21)

Christian and pagan: the one *iter* supersedes the other, but in so doing arises from and incorporates its predecessor.[14]

---

[11] Charles Singleton, "The Three Lights," *Dante Studies* 2: *Journey to Beatrice* (Cambridge, Mass. 1958) 15.

[12] *Ibid.*, esp. 26-31. A basically bipartite division of the poem is also suggested by Dante's use of classical mythology: see C. A. Robson, "Dante's Use in the *Divina Commedia* of the Medieval Allegories on Ovid," in *Centenary Essays on Dante*, by members of the Oxford Dante Society (Oxford 1965) 1-38.

[13] Quoted by Singleton, *Journey* 23; and by Silverstein (n. 4 above) 78.

[14] Cf. Davis (n. 3 above) 33: "Christ came, and Peter established the see of Rome, not to interrupt the tradition, but to fulfil it." Davis 138 cites *Purg.* 30.19-21 to illustrate Vergil's "dual role" as intermediary between the two Romes (see also my essay on "Dante's Ulysses and the Allegorical Journey," *Dante Studies* 85 [1967] 33-58). But the historicity and historical importance of Vergil and Aeneas do not preclude allegorical significances, for in Dante's view a figure could be both historical *and* allegorical (see, for example, his

Before flying aloft to see God face to face, Dante undergoes a *descensus*, a *conversio* and an *ascensio*: he travels the same spiritual path along which the Sibyl had led Aeneas. Both journeys have the same pattern and the same basic epistemology. So despite his initial protestation, Dante becomes both an Enea and a Paolo, in quest of the heavenly *patria*, "quella Roma onde Cristo è romano" (*Purgatorio* 32.102). And it should be little cause for wonder if Bernard's mystic Vergil acts as his first guide, along that "cammino alto e silvestro" (*Inferno* 2.142).

Department of Romance Languages and Literature
University of Washington
Seattle, Washington 98105, U.S.A.

----

discussion of Cato's wife, Marcia, in *Convivio* 4.28: there is no doubt of her historical reality, yet in Lucan's poem she can also represent "la nobile Anima"). The historical process is development, metamorphosis; and the same holds for a man's psychological progress: cf. *Purg.* 10.124-126; *Par.* 1.67-72; and Singleton, *Journey* 28-29.

THE LIBRO DEL CAVALLERO ZIFAR
AND THE MEDIEVAL SERMON

•

by James F. Burke

Critics have been aware for some time of the importance of the sermon for English literature of the Middle Ages;[1] yet very little interest has been shown in this genre in regard to the literary culture of the Spanish peninsula, despite an obvious Hispanic involvement with homiletics. Such works as the *Libro de los gatos* and the *Libro de los exemplos por A. B. C.* may have been written as source books for preachers. But even if they were conceived as entertainment and not primarily as moral storehouses,[2] they demonstrate the influence of the sermon upon the nascent literature of this area. The *Libro de buen amor*, only a few years later in date than the *Zifar*, even begins with a mock homily modeled upon the structure of the university sermon.[3] It is thus feasible that we look to the sermonic form as a possible prototype for a work that has always puzzled critics owing to its strange structure—the *Libro del Cavallero Zifar*.

Few scholars of medieval Spanish literature would question the importance of the anonymous early fourteenth-century *Zifar*. Since it does not seem to have been copied directly from any one source (as so much of medieval

---

[1] The two basic works concerning the subject are those of G. R. Owst, *Preaching in Medieval England* (Cambridge 1926), and *Literature and Pulpit in Medieval England* (Oxford 1961). Walter Schirmer, *John Lydgate*, trans. Ann E. Keep (London 1961) 85-88, demonstrates that *The Serpent of Division* is based upon sermon structure. Margaret Williams, *The Pearl-Poet* (New York 1967), shows that the same is true in regard to the poems *Cleanness* and *Patience*. A. Spearing, *Criticism and Medieval Poetry* (London 1964) 68-95, suggests that even *Piers Plowman* might be an evolution of the medieval university sermon. Coolidge Otis Chapman in two articles, "*The Parson's Tale*: A Mediaeval Sermon," *Modern Language Notes* (MLN) 43 (1928) 229-234 and "*The Pardoner's Tale*: A Mediaeval Sermon," MLN 41 (1926) 506-509, proves that Chaucer relied upon sermon structure for the plan of these two works. Chapman discusses Chaucer's knowledge and use of the *artes praedicandi* in "Chaucer on Preachers and Preaching," *Publications of the Modern Language Association* (PMLA) 44 (1929) 178-185.

[2] As John E. Keller believes. See his edition of the *Libro de los exenplos por A. B. C.* (Madrid 1961) 18-19.

[3] Juan Ruiz, *El libro de buen amor*, ed. J. Cejador, Clásicos Castellanos 14 (Madrid 1960) 1.6-14.

208   JAMES F. BURKE

Spanish literature has been), it probably is one of the first, if not the first,
original literary prose works in the Spanish language. It vies with the *Amadís
de Gaula* not only for that honor,[4] but also as the earliest of the novels of
chivalry, a genre that was to have a long and far-reaching influence upon
literature in the peninsula.

From the time of Menéndez Pelayo, who commented "la composición de
esta novela es extrañísima,"[5] scholars have been both fascinated by the *Zifar*
and bothered by its apparent lack of organization.[6] The result has been that
most have doubted the literary worth of the book and have subsequently
ascribed its importance to its early date and the interesting, if perplexing,
mixture of literary types found in its pages. The suspicion has remained
in the minds of those interested in the *Zifar*, however, that the work must
have had a purpose and that that purpose would have necessitated some
sort of plan on the part of the author which should be discernible to the critic.

With the publication of an excellent article by Roger Walker, who demonstrated remarkable parallelisms within the various divisions of the *Zifar*,[7]
the question of the unity of the work was again raised. The implication of
Walker's article is that the author must have organized his work in a logical
sequence and that the parallelisms evident on the surface are reflections of
this organization. The object of my study is to demonstrate that, indeed,
the *Zifar* does follow a pattern that the author conceived by imitating a
familiar medieval phenomenon—the university sermon.

The *Zifar* is divided into a prologue and three major sections. The prologue
relates how Ferrant Martínez, archdeacon of Madrid in the Cathedral of
Toledo, went to Rome for the Jubilee of 1300 and met there his old mentor
Gonzalo Gudiel, previously archbishop of Toledo, who had been made cardinal of Albano by Boniface VIII.[8] Cardinal Gonzalo wished to be buried
not at Rome, as was customary when a cardinal died there, but in Toledo.

---

[4] See Edwin B. Place, "Cervantes and the *Amadís*," in *Hispanic Studies in Honor of
Nicholson B. Adams*, University of North Carolina Studies in Romance Languages and
Literatures 59 (Chapel Hill 1966). Place believes that the *Amadís* was probably written
between 1312 and 1350, while the most probable date for the *Zifar* is 1301. See Erasmo
Buceta, "Algunas notas históricas al prólogo del 'Cavallero Cifar,'" *Revista de filología
española* 17 (1930) 18-36.

[5] M. Menéndez Pelayo, *Orígenes de la novela* (Madrid 1943) 1.295.

[6] See Roger Walker, "The Unity of *El libro del Cavallero Zifar*," *Bulletin of Hispanic
Studies* 42 (1965) 149-159, who gives an excellent study of the long and interesting controversy
concerning the unity of the *Zifar*. There is no need here to repeat the bibliography concerning
the question that he presents.

[7] *Ibid.*; see also n. 3.

[8] T. S. R. Boase, *Boniface VIII* (Toronto 1933) 197, says that Archbishop Gonzalo was
summoned to Rome because he had consecrated a bishop who had supposedly obtained
his see through the intervention of King Sancho. Boniface evidently found Gonzalo so
pleasing that he not only dismissed the charge against him, but also made him a cardinal.

He asked Ferrant Martínez to see, in the event of his death in the Eternal City, that his body be returned to Toledo for interment in the cathedral there. When the Cardinal did indeed die at Rome, the author of the *Zifar* relates how Ferrant Martínez fulfilled his promise at great hardship to himself.

After the prologue begins the first section; it treats the adventures of the knight Zifar and his family after they are forced to leave their home due to a series of misfortunes. Following many hazardous undertakings, Zifar becomes king of Mentón and the work switches to a new tenor. In the second section Zifar advises his sons Garfín and Roboán concerning the ways of religious chivalry and the duties of kingship. When this long "mirror of princes" is completed, the youngest son, Roboán, begs leave of his father to set out on another series of adventures that in some ways parallel those of his father, yet are uniquely different. These adventures comprise the third section.

Since the literary cement that joins the prologue and the three sections seems contrived, it is not surprising that scholars have suspected that the author of the *Zifar* had done nothing more than place together three separate literary pieces with the story of Ferrant Martínez to serve as an introduction. Although the *Zifar* lacks unity in the traditional Aristotelian sense of passing from beginning to middle to end, its structure does recall that of the medieval university sermon.

The form of the university sermon is well known; nevertheless, it may be appropriate to give here a brief outline of its more salient points. Two sermon patterns were common in the Middle Ages. The earlier of the two, examples of which abound in Saint Augustine, was really nothing more than a point-by-point commentary upon a chapter from the Bible. The second, which probably originated in the university communities of Oxford and Paris in the early thirteenth century (hence its name), is an evolution of the Roman oration. Its structure, due to the arrangement of its classical predecessor, was infinitely more complicated than the simple commentary sermon. To the end of teaching young preachers how to conceive such a sermon, elaborate *artes praedicandi* were composed,[9] which the student might use as a guide when he was unsure of himself.

---

[9] Probably the best analytical study of the *artes praedicandi* is T. M. Charland, *Artes praedicandi* (Paris and Ottawa 1936). Additional information may be obtained concerning the preaching manuals and the sermons themselves by consulting the following works: Louis Bourgain, *La chaire française au XIIᵉ siècle d'après les manuscripts* (Paris 1879); A. Lecoy de la Marche, *La chaire française au moyen âge* (Paris 1886); Homer G. Pfander, *The Popular Sermon of the Medieval Friar in England* (New York 1937); Étienne Gilson, "Michel Menot et la technique du sermon medieval," *Revue d'histoire franciscaine* 2 (1925) 301ff. Harry Caplan, *Mediaeval Artes praedicandi* (Ithaca 1934), lists only two manuscripts (31, 140) which could have been known in Spain prior to the date of the *Zifar*. But considering the lack of accurate catalogues and indexes to Spanish libraries, it is more than likely that others exist but have not been found.

The university sermon opened with the statement of a theme, usually a verse from scripture, which was to serve as the basis of the homily. The preacher then proceeded to the protheme, or in classical parlance the *exordium*, where the importance of the ideas implicit in the theme were demonstrated, and where the preacher attempted to gain the sympathy of his listeners. At the end of the protheme there was a brief prayer to implore God's aid to the preacher and the listeners, not only in regard to the sermon, but in all things. Following the prayer, the theme would be repeated, in case latecomers had not heard it at the beginning and would not, therefore, be aware of the intent of the sermon.

With these preliminaries out of the way, the preacher would begin the "introduction of the theme." Here he was constrained to tie the theme and protheme, the bases of the sermon, to the remainder, which was called the *depositio* or *dilatio*, and which was generally a discussion of three important points that he would draw from the theme. Various methods are suggested in the *artes praedicandi* by which the preacher could unite his theme and *dilatio*, but the one that seems relevant to the structure of the *Zifar* is based upon two tenets of ancient legal oratory—*narratio* and *argumentatio*.[10] *Narratio* in the classical oration was nothing more than a statement of the facts about the speaker's subject, or case.[11] The *argumentatio* or *status* occupied itself with interpreting the facts listed in the *narratio*. A tripartite division of the *argumentatio* allowed the orator to direct the attention of his audience to whatever position in regard to the facts and, more important, the interpretation of the facts, that he might deem necessary for clearer comprehension of what he was going to explain. Thus the *argumentatio* had to (1) decide whether the facts were to be admitted as true, (2) define what they meant, and (3) interpret these facts in a broad general sense.[12]

The preacher, having established the veracity and relevance of the main points that would constitute the sermon, then proceeded into the *dispositio* or body. The usual practice was to expand the three points or ideas, drawn from the theme, by various means of rhetorical *amplificatio* until a sermon of suitable length was achieved. When the *dispositio* was finished, the theme was again repeated and the listeners were exhorted to profit by the message implied in it. With this *peroratio* the sermon ended.

In the prologue of the *Zifar*, after the author has finished the tale of Ferrant Martínez's great deed, he moralizes on the story and concludes that the archdeacon was willing to perform such a task because he owed so much to the cardinal:

---

[10] J. W. Blench, *Preaching in England* (Oxford 1964) 73.
[11] C. S. Baldwin, *Ancient Rhetoric and Poetic* (Gloucester, Mass. 1959) 35.
[12] *Ibid.* 50.

> E çiertas sy costa grande fizo el Arçidiano en este camino, mucho
> le es de gradesçer porque lo enpleo muy bien, reconosçiendo la
> merçed que del Cardenal resçebiera e la criança que en el feziera, asy
> commo lo deuen fazer todos los omes de buen entendimiento e de buen
> conosçer e que bien e merçed resçiben de otro.[13]

Ferrant Martínez probably received his appointment as archdeacon of Madrid
from the hand of Cardinal Gonzalo himself when he was archbishop of Toledo,[14] and would, thus, in a very real sense have been beholden to him. An
archdeacon was the vicar of a bishop in the area under his authority[15] and
was thereby the servant and even the vassal of this bishop. Service rendered
after death to the overlord, as in the case of Ferrant Martínez, would certainly be exemplary.

The author of the *Zifar* begins with this historical episode, presented in
exemplum fashion, because he wishes to emphasize the idea that all men
granted *buen entendimiento* and *buen conosçer* should repay *bien e merçed*
that they receive from another. This point is important for him because
he is going to use it as the basis or theme (in the sense of a sermon) for the
entire work. In other words, the deeds of the knight Zifar, and later those
of his son Roboán, would illustrate this principle in much the same way that.
Ferrant Martínez's fulfillment of his promise to Cardinal Gonzalo had.

This principle, of great importance for medieval man, is basically the idea
of *redde quod debes*.[16] The Christian must always keep his moral scales in
balance: if he owes a debt, he should pay it; if he has sinned, he must do penance. The protection offered by an overlord required service in return.
In effect the principle of *redde quod debes* was what made the medieval system
of hierarchies function. It required that the man who would live justly in
the manner implied by Christian doctrine should always maintain an equili-
brium in his affairs, never allowing himself to fall into permanent debt, real
or moral. Not only did this principle apply between man and man but also
between man and God—hence the necessary penance for sin.[17]

---

[13] *El libro del Cavallero Zifar*, ed. Charles Philip Wagner (Ann Arbor 1929) 6.

[14] That Gonzalo while archbishop of Toledo had been solicitous of the welfare of his
clergy is shown by a letter quoted in in José Amador de los Ríos, *Historia de la villa y corte
de Madrid* (Madrid 1860) 1.118 in which the archbishop directs that each cleric in his diocese
receive ample funds for his needs.

[15] *Siete Partidas* 1.6.4.

[16] For an excellent discussion of the principle *redde quod debes* and its importance for
medieval literature, see Morton Bloomfield, *Piers Plowman as a Fourteenth-Century Apo-
calypse* (New Brunswick, New Jersey 1962) 130-134.

[17] One of the characteristics of the theme of a university sermon is that it generally
occurs several times in the *depositio*, often in slightly altered form, as a kind of reminder
to the listeners of the preacher's central point. Thus Zifar, during his long dialogue-debate
with el Ribaldo, when he first meets him in the hermit's hut, gives the theme of the work

The theme, given by the author of the *Zifar*, and its concomitant idea of *redde quod debes* would also have grave eschatological implications for medieval man which would go far beyond mere personal restitution made by one individual to another. As Bloomfield points out, *redde quod debes* is a summation of Christian justice, and no reformation or perfecting of medieval society was considered possible unless each *status* accepted this justice as its guiding principle and functioned according to it. Thus the perfecting of society, with which I think the author of the *Zifar* to have been concerned,[18] could only be possible through justice that depended upon the concept *redde quod debes*.

From the eschatological side, the theme of the *Zifar* reflects the admonitions of Jesus apparent in his parable of the good servants in Matthew 25. The master, returning from his trip, is pleased with the servants who used the talents given to them to good advantage, but is most displeased with the one who only preserved what he had received and orders that he be "cast . . . into outer darkness" (25.30). Jesus shows by this parable that those who do not use profitably the "talents" entrusted to them will be damned, and those who do will inherit the kingdom of God.

This is all common knowledge today, even to a nominal Christian, as it must have been in the Middle Ages. The important concept for the author of the *Zifar* is the interpretation given to the remainder of Matthew 25 where Jesus begins by saying: "For I was an hungred, and ye gave me meat: I was thirsty, and ye gave me drink: I was a stranger, and ye took me in" (25.35). What this means, according to Ray C. Petry, is that "each soul is admonished to remember that if he would stand at the Judgment within the community of the righteous, he must identify himself on earth with the community of the just. If he would do this, he must be in preparation always, to serve others."[19]

The Christian, then, who receives reason and common sense as a gift from God must be prepared to use these gifts to aid in establishing a "just society" here upon this earth which will be a kind of foretaste of that celestial kingdom that is to follow. Since this idea would be of such compelling importance to

---

in terms of the formula *redde quod debes*: "Çertas ley es entre las gentes establesçida, de tonrar ome lo que deue a aquel de quien lo resçibe. E asy lo de Dios resçebimos de Dios, e despues deuemos gelo tornar; e lo que resçebimos de la tierra deuemos lo tornar a la tierra: ca el alma tiene el ome de Dios e la carne de la tierra" (115). This dialogue, as C. P. Wagner pointed out, is basically derived from the twelfth century *Moralium dogma philosophorum*, "The *Caballero Zifar* and the *Moralium dogma philosophorum*," *Romance Philology* 6 (1952-1953) 309-312. Thus we find in the *Moralium* "Lex gentium est reddere quod acceperis" (PL 171.1028). The author has translated this commonplace into Spanish but, more important, he has used it as the theme of his work.

[18] This may be seen in the description of the kingdom of Mentón which, after Zifar becomes king, is glowingly described as a kind of terrestrial paradise. *Zifar* 172-174, 202-204.

[19] *Christian Eschatology and Social Thought* (New York 1956) 301.

medieval man, not only for the sake of his soul, but secondarily because of the effect that it would have upon his way of living, one would expect it to be heard from the pulpit as a constant reminder. We find it, for example, in a vernacular sermon by Maurice of Sully which is based upon the parable of the good servants. It is a homily of the older type in which the preacher simply recounted the parable in the vernacular and then proceeded to explain its significance allegorically:

> Li hom qui ala el lontain païs en pelerinage, ço est Deus Nostre Sire qui corporelment ala de terre el ciel. Li serjant, ço sont li crestien. . . . Li avoirs est li sens e li savoirs que Deus a mis en nos, que nos devons mutepliier, en nos meismes par bone vie demener . . . e quant nos faisons bien e nos donons as autres bone essample e lor ensegnons le bien a faire, lores est mutepliiés li biens Nostre Segnor en nos.[20]

After explaining that the bad servant is the sinner who wastes *l'entendement* given to him by God on *covoitise* and the like, the preacher demonstrates that the return of the master means the return of the Lord who will see what his servants have done with that entrusted to each and "as buens dira il: 'Venite, benedicti Patris mej,' e as malvais. . . . ' Ite, maledicti."[21]

In the *Zifar* the author is not primarily speaking to everyman, although his conclusions are just as valid for him, but to that individual who is a king or would be a king. Of course the role of the king in creating a "community of the just" upon the earth would be far more important than that of lesser individuals. The king is looked upon in countless medieval tracts as the vicar of God on earth and is thus conceived as a servant of God. The parable of the servants could be expected to apply more directly to him. The theme of the *Zifar*, drawing upon the faithfulness of Ferrant Martínez as an example, shows that *buen entendimiento* and *buen conosçer, bien e merçed* are talents given by God to only a few. If one of this chosen few should be further honored by being made a king, he must, to repay God, exert himself to the utmost to create a "community of the just" on this earth as a preparation for the heavenly kingdom. If he failed to do this, he would be in dire danger of losing his soul. This lesson is obvious in the *Zifar* because the kingdoms that both father and son come to rule are presented as types of the earthly paradise.[22] The author even refers to the kingdom of Triguida, after Roboán accedes to the throne, as *tierra de bendiçion*.[23]

---

[20] Sermon 63, quoted in C. A. Robson, *Maurice of Sully and the Medieval Vernacular Homily* (Oxford 1952).

[21] *Ibid.* 192.

[22] See n. 18 above.

[23] *Zifar* 515.

Of course the theme of a university sermon was supposed to be drawn always from scripture, but examples are extant of a preacher's having taken his text from other sources.[24] Stephen Langton based one of his sermons upon the refrain of a well-known ditty.[25] Even Saint Francis of Assisi wrote a sermon that has as its text the couplet of a popular love song. Lecoy de la Marche's statement concerning the renowned preacher who always began his sermons with an "histoire" describes a practice which was probably wide-spread in the Middle Ages especially in sermons preached in the vernacular to laymen who needed something with a "punch" to gain their interest. One would not expect, and does not find, much reference to such sermons in the *artes praedicandi* for the simple reason that they were written for more learned readers who would prefer to take a scriptural verse as the theme and analyze it in the approved manner.

After giving the theme, the basis of the work, the author of the *Zifar* moves into what corresponds to the protheme of a sermon. It must be remembered that the homiletic protheme had some connection with the *exordium* of an oration and was even occasionally referred to by that name. In the sermon the *exordium*-protheme usually served a definite purpose that we need not enter into here,[26] but many times it was no more than a "transitional"[27] section that helped to put the listener into the right frame of mind. In this respect it would have been almost identical in concept to the *exordium* of an oration. A whole set of "topics" for gaining the interest of the listener were evolved and used[28] in the *exordium*, which often became nothing more than a ritualistic recitation of these commonplaces. The protheme of the *Zifar* resembles this kind of *exordium* in that it is composed of three such *topoi*. The first, found also in the *Libro de buen amor*,[29] runs to the effect that men have to write things down due to weakness of memory:

> E porque la memoria del ome ha luengo tienpo, e non se pueden acordar los omes de las cosas mucho antiguas sy las non fallan por escripto, e porende el trasladador de la estoria que adelante oyredes, que fue trasladada de caldeo en latin e de latin en romançe, puso e ordeno estas dos cosas sobredichas en esta obra, porque los que venieren despues de los deste tienpo, sera quando el año jubileo a

---

[24] "Un célèbre orateur de l'antiquité commençait, dit-on, toutes ses harangues par une histoire. Dans la chaire du moyen âge les histoires ou, pour parler le langage du temps les *exemples*, sont au contraire réservés ordinairement pour la fin," Lecoy de la Marche 298.

[25] Owst, *Preaching in Medieval England* 231.

[26] See for example the treatment of the protheme in Charland 125-135.

[27] Spearing 75.

[28] See E. R. Curtius, *European Literature and the Latin Middle Ages*, trans. Willard Trask (New York 1953) 82-89.

[29] *Libro de buen amor* 1.10.

de ser ... e que sepan que este fue el primer cardenal que fue en-
terrado en España.[30]

The author of the *Zifar* uses this *topos* as his reason for having mentioned
the Jubilee of 1300 and the translation of the cardinal's body. Since his
primary interest is not in these events but in the "message" of the body of
the work, it is likely that *estas dos cosas* also refers to the two parts of the
theme given immediately before, that is, that all men with good common
sense will endeavor to repay the kindness received from their lord. The author
would suggest that it is necessary to write down examples of basic truths
(in this case the theme) so that the memory of man might be constantly re-
freshed by them.[31] He would imply thereby that the reader should see the
adventures of Zifar and his family as an illustration of *estas dos cosas*.

The second *topos* is what Curtius calls "a topic of affected modesty"[32] wherein
readers are invited to correct and emend the work if they feel that they can
improve it:

> Pero esta obra es fecha so emienda de aquellos que la quesieren
> emendar. E çertas deuenlo fazer los que quisieren e la sopieren
> emendar sy quier; porque dize la escriptura: "Qui sotilmente la cosa
> fecha emienda, mas de loar es que el que primeramente la fallo." E
> otro sy mucho deue plazer a quien la cosa comiença a fazer que la emien-
> den todos quantos la quesieren emendar e sopieren; ca quanto mas
> es la cosa emendada, tanto mas es loada.[33]

It seems possible that the author of the *Zifar* might also be referring here
to the medieval exegetical tradition of "glossing" the text. Leo Spitzer[34]

---

[30] *Zifar* 6.

[31] D. W. Robertson, *A Preface to Chaucer* (Princeton 1962) 72, suggests that Matthew
5.28, "Whosoever shall look on a woman to lust after her, hath already committed adultery
with her in his heart," meant the following to medieval man: When the corporal senses
place an image in the memory, it may be contemplated in a positive or negative manner.
If it is considered in a negative manner, that is, with the end of cupidinous satisfaction,
the result is evil. Of course certain images are more likely than others to tempt the mind
into sin. Thus the whole problem can be avoided if there is such a store of virtuous examples
in the memory that there is little or no room for unworthy ones. After the second *topos*
of the protheme, the author of the *Zifar* returns to this idea: "E non se deue ninguno es-
forçar en su solo entendimiento nin creer que todo se puede acordar; ca aver todas las cosas
en memoria e non pecar nin errar en ninguna cosa, mas es esto de Dios que non de ome. . . .
Ca por razon de la mengua de la memoria del ome fueron puestas estas cosas a esta obra"
(*Zifar* 6). Surely he is not merely concerned that the reader remember the Jubilee and the
translation of the cardinal's body. He wants the reader to be aware of the import of the
message implied in the theme so that it can serve as a worthy example to the memory.

[32] Curtius 83-85.

[33] *Zifar* 6.

[34] "The Prologue to the *Lais* of Marie de France and Medieval Poetics," *Modern Philology* 41 (1943-1944) 96-102.

has shown that if a work were considered to have a meaning demonstrating Christian doctrine, then this meaning, while imposed by the author, would only become fully developed over the centuries by the readers—"the progress achieved by the latest readers being foreseen, as it were, by divine inspiration" (96). The author of the *Zifar* does claim such a signification to be present in his work (10). Thus he would invite skilled readers subtly to search out and apprehend the full doctrinal import of the book.[35]

The problematic word is *emendar*, which normally means only "to correct" in Old Spanish. I would suggest that it might also have carried the implication of "glossing a text" or giving it an interpretation consonant with Christian doctrine. For example, Berceo, while allegorically explaining the *locus amoenus* in the introduction to the *Milagros*, tells us that the Virgin worked in concert with the four evangelists while they were writing the gospels. "Quanto escrivien ellos, ella lo emendava" (22). Does he mean, in the strictest sense, that she only corrected the grammar and punctuation of what they wrote or, rather, does he not wish to imply that she aided them in filling the gospels with the correct shade of Christian truth?

The same use of *emendar* seems to occur in Montalvo's prologue to the *Amadís*: "en los quales cinco libros como quiera que hasta aquí más por patrañas que por crónicas eran tenidos, son con las tales *emiendas* [italics mine] acompañados de tales enxemplos y doctrinas, que con justa causa se podrán comparar a los liuianos y febles saleros de corcho, que con tiras de oro y de plata son encarcelados y guarnescidos" (Place edition 9).

Montalvo must be comparing the literal story of *Amadís* to the worthless *salero de corcho* while equating the *enxemplos y doctrinas* with the gold and silver garnishments. Just as the smith surrounds the *salero* with precious metals, so the author, by means of the *emiendas*, imposes or finds a shadowing of Christian doctrine in the story of *Amadís*. Many critics[36] believe that such a statement as this, and likewise the one in the *Zifar*, are only justifications for *belles lettres* and refer at most to very generalized moralities and not to doctrinal meanings. However this may be, the authors are obviously *claiming* that the doctrinal signification is present and are thereby hoping to place their works within the context of the exegetical tradition. If the author of the *Zifar* is only pretending that the work adumbrates Christian truths, then his asking the reader to search for and develop these truths can only be a commonplace. On the other hand, if he is serious, then the critic

---

[35] The word "sotil" is used often in medieval literature in connection with the allegorical method, but it is extremely difficult to understand just what an individual author may have meant by the term since the implication probably switches from work to work as Anthony Zahareas, *The Art of Juan Ruiz* (Madrid 1965) 43-47, demonstrates by contrasting the meaning of the word in the *Libro de buen amor* and in the *Disciplina clericalis*.

[36] Cf. Rosemund Tuve, *Allegorical Imagery* (Princeton 1966) 394.

must consider this *topos* as a very important guide to the interpretation of the book.

The final topic is one that runs like a thread through all the *artes praedicandi*—the widespread maxim that a work should be both *dulce* and *utile*. "Ca todo ome que trabajo quiere tomar para fazer alguna buena obra, deue en ella entreponer a las vegadas algunas cosas de plazer e de solas."[37] It is necessary to sugarcoat the pill so that the patient will take it with gusto.

A prayer usually follows the protheme in a university sermon. There is nothing of the order of an *orate fratres* after the protheme in the *Zifar*; but the author does exhort his reader to place God at the beginning of all his affairs just as he is placing Him at the beginning of this work. "Ca Dios es comienço e acabamiento de todas las cosas, e syn el ninguna cosa non puede ser fecha."[38]

The theme is now repeated as would be expected at this point, in a slightly expanded version, with God as the overlord and the Christian as the vassal: "onde a quien Dios quiso buen seso dar puede començar e acabar buenas obras e onestas a seruiçio de Dios."[39] Then the author begins the "introduction of the theme" by means of *narratio* and *status-argumentatio*. Zifar's forthcoming misfortunes and adventures are sketched in brief outline form (the *narratio*),[40] which is followed by an explanation of facts in the *argumentatio*. The first premise to be clarified in the classical *status* was whether or not the facts of the situation could be taken as true. The author of the *Zifar* claimed in the protheme in conjunction with the *topos* on memory, as medieval authors were wont to do, that he was reworking a story that he had found in another version. "E porende el trasladador de la estoria que adelante oyredes, que fue trasladada de caldeo en latin e de latin en romance."[41] How could he thus assert that the facts found in the *Zifar* were true when he admitted that he was copying from source material? He avoids the problem first by agreeing that the facts of the story might be fictitious; he then goes on to say that this would be of no consequence, since the moral lesson implicit in the tale is the same whether the elements of the episode happened or not. "Pero commoquier que verdaderas non fuesen, non las deuen tener en poco . . . ca atal es este libro para quien bien quisiere catar por el, como la nuez, que ha parte de fuera fuste seco e tiene el fruto ascondido dentro."[42]

The second premise of the classical *status*—the definition of facts accepted as true—would have to be avoided if the author were not sure that they really happened. The third premise was the interpretation of facts. There might be no true facts in the *Zifar* as such, but the reader, nevertheless, could receive

[37] *Zifar* 6.
[38] *Ibid.*
[39] *Ibid.*
[40] *Ibid.* 8-9.
[41] *Ibid.* 6.
[42] *Ibid.* 10.

the same benefit, provided he interpreted the work correctly. The author uses the well-known medieval image of the kernel and shell to exhort his readers to go beneath the surface of the letter and survey the allegorical landscape implied by surface events. The reader should pass beyond the literal meaning and find the deeper moral or doctrinal significance bound up in the symbolism and allegory of the work. There was no need for the author of the *Zifar* to prove that his story was true; his purpose could be achieved once he had established a proper path for the reader to follow in understanding the work.

With the end of the *argumentatio* began the *depositio* of the sermon. The simplest way for a preacher to get the three points called for by the *artes praedicandi* was to divide the theme, if it were a Bible verse, into three portions. He would then explain the theological implications of each word or groups of words within these three portions. But this division of the verse and the subsequent explanation of its words and phrases was normally used only if the audience consisted of clerks themselves skilled in the ways of the university sermon.[43] If the listeners were not so learned, it was better to interpret the three portions of the verse in terms of experiences that the congregation could appreciate and to which they might relate. For example,[44] a sermon written at Paris for the Feast of Saint Nicholas in 1230 takes as its theme Ecclesiasticus 50.2:

> Quasi oliva pullulans et quasi cupressus in altitudinem se extollens;
> in accipiendo ipsum stolam gloriae, et vestiri eum in consumma-
> tionem virtutis gloriam dedit sanctitatis amictum.[45]

As we might expect, there are three principal divisions in the *depostio* of the sermon which derive from three facets of this theme. In the first the preacher compares the youth of Saint Nicholas to the olive tree, in the second his adolescence to the cypress, and in the third he winds up the sermon by demonstrating that the words of the verse, "he put on his splendid vestments," relate to Saint Nicholas's becoming a priest. The preacher is pushed at times to make his comparisons ring true. This does not matter as the purpose of the sermon is to stimulate the listener by the vision of the exemplary life of Saint Nicholas, hence the importance of the theme is not the meaning of the theme itself, but what it can imply when used by a clever preacher.

The author of the *Zifar* has adopted this "division prise de l'extérieur" as Charland calls it, as a means of dividing and explaining his theme. He

---

[43] Charland 163.

[44] I do not mean to imply that this sermon was written for the unlearned. I use it because it is an example of a sermon in which the explanation applied to the theme is not found within the theme itself.

[45] Quoted in M. M. Davy, *Les sermons universitaires parisiens* (Paris 1931).

thus illustrates with the three major divisions of the work—the *Cavallero de Dios y rey de Mentón* section plus the *Castigos del rey de Mentón* and the *Hechos de Roboán*—three ways of looking at or interpreting his theme.

The final phase of a university sermon is the peroration where the preacher repeats the theme once more and exhorts his listeners to profit by the example implied therein. He has now illustrated it by means of the *depositio* and can hope to have made it more fully clear and comprehensible to his audience. If the sermon was a good one, the basic truth of the theme, often somewhat hackneyed through familiarity, should have been given new luster and appeal. Thus in the *Zifar*, after the three major examples are finished, the author returns for the final time to his primary idea:

> Onde dize el traslaudador que bien auenturado es el que se da a bien, e se trabaja sienpre de fazer lo mejor; ca por bien fazer puede ome ganar a Dios e la los omes, e pro e onrra para este mundo e para el otro . . . e acabemos tales obras que sean a seruiçio de Dios, e a pro e a onrra de nuestros cuerpos, e a saluamiento de nuestras almas.   Amen.[46]

In exhorting the listener to *fazer bien*, the author obviously feels that he has provided an excellent example, in the preceding story of *Zifar* and his family, of the earthy benefits that would accrue to one who did so. In addition he reminds us that these "doers of good" can expect salvation and eternal life as the greatest of rewards for their service.

It thus seems from examining the structure of the *Zifar* that it may well be based upon the university sermon. It should be borne in mind, however that the methodology that I have used for explaining the organization of the work is drawn from several sources dealing with medieval homiletics. No one reference in itself provides a plan to which the *Zifar* might be compared.[47]

If one accepts the homiletic origins of the work as true, he might then seek to understand the creative process by which the author advances from sermon to literary artistry. The theme, protheme, and introduction to the theme only lead to and prepare for the important part of a sermon—the *depositio*—while the peroration is no more than a restatement of the basic idea that launched the preacher on his course. Within the *depositio* is found the essence of what the preacher wishes to say. Here he must organize and display to the greatest extent possible his intellectual and oratorical talents or fail to convince his listeners. In a literary work drawn from a sermon pattern,

---

[46] *Zifar* 516.

[47] This is not important as medieval preachers commonly diverged considerably from the model of the *artes praedicandi* in the preparation of their sermons. See the discussion in Spearing.

the major *exempla* of the *depositio* would have to be likewise most carefully and artistically conceived if the author were to be convincing in his thesis.

In the *Zifar* the three major divisions of the work stand as the major *exempla* illustrating various ways of looking at or interpreting the theme. In order fully to understand the book as a literary piece depending upon sermonic form, it is necessary to perceive the way in which each of the three *exempla* serves to make clear the important implications of the theme. The problem involved in doing this can perhaps be even better seen in the Middle English poem *Cleanness*, also thought to be based sermon structure,[48] which begins with a protheme exalting the virtue suggested in the title and then moves in the *depositio* to three major examples—Noah's flood, Sodom and Gommorrah, and Belshazzar's feast. The questions of interest to the critic concern why the poet chose these particular biblical stories, what facets of the theme of cleanliness they typify and explain, and, even more important, what literary development there is of other concepts and ideas of wider significance than the theme.

It would seem logical and necessary, when examining a work probably derived from the *artes praedicandi*, to use the sermonic form as a point of departure from which to examine critically the work as a whole. Before this can adequately be done, certain criteria need to be established which would aid the critic in answering questions such as those which I have posed above concerning *Cleanness*. Obviously these questions and their answers are as relevant to the *Zifar* or any other medieval work related to sermon structure as they are to *Cleanness*.

In the past few years interesting studies have come forth which treat both the *artes praedicandi* and the sermons that derive from them.[49] They provide us with a variety of examples of the methodology by means of which the preacher spun out his homily. It should be possible for the scholar, taking this sermon-making process as a basis, to bridge the gap between preacher and writer and to show how, for example, the latter used homiletic rhetorical devices in new fashion to produce long literary prose works.

It is helpful to know that the *Zifar* is based upon preaching tracts. Even a cursory study of the methodology of the *artes praedicandi* allows one to appreciate the philosophy behind the composition of the university sermon and thereby to see that a literary work that reflects this methodology is not

---

[48] Margaret Williams at the end of her study of *Cleanness* gives a very interesting schematic outline of the poem showing how the poet expanded from his sermon-form base to the full poem.

[49] See for example Otto A. Dieter, "*Arbor Picta*: the Medieval Tree of Preaching," *Quarterly Journal of Speech* 51 (1965) 123-144. Pierre Ullman, "Juan Ruiz's Prologue," MLN 82 (1967) 149-170, studies the prologue of the *Libro de buen amor* and definitively proves that the introduction of this work is based upon the structure of the university sermon.

necessarily amorphous or badly written. The *Zifar* lacks a pleasing form if it is considered only in the light of Romantic and post-Romantic ideals. On the other hand, the critic taking into account what was deemed proper for the period in which it was written may find much more to praise in the work than has been previously been found by others.

Department of Italian and Hispanic Studies
University of Toronto
Toronto 5, Ontario, Canada

TWO CONTEMPORARY ARMENIAN ELEGIES
ON THE FALL OF CONSTANTINOPLE, 1453

•

by Avedis K. Sanjian

The Ottoman conquest of Constantinople in 1453 had a shocking effect upon the Christian world, as attested by the considerable number of contemporary accounts of the episode in various languages. In addition to the works written by professional historians, there are journals or hastily composed reports written by individuals who were in Constantinople at the time of the siege.[1]

Since the demise of the Bagratuni kingdom in Armenia in 1071 and the fall of their kingdom in Cilicia in 1375, the Armenians had looked upon the Christian West as the future liberators of Armenia from the tyrannical yoke of its Muslim conquerors. Hence, the fall of Constantinople, the last bastion of Christianity in the East, produced a most profound effect upon the Armenians as well. This momentous event inspired two contemporary Armenian poets, Abraham Ankiwrac'i and Aṙak'el Baḷišec'i, to compose laments on the catastrophe in terms that unmistakably reflected not only the authors' own feelings but also those of the Christian Armenians in general. The present study provides, for the first time, English translations of the two elegies; it also analyzes their contents, stylistic and other characteristic features, and the respective points of view of their authors.

Long before the composition of these two works, the Armenians had already developed a significant elegiac literature both in prose and in verse. Some of the latter were inspired by the martyrdom of certain Armenians for their Christian faith; others were inspired by the tragedies resulting from the Muslim capture of a number of important Christian cities. Of interest to the present study are: (1) the elegy written by Catholicos Nersēs Šnorhali (1166-1173) on Edessa following its capture by Amir Zangi of Aleppo in 1144;[2]

---

[1] For a bibliography, with critical comments, of the major Greek, Slavonic, Western and Turkish sources, consult Steven Runciman, *The Fall of Constantinople, 1453* (Cambridge 1965) app. 1, 192-198. Cf. also A. A. Vasiliev, *History of the Byzantine Empire, 324-1453*, 2 vols. (Madison 1961) 2.648-649, which gives the major Greek, Latin, Italian, Russian and Turkish sources. The Christian sources were collected by A. Dethier in the *Monumenta Hungariae historica* (Budapest 1872) 21-22.1-2.

[2] Nersēs Šnorhali's elegy, entitled "Oḷb Edesioy" [Elegy on Edessa], has had four publications: Madras 1810; Paris 1828, with an introduction by J. Saint-Martin; Tiflis 1829; and

(2) the elegy by Catholicos Grigor Tłay (1173-1193) on Jerusalem written after its conquest by Salāḥ al Dīn (Saladin) in 1187;[3] (3) the elegy by Xačʻatur Kečʻarecʻi which describes the destruction of eastern Armenia by the Mongols during the reign of Ghāzān Khān in 1295;[4] (4) and the elegy by Stepʻannos Ōrbelean composed in 1300 which laments the deplorable condition of Vagharshapat, the ancient capital of Armenia, and foreign rule in the author's native homeland.[5]

The biographical data concerning Abraham Ankiwracʻi and Aṙakʻel Bałišecʻi are extremely meager. Judging by his surname *Ankiwracʻi* (lit., "of or from Ankara"), Abraham was probably born in or near the central Anatolian town of Ankara. Some scholars erroneously assert that Abraham was also nicknamed "Łablan" (from Turkish *kaplan*, "tiger, leopard");[6] but it is now certain that this name resulted from a deliberate forgery.[7] Neither the date

---

Calcutta 1832. The first half of the text was published with a translation by É. Dulaurier, "Élégie sur la prise d'Édesse," in *Recueil des historiens des croisades, Documents arméniens* (Paris 1869) 1.223-268. See also Russian translation by Valeria Brusov, "Elegia na vzyatie Edessii: Otriivok iz poemii Nersesa Shnorali (Blagodatniiy)," in *Poezia Armenii* (Moscow 1916) 171-178.

[3] A translation of this text, entitled "Élégie du Patriarche Grégoire Dgh'a, Catholicos d'Arménie, sur la prise de Jérusalem," will be found in Dulaurier (n. 2 above) 1.269-307.

[4] See text of this work, entitled "Ołb vasn awerman tans arewelean" [Elegy on the destruction of our Eastern land], in M. Tʻ. Avdalbegyan, *Xačʻatur Kečʻarecʻi* (Yerevan 1958) 129-133.

[5] Stepʻannos Ōrbelean's elegy, entitled "Ołb i Surb Katʻulikēn" [Elegy on the Holy Cathedral], was published, with an introduction and annotations, by Karapet Kostaneancʻ at Tiflis in 1885.

[6] See H. Ačaṙyan, *Hayocʻ anjnanunneri baṙaran* [Dictionary of Armenian personal names], 5 vols. (Yerevan 1942-1962) 3.139.

[7] The circumstances of the forgery are discussed in H. S. Anasyan, *Haykakan matenagitutʻyun* [Armenian bibliology] 1 (Yerevan 1959) 82-83. Briefly stated, the true Łablan was a sixteenth-century Armenian author who, in the course of copying Abraham Ankiwracʻi's elegy in 1583, inserted his own name instead of Abraham's in the third stanza (line 381) from the end of the text. He also failed to reproduce the last two stanzas of the original (385-392), thus ending the text with the stanza containing his falsified name. He then composed an elegy, in imitation of Abraham's, on the capture of the Crimean city of Kafa by the Ottomans in 1475. This work will be found in Kʻ. Patkanean, *Nšxarkʻ matenagrutʻean Hayocʻ* [Anthology of Armenian literature] (Saint Petersburg 1884) 65-66. At a later date, another scribe, who made a copy of the manuscript done by Łablan, copied Abraham's and Łablan's elegies one after the other and, despite the obvious chronological discrepancy in their composition, attributed them both to one author, namely Abraham Ankiwracʻi. This is evident in MS 286 (Supplément arménien 62) in the Bibliothèque Nationale in Paris. The entry describing this manuscript—see Frédéric Macler, *Catalogue des manuscrits arméniens et géorgiens de la Bibliothèque Nationale* (Paris 1908) 148-149—reads as follows: "Fol. 47. Élégie sur la prise de Constantinople, par Abraham d'Ancyre. Fol. 58. Du même, élégie sur la prise de Caffa, en 1583." In publishing Abraham's text from this manuscript, Patkanean (see 59-64) used the title: "Abraham Ankiwracʻwoy, Łablan kočʻecʻeloy, Ołb i veray aṙman Kostandnupolsoy i Tačkacʻ" [Elegy by Abraham Ankiwracʻi, *Called Łablan*,

of his birth nor the year of his death is known. Lines 381-386 of his elegy indicate that he had sojourned in Constantinople for three months; and the detailed description of the siege and capture of the city substantiates the fact that he was an eyewitness of this historic event. Apart from the elegy, Abraham Ankiwrac'i is also the author of three hymns for Christmas, and of an unpublished chronology of Armenian history.[8]

Although not much more information is available about Aṙak'el Baliśec'i, he is nevertheless known in Armenian literature as a prolific poet and prose writer. He was born in the 1380s in the village of Poṙ near the city of Bitlis (Armenian Baḷēš, hence the surname Baliśec'i, lit. "of or from Baḷēš"), situated southwest of Lake Van in eastern Turkey. As mentioned in his elegy, Aṙak'el's parents were Nersēs and Lut'lumelik'. He was the nephew, as well as the pupil, of the well known medieval Armenian ecclesiastic and author Grigor Xlat'ec'i, surnamed Cerenc'. Aṙak'el was at first associated with the monastery of Ḷazar, located near the town of Mush in the district of Taron; he subsequently became abbot of the monastery of Erkayn-Enkuzeac' in the district of Č'mškacag.

Besides his elegy, Aṙak'el composed numerous works in verse and in prose. His poetic writings can be divided into four major categories: (1) narrative and panegyrical poems, such as those on the life and activities of Saint Gregory the Illuminator (302-325) and Catholicos Nersēs I the Great (353-373); an elegy on the martyrdom of his uncle and mentor, the vardapet Grigor Xlat'ec'i Cerenc', who was murdered by the Rūzagī Kurds in 1426; and an ode on the Cathedral of Holy Etchmiadzin;[9] (2) legendary and allegorical poems, including the story of Johashaphat and Barlaam; (3) moralistic odes; and (4) spiritual and religious hymns and canticles. His prose works, on the other hand, consist of martyrologies and panegyrical-religious treatises.[10] The martyrologies include: the story of the martyrdom of Vardan Datuanc'i or Baliśec'i who, following a religious debate with the Kurdish Amīr Shams al-Dīn of Bitlis, was murdered by the latter in 1421;[11] the martyrdom of two

---

on the capture of Constantinople by the Tačiks], despite the fact that the manuscript does not contain the italicized words. Thus, by erroneously assuming that Lablan was Abraham's nickname and by interpolating it without any justification, Patkanean compounded the initial forgery.

[8] For a bibliography of the hymns composed by Abraham consult Anasyan (n. 7 above) 1.86-87. The text of his historical work will be found in Bibliothèque Nationale MS 233 (Supplément arménien 77); it is listed as "Chronologie de l'histoire d'Arménie, par Abraham d'Ancyre (XVe siècle)." See Macler (n. 7 above) 123-124.

[9] A translation of this ode, entitled "Chant sur Etchmiadzine," will be found in A. Tchobanian, La Roseraie d'Arménie 3 (Paris 1929) 95-103.

[10] For a complete bibliography of Aṙak'el's prose works, consult Anasyan (n. 7 above) 1.1133-1142.

[11] See a French translation of this martyrology by G. Bayan, "En ce jour martyre du nouveau martyre Vardan," Patrologia orientalis 18 (Paris 1924) 181-184.

Armenian clergymen, Step'annos Vardapet and Petros K'ahanay, who, having recanted their conversion to Islam, were put to death by the Muslim judge at Khizan in 1424; a prose version of the martyrology of Grigor Xlat'ec'i Cerenc'; and the martyrology of an eighteen-year-old youth, Amirza Spartkertc'i, who was slain by the Turks in 1432 for refusing to adhere to the Muslim faith. Aṙak'el is also the author of ten treatises on such subjects as the presentation of Jesus to the Temple, the resurrection of Christ, Saint John the Baptist, the Virgin Mary, the raising of Lazarus, and so forth. In all, he is the author of at least eighty works in prose and in verse, which ranks him among the most prolific medieval Armenian authors.

In 1957 the scholar and bibliographer H. S. Anasyan published the critical editions of the original texts of the elegies by Abraham Ankiwrac'i and Aṙak'el Bałišec'i on the capture of Constantinople.[12] Abraham's text is based on twelve manuscripts found in the Matenadaran (Library of Manuscripts) in Yerevan, as well as five printed editions.[13] Nine of these manuscripts represent the complete texts of the elegy; the others lack a varying number of stanzas or lines. Six of the complete texts are from manuscripts copied in the seventeenth century; the oldest dates back to the year 1617. Anasyan's critical edition of Aṙak'el Bałišec'i's elegy, on the other hand, is based on fourteen manuscripts in the Matenadaran, of which only two are complete texts, and one printed version.[14] The oldest manuscript was copied in the year 1556.

Abraham Ankiwrac'i's work, entitled "Ołb i veray aṙman Kostandinupolsoy" (Elegy on the Capture of Constantinople), consists of 392 lines, divided into 98 stanzas of 4 lines each. On the other hand, Aṙak'el Bałišec'i's lament, entitled "Ołb mayrak'ałak'in Stōmpolu" (Elegy on the Capital City of Stamboul), consists of 320 lines, divided into 80 stanzas of 4 lines each.

From the standpoint of style, content, and point of view, these two works have few common characteristic features. In general, they follow the tradition of Armenian elegiac literature, which, with the notable exception of Nersēs Šnorhali's "Lament on Edessa," never distinguished itself as an outstanding literary genre. In the main, this branch of Armenian literature served a didactic purpose, with major emphasis upon content designed to

---

[12] This work is entitled, *Haykakan albyurnerð Byuzandiayi ankman masin* [The Armenian Sources on the Fall of Byzantium], published by the Institute of History, Armenian SSR Academy of Sciences (Yerevan 1957). In addition to the two contemporary elegies by Abraham and Aṙak'el, this monograph also includes an excerpt, consisting of 168 lines, dealing with the fall of Byzantium from a long narrative poem by the seventeenth-century Armenian author Eremia Č'ēlēpi K'ēōmiwrčean devoted to the history of the Ottoman sultans. The Armenian text and the Russian translation of the excerpt will be found in *ibid*. 82-88, 141-147.

[13] For a description of these manuscripts and the printed versions, consult *ibid*. 29-34.

[14] For a description of these manuscripts and the printed text, see *ibid*. 60-63.

arouse the readers' emotions. As a corollary of this, it also sought to engender a strong feeling of hope for the future. In terms of poetic quality, therefore, these two elegies cannot be classed among the great medieval Armenian creations; they lack spontaneity of inspiration, sublimity of thought and expression, and literary inventiveness—ingredients that elevate prosody into great poetry.

Yet the two poems give genuine expression to the intensity of feeling occasioned by the catastrophic demise of the great center of Christendom. Not unlike many other medieval Armenian authors, both Abraham and Aṙakʻel tried in their respective poems to emulate the language and style of the classical period of Armenian literature, but with little success. As a matter of fact, the two elegies, particularly Abraham's, are replete with colloquial and dialectal forms, including a considerable number of foreign terms of which only a few have become part of the Armenian literary vocabulary. As such, they are of great interest to those who are concerned with the historical development of the Armenian language, as well as with Middle Eastern linguistics and philology. Moreover, consonant with the religious and moral concepts that prevailed in the Middle Ages, the two poems also contain a significant number of direct biblical quotations or paraphrases and parallelisms. This was a stylistic device frequently employed to underscore the intensity with which authors experienced calamities.

In terms of content, the two elegies are markedly different. Although both Abraham and Aṙakʻel wrote their respective poems about the capture of Byzantium and in general reflected the impact of this momentous event upon the Armenians, their treatments of the subject are quite dissimilar. Moreover, although both authors shared a common feeling of intense grief occasioned by the stunning victory of the Ottoman Turks, their points of view regarding the underlying reasons for the fall of the Byzantine capital and the prospects for its future represent two radically contrasting religious and political orientations.

As the account of an eyewitness, Abraham Ankiwracʻi's elegy is of special significance. Abraham's poem, unlike that of Aṙakʻel, provides a detailed description of the siege and capture of Constantinople, the slaughter and looting that followed, Ottoman Sultan Mehmet II Fatih's triumphant entry into the city, and its consequences. As a typical medieval author, Abraham attributes the calamity which befell Byzantium to the wrath of God as a punishment for the manifold sins of its leaders (lines 337-352). Yet, in a more realistic vein, Abraham points to certain historical facts that played a decisive role in the final chapter of the history of the imperial city. Referring to the siege and Emperor Constantine XI's appeal for aid to the West, he bitterly castigates the "merciless Latins" for having laid down the "improper condition" of the conversion of the Greeks to Catholicism and the surrender of the city to the Franks—conditions that brought about grave dissension

among the populace of the besieged city (lines 33-34). These assertions refer,
of course, to the conclusion of the famous Union of Florence in 1439 and especially to the Greco-Latin church union proclaimed on December 12, 1452,
the resultant agitation in Constantinople, and the division of the city's population into two factions, the one favoring and the other opposing the union.

Historians are agreed that the last emperor of Byzantium, Constantine XI,
fought heroically as a simple soldier and fell in battle. Since exact information regarding the circumstances of his death and the fate of his body was
wanting, this became the subject of a number of legends that have obscured
the historical facts. Among these legends, it was rumored—presumably by
the Greeks who favored union with Rome—that the emperor had fled to
Europe. Abraham also, who remained in Constantinople at least until October, 1453 (267-268), reiterates the rumor (101-108):

When the King saw this,	Someone from among the Franks,
And powerless in the combat,	Whom they called Captain,
He decided to take to flight,	Took the King and the notables,
For smitten was he by affliction.	On a ship they fled by sea.[15]

Finally, as one sympathetic to the nationalist or antiunionist Greek Orthodox party, Abraham (unlike Aṙakʿel) does not voice the hope that Byzantium
and the eastern lands would eventually be delivered by the West; rather, he
wonders whether God will in the end have mercy and deliver the city from
the "wicked Satan" and the infidels' evils and oppressions.

In contrast, the importance of Aṙakʿel Baḷišecʿi's elegy lies essentially
in the depiction of the event's emotional impact on Christians in general
and Armenians in particular. His is not an eyewitness but a contemporary
account, as evidenced in the stanza that reads (81-84):

> Woe and alas unto that moment
> When we learned the news, Stamboul,
> That "the Turks captured
> And enslaved the great Stamboul."

In the first forty stanzas of his poem, Aṙakʿel eulogizes the past glory of
Constantinople and contrasts this with the tragic fate meted out to it follow-

---

[15] It is interesting to note that the same legend, with considerable embellishment, is
echoed in the colophon of an Armenian Menology copied by Bishop Dawitʿ at Xarberd
(Harput) in 1453: "The patriarch and the king . . . boarded a large ship and, together with
numerous people, numbering some 20,000 men, fled to Rome; and they took with them all
the sacred objects, because they had a month earlier already made preparations to flee."
(See text of colophon in *XV dari Hayeren jeṙagreri hišatakaranner, Masn erkrord, 1451-
1480* [Colophons of Armenian manuscripts of the fifteenth century, Part Two, 1451-1480],
ed. L. S. Xačʿikyan (Yerevan 1958) 30-31 n. 38.

ing its capture by the Ottoman Turks. He even implores the great emperors and holy fathers, who respectively occupied the imperial and patriarchal thrones, to join with him in his lament. Nevertheless, Aṙakʿel was confident that Byzantium would eventually be delivered by the Franks from the "tyrannical yoke of the infidels." The predictions of ultimate Christian victory, Aṙakʿel asserts, were "foretold in days gone by / By the holy and pious fathers" who, speaking by the Holy Spirit, prophesied "the arrival of the Franks in subsequent times and days" (165-172).

According to these prophecies, a countless multitude of Franks will arrive in the East; they will first capture Constantinople and then Jerusalem; they will vanquish the former Byzantine territories and reach as far as Egypt in the south, and Tabriz and Khurasan in the east. As a result, the Christian faith will again flourish throughout the world and the heathen nations shall perish. According to the same prophetic literature, the victorious Frankish armies will be led by the descendants of Armenian troops retained at Rome by Emperor Constantine I the Great. These troops will not only recover Armenia but also will restore the ancient Armenian Aršakuni (Arsacid) kingdom and the Partʿew (Parthian) ecclesiastical dynasty at Vagharshapat. Since the prophetic section (165-260) constitutes an important aspect of Aṙakʿel's elegy, it is necessary to examine the apocalyptic genre of Armenian literature which was developed in the Middle Ages.

The primary objective of the Armenian prophetic literature was to instill and perpetuate among the Armenians the hope for the restoration of their political independence. This literature took the form of visions, often combined with predictory or prophetic pronouncements, attributed to some well-known Armenian church leader. Such works were edited and reedited—in conformity with varying political circumstances—and inserted in a number of well-known Armenian historical works. I shall summarize and examine here the major prophetic writings that have a close bearing on the composition of the relevant section in Aṙakʿel's elegy.

Chronologically, the first of these is the prophecy attributed to Saint Sahak I Partʿew (387-436), catholicos of the Armenian church. The present text of the *Patmutʿiwn Hayocʿ* (History of Armenia) by the fifth-century Armenian historian Łazar Pʿarpecʿi (Lazar of Pharpi) includes a chapter that describes an alleged vision by the catholicos; it also provides an extensive interpretation of this vision.[16] In summary, the catholicos prior to his death is said to have predicted the end of the ruling Aršakuni dynasty in Armenia, as well as the termination of the Partʿew ecclesiastical hierarchy of the Armenian church founded by Saint Gregory the Illuminator, to which family the catholicos

---

[16] For a translation of this text, see Victor Langlois, *Collection des historiens anciens et modernes de l'Arménie* 2 (Paris 1869) 253-368. The translation, entitled "Lazare de Pharbe: Histoire d'Arménie," was done by Samuel Ghésarian.

himself belonged. The vision also forecast the restoration of these two dynasties shortly before the end of the world. It has been definitively established, however, that this particular chapter was not part of the original text of Łazar's work; rather, it was interpolated in the work in the beginning of the eighth century.[17]

The second prophecy is ascribed to Catholicos Nersēs I the Great (353-373), a tale contained in the biography of this hierarch written by Mesrop Erēcʻ Vayocʻ-Jorecʻi in A.D. 967.[18] The historical data in this work were drawn from the *Patmutʻiwn Hayocʻ* (History of Armenia) of Pʻawstos Biwzandacʻi (Faustus of Byzantium)[19] and from other works, now lost, written in the fifth century of our era. Briefly stated, the author of this biography describes the circumstances that led to the fall of the Aršakuni dynasty in A.D. 428. Not found in the aforementioned sources but included in the biography is a prophecy attributed to Catholicos Nersēs. According to this account, shortly before his death by poisoning at the instigation of King Pap, Nersēs prophesied that, after the fall of the Armeno-Parthian Aršakunis, the Persians would capture Jerusalem. Later, the Armenians would be overrun by the Greeks, but the latters' hegemony would be shortlived for they would be destroyed by the "archers." Armenia would be completely devastated by the "archers," and its church for a long time to come would remain powerless. The biography also refers to the kingdom that would be established by Antichrist. These calamities would be followed by the liberation of the Christian world at the hands of the "Romans" or "Franks"; the "lawless peoples" would be subjected to Roman rule; the liberated lands would be transformed into a virtual paradise; and peace, prosperity and justice would reign everywhere.

[17] See N. Akinean, "Kʻnnutʻiwn tesleann S. Sahakay" [An examination of Saint Sahak's vision), *Handēs Amsoreay* (Vienna 1936) 467ff., and *ibid.* (1937) 5ff; cf. A. Hovhannisyan, *Drvagner hay azatagrakan mtkʻi patmutʻyan* [Episodes for the history of Armenian literature on freedom] 1 (Yerevan 1957) 17, 36-37.

[18] This work exists in at least two versions, the first of which will be found in "Patmutʻiwn Srboyn Nersisi Partʻewi Hayocʻ Hayrapeti" [History of Saint Nersēs Partʻew, Catholicos of Armenia], *Sopʻerkʻ Haykakankʻ* [Armenian literary works] 6 (Venice 1853) 89-104. The French translation of this version can be seen in Langlois (ed.), "Généalogie de la famille de Saint Grégoire Illuminateur de l'Arménie, et Vie de Saint Nérsès, patriarche des Arméniens, par un auteur du Vᵉ siècle; Ouvrage traduit pour le première fois en français, par Jean-Raphaël Emine," in *Collection des historiens* 2.17-44. The second version has been published twice: (1) *Patmutʻiwn erjanik varucʻ ew mahuan eraneli ařn Astucoy surb mecin Nersēsi* [History of the blessed life and death of the blessed man of God, Saint Nersēs the great] (Constantinople 1737); and (2) *Patmutʻiwn mnacʻordacʻ Hayocʻ ew Vracʻ, Arareal yumemnē Mesropay Kʻahanayē i Hołocʻ gełjē i Vayocʻ-Joroy yašxarhē i Siwneacʻ* [Armenian and Georgian paralipomena, by the priest Mesrop from the village of Hołocʻ in the district of Vayocʻ-Jor in Siwnikʻ] (Madras 1775).

[19] For a translation of this work, "Faustus de Byzance: Bibliothèque Historique en Quatre Livres," by J. B. Emine, see Langlois (ed.), *Collection des historiens* 1 (Paris 1867) 210-310.

In their essential features, the vision and prophecy attributed to Saint Nersēs are a reflection of the frustrations that the Armenians had experienced in their centuries-long association with the Byzantines, as evidenced in the following quotation from the document: "And Jerusalem shall no longer remain under Greek rule and the Ismaelites shall gain control over it. And, until the arrival of the mighty nation, the Greeks shall become tributaries; then the Romans, who are called Franks, shall take Jerusalem, and remove from it the Greek forces."[20] The reference here to the "Franks" as liberators attests to the fact that the original biography written by Mesrop Erēcʿ was subsequently tampered with and edited to conform to the demands of the new circumstances. This is substantiated further by the discrepancies—both in content and style—found in the extant manuscripts of this work. The allusions to the "Franks" must have been interpolated after the First Crusade, that is at the time when the Armenians had become convinced that their liberation from the yoke of both the "archers" (that is, the Seljuqs) and the Greeks would be achieved with the help of the Crusaders.

As a matter of fact, an examination of the extant manuscripts of the biography of Saint Nersēs reveals elements peculiar to various historical periods, and reflects the political aspirations of the Armenians in various eras. Some manuscripts indicate that, apart from the aforementioned interpolations, the biography and its prophetic section in particular were considerably expanded, thereby producing another version of the text.[21] This revised version, which was made during the hegemony of the Seljuqs in Asia Minor and sometime after the First Crusade, foretells the arrival from the east of the "archers," who are referred to as the "progeny of the Ismaelites born of Hagar and the scions of the erstwhile Elamite race [that is, the Persians]." The text goes on to state that Armenia, after being vanquished and destroyed by the kings of the archers, would be ruled by a peace-loving king from Khurasan, who is said to be a protector of the Christians. The reference here is to Malik-Shāh, who succeeded the Seljuq rulers Tughril and Alp-Arslan. Following Malik-Shāh's beneficent reign, the archers would for four years cause havoc in Armenia, that is, until the arrival of their liberators, the "mighty Romans," who are called *Ormankʿ*, *Aramankʿ*, or *Aramanankʿ*. According to the revised text, the latter were the descendants of Armenian troops who accompanied King Tiridates III of Armenia and Saint Gregory the Illuminator on their alleged journey to Rome during the reign of Emperor Constantine the Great. Upon the Greeks' refusal to permit their landing at Constantinople, the *Ormankʿ* would capture the Byzantine capital, and proceed to vanquish the lands held by the Arabs, including the cities of Damascus and Jerusalem; they would also occupy Tabriz, the capital of Persia. As a result of these

[20] See *Sopʿerkʿ Haykakankʿ* [Armenian literary works] 6.90ff.
[21] See n. 18 above.

victories, "all these territories, like Paradise itself, shall belong to the Christians; [and] the nation of archers shall be exterminated from the face of the earth by the mighty Roman nation. Peace and goodwill shall reign on earth; the believers shall flourish and the sanctuaries of the saints shall be restored; [and] the lands of the lawless peoples shall come under the domination and servitude of the Armenians."[22]

The inclusion of Tabriz among the cities to be liberated by the Romans (that is, the Crusaders)—also reiterated in Aṙakʻel's elegy—is explained by an often repeated tradition in ancient Armenian sources. According to this, the city was built in the third century after Christ by the Armenian King Khosrov I. To avenge the murder of his nephew, Artawan, by the Sassanian King Artashir, he waged a war against the Persians, and upon his victorious return from the campaign he allegedly stood before the site of the future city and exlaimed, *Da ē vrēž* (lit., "that is revenge"), from which derived the name *Tabriz*.[23] Hence, even in medieval times, Armenian authors frequently referred to it as an Armenian city, and in the prophetic literature concerning the political liberation of Armenia Tabriz was mentioned as the farthest point.

The reference to the Armenian origin of the *Ormankʻ* also recurs in a number of other medieval prophetic works, among which the predictions attributed to the "invincible philosopher" Agadron (or Agatʻon) are of particular interest. The identity of this author is unknown. H. Ačaṙyan suggests that he was of Armenian origin and that he used a Greek pseudonym.[24] The oldest extant manuscript of his work refers to him as *Atʻenacʻi* (Athenian); hence, the Mekhitarist scholar Barseł Sargisean surmises that the text attributed to Agadron is the Armenian version of a work written by the Greek author Methodius.[25] To the best of our knowledge, however, the work in question is unknown in non-Armenian literatures; on the other hand, it seems entirely possible that it was adapted into Armenian from an unknown foreign source. In any event, the thirteenth-century European traveler William of Rubruk asserts that during his travels in Armenia in 1255 Agadron's prophecy was widely related throughout the country.[26]

Agadron's work has close affinities to the prophetic writings discussed thus far and to others that will be examined later.[27] In summary, the do-

---

[22] This is an excerpt from the text in MS 1912. 309-312, in the Matenadaran (Yerevan).

[23] See Sukʻias Ēpʻrikean, *Bnašxarhik baṙaran* [Dictionary of natural geography] 1 (Venice 1900) 579-580; cf. J. Saint-Martin, *Mémoires historiques et géographiques sur l'Arménie* 2 (Paris 1819) 422.

[24] See Ačaṙyan (n. 6 above) 1.45-46.

[25] Consult Barseł Sargisean, *Usumnasirutʻiwn hin ktakarani anvawer grocʻ vray* [A study of the Old Testament apocryphal books] (Venice 1898), 174-219.

[26] See Anasyan (n. 7 above) 1.145; and Sargisean 179.

[27] There are many manuscripts of Agadron's text, which are divided into three groups

cument ascribed to Agadron claims that, subsequent to the proclamation of Christianity, Emperor Constantine the Great and Pope Sylvester I went on a pilgrimage to Jerusalem, accompanied by King Tiridates III and Saint Gregory the Illuminator of Armenia. While in the Holy Land, Constantine built the Cathedral of the Holy Sepulcher in Jerusalem, and Tiridates constructed the Church of the Nativity in Bethlehem. At the behest of the emperor, Tiridates and Saint Gregory journeyed with him and the pope to Rome, accompanied by some 64,000 (according to the printed text 70,000) Armenian troops, 200 of whom were retained in Rome by Constantine after the departure of his guests to their native country. The *Ormankʿ* or *Armankʿ* were descended from these 200 Armenian troops. In subsequent times, a new Constantine would come forth from among the latter. Acceding to the pleas of twelve Christian kings under his suzerainty, Constantine would launch a universal campaign against the "archers" and liberate the Christians, including the Armenians, from their bondage. After landing at Constantinople, he would proceed as far as the city of Tabriz built by Tiridates (not Khosrov I), he would reassemble the Armenians dispersed hither and thither, and he would restore the Armenian princely families and their domains. Emperor Constantine would then appoint as commander the royal scion Vałaršak who, after restoring his ancestral throne, would wage a war against Byzantium and thus avenge the sufferings of his ancestors at the hands of the Byzantine Greeks. Vałaršak would reestablish the ancient frontiers of Armenia; and, by appointing a descendant of Saint Gregory as catholicos, he would also restore the ecclesiastical authority of this family. In the meantime, Constantine would be succeeded on the imperial throne by Tiberius and Vizand.[28] During the latter's reign, the Ismaelites would reappear; they would reestablish idolatry, and sacrifice numerous Armenians to the pagan gods, to such an extent that only a few Armenians would survive in their native homeland. Vizand would then avenge the Armenians by waging a successful campaign against the twenty-four races who had invaded Armenia from the north. He would be succeeded by Tʿēodēn (in the printed text Tʿēodos), during whose reign Antichrist would be born; but the latter's hegemony would come to an end with the second coming of Christ.

Written in a fictional style, Agadron's predictions are reminiscent of that period in history when the Armenians nurtured strong hopes of liberating themselves from the rule of the Ismaelites (that is, the Arabs) with the help of the Romans (that is, the Byzantine Greeks). They also aspired, through

---

on the basis of their different titles and introductory sections. (For a complete bibliography of these manuscripts, consult Anasyan (n. 7 above). 1.145-147.) The only printed version of the text was published by M. Awgerean, "Agatʿon kam Agadoron" [Agatʿon or Agadoron] in *Bazmavēp* (Venice 1913) 396-400.

[28] The name "Vizand" probably corresponds to "Byzas," the Megarian chief after whom was named the ancient city of Byzantium. See Vasiliev (n. 1 above) 1.57.

the same means, to the restoration of the Aršakuni kingdom of Armenia
and the Armeno-Parthian catholicosate. As a matter of fact, the selection of
the name Vałaršak itself appears to have been designed to recall the founding
of the Armenian Aršakuni dynasty by Vałaršak I.

The text of Agadron's prophetic writing also contains a number of significant contradictions, attesting to the fact that the original version was subsequently tampered with. For instance, after some sharply critical and even
hostile comments about Byzantium, the text proceeds to state:

> After learning about the invasion and destruction of our land and
> country by the nation of Hagar and the defeat of the divinely crowned
> servant [King Vałaršak], King Vizand assembled his mighty and
> stout, courageous and combatant troops, and with the blessing of
> the uncreated God attacked the nation of Hagar and pounced
> upon them like lions . . . and thus, destroying the nation of Hagar
> and the children of Ismael, King Vizand avenged King Vałaršak.[29]

Since this statement cannot logically follow the spirit evidenced toward Byzantium in the preceding sections, it can be assumed that it was a later interpolation.

Another prophetic work, entitled "A Narrative of the Birth, Upbringing,
and Evil Deeds of Antichrist," is attributed to Agat'angel, whose identity
also is unknown. Agat'angel appears to be a pseudonym, borrowed perhaps
from the name of the Basilian monk Hieronymus Agathangelus, who lived
in Sicily in the thirteenth century. This contention is substantiated by a
work translated into Armenian in 1816 entitled "The prophecy of the blessed
and holy priest Hieronymus Agathangelus, from the order of the holy and
great Basil, written at the city of Mesek'is on the island of Sicily in the year
of the Lord 1279."[30] This work, which contains the story of the vision of
Hieronymus Agathangelus, predicts the capture of Byzantium by the Ottomans
and its eventual liberation. Agat'angel's work, on the other hand, concerns
the arrival of Antichrist, which would coincide with the fall of the "Roman"
kingdom. Antichrist's reign would last until the second coming of Christ.
In its essentials, Agat'angel's prophecy differs from the corresponding predictions of Agadron regarding the appearance and demise of Antichrist.[31]

---

[29] See Matenadaran (Yerevan) MS 3839.209a.

[30] The subtitle of the Armenian version indicates that Hieronymus Agathangelus's
work was translated, presumably from the Latin original, into Italian and published in
1555; subsequently, a Greek translation was done from the Italian version; and finally the
Armenian translation was made from the Greek version. See Anasyan (n. 7 above) 1.150 n. 1.
There are three manuscripts (6297, 6395, 8999) of the Armenian translation in the Matenadaran. I have not been able to identify the city of Mesek'is mentioned in the title of Agathangelus's work.

[31] Agat'angel's text has a long descriptive title that in translation reads: "History of
the Birth, Upbringing and Evil Deeds of Antichrist; the Resurrection of Elijáh and Enoch;

Finally, there is a vision and a prophetic work, allegedly written by the vardapet Yovhannēs Kozeṙn in 1033. This text claims that, subsequent to an earthquake and a total eclipse of the sun in 1023, Kozeṙn explained these phenomena as an indication that the time was imminent when, according to the Revelation of Saint John, Satan would be released from bondage; the Turks would rule in Armenia for sixty years; then the Franks would capture Jerusalem; and fifty years later the Christians everywhere would be delivered. Needless to say, this too is an apocryphal work, and its various editions attest to the influence of historical developments peculiar to the Armenian kingdom of Cilicia.[32]

In predicting the recapture of Byzantium by the Franks and the liberation of the Christian East, Aṙakʿel also assigns an important role to the Armenians, who would be responsible for the restoration of their ancient kingdom and catholicosate (lines 233-260). These assertions were, of course, inspired by a number of the previously described unauthentic works. More important, however, Aṙakʿel was influenced by an apocryphal document, known as the *Dašancʿ Tʿułtʿ* (Letter of Concord),[33] fabricated by some Latinophile Armenians in Cilicia at the time of the Third or Fourth Crusade and interpolated in the manuscripts of the *History* of Agathangelos.[34] As will be seen below, this work contains elements found in the prophetic texts discussed above; it differs from them not only in matters of detail but especially in the creation of new legends.

The document alleges that a "pact of mutual love and union" was concluded between Emperor Constantine the Great and Pope Sylvester I on the one hand, and King Tiridates III and Saint Gregory the Illuminator on the other. Thus, in reiterating the legend concerning the latters' journey to Rome, it intro-

---

the Growth of the Power of the Franks and their Conquest of the Great Cities of Constantinople and Jerusalem; and the Elimination of the Kings, the End of the World, and the Last Judgment; by the Holy and Invincible Philosopher Agatʿangel." The Matenadaran has four manuscripts of this text, all copied in the seventeenth century: 6961.62a-91b; 3506.84a-93b; 641.235a-251b; and 2004.112b-133b. Another manuscript is found in the British Museum: 108 (or. 4580) fols. 222-240, copied in 1680; see F. C. Conybeare, *A Catalogue of the Armenian Manuscripts in the British Museum* (London 1913) 278-279. There is also a translation of the text in modern Armenian done by Simēon Karnecʿi in 1875. (See Matenadaran MS 6891.120b-127a.)

[32] For additional details concerning Kozeṙn's prophecy consult Hovhannisyan (n. 17 above) 1.45-47.

[33] The text of this document, together with its Italian translation, was first printed in *Lettera dell'Amicitia e dell'Vnione di Costantino gran cesare. . . . scritta nell'Anno del Signore 316* (Venice 1683). The same text was reprinted at Padua in 1690, and at Venice again in 1695 and 1700.

[34] For a translation of this work—which should not be confused with the text attributed to Hieronymus Agathangelus—see Langlois (ed.), "Agathange: Histoire du règne de Tiridate et de la prédication de Saint Grégoire l'Illuminateur," in *Collection des historiens* 1.97-200.

duces the new legend of a pact. The text asserts that the pope, as the vicar of the apostles Peter and Paul, wields authority over all Christian nations in the West and in the East; even the Roman emperor is portrayed as the pope's vassal. The document alleges that, while at Rome, Sylvester ordained Saint Gregory as catholicos and proclaimed the Armenian ecclesiastical hierarchy as the "coequal of the great sees of Jerusalem, Antioch, and Alexandria." The pope is said to have empowered Saint Gregory and his successors to ordain the catholicoses of Georgia and Caucasian Albania; he even proclaimed that the patriarchs of both sees would be selected by and would be ordained with the consent of the Armenian catholicos, to whom they would also profess their faith as the "chief vicar" and "commander" of the pope in the East. Emperor Constantine, on the other hand, is alleged to have crowned Tiridates as king of Armenia, offered him various gifts and privileges, and placed Bethlehem, the birthplace of Christ, under his authority. Tiridates, in return, is claimed to have left Armenian troops in Rome at the disposal of the Emperor, who is quoted as having said:

> I asked King Trdat [Tiridates] for 300 men magnificent in stature and valor, whom I named *Armenkʿ*, and I appointed them to serve my royal throne and to protect it by day and by night, and to serve as outposts in time of war. It is now time to inform you of the vision which was revealed to me by the Lord. After many years, the princes of Armenia will drive away the house of Trdat . . . and they themselves will come under the servitude of the aliens for many long years . . . the Armenian nation will be subjected to much suffering, and their salvation will come from the Lord with the help of my own progeny.[35]

In this manner, Emperor Constantine is said to have predicted the fall of the Aršakuni dynasty and the captivity of the Armenian people, at the same time assuring them of their eventual deliverance at the hands of his successors, the Roman emperors.

The apocryphal character of the Letter of Concord was recognized a long time ago.[36] Ancient historians (Tacitus, Pliny, and Dio Cassius) give accounts of the journey to Rome of the *pagan* King Tiridates I (A.D. 53-59, 66-100)—not the Christian King Tiridates III, A.D. 298-330—to receive the royal crown from Emperor Nero. He was accompanied by the royal family, all the chief lords of the kingdom, and an escort of three thousand "Parthian" horsemen.

---

[35] See Agatʿankełos, *Girkʿ vipasanutʿean* [Book of history] (Constantinople 1709) 406.

[36] See Sr. De Moni, *Histoire critique de la créance et des coutumes des nations du Levant* (Frankfurt 1631) 134. The document was methodically analyzed and refuted by Karapet Šahnazareancʿ, *Dašancʿ tʿłtʿoy kʿnnutʿiwnn u herkʿumð* [An examination and refutation of the Letter of Concord] (Paris 1862). A more recent study of the text will be found in Hovhannisyan (n. 17 above) 1.65-80.

When he crossed into Roman territory, Tiridates I was welcomed in every city with signal honors, and his coronation took place at Rome. It is obvious that the anonymous author or authors of the Letter of Concord deliberately falsified this historical event by attributing it to the Christian Tiridates who reigned over two centuries later. Moreover, only a tendentious fabrication could have associated the origin of the Armenian church hierarchy with the Roman papacy and also ascribed to it the kind of position within the universal church which in fact it never enjoyed. The Armenian hierarchy was not only not preeminent in the East; it was never even recognized as the coequal of the patriarchates of Jerusalem, Antioch, and Alexandria. It is also not a mere oversight that the document makes no mention of the patriarchate of Constantinople; and equally significant is the enumeration of the patriarchate of Jerusalem among the major hierarchical sees in the East, despite the fact that it gained prominence only with the hegemony of the Crusades.

These historical inaccuracies suggest that the apocryphal document was composed sometime during the twelfth or thirteenth century, and that the falsification was motivated by religio-political considerations. The associations of the Armenians with the Roman papacy began in the twelfth century, as a direct result of the friendly relations between the Crusaders and the Armenian barony (later kingdom) of Cilicia. The Latins found a natural ally in the Armenians, both against the Byzantines and against the Muslims, particularly so long as the Franks evidenced a spirit of religious toleration toward the Armenian church. These friendly relations were at times exacerbated, however, chiefly by political, military, and economic rivalries, and by the growing determination of the papacy to Latinize the Armenian church.

As early as the first half of the twelfth century, the church of Rome sought to bring the Armenians into communion with her. By conferring a royal crown upon King Leon II of Cilicia in 1198, the papacy established a sort of protectorate over the Armenian kingdom, which it was long to exploit in the interest of its religious and political designs. Subsequent to the collapse of the Latin principalities in the Levant, the Armenian kingdom of Cilicia, which had become the target of the Mamelukes' periodic invasions, still continued to rely on the papacy for help; but the Roman see would not pledge any military assistance unless the Armenians were converted to the Catholic faith. The Armenian royal family had through intermarriage become increasingly Latinized by this time. In 1342 the Latinophile Armenian monarchs of Cilicia were succeeded by the Latin kings of the French Lusignan dynasty, who persisted in their policy of Latinizing the Armenian church. In consequence of these developments the Cilician Armenian church acquired a character peculiar to the region. While the Cilician church officially adopted certain characteristic features of the Latin church, she did not become fundamentally Latinized, nor did she definitively declare herself in full communion with Rome. The concessions that she was forced to make to the papacy were essentially dictated by the ruling class, which never abandoned its hopes for European aid against the Muslims.

The fabrication of the Letter of Concord must, therefore, be explained within the context of the developments described above. The document was obviously designed to promote the papal policy of subordinating the Armenian church to Rome, as the primary condition to secure Western military help. In pursuance of this objective, the author of the document resorted to the falsification of the historical facts, without regard to chronological discrepancies, and embellished them with additional details by distorting the old and new legends that were then current among the Armenians. In line with these legends, the Letter of Concord reiterated the story of Tiridates III's and Saint Gregory's alleged journey to Rome, reasserted the legend concerning the conclusion of the pact, and revived the fiction of the Armenian origin of the Romans who would liberate the Christians of the East.

The prophetic literature described above was not peculiar to the Armenians alone; rather, it forms a part of the general body of eschatological and messianic literature developed among the Christians both in the East and in the West. In the case of the Armenians, however, the development of this literary genre was closely associated with the political aspirations of the people, first in historic Armenia itself and then in Cilicia. Although fundamentally all of the Armenian prophetic works were motivated by the overriding hope for the deliverance of the Armenians from foreign rule, the agents of this liberation varied in conformity with the actual historical developments, as attested by the various extant versions of the texts.

Insofar as Aṙakʻel Baḷišecʻi is concerned, he was obviously influenced by the popular prophetic legends and traditions associated with the names of highly revered church leaders, and especially by the apocryphal Letter of Concord. In reiterating the predictions that Byzantium and the Eastern lands would be delivered from Muslim bondage by the Franks, he was of course reviving the hopes for a new Crusade. In asserting the alleged journey to Rome of Tiridates III and Saint Gregory and the conclusion there of a "pact of mutual love and union," and in claiming the Armenian origin of the Frankish liberators, Aṙakʻel provides concrete evidence not only of the popularity of the apocryphal Letter of Concord, but also of the Armenians' persistent hope for the restoration of the Aršakuni kingdom and the Armeno-Parthian dynasty of catholicoses at the ancient capital of Vagharshapat.[37]

---

[37] It is interesting to note that this theme recurs in one of Aṙakʻel's panegyrical poems dedicated to Etchmiadzin. After eulogizing this "holy of holies" of the Armenian church, and referring to the visions of Saint Gregory and Saint Sahak, Aṙakʻel asserts that Etchmiadzin would once again be revived and become the "assembling place" of the Armenians dispersed in near and distant lands. The text of this poem will be found in N. Kʻaramean, "S. Ējmiacinð Hay ergičʻneri taḷerum" [Etchmiadzin in the lyrics of Armenian poets], *Ararat* (1895) 190ff.

The view that the liberation of Byzantium and its former territories, as well as of Armenia, would be achieved with the help of the Franks or Europeans was of course not shared by Abraham Ankiwrac'i, whose sympathies were not with the Latins but with the antiunionist and nationalist Orthodox Greek party in Byzantium.

The contrasting political and religious points of view expressed by the two poets brings into sharp focus the divergent feelings that the demise of the great center of Christianity had engendered. It is equally clear that these elegies are as much a reaction to the Council of Ferrara-Florence as to the fall of Constantinople. The passionate difference of opinion between Abraham and Aṙak'el about the reason for the "catastrophe of 1453" would also seem to be a strong indication of the sort of unity of concern stretching from Armenia and the Caucasus to the Atlantic—a fact that, conceivably, underlay practically all the conflicts of the Middle Ages.

It is hoped that the foregoing discussion, albeit brief, has underscored the historic significance of these two Armenian elegies on the fall of Constantinople, and that their present translation will be an important contribution to our expanding knowledge of the Middle Ages, as well as a significant addition to the large mass of international literature on an event that produced world-wide repercussions.

There are a number of translations of Abraham Ankiwrac'i's and Aṙak'el Bałišec'i's elegies into French and Russian, but only the Russian translations are based on the critical editions of the texts published by Anasyan. The French translations of Abraham's work are: (1) "Touchante élégie sur la prise de Constantinople, arrivée l'an 902 de notre ère, époque fatale et douloureuse, où le Seigneur fit encore éclater violemment sa colère contre la nation des Latins et des Grecs," trans. E. Boré, *Nouveau journal asiatique* 15 (Paris 1835) 275-292;[38] (2) "Mélodie élégiaque sur la prise de Stamboul," trans. M. Brosset, in C. Lebeau, *Histoire du Bas-Empire*, ed. Saint-Martin, 21 (Paris 1836) 307-314; (3) "Abraham prêtre arménien: Mélodie élégiaque sur la prise de Stamboul," trans. A. Dethier, *Monumenta Hungariae historica* 22.2 (Budapest 1872) 225-248. The French translation of the elegy composed by Aṙak'el Bałišec'i, entitled "Lamentation sur la prise de Constantinople," will be found in A. Tchobanian, *La Roseraie d'Arménie* (Paris 1929) 3.109-118.

The Russian translations of the two elegies were done by S. S. Arevshatyan, and were published with an accompanying study by H. S. Anasyan: "Abraam Ankirskii: Plach na vzatie Kostantinopolia," in *Vizantiiskii Vremennik* 7 (Moscow 1953) 452-460; and "Arakel Vageshskii: Plach o stolitse Stimbole," *ibid.* 460-466. Both translations are also reprinted in Anasyan, *Haykakan*

[38] This translation was based on the text found in MS 140 (formerly 80) in the Bibliothèque Nationale in Paris. See description in Macler (n. 7 above) 75-76.

ałbyurnerə Byuzandiayi ankman masin (Yerevan 1957) 113-140. The translation of Aṙakʿel's elegy, in both publications, does not contain the last nine stanzas of the original Armenian text.

In this first translation of the two elegies into English an attempt has been made to render the style and language of the originals as closely as possible. Although the poetic lines have been retained, the primary objective was to render the meaning of the texts rather than to reproduce the prosody. With very few exceptions, foreign terms used in the Armenian texts have been translated; this also applies to the personal and place names that are, for the most part, rendered in their common English forms. Finally, comments regarding the texts, as well as explanations of particular problems and etymologies, are provided in the notes.

ELEGY ON THE CAPTURE OF CONSTANTINOPLE

by Abraham Ankiwracʿi

1   In the year nine hundred and two,[39]
    In bitter and in wicked times,
    The Lord was angered much again
    By the Greek and Rūm nation.[40]

5   There arose a terrible sultan,
    Whom they called Mehmet;[41]
    He was a descendant of Osman,[42]
    And son of Murad,[43] the great *xondkʿar*.[44]

9   He first conceived a small plan,
    Which he accomplished at great expense;
    A fort he began to build on the seashore,
    At the Strait of Alexander.[45]

[39] This date is according to the "Great Armenian Era"; it corresponds to (902 + 551) A.D. 1453.

[40] The text reads *azgin Hṙomocʿ*, "the nation of the Rūm," that is, the Greeks.

[41] The form in the text is "Mahamat": the Ottoman Sultan Mehmet II Fatih (1451-1481), the conqueror of Constantinople.

[42] The form in the text is "Ōtʿman": Sultan Osman (ʿUthmān) I, founder of the Ottoman dynasty. In the text, Abraham Ankiwracʿi refers to Mehmet II Fatih as the *tʿoṙn* of Osman. The Armenian term *tʿoṙn* means "grandson, grandchild"; in the context, however, it is used in the sense of "descendant." This is substantiated by the fact that Mehmet II was actually the son of Murād II and the grandson of Mehmet (Muḥammad) I.

[43] The Ottoman Sultan Murād II (1421-1451), son and successor of Mehmet (Muḥammad) I.

[44] This term is derived from *khunkiār* (apparently an abbreviation for *khudāwendigiār*), a title given to all the Ottoman sultans, at least until the seventeenth century, along with that of *Pādishāh*. See J. H. Kramers, "Khudāwendigiār," *Encyclopaedia of Islam*, ed. 1, 2.971.

[45] This fortress, on the Bosphorus, was then known to the Turks as *Boğaz-kesen* and now

13   What he began he soon completed,
     In one summer, in three months;
     Five miles it was distant
     From the Frankish city of Galata.

17   He then returned to whence he came,
     To his throne[46] at Edirne,[47]
     And conceived a plan of perfidy
     Against the great city of Byzantium.[48]

21   He planned all through the winter,
     Made preparations for war;
     He issued orders everywhere,
     "Come you all to wage holy war."[49]

25   In the second week of Lent,[50]
     He set forth and came upon the city;
     He assembled countless horsemen,
     Seven hundred thousand in number.

29   They laid siege[51] to it from all sides;
     By sea and land they pressed;
     The number of Turkish troops swelled,
     Those of the Christians diminished.

33   But the King[52] of Stamboul[53]
     Was altogether powerless;
     He cast his eyes upon the Franks,
     Expecting them to come to his aid.

Rumeli Hisar, and was completed on August 31, 1452. It is not known why Abraham Ankiwracʿi refers to the narrows as the "Strait of Alexander."

[46] The form in the text is *tʿaxtʿ*, borrowed from Persian *taxt*, "throne"; see H. Ačaṙyan,
Hayocʿ lezvi patmutʿyun [History of the Armenian language], 2 vols. (Yerevan 1940-1951)
1.258.

[47] Also known as Adrianople; now capital of Edirne province in European Turkey. See
M. Tayyib Gökbilgin, "Edirne (Adrianople)," in *Encyclopaedia of Islam*, new ed., 2. 683-684.

[48] The form in the text is *Biwzandia*, one of several forms by which the Armenians referred to Byzantium.

[49] The form in the text is *taza*, from Arabic *ghāzāh*, "the raids made by the Ghāzīs against
the infidels." For a discussion of the Ghāzī's raids of Rūm, consult M. F. Köprülü, *Les
origines de l'empire ottoman* (Paris 1935) 101-107. In Armenian it was used in the sense
of "holy war."

[50] This line can also be rendered: "On the second Saturday of Lent." According to the
Armenian church calendar, the second Saturday of Lent in the year 1453 fell on February
24. See Anasyan, *Haykakan albyurnerð* (n. 12, above) 56.

[51] The term used in the text is *xsarecʿin*, "they laid siege." The stem *xsar* is derived from
Arabic *ḥiṣār*, "besieging, encompassing; a fortified town, a fort, castle." See H. Hübschmann,
Armenische Grammatik, ed. 2 (Darmstadt 1962) 269 no. 85; also F. Steingass, *Persian-
English Dictionary*, ed. 3 (London 1947) 421.

[52] The reference here and in subsequent stanzas is to Constantine XI Palaeologus (1449-
1453), the last of the Byzantine emperors.

[53] That is, Istanbul.

37   But the cruel Latin nation
      Laid down an improper condition:
      "Convert to our own faith,
      And to us your city relinquish."

41   And King Constantine
      Acquiesced in their demand;
      The city was split into two,
      Half Greek[54] and half Latin.[55]

45   And misfortune befell
      The Greek and Frankish nations;
      The northern wind blew intensely,
      And cut off the south wind.[56]

49   The galleys[57] and ships
      That came to render help,
      Floundered and rocked back and forth,
      And remained where they were.

53   And the evil Sultan Mehmet
      Placed a great and huge cannon,[58]
      Causing wonderment to those who saw it,
      And amazement to those who heard it.

57   He demolished the city's five towers,[59]
      And leveled them with the ground;
      He built a road on the sea,
      And they marched on it as on land.

61   A speech he made before his large army,

---

[54] The term used in the text is *Hoṙom*, that is "Greek"; the reference is to the Greek Orthodox faith.

[55] The last two lines refer to the two Greek factions in Constantinople: the one which favored union with Rome, and the other which remained faithful to the Greek Orthodox faith.

[56] The term used in the text is *lotos*, from Turkish *lodos*, "south wind," itself derived from Greek *nótos*. See H. and R. Kahane and A. Tietze, *The Lingua Franca in the East* (Urbana 1958) 547-548 no. 818. See also S. Malxaseanc̣, *Hayerēn bac̣atrakan baṙaran* [Descriptive dictionary of Armenian], 4 vols. (Yerevan 1944-1945) 2.209; 3.489.

[57] The term used in the text is *latòrła*, from Ottoman Turkish *qadirga* (itself derived from Byzantine *kátergon*), a common designation of the "galley" in the eastern Mediterranean. See Kahane-Tietze 523-526 no. 785.

[58] The term in the text is *t῾op῾*, borrowed from Turkic *top*, "cannon, gun; artillery." See Gerhard Doerfer, *Türkische und mongolische Elemente im Neupersischen* (Wiesbaden 1965) 2.596-601 no. 948; also J. T. Zenker, *Dictionnaire turc-arabe-persan* (Leipzig 1866-1876) 604a. The reference is, of course, to the famous cannon used by Mehmet II for the capture of Constantinople. See Runciman (n. 1 above) 77ff.; and G. Schlumberger, *Le siège, la prise et le sac de Constantinople en 1453* (Paris 1926) 57-62.

[59] The term in the text is *purč*, borrowed from Arabic *burdj*, "tower, castle." See Hans Wehr, *A Dictionary of Modern Written Arabic* (Ithaca, N.Y. 1961) 50; and Ačaṙyan (n. 46 above) 2.202. In the present context it refers to the towers on the city walls of Constantinople.

Words of encouragement he uttered to them,
Saying: "Hearken, musulmans,[60]
You shall hear great and good tidings.

65 The great city of Stamboul
Shall be your spoil[61] and share;
Men, animals and all fortune[62]
Whoever takes shall be his own."

69 And in the month of May,
On the twenty-eighth day,
And on the day that was Monday,
When the feast of the Hṙip῾simians[63] was held.

73 Towards the evening they arrived,
And reached the bank of the fosse;[64]
They brought the boats[65] together,
And ladders they erected.[66]

77 They took to battle and fought
Until the hour of daybreak;
Half of them boarded the ships
And surrounded [the city] from the sea.

81 And at the breaking of the sun,
On Tuesday of the week,
On the third of the Armenian month of Mehek,[67]

[60] The term in the text is *mȯsȯlmankʿ*, from Persian *musulmān* (itself derived from *muslimān*, the Persian plural of Arabic *muslim*), "a follower of the religion of Islam." See Zenker (n. 58 above) 848a. The Armenian form has the plural suffix -*kʿ*.

[61] The term in the text is *tʿaxtan*, derived from Persian *takht*, "spoil, plunder, prey." See Steingass (n. 51 above) 273; cf. Ačaṙyan (n. 46 above) 1.258.

[62] The term in the text is *ȯṙzak*, derived from Arabic *arzāḳ* (sing. *rizḳ*), "livelihood, subsistence; property, possessions, wealth, fortune." See Wehr (n. 59 above) 336-337; also Ačaṙyan, (n. 46 above) 2.192. It is used here in the sense of "fortune."

[63] That is, "of or belonging to the group of Hṙip῾simē." According to Armenian tradition, Hṙip῾simē and Gayianē were the leaders of a group of virgins who, having been persecuted by the Roman Emperor Diocletian because of their Christian faith, left Rome and finally arrived in Armenia. In A.D. 301 these virgins were put to death by King Tiridates III of Armenia. See M. Ōrmanean, *Azgapatum* [National history], 3 vols. (Constantinople-Jerusalem 1913-1927) 1.51-52.

[64] The term in the text is *xantak*, borrowed from Arabic *khandaḳ*, "fosse, ditch, moat." See Steingass (n. 51 above) 477; Hübschmann (n. 51 above) 267 no. 64; and Ačaṙyan (n. 46 above) 2.193.

[65] The form used in the text is *santalun*, derived from Greek *sandálion*, "boat." See Kahane-Tietze (n. 56 above) 564-567 no. 839.

[66] The reference is to the scaling ladders used by the Turks. See Runciman (n. 1 above) 119, 134-137 passim.

[67] *Mehek* or *Mehekan* is the name of the seventh month of the ancient Armenian calendar. See *Baṙgirkʿ nor Haykazean lezui* [New dictionary of the Armenian language], 2 vols. (Venice 1836-1837) 2.245.

On the feast of the holy Gayianians,[68]

85   The Lord arose in great wrath
      Upon the city of Constantinople,
      Delivered it into the hands of the hated,
      Wicked enemies surrounded it.[69]

89   The King and his troops
      Joined in battle with all their might;
      But they failed in their resistance,
      For the Lord denied them His aid.

93   For they were split into two;
      They failed to achieve unity;
      Some were loyal to the King,
      Some said we will surrender to the Turks.

97   Like the torrents of a flood,
      The Tačiks[70] broke through the city;
      Many scrambled up the ramparts,
      Others pulled each other up by rope.

101   When the King saw this,
      And powerless in the combat,
      He decided to take to flight,
      For smitten was he by affliction.

105   Someone from among the Franks,
      Whom they called Captain,[71]
      Took the King and the notables,
      On a ship they fled by sea.

109   And when the musulmans came in,
      They poured in upon the city;
      They first captured the palace[72]
      Which was the court[73] of the King.

113   Then they left there and proceeded
      To the cathedral church,

[68] In 1453 the third of Mehek, according to the Armenian calendar, corresponded to May 29 of the Christian calendar; this day was Tuesday, on which day was held the feast of the Gayianians. See Anasyan (n. 12 above) 57. For the Gayianians, see Gayiane (n. 63 above).

[69] Cf. Psalms 106.40-41.

[70] A generic term used for the Muslims in general; it is derived from Pahlevi *tāčik*, "Arab"; see Hübschmann (n. 51 above) 86-87 no. 205. In the present context it refers to the Ottoman Turks.

[71] The term in the text is *łap'utan*, borrowed from Ottoman Turkish *kapudan* (itself derived from Italian *capitano*), "captain." See Kahane-Tietze (n. 56 above) 139-145 no. 152.

[72] The reference is probably to the palace of Blachernae. See Vasiliev (n. 1 above) 2, Index 806.

[73] The term in the text is *darbas*, borrowed from Persian *darvās* or *darvāza*, "gate, large door." See Hübschmann (n. 51 above) 137 no. 175. In Armenian usage it came to mean "royal or princely palace," see Ačaṙyan (n. 46 above) 1.253, corresponding to the Turkish *kapu* or *seray*. In the present context it is best rendered as "court."

Which was called [Aya] Sofya
And where the patriarch had his seat.

117   The numerous male Christians
There assembled joined in battle;
They were inflamed with intense fervor,
Like children for their parents.

121   They gave up their lives,
They went like sheep to the slaughter,
Countless fell victim to the sword,
And blood flowed like a brook.

125   And the wicked Sultan Mehmet,
Entering the great cathedral,
Rejoiced exceedingly
Having attained his desired goal.

129   The countless troops who entered with him
Scattered about in the streets;
They roared like wild beasts
Who are thirsty for blood.

133   The warriors, whom they found,
They slaughtered one and all;
But the other men and women
Into captivity they led away.

137   The young children they tore away
From the bosoms of their mothers,
And crushed them against the rocks,
The aged they pierced with swords.

141   Their cries and laments,
Their wailing and moaning,
No one can describe by mouth,
No one can relate with words.

145   As many monks as there were,
Whom they called *kalogerosk῾*,[74]
And many of the female sex,
Who were called *kalogriayk῾*,[75]

149   They seized and dragged them cruelly,
Tied them up and carried them off;
And those who by force resisted them
Were smitten to the ground and rolled over.

153   Many fell upon their knees
And willingly offered their necks to the sword,
With a martyr's voluntary death

---

[74] This term is from vernacular Greek *kalógeros*, "monk"; see D. Demetrakou, *Mega lexikon tes ellenikes glosses* (Athens 1938) 4.3576-3577. The Armenian form has the plural suffix *-k῾*.

[75] This term is from vernacular Greek *kalógria*, "nun" (see *ibid.* 4.3577). The Armenian form has the plural suffix *-k῾*.

They breathed their last and died.

157   The divinely ornamented churches
      They mercilessly plundered;
      They denuded them of their
      Precious vessels and ornaments.

161   The sacred relics of the martyrs,
      Hitherto guarded with reverence,
      They dispersed them everywhere,
      They trampled them underfoot.

165   The graves of the kings
      Covered with marble sarcophagi,
      They opened and plundered,
      And crushed all the bones.

169   Yet none of these sacred relics
      Wrought any miracles;
      Because of their multitudinous sins,
      They all remained intensely mute.

173   They hurled the church bells down,
      The bell ringers they slew,
      They annihilated the Cross,
      The holy communion they scattered about.

177   They removed out of the city
      The booty and captives which they took;
      From the hour of three until nine,
      They left nothing in the city.

181   As for the great prince of the Greeks,
      Whom they called Kir Luka,[76]
      They found him and they seized him,
      And brought him before the wicked Sultan.

185   And he honored him exceedingly
      Until he found out his secret;
      Then he had him beheaded,
      Together with his two sons.

189   All the musulmans who were there
      Revelled with great rejoicing,
      They rejoiced with great satisfaction,
      They told one another the great tidings.

193   They said, "Stamboul the eternal,
      Which the Tačiks had never captured,
      Now in these latter times
      God gave to us to be our own."

197   But all the Christian nations

---

[76] The reference is to the Emperor Constantine XI Palaeologus's senior minister, namely the Megadux and Admiral of the Fleet Lucas Notaras.

Were grieved with deep sadness;
Because the city of refuge was delivered
Into the hands of the Muslims.

201 They carried off much booty,
Silver, gold, and pearls,
Exquisite and precious gems,
Never before seen by the nation earthborn.

205 The choice, pearl-studded and precious
Vessels found in the churches,
Gospels bound with silver and replete
With exquisite illuminations.

209 All these they took to Edirne;
With them they made Bursa[77] abundant;
They took much goods to Ankara;
They scattered them all over the world.

213 They carried off countless books;
The Tačiks who saw them were wonder-struck;
The Christians recovered [books] without number,
Yet the majority remained with the Tačiks.

217 As for the people whom they took captive,
The notables and the commoners,
And so many from the clerical class,
No accounting of the common folk.

221 The old and the young, the youth,
Numerous women and their daughters,
They dispersed them like the dust
To all the corners of the earth.

225 In the small city of Galata,
Which was under Frankish rule,
The notables boarded a ship
And fled across the sea.

229 The remainder of its residents,
And the leaders who were left behind,
In terror and trembling they came
And prostrated at the feet of the Sultan.

233 And he demanded from them,
"Submit to my command,
Demolish the city's ramparts,
And the strong tower[78] of the clock."[79]

---

[77] The ancient town of *Prusa* or *Prusia* in the northern foothills of Mysian Olympus; capital of the Ottoman state from 1326 until 1402. See H. Inalcik, "Bursa," in *Encyclopaedia of Islam*, new ed., 1.1333-1336.

[78] See n. 59 above.

[79] The term in the text is *sahatʿ*, derived from Arabic *sāʿat*, "clock," with substitution of glottal stop by ẖ, as e.g. in Kipčak. See K. Grønbech, *Komanisches Wörterbuch: Türkischer Wortindex zu Codex cumanicus* (Copenhagen 1942) 210.

237   And they acquiesced,
      They carried out his command;
      They demolished [the walls by] the seacoast,
      They leveled them with the ground.

241   He changed the name of Stamboul,
      Which meant "to the city."
      He said, "It shall be called Islampol,"[80]
      Which means "multitude of Tačiks."

245   The renowned Sofya,
      Which means "wisdom,"
      He converted into the main mosque[81]
      And retained its name Sofya.

249   A prince he appointed for the city,
      Suleyman[82] was his name;
      He gave him numerous troops;
      And [appointed] Łara-Łati[83] as judge.

253   He also issued a stern order,
      Causing anguish to all who heard it,
      To all the cities in Rūm[84]
      Which were under his dominion.

257   He said to remove men with their families,
      To bring and settle them in this city;
      This brought great grief to the Turkish nation,
      Who are lamenting with bitter tears.

261   For they separated fathers from sons,
      They separated daughters from mothers,
      They separated brothers from one another,
      They deprived many of their ancestral homes.

265   Not only Tačiks but also
      Christians they brought here;
      On the twenty-eighth day of October
      They brought four Armenians from Ankara.

[80] This corresponds to Turkish *Islāmbol*, lit. "Islāmfull." It is a variant form of *Istanbul*, describing the ethnic character of Constantinople after its capture by the Ottomans. See J. H. Mordtmann, "Constantinople," in *Encyclopaedia of Islam*, ed. 1, 1.867-876. Mordtmann suggests that the form *Islāmbol* appeared in the sixteenth century; the present text indicates that it was used as early as the year 1453. See Anasyan (n. 12 above) 58-59.

[81] The text reads *mǒzkit'*, derived from Persian *mazgit* or *mizgit*, "small mosque." See Steingass (n. 51 above) 1223; cf. Hübschmann (n. 51 above) 271 no. 96; and Ačaṙyan (n. 46 above) 1.272. In Armenian usage it means a Muslim place of worship in general, regardless of its size.

[82] In Turkish and Arabic transcription *Sulaymān*; the identity of this official is unknown.

[83] This should probably be transcribed as *Kara-Kāḍī*; the identity of this official is unknown.

[84] The reference is to the territories formerly held by the Greeks, and now under Turkish rule.

269   Astuacatur Sat῾ōlmiš,
      And Siměon Barip῾aš,
      And Ayvat son of Papa,
      And baron Gorg, the *hěšim hači*.[85]

273   We must now bring our narrative to a close,
      For the more we write the more we pain;
      In the year nine hundred and two,[86]
      The Tačiks captured Byzantium.

277   And we cry out with intense laments,
      And we sigh tearfully,
      We groan and mourn grievously,
      And anguish for the great city.

281   Come, believer brothers,
      Fathers and dear chosen ones,
      Let us compose this tearful lament,
      On these events that have transpired.

285   Constantinople the exalted,
      The former throne for kings,
      How could you be overthrown
      And be trampled by infidels?

289   You, chosen Constantinople,
      Mother of cities you were called,
      To the enemies you were delivered,
      Your tormentors now dominate you.

293   Constantine, the great king,
      Who reigned in the city of Rome,
      And together with the pontiff Sylvester[87]
      He believed in Christ.

297   He encountered you during his travels,
      He beheld you and loved you much,
      He erected a place for his throne,
      And named you the New Rome.

301   Theodosius the Great sat on your throne,
      With his two sons he sojourned within you,
      You were chosen by Arcadius and Honorius,
      As well as by Theodosius the Younger.

---

[85] The first of the two italicized terms cannot be identified. The second is derived from Arabic *ḥadjdjī*, an epithet used for individuals who have performed the pilgrimage to Mecca. The text refers to an Armenian, Gorg, from Ankara, and in Armenian usage the applicable epithet would be *mahtesi* (derived from Arabic *maḳdisī* or *muḳaddasī*, "holy, sacred, sanctified"), referring of course to the pilgrimage to Jerusalem.

[86] This date is according to the "Great Armenian Era"; the corresponding date according to the Christian calendar would be (902 + 551) A.D. 1453.

[87] The reference is to Pope Sylvester I (314-335), who was a contemporary of Emperor Constantine I the Great. The spurious *Donation* of Constantine was supposedly made to Sylvester.

305   Justinian reigned here,
       A most renowned emperor he was,
       Your stature he elevated
       And erected the [Aya] Sofya.

309   Across from the church's gate
       He erected a colossal statue,
       He set up a replica in copper
       Of himself mounted on a horse.

313   The heathens have come into you,
       They have defiled your holy temple,
       They turned you into a cell of gardeners,
       And threw the corpses to the birds.[88]

317   Their blood flowed all around you,
       And no one buried them;
       They made you a taunt to your neighbors,
       You were mocked by those round about you.[89]

321   The fire devoured your young men,
       Your virgins no one mourned,
       Your priests fell by the sword,
       No one wept for your widows.[90]

325   The sound of psalms is no longer heard,
       The clerics have been reduced in number,
       Sweet melodies have been silenced,
       The sound of the bells no longer resound.

329   The divine liturgy has been silenced,
       The Lord's body and blood are no longer dispensed,
       The sweet songs of hallelujahs
       Were reduced much and have expired.

333   Oh, would that the Lord had awakened,
       Like a strong man shouting because of wine,
       And put your adversaries to rout,
       And restored you eternally.[91]

337   Brothers, and this we must remember,
       Why did this happen to them?
       Because the pious diminished in number,
       And the truth had pined away.

341   And their leaders went astray,
       Far removed they were from sanctity,
       The services and prayers
       They performed without chastity.

345   Their princes adjudged unjustly,

---

[88] Cf. Psalms 79.1-2.
[89] Cf. Psalms 79.3-4.
[90] Cf. Psalms 78.63-64.
[91] Cf. Psalms 78.65-66, 69.

They caused grief to the orphan and widow;
And the people in general
Committed acts of great wantonness.

349   Because of this, God was intensely angered
And punished them most severely,
He smote them with bitter blows,
And scattered them like dust.

353   Remembering all of this,
Let us have done with sins,
Abandon the familiar evils,
Tenaciously persevere in good deeds.

357   Let us turn to the church with hope,
Say prayers more frequently,
Observe the fasts with chastity,
And give alms incessantly.

361   Confess our sins more properly,
And do penance with tears;
And witnessing them, spare ourselves,
And avoid being like them.

365   Perhaps the Lord will have mercy
And deliver us from evil,
Spare us and take pity,
And prevent calamity.

369   Protect us hence from temptation,
Deliver us from the wicked Satan,
Save us from the infidels' evils,
And deliver us from oppressors.

373   Give us succor on the hour of death
By sending a good angel,
And communing with the Lord's body and blood
Be buried in blessed soil.

377   On the day of the great judgment,
To hear His holy voice saying, "Come to me";[92]
To be seated among those on His right
And eternally praise the Lord.

381   I, Abraham, abundant with sin,
Composed this lament with great grief,
Because Constantinople I have seen
In its days of prosperity.

385   For three months I sojourned there,
And before the sacred relics prayed;
The garment of Christ I saw yonder
Many times with mine own eyes.

[92] Cf. Matthew 11.28.

389   I plead with you most tearfully,
        Who might read my elegy,
        That should you find errors therein
392   Be forgiving and not reproving.

ELEGY ON THE CAPITAL CITY OF STAMBOUL

by Aŕakʻel Baɫišecʻi

  1   All nations and peoples
       Lament you, city of Stamboul,[93]
       For to all creatures you were
       The glory and honor, Stamboul.

  5   You were the habitat of divinity,
       And the resting place, city of Stamboul;
       Today you have become the heathens'
       Dwelling place, city of Stamboul.

  9   Heaven and earth in unison
       Compose a lament for you, Stamboul;
       By the celestial and terrestrial
       You were protected, city of Stamboul.

13   Heavenly angels spread your fame,
       Peerless city of Stamboul;
       You were protected by celestial powers,
       Magnificent city of Stamboul.

17   The resting-place of evil doers
       You became today, Stamboul;
       And all your glory and honor
       Vanished, city of Stamboul.

21   You were a second Jerusalem,
       Renowned city of Stamboul;
       To you all were drawn
       To see your glory, Stamboul.

25   Imperial city of Stamboul,
       Called mother of cities, Stamboul,
       You are the glory of sea and land,
       Harbor city of Stamboul.

29   The mighty King Constantine
       Made you famous, great Stamboul;
       And he named you after himself
       Polis of Constantine, Stamboul.

33   Today he mourns and laments,

---

[93] The term *Stômpol* in the text, used in this and in subsequent stanzas, represents one of the popular Armenian forms for Istanbul or Constantinople.

For they enslaved you, Stamboul;
For the body adorned by God
Was preserved within you, Stamboul.

37 Gratian and Theodosius,
Compose a lament for Stamboul;
Honorius and Justinian,
Shed tears over Stamboul.

41 Holy patriarchs and divines
Who bestowed blessings upon Stamboul,
Today turn over to malediction
The holy and great city of Stamboul.

45 Saint John Chrysostom,
Come and behold Stamboul;
And utter woes over your throne
In the great city of Stamboul.

49 You were brilliant, Stamboul,
Like the sun, Stamboul;
At noontime you became dark
At the hands of infidels, Stamboul.

53 You were the spring of life, Stamboul,
For the thirsty, you Stamboul;
Your water of life was dried out
Because of the infidels, Stamboul.

57 Like the paradise of Eden, Stamboul,
By the Lord's hand planted, Stamboul;
Abundant fruits of immortality
Were gathered within you, Stamboul.

61 You were destroyed by the infidels,
You were trampled underfoot, Stamboul;
And all your glory and honor
Vanished, Stamboul.

65 The treasure trove of the Lord's
Spiritual gifts,[94] Stamboul,
You were suddenly plundered
By the infidels, Stamboul.

69 You pearl, the herald of the Lord's
Kingdom on earth, Stamboul;
Which all the believers
Yearned to behold, Stamboul.

73 They came to you with yearning
City of holy vows, Stamboul;
Just as they went to Holy Jerusalem
So also to you, city of Stamboul.

[94] Cf. Nehemiah 12.44.

77   You were the abode of blessings
     And the subject of praises, Stamboul;
     Today you have become detestable,
     A place of shame, Stamboul.

81   Woe and alas unto that moment
     When we learned the news, Stamboul,
     That "the Turks captured
     And enslaved the great Stamboul."[95]

85   When the bells tolled
     In your churches, Stamboul,
     The heavenly host descended
     And danced within you, Stamboul.

89   In place of the services and bells,
     The reciters[96] chant within you, Stamboul;
     In all your churches now
     They conduct [Muslim] services,[97] Stamboul.

93   The heavenly host mourned
     When they captured you, Stamboul;
     And the whole universe bewailed
     When they heard of it, Stamboul.

97   Because for all the Christians
     You were a joy, Stamboul;
     And the infidels were enraged
     When we spoke of you, Stamboul.

101 Today you are the object of ridicule
     To all the heathens, Stamboul;
     And you have caused grief
     To all the Christians, Stamboul.

105 I call you by your real name,
     Chosen city, Byzantium;[98]
     The infidels surrounded you
     And declared holy war[99] against you.

109 Divinely wrought Byzantium,
     Miraculous Byzantium,
     By God you were chosen
     As the city of saints, Byzantium.

---

[95] This stanza indicates that Aṙakʿel Baḷišecʿi, the author of the elegy, was not in Constantinople at the time of its capture by the Ottomans.

[96] The term used in the text is *muṭrikʿ*, from Arabic *muḳrī*, "reciter or reader of the Qurʾān." See Ačaṙyan (n. 46 above) 2.199. The Armenian form has the plural suffix *-kʿ*.

[97] The term in the text is *namaz*, from Persian *namāz*, "prayers, those especially prescribed by [Islamic] law"; see Steingass (n. 51 above) 1425. It is used in Armenian exclusively for Muslim worship or prayers; see Malxaseancʿ (n. 56 above) 3.440.

[98] The term used in this and in the following eleven stanzas is *Biwzandia*, one of several forms by which the Armenians referred to Byzantium.

[99] See n. 49 above.

113 Magnificent Byzantium,
     And marvellous Byzantium,
     The jewel of the world, Byzantium,
     Renowned Byzantium.

117 Strong city, Byzantium,
     Built on seven hills, Byzantium,
     All the saints came to you
     And assembled here, Byzantium.

121 Elegant abode, Byzantium,
     A strong rampart, Byzantium,
     The joy of the celestial
     And of the terrestrial, Byzantium.

125 Eulogized in all tongues
     And a victorious name, Byzantium;
     All nations and peoples
     Always respected you, Byzantium.

129 Today you are lamentable
     And deserving of tears, Byzantium;
     The woe that befell you
     Was heard everywhere, Byzantium.

133 Your rejoicing was transformed
     Into sadness, Byzantium;
     And throughout the world you became
     The subject of discourse, Byzantium.

137 You were surrounded and defiled
     By the infidels, Byzantium;
     You became an object of ridicule
     To your heathen neighbors,[100] Byzantium.

141 Like a gorgeous vineyard,
     You flourished with vines, Byzantium;
     Today your fruit is changed to thorn,
     It has become worthless, Byzantium.

145 Byzantium! Byzantium!
     City of Stamboul, Byzantium!
     Called the polis of Constantine,
     Filled with blood, Byzantium.

149 The abode of angels and also
     Of the celestial host, Byzantium;
     Today you are the abode of demons,
     Because of [your] sins, Byzantium.

153 The gathering place of the clergy
     And of hymns of praise, Byzantium;
     Today you are the assembling place
     For the Tačik nation, Byzantium.

[100] Cf. Paslms 79.1, 4.

157   The healer of wounds, Byzantium;
      The remitter of sins, Byzantium;
      And the giver of health
      To all the weak, Byzantium.

161   I am hopeful that before the end
      You will be revived and will shed
      The tyrannical yoke of the infidels,
      Byzantium! Byzantium!

165   For the Franks[101] will set forth
      By the will of the immortal King,
      As foretold in days gone by
      By the holy and pious fathers.[102]

169   They spoke by the Holy Spirit
      And told of things to come,
      The arrival of the Franks
      In subsequent times and days.

173   In unison and one and all,
      The valiant nation shall move forth,
      United unto one another
      Burning with divine love.

177   By sea and land they shall come,
      Countless like the stars,
      Urging one and all
      To the war ordained by God.

181   First they shall take the city of Stamboul,
      By the will of the Almighty Savior;
      Then they shall venture further
      And spread throughout the world.

185   They shall proceed to the eastern land
      And cut everyone to pieces,
      And roaring like lions,
      They shall triumph over the infidels.

189   They shall capture the city of Jerusalem,
      And the holy dominical places;
      They shall adorn with gold
      The gate of the Holy Sepulcher.

---

[101] The text reads *Frankac' azgôn*, lit. "the nation of the Franks." This is a general term applied to the Christians of Europe or the Latin West. For various uses of the term in Armenian sources consult Malxaseanc' (n. 56 above) 4.629; see also *Baṙgirk'* (n. 67 above) 2.963, 1037.

[102] The reference here is to the prophetic literature developed by the Armenians in the Middle Ages. This literature, which influenced Aṙakʿel Baḷišecʿi in the writing of the prophecy regarding the future liberation of Constantinople by the Franks, is discussed in the introduction of the present study.

193 For their time has now come,[103]
   According to the command of Christ,
   As foretold long ago
   In the Gospel by the Son of God.

197 The Christians shall rejoice
   In the Holy City of Jerusalem;
   And the heathens shall perish
   And vanish like dust.

201 Blessed are those who shall see
   That day of infinite glory,
   Like the old man Simeon[104]
   Who yearned to see the Savior.

205 The power of the Cross shall increase
   Through the glory of the crucified King;
   And all the heathen nations
   Shall be destined to perish.

209 Countless shall be the Frankish troops,
   Like the sands of the seashore;
   And no one shall be able to defeat
   The valiant Frankish nation.

213 Like a lightning bolt among the reeds,[105]
   They shall descend upon the Muslims;[106]
   They shall drive out the Tačiks,[107]
   The adversaries of the Holy Cross.

217 They shall vanquish all of Rūm,[108]
   And reach as far as Egypt;
   They shall demolish the demons' abode,
   The sanctuary of the infidels.

221 They shall reach as far as *šahastan*,[109]

---

[103] Cf. Romans 11.25.

[104] The reference is to Simeon, the righteous and devout man who took the infant Jesus in his arms and blessed Him when He was presented in the Temple (see Luke 2.25-35).

[105] Cf. Isaiah 5.24.

[106] The term used in the text is *aylazgik'*, plur. of *aylazgi*, lit. "belonging to a different nation, race, people, tribe, etc." In Armenian sources it was originally applied to non-Jews; later it was used generally for non-Christians; and in the present text the term was applied to the Muslims in general. See *Baṙgirk'* (n. 67 above) 1.85; Malxaseanc' (n. 56 above) 1.76.

[107] See n. 70 above. In the present context it refers to the Muslims in general.

[108] The text reads *zhoṙmoc' ašxarhn*, lit. "the land of the Rūm," that is, the territories of the Greeks in Asia Minor. See F. Babinger, "Rūm," in *Encyclopaedia of Islam*, ed. 1, 3. 1174-1175.

[109] This term is borrowed from Persian *šahristān*, "large fortified city"; see Steingass (n. 51 above) 770; Ačaṙyan (n. 46 above) 1.276; Ačaṙyan, *Hayerēn armatakan baṙaran* [Etymological Dictionary of Armenian], 7 vols. (Yerevan 1926-1935) 5.230-231. In the present text it appears to have been used in the sense of the "land of the shāh," that is "Persia." See Anasyan (n. 12 above) 79.

And advance as far as Tabríz;[110]
They shall penetrate Khurasan[111]
And carry off all into captivity.

225   The whole world shall be illumined
       By the Christian faith,
       And all the heathen nations shall be
       Driven from the face of the earth.

229   Demolished churches everywhere
       Shall be restored again,
       And the whole world shall be glorified
       By hymns of praise of Christ.

233   Our Armenian nation shall flourish,
       For it shall be delivered from the Muslims;
       And everyone shall rejoice
       As in the days of the Illuminator.[112]

237   For when Tiridates[113] and St. Gregory
       Made their journey to Rome,[114]
       There were seventy thousand
       Who entered Rome with them.

241   The Illuminator and Tiridates
       Remained there for a whole year;
       And Constantine [the Great], every day,
       Presented their horsemen with royal robes.[115]

245   Then they concluded an agreement
       And they signed a treaty;
       The Armenians and the Franks

[110] The city of Tabriz is located in northwestern Iran and is the capital of the province of Ādharbaydjān or Azerbaijan. For its history consult V. Minorsky, "Tabriz," in *Encyclopaedia of Islam*, ed. 1, 4.583-593. For the tradition concerning its founding by King Khorsov I of Armenia, see p. 232.

[111] The reference is to the country of Khurasan, comprising the lands situated south of the river Āmū-daryā and north of the Hindū-kush; politically, it also embraced Transoxiana and Sidjistān. See C. Huart, "Khurasan," in *Encyclopaedia of Islam*, ed. 1, 2.966-967; consult also B. Spuler, *Die Mongolen in Iran: Politik, Verwaltung und Kultur der Ilchanzeit, 1220-1350*, ed. 2 (Berlin 1955) Index 526.

[112] The reference is to Saint Gregory the Illuminator, the first catholicos (302-325) of the Armenian church. For his biography see Langlois, *Collection des historiens* 1.97-200; consult also Ōrmanean (n. 63 above) 1.44-81.

[113] This is King Tiridates III (298-330) of Armenia who, after his conversion at the hands of Saint Gregory the Illuminator, proclaimed Christianity as the official religion of Armenia. See Langlois (n. 19 above) 1.97-200; also Ōrmanean (n. 63 above) 1.44-81.

[114] See n. 116 below.

[115] The term in the text is *xilatʿ*, derived from Arabic *khilʿa*, a robe from the wardrobe of the sovereign which he bestowed, as a gift, on the person whom he wished to honor. See C. Huart, "Khilʿa," in *Encyclopaedia of Islam*, ed. 1, 2.955; also *Baṙgirkʿ* (n. 67 above) 1.945-946.

Concluded a pact of mutual love.[116]

249 They left four hundred men yonder,
Pahlawuni[117] Aršakunis,[118]
To remain there and to multiply,
Thus to unite the Franks and Armenians.

253 They shall now serve as guides
To the brave Franks;
They shall come by sea and land
And render us assistance.

257 They shall take the canton of Ararat,
Where the Illuminator had his seat;[119]
They shall reign at Etchmiadzin,[120]
In the holy city of Vagharshapat.[121]

261 Glory to God the Father on high
And to His Only-Begotten, His Word,
To the Holy Ghost, giver of life
And the bestower of peace.

265 In the year nine hundred and two
Of the Great Armenian Era,[122]
When they captured the city of Stamboul
And the Christians they slaughtered.

269 I, Aṙak'el, abundant with sin,

---

[116] Concerning King Tiridates III's and Saint Gregory's alleged journey to Rome and the conclusion there of a "pact of mutual love and union," see the introduction of the present study.

[117] In ancient and medieval Armenian sources the term *Pahlawuni* (also *Palhawuni*) was used synonymously with "Parthian," the Armenian form of the latter being *Part'ew*. See Hübschmann (n. 51 above) 63-65 no. 140. In the present text the term *Pahlawuni* is used to indicate the Parthian origin of the Armenian Aršakuni or Arsacid dynasty.

[118] Aršakuni is the name of the Parthian Arsacid dynasty, a branch of which ruled in Armenia from A.D. 54 to 428. For the etymology of the term consult Hübschmann (n. 51 above) 27 no. 24. In the present text the reference is to the Armenian Arsacids of Parthian origin.

[119] The reference is to the seat of the catholicosate of the Armenian church founded by Saint Gregory the Illuminator at Etchmiadzin in A.D. 301.

[120] The term "Etchmiadzin" literally means "Descent of the Only-Begotten." Originally, it was the name of the church erected by Saint Gregory the Illuminator on the spot designated in a vision by Jesus. The monastery and cathedral by the same name are situated south of the ancient Armenian capital of Vagharshapat, in the canton of Aragacotn in the the province of Ararat. It is the original seat of the Armenian catholicosate which, after many peregrinations, was transferred again to Etchmiadzin in 1441, where it has since remained.

[121] The capital of Armenia, in the plain of Ararat, during the reign of King Tiridates III and the pontificate of Saint Gregory the Illuminator; now the town of Etchmiadzin, situated West of Yerevan.

[122] This date is according to the "Great Armenian Era"; it corresponds to (902 + 551) A.D. 1453.

Filled with calamitous evils,
Wrote these words of lamentation
On the great city of Byzantium.

273 Called the polis of Constantine,
Named after the great king,
Before which the angels hovered
And always steadfastly served.

277 I, the totally unworthy,
Who am called a vardapet,[123]
But wanting in deeds so much,
Brainless, foolish, and worthless.

281 These words I arranged
As a memorial to me on earth;
That whoever may encounter my ode,
With goodwill shall remember me.

285 That they may say, "Lord have mercy"
Upon the most sinful Aṙakʿel,
Who put these words together,
A lament on the polis of Constantine.

289 Also for my worthy parents,
Łutʿlumelikʿ and Nersēs,
Who gave birth to this wretched child,
Captive of manifold sins.

293 And for my mentor[124] Grigor,
Who is surnamed Cerencʿ,
A blessed martyr he was,
And an eloquent vardapet.[125]

297 And for my own beloved son,
Tēr Yovhannēs the priest,
Who at a tender age
Passed away into the living world.

---

[123] The term "vardapet" means "doctor, lecturer, master, preceptor, archimandrite." See É. Benveniste, "Études iraniennes," *Transactions of the Philological Society* (London 1945) 39-78; also consult R. W. Thomson, "*Vardapet* in the Early Armenian Church," *Le Muséon* 75 (Louvain 1962) 367-384. In medieval times the term was employed as a title, corresponding to "doctor of theology," and was generally applied to clergymen who distinguished themselves as scholars or pedagogues.

[124] The term in the text is *rabuni*, borrowed from Hebrew through the medium of Greek *rabbouni*, "rabbi, master, doctor, instructor." See Hübschmann (n. 51 above) 376 no. 367; also Ačaṙyan (n. 109 above) 5.1249-1250. In the present context the term is used in the sense of "mentor."

[125] Grigor Xlatʿecʿi Cerencʿ is the author of a number of religious works and of a historical chronicle; see Anasyan, *Haykakan matenagitutʿyun* (n. 7 above) 1.1135-1138. He was murdered by the Rūzagī Kurds in 1426. Aṙakʿel Baḷišecʿi also wrote an elegy on the martyrdom of Grigor, who was his paternal uncle and mentor.

301   And for Yakob the monk,[126]
      The scribe who with gold embroidered,
      Who wrote on paper
      The song which I composed.

305   And for whom who sings with fervent love,
      And for the sympathetic listener,
      And for him who renders this lament,
      And for him who recalls what I have written.

309   May the Lord have mercy upon all,
      For He is magnanimous towards all;
      And He is charitable towards those
      Who repent[127] their sins.

313   For the Son of God promised
      To His servant in the Gospel,
      "I have come for the sinful,
      For I am the healer of the sick."[128]

317   Glory to the Creator of everything,
      To the Father and His Only-Begotten Son,
      To the Holy Ghost, giver of all grace,
320   In the past, present, and future.

Department of Near Eastern Languages
University of California
Los Angeles, California 90024, U.S.A.

---

[126] The reference is to the vardapet Yakob Łrimecʿi, known as the author of calendrical, grammatical and other literary works. For a bibliography of his works consult Ačařyan, *Hayocʿ anjnanunneri baṙaran* (n. 6 above) 3.502 no. 198. He had also served, as indicated in this stanza, as a scribe to Aṙakʿel Bałišecʿi.

[127] The term used in the text is *pʿošiman*, borrowed from Persian *pashīmān*, "remorseful, rueful, sorry, regretful, penitent." See S. Haïm, *New Persian-English Dictionary*, 2 vols. (Teheran 1934-1936) 1.365.

[128] Cf. Mark 2.17.

SOME NEGLECTED COMPOSERS IN THE FLORENTINE CHAPELS, CA. 1475-1525

•

by Frank A. D'Accone

Chapels of polyphonic music, emulating those of northern Europe, were first established at the Florentine cathedral and baptistry in 1438. During the next century, despite brief periods of inactivity, these institutions provided a focal point around which much of the public musical life of Renaissance Florence revolved. Though modestly staffed at first, the chapels grew steadily both in numbers and in prestige, for under the enlightened patronage of the Medici no effort was spared in securing the services of the finest musicians of the day, foreign as well as Italian. The presence of these musicians, particularly those trained in the north, was to have a pround effect on the course of Florentine musical history. As a result of their contributions, not only did the new polyphonic style of the Franco-Netherlanders gain wide acceptance in the city's cultural life, but native forms, such as the carnival song and the ballata, were also further developed. More important, however, was the didactic role these musicians played, since it was through their teaching and influence that the foundations were laid for later Florentine schools of polyphonic composition.[1]

A particularly brilliant moment in the history of the chapels was reached during the closing decades of the fifteenth century, when several musicians of international reputation found employment in Florence. Chief among these were the composers Heinrich Isaac, Alexander Agricola and Johannes Ghiselin. The moment was short-lived, however, for with Savonarola's rise to power the chapels were disbanded, and most musicians were forced to leave the city in search of positions elsewhere. Reestablished early in the sixteenth century, the chapels were to continue as independent institutions until the end of the Republic. In these years they were staffed for the most part with local musicians. Nevertheless, a semblance of former glory was

---

[1] For further information on the musicians employed in the Florentine chapels, see my "The Singers of San Giovanni in Florence during the Fifteenth Century," *Journal of the American Musicological Society* 14 (1961) 307-358. (Hereinafter the article is referred to as "Singers.")

regained under the leadership of such younger composers as Bernardo Pisano, Mattia Rampollini and, above all, Philippe Verdelot.[2]

In addition to these well-known figures, there were a number of composers of lesser fame associated with the Florentine chapels during this period of fluctuating splendor and decline. A few of them are known to have composed several works. Others are not so well represented. According to extant documents, however, all of them played an active part in the city's musical life. My purpose here is to bring together all of the known materials relating to some of these composers and to give a survey of their surviving works. I pay particular attention to the compositions with Italian texts, which are without exception preserved in manuscripts of Florentine provenance and were doubtless written for Florentine audiences.

SER ARNOLFO GILIARDI

A few works by one Arnolfo have come down to us in manuscripts of the late fifteenth and early sixteenth centuries. All but one of these sources give the composer's first name only, the exception being MS Magliabechi XIX, 176 of the National Library in Florence. In her catalogue of the library's holdings Bianca Becherini gives the name appearing on folio 127v of the manuscript as *Arnolfo Schard*.[3] Although her reading seems correct taken alone, a comparison between the script of this difficult spot and other more easily read portions of the manuscript indicates that the name is *Arnolfo Giliardi*.[4] This solution in turn fits in well with the initial of the composer's surname as given in the Vatican Library MS Cappella Giulia XIII, 27—also of Florentine origin—where he is referred to as *Arnolfo G.* An *Arnulphus Gilardus* is reported by the theorist Johannes Hothby, writing about 1480, to have been in the en-

---

[2] G. Reese's *Music in the Renaissance*, rev. ed. (New York 1959) gives excellent summaries of the lives and works of most of the musicians mentioned here. Other recent biographical studies include: A. Bragard, "Verdelot en Italie," *Revue belge de musicologie* 11 (1957) 109-124; C. Gottwald, "Johannes Ghiselin-Janne Verbonnet: Some Traces of His Life," *Musica disciplina* 15 (1961) 105-111; F. A. D'Accone "Bernardo Pisano—An Introduction to His Life and Works," *Musica disciplina* 17 (1963) 115-135; idem, "Heinrich Isaac in Florence: New and Unpublished Documents," *The Musical Quarterly* 49 (1963) 464-483; C. Sartori, "Rampollini, Mattia," *Die Musik in Geschichte und Gegenwart* 10.1913. Recent editions of music, all published by the American Institute of Musicology, include: Alexander Agricola, *Opera omnia*, ed. E. R. Lerner (4 vols. to date); Johannes Ghiselin—Verbonnet, *Opera omnia*, ed. C. Gottwald (3 vols. to date); Philippe Verdelot, *Opera omnia*, ed. A. Bragard (1 vol. to date); Bernardo Pisano, *Collected Works*, ed. F. A. D'Accone, Music of the Florentine Renaissance 1 (1966).

[3] Bianca Becherini, *Catalogo dei manoscritti musicali della Biblioteca nazionale di Firenze* (Kassel 1959) 75. Professor Becherini's reading of the surname has been questioned by a few scholars, but to my knowledge an alternate reading of it has yet to be advanced.

[4] I record here my thanks to Professor Gino Corti of Florence for his help in deciphering the name.

tourage of Cosimo de' Medici (d. 1464).[5] Is it possible that this Arnolfo and the composer are one and the same person? I am inclined to think so for several reasons. The presence of a composer in Cosimo's circle is not surprising in the light of our knowledge of Cosimo's interest in music. Other Florentine documents, moreover, reveal that a musician named Arnolfo was associated with the Florentine chapels over a number of years and that he was on friendly terms with Cosimo's grandson Lorenzo, whom he was later to assist in recruiting singers.

Among the documents that I have been able to uncover, Arnolfo's name is first mentioned in a letter written by Braccio Martelli to Lorenzo the Magnificent on 3 September 1473.[6] At the time Lorenzo was staying at the Medici villa in Caffagiolo, and Martelli's purpose in writing was to present Arnolfo, who was "coming there in order to be appointed as a singer in San Giovanni." Several other singers, apparently newly arrived from the north, were accompanying Arnolfo to Caffagiolo, and Martelli urged Lorenzo to expedite the appointment of all of them to the baptistry's chapel. Although Lorenzo was actively involved in the chapel's management, personnel matters had evidently got out of hand during his brief absence from Florence. Consequently, Martelli also exhorted him to write the responsible parties from Caffagiolo, while promising to do what he could in Florence: "In any case recommend Arnolfo, the bearer of this letter, and I shall attend to the rest here." From the tone of the letter it appears that Arnolfo himself had just arrived in the city. This does not lessen the possibility, however, that he is the same person as the Arnolfo who was in Cosimo's service some ten years earlier. Subsequent documents show that quite a few musicians, including Arnolfo, were in and out of Florence several times during the next two decades.

The baptistry's account books from the period under consideration are not extant, so we have no way of knowing the length of Arnolfo's service in the chapel at this time. Later records indicate that he was employed there again from 1483 to 1485.[7]

Arnolfo is first mentioned in extant documents from the Santissima Annunziata dated August 1478, though not in connection with the chapel.[8] His duties consisted of "teaching the [convent's] novices figural music," that is, the principles of reading, writing and performing polyphony.[9] This

[5] A. Seay, "The *Dialogus Johannis Ottobi Anglici in arte musica*," *Journal of the American Musicological Society* 8 (1955) 92, 99.

[6] The letter is printed with an English translation in "Singers" 326, 354-355.

[7] See n. 15.

[8] In the early 1480s, however, many of the musicians employed at the baptistry also began serving at the Annunziata. See "Singers" 331.

[9] Abbreviations used in citing documentary sources here and in the following notes are:
ASF   Archivio di Stato, Florence
AC   ASF, Archivio dell'Arte di Calimala

is a clear indication that Arnolfo was a composer as well as a performer, further substantiation of which is furnished in a document to be mentioned presently.

A few other records from the Annunziata, including receipts with his signature, show that Arnolfo retained his position there through the beginning of January 1479, when he was succeeded by ser Antonio di Marco da Montughi.[10] Previously, on 1 February 1478, *ser Arnolfo da Francia, contratenore*, had been engaged, along with ser Antonio and several other singers, to perform in the newly reconstituted chapel at the cathedral.[11] He left the cathedral's service in December of the same year.[12]

Further information about Arnolfo's activities during this period is provided by a document in the cathedral archives which states that on 26 March 1479 the cathedral's overseers directed that one florin be paid to "ser Arnolfo, a singer and chaplain in San Lorenzo, for his work in having composed vocal pieces."[13] Besides establishing the fact that singer and composer are the same person, the document reveals that meanwhile Arnolfo had also obtained a chaplaincy in the Medici's family church, doubtless as a result of Lorenzo's influence. Unfortunately, none of San Lorenzo's account books for the decade 1480-1490 which I was able to examine contains any reference to Arnolfo.

Arnolfo left Florence sometime during the year following the date of the cathedral document. The record of a letter written on 2 August 1480 states that Lorenzo requested him "to defer to another time sending the singers

---

SMDF   Archivio dell'Opera di Santa Maria del Fiore, Florence

SSA   ASF, Corporazioni Religiose Soppresse 119, Santissima Annunziata

The document recording Arnolfo's duties is found in SSA 697, *Entrata & Uscita, 1477-1478*, fol. 54v.

Agosto 1478

A ser Arnolfo, chantore, a dì 13 detto L. due sono per parte di suo salario per insegnare chantare a' novizi canto figurato.

[10] SSA 197, *Debitori & Creditori, 1478-1484*, fol. 30:

1478 [1479]

Ser Arnolfo di [gap], chantore. . . . de' avere a dì V di giennaio 1478 [1479] L. 8 s. X per tanto gli si dà d'achordo per insegnare a' nostri noviti chantare.

The Florentine new year began on March 25, and documents recorded before that day usually carry the date of the preceding year. In the course of the text such dates have been changed to conform to our modern system.

[11] A. Seay, "The Fifteenth-Century Capeplla at Santa Maria del Fiore in Florence," *Journal of the American Musicological Society* 11 (1958) 49.

[12] *Ibid.* 50.

[13] SMDF 8.1.65, *Quaderno Cassa, com. Gennaio, 1478/79*, fol. 55v:

Spese d'opera de' dare. . .

E de' dare a dì 26 di marzo [1479] Fl. uno largho per loro a ser Arnolfo di Arnolfo, chantore e chappellano di San Lorenzo, i quali gli danno gli operai per sua faticha di chonpore canti, porto e' detto. Fl. 1

Coming as it does a few weeks before Easter, which occurred on April 11 of that year, the payment suggests that the pieces were commissioned for use during Holy Week. Evidence that such works by Arnolfo were in the repertory of the cathedral chapel is given below.

here" (to Florence).[14] Whether this was merely a short trip in order to recruit singers for the chapels or one of longer duration is difficult to determine. Musical evidence—in this case a dedicatory motet—suggests that Arnolfo spent some time in Siena during these years, and it may well be that his sojourn there took place in this period. He was back in Florence serving in the baptistry's chapel sometime around the end of 1483. On 20 January 1484 it is recorded that *ser Arnolfo d'Arnolfo, cantore in San Giovanni*, signed an agreement with the Annunziata to sing polyphonic music there at Saturday morning mass throughout the year, in return for a room, clothing and personal services.[15] He received, in addition, a salary of one florin per month, payments of which are recorded in his name from 26 February 1484 to 2 July 1485.[16] The absence of further payments after the latter date and the record of another of Lorenzo's letters written shortly beforehand—a "general" one "in behalf of ser Arnolfo"—suggests that he once again departed from Florence.[17] He returned a few years later, rejoining the cathedral chapel on 1 October 1492.[18] This was the shortest of his stays, for he is recorded as being there only through the end of the following December.[19] After that time no further mention of him is made in the archives of the various Florentine musical establishments.

Arnolfo's works continued to be performed in Florence long after his departure, indeed, for almost a century after his death. Francesco Corteccia, in the preface to his *Responsoria* (Venice, Gardano, 1570), states that he had been "strongly urged" to have his own compositions for Holy Week printed

> because there were almost none of them left for us [to use here in Florence] except for those most ancient ones by a certain Arnolfo, which almost never cease insisting on the similarity of voices and for that reason are not very highly esteemed, since in everything, repetition is the mother of satiety.

In the light of Corteccia's remarks, unflattering as they are, it is surprising that none of Arnolfo's responsories seems to have survived either in Florentine or in other musical sources. In fact, only two of Arnolfo's sacred works, both settings of the Magnificat, are known at the present time. These simple pieces present an embellished version of the chant tone in the cantus, and in conformity with *alternatim* practice set only the even numbered verses of the canticle. The first setting, in the sixth tone, is for three voices of which

---

[14] M. del Piazzo, ed. *Protocolli del carteggio di Lorenzo il Magnifico per gli anni 1473-74, 1477-92*, Deputazione di storia patria per la Toscana, Documenti di storia italiana 2.2 (Florence 1956) 113.

[15] "Singers" 334-335, 356-357.

[16] *Ibid.* 335.

[17] M. del Piazzo 372.

[18] "Singers" 345.

[19] *Ibid.* 346.

the upper and lower only are written out.[20] The middle voice is to be improvised by the performer, as is indicated by the title "a faulx bourdon" and by
the accompanying rubric "qui habet aures audiendi audiat." The second
setting, in the eighth tone, is for four voices, all of them written out. Two
versions of this piece survive in two manuscripts of north Italian origin dating
from around the turn of the sixteenth century.[21] Perhaps this is an indication
that Arnolfo spent some time in other Italian cities after leaving Florence.

Sena vetus, Arnolfo's paean to the glories of Siena and the beauty of its
women, provides more direct evidence of his activities elsewhere in the peninsula. The piece, preserved in a handsomely decorated parchment manuscript
of the late fifteenth century, was probably commissioned by the Sienese
government or some civic minded patron, for its text also stresses the city's
ancient tradition of liberty and its enjoyment of continuous and prosperous
peace.[22] The three-part *Le Souvenir* is the only one of Arnolfo's works with
French text known at the present time. It is found, as far as I can ascertain,
in two manuscripts of Italian origin,[23] which suggests that it also dates from
his years in Italy. The opening of Arnolfo's piece begins exactly like a setting
of the same name by the mid-fifteenth century English composer Morton.
If the pieces are nearly contemporaneous, as seems likely, Arnolfo's "is a very
early example of the parody and represents a primitive stage in the development of that technique."[24]

Two of Arnolfo's works with Italian texts appear in the previously mentioned Florentine MS Magliabechi XIX, 176[25] (see musical supplement, nos.
1, 2). Though they present certain problems of interpretation and transcrip-

---

[20] The piece is preserved in MS Rés. Vm.[7] 676 of the National Library in Paris. See
N. Bridgman, "Un manuscrit italien du début du xvi⁰ siècle à la Bibliothèque Nationale,"
Annales musicologiques 1 (1953) 183-184, 228-229.

[21] It appears anonymously in MS Rés. Vm.[7] 676 (*ibid.* 216-217), but with ascription to
Arnolfo in MS Liber Capelle Franchini Gafori, vol. 1 of the Cathedral Archives in Milan.
For the latter source see C. Sartori, *Le musiche della Cappella del Duomo di Milano, Catalogo*
(Milan 1957) 44.

[22] The piece is printed in a faulty modern edition by S. A. Luciani, *La musica in Siena*
(Siena 1942) 38-41.

[23] With ascription to Arnolfo in MS Cappella Giulia XIII, 27; anonymously in MS Q
16 of the Conservatory Library, Bologna. See A. Smijers, "Vijftiende en zestiende eeuwsche
muziekhandschriften in Italië met werken van Nederlandsche componisten," *Tijdschrift
der Vereeniging voor nederlandsche Muziekgeschiedenis* 14 (1935) 168.

[24] H. M. Brown, *Music in the French Secular Theater, 1400-1550* (Cambridge, Mass.
1963) 134.

[25] On fols. 40v-42 (*O invida fortuna*) and 127v-129 (*Piagneran gli occhi mey*) respectively.
At one time the second piece also formed part of the contents of MS 2356 of the Riccardiana
Library in Florence. See D. Plamenac, "The 'Second' Chansonnier of the Biblioteca Riccardiana," *Annales musicologique* 2 (1954) 112, 114. Both pieces are discussed briefly
in B. Becherini, "Autori minori nel codice Fiorentino Magl. XIX, 176," *Revue belge de musicologie* 4 (1950) 24-25.

tion, both works are of great interest, poetically as well as musically, for the student of Italian quattrocento music. The three-part *Piagneran gli occhi mey* consists of two sections of music, the first marked "verte" at its close on the tonic, the second containing a *signum congruentiae* that indicates an ending on the dominant in bar 35, as well as another ending on the tonic in the next bar. As they stand, the musical structure of the sections and of their endings gives little indication of the form of the piece; nor does the poetry to which both sections are set.

The entire text consists of four strophes, each formed of four heptasyllabic lines with the rhyme scheme *a b b a*. In the first section one strophe is given line by line under the cantus part, a second strophe appears complete in the remaining space at the close of the contratenor part. The process is repeated for strophes three and four in the second section. Since textual continuity between strophes three and four is quite clear, a logical assumption is that the first two strophes are to be performed one after the other to the music of section one, the final two strophes to the music of section two, and that the piece is structured in an *A A B B* form. This solution, however, fails to take into account the "verte" marking at the end of section one, the two endings of section two (typical of the musical form of the trecento ballata) and the thought expressed in strophe two, which stands by itself as a closing apostrophe.

In my opinion the "verte" marking at the end of section one does not signify an immediate repetition of that section after strophe one. Rather, it serves as an indication that the performer is now to proceed to section two and continue with strophes three and four, utilizing the two different endings provided by the composer. Here, however, melodic and textual considerations point to the ending of the last bar as the appropriate close for strophe three, the ending at the *signum congruentiae* in bar 35 as that of strophe four.[26] After this a return is to be made to section one for the poetry of strophe two and the end of the piece. The text is thus treated as a ballata, though it is not one; and the musical form, thoroughly satisfying from a melodic, harmonic and structural point of view, also approximates that most widespread and enduring of all Italian polyphonic forms.

Quite apart from these problematic aspects, *Piagneran gli occhi mey* contains several passages of very beautiful music. At the opening of the piece, for example, the cantus presents a phrase on the syllable "pia" which encompasses the upward leap of a sixth and then comes almost immediately

---

[26] In returning to the opening of section two (for the text of strophe four) an awkward melodic interval (G-C-sharp) is avoided if strophe three ends on the A of the last bar. Furthermore, an ending on G at the *signum congruentiae* for strophe four ensures a smooth return to the opening note (A) of section one. With regard to the text, the last line of strophe three cannot be fitted easily to the last phrase of music if the ending is at the *signum congruentiae*.

to a cadence on the sharped leading tone. After a rest of one beat the phrase is resumed on the same syllable and the entire word, "piagneran," as well as the rest of the line follow. This abrupt halt in the middle of the first phrase not only serves to heighten the dramatic impact of the word, but also introduces almost literally into the musical structure the idea of a sob. The following phrase makes use of equally effective devices. Here the cantus rises in sequences of ascending fourths until it reaches a climax a full octave above its first note; it then descends to a deceptive cadence on the minor dominant, all the while having formed a series of poignant seven-six suspensions with the lower parts.

The composer's sensitivity to harmonic color is much in evidence throughout the rest of the piece. In the untransposed Aeolian mode on A, in which both sections begin and end, intermediary phrases are constructed so as to cadence on such widely divergent areas as e, a, B-flat and F; in the meantime ample use has also been made of notated chromatics such as G-sharp, C-sharp, B-flat and E-flat. Altogether, *Piagneran gli occhi mey* shows Arnolfo to have been a composer of no mean gifts, one who knew how to combine the clarity of Franco-Netherlandish part-writing with expressive Italian melody.

The three-part *O invida fortuna* also contains two musical sections, the first of which is marked "verte folium" at its close. The rubric in this case clearly means that the second section is to follow immediately upon the first. Both sections begin in the tonic, but only the second section ends there. The close of the first section, instead, first cadences deceptively on VI and then inconclusively on IV. This is another indication that the final cadence is that of the second section and that the musical form of the piece is a simple *A B*.

The poetry is divided into two sections which, like the music, must be read through from beginning to end. The first section consists of four lines with the rhyme scheme *a b b A*, the second of five lines with the rhyme scheme *c c d d C*.[27] Despite the fact that the first four lines form a complete statement and could be thought of as a ripresa, the poem cannot be classified as a ballata because none of the rhymes of the first section recurs in the second. Actually, as it is presented here, the poem does not correspond to any of the traditional Italian forms of the time. It is cast, rather, in a free scheme, one that is exactly mirrored in the straightforward structure of the music.

The only hindrance to a correct reading of the piece at first sight is caused by a copyist's errror. At the beginning of the second section lines five and six of the poetry should be sung to the same music. The copyist, however, neglected to repeat the music in his score, and it was apparently only after he finished that he realized his omission. Accordingly, he went back and placed one line of text below the other, with the clear intention of correcting his error. But in doing so he failed to give a sign of repetition in the musical score, with

---

[27] Lower case letters indicate heptasyllabic lines; capitals, lines of eleven syllables.

the result that, as it now stands, the piece seemingly does not have enough music to accomodate the text. By repeating the music of line five for line six of the text the mistake is easily rectified.

O invida fortuna is in the transposed Ionian mode on F, with all parts carrying a flat in the signature. Major cadential points occur on closely related degrees of the scale such as d and C, as well as on the tonic. The harmonic variety with which Arnolfo infused *Piagneran gli occhi mey* is not so apparent here, the only extra accidental introduced being an E-flat, which would have been supplied in any case by the performers because of the rules of *musica ficta*. Nevertheless, the piece is a worthy companion to its fellow, not only because of its well-designed contrapuntal passages and carefully planned harmonic scheme, but also because its phrase structure effectively reproduces the rhythms and accents of the text.

RUBINETTO, STOCHEM, PIETREQUIN

Only fragmentary information about these composers has survived in Florentine archives. *Rubinetto francioso, cantore*, is first recorded at the Santissima Annunziata on 7 February 1482, and payments to him for serving in the chapel there are listed in the convent's accounts until the end of the following April.[28] Two other payments, dated May 6 and 10 of the same year, give the expenses for a robe that the convent had had made for him.[29] There is no further mention of him after this time. Another "frate Rubinectus franciosus," who may or may not be the same person, is recorded in Florence twenty-four years later. This musician received an appointment to the cathedral chapel on 26 June 1506 and served there for a little over a year, leaving sometime before 13 August 1507.[30] One or the other of these men is probably the *F. Rubinet* to whom several chansons are ascribed in the Florentine manuscript Banco rari 229 and a few other manuscripts of the period.[31]

---

[28] "Singers" 332.

[29] SSA 246, *Entrata & Uscita, 1479-1482*, fol. 249v.

6 maggio 1482

A Rubinetto, cantore, a dì detto L. una s. sedici sono per cinque braccia di tella per fodrare la sua tonica e per fillo a cuxilla.

Ibid. fol. 250:

10 maggio 1482

A Rubinetto a dì detto L. una s. quattro sono per facitura dela sua tonica, portò il sarto.

[30] SMDF 2.2.9, *Deliberazioni, 1498-1507*, fol. 148v:

26 junii 1506

Item . . . elegerunt in chantorem fratem Rubinectum Franciosum loco Ciarles Premerani [?] pro contro alto et ad rationem L. quinque pro quolibet mense, prout solvebatur dicto Ciarles.

Rubinectus is not mentioned in a deliberation dated 13 August 1507, in which the chapel members are named. (*Ibid.* fol. 188).

[31] It is unclear whether Rubinet is the same composer as the Rubinus of the *Glogauer*

Johannes Stochem, whose works have come down to us in several well-known printed and manuscript collections of the time, was attached to the court of Matthias Corvinus, king of Hungary, during the early 1480s.[32] From 1487 to 1489 Stochem was in Rome, serving in the papal chapel of Innocent VIII.[33] While en route to Rome, Stochem stopped in Florence and received temporary employment in the Annunziata's chapel. Given the informal nature of his appointment, it is not surprising that his name is lacking in the account books that list the musicians regularly employed at the convent. His signature, however, appears twice in one of the Annunziata's receipt registers, under the entries for 31 July and 5 September 1486, in acknowledgement of his salary for the months of July and August 1486.[34] He must have left Florence shortly after this time, since he began serving in the papal chapel the following February.

Pierre Bonnel of Picardy, otherwise known as Pietrequin (Pietrachino), first arrived in Florence in the spring of 1490. He was employed at the Annunziata from 3 April of that year through 6 June 1491 and then again from 9 October 1492 to 20 March 1493.[35] His signature is also preserved in receipts from the convent's registers carrying the dates 3 July and 2 September 1490.[36] Although he is not identified as a singer of San Giovanni in the Annunziata's account books, it seems likely, given the length of his stay in Florence, that he was employed at the baptistry as well. Pietrequin joined the cathedral

---

Liederbuch. See G. Reese (n. 2 above) 48, 635. Five chansons, all of them apparently unique, are given to Rubinet in Banco rari 229. Another chanson, also attributed to him in this manuscript, is ascribed to Isaac in the Segovia manuscript and appears anonymously in Washington, Library of Congress, M2. 1. M6. A chanson by Stochem, preserved among other places in Banco rari 229 and the Cappella Giulia manuscript, is ascribed to Rubinet in MS Q 18 of the Conservatory Library, Bologna. I am indebted to Professor Howard M. Brown of the University of Chicago, who kindly communicated this information about Rubinet's works. Professor Brown's edition of MS Banco rari 229 is now in preparation and will be published by the University of Chicago Press in the "Monuments of Renaissance Music" series.

[32] For a summary of this composer's life and works see A. Seay, "Stochem, Johannes," *Die Musik in Geschichte und Gegenwart* 12.1392-1393.

[33] F. M. Haberl, "Die römische 'schola cantorum' und die päpstlichen Kapellsänger bis zur Mitte des 16. Jahrhunderts," *Vierteljahrsschrift für Musikwissenschaft* 3 (1887) 244.

[34] SSA 1050, *Ricevute, 1486-1493*, fol. 5v ("Ego Johannes Stochem recepi 31 julii ducato 1"); fol. 6v ("Ego Johannes Stochem recepi ducato 1").

[35] SSA 198, *Debitori & Creditori, 1488-1493*, fol. 279v:
Piero di Bonello, cantore, de' dare a dì 3 d'aprile 1490 Fl. uno largho. . . .
E de' dare a dì 6 di giugno 1491 Fl. uno largho.
Ibid. fol. 357v:
Pietro di Bonello, chantore, de' dare a dì 9 d'ottobre 1492 Fl. uno largho. . . .
E a dì 28 di marzo 1493 Fl. uno largho.

[36] SSA 1050, *Ricevute, 1486-1493*, fol. 96 ("Ego Pietrequinus de Piccardia recepi per sallario mensium III di aprile, maii, junius Fl. 3 la"); fol. 99v ("Ego Petrus Bonnel de Picardia recepi a di duo settembris duos ducatos pro salario mensium 2").

chapel on 1 April 1490 and served there through December of the same year.[37] After an absence of a few years he resumed service at the cathedral on 1 July 1492.[38]

Another glimpse of Pietrequin's activities at this time comes from an account recording the clothing expenses of the entourage that accompanied Piero de' Medici to Rome in September 1492, on the occasion of his journey there to congratulate the newly elected Pope Alexander VI. Apparently no expense was spared in providing suitable attire for the Medici party, which, among others, included three members of the Florentine chapels who also served as Piero's personal musicians:

> For the three singers, that is, Arigho [Isaac], Charletto [de Launoy] and Petrachino, for each of them a robe . . . and a beret . . a tunic . . . a hat . . . the sum of 32 1/2 florins for each of them, in all Fl. 97 s. 10[39]

Besides indicating a hitherto unknown aspect of Pietrequin's activities while he was in Florence, the document is of great interest for the information it brings to bear on another point. It suggests that even at a time when the concept of choral polyphony was well established at public services in Florence, the Medici continued the time-honored, princely practice of retaining a smaller group of musicians for more intimate performances at home or in the family chapel.

Upon his return to Florence, Pietrequin rejoined the cathedral chapel, serving there until the end of March 1493, when the chapel was disbanded.[40] After that time he is no longer mentioned in Florentine musical archives. Six works are attributed to him in several manuscripts and a print of the late fifteenth and early sixteenth centuries. Among them is the delightful farewell chanson, *Adieu Florence la iolye*, a piece that perhaps was composed at the time of his trip to Rome.[41]

---

[37] "Singers" 342.

[38] SMDF 8.1.90, *Quaderno Cassa, com. Luglio, 1492*, fol. 40v:
La chapella del chanto fighurato de' dare. . . . a dì 8 di detto [agosto] Fl. due larghi d'oro in oro per lui a Petrichino di Pichardia. . . . per suo salario del mese di luglio. Fl. 2.

[39] ASF, Medici Avanti il Principato, 104, fol. 583:
Spese per vestire la famiglia del Mangnifico Piero per la gita di Roma. . . . A' tre chantori, cioè Arigho, Charletto, Petrachino, a ciaschuno uno robone. . . . e uno beretto. . . . una robetta. . . . uno chapello. . . . somma Fl. 32 larghi e 1/2 per ciaschuno, monta in tutto Fl. 97 s. 10.
I am indebted to Professor Gino Corti of Florence for the transcription of this document.

[40] "Singers" 346.

[41] Four chansons are found in MS 2794 of the Riccardiana Library, Florence. See B. Becherini, "Alcuni canti dell' Odhecaton e del codice fiorentino 2794," *Bulletin de l'Institut historique belge de Rome* 22 (1950) 338-339; D. Plamenac (n. 25 above) 105-106. A fifth chanson, *Mais que ce fut secretement*, appears, among other places, in the Cappella

PINTELLI

Two musicians, Giovanni di Giovanni Pintelli and his brother Tomaso di Giovanni, are recorded as having served in various Florentine chapels during the 1480s. Direct evidence is lacking as to which of them is the composer represented in musical sources by two works, the ballata *Questo mostrarsi adirata di fore* (text by Poliziano) and the mass *Gentilz gallans de France*. Unfortunately, only the composer's surname is given at the beginning of each of these works—a practice that is not unusual for the time. Nevertheless, for reasons to be cited below, extant Florentine documents make it appear that it was Giovanni who composed the works in question.

Due to the loss of the baptistry's accounts for the 1470s and 1480s, we cannot know exactly when Giovanni joined the chapel in San Giovanni. But he must have been employed there before entering the chapel at the Santissima Annunziata because in his first payment from that church, dated 10 October 1484, he is listed as *Giovanni di Giovanni Pintelli, cantore in San Giovanni*.[42] He was associated with the Annunziata over the next several years, the last record of payment in his name being issued on 5 February 1491.[43] Presumably, as with most other singers, he was simultaneously employed at the baptistry throughout these years. Meanwhile, on 15 June 1488, he had also become a member of the cathedral chapel, his tenure there continuing until 1 April 1490.[44] After the date of his last payment from the Annunziata his name does not appear again in the archives of the various chapels.

Tomaso di Giovanni Pintelli joined his brother in the cathedral chapel on 1 August 1488.[45] He was there for less than a year, leaving the church's service on or before 1 July 1489.[46] Several months earlier, on 2 December 1488, it is recorded that *Tomaso di Giovanni Pintelli, cantore in San Giovanni*, was appointed to the Annunziata's chapel.[47] He was employed there until

---

Giulia manuscript, Banco rari 229 and the *Odhecaton*, in the latter source with attribution to Compère. See H. Hewitt, ed., *Harmonice Musices Odhecaton* (Cambridge, Mass. 1942) 165-166, 400. *Adieu Florence la iolye* is preserved in Banco rari 229; MS Magliabechi XIX, 178 of the National Library, Florence; and MSS 328-331 of the University Library, Munich (communication from Professor H. M. Brown).

[42] "Singers" 336.

[43] SSA 198, *Debitori & Creditori, 1488-1493*, fol. 149v:
Giovanni di Giovanni, chantore, de' dare. . . .
E a dì 5 di febbraio [1491] de' dare Fl. uno largho.

[44] "Singers" 341-342.

[45] *Ibid.*

[46] *Ibid.*

[47] SSA 198, *Debitori & Creditori, 1488-1493*, fol. 270v:
Thomaxo Pintelli, cantore in San Giovanni, de' dare a dì 28 di dicembre 1488 Fl. uno largho.

15 October 1491.[48] As in the case of his brother, nothing further of him is known after the date of his last payment from the Annunziata.

Another question, that of the national origin of the Pintellis, should be considered before attempting to establish the composer's identity. Very little music by Italian composers from this period survives; the situation is echoed by archival sources, where lack of reference to native composers seems to indicate that around the middle of the fifteenth century creative musical activity on the peninsula went into an eclipse. Whatever the reasons for this,[49] recent scholarship has shown that toward the end of the century Italian composers began to appear on the scene once again. In Florence the emergence of a native school of composition at the turn of the sixteenth century is reflected in the works of Alessandro Coppini, Bartolomeo degli Organi and, slightly later, in those of Bernardo Pisano and Francesco de Layolle.[50]

One might suppose that Pintelli was an older member of this group. Certainly, the setting of a Florentine text by a composer with an Italian surname who lived and worked in Florence presents a convincing argument in favor of his Florentine, or at least Italian, origin. The Pintelli surname is even found in Florentine tax registers of the time.[51] I was not able, however, to locate the names of Giovanni and Tomaso in any documents pertaining to various branches of the Pintelli family.[52] There is, of course, the possibility that the brothers were priests and therefore not liable to be listed in tax registers; but the absence in their payments from the Annunziata and the cathedral of the titles "ser," "messer" or any other clerical distinction suggests otherwise. This perplexing situation was finally clarified by the chance discovery of a few documents from the convent church of Santo Spirito.

Surviving account books from the mid-1480s show that the musical establishment at Santo Spirito was hardly comparable to those of the baptistry or of the Annunziata. The Augustinian convent, however, did employ an organist, and there is some evidence that vocal polyphony was also performed

---

[48] *Ibid.* fol. 318v:

Tommaso Pintegli, cantore in San Giovanni, de' dare. . . . a dì XV d'ottobre [1491] Fl. mezzo largo.

[49] An excellent discussion of the problem is found in N. Pirrotta, "Music and Cultural Tendencies in Fifteenth-Century Italy," *Journal of the American Musicological Society* 19 (1966) 127-161.

[50] Modern editions of the collected works of these composers have been prepared by the present writer and are being published by the American Institute of Musicology in the series "Music of the Florentine Renaissance."

[51] For example, in ASF, Decima della Repubblica 6, *1498, Santo Spirito, Ferza*, fol. 253, wherein is found a tax report filed by Jachopo, Giovambatista, Gherardo, Bernardo and Piero, the sons of Piero di Jachopo Pintegli. The family had filed a previous report in 1481.

[52] Further information is found in Gargani's monumental *Poligrafo* no. 1566 ("Pintelli") in the National Library, Florence; in ASF, Archivio dell' Ancisa, HH. fols. 253v, 687; *ibid.* MM fol. 535v; and in ASF, Monte delle Graticole 977 fol. 259.

there. A payment in the convent's account books, dated 20 March 1488, for example, lists the cost of a "volume of figural music" for use by the choir.[53] Another entry shows that the novices were given instruction in music by a professional, who was also expected to assume the duties of *maestro di cappella:*

> I record that Carlo de Burgis came to stay with us [at the convent] on the 1st of September, 1486 at the instance of frate Giovanni, our prior, with the stipulation that he teach the novices plainchant and polyphony and sing in church with them, at a salary of four lire a month, which amounts to forty-eight lire a year.[54]

Payments to Carlo de Burgis are recorded until 10 January 1488, when it is stated that he received three lire and three soldi in severance pay.[55] A little over a month later another musician was engaged to replace him:

> I record that on the 19th of February, 1488 *Giovanni Pintelli francioso* [italics mine] came to stay with us in the capacity of singing master and to teach the novices figural music and to sing with the others [in chapel] at a salary of four lire a month, with expenses and living quarters.[56]

The significance of the document is twofold: it suggests that Giovanni, by reason of his position as singing master and teacher of polyphonic music,

---

[53] ASF, Corporazioni Religiose Soppresse 127, Santo Spirito 8, *Entrata & Uscita A. 1488-1498*, fol. 79v;
marzo 1487 [1488]
Item a dì 20 a frate Agnolo di Certaldo Fl. tre d'oro in oro & per lui dua a frate Francesco & uno al baccielliere cathelario per uno libro di chanto figurato, valsono lire diciotto e soldi diciotto.
[54] *Ibid.* 1, *Libro campione AA, 1475-1494*, fol. 118v:
Ricordo come Carlo de Burgis venne a stare con noi a dì primo di septembre 1486 per mezzo di frate Giovanni, pater noster, con patto ch'egli insegnassi a' novitii canto fermo & figurato e cantare in chiesa con loro con salario di quatro lire il mese, che monta un anno lire quaranta otto.
[55] *Ibid., Entrata & Uscita A. 1488-1498*, fol. 78v:
gennaio 1487 [1488]
Item a dì 10 a maestro Carlo de Burgis lire tre e soldi tre per ogni suo resto avessi avuto a ffare col convento.
[56] *Ibid.* 1, *Libro campione AA, 1475-1494*, fol. 178v:
Ricordo chome per insino a dì 19 di febraio 1487 [1488] venne a stare con noi Giovanni Pintelli francioso per magistro del canto e per insegnare a' novitii canto figurato e per cantare insieme cogli altri, dandogli per ciascheduno mese lire quatro colle spese e la tornata di chasa.
Pintelli evidently remained at Santo Spirito for only a few months. In the continuation (fol. 179) of the above account, written in the margin are the words "stette per insino a dì 20 di giugno 1488." A payment to him, however, is listed below this with the date 20 September 1488.

was a composer as well as a performer; it also leaves no doubt that the Pintellis' origins were either French or Netherlandish. Clearly, whatever the original version of the name, its sound was familiar enough to Florentine ears to be Italianized into Pintelli.

Pintelli's four-part *Missa Gentilz gallans de France*, based in part on the tune of the same name, has survived, lacking portions of the first Kyrie and the Gloria, in an apparently unique source, MS Cappella Sistina 41 of the Vatican Library.[57] A few sections of the Mass also draw on the materials of two polyphonic chansons, the four-part *Gentil galans de Franza* of Prioris (?) and Agricola's three-part *Gentil galans*. The Patrem, for example, reproduces the duet between the cantus and altus (bars 3-6) of Prioris's chanson, first in its cantus and tenor, then in its altus and bassus, before enlarging upon the rest of the chanson's first phrase. Less obvious are the quotations, in the Sanctus and the Benedictus, of the descending fourth motive that appears at the opening and toward the close of the tenor of Agricola's chanson. Both of these chansons are preserved, among other places, in manuscripts of Florentine provenance,[58] and one might speculate that Pintelli drew on these materials because they were current in Florence at the time he was there.

The text of Pintelli's only known secular work, *Questo mostrarsi adirata di fore*, was also set by Isaac, who was his colleague in Florence for a number of years.[59] Pintelli's music, like Isaac's, was doubtless written for the court of Lorenzo the Magnificent and probably dates from the late 1480s. (The piece is given in the musical supplement, no. 3.) In its broad outlines it is similar to many of Isaac's Florentine works: it is in three parts, each of which is vocally conceived; its melodies, though simple, are constructed neatly and they closely follow the rhythms of the text; its prevailing duple meter is varied with the usual dancelike section in triple time appearing toward the end. Both Isaac's and Pintelli's settings are in the transposed Dorian mode on G. The music is provided with text only for the first stanza of the poem, the additional stanzas of which are written out at the close. Unlike Isaac's version, however, Pintelli's is through-composed. Frequent cadences, generally at the end of each line of text, occur on the tonic, the dominant and the submediant, with both ripresa and strophe beginning and ending in the tonic.

---

[57] See J. M. Llorens, *Capellae sixtinae codices* (Vatican City 1960) 81.

[58] The first is found anonymously in the Florentine manuscripts Banco rari 229 and Magliabechi XIX, 164-167, but with attribution to Prioris in manuscripts at Cortona and Regensburg and with attribution to Stappen in Petrucci's *Canti C*. Agricola's chanson is apparently preserved only in the Florentine manuscripts Magliabechi XIX, 178 and Banco rari 229.

[59] Both works are preserved in MS Banco rari 230 of the National Library, Florence. Isaac's setting is printed in a modern edition in J. Wolf, ed., *Heinrich Isaac: Weltliche Werke*, Denkmäler der Tonkunst in Österreich 14.1, 28.42.

Unity is obtained in the ripresa by stressing a rhythmic figure from the opening once again toward the close. The figure itself is first introduced in the tenor as part of a melodic sequence that is repeated three times in the first phrase. A sequential pattern also appears briefly in the setting of the volta and provides, perhaps fortuitously, a link with the structure of the ripresa. Another notable feature of the work is the presence on a number of occasions of notated accidentals—E-flats and A-flats—a practice that is somewhat rare in Florentine sources of this period. Altogether, Pintelli's ballata furnishes a charming example of the kind of music that was much in vogue during Lorenzo's day, and knowledge that its composer was another Italianized Franco-Netherlander serves to underline the international character of Florentine polyphony at the time.

SER MATTEO, SER FELICE, SER VIRGILIO

No music by ser Matteo, whom documentary sources mention as a composer, is known to have survived. One work each is ascribed to ser Felice and ser Virgilio in the previously mentioned Cappella Giulia manuscript. All three musicians were apparently native Florentines.

Matteo di Paolo is first recorded in cathedral archives in a document, dated 26 June 1478, which names him among the choristers who assisted the adult singers of polyphonic music in the chapel.[60] He was ordained and appointed a substitute chaplain in Santa Maria del Fiore shortly after that time.[61] On 1 January 1479 *ser Matteo di Paolo, contralto,* began serving as an adult member of the cathedral chapel and received an official appointment to the position on the fifth of the following month.[62] He was employed in that capacity until 19 January 1485, when the chapel was temporarily suspended.[63] Information about his activities as a composer is found in another document

---

[60] SMDF 2.2.5, *Deliberazioni, 1476-1482*, fol. 38v:

26 junii 1478

Item deliberaverunt quod salarium quatuor florenorum assignatum quatuor clericis cantare debentibus in cappella cori maioris ecclesie Florentine, solvatur Matheo Pauli, clerico sacrestie; et dictum salarium dicto Matheo assignaverunt.

Ibid. fol. 39:

26 junii 1478

Stantiamenta operariorum . . . Johanni Laurentii, clerico; Laurentio ser Verdiani, clerico; Matteo Pauli, clerico; Francesco Jacobi, clerico.

[61] As indicated in a document, dated 29 April 1480, given below in n. 64.

[62] SMDF 2.2.5, *Deliberazioni, 1476-1482*, fol. 49v:

1478 [1479]

Die quinta mensis februarii.

Prefati domini operarii . . . volentes dare operam efficacem ut cantores deputati ad canendum canto figurato in coro nostre ecclesie sint copiosi et experti . . . conduxerunt in cantores . . . ser Matheum Pauli pro contro alto, cum salario Fl. octo quolibet anno.

[63] A. Seay (n. 11 above) 52.

MUSICAL EXAMPLES

Florence, National Library
US Magliabechi XIX, 176
fols. 127^V - 129^2

1.   Arnolfo Giliardi
Piagneran gli occhi mey

[1] Pia — pia-gne-ran — gli oc-chi
[4] Don — na [don-na] fe-li-ce —

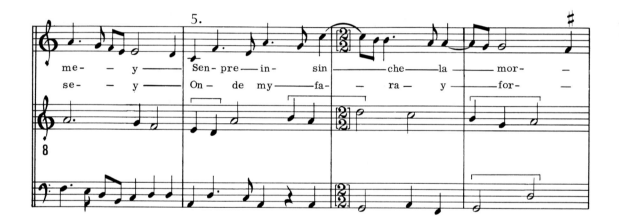

me-y — Sen-pre-in sin — che-la — mor —
se-y — On-de my — fa-ra — y — for-

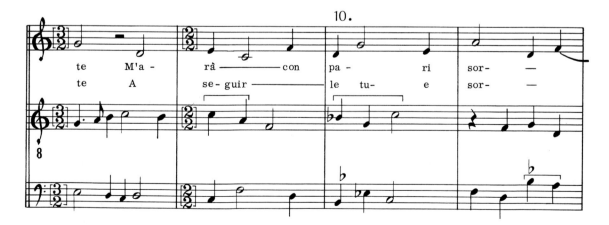

te M'a-rà — con pa-ri sor —
te A se-guir — le tu-e sor —

15.

te Ri u ni to
te Che mor to

20. VERTE

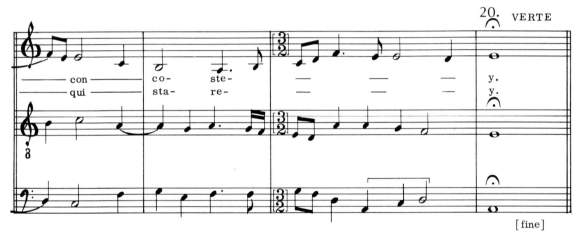

con co ste re y.
qui sta re y.

[fine]

Vi ver più non po tre y San
E sem pre son co' lle i Tut

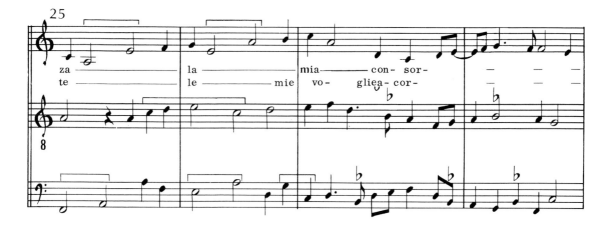

za—————— la—————— mia————— con- sorte————— le——— mie vo—— gliea- cor-

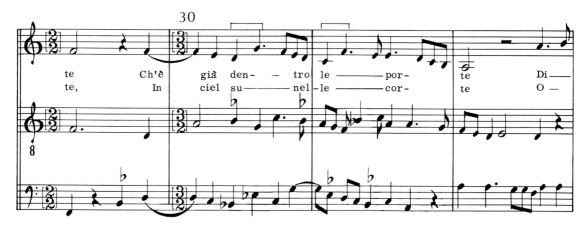

te, Ch'è già den- tro le ——— por-
In ciel su —— nel- le ——— cor-

te Di —
te O —

Gio- ve in- fra gli ——— de- y —— — —
ve vi- vo sa- re- —— y.

.S. da capo
al fine

Florence, National Library
MS Magliabechi XIX, 176
fols. 40V - 42R

2. Arnolfo
O invida fortuna

O in-vi- - da—— for-tu- na, Per-

O invida fortuna

O invida fortuna

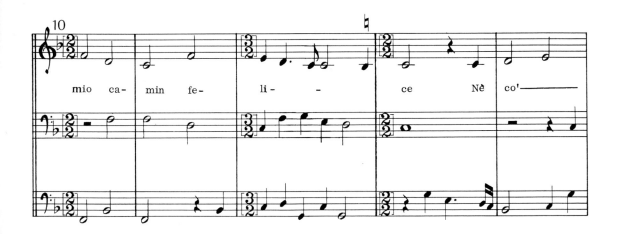

cui tor- - nar non li- - ce Al

mio ca- min fe- li- - ce Nè co'——

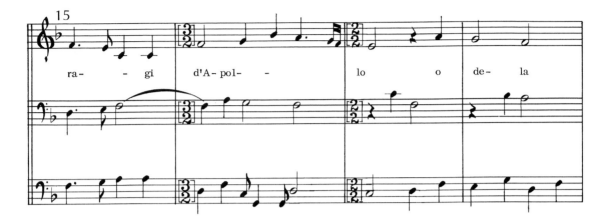

ra- - gi d'A-pol- - lo o de-la

lu- - - - - - na. Verte folium

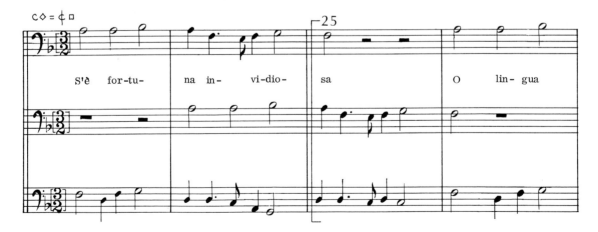

S'è for-tu- na in- vi-dio- sa O lin- gua

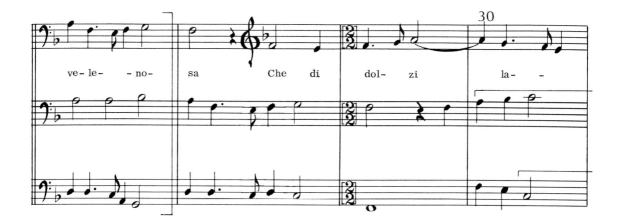

ve- le- -no- sa   Che di dol- zi la- -

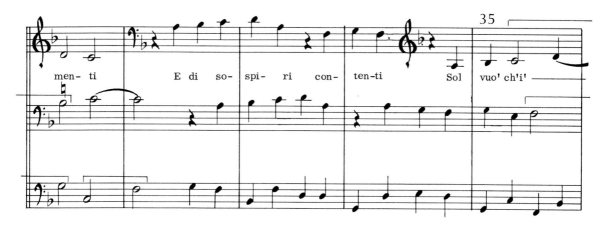

men- ti   E di so- spi- ri con- ten- ti   Sol vuo' ch'i'

—— vi -va   vi - - ta la-gri- mo- - -

- — sa.

3. Pintello'
Questo mostrarsi adirata di fore

Florence, National Library
MS Banco rari 230,
fols. 50V - 51R

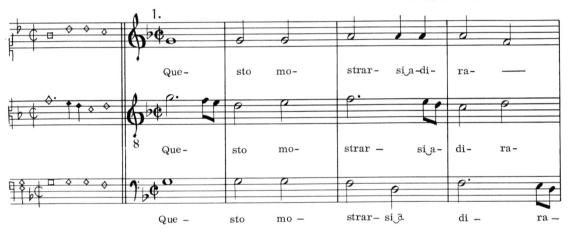

Que- sto mo- strar- si_a-di- ra- ——

Que- sto mo- strar — si_a- di- ra-

Que — sto mo — strar- si_a di — ra —

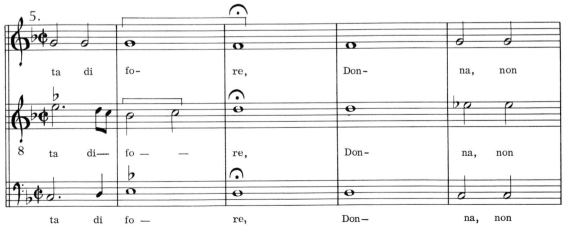

ta di fo- re, Don- na, non

ta di— fo — — re, Don- na, non

ta di fo — re, Don— na, non

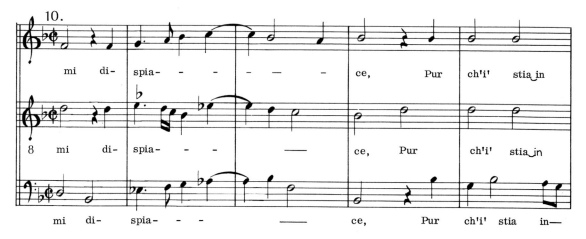

mi di- spia- - - - - - ce, Pur ch'i' stia in

mi di- spia- - - - ce, Pur ch'i' stia in

mi di- spia- - - - - ce, Pur ch'i' stia in—

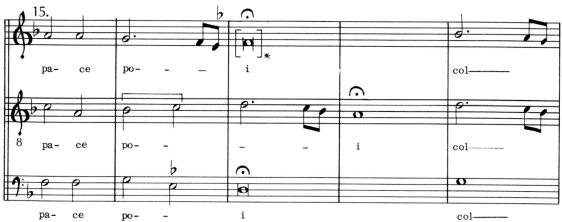

pa- ce po- - - i col————

pa- ce po- - - - i col————

pa- ce po- - i col————

vo- stro co - - - - - - - re-

vo- stro co - - - - - - - re-

vo- stro co - - re... co - - - re.-

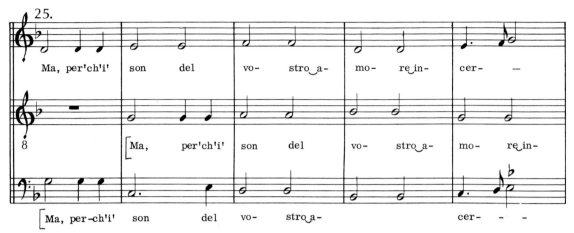

Ma, per'ch'i' son del vo- stro a- mo- re in- cer- —

Ma, per'ch'i' son del vo- stro a- mo- re in-

Ma, per-ch'i' son del vo- stro a- cer- - -

* MS gives a breve here instead of a long.

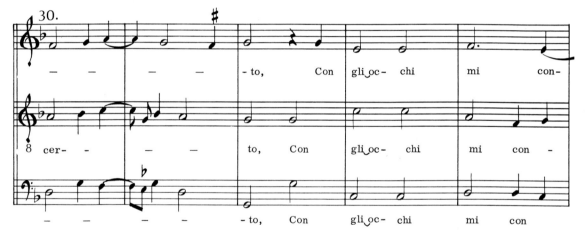

— — — — -to, Con gli oc- chi mi con-

cer- - — — to, Con gli oc- chi mi con -

— — — — -to, Con gli oc- chi mi con

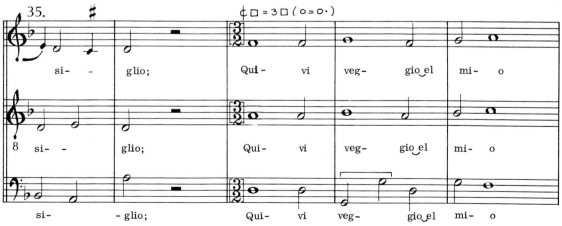

si- - glio; Qui- vi veg- gio el mi- o

si- - glio; Qui- vi veg- gio el mi- o

si- -glio; Qui- vi veg- gio el mi- o

Se poi vi veggio in acto disdegnosa,
Par che el cor si disfaccia;
Et credo allor di non poter far cose,
Donna, che mai vi piaccia:
Così s' addiaccia el core a tutte l' ore.

Ma, se talhor qualche pietà mostrassi
Negli ochi, o diva stella,
Voi faresti d' amore arder e saxi:
Pietà fa donna bella
Pietà è quella onde amor nasce et more.

from cathedral archives which states that on 29 April 1480 the church's over-seers ordered that a payment be made to him

> for settings in figural music of the Lamentations of Jeremiah, the responsories of the same lamentations and of other things which he composed for the said church for the days of Holy Week.[64]

In the following century the performance of polyphony during the last days of Holy Week became a tradition at the cathedral and it is unfortunate that ser Matteo's works do not survive, since they would have furnished us with the oldest recorded Florentine settings of those texts.

Ser Matteo joined the Annunziata's chapel sometime around the end of 1481.[65] His name is listed in the convent's account books until 25 September 1482, when it is reported that he was given two florins, "the remainder of any claim he might have against the convent."[66] A few weeks later he was given another two florins "because the convent felt responsible."[67] He had evidently been discharged abruptly, and with this payment the convent hoped to settle the matter once and for all.

About this same time his name begins to appear in the lists of chaplains associated with the church of San Lorenzo. In one roll from 9 August 1484 he is called ser Matteo, *cantore*, and the inference is that he was also serving as a singer; in another of 1485 his full name, ser Mattheo di Pagholo, is given.[68] On 5 September 1494 it is reported that an agreement, rectifying "certain differences," was reached between the Canons and Chapter of San Lorenzo and ser Matteo di Pagolo, "chaplain of San Lorenzo, titulary of the chapel

[64] SMDF 2.2.5, *Deliberazioni, 1476-1482*, fol. 68:

Die XXVIIII aprilis 1480

Prefati operarii deliberaverunt et deliberando stantiaverunt quod camerarius dicte eorum opere det et solvat et dare et solvere possit et debeat ser Matteo Pauli, cappellano substituto dicte eorum ecclesie, libras octo s. quindecim d. X parvorum pro scripturis et intonaturis cantus figurati pro Lamentationibus Hieremie et responsis ipsarum lamentationum et aliarum rerum compositarum [sic] pro diebus ebdomode sancte pro dicta eorum ecclesia.

[65] "Singers" 332.

[66] SSA 246, *Entrata & Uscita, 1479-1482*, fol. 271:

25 settembre 1482

A ser Matteo di Pagolo, piovano chapellano in San Lorenzo, a dì detto Fl. due larghi d'oro in oro per resto d'ogni ragione avesse col convento.

[67] *Ibid.* fol. 274:

5 ottobre 1482

A ser Matteo di Pagolo, chappellano in San Lorenzo, a dì detto Fl. due larghi d'oro in oro i quali si gli danno perchè . . . el convento si sentiva gravato s'e' licentiato; e detti danari si gli danno per satisfacimento d'ogni suo danno benchè n'abia auti dua altri fiorini.

[68] Florence, Archivio Capitolare di San Lorenzo 74, *Liber Camerarii A, 1484*, fol. 10; *Ibid.* 75, *Liber Camerarii, 1485*, fol. 9v.

of San Lorenzo."[69] A final document from the church's archives, dated 10 July 1499, states that he was given leave to visit the baths at Monte Catini, probably because he was in poor health.[70] No further mention of him is made in the next few years, so it may be that he settled outside the city after that time.

Ser Felice di Giovanni Martini, contratenore, was appointed to the cathedral chapel on 26 January 1478. He had been associated with Santa Maria del Fiore for several years before, however, and his name figures in lists of the church's chaplains dating from as early as July 1469.[71] A document of 26 June 1478 records the salary paid him for his services as a singer during the previous five months.[72] He died shortly after that, and on 14 August 1478 his position as a chaplain was assigned to ser Antonio di Marco da Montughi.[73]

Ser Felice can probably be identified with the *Felice* who is named in the Cappella Giulia manuscript as the arranger of a five-part version (the original *a tre* with two added parts) of the well-known chanson *Fortuna desperata*.[74] Since one of the added parts (the altus) is found together with the original three-part version in musical sources presumed to be earlier than the Cappella Giulia collection, there is good reason to believe that Felice composed only the fifth part (the second bassus) which, interestingly, is preserved only in that manuscript.[75] If this is so, it appears that Felice was an amateur. Taken

---

[69] *Ibid.* A 2, *Partiti, 1482-1501*, fol. 52:

Ricordo come a dì 5 di septembre 1494 per cagione di certa differentia exorta fra 'l capitolo nostro e ser Matteo di Pagolo cappellano di San Lorenzo al titolo a cappella di San Lorenzo per se come cappellano di dicta e predicta cappella ... d'accordo fecono general compromesso.

[70] *Ibid.* fol. 77v:

10 luglio 1499

Item dicto dì si die licentia a ser Matteo di Pagolo, nostro cappellano, d'andare al bagno Monte Catini lasciando ongni dì la messa in suo luogo.

[71] SMDF 8.1.50, *Quaderno Cassa, com. Luglio, 1469*, fol. 34v; *Ibid.* 8.1.61, *Quaderno Cassa, com. Luglio, 1475*, fol. 4.

[72] Seay (n. 11 above) 49; the record of his appointment to the chapel is also printed here.

[73] ASF, Archivio dell'Arte della Lana 223, *Partiti, 1478*, fol. 76:

MCCCCLXXVIII, die XIIII mensis Augusti

Supradicti domini consules ... audita morte ser Felicis Johannis Martini, olim cappellani ... elegerunt ... in cappellanum dicte cappelle, loco dicti ser Felicis, honestum et religiosum virum ser Antonius Marci de Montuchio, cum prebendis, distributionibus, emolumentis et aliis.

[74] The original version by A. Busnois also served as the basis for Mass compositions by Josquin and Obrecht. See G. Reese, (n. 2 above) 102.

[75] A list of concordances for the four-part version is given by D. Plamenac, "A Reconstruction of the French Chansonnier in the Biblioteca Colombina" 3, *The Musical Quarterly* 38 (1952) 262. Three sources give the same altus part as the Cappella Giulia manuscript; two other sources have an altus part very similar to it. I am grateful to Mr. Allan Atlas of New York University, who is at present preparing a doctoral dissertation on the Cappella Giulia manuscript, for this information.

alone, the added part is rather monotonous because of its frequent repetition of similar rhythmic patterns; within the polyphonic complex it creates several awkward harmonies and on occasion even lapses into ungainly parallel octaves. What reasons prompted the compiler of the Cappella Giulia manuscript to include Felice's added part to the collection can, naturally, only be surmised. It is worth noting, however, that the manuscript, long thought to have belonged to Pope Leo X, contains works by Isaac, Agricola, Arnolfo and Stochem, all of whom were associated with Florence. It may be that the collection represents a group of works that the compiler presumed were familiar to Leo X; or it may be that the collection was planned to contain works by those composers who were known to have been personally connected with the Medici. In any case the inclusion of a chanson with an added part by a sometime composer would probably have appealed to the music-loving Leo X, who himself was the composer of a work based on another well-known chanson of the time.[76]

Ser Virgilio, contralto, is first mentioned in a personnel list of the cathedral chapel dating from 13 August 1507.[77] The cathedral's account books do not mention the exact date of his entrance into the chapel; but since his name is lacking in an earlier list, dating from 25 February 1502, it is obvious that he began serving during that five-year period.[78] Another document shows that on 6 January 1513 twenty-four lire were paid to *prete Vergilio, cantore,* part of his salary for the past six months.[79] Previously, on 22 August 1510, he had been engaged, along with his colleagues in the cathedral chapel, to perform at the baptistry.[80] On 4 July 1515 the cathedral singers, among

---

[76] See G. Reese (n. 2 above) 286.

[77] SMDF 2.2.10, *Deliberazioni, 1507,* fol. 5v:

Die 13 augusti 1507

Prefati operarii desiderantes cappellam cantus figurati eam in aliqua parte corrigere . . . deliberaverunt etc. ser Raffaelem debere in dicta cappella canere et servire, serviendo [?] cum famulis vel fanciullis pro sobranis . . . ser Franciscum Boscherinum et ser Ioangualbertem chericum pro tinoribus; ser Iacobum Bonaiuti et ser Niccolum Pedoni et ser Davit Sandri pro cantori bassi; ser Magdolum de Aretio et ser Ioanfranciscum et Vergilium pro cantori alti; Serraglium vero voluerunt esse magistrum cappelle.

[78] *Ibid.* 2.2.9, *Deliberazioni, 1498-1507,* fol. 41.

[79] *Ibid.* 8.1.128, *Quaderno Cassa, com. Luglio 1512,* fol. 53v:

La chapella del chanto fighurato de' dare . . . a dì 6 di gienayo [1513] L. 24 piccioli per lui a prete Vergilio, chantore, per suo salario.

A subsequent payment to him dates from 1516: *Ibid.* 8.1.135, *Quaderno Cassa, com. Luglio 1516,* fol. 40v:

Cappella e cantori di canto figurato de' dare . . . a dì 25 detto [settembre] Fl. due in oro larghi per loro a ser Vergilio cantore, portò lui detto.

[80] AC 23, *Deliberazioni, 1508-1513,* fol. 78:

Die XXII augusti 1510 . . . pertanto per la presente provisione . . . ordina che in decta chiesa et oratorio di San Giovanni Baptista si possi et debbi fare una cappella di cantori, et che in detta et per detta cappella da ora s'intendino essere et sieno electi tutti gl'in-

them *ser Virgilio di Domenico*, received an increment in salary from the baptistry's overseers.[81]

Subsequent documents from San Giovanni make it appear that he also received a chaplaincy there. Some confusion, however, is evident in the baptistry's records which name a *ser Virgilio d'Antonio, cappellano*, in a document from 22 August 1515; the next list of chaplains, dating from 26 April 1516, merely calls him *ser Virgilio*.[82] It is difficult to determine whether the difference in patronymic was a slip of the pen on the part of the clerk who copied the records or whether there was another Virgilio in the baptistry's service at the time. Later lists of San Giovanni's chaplains, dating from 11 December 1522 to 17 December 1527, do little to clarify the situation, for in these documents there appears yet another Virgilio, *ser Virgilio di Guasparre*.[83] Further information about ser Virgilio the musician is found in a letter, dated 5 August 1518, which begins:

> The present bearer is sent especially to tell you on behalf of the Magnificent [Lorenzo de' Medici, duke of Urbino] that you should send Baccio the organist and ser Virgilio here early tomorrow morning, and tell them to bring a soprano and singing books with them.[84]

Evidently ser Virgilio had been in the duke's personal service even prior to this time, since three payments in his name are recorded in the ducal accounts of 1516.[85]

---

frascripti otto cantori . . . ser Iacopo di Bonaiuto et ser Niccolaio Pedoni per due contrabassi; ser Francesco Boscholi et ser Giovanni Serragli et ser Davit per tre tinori; ser Giovanfrancesco d'Antonio et Vergilio per due contrialti; ser Raffaello di Piero per sovrano insieme con sei cherici almeno, o que' più che vi cantassino a electione di decto ser Giovanni Serragli, maestro della vostra scuola de' cherici.

[81] *Ibid.* 26, *Deliberazioni, 1514-1515*, fol. 79.

[82] *Ibid.*, 84v; *ibid.* 24, *Deliberazioni, 1514-1522*, fol. 114.

[83] *Ibid.* 28, *Deliberazioni, 1522-1528*, fol. 11v; fol. 85v; fol. 210.

[84] ASF, Medici avanti il Principato 111 fol. 407; quoted in G. Pieraccini, *La stirpe de' Medici di Cafaggiolo* (Florence 1924) 1.260.

[85] ASF, Medici avanti il Principato 132, *Entrata & Uscita di Lorenzo, Duca d'Urbino*, fol. 32v:

febbraio 1515 [1516]

E a dì detto [28] Du. LXXV per tanti pagati a ser Gherardo e Giovambatista musico e ser Virgilio per vestirsi di paonazo che li dette loro per conto della mancia di natale. Du. 75.

Ibid. fol. 42v:

maggio 1516

Et a dì XXVIII di detto Fl. uno s. XII d'oro pagati per mandato di Pagolo de' Medici a ser Virgilio cappellano per le spese da Firenze in campo. Fl. 1 s .12

Ibid. fol. 44:

luglio 1516

Et a dì detto [8] L. V piccioli per resto di vettura d'uno cavallo per ser Virgilio quando andò a Urbino. S. 14. 4

One work, *a tre*, *Nec mihi nec tibi*, is ascribed to *Virgilius* in the Cappella Giulia manuscript. Given the pronounced Florentine character of the collection, it seems reasonable to suggest that the composer named there is the same person as the Florentine musician. Ser Virgilio's connections with Leo X's nephew Lorenzo offer further confirmation of this suggestion. Objections to accepting the ascription, however, can be raised on several grounds. There are both two-and three-part versions of the piece in five other manuscripts, one of which was compiled during the 1490s—at least a decade before we have any record of the Florentine musician's activities.[86] Another of these sources names Obrecht as the composer of the three-part version of the work.[87]

With regard to the first point, it may be noted that ser Virgilio could have been a practicing musician long before he joined the cathedral chapel, even though we lack information about him before that time. In fact, one could assume that he had already had a certain amount of experience before being appointed to the chapel. His authorship, therefore, cannot be discounted on the grounds that on the basis of known documents he was too young to have composed a work that dates, at the latest, from the early 1490s.[88]

The conflicting attribution to Obrecht, on the other hand, does provide sufficient reason for questioning the Cappella Giulia ascription. Since the piece exists also in a two-part version and since no other works by Virgilio are known, one might assume that he, too, was an occasional composer and that in this case the Cappella Giulia collection again contains an arrangement of a preexisting work by a Florentine who was associated with the Medici. An examination of the three-part version offers strong support in favor of this assumption.[89] The bottom part, for example, gives the impression of being an added rather than an integral member of the polyphonic complex, for it leads an existence noticeably independent of the others. It does not contribute to the contrapuntal development of the various motives that

[86] The piece is also preserved in Florence (MS Banco rari 229); Hradec Králové (Museum, Codex Speciálník); Segovia (Cathedral, MS without number); and in a two-part version in Perugia (Communal Library, MS 431); and Turin (National Library, MS I 27). The Florence manuscript is believed to date from ca. 1491.

[87] H. Anglès, "Un manuscrit inconnu avec polyphonie du xve siècle conservé à la cathedrale de Ségovie (Espagne)," *Acta musicologica* 8 (1936) 14.

[88] Various other musicians named Virgilio, however, can be discounted on these grounds. These musicians, mentioned among the personal of the Papal and Julian chapels during the 1530s and 1540s, are obviously too late chronologically to be connected with the piece in question. For information on these musicians see F. X. Haberl (n. 33 above) 274, 267, 269; R. Casimiri, "I diarii Sistini," *Note d'archivio* 4 (1927) 258; A. Ducrot, "Histoire de la Cappella Giulia au xvie siècle," *Mélanges d'archéologie et d'histoire* 85 (1963) 195, 199, 209, 514. Yet another Virgilio is recorded in the Julian chapel in 1524, during the Pontificate of the Medici Pope Clement VII (*ibid.* 191). Could this be the Florentine Virgilio? Other Florentine musicians are known to have been employed in Rome by the Medici Popes.

[89] The piece will be published in H. M. Brown's edition of MS Banco rari 229, mentioned above, n. 31.

appear in the upper parts and generally serves merely to complete triadically the harmonies implied there. Moreover, the two-part version, though not a very distinguished work, does stand as a complete piece in its own right. Aside from these considerations, however, the problem remains: it is the three-part version that is attributed to both Obrecht and Virgilio, and until more information becomes available, it is impossible to say with certainty which was the original version of *Nec mihi nec tibi* and who was its composer.

SER GIOVANNI SERRAGLI

Ser Giovanni Serragli was one of the group of Florentine composers active around the turn of the sixteenth century to whom reference has been made above. Although manuscripts containing works of his have been cited often in musicological literature, until recently the composer's name was completely unknown to the history of music. Documents from various Florentine archives disclosed the existence of a singer of this name who was also a music teacher at the cathedral and baptistry schools. A subsequent search through Florentine musical sources revealed that five complete and six incomplete works of his are extant. These sources present his name in such a way, however, that a positive identification of the composer would have been impossible had the name not appeared elsewhere. One manuscript from the cathedral, for example, gives his name as *Johannes Serra*; a second manuscript, also of Florentine origin, shortens it further to *Johannes Ser*; a third Florentine collection, using a common scribal abbreviation of the time, merely records it as & *Jo.* & = ser Jo[hannes] Ser[ragli].[90] Clearly, in his own day the composer was well enough known by both Florentine music copyists and persons for whom these manuscripts were prepared that more precise identification was evidently thought unnecessary.

Serragli was probably a member of the prominent Florentine family of that name. None of the documents relating to the family that I have been able to see, however, makes reference to him.[91] Born perhaps about 1480, he must have been educated at the Cathedral School of Chant and Grammar and ordained at the turn of the new century, for a document of 25 February 1502 gives him the title "ser." The document records his appointment to the cathedral's newly reconstituted chapel and shows that at the time he was already employed as one of the two music teachers in the cathedral school.[92]

---

[90] B. Becherini (n. 3 above) 109, 110, 111, reads the abbreviation as Ser Jo. Francesco.

[91] The sources consulted are listed in nn. 51, 52 above.

[92] SMDF 2.2.9, *Deliberazioni, 1498-1507* fol. 41:

Die 25 februarii 1501 [1502]

Spectabiles viri consules artis lane . . . elegerunt in cantores pro dicta ecclesia . . . magistros qui docent clerichos musicam . . . qui sunt duo videlicet ser Franchus et ser Ioannes de Serraglis.

Payments to him for his services as a singer are listed in cathedral account books over the next several years.[93] One of them, dated 21 February 1508, indicates that he subsequently became master of the chapel.[94] He continued in this capacity until the fall of 1512, when he was replaced by Bernardo Pisano. Serragli continued as a singer in the chapel, however, and later also served under Rampollini and Verdelot.[95]

Some years previously, on 22 August 1510, the cathedral singers, among them *ser Giovanni Serragli, tinore*, had been engaged to perform at the baptistry.[96] The document that records their appointment shows that, even prior to being replaced by Pisano as master of the cathedral chapel, Serragli had begun to be more closely associated with the baptistry. He assumed the position of "master of the boys" at its school, established on 26 August 1508.[97] He also obtained a chaplaincy in San Giovanni around the same time, and later, on 12 December 1512, it is reported that ser Giovanni Serragli, "a chaplain and master of the school," was granted a month's leave of absence by the baptistry's overseers.[98]

A few other documents record his continuing service at San Giovanni during the next several years.[99] The most interesting of these is one dated 1 July 1523, which states that on that day the baptistry's overseers granted "maestro Verdelotto, ser Giovanni Serragli and Brueto, singers in the church of San Giovanni," permission to take a month's leave of absence.[100] Serragli

---

[93] *Ibid.* 8.1.109, *Quaderno Cassa, com. Luglio, 1502,* fol. 52v:

Ser Francho e ser Giovanni Serraglio, chantori di duomo, deono dare a dì 22 d'ottobre L. quindici, portò ser Francho chontanti.

Ibid. 8.1.115, *Quaderno Cassa, com. Luglio, 1505,* fol. 17v:

Chappella del chanto fighurato de' dare . . . a dì 13 di settembre L. cinquantatre, portò ser Giovanni di Iacopo Seragli, distribuitore agli altri cantori.

[94] *Ibid.* 8.1.120, *Quaderno Cassa, com. Gennaio 1507/08,* fol. 28v:

La chapella del chanto fighurato de' dare a dì 21 di febbraio 1507 [1508] L. settanta piccioli, portò ser Giovanni Serragli, maestro della chappella.

An earlier document (n. 77 above) suggests that he was already master of the cathedral chapel in August 1507.

[95] Rampollini is mentioned as master of the chapel for the first time in an account book begun July 1520; Verdelot, in one begun January 1523.

[96] See n. 80 above.

[97] G. Baccini, "L'antica cappella dei musici di San Giovanni," *La Cordelia* 14 (1894); offprint (Rocca San Casciano 1895) 23. Baccini apparently drew his information from a volume of the AC that has since disappeared.

[98] AC 24, *Deliberazioni, 1514-1522,* fol. 25v:

Die XII settembris 1512

Prefati domini consules . . . concesserunt licentiam ser Johanni [gap] de Serraglis, cappellano et magistro schole, pro uno mense proxime futuro.

[99] *Ibid.* 26, *Deliberazioni, 1514-1515,* fol. 79; *ibid.* 28, *Deliberazioni, 1522-1528,* fols. 11v, 20v, 28v.

[100] The document is printed in A. Bragard (n. 2 above) 121, where the name of the third musician is given as "Bracio (?)."

had been serving under Verdelot in the cathedral and baptistry chapels since the latter's arrival in Florence, but this is the only evidence extant that shows him to have been on friendly terms with one of the most gifted composers of the age. The details of Verdelot's Florentine period have only recently been uncovered and it now seems quite certain that his stay in Florence contributed immeasurably to the formation of his madrigal style. Whether Serragli was in any way connected with Verdelot's first efforts in the new genre, or whether Verdelot, a master composer in the Franco-Netherlands tradition, had some influence on Serragli's work, are questions that unfortunately can only be asked for the moment.

Although Verdelot resumed service at the baptistry after his month's leave, the absence of Serragli's name in the lists of San Giovanni's chaplains, dating from 22 April 1524 and 16 December 1525, suggests that he did not.[101] He must have returned later, however, for a final document from the baptistry states that on 2 March 1526 ser Giovanni Serragli was relieved of his duties as a singer and appointed instead to the less prestigious job of keeping the chapel's attendance records.[102] The lack of any other information about him in San Giovanni's account books from the following years indicates that he did not accept the position. Perhaps he received an appointment in another city, since no further mention of him is found in Florentine musical archives. The date and place of his death remain unknown.

Serragli's only known sacred work, *O redemptor sume carnem*, exists in two versions, one for two parts, the other for four, in an early sixteenth-century Florentine manuscript now in the cathedral archives.[103] Some of the other polyphonic works in this predominantly monophonic collection may also be his, but only the four-part version of the piece carries his name.

Four complete secular works are found—three anonymously, another with an abbreviated version of his name—in MS Banco rari 230 of the National Library in Florence.[104] The bass parts of these four works, as well as those of six others, are attributed to him in another Florentine collection, MS Banco rari 337.[105] Serragli is the most frequently represented composer in the latter

---

[101] AC 28, *Deliberazioni, 1522-1528* fols. 85, 151.

[102] *Ibid.*, fol. 163v:

2 marzo 1525 [1526]

Item simili modo cassaverunt de officio cantoris dumtaxat ser Iohannem de Seraglis, et eumdem elegerunt in coristam dictorum cantorum, cum auctoritate apuntandi dictos cantores in illis apuntaturis et prout dispositum fuerit per dictos dominos consules et officiales musaici.

[103] His name here is given as *Johannes Serra*. The manuscript is described by F. Ghisi, "Un processionale inedito per la settimana santa nell'Opera del Duomo di Firenze," *Rivista musicale italiana* 55 (1953) 362-369. The work is printed in a modern edition in "Music of the Florentine Renaissance" 2.121-122.

[104] The one ascribed work gives his name as *Johannes Ser*.

[105] By means of the scribal abbreviation mentioned above.

manuscript, which, judging from its format and contents, must have been compiled during the period between 1515 and 1525. For this reason, as well as from what we know of his biography, it appears that his surviving secular works were written sometime around the end of the first decade of the sixteenth century.

Two pieces *a quattro*, *Per non trovare* and *Quel principe*, are typical examples of the Florentine polyphonic carnival song.[106] In duple meter with contrasting sections in triple time, both works are predominantly homophonic in texture, but varied occasionally with short sections in imitation. All parts are vocally conceived and carefully fitted to the text. The formal variety observable in other Florentine settings of this type is also present in these works. *Per non trovare*, poetically a ballata, provides new music for each line of text except for the second pair of piedi, which are repeated to the music of the first pair. The seven-line stanza of *Quel principe* is, on the other hand, through-composed. As was customary, only the first stanza of each poem is set, the remaining stanzas being sung to the music of the first.

With its low vocal ranges and sombre G dorian modality, *Per non trovare* is generally successful in depicting the text of the "Song of the Baptized Jews." Solemn declamatory phrases such as "et battezati siano" and "che tre di qui da voi fumo accettati" are skillfully contrasted with imitation on the words "l'ebrea lasciata abbiano" and the more joyous, dancelike section in triple time that sets the words "colle donn'e figliuol sanza paura." The piece, however, is the least defined tonally of Serragli's works. The ripresa ends in the dominant instead of the usual tonic, and intermediary cadences on the tonic, subdominant and mediant do little to relieve the meandering structure of the whole.

Quel principe, a *trionfo* whose text celebrates the four temperaments, has a tightly organized tonal structure. It begins and ends in the untransposed mixolydian mode on G, and its intermediary cadences are contrived to stress only the tonic, dominant and subdominant chords. Imitative sections for two and three voices provide variety within the prevailing four-part chordal texture. The well-spaced sonorities, the bright quality of the high tessituras employed in the upper voices and the clear harmonic progressions outlined in the bass also contribute to the general appeal of the setting.

Donna, el pianto is at present the only known example of a frottola set by a Florentine in this period.[107] Traditionally, this type of poetry was set by the North Italian composers, the Florentines generally preferring the more literary ballata or the various forms of the native carnival song. Emulating the North Italians, Serragli furnishes his setting with a sprightly melodic cantus whose phrase structure and rhythms unerringly reproduce those of

---

[106] Both works are printed in a modern edition in "Music of the Florentine Renaissance" 2.44-46.

[107] Printed in a modern edition in "Music of the Florentine Renaissance" 2.39-40.

the octosyllabic verses. In contrast to the North Italian prototypes, however, the lower parts of Serragli's setting are eminently singable, conforming more to the Florentine concept of vocal part writing. The piece is firmly grounded in a bright F major tonality, which is emphasized at the end by the addition of a seven-measure coda outlining the submediant, subdominant and tonic chords.

Grato ognora, the longest of Serragli's works, is also the most ambitiously planned.[108] The text, in ballata form, is set to new music in the ripresa and in the first pair of piedi. The second pair of piedi has the same music as the first pair while the volta, which begins with new material, returns to the final part of the ripresa at its close. In this case the symmetrical musical structure of ripresa and volta mirrors exactly the form of the poetry in which the two final lines of the ripresa text also serve to close the volta. As might be expected, the musical setting closely follows the rhythms and accents of the text. Some attempt at word painting is also present in the juxtaposition of the static, low-voiced phrase on the words "Poi che tu, signora, in terra" with the brighter, more rhythmically active, then finally plaintive setting of the following line "Cagion sei del mio martire."

At the outset all of the voices share in lively imitation before moving into the homophonic texture that characterizes the piece as a whole. The basic homophony, however, is occasionally varied by quicker moving figures in the inner voices as well as by a few passages *a tre* that are more freely contrapuntal in nature. The four parts, each encompassing the range of a ninth, are vocally conceived. Melodic jumps of more than a fifth are rare, larger leaps generally occuring between phrases. At times individual melodic phrases outline the interval of a seventh or of an octave, but these are so constructed that no difficulties arise in vocal execution. Serragli's concern for well-defined tonal organization is also evident here. The piece is in the transposed dorian mode on G, in which the ripresa begins and ends. Intermediary cadences on the subdominant and dominant occur in ripresa and strophe, both of which close with a two-measure coda whose simple plagal cadence effectively echoes the words "del mio martire."

With this discussion of Serragli and his music I close this survey of certain still obscure composers in the Florentine chapels. In fact, it was during Serragli's lifetime that the course of Italian polyphony began to undergo radical changes that, in the hands of composers such as Serragli's colleagues Pisano and Verdelot, were soon to lead to the formation of the madrigal style— and to a new era in the history of Italian secular music.

Department of Music
University of California
Los Angeles, California 90024, U.S.A.

[108] Printed in a modern edition in "Music of the Florentine Renaissance" 3.40-42.

THE EGYPTIANS IN SCOTLAND: THE POLITICAL HISTORY OF A MYTH[1]

•

by William Matthews

Some years ago, in an engaging essay entitled "The Trojans in Britain,"[2] the late George Gordon—a Scotsman—recalled a boyhood grudge that I suspect may be shared by a lot of Englishmen. It was against the dispiriting way in which histories of England usually begin, with the invasion led by that most marmoreal of celebrities, Julius Caesar. As a substitute, Gordon considered the merits of earlier historical practice, of injecting into the island story the picturesque legends that for five centuries following Geoffrey of Monmouth's *Historia* (1137) had set off most English chronicles with a heroic fanfare. The wanderings of Brutus the Trojan, his founding of Britain and division of the kingdom among his three sons, the slaying of Gog Magog and the giants, the lively exploits of Merlin, Uther Pendragon and his son King Arthur, and the related stories of Lear, Cymbeline, and Cadwallader may represent an order of truth now unacceptable to serious historians. But they have nourished English imaginations for eight centuries and more, and for much of that time they also served important national purposes.

The same plea might also be urged on historians of George Gordon's own Scotland. Since the eighteenth century, Scottish histories have generally begun cautiously, following the English pattern, in A.D. 80 with the Roman occupation under Agricola, or sometimes with Kenneth McAlpin's subjugation of the Picts in A.D. 843. The abundant earlier assertion of a remoter, more heroic origin is now ignored by all but an occasional scholar.[3]

---

[1] Originally delivered as the Annual Faculty Research Lecture at the University of California, Los Angeles, 23 April 1968.

[2] *Essays and Studies* by Members of the English Association 9 (1924) 9-30.

[3] The following modern histories begin with Agricola: Thomas Wright, *The History of Scotland* (London 1852-1855) 3 vols.; John Hill Burton, *The History of Scotland* (Edinburgh 1873) 8 vols.; Patrick Fraser Tytler, *History of Scotland*, ed. Sir Archibald Allison (London 1873-1877) 4 vols.; John S. Keltie, *A History of the Scottish Highlands* (Edinburgh 1875) 3 vols.; Peter Hume Brown, *History of Scotland* (Cambridge 1899) 3 vols.; Andrew Lang, *A History of Scotland*, ed. 5 (Edinburgh 1929) 4 vols.; William Croft Dickinson, Gordon

Thanks to the earlier English poets, Brutus the Trojan is familiar enough to students of English history and literature, and it is still a compliment to call an Englishman a Trojan. But, to judge from my own inquiries over several years, it is rather rare to find a scholar, even a Scottish scholar, who is similarly aware that Scotsmen once claimed an ancestry more ancient and glorious than that of any Trojan Englishman, or that for several centuries the Scottish legend and the British one were mortal rivals. My present purpose, therefore, is to dust off the medieval legend of Scotland's origins and to outline the course of its rivalry with the British legend. In the interests of space and novelty, I propose to restrict myself as narrowly as possible to Scottish materials and Scottish points of view, ignoring the Irish concern in the matter and all but a necessary modicum of the English and Welsh advocacy of the legend of Trojan and Arthurian descent.

In its many retellings, the Scottish story differs considerably in detail. But here are the bare bones of the version that was enthusiastically set forth in 1527 by an eminent Aberdonian, Hector Boece.[4]

Donaldson, and Isabel A. Milne, eds., *A Source Book of Scottish History* (London 1958) 3 vols.

William Orr Anderson, *Early Sources of Scottish History* (Edinburgh 1922) 2 vols., begins at A.D. 500 and briefly mentions King Arthur, but it contains nothing about the Scottish migration myth, and neither does William Croft Dickinson, *Scotland from the Earliest Times to 1603* (London 1965), although it contains a short chapter on the prehistoric people of Scotland.

The Scottish myth is dealt with briefly in three specialized studies by William F. Skene: *Chronicles of the Picts*, *Chronicles of the Scots* (Edinburgh 1867), *The Coronation Stone* (Edinburgh 1869), and *Celtic Scotland* (Edinburgh 1890) 3.94. It is also mentioned in James Hilton, "The Coronation Stone at Westminster," *Archaeological Journal* 59 (1897) 201-224, and George Watson, "The Coronation Stone of Scotland," *Trans. Scottish Ecclesiological Soc.* 3 (1909-1912) 21. Apparently the only general modern history of Scotland that refers to it is James Mackinnon, *The Constitutional History of Scotland* (London 1924) 1-4, 106.

Earlier Scottish histories and treatises are not so neglectful but tend to mention the legend only to reject it. The eccentric Sir Thomas Urquhart (1611-1660) in his *Pantochronachanon* (*Works*, Edinburgh 1830) traces his own family tree back to Gathelus; William Neilson, *The Scottish Historical Library* (London 1702) 87, 104-105, comments ironically on two of the medieval propagators of the myth, Fordun and Boece; James Anderson, *An Historical Essay* (Edinburgh 1705), attacks the British story of Trojan descent but makes no use of the Scottish migration myth; Sir Robert Sibbald, *An Account of the Writers of Scotland* (Edinburgh 1710), praises Buchanan for condemning Boece's credulity; Matthew Duncan, *The Catalogue of the Kings of Scotland* (1722) iii, rejects the story of Scottish descent from Scota; David Scott, *The History of Scotland* (Westminster 1727), relates the Gathelus story fully; Thomas Innes, *The Civil and Ecclesiastical History of Scotland* (Aberdeen 1853) written in 1735, begins with Agricola; and John Macpherson, *Critical Dissertations on the . . . Ancient Caledonians* (London 1768) 15, regards the Scottish migration myth as a folly that the Scots shared with other peoples.

[4] *The Chronicles of Scotland*, compiled by Hector Boece, translated into Scots by John Bellenden, 1531, ed. R. W. Chambers and Edith C. Batho, Scottish Text Society (STS), (Edinburgh 1938-1941) 1.21-382 (see esp. 21-30, 359-382).

In the time of Moses, there was a spirited young Greek, Gathelus of Athens, who after running into troubles at home, decided to try his fortunes abroad. Egypt was then under attack by Indians and Moors, so Gathelus and his friends offered their services to Pharaoh, and under the command of Moses they helped defeat the invaders. Soon after this, when Moses fell into disfavor, Gathelus was made general of the Egyptian army. Moreover, because he was "ane lusty persoun, seymlie, and of hye blude riall of Grece," he was also given the hand of Pharaoh's daughter Scota. From this marriage it is that Gaels and Scots trace both their names and their descent.

A few years later, when Egypt was stricken by the plagues, Gathelus resolved to seek a new home. With Scota and his children, and a multitude of Greeks and Egyptians, he set forth from the mouth of the Nile in the year 3643 after the creation. Their oddyssey along the Mediterranean and Atlantic shores was hazardous and prolonged. At length, however, they settled in Galicia in northern Spain, where the natives believed a strange people would come to live among them. There Gathelus founded Brigance, later known as Compostella, called his followers Scots in honor of his wife, and administered justice from a chair of marble which bore the Latin inscription:

> Ni fallat fatum, Scoti quocumque locatum
> Inuenient lapidem, regnare tenentur ibidem.

> The Scottis sall ioyss and brouke the landis haill
> Quhair thai fynd it, bot gif weirdis faill.

This chair, later known as the Stone of [Skun]—[Skon] to the vulgar—accompanied the Scots in all their further migrations.

In time, the proliferation of his followers became a problem, and Gathelus, too respectful of his word and his neighbors' rights to engage in expropriation, resolved to send out explorers to check the truth of reports that there was an island north of Spain which was sparsely occupied by primitive people. The expedition, led by his son Hiber, arrived on the fifth day, and the barbarous inhabitants fled into caves. Hiber offered to spare the natives if they would submit, and so touched were they by his clemency that they surrendered their persons and their goods and were thereafter permitted to increase with Hiber's own people. Leaving the island in charge of a garrison, Hiber returned to Galicia, to find that his father had died. Hiber succeeded and proved a strong king, enlarging his territory and maintaining firm control over the land that was now called Iberia in his honor. And so the descendants of Scotia continued in Spain until the time of Symon Brek.

In the island colony, named Hibernia in honor of its founder, relations between the natives and the settlers ultimately broke down, and after a series of wars it was decided to seek a new ruler who was uninvolved in the local quarrels. The choice was Symon Brek, a man of great sobriety and justice, lineally descended from Gathelus and Scota. Brek accepted, brought the marble chair from Galicia, and was crowned in 695 B.C., the first king to reign over the Scots in Hibernia. His reign lasted sixty years.

A few generations later, his successor Rothesaus sent explorers to survey the islands to the north. They came first to lands that they called Argaeill after Gathelus and Rothesay after their present king, and they spread out from there, each clan under its own captain. In this way, in 579 B.C., began the settlement of the land that came to be known as Scotland. Two hundred and fifty years later, Picts came and settled down peacefully with the Scots, the Picts concentrating on urban arts, the Scots on country occupations, each race marrying its daughters to the other in peaceful harmony.

To the descendants of Brutus the Trojan, who had occupied the south some time before, the idyllic happiness of their northern neighbors was a matter for continuous envy. Coilus tried various evil stratagems to turn Scots and Picts against one onother, and when these failed he invaded with a large army—only to be massacred in a battle in which the Scottish women were even more terrifying than their men, "havand na mercy quhare thay were victorious."

During succeeding centuries, although the Scots and Picts often came to the rescue of the Britons against invading Romans and Saxons, the Britons persisted in malevolence. Against the odds, however, the Scots always preserved the freedom that had been theirs from the beginnings in Egypt.

Matters came to a head in the reign of the British king Arthur, whose story Boece relates from an unsympathetic Scottish point of view. In those days, says he, Britain was thoroughly degenerate, given over to idleness, pleasure, adultery, murder, Pelagian heresies, and Christmas gluttony. It was in this moral sink that Arthur was born. Uther Pendragon first saw Igraine at a riotous, unchristian Christmas feast, pursued her into Cornwall, and there, while her husband was away, begot Arthur "in maist schaymful lust."

Upon Uther's death, the king of the Picts laid claim to the British throne on behalf of his son Mordred. Arthur was a bastard, he urged; his own son, lawfully begotten of Uther's sister, was the rightful heir. The claim was rejected, however; the British made Arthur their king as Uther had demanded.

At first, Arthur's career was praiseworthy, but then moral decay set in. His army grew soft, incapable of stopping the Saxons. In these sorry circumstances, the bounty of northern compassion flowed once more. On the proviso that his sons should succeed Arthur, the Pictish king sent reinforcements, and in a great battle in which the bravery of Mordred was decisive, the Saxons were driven out and Arthur's rule maintained.

During the long peace that followed, the Britons had second thoughts about the agreement whereby Mordred should succeed Arthur, and on their insistence Arthur broke faith and named a British heir. Mordred was informed, as soon as his father died, that the pact was no longer valid; that Britons would never be ruled by one of their old enemies of the north. Resenting this treason, Mordred sought justice in the only way left open. His army marched south into Britain, Arthur's came to meet it, and the two forces engaged near the River Humber in Yorkshire. The Scots and Picts gained a victory, but the day was tragic for both sides; Arthur and Mordred were both slain, and so was Mordred's brother Gawain, "fechtand that day for the lufe of King Arthure aganis his native pepill."

Despite Hector Boece's eminence—he was the first Principal of the University of Aberdeen and a scholar highly praised by Erasmus—the story he tells and the elusive authorities he cites may be thought somewhat suspect. Indeed, even in his own time, John Leland wrote rather sourly:

> Hectoris historici tot quot mendacia scripsit
> Si vis ut numerem, lector amice, tibi,
> Me jubeas et[i]am fluctus numerare marinos
> Et liquidi stellas connumerare poli,[5]

Which might be translated into the modern idiom, "Hector the historian, he'll tell you more lies, than the crossties on the railroad or the stars in the skies." Leland, Henry VIII's librarian and antiquary, was no impartial critic, however; he was busy on the other side of this mythical fence, vigorously engaged in defending the historicity of King Arthur, and thereby implicitly supporting Henry VIII's claim to Trojan and Arthurian descent, and so to dominion over Scotland.[6] Now that Anglo-Scottish relations are reasonably peaceful, it is possible to be evenhanded and to acknowledge a truth that has always been patent, that the legend of Brutus and the legend of Gathelus are in fact cast from the same mold. There are many differences in detail, but the design of the two migration myths is the same in general pattern and even in details. What really distinguishes them is that they were framed to opposing political objectives.

The legend of Gathelus and Scota and their descendants is a variant of an Irish migration myth which is told briefly in an eleventh-century Irish version of Nennius's ninth-century *Liber Brittonum*[7] and related fully in the twelfth-

---

[5] "De Hectore Boethio," in John Leland's *Principes ac illustres aliquot et eruditi in Anglia viri* (London 1589) 66.

[6] John Leland, *Assertio inclytissimi Arthurii regis Brittaniae* (London 1544); trans. Richard Robinson, *A Learned and True Assertion* (London 1582). Two years before, Henry VIII's *A Declaration conteyning the ivst cavses and consyderacions of this present warre with the Scottis* (1542), had cited Brutus's division of Britain in support of the claim to English sovereignty and had mentioned Arthur in the succession. Leland's work was dedicated to Henry VIII.

[7] *Leabhar Breatnach anno sis. The Irish Version of the Historia Britonnum of Nennius*, ed. James H. Todd (Dublin 1848) Section 11.

century *Lebor Gabála Érenn*.[8] But the story must have come to Scotland
early; a few allusions in Scottish records show that the essentials were current
there by the tenth century. A Pictish chronicle of 971-995, for example,
states that the Scots derive their name either from Scythia or from Scota,
daughter of Pharaoh.[9] Political use of the legend may also be quite early, in
the reign of the Scottish king William the Lion, 1165-1214, for two royal ge-
nealogies of his time are taken back to Gathelus, and a brief chronicle of 1187
arranges the Scottish and Pictish kings to establish the Scottish line in 443
B.C., nine centuries before King Arthur.[10] All three documents may possibly
reflect Scottish feeling about the oath of vassalage that William the Lion
had to give to Henry II in order to secure release from prison.[11]

It was a century later that political use of the myths became active, however, when a succession of English kings, Edwards I, II, III, vigorously pursued their claim to dominion over Wales and Scotland. In the process of
justification, one of the gambits was to appropriate the myths of their opponents. Edward I, as soon as he had vanquished the last of the Welsh princes
who might claim Arthurian descent, fostered the fiction that he himself was
Arturus redivivus, dramatising the claim in 1284 in a great Round Table at
Nefyn in Carnarvonshire at which the chivalry of Europe competed and
feasted and the king was presented with the crown of King Arthur.[12] In
1290, he supported his claim to lordship over Scotland by having his scholars
assemble from monastic records a dossier that went back to Arthur and Brutus.
And soon afterwards he endeavored to weaken the legend of his opponent
by impounding its main symbol. In 1296 he marched into Scotland, and after
stripping John Balliol of the kingship and taking homage from the barons,
he seized the Stone of Destiny that had been brought from Spain (or Egypt)
and transported it to Westminster, where it was soon to become the coronation
seat for English kings:

---

[8] *Lebor Gabála Erenn* 1-5, ed. and trans. R. A. Stewart Macalister, Irish Texts Society
(Dublin) 138-156, The whole work relates to the settlement of Ireland; the Gathelus-Scota
part of the story appears in Part 2.

[9] See William H. Gregg, *Controversial Issues in Scottish History* (New York 1910) 226-
233, and Skene, *Chronicles* (n. 3 above) item 1.

[10] Skene, *Chronicles*, items 16, 23. See also Mackinnon (n. 3 above) 4.

[11] In 1174 William the Lion invaded Northumbria and on 14 July he was taken prisoner
at Alnwick. Next year he made peace with Henry II by giving him homage and allegiance
for all his land, as to his proper lord, and conceded that all the bishops, abbots, earls, and
barons should do the same: cf. Robert of Torigni, *Chronici*, Rolls Series 82, 4.267-268.
The Scots later asserted the oath applied only to Lothian: Giraldus Cambrensis, *De prin-
cipis instructione* 2.1, *Opera*, Rolls Series 21, 8.156-157.

[12] W. Rishanger, *Cronica*, ed. H. T. Riley (London 1865) 110; see also, R. S. Loomis,
"Edward I, Arthurian Enthusiast," *Speculum* 28 (1933) 114-127; F. M. Powicke, *The Thirteenth Century* (Oxford 1956) 429, 515-516.

> The croune he tuk upon that sammyne stane
> At Gadelos send with his sone fra Spane,
> Quhen Iber Scot fyrst in till Irland come
> At Canemore syn King Fergus has it nome;
> Brocht it till Scwne, and stapill maid it ther,
> Quhar kingis was crowned, viij hundyr ꝫ^{er} and mar,
> Befor the tyme at King Edward it fand.[13]

Those are lines from the epic in which Blind Henry the Minstrel celebrated the almost immediate revolt of the Scots under Sir William Wallace. They had already opposed their legend to Edward's: the earliest extended version of their migration from Egypt can be dated 1280 and is inserted into the account of Edward I's campaigns in Gray's *Scalacronica*.[14] Now, when Edward responded to Wallace's revolt by devastating Scotland, the rival claims were brought to Rome and solemnly argued before the curia in the year 1301.[15]

The English case, supported with copious excerpts from monastic chronicles, instructed the curia, *inter alia*, in the story of Brutus the Trojan and his conquest and division of Britain, Arthur's conquest of Scotland and installation of its king, and the homage that the Scottish king rendered at Caerleon, the British capital. The Scottish case, similarly substantiated by ancient records, asserted that the Scots were a more ancient people than the Britons, being descended from Scota and Gathelus, who had sailed from Egypt considerably before Brutus arrived in Britain. Scots had settled in Ireland and Scotland in remote times and had always been free. During the Roman occupation of Britain, Picts and Scots had helped the Britons on the understanding that the sons of the Scottish king should succeed to the throne. Arthur was a bastard, disqualified from ruling; his lordship in Scotland was won by cruel violence, and Mordred the Pict rightly slew him in the course of restoring the original liberty of his native land. Finally, Edward I was not even a descendant of Brutus; his line must be traced to the Normans who conquered England.[16]

This diplomatic exchange had precisely the effect that might have been expected—none. English Trojans continued to attack, Scottish Egyptians continued to resist—at Bannockburn most successfully—but the formulas of justification continued unchanged. British claims from Brutus and Arthur

---

[13] *The actis and deidis of . . . Schir William Wallace*, ed. James Moir, STS (Edinburgh 1889) bk 1, lines 121-127.

[14] Sir Thomas Gray, *Scalacronica*, ed. J. Stevenson (Edinburgh 1836) 112-118; see also Skene, *chronicles*, item 32.

[15] Documents relating to the English claims in this inquiry are published in Skene, *Chronicles*, item 35. An account of the inquiry appears in John of Fordun's *Scoticronicon* (cf. n. 20 below) 325. See also Watson (n. 3 above) 13-21.

[16] *Chronicles of the reigns of Edward I and Edward II*, ed. W. Stubbs (London 1882) 1.104.

were symbolized, for instance, by the Round Table that was held at Falkirk in 1302, possibly in commemoration of the English victory there four years before,[17] Scottish adherence to their own migration myth was proclaimed at the Arbroath assembly of 1320,[18] when the barons drew up a letter to the pope which listed an uninterrupted succession of 113 Scottish kings, all independent, and recited their origins in Scythia and residence in Spain; and again at the conference at York in 1323, when Robert the Bruce demanded restoration of the Stone of Scone that Scota had brought from Egypt.[19]

The conflict was also taken up in a battle of the books, and notably in the Scottish chronicles of John of Fordun and Andrew of Wyntoun.

Fordun's *Scoticronicon* (1385)[20] is generally a scholarly work, careful to report its sources and any discrepancies and variations in the evidence, grave in style. His weapon for fighting the battle of the myths was a buttoned foil. Yet for all its delicacy, Fordun's history is thoroughly Scottish. Its account of Scottish migrations not only lays out the legend in full, but also bedecks it with instances of all those public and private virtues that Scotsmen perceived in their national mirror: the devotion to justice that led Gathelus to teach his people the laws of Greece, the simple piety of Scots even when they were pagans, the love of freedom that led them to reject obedience to a strange king in favor of a life of barefoot independence, the peace and charity they ever displayed towards any neighbor who would reciprocate. It cites English authorities in support of the view that Scotland was always a distinct kingdom, separate from England: statements to the contrary it blames on the corruption of political scribes. Toward the British myth, however, Fordun's manner is quizzical. He points out that some writers assert that Britons get their name from Brutus the consul, not from Brutus the Trojan, and that others declare they get it from their brutish manners. But Fordun himself is more gracious, preferring to report Geoffrey of Monmouth's better-

---

[17] On New Year's Day, the king sent heralds with invitations into the courts of France, Burgundy, Hainault, Scotland, Flanders, Brabant, and Germany. The celebrations lasted four days, beginning on Saint George's day. On the fifth day, the king swore solemnly to restore Arthur's Round Table and to hold a celebration at Windsor every Pentecost. See Adam Murimuth, *Continuatio chronicarum*, ed. E. M. Thomson, Rolls Series (London 1889) 155-156, 231-232; Froissart's *Chroniques*, chap. 100; Thomas Walsingham, *Historia anglicana*, ed. H. T. Riley, Rolls Series (London 1863) 1.263; Laura Keeler, *Geoffrey of Monmouth and the Late Latin Chroniclers* (Berkeley 1946) 136-137. Froissart states, but is not confirmed by other historians, that it was at this celebration that the Order of the Garter was instituted.

[18] See, Dickinson, Donaldson, and Milne (n. 3 above) 1.156-158; also P. F. Tytler, *The History of Scotland* (Edinburgh 1866) 1.318-319.

[19] Tytler, (n. 18 above) 333; Watson (n. 3 above) 19, 22.

[20] Johannis de Fordun, *Scoticronicon*, ed. W. F. Skene (Edinburgh 1871); trans. F. J. H. Skene, *John of Fordun's Chronicle of the Scottish Nation* (Edinburgh 1872) 1.8-37; 2.5-6; 3.25; Annals 106.

known story. So he summarizes the Brutus legend, but in a Scottish style, injecting into it a variety of details favorable to the Scottish image and the Scottish cause. Their drift is shown by his opinion on the 1301 investigation in Rome: the Scottish representative, he declares, showed that British claims "were utterly devoid of truth."

Wyntoun's versified *Original Chronicle* (about 1420)[21] is less scholarly and also less political. It raises no protest against Edward I's seizure of the Stone of Scone, and its versions of the two national legends are simple and noncompetitive. The migrations of Gathelus are recounted as part of a summary of marvels in Old Testament history and the later migrations of Brutus as a parenthesis in classical history, without the least indication of any political rivalry between them. Still more surprising is the noncombativeness of its biography of King Arthur; it reports his mighty conquests without questioning their actuality or their justification, shows no awareness of the problem of Arthur's legitimacy, and regards Mordred as a traitor—though it makes no mention of Mordred's being either Scot or Pict. This failure to apply the legends to national interests is striking in a fifteenth-century Scottish historian who could scarcely have been ignorant of the political implications. Although Wyntoun too scorns the claims that Edward I made before the pope in 1301, for him, it would seem, Brutus and Gathelus were personages apart from contemporary national conflicts, their legends interesting, but not matters for passionate argument. Although he feels assured that the Scots came from Spain, concerning their ultimate origin he prefers to be noncommital; he reports the various theories and says (2.9.835-836):

> I wold noucht hald thir oppynnyownys ale
> Contrary, for thai mycht weylle fale.

So cautious an attitude is somewhat out of the medieval swim, but it is not entirely unmedieval. William of Newburgh, Giraldus Cambrensis, Ralph Higden, and John of Whethamsted are witnesses that some medieval historians regarded the Arthurian legend as fictional in whole or in part.[22]

---

[21] Andrew of Wyntoun, *The Oryginald Chronykil of Scotland*, ed. F. J. Amours, STS (Edinburgh 1903-1914) 2 lines 90-213, 304-316; 4.18-26; 8.2379-2400.

[22] William of Newburgh in the *Proemium* to his *Historia Rerum Anglicarum* (*Chronicles of the Reigns of Stephen, Henry II and Richard I*, ed. R. Howlett, Rolls Series, 1884-1885, 1.11-19) launches a full scale attack on Geoffrey of Monmouth's credibility about Arthur; Giraldus Cambrensis in his *Itinerarium Kambriae* 1.5.57-58, *Opera* 6, ed. James F. Dimock, Rolls Series 21 (1868), tells the story of the monk who was beset by lie-revealing devils when a copy of Geoffrey's *Historia* was laid in his lap; Ralph Higden, although accepting much of Geoffrey, records his astonishment that Arthur's conquests were not recorded by Gildas or Bede or by any French or Roman historian (*Polychronicon* 5.336); and Thomas Rudborne similarly attacks the credibility of Arthur's Roman campaign, *Historia maior*, ed. Henry Wharton (London 1691) 187-188. John of Whethamstede in his *Granarium de*

So far I have drawn evidence mostly from medieval chronicles. But imaginative writers were not indifferent to the controversy, and its reflex may perhaps be found in the remarkable flourishing of Arthurian romance that occurred in the later fourteenth century. What is most significant about these romances for our present interest is: first, that most of them were composed in the north of England, some very near the Scottish border; second, that the hero who is celebrated by far the most often is Gawain. In Continental romances of this time, Gawain often appears as a degenerate knight, vengeful, faithless, murderous. In these English romances, however, he is the ideal knight, almost *sans peur et sans reproche*.[23] French influence on English romance was strong, so to find this idealized characterization of Gawain in such romances as *Sir Gawain and the Green Knight* or *Awntyrs off Arthure* seems somewhat strange, and not less so because he was a Scot, son of King Lot and brother of Mordred. It may of course simply represent a continuance of the pre-romance way of depicting Gawain, but another possible explanation is that, like the Saracen heroes of romance who were popular because they abjured Islam and fought for the Christian faith, Gawain may have endeared himself to Englishmen by being a Scot who abandoned the descendants of Gathelus and fought for King Arthur: few heroes are more appealing than those who have reneged from the enemy.

As for Scottish romance, the legend of Gathelus offered no such tales for retelling as had accumulated about Arthur and the Round Table; the Scottish fondness for the story of Alexander—it is still apparent in the Scotsman's nickname, "Sandy," earlier "Sawney"—may be something of a substitute. But Scottish poets also occasionally told tales of Arthur and his knights, and when they did so it is clear that their opinion of the king was dictated by the battle of the myths. In *Lancelot of the Laik*,[24] a fifteenth-century Scottish romance, Arthur is a poltroon, who is terrified by dreams, bullies his bishops into interpreting them, and is told that those on whom he relies will fail him. Later he is defeated in combat, only the intervention of Lancelot and Gawain saving him. And finally a clerk reads him an interminable lesson, reminding him that he is a bastard, not the true heir to the throne, and declaring that he is so far gone in wickedness that God will destroy him. Instead of main-

---

viris illustribus (quoted in William Camden's *Britannia*, 1586) characterizes Geoffrey's story of Brutus as a poetical fiction. More commonly, howevei, medieval chronicles proceed from Geoffrey in this matter. For accounts of the medieval response to his *Historia*, see Laura Keeler (n. 17 above), and R. H. Fletcher, *The Arthurian Material in the Chronicles* (Boston 1906).

[23] See B. J. Whiting, "Gawain: His Reputation, His Courtesy, and His Appearance in Chaucer's 'Squire's Tale,'" *Mediaeval Studies* 9 (1947) 189-234. In Sir Thomas Malory's *Le Morte Darthur*, Gawain is an inconsistent character, partly heroic in the English style, but largely debased as in the French.

[24] *Lancelot of the Laik*, ed. M. M. Gray, STS (Edinburgh 1912).

taining justice, he has sought only pleasure; widows, children, and the poor have suffered under his rule; he has lost the people's hearts. *Golagros and Gawain*,[25] another fifteenth-century romance, gives a similarly partisan portrait. This Arthur is engaged in an unjustified war, an imperialistic campaign, in the course of which he is determined to impose his will and power upon Golagros, whose ancestors had not been conquered even by Alexander. Two characterizations are drawn in complete contrast: a tyrannical Arthur in whom ruthless cruelty is joined to sniveling cowardice; a stalwart, freedom-loving Golagros who might have been drawn in the pattern of Scotland's real-life heroes, the Wallace and the Bruce. There are many different portraits of Arthur in medieval literature, but nowhere else is there anything to match the contemptible tyrant who is presented in these Scottish romances, clearly as a reaction to the political implication of the legend of Brutus and Arthur.

Reactivated when Henry VII came to the English throne in 1485, the controversy gradually took on some traits of Renaissance scholarship and also shifted to new positions. Since some medieval writers had transcended their times to note what should always have been obvious to any nonpolitical scholar—that both these myths affront the evidence of general historical record—the same conclusions should have been apparent to the new historians. With some they were. It is ultimately to such sixteenth-century historians as Polydore Vergil and George Buchanan that can be traced the histories that were the bane of George Gordon's youth and the beginnings of conclusions that are our own: that the legends of Gathelus and Brutus are political fictions, that Englishmen are mainly English, that Arthur probably existed but neither as imperial conqueror nor leader of chivalry, that the histories of England and Scotland proper begin with the Anglo-Saxon migrations and Kenneth McAlpin's unification of the north, that the inscribed marble chair from Egypt, Spain, or the bottom of the sea is really a block of red sandstone of a kind found around Scone.[26] Such scholarly objectivity, however, was very far from being the sixteenth-century rule, and many scholars contemporary with Vergil and Buchanan continued to argue for and against this legend and that, arguing indeed with even more zest than their medieval forebears.[27]

The motivations that prompted so many good scholars to fervent defense of patent absurdity were more complicated than before; during the reign of Elizabeth particularly, Catholic and Protestant rivalry was responsible for adding a new tinge to the debate. It is therefore a reflex of many considerations and typical of the tangled politics of the time that the principle of race

[25] In *Scottish Alliterative Poems*, ed. F. J. Amours, STS (Edinburgh 1891) 1.

[26] Watson (n. 3 above) 30, quotes geological opinion on the Stone of Scone.

[27] For the Arthurian legend in English politics and English literature during the fifteenth and sixteenth centuries, see Charles Bowie Millican, *Spenser and the Table Round* (Cambridge, Mass. 1932).

that formerly determined the composition of the opposing forces did not always apply. Among the Scottish participants, some continued to fight under the flag of Gathelus and Scota, some were diplomatically inspired to fire their broadsides in directions contrary from those that would once have been dictated by their birth and upbringing, a few satisfied the claims of both truth and diplomacy by firing both ways.

Imperial claims based on Arthurian descent had not ceased with Edward III. At Henry V's funeral in 1422, for example, Arthur's arms were displayed, three crowns *or* in a field *azure*, token of his having united three kingdoms in one.[28] The Tudors, similarly bent on works of island unity, embraced the old legend with more zeal than anyone had shown since Edward III's days. In proclamation to the Welsh, Henry VII reminded them of an ancient prophecy that one of true Arthurian blood would succeed to the British throne; genealogists traced his own line back to Cadwallader and so to Arthur, Uther Pendragon, and Brutus; and he himself named his first son Arthur, greatest of British names.[29] So renewed, the legend was the legacy of all the Tudors, a theme for their poets and pageanteers, their justification for tenure of England and Wales, their sanction for efforts to bring Scotland and Ireland under the dominion of Britain, their support for claiming independence from Rome.

Henry VII's expansiveness was limited and cautious, however, Wales was safely in the fold, a Welshman the king, ancient prophecy fulfilled. Scotland was more obdurate, and Henry's approach was diplomatic, to marry his daughter Margaret to James IV of Scotland. This marriage, the basis of the ultimate union of the two crowns, was solemnized in 1503, and among the festivities was an Arthurian tournament.[30] From the British point of view, the marriage was doubly blessed, for both bride and groom could lay claim to Arthurian descent, Margaret Tudor by her father's device, James IV by a fiction that is remembered by several Elizabethans, including Shakespeare: that Banquo's son Fleance, who escaped from Macbeth's murderous hand, made his way to Wales, there married Griffith ap Llewellyn's daughter, and so passed on to the Stuarts the blood of King Arthur.[31] Another century was to elapse before the union of the crowns was actually effected, however, and during much of that time the two nations and many of their propagandists were as hostile as ever. Henry VIII's demand for homage from Scotland,[32] for example, was supported by a statement of Arthurian precedent and it led to the Scottish disaster at Solway Moss in 1542 and to the sack of Edin-

---

[28] John Speed, *The Historie of Great Britaine* (London 1611) 648; see also A. E. Parsons, "The Trojan Legend in England," *Modern Language Review* (MLR) 24 (1929) 396.

[29] See Lilian Winstanley, "The Arthurian Empire in the Elizabethan Poets," *Aberystwyth Studies* 5 (1922) 59-66; Millican (n. 27 above) 10-11.

[30] William Drummond, *The History of Scotland* (London 1655) 133.

[31] See Winstanley (n. 29 above) 62-63.

[32] Henry VIII, *A Declaration* (n. 6 above).

burgh in 1544. But when at length, in 1603, James VI of Scotland became also James I of England, not only were two crowns united, but so also were the two legends that divided them. Along the Stuart line, James I was a descendant of Gathelus and Scota; along the lines of Margaret Tudor and Fleance, he was also a descendant of Brutus, *Arturus redivivus*.

Progress toward this union goes far to explain the outcrop of writing relating to the national myths during this century. In England, political and religious concern had the result that the British story as it had been related by Geoffrey of Monmouth became a major quarry for writers of many kinds: poets, playwrights, historians, antiquaries, writers of pageants and masques all discovered in it a rich treasure of symbol and story. Nor was the vogue directed solely toward politics and the court; broadsides, chapbooks, and the revels of the three hundred London merchant-archers who made up Sir Hugh Offley's Fellowship of the Round Table bear witness to the wideness of its appeal.[33]

No such efflorescence can be claimed for the legend of Gathelus and Scota, however. Neither in Scotland nor in Ireland was there anything to match the royal Arthurian revels offered to Elizabeth at Kenilworth Castle or the bourgeois Arthurianism of Offley and his friends in London. Nor did Gathelus and Scota ever join the Wallace and the Bruce in the Scottish hall of poetic fame. Indeed, from John Barbour in the fourteenth century to Sir William Alexander in the seventeenth, their legend is rarely mentioned by Scottish poets. Henry the Minstrel's *Schir William Wallace* briefly summarizes the history of the Stone of Scone.[34] David Steele's *Ring of the Roy Robard*[35] recounts Henry IV's demand for Scottish homage on the basis of "sonnis of auld brutus" and the Scottish king's rejection (59-60):

> Scotland euir ʒet hes bene fre
> Sen Scota of Egipt tuik the see.

In the *Flyting of Dunbar and Kennedie*, Dunbar's dislike of "Irsch" speech (i.e. Gaelic) is attacked on the score that it was also the good language of Scotland, "And Scota it causit to multiply and sprede."[36] Unless one adds Polydore Vergil's recollection of how Gawin Douglas urged him not to follow the example of a Scottish historian who had poured contempt on the story of Gathelus,[37] this seems to be all. Even Gaelic poetry was no more responsive. There are only two minor allusions, both Irish in origin, in the Dean of

[33] For Sir Hugh Offley's fellowship, see Millican (n. 27 above) 60-61; also, John Nichols, *Progresses . . . of Queen Elizabeth* (London 1823) 1.529.

[34] Henry the Minstrel, see n. 13 above.

[35] In W. A. Craigie, ed., *The Maitland Folio Manuscript*, STS (Edinburgh 1919) 1.127-133.

[36] W. Mackay Mackenzie, ed, *The Poems of William Dunbar* (Edinburgh 1932) 15 lines 347-348.

[37] Sir Henry Ellis, *Polydore Vergil's English History*, Camden Society 1.36 (London 1846) 105.

Lismore's book:[38] one praises John MacGregor as the star of valor among the Grecian Gael; the other refers to Lugh who set Ireland under the rule of the Gael from Greece. The entire harvest is pitiful, and its only interest is its proof that although poets were not ignorant of the legend, nothing about it stimulated their fancy: what was lacking was anything to match the romantic appeal of the Arthurian story as it had been developed by Geoffrey of Monmouth and the romance writers who followed him.

With polemical historians it was far different, however, and the importance they attached to the legends and the diversity of their political attitudes may be judged from two of the most important early Scottish histories, John Major's *Majoris Britanniae historia*, 1521,[39] and Hector Boece's *Scotorum historia*, 1527.[40] Each historian sets the tone for his treatment of recent events with a full version of the stories of ancient origin. But while Boece is enthusiastic about both legends, about the Gathelus story as witness to ancient and unchanging Scottish virtues and independence, about the Brutus story as a record of unchanging British baseness, Major carefully distinguishes between them. On the authority of Geoffrey of Monmouth, he grants the truth of the Trojan settlement of Britain, although for his own unstated but presumably Scottish reasons he denies the historicity of Brutus's division of the island between his three sons. Rival stories are given short shrift. Major declares that the legend related by Caxton that Albion was originally settled by Albina and her ladies was fabulous and absurd. And as for the Scottish story of Gathelus, he counted it a fable: the Scots and the Irish were both descended from migrants from Spain, but since "their English enemies had learned to boast of an origin from the Trojans, so the Scots claimed an original descent from the Greeks who had subdued the Trojans, and then bettered it with this about the illustrious kingdom of Egypt."[41]

These opposing attitudes of the two Scottish historians mirror the uncertainties of Scottish policy during the minority of James V. Boece must relate to the drift towards the old French alliance: indeed, his work may have been meant to encourage that drift. Major's discrimination, scholarly in one case, unscholarly in the other, apparently stems less from learned considerations than from the aims of the pro-English party led by the queen mother, Margaret Tudor. The delicate role that Major set himself was to remove or minimize historical impediments to an Anglo-Scottish entente under English leadership, a role that gave him only one politic choice between the rival myths. The history he managed to trace was flattering to both peoples,

[38] William J. Watson, ed., *Scottish Verse from the Book of the Dean of Lismore*, Scottish Gaelic Texts Society (Edinburgh 1937) 160-161, 204-205.

[39] John Major, *Majoris Britanniae historia* (Paris 1521); trans. Archibald Constable, Scottish Historical Society (SHS) (Edinburgh 1892) 1-4, 52-53, 81-85.

[40] Hector Boece (n. 4 above).

[41] Major (n. 39 above) 151-152.

however, one of independence and heroism, marred only by occasional excess. As Major states, the two countries had a common interest in removing ancient hostilities. His own plan was to unite them peacefully as one Great Britain and to make firm the union by a system of royal marriages. "For thus and thus only," he writes, "could two intensely hostile peoples, inhabitants of the same island, of which neither can conquer the other, have been brought together under one and the same king. And what although the name and kingdom of the Scots had disappeared—so too would the name and kingdom of the English no more have had a place amoug men—for in the place of both we should have had a King of Britain."[42]

Less temperate statements appear in a *Chronicle of the Scots*, 1482-1530,[43] and James Harryson's *An Exhortacion to the Scottes*, 1547.[44] The anonymous chronicler hoots at the notion that Scotsmen were descended from the traitors of Troy. Their forebears were Greeks, the only people who had conquered the world twice. If on the distaff side they also came from Egyptians, that misfortune might be minimized by remembering that Christ was descended from Jews. Scotland's name was founded and its land inhabited "lang tymme on to Troy was distroyt, and or Brutus was bornne." As for Arthur, stories told by Walter Napillis [Map] in *Lancelot de Lac*, that he slew Stallo [Frollo] of France and Lucius of Rome were "fenzit" and "lesinges," pretenses and falsehoods. In fact, Arthur was "spurius, yat is bastard and ane hureis sonne, saife revirence," and came to the throne only through Merlin's deviltry. The true heir was Mordred of Lothian, so that when during Arthur's absence Mordred made himself king over the Britons, who "war oure naturall enemys," and later slew Arthur, he was actuated only by righteousness. The chronicler was Scottish indeed, perhaps reacting against Henry VIII's demands and incursions against his native land; but that even he was not unaffected by the desire for a peaceful composition may be indicated by his surprising conclusion from Mordred's revenge. Since that time, he declares, there had been "true friendship betwyxt ws and ye Bryttanis to yis day."

Harryson, on the other hand, although he was a Scotsman addressing compatriots, displayed more Anglophilia than even John Major. His *Exhortacion* wears his politics on its sleeve, for it is dedicated to Edward, Duke of Somerset, the Lord Protector who sought to marry Edward VI of England to the infant Mary of Scotland. The pamphlet itself is a plea for Anglo-Scottish union, and its principal gambit is to stress the original and continuing unity of Scotland and England. It characterizes the Scottish legend of Gathelus and Scota as "lesynges and vanities" put forth by monks and friars under the devil's inspiration, and trains on its absurdities the resources of chronological, lin-

---

[42] *Ibid.* 189. This marriage theme is one that he emphasizes whenever his history gives him the chance.

[43] Skene, *Chronicles* (n. 3 above) item 50.

[44] James Harryson, *An Exhortacion to the Scottes* (London 1547), pamphlet.

guistic, and logical argument. Harryson's scholarship, like John Major's, was not for all seasons, however. It led him to no comparable doubt about the Brutus legend, nor did it prompt him to dispute the Tudor claim. Whether or not Brutus was an exile from Italy, Harryson claims, he was the first king of the whole island, and divided it among his three sons. Picts entered Britain about A.D. 72 and later, with the help of Irish-Scots, raided on the Britons. Before then "the first inhabitors of this island were al Britaines, more then vi C yeres afore Scottes had any kyngdom there." Most Scotsmen were English, as their language shows, and the unnatural discords that had existed between the two peoples were in fact "a Ciuill warre" (preface).

Association of the legends not only with union but also with religious conflict is still more apparent in two major histories that were written during Mary Stuart's last years. They are John Lesley's *De origine, moribus, et rebus gestis Scotorum*,[45] published in Rome in 1578, and George Buchanan's *Rerum scotticarum historia*, 1582.[46] Lesley, Bishop of Ross, a champion of Catholicism, and one of the Scottish queen's most devoted followers, compiled his work while he was resident in England, sometimes as a diplomat, sometimes as a prisoner, and in 1571 he presented the English version of it to his captive queen. Buchanan, the great humanist, once tutor to Mary but from 1562 an advocate of reform, wrote his history during years when he was leader of the Reformed Church and mentor to Mary's rebellious son James; and when it was published in Edinburgh it was dedicated to his pupil, then king of Scotland, and a Protestant who was reasonably sure of becoming the first wearer of the united crowns of Great Britain.

Lesley raises no scholarly doubts while retelling from Hector Boece the full story of Scottish migration from Egypt; but his version of British affairs is strongly modified by learned reasoning. The Trojan origin of Britain he briefly dismisses as fables and "clattiris"; Britons come first into his record when they are conquered by Julius Caesar and when Picts and Scots help them against the Saxons. Concerning the legends about Merlin and Uther Pendragon, he is also silent; and as for Arthur, he regards the tales of his great imperial conquests of Scotland, Ireland, France, and most of northern Europe as cock-and-bull stories—although, having seen the Round Table at Winton, he is not altogether sure about the exploits of the knights of the Round Table. What he is certain of, however, is that Arthur was ultimately brought to his doom by Picts and Scots.

Buchanan's preferences were to associate Arthur with religion and reform and to make more drastic use of the new scholarship. Referring to Polydore

[45] John Lesley, *De origine, moribus et rebus gestis Scotorum*, (Rome 1578); trans. James Dalrymple, *The Historie of Scotland*, 1596, STS (Edinburgh 1888) 68-82, 214-224.

[46] George Buchanan, *Rerum scotticarum historia* (Edinburgh 1582); trans. John Watkins (London 1827) pp. 26-33, 102-106.

Vergil, he dismisses out of hand, although for sound linguistic and textual reasons, both the southern legend of Brutus and the northern legend of Gathelus. The former he characterizes as a monkish forgery, of which even the inventor seems to have realized the absurdity. As for the Gathelus fable, he stresses its linguistic absurdity, points out the fact that Gathelus was quite unknown to any Greek author, wonders why the inventors should have chosen so ignoble a founder—ignorance of the ancients might explain the choice, he suggests—and contemptuously apologizes for having pursued the subject longer than necessary, simply because others had pertinaciously defended the story "as though it were a palladium dropped down from heaven."

Beginning his own history with Fergus in the fourth century before Christ, Buchanan rapidly runs over the story of eighty Scottish kings before Kenneth III, who came to the throne in A.D. 970. In the course of this scurry, his only pause is over British-Scottish affairs in the reign of Goranus, A.D. 501-535, a stay long enough to pass on some information that could do only good for the cause of union and the self-esteem of both Scotland and England. He raises the possibility that Mordred's mother Anna, as well as her brother Arthur, may have been natural-born, children of Uther Pendragon by a concubine.[47] Merlin was a cheat but no magician, and the story of his supernatural assistance in the begetting of Arthur was forged to conceal Uther Pendragon's adultery. Arthur came to the throne despite Scottish protests, but as soon as he was king he showed his liberality and greatness of mind by renewing the alliance of Scots, Picts, and Britons that drove out the Saxons. Arthur regarded Mordred of Lothian, his nearest of kin, as his rightful successor, but during the king's absence in France, Constantine plotted to gain the succession and persuaded the majority of the British nobles to favor him over Mordred. Presented with this decision, Arthur democratically decided to give way to it. This had the natural though unfortunate effect of alienating Mordred, and the battle that followed in 542 was tragic for both sides, a victory for neither. And with this discreet rationalization of Arthurian obstacles that had divided Englishmen and Scotsmen for several centuries, Buchanan turns to praise his royal pupil's forebear. Arthur, he declares, despite the fictions that had clustered about him, was not only a great and valiant man, he was also a religious man, who reformed his country and restored the true worship of God.

In 1603, the year of James I's accession to the British throne, Samuel Daniel exhorted in his *Panegyric*:

> Shake hands with Union, O thou mighty State!
> Now thou art all Great Britain and no more;
> No Scot, no English now, nor no debate.[48]

---

[47] Buchanan inclines, however, to the opinion that Anna was Uther's sister.
[48] James Nichols, ed. *The Progresses of King James the First* (London 1828) 1.133.

As regards the battle of the myths at least, it was pretty well true. The actual political problem having been solved apparently, there was no more call for propagandist use of the ancient legends, and the way was free for more scholarly considerations. In England, after an initial flurry of masques and entertainments identifying James with Brutus and Arthur, Saxon origins were soon to become the vogue and King Alfred was to come to rival King Arthur as the national hero. Similarly in Scotland. On the eve of the union, Andrew Melville[49] once more traced the Stuarts back to Gathelus; six years later Habbakuk Bisset[50] retold the Gathelus story; and in 1612 John Monipennie[51] recounted both legends in a fashion that would displease neither nation. But these are near the fag end of the conflict. Sir Thomas Craig, one of the Scottish commissioners for the union, voiced the more general opinion: "what our own Boece, following Veremundus, says about the origin of the Scots I regard as pure romance, as I also hold Brutus, the mythical ancestor of Britain's inhabitants. . . . Every nation indeed is in the habit of ascribing its origin either to the Trojans or to the Greeks or to the gods themselves."[52] Before many years, the new histories of both England and Scotland were either dismissing the now useless legends or ignoring them, filling their ancient places with the nearer and drier beginnings of which George Gordon complained. The only variations seem to be Sir Thomas Urquhart's engagingly outrageous claim to descent from Gathelus and Scota and a brief flurry of historical interest early in the eighteenth century which may be related to the Old Pretender's pathetic aspirations and endeavors.[53]

Three centuries of such silence in the national histories has had a predictable result. Had it not been for Malory's and Spenser's King Arthur, Englishmen might well have forgotten that they once claimed to be Arthurians and Trojans. Scotsmen, lacking any figure as striking as Arthur, have generally forgotten that they once thought they came from Egypt.[54]

Department of English,   Univ. of Calif.
Los Angeles, California 90024, U.S.A.

[49] [Andrew Melville], *A trewe description of the nobill race of the Stewards* (Edinburgh 1603, STS 12886).

[50] Habbakuk Bisset, *Rolment of Courtis*, ed. Sir P. Hamilton-Grierson, STS (Edinburgh 1920-1926).

[51] John Monipennie, *The Abridgement or Summarie of the Scots Chronicles*, 1612.

[52] Sir Thomas Craig, *De unione regnorum Britanniae tractatus*, c. 1605 SHS (Edinburgh 1909) 357.

[53] See n. 3 above, par. 4.

[54] The last popular allusions I have found are two Gaelic songs by Alexander Macdonald (1700-1770) relating to the 1745 rebellion; published in John Lorne Campbell, ed., *Highland Songs of the Forty-Five* (Edinburgh 1933) 5.80-81 and 11.46. The substantial account of the Gathelus myth which is presented as "Historical Tradition" in David Scott's *The History of Scotland*, Westminster, 1727 (dedicated to the Duke of Hamilton) may also have a Jacobite connection.

PROFITABLE STUDIES: HUMANISTS AND GOVERNMENT IN EARLY TUDOR ENGLAND

•

by Arthur J. Slavin

There was in early Tudor England an incipient civic humanism. Humanist concern for the commonwealth has recently been the subject of intensive investigation, especially inasmuch as some of the greatest writers of the age, Sir Thomas More, Dean Colet, and Thomas Starkey, made their mark in part by asking who the good citizen and what the true polity were. While not wishing to draw attention away from the ideas of those for whom stars danced, I suggest that our image of English humanistic activity would be more realistic if, as an experiment, we forgot that that trio ever wrote about reform in church and commonwealth, and especially that one of them was martyred. By so doing we will be able to look at the work of the humanists in another sense and ask what use Henry VIII made of humanists in governing the commonwealth as it existed.

There is, of course, much to be learned from the studies that relate behavior to attitudes. A good deal also may be learned, however, about humanists and humanism by asking simpler questions and finding answers in direct observations on their backgrounds and careers, taking our cue in this from Hugh Latimer:

> So that I think many one nowadays professeth the gospel for the livings sake. . . . They are so troubled with lordly living, they be so placed in palaces, couched in courts, ruffling in their rents, dancing in their dominions, burdened with ambassages, pampering of their paunches, like a monk that maketh his jubilee, munching in their mangers, and moiling in their gay manors and mansions, and so troubled with their loitering in their lordships, that they cannot attend it. They are otherwise occupied, some in the King's matters, some are ambassadors, some of the Privy Council, some to furnish the Court, some are lords of the Parliament, some are presidents, and some comptrollers of mints. Well, well!

The first of our direct observations is of a lack evident in Conyers Read's bibliography of Tudor history. One scans the index in vain for a single entry

under the heading "patronage." While striking essays illuminate the conditions of Elizabethan politics and patronage,[1] the study of the inwardness of
early Tudor politics and avenues of patronage in no way is as advanced.[2]
Despite the recent publication of excellent studies of the humanist tradition
and its relations to reform and Reformation,[3] we have as yet for England no
study parallel to Lauro Martines's work on the social world of the Florentine
humanists.[4] While James K. McConica[5] made an important start in the right
direction, we are for the most part still bound to a tradition in which humanism
in England is studied chiefly by faculties of English and not by faculties of
History, with this unhappy result: we know more about humanist ideas about
politics than we do of their participation in politics. This is worth noting
when we consider their bold rallying cry, *Numquam privatus est sapiens*![6]

To throw some light on the social world of early Tudor humanists and their
participation in government and public life in brief compass brings one face
to face with the difficulty of sampling. The more remote the past is with
which we concern ourselves the more difficult exact sociological sampling
becomes. What survives in our records is the merest debris of the former
activities of Tudor humanists. The historian is thereby compelled toward a
selectivity which is "arbitrary" in terms of his best judgment. Which humanists
among the scores who lived between 1500 and 1550 will help us understand
the pattern of humanist participation in government is a question that admits
of no exact answer.

I originally selected several dozen writers, scholars, artists and teachers
for detailed study. From this list I have chosen to present here material
concerning about half my original sample. In the course of my work it became
clear that nothing could be won for understanding by artificially inflating
the sample or by providing all of the data about all of the men studied. In-

---

[1] Sir John E. Neale, "The Elizabethan Political Scene," in *Essays in Elizabethan History*
(London 1958) 59-84; S. T. Bindoff, Joel Hurstfield and C. H. Williams, eds., *Elizabethan
Government and Society* (London 1961), esp. Wallace MacCaffery, "Place and Patronage
in Elizabethan Politics" (95-126) and G. R. Elton, "The Elizabethan Exchequer: War in
the Receipt" (213-248).

[2] Elton's *The Tudor Revolution in Government* (Cambridge 1953) has illuminating comments on this problem scattered throughout; see also A. J. Slavin, *Politics and Profit* (Cambridge 1966) chaps. 1-4, 8, 9, as well as his "Sir Ralph Sadler and Master John Hales at the
Hanaper," *Bulletin of the Institute of Historical Research* 38 (1965) 31-47

[3] See especially Fritz Caspari, *Humanism and the Social Order in Tudor England* (Chicago
1954); Arthur B. Ferguson, *The Articulate Citizen and the English Renaissance* (Durham,
N. C. 1965); and W. Gordon Zeeveld, *Foundations of Tudor Policy* (Cambridge, Mass. 1948).

[4] *The Social World of the Florentine Humanists* (Princeton 1963).

[5] *English Humanists and Reformation Politics* (Oxford 1965).

[6] On the application of humanist ideas see the many works of Hans Baron, especially
"Secularization of Wisdom and Political Humanism in the Renaissance," *Journal of the
History of Ideas* 21 (1960) 131-150; also, Paul Oskar Kristeller, "The Humanist Movement,"
in *The Classics and Renaissance Thought* (Cambridge, Mass. 1955).

stead, I chose to concentrate on men who had published some important work before the death of Henry VIII, or those who had won some fame in their art or by their learned discourse. Even among these there was much duplication of data, so that Howard, Wyatt, Fabyan, Hall, Copeland, Coverdale, Rhodes, Tyndale, and Record need not be put forward in order to balance the picture. Those we have selected for inclusion well enough illustrate distinguished achievement: Elyot's celebrated *Latin-English Dictionary*,[7] Barclay's rendering of Brant's *Narrenschiff*,[8] Lord Berners's translations of Froissart's *Chronicles*[9] and Ascham's *Toxophilus*.[10] I have excluded some like More and Skelton in the belief that by avoiding their giant shadows we may more easily see essentials. I have also omitted some whose floruit places them primarily in the reign of Henry VII or after the time of Henry VIII. Finally, I have been especially conscious of the need to present material about men of very different social backgrounds, in the hope of learning something about the relations between humanistic learning, public service and mobility. This is very important, for unlike the Florentines studied by Professor Martines, our English humanists exhibit no strong homogeneity of class.[11]

The birth and family background of a quarter of the men studied here is obscure, by which I mean that little reliable data exists about their origins or any other thing pertinent to placing them in the Tudor social hierarchy. Among this number are the Scot Alexander Barclay, who made his way early in the century to Lincolnshire and then to court; and the Englishmen Richard Cox, Simon Heynes, John Ponet, Stephen Hawes, and William Baldwin. It is very likely that they came of humble families. John Bale sprang from a family of village peasants, while of John Mason we have only the tale that his father was a cowherd. A step above these men of obscure or peasant origins, we have several men from the middling ranks of rural society: Roger Ascham, whose father was a Yorkshire yeoman; Leonard Coxe, the second son of a yeoman; Hugh Latimer's father was a prosperous Leicestershire yeoman of gentry pretence, a status similar to that of the father of William Tyndale. Some of our people came from firmly established gentry families. This is unambiguously the case with John Cheke, George Ferrers, Thomas Smith, Thomas Linacre, George Cavendish, Thomas Elyot, and John Lyly. The ranks of the landed aristocracy are represented by Lord Berners and

---

[7] Published in 1538, with a dedication to Henry VIII.

[8] Published in 1509, with a dedication to Henry VIII.

[9] Published in 1525, with a dedication to Henry VIII.

[10] Published in 1545, with a dedication to Henry VIII.

[11] Summary lives are in the *Dictionary of National Biography* (DNB). For that reason I have not encumbered these pages with references to Wood, Cooper, Venn and Venn, or other specialized biographical guides. Instead, in the following notes I have tried to present a guide to some recent works and published documentary materials relevant to my twenty-five.

Reginald Pole. A full third of our men had origins that can fairly be called "bourgeois," either in an artisan, mercantile or professional sense. Among those of merchant family status were Thomas Lupset, who was the son of a London goldsmith; John Heywood, whose family owned land in Hertfordshire but thrived mainly on London legal and commercial ties; Richard Grafton, the son of a well-to-do merchant and mercer, and his partner in printing Edward Whitchurch, both seem to have come from London families engaged in wholesale trade. Nicholas Lyzarde presents a difficult case. He seems to have been a Frenchman of artisan background about whom little is know before he appears in England. Rounding out our two dozen are three men whose family ties seem to oscillate between the yeomanry and London merchant origins: Henry Brinkelow, Robert Fabyan, and Edward Hall.

Whatever the condition of their birth, education at the two universities of England was an experience shared by nineteen of the twenty-four men under study. Taking a degree at Cambridge helped on the way to preferment Ascham, Bale, Barclay, Cheke, Leonard Coxe, and the future bishop Richard Cox, Ferrers, Heynes, Latimer, Lupset, Ponet, and Smith. All but Barclay took a B.A. there. Seven were hooded masters of arts in Cambridge colleges, while two were made bachelors of divinity and three doctors of things divine. Richard Cox, Bale, and Latimer earned the tripod of degrees upon which their careers stood in the precincts of the Cam. Nine Oxonians are in our group. Barclay took his B.A. there, joining Lord Berners, Leonard Coxe (B.A. Cantab.), Hawes, Heywood, Linacre, Lupset (another ambivalent fellow), Mason, and Pole. Four of our nine could write *magister artium Oxoniensis* after their names. Linacre took a degree in medicine at Oxford after an extended period of study abroad. In all, only eight of the nineteen were content with their first earned degree.

The bachelors are thus nearly evenly divided between the ancient English universities, while only Brinkelow, Cavendish, Grafton, Lyzarde, and Elyot seemed to lack the benefits of university training. Cambridge which was to be notorious for the radicalism of the religious ideas imbibed there, was for our men a place more excellent for advanced studies than was Oxford, though the Oxonians Barclay, Linacre, and Pole have not suffered in reputation from having gone to the older university. More worth noting is the fact that few of our two dozen had special training in law at the London Inns, whether civil or common, the exceptions being Ferrers and Smith.

So much for prologue. What, then, were the avenues of patronage? Scholars were employed as tutors to royal children, as all know who can recall Erasmus's frustration and anger with More, when Thomas took him unaware and introduced him to Prince Henry at Eltham, near Lord Mountjoy's country house—a hurt repaired by the hasty composition and dedication of a poem.[12]

[12] P. S. Allen and H. M. Allen, editors, *Opus epistolarum* (Oxford 1906-1965) 1 no. 103,

Our writers served also in foreign embassies, as clerks of assize and of the council, as royal councillors, sheriffs, members of parliament and commissioners for sewers. There is even a Latin secretary, a lord deputy of Calais, a chancellor of the Exchequer and a chancellor of England in our company. State offices, then, were given in plenty. Our men also held posts as deans, vicars, rectors, prebends, canons-regular, priors. And they served on ecclesiastical commissions as well. Furthermore, among the clerks there were bishops, and even a cardinal-archbishop, Pole, who owed his education and subsequent position, ironically enough, to his royal cousin Henry VIII.[13]

Ascham,[14] Richard Cox,[15] Cheke,[16] Linacre,[17] and Lupset[18] all served in tutorial positions. Elyot,[19] Berners,[20] Heynes,[21] Mason,[22] and Smith[23] were

---

for Erasmus's account of the meeting; and *ibid.*, no. 1 p. 6, for the poem given by Erasmus three days later to the King. Hereafter cited as *Opus epist.*

[13] On Pole see Ludovico Beccadelli, *The Life of Cardinal Reginald Pole* (London 1766); F. A. Gasquet, *Cardinal Pole and his Early Friends* (London 1927); Kenneth B. McFarlane, *Cardinal Pole* (Oxford 1925); and Wilhelm Schenk, "The Student Days of Cardinal Pole," *History* 33 (1948) 211-225, as well as his *Reginald Pole, Cardinal of England* (London 1950).

[14] On Ascham's connections with courtiers, among them Norfolk, Gardiner, Denny, and Cranmer, and his tutorial work in Norfolk's household and that of Prince Edward, see Larry Ryan, *Roger Ascham* (Stanford 1963) and also W. Giles, ed. *The Whole Works of Roger Ascham* (London 1864-1865) 1 nos. 32, 34, 46, 44; also nos. 38, 40, 41, 42, 45. Hereafter cited as *Works.*

[15] He was royal almoner as well as one of the directors of Prince Edward's education, along with Cheke. For his role in that capacity see J. G. Nichols, ed., *The Literary Remains of King Edward VI* (Edinburgh 1857) 1.xxxix. Apart from C. H. and T. Cooper, *Athenae cantabrigienses* (London 1858-1861) 1.437-445, nothing has been written since Strype and Burnet printed several of the tracts by him. His works were chiefly biblical translations and catechetical books.

[16] Cheke first came to Edward VI's service as "a supplimente to Mr. Coxe," in a tutorial role: Nichols 1.xxxix. The best life fitting Cheke into the humanist movement in England is that by Walter Nathan, *Sir John Cheke und der englische Humanismus* (Bonn 1928).

[17] On the court career of Thomas Linacre see J. F. Fulton, "Early Medical Humanists," *New England Journal of Medicine* 205 (1934) 141-146; John N. Johnson, *Life of Thomas Linacre* (London 1835); Charles D. O'Malley, *English Medical Humanists* (Lawrence 1965); and R. Weiss, "Letters of Linacre," *Times Literary Supplement* (TLS) (26 September 1936) 768. On his relation to Mary Tudor see McConica (n. 5 above) 54, and R. W. Chambers, *Thomas More* (Ann Arbor 1962) 83, for his role in teaching Greek to More.

[18] Lupset's court-connected tutorial work grew out of his employment as the teacher of Wolsey's bastard son Thomas Winter. For this and related work by Thomas Lupset see John A. Gee, *The Life and Works of Thomas Lupset* (New Haven 1928) 124-126.

[19] Thomas Elyot's ambassadorial work was the result of his place in the Boleyn connection before 1531, at which time he served in the Imperial Embassy. His earlier involvement in a mission to Antwerp in which he was to aid Stephen Vaughan in apprehending Tyndale is discussed in Walter C. Richardson, *Stephen Vaughan* (Baton Rouge 1953) 33. See also McConica (n. 5 above) 122-123; and Stanford Lehmberg, *Sir Thomas Elyot, Tudor Humanist* (Austin 1961) *passim*; on the Imperial mission see H. W. Donner, "The Emperor and Sir Thomas Elyot," *Review of English Studies* (RES) 2 (1926) 55-59.

[20] On Lord Berners (Sir John Bourchier) see John Sharon Brewer, *The Reign of Henry*

sent abroad in diplomatic capacities. Cheke, Elyot,[24] and Mason were privy councillors, all having had earlier experience as clerks of the council.[25] George Ferrers, reader in law at Lincoln's Inn, served in the House of Commons, as did many others on our list, among them Mason, Elyot, Smith, and Cheke. Ferrers, the translator of *Magna carta* and the author of several crucial tales in *A Mirror for Magistrates*, however, also holds a place in English constitutional history, as the burgess for Plymouth whose arrest in 1543 on a condemnation for debt resulted in Ferrers Case—a landmark of parliamentary privilege.[26] Lord Berners was chancellor of the Exchequer in 1516 after holding the reversionary rights to that office for several years; he continued to serve as lord deputy at Calais.[27] Cheke was at one time secretary of state

---

VIII (London 1884) 1.190; and *Letters and Papers, Foreign and Domestic, of the Reign of Henry VIII*, ed. Brewer, James Gairdner and R. H. Brodie (London 1856-1929) 2.2.4135. Hereafter cited as LP, with numbers referring to volume and number of document, unless page is specified. See also the appreciation of Berners by J. H. McDill, "The Life of Lord Berners," TLS (17 April 1930).

[21] See DNB 26.325-327, where the mission to Spain of 1538 is fully discussed. Simon Heynes is a totally obscure figure; for his "Instructions" in 1538 see LP 13.1.140 (3). Other references to Heynes's mission to Barcelona in tandem with Edmund Bonner are in *ibid*. 13.1.671, 695-696, 710-712, 766, 840, 915, 1146, 1512; *ibid*. 2.59, 60, 130-131, 144, 269, 270, 615, 1231, 1280.

[22] John Mason had been king's scholar in Paris. His diplomatic service began under Sir Thomas Wyatt, whose secretary he was and with whom he served in Spain and elsewhere: see LP 20.1.257, 282, 710, 1146, 1165, 1213, 1426; *ibid*. 2.144, 191, 270, 348, 615 and 786. For his long and varied administrative career see DNB 36.425ff.

[23] John Strype's *Life of the Learned Sir Thomas Smith* has at last been superseded by Mary Dewar, *Sir Thomas Smith: A Tudor Intellectual in Office* (London, 1964) where his embassies in France and elsewhere are fully treated: 88-114, 129-148.

[24] For Cheke and Elyot in this capacity see the references given in nn. 16-17 above.

[25] On Mason as council clerk see LP 17.131, 138, 399, 523, 718, 843 (2), 986. The only unambiguous reference is 1015, where is notice of his style "clerk of the council," and 1012 (24), letters patent 20 September 1540, appointing "John Mason, clerk of the council, the King's Secretary for the French Tongue." Here we have a good example of the repayment of royal generosity by a former exhibitioner in Paris. For Mason's hand in drafting French translations of royal letters see British Museum, Cotton MS Caligula E IV 112.

[26] George Ferrers's translation of *The Boke of Magna Carta* appeared in 1534, while the *Mirror* was published in 1559 and in many subsequent editions. There is little more to record of him, with the important exception of his connection with the Cromwellian reforms. He was apparently one of that minister's advisers and servants: see Howard J. Graham, "*Our Tong Maternall Maruellously Amendyd and Augmentyd*: The First Englishing and Printing of the Medieval Statutes at Large, 1530-1533," *UCLA Law Review* 13 (1965) 58-98, esp. 87-91. The account of Ferrers Case by Holinshead appeared while the principal was still alive (1577): *Chronicle* 3.824-826. It is supported by the briefer record in Hall's more contemporary *Chronicle* 843. The fullest account of Ferrers's life is by Lily Bess Campbell, in the introduction she wrote to *The Mirror for Magistrates* (Los Angeles 1938) 25-33.

[27] On Berners's official career see LP 1-6, where there are hundreds of references; see also *Patent Rolls of Henry VII* 1.16, 368; 2.40, 114, 161, 326, 661. The appointment of Berners

and at another served as chamberlain of the Exchequer.[28] Elyot, who had a decided administrative talent, served on numerous commissions and was at one time or another sheriff in various shires, when statute loaded upon statute broadened the business of that office and burdened its holders.[29]

Some held household positions, offices which had not yet "gone out of court," in Tout's fine phrase. Hawes was for both Henry VII and Henry VIII a groom of the chamber.[30] Grafton was printer to the king.[31] Linacre was physician royal.[32] Heywood, a minor poet and important dramatist, was a singer in the chapel royal.[33] Lyzarde was second court painter,[34] while Ponet—

---

as chancellor of the Exchequer relates the details of the reversion: LP 2.1.1946, a signet bill dated 28 May 1516, warranting the issue of letters patent.

[28] He held the posts after 1547, but before Henry VIII's death early in that year his preferments were many, including the Cambridge professorship (1540-1551), his canon's post in King's College, Oxford and a Royal Pensioner's award (1545): see LP 19.1.864, 610 (35); 20.2.579; and 21.1.643.

[29] His administrative career may be traced in LP, where evidence of his clerkship of assize on the western circuit, his justice-of-the-peace office in Oxfordshire, his clerkship of the council and many other commissions and appointments are calendared: 1.1.1266 (26-27), 804 (36), 833 (2), 1083 (8), 1316 (3, 14), 1662 (1, 28); 3.1.102, 405, 644, 933; 4.3.6490 (1), 6598 (1), 6803 (6); 5.1694 (ii), app. 15; 6.1292; 8.149 (52); 9.1217 (20); and dozens of mentions in vols. 12-21. Sir Richard Elyot, Thomas's father, was a promient early Tudor lawyer who rose to be attorney general to Henry VII's queen and a frequent sitter in parliaments.

[30] Stephen Hawes, of whom Bale once wrote that his life was "an ensaumple of vertue," wrote poems ih the cardinal virtue tradition without much poetic inspiration. For his career and works see J. H. W. Atkins, *English Literary Criticism: The Medieval Phase* (London 1951); C. W. Lemmi, "The Influence of Boccaccio on Hawes' *Pastime*," RES 5 (1929) 195-198; H. Sellers, "The Poems of Stephen Hawes and an Early Medical Tract," *British Museum Quarterly* 13 (1939) 7-8; and W. Wells, "Stephen Hawes and *The Court of Sapience*," RES 6 (1930) 47-58. *The Joyfull Medytacyon* (1509), written to celebrate the accession of Henry VIII, is perhaps Hawes's best poem.

[31] On Grafton's career as a London grocer, merchant adventurer and royal printer see Foxe's *Acts and Monuments* and Hall's *Chronicle*, as well as A. G. Dickens, *The English Reformation* (New York 1964) 132-133, for a summary. His chief work was the lively continuation of Hardyng's *Chronicle*. Stow charged him with garbling editions of Hall and Hardyng issued in 1548 and 1543 respectively. Moreover, he compiled an *Abridgement of Chronicles* issued in his own name.

[32] Linacre's functions at court were chiefly medical, despite the fact that he tutored Princess Mary. By 1521 we have Erasmus's letters as a reliable guide to Linacre's place in the royal household, where he was senior medical officer. Before that year Linacre is always styled *medicus regius*, while after the Summer of that year he is invariably called *serenissimi Anglorum regis medicus primarius*. See Allen, *Opus epist.* (n. 12 above) 2.247, 4.570. No official contemporary document records the change. Apart from *Opus epist.*, George Lily ambiguously spoke of an appointment *renovatio patris exemplo*, in Paulo Giovio, *Descriptio Britanniae* (London 1548). This can refer to his tutorial work as well.

[33] On John Heywood see R. de la Bere, *John Heywood: Entertainer* (London 1937); Robert Bolwell, *The Life and Works of John Heywood* (New York 1921); K. W. Cameron, "John Heywood and Richard Stanley," *Shakespeare Association Bulletin* 14 (1938) 51-56;

in what capacity we do not know—designed Henry VIII's favorite sun parlor and an ingenious sundial at Lambeth Palace.[35] For the author of the *Short Treatise on Political Power*, where the word "puritan" was first used in a later standard sense, that was a virtuoso display dear to Henry VIII's heart. Even Thomas Cromwell catered to the king's taste for novelties; on one occasion sending him a cleverly made lock with which the king was much pleased.[36]

Together these men held more than forty offices under Henry VIII, all with salaries attached. Court painters drew various sums,[37] while that given tutors ranged from £ 10 to double that.[38] Councillors drew a salary and diet for the support of the burdens of office.[39] The king's secretaries for Latin and French had salaries varying between £100 and £200.[40] Berners, who held the Exchequer chanceliorship apparently *sine cura*, had an allowance for his deputyship at Calais of £100.[41] Gentlemen and grooms of the chamber had a minimum competence of £10.[42] Smith drew a "rent" for his Regius Professorship of Civil Law worth £40.[43] Heywood, who, we are told, had a "golden

---

and R. J. Schoeck, "Anthony Bonvisi, the Heywoods, and the Ropers," *Notes and Queries* 197 (1952) 178-179 and the same writer's "William Rastell and the Prothonotaries," *ibid.* 398-399.

[34] Little is known of Nicholas Lyzarde (d. 1570). He was sergeant painter to Mary I and Elizabeth I after earlier serving Henry VIII as second court painter, a post he also held under Edward VI. He apparently was a skilled painter of miniatures: see Erica Auerbach, *Tudor Artists* (London 1954) 91-92, and Eric Mercer, *English Art, 1553-1625* (Oxford 1962) 195.

[35] See the introductory matter in Winthrop S. Hudson, *John Ponet, Advocate of Limited Monarchy* (Chicago 1942).

[36] Public Record Office (PRO) SP 1/101 fols. 57-58, Ralph Sadler-Thomas Cromwell, 11 January 1536: "I delyveryd your locke unto hys grace and openyd all the ginnes of sam whych hys grace lyketh maruellouslie well."

[37] PRO, E 351/3100-3258, Paymaster of the Royal Works (Tudor period accounts), ca. 1500-1625, for sums paid out. See also A. Feuillerat, *Documents Relating to the Office of Revels* (Louvain 1908) 175.

[38] For tutorial annuities and wages see Giles, *Works* (n. 14 above) 1.46. See also the references in nn. 14-18 above, for Cox, Cheke, Linacre and Lupset, as well as LP 19.1.846.

[39] For examples of such payments see PRO, E 101/421/6, nos. 34, 48; and LP 1.1557; 10.217. On the subject of diets see *ibid.* 4.1.281, 1577 (11), 1097.

[40] On secretarial fees see British Museum, Stowe MS 163 fol. 168, and Sloane MS 1520. F. M. G. Evans, *The Principal Secretary of State* (Manchester 1923) 352, prints excerpts from the manuscript fees schedules cited above and others as well.

[41] See LP 1.1.190 (39) for the deputy's post. During most of his tenure at Calais, Berners also held the chancellorship of the Exchequer, which he apprently converted into a sinecure. At any rate, he rarely visited England for any long time: see LP 5.787, 857, 1041, 1219, 1543, all related to Calais, and *ibid.* 1710, the single reference to the office at the Exchequer.

[42] For the significance of positions in the chamber see A. J. Slavin, *Politics and Profit* (n. 2 above) 28-32, and also British Museum, Additional MS 38136 fols. 77-78v, annuities "in consideracione boni et veri et fideli servicii."

[43] Dewar (n. 23 above) 29.

voice"—drew eight shillings a day, or about £140 per annum for more than twenty years.[44] Linacre, for attending the king's body, had a free of £50 per annum,[45] while Mason, who was employed to "plainly set forth to the world" English claims to suzerainty over Scotland, was handsomely rewarded in his antiquarian labors.[46] Those who held the title of "Crown Scholars" drew various allowances; Pole's grew from £12 per annum to £100 per annum for the period 1521 to 1530, while he studied and kept a remarkable academy in Paris and at Padua, to which flocked men who later made their mark as apologists of Reformation.[47] Diplomats were perhaps the most exploited and underpaid learned servants, if we listen to their own constant complaints about the difficulties and expenses of embassies abroad. They were, nonetheless, paid agents of the crown. They collected sums that varied from a few pounds a year to £2 per diem[48] while seeing to his master's interests at a foreign court, perhaps anticipating the famous later jest, that ambassa-

[44] For Heywood's rewards see LP 3.1.1186, 1262; 14.1.1326 (2); 16.379 (10), 1226 (14); 19.1.442 (10), 444 (6), 812 (109); 20.1.1335 (18); 20.2.1068 (50); and 21.1.504 (1). See also *State Papers of Henry VIII* (London 1838) 3.1186; J. P. Collier, *History of English Dramatic Poetry* (London 1879) 1.94, 116; and Sir F. Madden, *Privy Purse Expenses of the Princess Mary* (London 1831) 12, 62, 239.

[45] His stipend can be traced only after 1516: LP 1.2.1472, and 3.1.491, 1114, 1535.

[46] See Slavin, *Politics and Profit* 98; LP 17.898, 1033. Mason was soon to be named clerk of the council: *ibid.* 18.1.450, in addition to his duties as French secretary (*ibid.* 754) His annuities appear in LP 18.1.635 (65).

[47] On Pole's exhibition in Paris and Padua as king's scholar see LP 3.1.198 (1519) and 3.2. p. 1544. On the Padua "academy" kept in his household see Zeeveld (n. 3 above) 11-13, 43-49. Mason had a similar but less generous exhibition in Paris (LP 2.2.747), while Ascham, William Petre and the future archbishop Thomas Cranmer also traveled that path into politics.

[48] Ambassadors by custom were entitled to a per diem from their own government while also allowed expenses for journeys and reimbursement for loss suffered in such missions. In defense of the crown and against such complainants it should be stressed that once accepted by a foreign court the mission normally received its support at the expense of the receiving government. Thus per diem and other allowances actually constituted a reasonable reward for state service. What really troubled ambassadors was the fact that such allowances were usually not payable until the completion of a mission. On all problems of diplomatic service and payment see Garrett Mattingly, *Renaissance Diplomacy* (London 1955) 35, 147-149, 231-236. On the medieval background see A. Larson, "The Payment of English Ambassadors," *English Historical Review* 54 (1939) 406ff. Surely the most elegant complaints were voiced by Tunstal in More's behalf: "Master More at thys tyme at a low ebb, desyres by your grace to be sett afloat agayn."—9 July 1516, Tunstal-Henry VIII, British Museum, Cotton MS Galba B III, fol. 293v. More, in his own behalf, had complained wittily to Erasmus: "When I am on leave I must support two households . . . but no consideration was made for those I had to leave at home; and although I am, as you know, a kindly husband and an indulgent father and a gentle master, still I have never had the least success in persuading the members of my family to do without food for my sake." Allen, *Opus epist.* (n. 12 above) 2.338; trans. from E. F. Rogers, *St. Thomas More, Selected Letters* (New Haven 1961) no. 5.

dors were men sent "to lie abroad" for their king.[49] Members of parliament
received no fee from the crown; nor did sheriffs. Yet they enjoyed enormous
possibilities of profit making, which depended on many variables, chiefly
their own scruples, their health, and the endurance of the Tudor *pax perpetua*.[50]

Naturally we would like to know exactly what such sums meant to the
men who got them. We must take care, however, in translating Tudor income
into modern terms. Perhaps it is simply best to recall that in good times
a quarter of wheat could be had for five shillings, while beef and pork were
fixed at a halpenny a pound in 1533 and strong beer was a penny a gallon.[51]
Beyond questions of price and profit, however, stands the fact that these
sums were primarily evidence of the king's willingness to part with cash in
exchange for the talents that wise men put at the disposal of the commonwealth. Such payments marked the obligations of the prince to favor minstrel and bard only in a secondary sense. First of all stood the fact that the
crown employed learned men out of a commitment to improving the well-
being of the realm.[52]

Henry VIII was, it seems, reluctant to reward in the "Continental manner,"
by giving large sums for particular works completed. That is understandable,
however, not simply on the grounds of his not depleting his resources, of a
kind of parsimony often charged to Elizabeth. Roger Ascham, for whom
Elizabeth so mourned as to claim she would rather have tossed £10,000 into
the sea—an expensive sentiment—collected £1,350 in annuities and salaries
between 1540 and 1568.[53] Rather, it was part of an overt attempt to attract
men of learning and civic spirit to the permanent service of the Tudor state.
Once they were so attracted, rewards might take many forms other than simple
money payments. While forty shillings were paid out of the privy purse for

[49] Sir Henry Wotten's epigram: "Legatus est vir bonus peregre missus ad mentiendum
Reipublicae causa," quoted in Mattingly (n. 48 above) 314 n. 7.

[50] See the references in n. 2 above, especially MacCaffery.

[51] On the prices of commodities in Henry VIII's reign see James A. Froude, *History of
England from the Fall of Wolsey to the Defeat of the Spanish Armada* (London n.d.) 1.20-26.
For a modern analysis of inflation in prices and value translations see E. H. Phelps Brown
and S. V. Hopkins, "Seven Centuries of Prices of Consumables compared with Builders'
Wage Rates," *Economica* 23 (1956) 296-314.

[52] See the valuable study of Elisabethan patronage by Eleanor Rosenberg, *Leicester,
Patron of Letters* (New York 1955) 3-14 and especially her remarks about Henry VII and
Henry VIII, 4-6.

[53] The remark is quoted with no source mentioned, in DNB 1.659. Ascham's dire poverty
was relieved by a series of grants and annuities commencing in 1540 and illustrated in the
list that follows: 1540-1544, for trans. *New Testament Commentaries*, £2 per annum. 1545-
1568, for *Toxophilus*, £10 per annum; 1550-1553, Latin Secretary to Edward VI and for
past services, £10 per annum; 1553-1568, Latin Secretary to Mary I and Elizabeth I,
£20 per annum; for tutorial work, £20 per annum; reward for various services, £20 per
annum; 1560-1568, portion of Wetwang Prebend in York Cathedral, value unknown;
1553-1558, for special services to Mary I, £27 per annum.

one of Bale's plays[54]—we would like to believe it was one of his antipapal interludes or that on King John's trials and tribulations—it was more usual for the king to show his appreciation in other ways. Cheke received a life annuity upon his appointment as Edward VI's tutor.[55] Heywood, the mellifluous and affluent singer, collected various annuities until his death in 1580.[56] More, it is useful to recall, was once in the king's book for an annuity of £100.[57] While Secretary Smith claimed a modest pension of ten marks, beginning in 1527, he was soon to enjoy large rewards in return for service in a variety of offices.[58]

That is not to say that the men mentioned were uniformly happy with their lot. Cheke, shortly after Henry VIII's death, was granted the site and house of Spalding Priory, Lincolnshire, worth £675, to which he added by purchase the property of Saint John Baptist *iuxta* Clare, in Suffolk. He was content with them,[59] as he doubtless was with his career, which led from a Greek professorship at Cambridge to the principal secretaryship in 1553. But Ascham abominated his "poverty" with wit, despite Elizabeth's lavish thoughts.[60] Bale complained always about his financial disabilities.[61] Bar-

---

[54] For Bale there are few references in LP: but see 1.1.1503, 1512, 731 (20); 1.3.1964 (35) and *addenda* 304; 3.1.138; 4.2.3064; 9.230; 11.111; 13.1.40, 230, 307; 14.1.403 (47); 17.177, 258; and 21.1.643. On Cromwell's exploitation of Bale's anti-Roman writings see H. Barke, *Bales Kynge Johan und sein Verhältnis zur zeitgenössischen Geschichtsschreibung* (Wurzburg 1937); Jesse Harris, *John Bale, A Study of the Minor Literature of the Reformation* (Urbana 1940); H. C. McCusker, *John Bale, Dramatist and Antiquary* (Bryn Mawr 1942); J. H. P. Pafford, "Bale's *King John*," *Journal of English and Germanic Philology* 30 (1931) 176-178, and his "Two Notes on Bale's *King John*," *Modern Language Review* 56 (1961) 553-555; Rainer Pineas, "John Bale's Non-Dramatic Works of Religious Controversy," *Studies in the Renaissance* 9 (1962) 218-233.

[55] LP 14.1.864.

[56] LP 3.1.1186 (4), 4 February 1521, a grant of ten marks per annum is the first of a, succession of annuities; see also *ibid*, 1262 (479); 14.1.1326 (2), and 2.781; also 16.379 (10) 1226 (14); 19.1.442 (10), 444 (6) and 812 (109); 20.1.1335 (18); and 21.1.504 (1).

[57] More received a pension of £100 in 1518, retroactive to Michaelmas 1517 (29 September) and charged upon the "little customs" of London. He resigned his undersheriff's office at that time, considering himself to be the king's man in a special sense: see LP 2.1.874, and 2.2.4247. The annuity was perhaps promised earlier, as is reflected in one of More's letters in which a "handsome gift" from the king is mentioned: Rogers (n. 48 above) no. 5. But see Enid Routh, *Sir Thomas More and his Friends* (London 1934) 92-93, for the date, of this annuity.

[58] Dewar (n. 23 above) 13, for Dr. William Butts's role in bringing Smith to court. On the subject of his growing prosperity, *ibid*. 29-35.

[59] Strype, in his *Life of Sir John Cheke*, ed. Parker Society (London 1820) 36-37, speaks of these acquisitions as "no question a good pennyworthe."

[60] Ascham's *Toxophilus* earned gifts for him, among them an annuity of £10, because the "kinge did so well lyke it." Giles (n. 14 above) 2 no. 87. For other examples of Ascham's professions of poverty, see *ibid*. 1 no. 170; 2.86-87, 171.

[61] His own sense of misfortune and injury is illustrated in *The Vocacyon of John Bale to the Bysshopperycke of Ossorie* (n.p. 1553), reprinted in *The Harleian Miscellany* 6.

clay, on the other hand, praised Tudor munificence in more than one of his *Eclogues*.[62] Leonard Coxe had £10 per annum by way of a pension, the income of which rested on the lands of Cholsey Manor, a parcel of Reading Abbey.[63] Payments made in that way were typical, both with regard to the actual gifts of land and the derivation of a pension or annuity therefrom· Elyot had manors in Cambridgeshire, once held by Thomas Cromwell, a fitting memorial to Elyot's ambiguity and dexterity in politics.[64] Ferrers received Flamstead, Hertfordshire, and held the demesne of the priory of Markgate, worth some £30 per annum.[65] Heywood enjoyed several pensions charged against two Northamptonshire manors held by the king.[66] While allowing for the dramatic current of inflation that so upset personal and royal economy, we must assess these facts of employment against the backdrop of Sir Thomas Smith's reckoning that a thousand pounds surely made a baronial competence; forty pounds a knight; and ten pounds a gentleman; providing of course that the fellow in question held a university degree, a liberal profession, or was at least cleansed of the stain of manual labor. By that standard, or by one employed at the Heralds' College, where ten pounds

[62] After writing against scholasticism in his version of *Ship of Fools* ("on unprofytabul studies"), Barclay went on to enjoy the fruits of his own more profitable ones under Henry VIII. Cardinal Morton was also his patron, and he is mentioned along with Henry VII and Henry VIII in various parts of *Eclogues*, ed. Sir Sidney Lee (London 1928) esp. nos. 1, 3, 4. On Barclay's life and work see J. M. Berdan, "Alexander Barclay, Poet and Preacher," *Modern Language Review* 8 (1912) 289-300; William Nelson, "New Light on Alexander Barclay," RES 19 (1943) 59-61; Oswald Reissert, "Die Eklogen des Alexander Barclay," *Verein f. n. Sprachen in Hanover* 1 (1886) 14-31; J. R. Schultz, "Life of Alexander Barclay, *Journal of English and Germanic Philology* 18 (1916) 360-368; and Beatrice White, "A Note on Alexander Barclay," *Modern Language Review* 33 (1938) 161-170.

[63] This grant to Cox is dated 6 February 1541, six months after the death of his patron Thomas Cromwell, and signifies the continuity of what McConica has called the Erasmian reform tradition that flourished under Cromwell's leadership: LP 16.580 (51). For Cox's early career and dependence upon Cromwell see LP 3.1.153 (24); 4.3.3129; 7.659; 15.614, 706; and 16.580 (51). He was primarily a translator and rhetorician and held the post preceptor at Reading Grammar School (*ludus literarius*). His career has not attracted much attention, though his *The Arte of Rhetoryke* was the first such English work in the period. For Cox's contributions to the important Renaissance debate on eloquence and rhetoric see McConica (n. 5 above) 140-141 and 193-194, as well as W. S. Howell, *Logic and Rhetoric in England, 1500-1700* (Princeton 1956) 94-95.

[64] LP 15.1027 (16). Elyot had actually made the bargain before Cromwell's execution, on March 14 1540, and had paid £489 14s. 6d. of the price of £789 14s. 6d. Elyot's caution and self-serving instincts can be seen in his rededication of *The Castel of Helth* (London 1539), which in the first edition was dedicated to Cromwell.

[65] Ferrers was another of Cromwell's recruits. In 1538 he is listed among "the Gentlemen most mete to be daily waiters upon my lord privie seale" LP 13.2.1184 (ii). See also LP 21.1.1280 (fol. 7). Grants made to him are fully listed in DNB 18.383, but I cannot find mention of them in the calendared patent rolls printed in LP.

[66] See nn. 33-34 above. The first grants rested on the issues of Makesy and Torpull manors, Northamptonshire, and were made 4 February 1521: LP 3.1.1186 (4)

in free tenure or three hundred in moveables allowed an approach to be made in the matter of a coat of arms, our scholars were caught up in the upward social mobility of the age.

Apart from grants of land, office or pensions, monopolies played a part. A statute of 1511 had created a city monopoly on the licensing of all physicians within a radius circumscribing London by seven miles.[67] The original privilege was superseded seven years later by a royal patent, at which time, Linacre, John Chamber, and Ferdinando de Vittoria were named partners in the enterprise. The monopolists had perpetual succession, a common seal, lands and tenements, the right of suit, and, apart from fees, the right to collect fines of £5 for each act of unlicensed practice.[68]

An even more striking example of monopoly is that of the Cromwellian agent, Richard Grafton. After arranging the edition of *Matthew's Bible*, Grafton was given a patent covering the printing and distribution of the work, at twelve shillings "the copy bound," and ten shillings for the unbound work. When in 1540 the government decreed that all parish churches obtain a copy before All Souls Day of that year, how lucrative such favor could be was demonstrated. On Father Hughes's calculation of 8,071 parishes administering the needs of the English and Welsh faithful, Grafton ought to have grossed £4035/1/10, if all parishes acquired the unbound edition, and £4842/1/10, if all bought the bound version. The truth was doubtless that some parishes did not get any copy, while the others compromised aesthetic and economic consideration in a medley forever hidden from us. Grafton also gained a monopoly of the printing of church service books on 28 January, 1543, while three years later he and his partner Edward Whitchurch had the exclusive right to publish English and Latin primers as well as to print the gospels for Sundays and Saints' days. Whatever Elizabeth did or did not do, monopolists were off to a good start under Henry VIII. John Rogers, the actual translator of the "official" Bible of 1540, who may have offended the

---

[67] *Statutes of the Realm*, 3 Henry VIII chap. 11. This first enactment touching the practice of medicine is analyzed in Sir G. N. Clark, *A History of the Royal College of Physicians* (Oxford 1964) 55ff. City companies enjoyed monopolies varying in extent from three to eight miles of radius, with seven being the limit within which the city had sole right to limit markets. Linacre was doubtless aware of the preliminary discussion upon which the statute rested. The bishop of London (Fitzjames), dean of St. Paul's (Colet) and others of the church hierarchy had the licensing power; the two chief licensers were, of course, friends of Linacre. Further, the machinery of enforcement rested on the undersheriff of London, who was Thomas More.

[68] According to Clark 58, the reasons for the royal patent creating a "President and College" of the faculty of medicine in London stemmed from a sincere desire to improve conditions of health, without at all discounting the immediate personal desires of the would-be monopolists. Among the four other grantees we find three physicians (Nicholas Halswell, John Francis, and Robert Yaxley) and the powerful Cardinal Wolsey, to whom Linacre was the personal physician.

king's taste in divinity, as apart from state policy, went unrewarded until death took his king in 1547.[69]

For the ostensibly orthodox and loyal, the church was a broad corridor to power and even great wealth. Ascham was a prebendary of Wetwang in York Cathedral.[70] Bale was in succession rector at Bishopstoke, vicar at Swaffham (where he never resided), and, finally, bishop of Ossory.[71] Barclay, both poet and priest, held two vicarages at the same time, at least one necessarily in absentia, multiplying the initial fault by a second one, perhaps avarice. But he was also rewarded by the dean of the cathedral chapter at Canterbury with the rectory of All Hallows, London, the latter being an especially handsome living.[72] By way of abbreviation, Berners, Brinkelow,[73] Cavendish,[74] Cheke, Leonard Coxe, Elyot, Grafton, Hawes, and Ferrers never held ecclesiastical offices.

[69] On Grafton's relation to Cromwell, who had Ł400 of his own money in the printing adventures mentioned, see LP 12.2.122 (2), 593; 13.1.1249 and 2.58, 336, 722, 972-973; 14.2.782 (p. 332). For the post-Cromwellian monopolies see LP 16.366, 422, 424; 17.177; 18.384, 489, 100 (31); and 21.1.149 (12). John Rogers, the Marian martyr, prepared the so-called Mathew Bible, signing himself Thomas Mathew: on his career see J. L. Chester, *John Rogers* (London 1861) and William A. Clebsch, *England's Earliest Protestants* (New Haven 1964) 110, 193-194, 227, 306-307, 231.

[70] Giles (n. 14 above) 2.lxxv. The prebend's portion was granted six years before occupancy of the living, the long delay being caused by a suit of the old incumbent who was ousted for nonconformity. Ascham had his own roots in Yorkshire and a long history of connections there. Lee and Holgate, archbishops of York were early patrons (*ibid*. 1.x, xix).

[71] His first preferment came in 1534, when he was given the living of Thornden, Suffolk. In 1547 Bishopstoke in Hampshire came his way. He apparently resided in each of these places, but not in Swaffham: see H. Christmas's introduction to Bale's *Works*, Parker Society (London 1849).

[72] Barclay was ordained by Bishop Cornish after which he received the benefice of the College of Ottery, Saint Mary's, Devonshire. *Ship of Fools* was dedicated to the bishop. By 1514 he refers to himself as "prest of Ely" in his dedication of *The Myrrour of Good Maners*, a move probably inspired by the death of Cornish. By 1534 he had abandoned the aristocratic and lax Black Monks and taken the Franciscan habit at Canterbury, where he had a prebendary, while also accumulating vicarages at Great Baddow, Essex, and Wokey, Somersetshire, where he was an absentee pluralist, though each involved cure of souls. His final preferment to the City Rectory of All Hallows, London, induced him to reside there, however. These and other facts of Barblay's pluralism are related in DNB 1.1078-1079, as well as in Warton's *History of English Poetry*, ed. William Hazlitt (London 1871) 3.189-203. Barclay enjoyed Colet's friendship (LP 3.1.259) and Wolsey's favor (*Eclogue* 4).

[73] Henry Brinkelow (d. 1546) was a renegade Franciscan monk turned satirist. Like Grafton, he also made a good career in a city company (Mercers) and early adopted reform opinions, which he published under the pen name of Roderigo Mors. Mention of him and his work occurs in LP 18.1.538 (ii); 19.2.527 (30); 20.2.733n, and 21.1.95, 105-106, 347 (p. 170). His works were edited with an introductory essay for the Early English Text Society by J. M. Cowper (1874).

[74] George Cavendish's *Wolsey*, ed. R. Sylvester (London 1959), and his less famous *Metrical Visions* (London 1825-1827) have been little studied. Joseph Hunter attached a "Life" to the Singer edition of *Metrical Visions*. See LP 8.149 (54); 11.354 (ii); 16.1308

Richard Cox went through a profitable *cursus*, which included the arch-deaconate and bishopric of Ely, a prebend's share in Lincoln Cathedral, and many other posts. Cox also served the king's fine impartiality on the ecclesiastical commissions attesting the Spanish and Cleves divorces, and was one of the commissioners appointed by Elizabeth to visit Oxford in 1559! Finally, he was bishop of Ely, wherein he gave proof of having learned some lessons of the court well; he alienated episcopal lands to a number of courtiers, before wearily, if not contritely, resigning his see in 1580.[75] Heynes, whose career was less spectacular, was rector of Barrow, vicar of Stepney, rector of Fullham, canon of the collegiate chapter at Windsor, prebendary of Westminster and dean of Exeter.[76]

Nor were clerical offices held only by clergymen. Linacre held a rectorship, the portion of a prebendary and a living at Hawkhurst before he was in holy orders. After being ordained priest, he held in addition three rectorships, a precentorship and three prebends. Since he was personal physician to Henry VIII for almost the entire period covered by these appointments, one cannot help questioning the relationship between precept and practice in Tudor society, even among the most reform-minded and civic-spirited crown servants.[77]

Clearly pluralism was a striking aspect of royal favor as it touched these men, though some among them helped make the case upon which the dissolution of the monasteries rested. Lupset, for example, upon whom part of the burden of reform in the "common wele" was cast by Starkey in the justly famous *Dialogue Between Reginald Pole and Master Lupset*, was the incumbent of more than one benefice with cure of souls and a prebendary in Salisbury Cathedral.[78] Pole, Henry VIII's cousin, the other speaker in

---

(34); 20.2.910 (82), 1086 (46); and 21.1.1280 (fol. 43). On his book about Wolsey, the best study is P. L. Wiley, "Cavendish's *Life of Wolsey*," *Studies in Philology* 43 (1946) 121-146.

[75] His many appointments include a commission to sit on the Anne of Cleves divorce proceedings and benefices as follow: archdeacon of Ely, prebend of Lincoln Cathedral; dean of Lincoln Cathedral; rector of Harrow; dean of Christ Church, Oxford; canon of Windsor; dean of Westminster; chancellor of the University, Oxford and several vicarages. He was deprived of all benefices and annuities by virtue of complicity in the Lady Jane Grey plot (*Grey Friars' Chronicle* 82), and shortly thereafter went into exile. He made a second career under Elizabeth and rose to episcopal rank. For that career and his subsequent disgrace see Strype, *Annals of the Reformation*, app. 1.23.

[76] Cooper (n. 15 above) 1.80, 542.

[77] In 1509 he received the rectory of Mersham, Kent, the first of a steady stream of benefices to come to him. Until 1520 he was precentor of York Cathedral and also rector of Wigan, Lancashire. Yet it is clear that he was not in priest's orders until 22 December 1520, though he may have been a deacon as early as 1511. At least there is a letter from Ammonius to Erasmus relating that he had taken deacon's orders (LP 2.1.136). There is no evidence that he was resident in any benefice until he entered the priesthood in 1520, at which time he gave up medical studies and practice in order to reside in his parish and devote himself to his own spiritual concerns and the cure of souls.

[78] Lupset's preference for academic life and study abroad has been stressed by Gee

that earnest debate, had the deaneries of Exeter and College Church, Wim-
bourne Minster, Dorset, in 1513, although he was but eighteen years old and
a layman to boot. He also was a prebendary of Westminster Cathedral. And
the future curial reformer held those posts until 1537, when the king, angered
by Pole's rejection of the Reformation in England, confiscated these offices
as well as Pole's other pensions and preferments. Pole, of course, did not
enter the clerical estate until 1536, at which time Paul III named him Cardinal
Archdeacon of Saint Mary in Cosmedin, Rome.[79]

Other examples are easily adduced. Hugh Latimer first was noticed in
1530 as one of the theologians listed, ironically, by Bishop Gardiner, as favoring the divorce of Henry VIII.[80] He gained further favor by his work on the
commission of the same year which scrutinized objectionable books.[81] Soon
after he appears as a court preacher, collecting £2 for each sermon, with
traveling expenses to and from Cambridge. In 1531 he secured benefices
worth nearly £20 in Wiltshire.[82] By 1535, and despite a charge of heresy
lodged against him, he was a member of the bishop's bench, the king having
assented to his appointment as bishop of Worcester on 12 August.[83] In the
light of the papal tax of 2,000 marks imposed on the see, which was supposed
to be one-third of the income attached to the bishopric, Latimer was well

---

(n. 18 above) 100-102. He was, however, beneficed by Henry VIII on 31 January 1522,
with a pension out of Saint Mary's, York, just before being granted "a competent benefice"
at Ashton, Derbyshire: LP 3.2.2029, and 4.2.1989. On 26 March 1523 he received the rectory
of Saint Michael, Stratford-le-Hope, Essex (Wood, *Athenae oxonienses* 1.72)—all doubtless
due to Wolsey's favor. He served as tutor to the Cardinal's bastard son Thomas Winter
while the latter studied in Italy and France, ensuring that he would be an absentee pluralist.
In the last two months of his life he received several additional preferments from Wolsey
(*Registrum Thome Wolsey* 181). See also LP 5.80 (2) and Anon., *Gentleman's Magazine*
n.s. 45 (1890) 120, as well as G. Hennesey, ed., *Novum reportorium ecclesiasticum* (London
1899) 292.

[79] On Pole's benefices and his deanery before 1527 see Zeeveld (n. 3 above) 76, and LP
2.2.3943 as well as 3.1.1544. When still abroad until 1532, Pole maintained his friendship
with Henry VIII, the king in turn maintaining his cousin's exhibition and preferments.
Pole refused the inducement of the archbishopric of York, if only he would support the
divorce (LP 5.737). On the break with Henry, his reaction, Pole's acceptance of a cardinal's
hat and Henry's declaration of Pole's treason, see LP 11.1353 and 12.1.760, 939, 987-988,
996. See also the list of benefices given in Henry M. Smith, *Pre-Reformation England*
(London 1938) 35. Pole was cardinal deacon until he entered the priesthood in 1554 prior
to his return to England as legate to England and archbishop of Canterbury under Mary I.

[80] LP 4.3.6247. Before Gardiner's visit to Cambridge, Latimer had been in trouble for
holding heterodox opinions on several matters hotly debated there: LP 4.3.6162, 6176.

[81] LP 4.3.6367, 6402, 6411.

[82] *Ibid.* 5.629, 912; also "Treasurer of the Chamber, Accounts," p. 317 (21 March 1530,
20s); pp. 749, 751, Privy Purse Expenses (16 March, 15 and 18 September, for costs to
Cambridge, etc.)

[83] The *congé d'élire* went out on 3 August: LP 9.236 (4). Latimer's election was made
official with Henry's assent on 12 August (*ibid.* 236 (12).

provided for. By his own account, some £4,000 passed into the cathedral treasury by 1538.[84] Subsequent work for the crown entailed a place on the commission that sat to consider the Six Articles, a fact that underlines the pragmatic aspect of royal patronage as Henry VIII sought the broadest possible range of support for official formularies. Finally, like other "radicals," Latimer was forced from court in the years after Cromwell's fall to emerge once more in favor under the Protestant regime of Edward VI.[85] And he was handsomely paid: sermons delivered for the last Tudor king before rapt audiences at Paul's Cross netted sums varying between £20 and £320.[86]

John Ponet was another clerical pluralist, the holder of several rectories in 1545 and also one of the canons of Canterbury Cathedral at that time. He did resign one of his trio of rectories when the Canterbury post came his way.[87] But this exemplary self-denial must be balanced against the actions of one of the great civic-minded humanists of the day, Sir Thomas Smith. While holding the Regius Professorship of Civil Law at Cambridge, that worthy also "served" as a prebendary of Lincoln Cathedral—something notable, since he was not only an absentee, but was never in holy orders. Where scholars once found a "renegade priest" giving up a clerical career for study and state service under Somerset, Mary Dewar has found only a studious but ambitious layman, with a finger in the clerical jam pot.[88]

Thus twelve of the men on our list held sixty-three church livings, varying in income from a few pounds a year to fabulous rent rolls and other revenues accruing to an episcopal incumbent. On our list are three bishops, five deans, two priors, thirteen rectors, six vicars, four canons of chapter, three royal chaplains, twelve prebendaries, five unclassified "livings," eight members of ecclesiastical commissions, with work touching the essence of church polity and religious reform and, finally, one precentor. The number of absentee positions is nearly half the total. While only some held office in violation of church law, almost all of the men involved were pluralists.[89]

---

[84] Latimer-Cromwell, 24 December 1538: LP 13.2.1133.

[85] On Latimer's place in the ecclesiastical politics of the 1530s see Dickens (n. 31 above) 176-178.

[86] Latimer's long association with Edward VI was foreshadowed in his letter to Cromwell written upon Edward's birth in 1537: LP 12.2.894. His high place under Somerset can be traced in his own *Sermons* and in Allan G. Chester, *Hugh Latimer, Apostle to the English* (Philadelphia 1954).

[87] See LP 17.611; 20.1.333 and 2.418 (72); also 21.1.1536 and 2.199 (17), 200 (27).

[88] On Smith's ecclesiastical preferments, all held without his ever taking orders of any kind (Elizabeth noted his "benet and Colet be but a matriculation into the University"), see Mary Dewar (n. 23 above) 29-31.

[89] From the thirteenth century on, pluralism in benefices with cure of souls has been condemned. But the provision of deans and administrative persons in priest's orders or administrators not in priest's orders was often allowed *in pluralitate*. This was the case with Pole, Cox and Smith's friend Ponet. But posts involving cure of souls, rectories and

It seems clear, therefore, that the church continued to be an avenue of advancement for learned but loyal men at Henry VIII's court and in his government after 1534. Any large claims about the Reformation driving clerics to cover, or their being replaced suddenly by bureaucrats and purely lay officials more suited to the business of reform in church and state, must remain doubtful. And it seems likely that when a fuller examination is made of the hundreds of lesser men helping in the government of England, that view will be further undermined.

While this essay has up to a point dealt with little details and arid statistics, its main purpose remains clear: to get some firm idea of the participation in government opened to learned men and also to understand the use to which their special skills were put in behalf of the Tudor commonwealth. We recall that our poets, scholars, historians, dramatists, translators and educators were also justices of the peace, ambassadors, church officials, servants of the crown in numerous capacities, and that a few of their fellowship held high public office, including the chancellorship of England and the secretary-ship of state.

Viewed in a different prospect, other interesting facts emerge. Only six men of twenty-five were first patronized by the king: Berners, Grafton, Heynes, Pole, Smith, and Leonard Coxe. Balanced against that quarter, we find a third brought to notice by a member of the bishops' bench, discovered either by Wolsey, Bainbridge, Morton, Lee, Warham, or Cranmer. And that number includes Ascham, Barclay, Cavendish, Richard Cox, Latimer, Lupset, and Ponet. The remainder owed their first advancement neither to the church nor to the king. The discerning eye of Dr. Butts, Henry VIII's shrewd physician, or Sir Thomas More, or John de Vere, the earl of Oxford, and, most notably, Thomas Cromwell, also scouted talent for the Tudor imperium.

It may also be said that Henry VIII's *court* actively patronized humanists and brought them into government. But it would certainly misrepresent the data to draw from it the conclusion that Henry VIII was a new Maecenas or to overpraise his personal role in the movement that brought humanists to serve the state in a time of unprecedented crisis. When we consider the data carefully, we shall perhaps agree with Professor Elton who gave Henry VIII high marks in Renaissance kingcraft while remembering that Cromwell and Wolsey did much to insure that the crown received more than good counsel from humanists. And we shall perhaps agree as well with Douglas Bush's

---

vicarages, for example, were not to be held by absentee pluralists. Statute created loopholes by which "choppe churche" clergy and nonclergy alike held plural benefices: donors and patrons were pleased with 21 Henry VIII chap. 13, ostensibly intended to support earlier legislation and canon law, but which allowed exceptions to be made in the case of royal chaplains, literati and other royal clerks, even if the benefice involved cure of souls. See Henry M. Smith (n. 79 above) 33-37, and Margaret Bowker, *The Secular Clergy of the Diocese of Lincoln, 1495-1520* (Cambridge, Eng. 1968) chaps. 1-3.

remark that Tudor humanism took a practical turn and that government was especially on the lookout for men who could bring something of value to public business and its conduct.[90]

Men like Barclay knew that their studies could be profitable and that counsel, service, and reward were interwoven strands in the thread of learning. They also knew that men reluctant to serve and out of sympathy with policy were more often broken than prized. The state was being made better by the work of men farmed by ministers, paid by the court, and adornments to England. But there was always the voice of More raising again the question who the good man and what the good state were. The road to government led through the academy by diverse paths of learning and patronage. There were danger signs along the way, however. And the study of patronage, public service, social origins and mobility is in reality part of a larger study.

That study might well be called a sociology of Tudor humanism. When we have pursued in greater depth than was possible here all of the questions about birth, education, marriage, wealth, and participation in government that now permeate the study of Italian humanism, we shall then want to go a step further. We shall want to know whether it is possible to explain why certain humanists put aside the civic ideal of participation in public life.[91] For alienation from government is the other side of the coin of participatión in an age that saw the waxing articulateness of the English citizen. Inasmuch as humanism embodied an ideal of civic virtue in England, we must in the future try to relate the changing temper of social and political life to humanistic ideas. We must try to understand participation and alienation in terms of the relations between ideology and action. Inasmuch as their social origins, education, and employment brought men to measure themselves against the humanistic ideal of an active concern for the commonwealth, we may hope to gain understanding of why some lived out their lives in harness while others sought exile or were reduced to sad and melancholy contemplation.

Department of History
University of California
Los Angeles, California 90024, U.S.A.

---

[90] Douglas Bush, "Tudor Humanism and Henry VIII," *University of Toronto Quarterly* 7 (1937) 162-167.

[91] Mark Curtis, "The Alienated Intellectuals of Early Stuart England," *Past and Present* 23 (1962) 25-49, made a start for an important period, and promptly drew critical fire in *Past and Present* 26 (1963) and 28 (1964) from Joan Simon and Hugh Kearney.

SIR THOMAS ELYOT ON PLATO'S AESTHETICS

•

by Morriss Henry Partee

Sir Thomas Elyot's discussion of poetry in *The Boke Named the Governour* (1531) and in *The Defence of Good Women* (1540) antedates by about fifty years the controversy in England over the value of poetry. His comments directly influenced such later critics as William Webbe and Sir Philip Sidney.[1] But Elyot's use of philosophic authority contains an apparent discrepancy. This man, who studied and revered Plato, cites the philosopher to defend poetry in the *Governour*. Later, with no apologies, he alludes to Plato to condemn poetry in *The Defence of Good Women*. Similar examples of this inconsistency abound. Thomas Nashe,[2] Stephen Gosson,[3] and Thomas Lodge[4] cite Plato's famous banishment of poetry from the well-run state. On the other hand, Sir Philip Sidney,[5] William Webbe,[6] and George Chapman[7] think that Plato generally approves of poetry. The confusion arises not from an unavailability of his dialogues, but rather from an ambiguity inherent in Plato's aesthetics. Although the spurious *Axiochus* was the only Platonic dialogue translated into English during the sixteenth century, Marsilio Ficino's translation of the dialogues into Latin, finished in 1468 and published in 1484, had made Plato readily accessible to Western scholars. Therefore, the present

---

[1] Theodore Stenberg in "Sir Thomas Elyot's Defense of the Poets," *University of Texas Studies in English* 6 (1926) 121-145 argues that Elyot should be considered as the first great literary critic in England, both for his influence and for the intrinsic merit of his discussion of poetry. The standard works on Elyot's Platonism in general are Friedrich Dannenberg, *Das Erbe Platons in England bis zur Bildung Lylys* (Berlin 1932) and Kurt Schroeder, *Platonismus in der englischen Renaissance vor und bei Thomas Eliot* (Berlin 1920).

[2] "Preface to R. Greene's *Menaphon*," in *The Works of Thomas Nashe*, ed. Ronald B. McKerrow (London 1910) 3.323.

[3] *The Schoole of Abuse*, ed. Edward Arber (London 1868) 20.

[4] *A Reply to Stephen Gosson's Schoole of Abuse : In Defence of Poetry, Musick, and Stage Plays*, in *The Complete Works of Thomas Lodge*, Hunterian Club (Glasgow 1883) 1.6, 7, 14. Indeed, Lodge calls upon almost exactly the same material to attack Plato that Sidney uses to defend him.

[5] *Prose Works*, ed. Albert Feuillerat (Cambridge 1963) 3.34.

[6] *A Discourse of Englishe Poetrie*, ed. Edward Arber (London 1870) 21, 22, et passim.

[7] "Preface to *Seaven Bookes of the Iliades of Homere*" (1598), in *Chapman's Homer*, ed. Allardyce Nicoll (New York 1956) 1.508.

examination of Elyot's ambivalent interpretation will illustrate the difficulty that Plato's aesthetics presented to the Renaissance and indeed to every critic since Plato's time.

The underlying tenets of Elyot's poetics as well as his citations of Plato reveal a basic sympathy with the philosopher's attitude toward art. The conflict between a love of poetry's beauty and a demand for morality in art leads both men into a complex and almost contradictory statement of aesthetics. Since Plato leaves no single work devoted to art, his thought has caused unusually diverse interpretations.[8] His aesthetics possesses a unity only within the context of the dialogues as a whole.[9] On one hand, Plato lauds the poet's divine inspiration (*Ion* 533-536, *Symposium* 209, *Phaedrus* 245), and recognizes a legitimate role for myths and selected excerpts of poetry in the education of the young.[10] On the other hand, he banishes poets from the best state imaginable (*Republic* 10.595).[11] Elyot's seeming contradiction in citing Plato comes simply from his endorsing the literal statements of these dialogues with little attempt to probe into their meaning or context. But Elyot maintains—as did Plato—a consistent attitude towards poetry's value to man and society. Although Elyot ultimately accepts art, he agrees with Plato's primary concern that poetry be judged by moral standards.

The use of Plato by such an eminent humanist and literary critic as Elyot illustrates the highest degree of sophistication toward this philosopher current in Tudor England. Plato's authority, along with that of Aristotle and Horace, provided the Renaissance with the classical background for their critical theories.[12] While they may read into Aristotle's *Poetics* and Horace's *Ars poetica* a dogmatism not originally present, Renaissance critics as a rule

---

[8] Bernard Weinberg in *A History of Literary Criticism in the Italian Renaissance* (Chicago 1961) 1.250, observes, "Unlike those Renaissance critics who attached themselves to Horace's *Ars poetica* or to Aristotle's *Poetics* as the basis for their critical thinking, the Platonic critic was essentially a man without a text. I mean by this that he was unable, as were his compeers, to derive his critical doctrine point by point from a central text, to concentrate his efforts of exegesis and commentary and interpretation upon that text, to discover within it all the answers to a host of artistic and technical questions."

[9] Minor inconsistencies can be readily found. For example, Plato condemns dithyrambic poetry as merely pleasurable in *Gorgias* 502, the writers of dithyrambs being ignorant imitators in *Apology* 22. Yet in *Republic* 3.394 and *Laws* 3.700, he finds this form of poetry highly praiseworthy.

[10] See Ludwig Edelstein, "The Function of Myth in Plato's Philosophy," *Journal of the History of Ideas* 10 (1949) 463-481.

[11] While he does recognize honorable tales of gods and noble men (*Republic* 10.607) Plato has banished his favored poet Homer, and recognizes no one to take his place. I have discussed this point more fully in "Plato's Banishment of Poetry," *Journal of Aesthetics and Art Criticism* 20 (1970) 209-222.

[12] See G. Gregory Smith, *Elizabethan Critical Essays* (London 1959) 1.lxxii and C. S. Lewis, *English Literature in the Sixteenth Century* (London 1954) 18-20. A much fuller study may be found in Weinberg (n. 8 above) 1.71-634, 2.635-714.

propose consistent and reasonable interpretations of their aesthetics. But the critics' oversimplified approach to the dialogues does a particular injustice to Plato's thought. Moreover, the direct indebtness of Renaissance critics to Plato bears little resemblance to the poets' indirect reliance on him in their art.[13] Plato's theory of love and beauty informs most Elizabethan love poetry after Spenser and Sidney.[14] To a lesser extent, his doctrine of poetic inspiration finds expression in Spenser's "October" eclogue[15] as well as in Sidney's *Defence of Poesie*. Thus, Plato—directly through the *Ion, Symposium,* and *Phaedrus* and indirectly through such works as Plotinus's *Enneads* 1.6 and 5.8—became the patron of poets in the Renaissance. Nevertheless, while most Renaissance defenders of poetry embraced Plato's doctrine of inspiration, few attempted to reconcile this element of his thought either with his censorship or with his ultimate condemnation of poetry.[16]

The complexity of Plato's statement on art has prevented even modern scholars from fully recognizing the basis for Elyot's interpretation of Plato. For instance, John M. Major argues that despite Elyot's broad knowledge of the dialogues, his comments on Plato's aesthetics show a mistaken reliance on the philosopher. Major assumes that Plato's expulsion of the poets in the *Republic* 10 represents a consistent position with regard to his other statements on poetry.[17] Then, referring to Elyot's apparently paradoxical interpretation of Plato, he states, "If ever there were proof of Elyot's almost instinctive deference to the authority of Plato, it is here in this fantastic split attitude of his toward poetry, in which he invokes the philosopher's name first in order to vindicate poetry and then to condemn it. In the process,

---

[13] It is generally recognized that various strains of Neoplatonism rather than Platonism influenced the poets of the sixteenth century. Recently, scholars have tried to distinguish the direct from the indirect Platonic influence on Renaissance theology and poetry. Among others, Paul O. Kristeller, *Renaissance Thought: The Classic, Scholastic, and Humanist Strains* (New York 1961) 48-69, Raymond Klibansky, *The Continuity of the Platonic Tradition During the Middle Ages* (London 1939) 13-47, and Robert Ellrodt, *Neoplatonism in the Poetry of Spenser* (Geneva 1960) 7-24, have pointed out the problems involved in the interpretation of literary Platonism. Many so-called "Platonists" may have had no direct access to the philosopher's thought; others may modify Plato's thought almost beyond recognition.

[14] Paul Shorey, *Platonism, Ancient and Modern* (Berkeley 1938) 178.

[15] Spenser describes the power that music and society have over man. Besides restraining the lawless impulses of youth, art may hold their minds entranced. E. K.'s gloss, however, moves further away from Plato's thought by mentioning the theory of inspiration here. E. K. states that the creator of heavenly beauty is the poet "at whose wonderful gyft al men being astonied and as it were rauished with delight, thinking (as it was indeed) that he was inspired from above, called him *vatem.*" Plato does not discuss the role of divine inspiration in the serious education of the young.

[16] And even within *Republic* 10 the consistency of Plato's argument may be questioned. See Carleton L. Brownson, *Plato's Studies and Criticisms of the Poets* (Boston 1920) 89-97.

[17] John M. Mayor, *Sir Thomas Elyot and Renaissance Humanism* (Lincoln, Nebr. 1964) 267.

incidentally, he manages to anticipate most of the key arguments used by both sides in the controversy over poetry that arose later in the century."[18] Elyot, however, no more has a "fantastic split attitude" than does Plato. Although rhetorically motivated, Elyot correctly states that the *Republic* banishes all poets.[19] But he does not grapple with Plato's argument in *Republic* 10 that poetry misleads the ignorant and arouses the baser emotions of the citizens. Immediately limiting his censure of poetry in The *Defence of Good Women* to the clearly immoral, Elyot's comments here are largely consistent with those in the *Governour*.[20] By not recognizing that Plato's explicit condemnation of poetry runs counter to his tacit sanction of its beauty, Elyot exposes a critical problem that even Sir Philip Sidney's more extensive examination of Plato in the *Defence of Poesie* does not resolve completely.[21]

I

First, the *Governour*. Here Elyot alludes to that side of Plato which endeared him to poets and to the defenders of poetry. After lamenting the fortunes of poetry in England, Elyot cites the respect that antiquity gave to poetry: "Poetry was the first philosophy that euer was knowen: wherby men from their childhode were brought to the raison howe to lyue well, lernynge therby nat onely maners and naturall affections, but also the wonderfull werkes of nature, mixing serious mater with thynges that were pleasaunt: as it shall be manifest to them that shall be so fortunate to rede the noble warkes of Plato and Aristotle, wherin he shall fynde the autoritie of poetes frequently alleged."[22] Elyot may have in mind either Plato's implicit respect for poets or his explicit theory of education. When quoting poetry in the course of an argument, Plato almost always gives poets and their work high praise.[23] In addition, although never admitting value to an entire work of

[18] *Ibid.* 268.

[19] Perhaps the best discussion of Plato's intent may be found in Eric A. Havelock, *Preface to Plato* (Cambridge, Mass. 1963) 3-19. See also N. R. Murphy, *The Interpretation of Plato's Republic* (Oxford 1951) 224-246.

[20] George Pace in "Sir Thomas Elyot Against Poetry," *Modern Language Notes* 56 (1941) 597-599, thinks that Elyot does not change his attitude toward poetry. He bases his argument on the assumption that Elyot is merely following a convention rather than expressing his personal beliefs.

[21] Sidney chooses to emphasize Plato's doctrine of inspiration. Slighting Plato's reasoning that poetry is an imitation of the physical world, he then can state that Plato condemns only poetry not useful to the state.

[22] Sir Thomas Elyot, *The Boke Named the Governour*, ed. H. H. S. Croft (London 1883) 1.121-122. Further references to the *Governour* will be given in the text.

[23] The *Lysis* 212-214, *Meno* 81 and *Laws* 3.682 give sincere praise to the poets; *Protagoras* 316, *Republic* 3.366, *Timaeus* 40 and *Theaetetus* 152, 179 refer ironically to their greatness.

art, Plato recognizes that some poetic sayings encourage a commendable harmony in the soul.[24]

Elyot then mentions Plato's doctrine of poetic inspiration, a theory that links Muse, poet, and audience in a chain of divine influence.[25] According to Elyot, Cicero and Plato hold that poetry springs from divine inspiration: "In poetes was supposed to be science misticall and inspired, and therfore in latine they were called *Vates*, which worde signifyeth as moche as prophetes. And therfore Tulli in his Tusculane questyons [*Tusculanae disputationes*] supposeth that a poete can nat abundantly expresse verses sufficient and complete, or that his eloquence may flowe without labour wordes wel sounyng and plentuouse, without celestiall instinction, whiche is also by Plato ratified" (*Governour*, 1.122). Although Plato indeed pays tribute to the inexplicable beauty of poetry, Elyot fails to recognize that Plato feels even the most noble inspiration to be beyond the poet's control. Evidence of Plato's reservations about poetry appears throughout his comments on inspiration. For instance, the *Ion*, a dialogue of great influence in the Renaissance, attacks the rhapsodist, the reciter of poetry, for presuming to have knowledge; the discussion of poetic inspiration is secondary. Similarly, the poet may have divine madness, but does not understand what he says.[26] Only the *Phaedrus* 245 and *Symposium* 209 attribute to the poet an understanding similar to that of the philosopher.

Thus, in the *Governour* Elyot legitimately cites Plato's major, if qualified, approval of poetry. In *The Defence of Good Women*, on the other hand, Elyot recognizes Plato's unqualified mistrust of poetry, a doctrine found only in *Republic* 10. He follows a Platonic argument perhaps known to the Renaissance chiefly through Saint Augustine.[27] In the *Defence*, Candidus, probably reflecting Elyot's attitude towards women, attacks Caninus's use of poetic authority against the honor of women:

> The authors whom ye so moche do set by, for the more part were poetes, which sort of persons among the latines & grekes were neuer had but in smal reputation. For I could neuer rede that in any weale publike of notable memory, Poetes were called to any honorable place, office, or dignite. Plato out of the publike weale whiche he had deuysed, wolde haue all poetes vtterly excluded. Tulli, who next vnto Plato excelled all other in vertue and eloquence, wolde not haue in his publyke weale any poetes admitted. The cause why they were soo lyttell estemed was, for as moche as the more parte of theyr inuencions consysted in leasynges, or in sterynge

[24] See, for instance, *Republic* 3.399-403.

[25] J. G. Warry's chapter, "The Poetic Process" in his *Greek Aesthetic Theory* (London 1962) 68-82 stresses Plato's linking of the true poet with the philosopher.

[26] Cf. *Apology* 22 and *Laws* 4.719.

[27] The eighth book of his *City of God* discusses Plato at some length. One popular version was a Latin text edited and annotated by Vives, published in 1522.

vp of wanton appetytes, or in pourynge oute, in raylynge, theyr
poyson of malyce. For with theyr owne goddes and goddesses
were they so malaparte, that with theyr aduoutries they fylled great
volumes.[28]

So Elyot not only states that Plato banishes poets, but echoes his chief objections—poets tell lies, they cater to base appetites, and they tell false tales
about the gods. Elyot even refers to the lack of respect which cities have
accorded to poets (*Republic* 10.599). Here, of course, Elyot qualifies his praise
of the poet's moral lessons in the *Governour*, by suggesting that some men
may incorrectly interpret the artistic presentation of immorality.

Nevertheless, Elyot, like almost all Renaissance critics, ignores the episte-
mological argument that Plato uses to attack poetry. When considering
poetry as imitation of the Forms of virtuous action rather than as a copying
of the physical world, Plato has given poetry qualified support.[29] But in
Republic 10.595-603 Plato analyzes poetry's relationship to the physical
world, and naturally he finds poetry lacking substance. Plato reasons that
a god makes the idea of a bed, a carpenter imitates this idea, and the artist
copies the carpenter's product.[30] Plato would—as Elyot states—"haue all
poetes vtterly excluded" when poetry deceives the young and the inexperienced.
After proposing this theory of imitation which demands complete exclusion of
poetry, Plato continues his argument by stating in *Republic* 10.603-608 that
all poetry, including that of Homer, panders to the lower part of man's soul.

Ignoring Plato's disparagement of poetry as an imitation of an imitation,
Elyot would answer the philosopher's objections to immorality in poetry.
Like Plato, he bases his mistrust of poets on the likelihood of their encouraging
vice. Poetry may, however, stimulate virtue as well. More tolerant than
Plato, Candidus condemns poets only "whan they excede the termes of honestye.
But if they make verses conteynynge quicke sentences, voyd of rybauldry,
or in the commendation of vertue, some praty allegory, or do set forthe any
notable story, than do I set by them as they be well worthy" (*Defence* 17-18).
Obviously not probing beneath the surface of Plato's final statement in *Republic* 10, Elyot's argument parallels the tentative acceptance of poetry in
Republic 2 and 3. In *The Defence of Good Women*, therefore, Elyot would
not banish all poets. He condemns only poetry devoted to the "sterynge vp
of wanton appetytes."

[28] Edwin J. Howard, ed. (Oxford, Ohio 1940) 13-14. All further references will be from
this edition.

[29] *Republic* 3.394-399. See J. Tate, "'Imitation' in Plato's *Republic*," *Classical Quarterly*
22 (1928) 16-23.

[30] Discussions of this perplexing argument may be found in R. G. Collingwood, *The
Principles of Art* (Oxford 1938) 46-52 and Rupert C. Lodge, *Plato's Theory of Art* (London
1953) 167-191.

II

Elyot has shown familiarity with three aspects of Plato's aesthetics: his love of poetry, his doctrine of inspiration, and his reservations about the value of poetry. An examination of his underlying principles shows, however, that Elyot consistently gives poetry more credit than does Plato. The *Governour*, like *The Defence of Good Women*, evaluates poetry in moral terms. But the *Governour* defends poetry against accusations of its occasional immorality like those suggested in the *Defence*. Despite their common orientation to morality, Elyot differs from Plato on the permissible amount of indiscriminate reading of the ancients. Plato would censure questionable passages from all past, present, and future poetry. Elyot would allow the reader to interpret and to censor for himself passages of dubious moral worth: "But sens we be nowe occupied in the defence of Poetes, it shall nat be incongruent to our mater to shewe what profite may be taken by the diligent reding of auncient poetes, contrary to the false opinion, that nowe rayneth, of them that suppose that in the warkes of poetes is contayned nothynge but baudry, (suche is their foule worde of reproche), and unprofitable leasinges" (*Governour* 1.123). He consistently recognizes—as does Plato—that poetry may contain material besides ribaldry and lies. Elyot uses the presence of some virtuous passages to defend poetry against a somewhat hostile environment. The comments of Plato, on the other hand, spring from his defense of philosophy against a culture that commonly regarded poetry as one of the highest authorities.[31] Accordingly, even morality in poetry cannot excuse its antagonism to philosophy.

Elyot assigns wider boundaries to the province of good poetry than does Plato. Throughout the *Republic* and the *Laws*, Plato attacks "realistic" art; only encomia and poetry directly encouraging excellence should be allowed. Elyot, on the other hand, gives the common man broader powers of interpretation. The imaginative presentation of evil deeds serves as a warning: "First, comedies, whiche they suppose to be a doctrinall of rybaudrie, they be undoutedly a picture or as it were a mirrour of man's life, wherin iuell [evil] is nat taught but discouered; to the intent that men beholdynge the promptnes of youth unto vice, the snares of harlotts and baudes laide for yonge myndes, the disceipte of seruantes, the chaunces of fortune contrary to mennes expectation, they beinge therof warned may prepare them selfe to resist or preuente occasion" (*Governour* 1.124-125). By relying heavily on man's critical ability, Elyot makes the presentation of vice an integral part of poetry's moral teaching. Plato, however, condemns representations of evil, for the soul has no faculty for rejecting false impressions once implanted.[32]

---

[31] The *Protagoras* 325 gives a description of the role of poetry in education during Plato's time. Werner Jaeger discusses this matter in *Paideia: The Ideals of Greek Culture*, trans. Gilbert Highet (New York 1943) 2.211-230.

[32] See *Republic* 4.431, 434-441, *Philebus* 39, and *Laws* 9.863.

Elyot allows poetry that contains some quantities of "ribaudry" if enough profitable matter is included. Comedy contains wise sayings as well as examples of vice. The manner of the presentation of vice, not the mere fact of portrayal, determines its moral value (*Governour* 1.125-126):

> Semblably remembering the wisedomes, aduertisements, counsailes, dissuasion from vice, and other profitable sentences, most eloquently and familiarely shewed in those comedies, undoubtedly there shall be no litle frute out of them gathered. And if the vices in them expressed shulde be cause that myndes of the reders shulde be corrupted: than by the same argumente nat onely entreludes in englisshe, but also sermones, wherin some vice is declared, shulde be to the beholders and herers like occasion to encreace sinners.

Elyot rhetorically assumes that "entreludes" present vice in the same manner as the sermons; art imaginatively reproves evil just as a sermon explicitly warns against sin. Plato, on the other hand, fears the effects of any artistic presentation of the trivial or the corrupt. Artistic beauty leads too often to mere pleasure. Even his dialogues must not be taken as literal truth; they point to a reality beyond the words. Otherwise, some of his own dialogues must be forbidden because, as Sir Philip Sidney observes, the *Phaedrus* and the *Symposium* seem to "authorize abhominable filthinesse."[33]

Furthermore, unlike Plato, Elyot attempts to justify even poetry of dubious merit. Denying the possibility of an objective response to poetry, Plato would protect the unwary and the uneducated from the ravishing pleasure of art. Elyot, on the other hand, begins with the man whose wisdom enables him to reject improper poetry (*Governour* 1.129-130):

> No wyse man entreth in to a gardein but he sone espiethe good herbes from nettiles, and treadeth the nettiles under his feete whiles he gadreth good herbes. Wherby he taketh no damage, or if he be stungen he maketh lite of it and shortly forgetteth it. Semblablye if he do rede wanton mater mixte with wisedome, he putteth the warst under foote and sorteth out the beste, or, if his courage be stered or prouoked, he remembreth the litel pleasure and gret detriment that shulde ensue of it, and withdrawynge his minde to some other studie or exercise shortly forgetteth it.

Here Elyot indirectly suggests the Platonic concept that the philosophical intellect should control the baser emortions. Nevertheless, while Plato analyzes poetry's function in educating the young and the ignorant, he does not discuss any profit in imaginative poetry for those who already possess wisdom.[34]

---

[33] *Defence of Poesie* 33.
[34] In his discussions of art in *Republic* 2 and 3, Plato does not recognize any period of

Therefore, Elyot brings to the forefront a theme only tentatively stated by Plato: knowledge leads to the proper response to poetry. The *Laws* 8.829 would allow the most virtuous of men to compose and to judge poetry, but reason and the laws must control their work. More leniently, Elyot makes a thorough knowledge of poetry essential to a full education: "So all thoughe I do nat approue the lesson of wanton poetes to be taughte unto all children, yet thynke I conuenient and necessary that, whan the mynde is become constante and courage is asswaged, or that children of their naturall disposition be shamfaste and continent, none auncient poete wolde be excluded from the leesson of suche one as desireth to come to the perfection of wysedome" (*Governour* 1.131). Both Elyot and Plato pay tribute to didactic sayings from the venerable past. But while Elyot accepts some immoral poetry in order to gain these wise sentences, Plato ultimately condemns all poetry except that which directly encourages noble deeds and moral excellence.

In short, Elyot agrees with Plato that poetry must be judged for its moral worth; beauty is a secondary consideration. They are acutely aware that bad poetry does exist, and both warn against ribaldry. Similarly, both men praise poetic inspiration to some extent. Finally, they attribute some authority to poets in education and tacitly approve of poetry by their frequent allusions. The two men disagree primarily on the proper scope of poetry. Elyot divides poetry into the good and the bad; Plato into that which reveals truth and that which only mirrors the physical world. As a result, Elyot can allow complex and ambiguous art, for the wise man will easily reject the irrelevant or the evil. Plato, on the other hand, allows only poetic excerpts which directly produce harmony and virtue in the hearers.

To conclude, Elyot's apparently contradictory citation of Plato stems from a problem inherent in the philosopher's statement of aesthetics. Like most Renaissance critics, Elyot recognizes that Plato acutely felt the power and beauty of poetry. Yet he is also aware of Plato's strict regulations against immoral or frivolous poetry. But because of the tendency of the Renaissance mind to synthesize diverse ideas, Elyot glosses over a distinction between the divine beauty of poetry and the effects of poetry on fallible men, a problem never fully solved even by Plato.

Department of English
University of California
Los Angeles, California 90024, U.S.A.

---

transition from childhood to maturity, the time that poetry might be expected to reinforce the partly aware intellect. *Republic* 7.537 speaks of some change, but does not recognize any gradual acquisition of knowledge. See R. Hackforth, "The Modification of Plan in Plato's *Republic*," *Classical Quarterly* 7 (1913) 267.

FOREIGN SOURCES FOR THE ELIZABETHAN NOTION OF THE SPANIARD

•

by Paul A. Jorgensen

"It is recorded of the Spaniard," declared Sir Francis Hastings late in Elizabeth's reign, "that in dissimulation he surpasseth all nations, till he have attayned to his purpose, and when he can once prevayle, he goeth beyond them all in oppression and tyrannie: also that in pryde and carnal voluptuousness, no nation cometh neer him, and these be his qualities."[1] The description is noteworthy, perhaps, not so much for its details as for its tone of utter conviction. And although this tone was challenged by the pro-Spanish Robert Parsons, Sir Francis was able to reply that all these "properties are imputed to [the Spaniards] by sundrie imprinted books," and that whereas the enemy "speaks of our land untrulie, . . . wee of them report nothing but knowne truth."[2]

Sir Francis was not alone in his assurance. In *The Three Lords and Three Ladies of London*, a morality depicting English preparation in 1588, Policy takes for granted that his audience is equally secure in its knowledge:

> I need not tel thee, they are poore and proud,
> Vaunters, vaineglorious, tyrants, truce-breakers,
> Envious, irefull, and ambitious.[3]

In fact, portraits of the Spaniard in the drama, a medium close to public opinion, assume that the Spanish people were readily characterized by a few unlucky traits: pride, poverty, military weakness, lechery, deceptiveness, and cruelty. Especially curious was the prevailing emphasis upon the less respectable features of so dangerous an enemy. Though treacherous and cruel, the Spaniard was considered neither substantial nor formidable. Whereas

---

[1] As he is quoted by his antagonist Robert Parsons in *A Temperate Ward-ward, to the Turbulent and Seditious Wach-word of Sir Francis Hastinges* ([Antwerp?] 1599) 104. Hastings acknowledges the statement in the work cited below (n. 2).

[2] Sir Francis Hastings, *An Apologie or Defence of the Watch-word* (London 1600) 197, 202.

[3] R[obert] W[ilson], *The Pleasant and Stately Morall, of the Three Lordes and Three Ladies of London* (London 1590) sig. F 4v, Tudor Facsimile Texts 145.

Italians earned a sinister distinction as villains in Elizabethan tragedy, Spaniards filled, when they were characterized as Spaniards, only frothy roles.[4]

This paper does not attempt to account fully for ways in which the English attained their knowledge of the Spaniard, and certainly not for the complicated and gradual infiltration that came through increasing familiarity with Spanish literature.[5] Nor can one underestimate the knowledge of Spain contributed by voyagers and soldiers. These, and other influences, must have been considerable. On the other hand, they do not explain the consistently grotesque version that the public got in Sir Francis Hastings's "sundrie imprinted books," with their "recorded" facts about the enemy. If we can identify these books, explain their purpose and bias, we may be better able to account for the warped, diminutive creatures that passed for Spaniards on the stage and in the popular mind.[6]

One might at first suppose, especially from a people so vigorous in language, that the books referred to by Hastings were original English invectives against Spain. But only two or three sustained examples, such as *A Fig for the Spaniard* (London 1591) and Sir Lewis Lewkenor's *The Estate of English Fugitives* (London 1595), became widely known,[7] and these appeared a year or more after *The Three Lords* and well after the crisis of the Armada period. Indeed, prepared by tradition to satirize France rather than Spain, the English possessed, when they most needed it, almost no native supply of anti-Spanish material. Cut off, furthermore, from free contact with Spain,[8] most English-

---

[4] R. V. Lindabury concludes that most frequently "the Spaniards are making themselves ridiculous, . . . or being made ridiculous by the good-humored abuse of others," *A Study of Patriotism in the Elizabethan Drama* (Princeton 1931) 89. Possibly "humorous" rather than "good-humored" might be the more generally applicable expression.

[5] The complexity of the subject may be seen in two major scholarly treatments of it: Martin Hume, *Spanish Influence on English Literature* (London 1905); J. G. Underhill, *Spanish Literature in the England of the Tudors* (New York 1899).

[6] The real Spaniards and their menace were understood by informed statesmen like Lord Burghley, who described them to Elizabeth as "a people all one-hearted in religion, constant, ambitious, politick, and valiant," "The Lord-Treasurer Burghleigh's Advice to Queen Elizabeth, in Matters of Religion and State," MS, printed in *Harleian Miscellany* (London 1808-1811) 2.282.

[7] I have cited several contemporary references to Lewkenor's book in "Enorbabus' Broken Heart and *The Estate of English Fugitives*," *Philological Quarterly* 30 (1951) 387-392. That the title at least of *A Fig for the Spaniard* had earned notoriety is shown by an envious allusion by H[enry] O[cland] in his remarks to the "Gentlemen Readers" (sig. A 2) prefacing Vasco Figuerio's *The Spaniards Monarchie, and Leaguers Olygarchie*, Englished by H. O. (London 1592). The audacity of giving the fig back to the Spaniard himself may be reflected in Ancient Pistol's assurance (*2 Henry IV* 5.3.123):

> When Pistol lies, do this; and fig me, like
> The bragging Spaniard.

Shakespeare references are to *The Complete Works*, ed. G. L. Kittredge (Boston 1936).

[8] For the meagerness of reports from Spain in the early eighties, see George B. Parks, *Richard Hakluyt and the English Voyages* (New York 1928) 100-101.

men had in the early 1580s an imperfect firsthand knowledge of the nation now opposing them.

I am suggesting in this essay that when a systematic knowledge of Spaniards did reach England, it came through translations; that it came not directly from Spain but from European countries that had already suffered intimate contact with conquering or "protecting" Spaniards; and that it had, at the hands of these countries, already received its final and authoritative distortion into satire. For Elizabethans, therefore, satire of the enemy passed without conscious falsification as an authentic portrait. Few other nations at war have acquired their invective so easily or so artlessly.

Not all translations, however, gave Englishmen what was to become the standard portrait of Spaniards. The results of a more disinterested observation had been transmitted to the English in 1575 by the translation of Turler's *De peregrinatione*. Stressing the ideal of objectivity in a traveler, Turler sketches the Spaniard in comparison with three other nationalities. Though "objectivity" leads to curiously unpleasant portraits of all four types, the Spaniard is seen as a fairly complete being, with but a few significant eccentricities. Courteous to strangers, wary in conversation, wakeful in affairs, excellent in navigation, he nevertheless has a "proude look" and "exquisite apparel," is crafty in counsel, and groans in his singing (the German howls and the Italian bleats).[9]

Unflattering to be sure, the picture lacks the systematic distortion of satire. And for portraits that deliberately shape the Spaniard into a ridiculous and ineffectual figure, we must turn to somewhat later Continental works distinguished by a political slant. Numbers of these appeared in translation from 1585 onward, mainly from French, but occasionally from Dutch, Portuguese, and Italian writers. It is to these works that authors of supposedly original English invective are primarily indebted. The author of *A Fig for the Spaniard* acknowledges the Continental influence by referring his readers to "the bookes that are daily printed" in the victimized countries "and sent abroad from them touching our present matter." "Having so many autentique witnesses," he argues, "what neede I more proofe in an open cause?"[10]

These "autentique witnesses" offered, furthermore, precisely the sort of information that the strong interventionists in England—conspicuously the War Party—happened to want: information suggesting a craftily expanding Spain, but one easily vulnerable to decisive tactics. English translators were

---

[9] *The Traveiler of Jerome Turler* (London 1575) 40-41. For a later nonsatirical portrait by a disinterested observer, see John Barclay's *Icon animorum*, trans. Thomas May under the title *The Mirrour of Mindes* (1631) 227-238.

[10] *A Fig* sig. B 3v. Even so early as 1589, Christopher Ockland cites as authorities in an anti-Spanish and anti-Romish work the books "written in French, Latin, and other languages," *The Fountaine and Welspring of All Variance, Sedition, and Deadlie Hate* (London 1589) 25.

not slow to recognize gold when they saw it. As a result, English readers, hitherto deprived of this solace, suddenly were offered an unlimited supply of anti-Spanish books written with gratifying insight.

The hurried scramble of translators and their eagerly worded prefaces suggest the value that they saw in this foreign material. *The Spaniards Mon-archie*—written by a Portuguese but prompted, like most of these tracts, by the current French crisis[11]—was offered by the translator as an urgent argument against unwise isolationism, and as an exposure of a "Spanish imitation of Machiavellized axiomes."[12] Still greater and more typical importance was seen in the *Discours politique, tres-excellent pour le temps present*, a work that two translators claimed almost simultaneously. The winner was Francesco Marquino who, though admittedly a foreigner like his original, piously confessed that he was moved to the labor by love of "this blessed Realme."[13] Robert Ashley, who had been urged by friends to postpone a major work in favor of this tract, was not unrighteously displeased to find that he had been anticipated by an Italian. But since the prior and somewhat alien version had been almost sold out, Ashley deigned to publish his own, with a title chosen to appeal more strategically to English readers: *A Comparison of the English and Spanish Nations*. In his hands, the treatise takes on emphatically an interpretation found generally in the foreign tracts: a plea not to fear but to scorn the "braveries" of a nation so inferior to the English. Readers, according to Ashley, will "learne to despise those magnificent *Dom Diegos* and *Spanish Cavalieros*, whose doughtiest deedes are bragges and boastinges, and themselves (for the most part) shadowes without substance."[14]

That there was a real basis for this view in the French document and in others of its kind we shall presently see, but first should be noted the parallel problem facing the translators of what attitude should be taken toward the French themselves, who appear in these treatises much more pleasantly than had been their fortune in most English books. It was necessary to learn to tolerate the new allies and their point of view if the full force of the tracts was to be felt. The translators approach this problem conscientiously. Ashley praises his original for its "roundnesse, and integritie" in demonstrating English prowess through "the memorable, and valiant deedes of our renowned Ancestors, in the noble Realme of France."[15] Mostly, too, the translators pass on with courteous silence the praises of the French which they find in the

---

[11] For a political consideration of the controversy about the Holy League, see J. W. Allen, *A History of Political Thought in the Sixteenth Century* (New York 1928) part 3, chap. 6.

[12] Henry Ocland (n. 7 above) sig. A 2.

[13] Francesco Marguino (trans.), *A Politike Discourse* (London 1589), "To the discrete and vertuous Reader," sig. A 2.

[14] Robert Ashley, *A Comparison of the English and Spanish Nations* (London 1589), sigs. A 2v-A 3.

[15] *Ibid.*, sig. A 2v.

originals. But they are alert for any slur upon the English. Thus, while the translator of *A Pleasant Satire* concurs eagerly with the author in denouncing the Spaniard (the expression "southernly divels" is marginally endorsed: "Spanyards wel set out"), the insinuation that the English resembled the Spanish in their ravishing of France sets off the marginal explosion: "False, and spoken like a Frenchman."[16] The coalition for invective, as for war, was a precarious one.

But if the English did not fully accept their allies, it was the French endeavor to accept the English rather than the Spanish that contributed materially to the derisive portrait of the latter in the tracts. One of the major arguments against the Holy League was that Spain was much less trustworthy than England as an ally. And the same point of view is found in invectives by other European nations threatened by the protectorship of Philip. Spain must be shown not as a fearful power, but as a vastly overrated nation, incapable of protecting members of the League. Few invectives, accordingly, portray Spain with serious alarm. Those that do are mainly translated newsletters from France, Holland, and the German states relating atrocities. These deplore Spanish tyranny, but give no credit to the Spanish power that made the tyranny possible.[17] And of course the English, who already had their translation of Las Casas's *The Spanish Colonie* and of Gonzales Montano's "Discovery" of the Inquisition, needed no new evidence of Spanish cruelty. What evidence they now had made the Spaniards seem sneakingly crafty rather than heroic.

The customary subordination of tragic to ridiculous qualities is well illustrated in *A Politike Discourse.* After a brief section on Spanish tyranny in the Indies, the author remarks, "But I tarrie too long upon so tragical a matter," and turns to his major business of setting forth "the Spaniardes in sport, as good Apothecaries, that is to saye, to make them to serve us for laughing stockes at there cost." "And who is the man," he adds, "so melancholicke, that coulde with-holde himselfe from laughing, seeing a porter, a cobler, and a carman, to play the Cavaliero: or a Cavaliero of Spaine, walking in the fields, and carrying the remnant of his dinner in his by-sacke: and doing a thousand such other villanies, of the which the porters, coblers, and carremen of this countrie would be sorrie to have thought upon."[18] Here we have the normal intention of the foreign invectives, which is to expose the groundless pride, the pretense, of the would-be protectors. The same contemptuous spirit informs the Dutch *A Pageant of Spanish Humours,* which

[16] *A Pleasant Satyre* (London 1595) 132, 146.

[17] See, *e.g., A True Discours of the Most Horrible and Barbarous Murthers and Massacres Committed by the Troupes of the Duke of Savoye. . . . Translated out of the French by A. P.* (London 1590), and *A Briefe Discourse of the Cruell Dealings of the Spanyards, in the Dukedome of Gulich and Cleve. . . . Translated out of the Dutch Copie* (London 1590).

[18] *A Politike Discourse* (n. 13 above) 23-24.

discusses "the naturall kindes of a Signor of Spaine" under the headings: "A Lyon in a place of Garrison," "A Hare in a besieged place," "A Peacocke on the streets," "A Foxe to deceive Women," and "Faithlesse and perjurous" —with a concluding section, "A happie estate to be free from Signor," which underlines the political import of the whole sketch.[19]

"I need not tel thee, they are poore and proud," Policy assured his countrymen from the stage. Yet it is this persistent attributing of poverty to the fabulously wealthy Spaniard that so careful a student as R. V. Lindabury finds inexplicable in Elizabethan plays.[20] It is, for example, the major theme in the longest description of the enemy found in the drama, that occurring in *Thomas Lord Cromwell*.[21] But one has merely to glance at any one of the foreign invectives to see why Policy did not have to tell the audience of Spanish poverty. In almost all the tracts it appears as a major reason for not looking to Spain for help. Philip may be rich in money, acknowledges the author of *A Discourse upon the Present Estate of France*, "but hee is at infinite charges, scarce having any countrie where hee is not forced to keepe a great garrison," and his neediness is evident in his failure to pay his troops in Flanders.[22] We can hardly expect him to give us money, argues the *Anti-Spaniard*, since the Netherlands rebellions have cost him as much gold as he got from the mines of Peru.[23] And *A Politike Discourse*, granting Spaniards primacy in "shamelesse bragging," especially "when they come to speake of their wealth and riches," estimates that "if they had the third part of the riches they imagine to have, they should be three times richer than they bee."[24]

It is partly the reputed poverty of Spain that led to another theme remarked by Lindabury in the drama: "the intoxicating possibility that the Spanish Empire would not long endure."[25] But the shakiness of Spain was explored still more fundamentally in the invectives. The *Anti-Spaniard* points out that the safety of Spain depends upon too many precarious threads: an aged king, the quiet of the Turk, and the continued submission of the conquered Flemings and Portugals.[26] Again, it was a favorite theory that, as Marquino expresses it, "although the Spaniard be greater [than England] in lands, and thereupon maketh great boastings and brags, yet is he to be compared to the Cipresse tree, the which though it be high, great and faire in sight, is never-

---

[19] *A Pageant of Spanish Humours. . . . Translated out of Dutch, by H. W.* (London 1599).

[20] Lindabury (n. 4 above) 88.

[21] *The True Chronicle Historie . . . of Thomas Lord Cromwell* (London 1602), sig. D 2v; see also *Blurt Master Constable*, or, *The Spaniard's Night Walk* 1.2.200, and Shakespeare's *Love's Labour's Lost* 5.2.710, both cited by Lindabury 88.

[22] [Michel Hurault], *A Discourse upon the Present Estate of France* (London 1588) 41.

[23] *The Coppie of the Anti-Spaniard* (n.p., n.d.) 9.

[24] *A Politike Discourse* (n. 13 above) 35.

[25] Lindabury 64.

[26] *The Coppie of the Anti-Spaniard* 4.

thelesse, weake, tender, slender, and unfruitfull." These and other reasons make Marquino join with his original in saying "that the Spanish nation, is at hir highest degree, and shalt therefore no more ascende but descend."[27]

Another surprising shortcoming of Spain was found in valor and military prowess. And here it is noteworthy that, although the Spanish captain had become associated in Italy with the *miles gloriosus* and with the Capitano of popular comedy, the satirical tracts ignore this literary vantage point in their absorbing concern with political strategy and evidence. Their aim is to diminish the reputation not of one eccentric type, but of an entire nation. Some will say, complains the *Anti-Spaniard*, that if we do not accept the protectorship, "we shall now be troubled with Spaniards, those great warriors, those great bug-beares." If "they be so mightie, how comes it to passe that they can not defende them selves better from the open enemies of all Christendome?" Why are they so slow in subduing the English?[28] Although most attacks on Spanish valor hunt cautiously through history for evidence, the author of *A Politike Discourse* employs Aristotle's correlation between geography and temperament as evidence "sufficient enough to displace the Spaniard out of the roome which hee pretendeth to have among warlike Nations."[29]

Instead, therefore, of portraits that acknowledge the Spaniard of wealth and refinement, there comes through the consistently biased pages of the Continental invectives only the figure of a poor wretch, dressed in his one brave suit, twisting his "mustachoes" and stroking his beard, glancing at "Su Signoria," and casting "a leering eie a side, to espie if the beholders admire him not."[30] Instead of the valorous Spaniard who for a time proved to be the ablest soldier in Europe, there is visible only a Signor bragging in a garrison, and cowering when he hears "the thundering rumer of *Los Ennemigos.*"[31]

Likewise we might run through the Continental tracts to find in them possible influences behind other attitudes adopted by the English. We might notice the persistent use of racial bases for determining Spanish traits: "They be Affricans, tanned, hot, parched subtill"; if one steps in your house, "you shall have an intollerable Maister, a necessarie concubmarie."[32] Their faith-

---

[27] Marguino (n. 13 above) sig. A 2.

[28] *The Coppie of the Anti-Spaniard* 16-17. Fiquerio (n. 7 above) relates (sig. D 2) how the French king met Parma so courageously "that the Spaniard for all his bravadoes, was so astonished at the sight of this valorous armie, that he never dared come to blowes. . . Thus in briefe behold, all the succours, and advancement, that France received of her great friend Philip king of Spaine, by the coming of the Prince of Parma." And see Hurault (n. 22 above) 39.

[29] *A Politike Discourse* (n. 13 above) 32-34.

[30] *A Pageant* (n. 19 above) sig. B 1.

[31] *Ibid.* sig. B 2.

[32] *The Discoverer of France to the Parisians. . . . Translated out of the French by* E. A[ggas] (London 1590) 8.

lessness, similarly, comes from the Moors, and their pride from the Sara-cens.[33]

It would also be instructive fully to note the complexity of nationalities often concealed behind the final English product (a product that some readers possibly mistook for an original work). Thus, an Italian translated the French *Discours politique* into English. *A Pleasant Satyre* is said to have been "written in the Italian tonge, by a Gentleman of Florence," reaching the English trans-lator through the French copy.[34] And *The Spaniards Monarchie* was licensed to be translated from a French version of the Spanish of Vasco Figuerio, a Portuguese who was writing to warn the French by the examples of his own country.

Or we might profitably extend the study to include the involuntary role played in invective by tracts issued by the Spaniards themselves. Numbers of these had been written to inform the world of Spanish strength, successes, and plans. These fell into the hands of English translators who published them, with vigorous irony and marginal catcalls, usually just after the Armada.[35]

Indeed, it is doubtful whether translation has ever played a more curious or complex role in providing propaganda during wartime, or whether the effect upon literature has ever been so contrary to what are considered the ideal intentions of translation. Louis B. Wright is surely paying the more famous Elizabethan translations their rightful due in saying that through them, primarily, "a knowledge of the culture and learning of other nations reached the great body of intelligent citizens."[36] But the tribute has only iron-ical relevance to the translations of invective. For even if these works did not originate all the satirical distortions that they utilized, they must have given to these biases the stamp of authority which, even today, is apt to come from "imprinted books."

Department of English
University of California
Los Angeles, California 90024, U.S.A.

[33] *A Politike Discourse* 18. The reflection of racial argumentation in English invective may be seen in Edward Daunce, *A Briefe Discourse of the Spanish State* (London 1590) 36 et passim, and in Lewkenor (above at n. 7) sig. I 2.

[34] *A Pleasant Satyre* (n. 16 above) sig. A 2.

[35] To mention a few: *A Packe of Spanish Lyes, Sent Abroad in the World: First Printed in Spaine in the Spanish Tongue, and Translated out of the Originall, Now Ripped up, Un-folded, and by Just Examination Condemned, as Conteyning False, Corrupt, and Detestable Wares, Worthy to be Damned and Burned* (London 1588); *A Libell of Spanish Lies* (London 1596); *An Answer to the Untruthes, Published and Printed in Spaine* (London 1589), which had the inestimable advantage of being produced by a reformed Spaniard; and *A True Discourse of the Armie Which the King of Spain Assembled. . . . Translated by Daniel Arch-deacon* (London 1588).

[36] Louis B. Wright, *Middle-Class Culture in Elizabethan England* (Chapel Hill 1935) 339.